חומש קורן מקראות הדורות
THE KOREN MIKRAOT HADOROT

פרשת אמר
PARASHAT EMOR

קורן ירושלים

THE ROHR FAMILY EDITION

חומש קורן מקראות הדורות
THE KOREN MIKRAOT HADOROT

THE KOPLOW FAMILY EDITION OF PARASHAT EMOR

פרשת אמר עם רש״י
PARASHAT EMOR WITH RASHI

TORAH TRANSLATION BY

Rabbi Lord Jonathan Sacks זצ״ל

RASHI'S COMMENTARY TRANSLATED BY

Rabbi Jonathan Mishkin

•

KOREN PUBLISHERS JERUSALEM

The Koren Mikraot HaDorot, The Rohr Edition
Volume 28: Parashat Emor
First Edition, 2024

Koren Publishers Jerusalem Ltd.
POB 4044, Jerusalem 9104001, ISRAEL
POB 8531, New Milford, CT 06776, USA

www.korenpub.com

The Tanakh translation is excerpted from the Magerman Edition of The Koren Tanakh.

The creation of this work was made possible with the generous support of the Jewish Book Trust Inc.

Printed in ISRAEL

ISBN 978 965 7760 83 3

KMDEM01

The Rohr Family Edition of
The Koren Mikraot HaDorot
pays tribute to the memory of

Mr. Sami Rohr ז״ל
ר׳ שמואל ב״ר יהושע אליהו ז״ל

who served his Maker with joy
and whose far-reaching vision, warm open hand, love of Torah,
and love for every Jew were catalysts for the revival and growth of
vibrant Jewish life in the former Soviet Union
and in countless communities the world over

and to the memory of his beloved wife

Mrs. Charlotte Rohr (née Kastner) ע״ה
שרה בת ר׳ יקותיאל יהודה ע״ה

who survived the fires of the Shoah to become
the elegant and gracious matriarch,
first in Colombia and later in the United States,
of three generations of a family
nurtured by her love and unstinting devotion.
She found grace in the eyes of all those whose lives she touched.

Together they merited to see all their children
build lives enriched by faithful commitment
to the spreading of Torah and *Ahavat Yisrael*.

Dedicated with love by
The Rohr Family
NEW YORK, USA

"לְמַעַן יֵדְעוּ דֹרֹתֵיכֶם..."

"So that future generations may know..."

Dedicated to our
children and grandchildren,
who are the future of the Jewish people.

The Meyer G & Ellen Goodstein Koplow Foundation

CONTENTS

FOR PARASHAT EMOR WITH COMMENTARIES AND THE BIBLICAL IMAGINATION
TURN TO THE OTHER END OF THIS VOLUME.

PUBLISHER'S PREFACE

The genius of Jewish commentary on the Torah is one of huge and critical import. Jewish life and law for millennia have been directed by our interpretations of the Torah, and each generation has looked to its rabbinic leadership for a deeper understanding of its teachings, its laws, its stories.

For centuries, *Mikraot Gedolot* have been a core part of understanding the Ḥumash; the words of Rashi, Ibn Ezra, Ramban, Rashbam, Ralbag, and other classic commentators illuminate and help us understand the Torah. But traditional editions of *Mikraot Gedolot* present only a slice in time and a small selection of the corpus of Jewish commentators. Almost every generation has produced rabbinic scholars who speak to their times, from Philo and Onkelos two thousand years ago, to Rabbi Joseph B. Soloveitchik, Rabbi Aharon Kotler, the Lubavitcher Rebbe, and Nehama Leibowitz in ours.

The Koren Mikraot HaDorot – Scriptures or Interpretations for the Generations – brings two millennia of Torah commentary into the hands and homes of Jews around the world. Readers will be able to encounter not only the classic commentators, but to gain a much broader sense of the issues that scholars grappled with in their time and the inspiration they drew from the ancient texts. We see, for example, how Philo speaks to an assimilating Greek Jewish audience in first-century Alexandria, and how similar yet different it is from Rabbi Samson Raphael Hirsch's approach to an equally assimilating nineteenth-century German readership; how the perspectives of Rabbi Soloveitchik and Rabbi Kotler differ in a post-Holocaust world; how Rav Se'adya Gaon interpreted the Torah for the Jews of Babylonia. It is an exciting journey through Jewish history via the unchanging words of the Torah.

The text of the Torah features the exceptional new translation of Rabbi

◀

Lord Jonathan Sacks, together with the celebrated and meticulously accurate Koren Hebrew text. Of course, with the exception of Rashi – for whom we present an entirely new translation in full – the commentaries are selected. We offer this anthology not to limit our reader's exploration but rather as a gateway for further learning of Torah and its commentaries on a broader and deeper level than space here permits. We discuss below how to use this book.

We must thank **Pamela and George Rohr** of New York, who recognized the unique value of the *Koren Mikraot HaDorot* and its ability to communicate historical breadth and context to the reader. For my colleagues here at Koren, we thank you; for the many generations of users who will find this a continuing source of new learning, we are forever in your debt.

We are honored to acknowledge and thank **Debra and David Magerman**, whose support for the Koren Ḥumash with Rabbi Sacks's exemplary translation and commentary laid the foundation for the core English text of this work.

Finally, I must personally thank **Rabbi Marvin Hier**, with whom I had a special breakfast some years ago at the King David Hotel. During the meal, he raised the problem that so few people knew the writings of Rabbi Joseph B. Soloveitchik and Rabbi Aharon Kotler on the Torah; and I, who had just read some of Philo's work, had the same reaction. From that conversation came the seed for this project.

HOW TO USE THE KOREN MIKRAOT HADOROT

The Koren Mikraot HaDorot will be a fifty-five-volume edition of the Ḥumash (one for each *parasha* plus a companion volume). Each of the fifty-four volumes of the *parashot* can be read from right to left (Hebrew opening side), and left to right (English opening side).

Opening from the Hebrew side offers:

- the full Torah text, the translation of Rabbi Sacks, and the full commentary of Rashi in both Hebrew and the new English translation
- all *haftarot* associated with the *parasha* of the volume, including Rosh Ḥodesh and special readings, both in Hebrew and English

Opening from the English side presents four sections:

- **THE TIME OF THE SAGES** – includes commentaries from the Second Temple period and the talmudic period

◀

- **THE CLASSIC COMMENTATORS** – quotes selected explanations by Rashi as well as most of the commentators found in traditional *Mikraot Gedolot*
- **CONFRONTING MODERNITY** – selects commentaries from the eighteenth century to the close of the twentieth century
- **THE BIBLICAL IMAGINATION** – features essays surveying some of the broader conceptual ideas as a supplement to the linear, text-based commentary

The first three of these sections each feature the relevant verses, in Hebrew and English, on the page alongside their respective commentaries, in chronological order, providing the reader with a single window onto the text without excessive page turning.

In addition to being a valuable resource in a Jewish home or synagogue library, we conceived of these volumes as a weekly accompaniment in the synagogue. There is scope for the reader to study each *parasha* on a weekly basis in preparation for the reading on Shabbat. One may select a particular group of commentators for study that week, or perhaps alternate between ancient and modern viewpoints. Some readers may choose to delve into the text through verse-by-verse interpretation, while others may prefer a conceptual perspective on the *parasha* as a whole. The broad array of options for learning means this is a series which can be returned to year after year, always presenting new insights and new approaches to understanding the text.

ACKNOWLEDGMENTS

The creation of this book was possible only thanks to the small but exceptional team here at Koren Jerusalem. We are grateful to:

- Rabbi Tzvi Hersh Weinreb, שליט״א, who conceptualized the structure of the project and provides both moral and halakhic leadership at Koren
- Rabbi Shai Finkelstein, whose encyclopedic knowledge of Torah and its interpreters is equaled only by his community leadership, formerly in Memphis and today in Jerusalem
- Rabbi Yedidya Naveh, whose knowledge, organizational skills, and superb leadership brought the disparate elements together
- Rabbi Jonathan Mishkin, translator of the commentaries, who crafted a fluent, accurate, and eloquent English translation

Our design, editing, typesetting, and proofreading staff, including Tani Bayer, Esther Be'er, Tomi Mager, Adina Luber, Rabbi Dr. Tzvi Sinensky,

Dr. Yoel Finkelman, Rabbi David Debow, Tali Simon, Nechama Unterman, Ben Zion Bokser, Debbie Ismailoff, Ilana Sobel, Dvora Rhein, and Carolyn Budow Ben David, enabled an attractive, user-friendly, and accurate edition of these works.

> "One silver basin" (Numbers 7:13) was brought as a symbol of the Torah, which has been likened to wine, as the verse states: "And drink of the wine which I have mingled" (Proverbs 9:5). Because it is customary to drink wine in a basin – as we see in the verse "that drink wine in basins" (Amos 6:6) – he therefore brought a basin. "Of seventy shekels, after the shekel of the sanctuary" (Numbers 7:13). Why? Because just as the numerical value of "wine" [*yayin*] is seventy, so there are seventy modes of expounding the Torah. (Bemidbar Rabba 13:16)

Each generation produces exceptional rabbinic, intellectual leadership. It has been our purpose to enable all Jews to taste the wine of those generations, in the hope of expanding the breadth and depth of their knowledge. Torah is our greatest treasure, and we need the wisdom of those generations to better understand this bountiful gift from God. We hope that we at Koren can deepen that understanding for all who seek it.

Matthew Miller, Publisher
Jerusalem, 5784 (2024)

A NOTE ON THE TRANSLATION OF RASHI

The translation of Rashi's commentary provided here is complete and unabridged, following the meticulously researched Hebrew version of the commentary published by Koren. This version omits some material published in other editions that was found likely to have been added later by Rashi's students and other authors. We have included all of Rashi's numerous grammatical and linguistic discussions, even though these tend to be of less interest to the English-speaking reader, for two reasons: First, we felt it important for the readership to be confident that they are holding a complete version of Rashi's commentary and to know that they are not missing any matter of potential interest it might contain. Second, we wished to impress upon the reader that the elegant Sacks translation of the Torah included in this volume represents only one reading among many possible interpretations. Rashi's inquiries into the meanings of individual words and phrases emphasize the ambiguity of the verses and the potential of any passage to be interpreted in several different ways. This multifaceted nature of the Torah is a central theme of *The Koren Mikraot HaDorot.*

The inclusion of these discussions – often technical and sometimes confusing – bears implications for the translation. Here the translator was often forced to insert himself into the discussion to clearly establish the grammatical difficulty or ambiguity in the Hebrew text that is troubling Rashi. Since these difficulties are not always conveyed in the Sacks verse translation, the reader will find bracketed editorial comments used more aggressively in these discussions. The editor's notes also serve to supply the English-speaking reader with relevant details regarding Hebrew grammar that Rashi assumes to be known to his audience, which are necessary to understanding his point.

◀

Here at the outset, we will provide a very brief overview of the Hebrew system of *binyanim*, or Hebrew verb forms, which is central to so many of Rashi's grammatical arguments.

Hebrew verbs, which are always conjugated by number, person, gender, and tense, are also divided into seven categories of verbs called *binyanim*. Three of these are in the active voice, three passive, and one in a reflexive voice that is neither active nor passive. In theory, any three-letter root (*shoresh*) in Hebrew can be conjugated in any one of these forms, with slightly different meanings in each one, though few roots exist in all forms. Readers who encounter one of Rashi's discourses analyzing to which class a given verb belongs can refer to the following chart to orient themselves.

BINYAN NAME	EXAMPLE (PAST/FUTURE)	VOICE	
Paal (Kal) – פָּעַל (קל)	*Katav/Yikhtov* – write	Active	Simple
Hifil – הִפְעִיל	*Hikdish/Yakdish* – consecrate	Active	Causative
Pi'el – פִּעֵל	*Giddel/Yegaddel* – promote or exalt	Active	Intensive
Hitpael – הִתְפַּעֵל	*Hitgaddel/Yitgaddel* – become great	Reflexive	Intensive
Pual – פֻּעַל	*Guddal/Yeguddal* – be promoted or exalted	Passive	Intensive
Hufal – הֻפְעַל	*Hukdash/Yukdash* – be consecrated	Passive	Causative
Nifal – נִפְעַל	*Nikhtav/Yikkatev* – be written	Passive	Simple

Each of the three active conjugations pairs with one of the passive ones, as seen in the above chart, such that the seven *binyanim* can be simplified into three more basic forms. The simple form (*paal/nifal*) denotes simple actions. The causative form (*hifil/hufal*) is reserved for actions induced by the subject in the object, e.g., to cause something to become holy (consecrate). The intensive form (*pi'el/pual*) describes a special form of the action, usually more significant or intense. The reflexive form is considered a third subgroup of the intensive form and is used for actions done to oneself.

Rashi's grammatical discussions also focus on the vocalization (*nikkud,* or vowel marks) of the Hebrew text. The reader can review the names of the vowel marks in the following chart, as well as see how these vowels are transliterated in this edition.

VOWEL MARK	NAME	TRANSLITERATION
בְ	*Sheva* (*Ḥataf* when combined with a *segol, pataḥ,* or *kamatz*)	*e* or silent
בֶ	*Segol* (in Rashi's language: *Pataḥ Katan*)	*e*
בַ	*Pataḥ*	*a*
בָ	*Kamatz*	*a* or *o*
בִ	*Ḥirik*	*i*
בֵ	*Tzerei* (in Rashi's language, also: *Kamatz Katan*)	*e* or *ei*
בֹ	*Ḥolam* (in Rashi's language: *Melafum*)	*o*
בֻ	*Kubbutz* (in Rashi's language: *Shuruk*)	*u*
בוּ	*Shuruk*	*u*

For Rashi's terms in Old French, we have been guided by Yisrael Gukovitzky's dictionary *Targum HaLaaz* (1985).

Yedidya Naveh, Managing Editor
Jerusalem, 5784 (2024)

פרשת אמר

PARASHAT EMOR

חומש עם רש״י

THE ḤUMASH WITH RASHI

21 1 The LORD said to Moshe, "Speak to the priests, Aharon's sons.
Say: No one of you shall render himself impure for any dead
2 person among his people except for his nearest relatives: his
3 mother, father, son, daughter, or brother; or his virgin sister
who has remained close to him because she has not mar-
4 ried – for her, he may render himself impure. But he shall not
become impure for those he is related to by marriage, and so
5 become profane. Priests shall not make bald patches on their
heads, or shave off the edges of their beards, or gash wounds

21 1 | **אֱמֹר אֶל־הַכֹּהֲנִים** – *Speak to the priests:* God instructs Moshe to both "speak to the priests" and to "say." The two verbs imply that adult priests are responsible [not only for keeping the purity laws themselves but] also for ensuring their observance by their minor sons.

כא א | אֱמֹר אֶל־הַכֹּהֲנִים. "אֱמֹר" "וְאָמַרְתָּ", לְהַזְהִיר גְּדוֹלִים עַל הַקְּטַנִּים:

בְּנֵי אַהֲרֹן – *Aharon's sons:* Does the prohibition against becoming impure from a corpse extend to *ḥalalim*? [A *ḥalal* is one born from the unlawful union of a priest to a woman he is forbidden to marry, such as a divorcée. The *ḥalal* enjoys no privileges of the priesthood, and is subject to none of its restrictions, as Rashi's present comment notes.] No, for the verse uses the term "the priests" [thus including only priests who have not lost their status].

בְּנֵי אַהֲרֹן. יָכוֹל חֲלָלִים? תַּלְמוּד לוֹמַר: "הַכֹּהֲנִים":

בְּנֵי אַהֲרֹן – *Aharon's sons:* These words are stated to include in the prohibition even those priests who are blemished.

בְּנֵי אַהֲרֹן. אַף בַּעֲלֵי מוּמִין בַּמַּשְׁמָע:

בְּנֵי אַהֲרֹן – *Aharon's sons:* However, the daughters of Aharon are not warned to avoid impurity.

בְּנֵי אַהֲרֹן. וְלֹא בְּנוֹת אַהֲרֹן:

לֹא־יִטַּמָּא בְּעַמָּיו – *No one of you shall render himself impure among his people:* The restriction applies as long as the corpse remains "among his people" [that is, the dead person is being tended to by his or her fellow Israelites]. This excludes a *met mitzva*. [The term refers to a dead person who has no relatives or friends to bury him. It is incumbent upon every Israelite, including priests, to tend to this corpse.]

לֹא־יִטַּמָּא בְּעַמָּיו. בְּעוֹד שֶׁהַמֵּת בְּתוֹךְ עַמָּיו, יָצָא מֵת מִצְוָה:

2 | **כִּי אִם־לִשְׁאֵרוֹ** – *Except for his nearest relatives:* This refers to the priest's wife.

ב | כִּי אִם־לִשְׁאֵרוֹ. אֵין "שְׁאֵרוֹ" אֶלָּא אִשְׁתּוֹ:

3 | **הַקְּרוֹבָה** – *Who has remained close to him:* The adjective serves to include a sister who is betrothed [but is not yet married].

ג | הַקְּרוֹבָה. לְרַבּוֹת אֶת הָאֲרוּסָה:

◀

כא א וַיֹּאמֶר יהוה אֶל־מֹשֶׁה אֱמֹר אֶל־הַכֹּהֲנִים בְּנֵי אַהֲרֹן יז
ב וְאָמַרְתָּ אֲלֵהֶם לְנֶפֶשׁ לֹא־יִטַּמָּא בְּעַמָּיו: כִּי אִם־
לִשְׁאֵרוֹ הַקָּרֹב אֵלָיו לְאִמּוֹ וּלְאָבִיו וְלִבְנוֹ וּלְבִתּוֹ
ג וּלְאָחִיו: וְלַאֲחֹתוֹ הַבְּתוּלָה הַקְּרוֹבָה אֵלָיו אֲשֶׁר
ד לֹא־הָיְתָה לְאִישׁ לָהּ יִטַּמָּא: לֹא יִטַּמָּא בַּעַל בְּעַמָּיו
ה לְהֵחַלּוֹ: לֹא־יִקְרְחָה קָרְחָה בְּרֹאשָׁם וּפְאַת זְקָנָם יְקָרֵחוּ

אֲשֶׁר לֹא־הָיְתָה לְאִישׁ. לְמִשְׁכָּב:

לָהּ יִטַּמָּא. מִצְוָה:

ד | לֹא יִטַּמָּא בַּעַל בְּעַמָּיו לְהֵחַלּוֹ. לֹא יִטַּמָּא לְאִשְׁתּוֹ פְּסוּלָה שֶׁהוּא מְחֻלָּל בָּהּ בְּעוֹדָהּ עִמּוֹ, וְכֵן פְּשׁוּטוֹ שֶׁל מִקְרָא: "לֹא יִטַּמָּא בַּעַל" בִּשְׁאֵרוֹ בְּעוֹד שֶׁהִיא בְּתוֹךְ עַמָּיו, שֶׁיֵּשׁ לָהּ קוֹבְרִין שֶׁאֵינָהּ מֵת מִצְוָה. וּבְאֵיזֶה שְׁאֵר אָמַרְתִּי? בְּאוֹתוֹ שֶׁהוּא "לְהֵחַלּוֹ", לְהִתְחַלֵּל הוּא מִכְּהֻנָּתוֹ:

ה | לֹא־יִקְרְחָה קָרְחָה. עַל מֵת. וַהֲלֹא אַף יִשְׂרָאֵל הֻזְהֲרוּ עַל כָּךְ? אֶלָּא לְפִי שֶׁנֶּאֱמַר בְּיִשְׂרָאֵל: "בֵּין עֵינֵיכֶם" (דברים יד, א), יָכוֹל לֹא יְהֵא חַיָּב עַל כָּל הָרֹאשׁ? תַּלְמוּד לוֹמַר: "בְּרֹאשָׁם". וְיִלְמְדוּ יִשְׂרָאֵל מִכֹּהֲנִים בִּגְזֵרָה שָׁוָה: נֶאֱמַר כָּאן "קָרְחָה" וְנֶאֱמַר לְהַלָּן בְּיִשְׂרָאֵל "קָרְחָה" (שם), מַה כָּאן כָּל הָרֹאשׁ

אֲשֶׁר לֹא־הָיְתָה לְאִישׁ – *Because she has not married:* This is a woman who has not had relations with a man.

לָהּ יִטַּמָּא – *For her, he may render himself impure:* It is an obligation [for the priest to become impure on behalf of his relatives. In contrast to the current translation, Rashi understands the text as not merely granting permission, but demanding that the priest bury his dead].

4 | **לֹא יִטַּמָּא בַּעַל בְּעַמָּיו לְהֵחַלּוֹ** – *But he shall not become impure for those he is related to by marriage, and so become profane:* A priest may not become impure by burying his dead wife whom he was forbidden to marry, and through whom he becomes profaned as long as he lives with her. Hence the straightforward meaning of this verse is: A husband may not make himself impure for his dead wife while she is among his people, meaning that she is not a *met mitzva*, as others are able to tend to her burial. And to which wife does this restriction apply? To one who profanes him from the priesthood by being married to him. [On the other hand, the priest has an obligation to bury a lawful wife even if her relatives are available to do it.]

5 | **לֹא־יִקְרְחָה קָרְחָה** – *Shall not make bald patches:* This may not be done as a sign of mourning for the dead. Now one might point out that the Torah also issues such a warning to the general Israelite public [when it states: *Do not make bald patches – korḥa – in the middle of your heads – bein eineikhem,* literally, "between your eyes" – *for the dead* (Deuteronomy 14:1), and surely priests as well are included in that prohibition]. And yet, because the phrase *bein eineikhem* is used in the general commandment, we might have thought that one would only be liable for tearing out his hair at that

6 into their flesh. They shall be holy to their God and not profane God's name, for they bring close the LORD's fire offerings,
foodstuff offerings to their God; therefore they shall be holy.
7 • They may not marry a woman made profane by immorality,
nor may they marry a woman divorced from her husband, for
8 they are holy to their God. You shall treat a priest as holy, for
he brings close the offerings of foodstuffs to your God. And he
shall be holy to you, because I, the LORD, am holy and make

אַף לְהַלָּן כָּל הָרֹאשׁ בְּמַשְׁמָע, כָּל מָקוֹם שֶׁיִּקָּרֵחַ בָּרֹאשׁ. וּמָה לְהַלָּן עַל מֵת, אַף כָּאן עַל מֵת:

specific spot, but not anywhere else on the head. Thus, the present verse states: *On their heads*. And although this phrase is stated specifically with regard to priests, we can infer that it applies to the rest of the nation as well, through the following *gezera shava* [linguistic analogy]: The Torah uses the term *korḥa* in both the present verse and in the later one. And so we infer that just as here the entire head is included in the prohibition, so too the subsequent text also refers to the whole head – that is, anywhere that a bald patch could be created. We also infer that just as there the prohibition is restricted to tearing out hair for the dead, that condition is necessary here as well.

וּפְאַת זְקָנָם לֹא יְגַלֵּחוּ. לְפִי שֶׁנֶּאֱמַר בְּיִשְׂרָאֵל: "וְלֹא תַשְׁחִית" (לעיל יט, כז), יָכוֹל לִקְּטוֹ בְּמַלְקֵט וּרְהִיטְנֵי יְהֵא חַיָּב? לְכָךְ נֶאֱמַר: "לֹא יְגַלֵּחוּ", שֶׁאֵינוֹ חַיָּב אֶלָּא עַל דָּבָר הַקָּרוּי גִּלּוּחַ וְיֵשׁ בּוֹ הַשְׁחָתָה, וְזֶהוּ תַּעַר:

וּפְאַת זְקָנָם לֹא יְגַלֵּחוּ – *Or shave off the edges of their beards:* Because the general warning to all of Israel states: *Do not destroy the edges of your beard* (19:27), we might have thought that one who plucks out hair with tweezers or uses a file would be liable for transgressing this prohibition. Hence the present verse says: *Or shave off the edges of their beards*. Combining these two statements we conclude that a violation only occurs if a man performs an act that is considered shaving, and which also destroys the hair [by completely uprooting it]. This is only achieved by using a razor.

וּבִבְשָׂרָם לֹא יִשְׂרְטוּ שָׂרָטֶת. לְפִי שֶׁנֶּאֱמַר בְּיִשְׂרָאֵל: "וְשֶׂרֶט לָנֶפֶשׁ לֹא תִתְּנוּ" (לעיל יט, כח), יָכוֹל שָׂרַט חָמֵשׁ שְׂרִיטוֹת לֹא יְהֵא חַיָּב אֶלָּא אַחַת? תַּלְמוּד לוֹמַר: "לֹא יִשְׂרְטוּ שָׂרֶטֶת", לְחַיֵּב עַל כָּל שְׂרִיטָה וּשְׂרִיטָה, שֶׁתֵּבָה זוֹ יְתֵרָה הִיא לִדְרֹשׁ, שֶׁהָיָה לוֹ לִכְתֹּב "לֹא יִשְׂרְטוּ" וַאֲנִי יוֹדֵעַ שֶׁהִיא "שָׂרֶטֶת":

וּבִבְשָׂרָם לֹא יִשְׂרְטוּ שָׂרָטֶת – *Or gash wounds into their flesh:* Because the general warning to all of Israel states: *Do not gash your body for the dead [veseret lanefesh]* [19:28, where the term *seret* – "gash" – is singular], we might have thought that one would be held liable for just one violation even if he gashed himself five times. Hence the present verse states: *Lo yisretu saratet* [where the term is doubled in order] to make one liable for each individual cut. Since the second word *saratet* is redundant – the text could have just said *Lo yisretu* – its presence is therefore used to teach the abovementioned point.

ו לֹא יְגַלְּחוּ וּבִבְשָׂרָם לֹא יִשְׂרְטוּ שָׂרָטֶת: קְדֹשִׁים יִהְיוּ
לֵאלֹהֵיהֶם וְלֹא יְחַלְּלוּ שֵׁם אֱלֹהֵיהֶם כִּי אֶת־אִשֵּׁי
ז יהוה לֶחֶם אֱלֹהֵיהֶם הֵם מַקְרִיבִם וְהָיוּ קֹדֶשׁ: · אִשָּׁה
זֹנָה וַחֲלָלָה לֹא יִקָּחוּ וְאִשָּׁה גְּרוּשָׁה מֵאִישָׁהּ לֹא
ח יִקָּחוּ כִּי־קָדֹשׁ הוּא לֵאלֹהָיו: וְקִדַּשְׁתּוֹ כִּי־אֶת־לֶחֶם
אֱלֹהֶיךָ הוּא מַקְרִיב קָדֹשׁ יִהְיֶה־לָּךְ כִּי קָדוֹשׁ אֲנִי

6 | קְדֹשִׁים יִהְיוּ – *They shall be holy:* Even against their will. This is an instruction to the courts to ensure that priests maintain their sanctity [by avoiding contact with corpses].

ו | קְדֹשִׁים יִהְיוּ. עַל כָּרְחָם יַקְדִּישׁוּם בֵּית דִּין בְּכָךְ:

7 | זֹנָה – *By immorality:* [The literal reading suggests two different categories of women whom a priest may not marry.] A *zona* is a woman who has had relations with an Israelite whom she is forbidden to marry. This includes those with whom intimacy warrants excision [such as a brother], and those with whom intimacy is merely a prohibition, such as a *netin* [a member of the Gibeonite nation who may not marry into the nation of Israel] or a *mamzer* [a child born out of an incestuous or adulterous union who can only marry converts or other *mamzerim*. A woman who engages in such unlawful relations attains the status of *zona* and may not subsequently marry a priest].

ז | זֹנָה. שֶׁנִּבְעֲלָה בְּעִילַת יִשְׂרָאֵל הָאָסוּר לָהּ, כְּגוֹן חַיָּבֵי כְרֵתוֹת אוֹ נָתִין אוֹ מַמְזֵר:

חֲלָלָה – *Profane:* A *ḥalala* is a woman whose father is a priest and whose mother was forbidden to marry him. For example, the daughter of a widow who married a High Priest, or the daughter of a divorced woman who married a common priest [or obviously, a High Priest] is a *ḥalala* [and cannot herself marry a priest]. Additionally, should a woman who may not marry into the priesthood nevertheless have relations with a priest, she herself becomes a *ḥalala* [and subsequently may not marry a priest – either the man through whom she became a *ḥalala* or any other priest].

חֲלָלָה. שֶׁנּוֹלְדָה מִן הַפְּסוּלִים שֶׁבַּכְּהֻנָּה, כְּגוֹן בַּת אַלְמָנָה מִכֹּהֵן גָּדוֹל אוֹ בַּת גְּרוּשָׁה מִכֹּהֵן הֶדְיוֹט, וְכֵן שֶׁנִּתְחַלְּלָה מִן הַכְּהֻנָּה עַל יְדֵי בִּיאַת אֶחָד מִן הַפְּסוּלִים לַכְּהֻנָּה:

8 | וְקִדַּשְׁתּוֹ – *You shall treat a priest as holy:* The priest should be forced to be holy. For example, if he marries a woman who is forbidden to him and refuses to divorce her, the court should administer lashes and admonish him until he complies.

ח | וְקִדַּשְׁתּוֹ. עַל כָּרְחוֹ, שֶׁאִם לֹא רָצָה לְגָרֵשׁ הַלְקֵהוּ וְיַסְּרֵהוּ עַד שֶׁיְּגָרֵשׁ:

◀

9 you holy. If the daughter of a priest profanes herself by immorality, she profanes her father also; she shall be burned with
10 fire. The priest, the highest among his brothers, on
whose head the anointing oil has been poured and who has
been ordained to wear the vestments, shall not dishevel his hair
11 or tear his clothes. He shall not go near the dead; even for his
12 father or mother he shall not render himself impure. He shall
not leave the Sanctuary, profaning his God's Sanctuary, for
the crown of his God's anointing oil rests upon him; I am the
13 14 Lord. ▸ He may marry a woman only in her virginity. He may
not marry a widow, a divorcée, or one profaned by immorality.

קֹדֶשׁ יִהְיֶה־לָּךְ – *And he shall be holy to you:* Treat the priest with holiness, and grant him the privilege of being first in all matters. For example, invite the priest to lead the blessings at meals.

קֹדֶשׁ יִהְיֶה־לָּךְ. נְהֹג בּוֹ קְדֻשָּׁה לִפְתֹּחַ רִאשׁוֹן בְּכָל דָּבָר וּלְבָרֵךְ רִאשׁוֹן בִּסְעוּדָה:

9 | כִּי תֵחֵל לִזְנוֹת – *Profanes herself by immorality:* The verse describes the daughter of a priest who profanes herself by having unlawful relations. Specifically, this woman was either betrothed to a man or married to him and was intimate with someone else. Now although our Sages debate the matter [that is, whether the case of a priest's daughter being burned relates to a woman who was betrothed or married], all agree that Scripture is not discussing a daughter who was single.

ט | כִּי תֵחֵל לִזְנוֹת. כְּשֶׁתִּתְחַלֵּל עַל יְדֵי זְנוּת, שֶׁהָיְתָה בָּהּ זִיקַת בַּעַל וְזָנְתָה אוֹ מִן הָאֵרוּסִין אוֹ מִן הַנִּשּׂוּאִין. וְרַבּוֹתֵינוּ נֶחְלְקוּ בַּדָּבָר, וְהַכֹּל מוֹדִים שֶׁלֹּא דִּבֵּר הַכָּתוּב בִּפְנוּיָה:

אֶת־אָבִיהָ הִיא מְחַלֶּלֶת – *She profanes her father also:* Through the daughter's behavior she has profaned and impugned her father's honor. For the neighbors will all say: Cursed be this man who fathered and who raised such a promiscuous daughter.

אֶת־אָבִיהָ הִיא מְחַלֶּלֶת. חִלְּלָה וּבִזְּתָה אֶת כְּבוֹדוֹ, שֶׁאוֹמְרִים עָלָיו: אָרוּר שֶׁזּוֹ יָלַד, אָרוּר שֶׁזּוֹ גִּדֵּל:

10 | לֹא יִפְרָע – *Shall not dishevel his hair:* The High Priest may not allow his hair to grow wild in mourning for the dead. And what constitutes an unacceptable length? More than thirty days' growth creates a violation.

י | לֹא יִפְרָע. לֹא יְגַדֵּל פֶּרַע עַל אֵבֶל, וְאֵיזֶהוּ גִּדּוּל פֶּרַע? יוֹתֵר מִשְּׁלֹשִׁים יוֹם:

11 | וְעַל כָּל־נַפְשֹׁת מֵת – *He shall not go near the dead:* The High Priest is cautioned not to enter a tent in which a corpse lies. [The preposition *al* suggests "within."]

יא | וְעַל כָּל־נַפְשֹׁת מֵת. בְּאֹהֶל הַמֵּת:

נַפְשֹׁת מֵת – *The dead:* [The superfluous term *nafshot* serves] to include a quarter of a *log* of blood. That amount of blood can transmit impurity to a priest who enters a tent [that is, a room] where it lies [even if the rest of the corpse is not there].

נַפְשֹׁת מֵת. לְהָבִיא רְבִיעִית דָּם מִן הַמֵּת שֶׁמְּטַמֵּא בְּאֹהֶל:

◀

ט יְהוָה מְקַדִּשְׁכֶם: וּבַת אִישׁ כֹּהֵן כִּי תֵחֵל לִזְנוֹת אֶת־
י אָבִיהָ הִיא מְחַלֶּלֶת בָּאֵשׁ תִּשָּׂרֵף: וְהַכֹּהֵן
הַגָּדוֹל מֵאֶחָיו אֲשֶׁר־יוּצַק עַל־רֹאשׁוֹ | שֶׁמֶן הַמִּשְׁחָה
וּמִלֵּא אֶת־יָדוֹ לִלְבֹּשׁ אֶת־הַבְּגָדִים אֶת־רֹאשׁוֹ לֹא
יא יִפְרָע וּבְגָדָיו לֹא יִפְרֹם: וְעַל כָּל־נַפְשֹׁת מֵת לֹא יָבֹא
יב לְאָבִיו וּלְאִמּוֹ לֹא יִטַּמָּא: וּמִן־הַמִּקְדָּשׁ לֹא יֵצֵא
וְלֹא יְחַלֵּל אֵת מִקְדַּשׁ אֱלֹהָיו כִּי נֵזֶר שֶׁמֶן מִשְׁחַת
יג אֱלֹהָיו עָלָיו אֲנִי יְהוָה: • וְהוּא אִשָּׁה בִבְתוּלֶיהָ יִקָּח:
יד אַלְמָנָה וּגְרוּשָׁה וַחֲלָלָה זֹנָה אֶת־אֵלֶּה לֹא יִקָּח כִּי

לְאָבִיו וּלְאִמּוֹ לֹא יִטַּמָּא – *Even for his father or mother he shall not render himself impure:* [The verse emphasizes that a High Priest may not become impure through contact with his deceased parents] to stress that in contrast, he may become impure in order to bury a *met mitzva* [someone who has no relatives or friends to tend to his or her burial].

12 | **וּמִן־הַמִּקְדָּשׁ לֹא יֵצֵא** – *He shall not leave the Sanctuary:* Should a High Priest's parent die, he may not follow the bier during the funeral procession. Furthermore, our Sages learn from here that the High Priest continues to offer sacrifices despite the fact that he is an *onen* [a mourner whose relative has yet to be buried.] This then is the sense of the verse: Even if the High Priest's father or mother dies, he need not leave the Temple, but may continue to participate in the sacrificial services.

וְלֹא יְחַלֵּל אֵת מִקְדַּשׁ – *He shall not…profaning his God's Sanctuary:* [If the High Priest serves in the Temple following the death of a relative] he does not thereby profane the services he performs, since the Torah has permitted him to act in the usual manner. However, the service of a regular priest would be disqualified if he works while he is an *onen* [a mourner whose relative has yet to be buried].

14 | **וַחֲלָלָה** – *One profaned by immorality:* This refers to a woman born to a mother who was disqualified from marrying a priest [and yet did].

לְאָבִיו וּלְאִמּוֹ לֹא יִטַּמָּא. לֹא בָּא אֶלָּא לְהַתִּיר לוֹ מֵת מִצְוָה:

יב | וּמִן־הַמִּקְדָּשׁ לֹא יֵצֵא. אֵינוֹ הוֹלֵךְ אַחַר הַמִּטָּה. וְעוֹד, מִכָּאן לָמְדוּ רַבּוֹתֵינוּ שֶׁכֹּהֵן גָּדוֹל מַקְרִיב אוֹנֵן, וְכֵן מַשְׁמָעוֹ: אַף אִם מֵתוּ אָבִיו וְאִמּוֹ אֵינוֹ צָרִיךְ לָצֵאת מִן הַמִּקְדָּשׁ, אֶלָּא עוֹבֵד עֲבוֹדָה:

וְלֹא יְחַלֵּל אֵת מִקְדַּשׁ. שֶׁאֵינוֹ מְחַלֵּל בְּכָךְ אֶת הָעֲבוֹדָה, שֶׁהִתִּיר לוֹ הַכָּתוּב, הָא כֹּהֵן הֶדְיוֹט שֶׁעָבַד אוֹנֵן, חִלֵּל:

יד | וַחֲלָלָה. שֶׁנּוֹלְדָה מִפְּסוּלֵי כְהֻנָּה:

15 He may marry only a virgin from his own people, so that he
will not profane his children among his people, for I, the LORD,
16 sanctify him." ◂ The LORD spoke to Moshe: "Tell SHENI
17 Aharon: Any of your future descendants who has a physical
blemish may not draw close to present foodstuff offerings to
18 his God. No one with a blemish shall approach: this includes
19 one who is blind, lame, disfigured, or deformed; or who has
20 a broken foot or hand; or who is a hunchback or a dwarf, or
who has a growth in his eye, a severe rash, scabs, or crushed

טו | וְלֹא־יְחַלֵּל זַרְעוֹ. הָא אִם נָשָׂא אַחַת מִן הַפְּסוּלוֹת, זַרְעוֹ הֵימֶנָּה חָלָל מִדִּין קְדֻשַּׁת כְּהֻנָּה:

15 | וְלֹא־יְחַלֵּל זַרְעוֹ – *So that he will not profane his children:* However, should a High Priest marry a woman he is ineligible to wed, his sons will be banned from the priesthood.

יז | לֶחֶם אֱלֹהָיו. מַאֲכַל אֱלֹהָיו. כָּל סְעוּדָה קְרוּיָה לֶחֶם, כְּמוֹ: "עֲבַד לְחֶם רַב" (דניאל ה, א):

17 | לֶחֶם אֱלֹהָיו – *Foodstuff offerings to his God:* The term *leḥem* here [literally, "bread"] connotes the food of God. Indeed, any meal can be referred to simply as "bread," as in the verse *Beleshatzar the king made a great banquet [leḥem rav]* (Daniel 5:1).

יח | כִּי כָל־אִישׁ אֲשֶׁר־בּוֹ מוּם לֹא יִקְרָב. אֵינוֹ דִּין שֶׁיִּקְרַב, כְּמוֹ: "הַקְרִיבֵהוּ נָא לְפֶחָתֶךָ" (מלאכי א, ח):

18 | כִּי כָל־אִישׁ אֲשֶׁר־בּוֹ מוּם לֹא יִקְרָב – *No one with a blemish shall approach:* It would be inappropriate for a blemished priest to serve in the Temple. The reasoning behind this is expressed in the verse *When you offer a blind animal to be sacrificed, is this no evil? And when you offer the lame and the sick, is this no evil? Offer it if you will to your governor* (Malachi 1:8).

חָרֻם. שֶׁחָטְמוֹ שָׁקוּעַ בֵּין שְׁתֵּי הָעֵינַיִם, שֶׁכּוֹחֵל שְׁתֵּי עֵינָיו כְּאַחַת:

חָרֻם – *Disfigured:* This refers to a person whose nose is sunken between his two eyes, allowing him to apply makeup to both eyes simultaneously.

שָׂרוּעַ. שֶׁאֶחָד מֵאֵבָרָיו גָּדוֹל מֵחֲבֵרוֹ, עֵינוֹ אַחַת גְּדוֹלָה וְעֵינוֹ אַחַת קְטַנָּה, אוֹ שׁוֹקוֹ אַחַת אֲרֻכָּה מֵחֲבֶרְתָּהּ:

שָׂרוּעַ – *Deformed:* A person with this blemish has one limb larger than the other. For example, he possesses one big eye and one small one, or one of his legs is longer than the other.

כ | אוֹ־גִבֵּן. שורצילו"ש בְּלַעַז, שֶׁגַּבִּינֵי עֵינָיו שְׂעָרָן אָרֹךְ וְשׁוֹכֵב:

20 | אוֹ־גִבֵּן – *Or who is a hunchback:* [Rashi's interpretation of this term is unlike the current translation.] The term in Old French for this part of the face is *sourcils* ["eyebrows"], and the condition described refers to a person with excessively long eyebrow hairs which lie over his eyes.

אוֹ־דַק. שֶׁיֵּשׁ לוֹ בְּעֵינוֹ דַּק שֶׁקּוֹרִין טייל"א, כְּמוֹ "הַנּוֹטֶה כַדֹּק" (ישעיה מ, כב):

אוֹ־דַק – *Or a dwarf:* [Rashi's interpretation of this term is unlike the current translation.] This refers to a person who has a *dok* [a membrane on top of his pupil], which is called *teile* ["eye web"] in Old French. We find this word in the verse *He spreads out the skies like a canvas [khadok]* (Isaiah 40:22).

◀

טו אִם־בְּתוּלָה מֵעַמָּיו יִקַּח אִשָּׁה: וְלֹא־יְחַלֵּל זַרְעוֹ
טז בְּעַמָּיו כִּי אֲנִי יהוה מְקַדְּשׁוֹ: ▸ וַיְדַבֵּר שני
יז יהוה אֶל־מֹשֶׁה לֵּאמֹר: דַּבֵּר אֶל־אַהֲרֹן לֵאמֹר
אִישׁ מִזַּרְעֲךָ לְדֹרֹתָם אֲשֶׁר יִהְיֶה בוֹ מוּם לֹא יִקְרַב
יח לְהַקְרִיב לֶחֶם אֱלֹהָיו: כִּי כָל־אִישׁ אֲשֶׁר־בּוֹ מוּם לֹא
יט יִקְרָב אִישׁ עִוֵּר אוֹ פִסֵּחַ אוֹ חָרֻם אוֹ שָׂרוּעַ: אוֹ אִישׁ
כ אֲשֶׁר־יִהְיֶה בוֹ שֶׁבֶר רָגֶל אוֹ שֶׁבֶר יָד: אוֹ־גִבֵּן אוֹ־דַק
אוֹ תְּבַלֻּל בְּעֵינוֹ אוֹ גָרָב אוֹ יַלֶּפֶת אוֹ מְרוֹחַ אָשֶׁךְ:

אוֹ תְבַלֻּל. דָּבָר הַמְבַלְבֵּל אֶת הָעַיִן, כְּגוֹן חוּט לָבָן הַנִּמְשָׁךְ מִן הַלָּבָן וּפוֹסֵק בַּסִּירָה, שֶׁהוּא עִגּוּל הַמַּקִּיף אֶת הַשָּׁחוֹר שֶׁקּוֹרִין פרוניל״א, וְהַחוּט הַזֶּה פּוֹסֵק אֶת הָעִגּוּל וְנִכְנָס בַּשָּׁחוֹר. וְתַרְגּוּם ״תְּבַלֻּל״: ״חִלִּיז״, לְשׁוֹן חִלָּזוֹן, שֶׁהוּא דּוֹמֶה לְתוֹלַעַת – אוֹתוֹ הַחוּט, וְכֵן כִּנּוּהוּ חַכְמֵי יִשְׂרָאֵל בְּמוּמֵי הַבְּכוֹר, חִלָּזוֹן נָחָשׁ עָנָב:

גָּרָב אוֹ יַלֶּפֶת. מִינֵי שְׁחִין הֵם. ״גָּרָב״ זוֹ הַחֶרֶס, שְׁחִין הַיָּבֵשׁ מִבִּפְנִים וּמִבַּחוּץ. ״יַלֶּפֶת״ הִיא חֲזָזִית הַמִּצְרִית, וְלָמָּה נִקְרֵאת ״יַלֶּפֶת״? שֶׁמְּלַפֶּפֶת וְהוֹלֶכֶת עַד יוֹם הַמִּיתָה, וְהוּא לַח מִבַּחוּץ וְיָבֵשׁ מִבִּפְנִים. וּבְמָקוֹם אַחֵר קוֹרֵא לְגָרָב שְׁחִין הַלַּח מִבַּחוּץ וְיָבֵשׁ מִבִּפְנִים, שֶׁנֶּאֱמַר: ״וּבַגָּרָב וּבֶחָרֶס״ (דברים כח, כז), כְּשֶׁסָּמַךְ גָּרָב אֵצֶל חֶרֶס קוֹרֵא לְיַלֶּפֶת ״גָּרָב״, וּכְשֶׁהוּא סָמוּךְ אֵצֶל יַלֶּפֶת קוֹרֵא לְחֶרֶס ״גָּרָב״, כָּךְ מְפֹרָשׁ בִּבְכוֹרוֹת (דף מא ע״א):

אוֹ תְבַלֻּל – *Or who has a growth in his eye: Tevallul* is something which muddles [*mevalbel*] a person's eye. It is like a white thread which extends from the white of the eye and pierces the iris – the round ring that surrounds the pupil, called *prunele* in Old French. This thread divides the iris and enters the pupil [so that the white and the black of the eye mingle]. The Targum renders the term *tevallul* as *ḥilliz* which derives from the word *ḥillazon* [a sea snail], since the thread resembles that creature. The Sages of Israel list the *tevallul* among the blemishes that disqualify a firstborn calf [from being sacrificed], referring to it as a *ḥillazon*, a snake, or a grape [since it resembles these entities].

גָּרָב אוֹ יַלֶּפֶת – *A severe rash, scabs:* These terms refer to various types of boils. A bout of *garav* makes the skin hard like earthenware [*ḥeres*] with boils which are dry both inside and out. The name *yallefet* relates to the Egyptian lichen. It is so called because it cleaves ever closer [*melappefet*] to the victim's skin as the condition worsens, until it kills him. This rash is moist on the outside while remaining dry on the inside. It is true that elsewhere the text refers to this type of boil as *garav*, in the verse *The Lord will afflict you with the boils of Egypt, with hemorrhoids, rashes [uvagarav], and scabs [uvḥares], from which you shall never recover* (Deuteronomy 28:27.) [Since the term *ḥeres* – usually "earthenware" – refers to boils which are dry externally and internally, *garav* implies boils which are dry on the inside but moist outside.] Hence, we must explain that when the text mentions *garav* together with *ḥeres*, it is

◀

21 testicles. No descendant of Aharon the priest who has a physical blemish shall draw near to present the Lord's fire offerings; because of his blemish, he shall not approach to present
22 an offering of foodstuffs to his God. He may eat the foodstuff
23 offerings of his God, the holy of holies as well as the holy. But
he may not come close to the inner curtain or approach the
altar, because of his blemish; he shall not profane My Sanctu-
24 ary; I am the Lord who makes them holy." Moshe told this to
Aharon, his sons, and all the Israelites.

the Egyptian boils [which are wet outside] which are called *garav*. However, when the term *garav* appears in conjunction with *yallefet*, then the word *garav* connotes the thoroughly dry type of boils. This is the explanation given in the Talmud (Bekhorot 41a).

מְרוֹחַ אָשֶׁךְ – *Crushed testicles:* The Targum renders this term as *meris paḥdin*, meaning that the sufferer's testicles are crushed. We find the word *paḥadin* referring to testicles in the verse *The tendons of his testicles [paḥadav]are woven together* (Job 40:17).

מְרוֹחַ אָשֶׁךְ. לְפִי הַתַּרְגּוּם "מְרִיס פַּחְדִּין", שֶׁפַּחְדָּיו מְרֻסָּסִין, שֶׁבֵּיצָיו שֶׁלּוֹ כְּתוּתִין. "פַּחְדִּין" כְּמוֹ: "גִּידֵי פַחֲדָו יְשֹׂרָגוּ" (איוב מ, יז):

21 | **כָּל־אִישׁ אֲשֶׁר־בּוֹ מוּם** – *No one who has a physical blemish:* This clause serves to include people with other defects [not listed here].

כא | כָּל־אִישׁ אֲשֶׁר־בּוֹ מוּם. לְרַבּוֹת שְׁאָר מוּמִין:

מוּם בּוֹ – *Because of his blemish:* The priest may not serve as long as he suffers from the blemish. However, if he recovers from his condition, he is eligible to work in the Temple.

מוּם בּוֹ. בְּעוֹד מוּמוֹ בּוֹ פָּסוּל, הָא אִם עָבַר מוּמוֹ – כָּשֵׁר:

לֶחֶם אֱלֹהָיו – *Foodstuff offerings to his God:* The word *leḥem* is a general term for food.

לֶחֶם אֱלֹהָיו. כָּל מַאֲכָל קָרוּי לֶחֶם:

22 | **מִקָּדְשֵׁי הַקֳּדָשִׁים** – *The holy of holies:* This refers to the sacrifices with the highest degree of sanctity [such as the purification offering and the guilt offerings].

כב | מִקָּדְשֵׁי הַקֳּדָשִׁים. אֵלּוּ קָדְשֵׁי הַקֳּדָשִׁים:

וּמִן־הַקֳּדָשִׁים יֹאכֵל – *He may eat the holy as well:* This refers to the sacrifices with a lower degree of sanctity [such as peace offerings. One might ask why this second category has to be specified, considering that the text has already allowed a blemished priest to eat the holier type of sacrificial meat]. Had mention not been made of the lower level of offering, we might have argued that in fact the Torah only permits the blemished person to partake of the most sacred sacrifices, since there was one occasion when that type of meat was

וּמִן־הַקֳּדָשִׁים יֹאכֵל. אֵלּוּ קָדָשִׁים קַלִּים. וְאִם נֶאֶמְרוּ קָדְשֵׁי הַקֳּדָשִׁים לָמָּה נֶאֱמַר קָדָשִׁים קַלִּים? אִם לֹא נֶאֱמַר הָיִיתִי אוֹמֵר, בְּקָדְשֵׁי הַקֳּדָשִׁים יֹאכַל בַּעַל מוּם, שֶׁמָּצִינוּ שֶׁהֻתְּרוּ לְזָר, שֶׁאָכַל מֹשֶׁה בְּשַׂר הַמִּלּוּאִים, אֲבָל בְּחָזֶה וָשׁוֹק שֶׁל קָדָשִׁים קַלִּים לֹא יֹאכַל, שֶׁלֹּא

כא כָּל־אִישׁ אֲשֶׁר־בּוֹ מוּם מִזֶּרַע אַהֲרֹן הַכֹּהֵן לֹא יִגַּשׁ
לְהַקְרִיב אֶת־אִשֵּׁי יְהֹוָה מוּם בּוֹ אֵת לֶחֶם אֱלֹהָיו
כב לֹא יִגַּשׁ לְהַקְרִיב: לֶחֶם אֱלֹהָיו מִקָּדְשֵׁי הַקֳּדָשִׁים
כג וּמִן־הַקֳּדָשִׁים יֹאכֵל: אַךְ אֶל־הַפָּרֹכֶת לֹא יָבֹא וְאֶל־
הַמִּזְבֵּחַ לֹא יִגַּשׁ כִּי־מוּם בּוֹ וְלֹא יְחַלֵּל אֶת־מִקְדָּשַׁי כִּי
כד אֲנִי יְהֹוָה מְקַדְּשָׁם: וַיְדַבֵּר מֹשֶׁה אֶל־אַהֲרֹן וְאֶל־בָּנָיו
וְאֶל־כָּל־בְּנֵי יִשְׂרָאֵל:

given to a non-priest. This refers to Moshe who was allowed to eat from the inaugural offerings [as stated in 8:29, despite the fact that those were a type of *kodshei kodashim*. This shows a leniency which might be extended to blemished priests]. Perhaps, however, a blemished person would not be permitted to eat the breast and thigh of the lesser types of sacrifices [the *kodashim kalim*] for we find no instance where a non-priest is given a share in these parts. This is why the Torah emphasizes that a blemished priest may eat even these. This is the interpretation found in the Talmud (Zevaḥim 101b).

מָצִינוּ זָר חוֹלֵק בָּהֶן, לְכָךְ נֶאֶמְרוּ קָדָשִׁים קַלִּים. כָּךְ מְפֹרָשׁ בִּזְבָחִים (דף קא ע״ב):

23 | אַךְ אֶל־הַפָּרֹכֶת – *But he may not come close to the inner curtain:* A blemished priest may not approach the inner curtain in order to sprinkle sacrificial blood toward it seven times. [That procedure is performed on rare occasions; see, for example, 4:17.]

כג | אַךְ אֶל־הַפָּרֹכֶת. לְהַזּוֹת שֶׁבַע הַזָּיוֹת שֶׁעַל הַפָּרֹכֶת:

וְאֶל־הַמִּזְבֵּחַ – *Or the altar:* This refers to the outer sacrificial altar. The Sifra (3:10) explains why both of these details need be mentioned. [After all, if a blemished priest cannot serve at the altar, then surely he may not enter the Sanctuary to work there. The Sages' explanation is that the casting of the blood inside might not be viewed as an actual sacrificial service.]

וְאֶל־הַמִּזְבֵּחַ. הַחִיצוֹן, וּשְׁנֵיהֶם הֻצְרְכוּ לִכָּתֵב, וּמְפֹרָשׁ בְּתוֹרַת כֹּהֲנִים (פרק ג, י):

וְלֹא יְחַלֵּל אֶת־מִקְדָּשַׁי – *He shall not profane My Sanctuary:* If such a priest unlawfully serves, the work he has performed is profane and disqualified.

וְלֹא יְחַלֵּל אֶת־מִקְדָּשַׁי. שֶׁאִם עָבַד, עֲבוֹדָתוֹ מְחֻלֶּלֶת לִפָּסֵל:

24 | וַיְדַבֵּר מֹשֶׁה – *Moshe told:* Moshe related this particular commandment [regarding the service of blemished priests].

כד | וַיְדַבֵּר מֹשֶׁה. הַמִּצְוָה הַזֹּאת:

אֶל־אַהֲרֹן... וְאֶל־כָּל־בְּנֵי יִשְׂרָאֵל – *To Aharon, his sons, and all the Israelites:* [It appears unnecessary to communicate these laws

אֶל־אַהֲרֹן וְגוֹ׳ וְאֶל־כָּל־בְּנֵי יִשְׂרָאֵל. לְהַזְהִיר בֵּית דִּין עַל הַכֹּהֲנִים:

22 1 2 The LORD spoke to Moshe: "Tell Aharon and his sons to take
great care with the sacred offerings that the Israelites consecrate to Me, so that they do not profane My holy name: I am
3 the LORD. Tell them: If any descendant of yours throughout
the generations comes near the sacred offerings that the Israelites have consecrated to the LORD while in an impure
state, he shall be severed from My presence; I am the LORD.

to the Israelites, who are not required to observe them.] This warning is intended for the courts, which are responsible for overseeing the priests.

כב ב | **וְיִנָּזְרוּ**. אֵין נְזִירָה אֶלָּא פְּרִישָׁה, וְכֵן הוּא אוֹמֵר "וְיִנָּזֵר מֵאַחֲרַי" (יחזקאל יד, ז), "נָזֹרוּ אָחוֹר" (ישעיהו א, ד), יִפְרְשׁוּ מִן הַקֳּדָשִׁים בִּימֵי טֻמְאָתָן: וְיִנָּזְרוּ מִקָּדְשֵׁי בְנֵי יִשְׂרָאֵל, אֲשֶׁר הֵם מַקְדִּשִׁים לִי, וְלֹא יְחַלְּלוּ אֶת שֵׁם קָדְשִׁי. סָרֵס הַמִּקְרָא וְדָרְשֵׁהוּ:

22 2 | **וְיִנָּזְרוּ** – *To take great care with:* The term *nezira* connotes "separation," as in the verse *For any man... who becomes estranged [veyinnazer] from me* (Ezekiel 14:7) and the verse *They fell away [nazoru aḥor]* (Isaiah 1:4). The present verse warns that priests must distance themselves from the sacrifices at times when they are impure [and may not eat sacrificial meat when in that state]. Those priests must desist from *the sacred offerings that the Israelites consecrate to Me*, and that which *they consecrate to Me*, in order that *they do not profane My holy name*. The clauses of this verse must be transposed to be understood correctly. [The Hebrew original reads literally: Tell Aharon and his sons to take great care with the sacred offerings (a) that the Israelites consecrate to Me, (b) so that they do not profane My holy name, (c) that which they consecrate to Me. The first clause refers to the sacrifices that the nation brings to God, while the third clause relates to those which the priests themselves offer. According to Rashi, (c) should be inserted between (a) and (b) to teach that the service of impure priests will also defile sacrifices brought by the priestly class.]

אֲשֶׁר הֵם מַקְדִּשִׁים לִי. לְרַבּוֹת קָדְשֵׁי כֹּהֲנִים עַצְמָן:

אֲשֶׁר הֵם מַקְדִּשִׁים לִי – *That which they consecrate to Me:* This refers to the sacrifices offered by the priests themselves.

ג | **כָּל־אִישׁ אֲשֶׁר־יִקְרַב**. אֵין קְרִיבָה זוֹ אֶלָּא אֲכִילָה, וְכֵן מָצִינוּ שֶׁנֶּאֶמְרָה אַזְהָרַת אֲכִילַת קָדָשִׁים בְּטֻמְאָה בִּלְשׁוֹן נְגִיעָה: "בְּכָל קֹדֶשׁ לֹא תִגָּע" (ויקרא יב, ד) אַזְהָרָה לָאוֹכֵל, וּלְמָדוּהָ רַבּוֹתֵינוּ מִגְּזֵרָה שָׁוָה. וְאִי אֶפְשָׁר לוֹמַר שֶׁחַיָּב עַל הַנְּגִיעָה, שֶׁהֲרֵי נֶאֱמַר כָּרֵת עַל הָאֲכִילָה בְּצַו

3 | **כָּל־אִישׁ אֲשֶׁר־יִקְרַב** – *If any descendant comes near:* "Coming near" in this context refers to eating [and not merely getting close to the sacred offerings]. Indeed, we find that the Torah warns against an impure person eating sacrificial meat by using the language of "touching," as in the verse *She [a woman who has given birth] must not touch anything holy or enter the Sanctuary* (12:4). That actually represents a prohibition against eating, as the Sages learn through a *gezera shava*

◀

ב א ב וַיְדַבֵּר יְהוָה אֶל־מֹשֶׁה לֵּאמֹר: דַּבֵּר אֶל־אַהֲרֹן
וְאֶל־בָּנָיו וְיִנָּזְרוּ מִקָּדְשֵׁי בְנֵי־יִשְׂרָאֵל וְלֹא יְחַלְּלוּ
אֶת־שֵׁם קָדְשִׁי אֲשֶׁר הֵם מַקְדִּשִׁים לִי אֲנִי יְהוָה:
ג אֱמֹר אֲלֵהֶם לְדֹרֹתֵיכֶם כָּל־אִישׁ ׀ אֲשֶׁר־יִקְרַב מִכָּל־
זַרְעֲכֶם אֶל־הַקֳּדָשִׁים אֲשֶׁר יַקְדִּישׁוּ בְנֵי־יִשְׂרָאֵל
לַיהוָה וְטֻמְאָתוֹ עָלָיו וְנִכְרְתָה הַנֶּפֶשׁ הַהִוא מִלְּפָנַי

["verbal analogy"]. Now it is impossible to interpret the text as saying that one who touches sacrificial meat is subject to the death penalty based on this reasoning: The Torah warns of excision with regard to eating sacred food in Parashat Tzav (in 7:20–21), a passage which twice mentions that punishment. And if a person deserved excision for merely touching holy items when impure, then surely there would be no need to refer to sentencing him for eating such foods [since eating is more severe than touching, and furthermore, one must touch food in order to eat it]. Additionally, the Sifra (4:7) argues as follows. Since one does not receive excision for touching sacred meat when impure, why does the text use the words *asher yikrav* – "who might come near"? What the verse thereby teaches is that if an impure priest eats the meat, he would only be held liable if that which renders the meat permissible for consumption [for pure priests] had already brought near [that is, had been offered on the altar. When portions of a sacrificial animal are given to the priests to eat, such as in the case of a purification offering, these may only be consumed once the relevant body parts have been sacrificed, and the blood has been cast against the altar]. The reader might wonder why the Torah threatens excision three times [that is, once in the present verse and twice in 7:20–21] with regard to an impure priest eating sacred food. The Sages explain this point in Shevuot 7a and maintain that one instance represents a general statement, and one a particular statement. [See Rashi's comments to 7:20 for a fuller analysis of this argument.]

אֶת אַהֲרֹן, שְׁתֵּי כְּרֵתוֹת זוֹ אֵצֶל זוֹ (לעיל ז, כ-כא), וְאִם עַל הַנְּגִיעָה חַיָּב, לֹא הֻצְרַךְ לְחַיְּבוֹ עַל הָאֲכִילָה. וְכֵן נִדְרַשׁ בְּתוֹרַת כֹּהֲנִים (פרשתא ד, ז): וְכִי יֵשׁ נוֹגֵעַ חַיָּב? אִם כֵּן מַה תַּלְמוּד לוֹמַר: "יִקְרַב"? מִשֶּׁיִּכְשַׁר לִקְרַב, שֶׁאֵין חַיָּבִין עָלָיו מִשּׁוּם טֻמְאָה אֶלָּא אִם כֵּן קָרְבוּ מַתִּירָיו. וְאִם תֹּאמַר, שָׁלֹשׁ כְּרֵתוֹת בְּטֻמְאַת כֹּהֲנִים לָמָּה? כְּבָר נִדְרְשׁוּ בְּמַסֶּכֶת שְׁבוּעוֹת (דף ז ע״א), אַחַת לִכְלָל וְאַחַת לִפְרָט וְכוּ׳:

וְטֻמְאָתוֹ עָלָיו – *While in an impure state:* The verse refers to the impurity of the human being [that is, the pronouns relate to the priest who is the subject of the verse]. Still, perhaps the text is discussing the impurity of the meat itself, meaning ◀

וְטֻמְאָתוֹ עָלָיו. וְטֻמְאַת הָאָדָם עָלָיו. יָכוֹל בַּבָּשָׂר הַכָּתוּב מְדַבֵּר, וְטֻמְאָתוֹ שֶׁל בָּשָׂר עָלָיו, וּבְטָהוֹר שֶׁאָכַל אֶת הַטָּמֵא הַכָּתוּב מְדַבֵּר? עַל כָּרְחֲךָ

4 Any descendant of Aharon who has a defiling blight of the
skin or a discharge may not eat of the sacred offerings until
he becomes pure. One who touches anything made impure
by contact with the dead, or who has had a seminal emission,
5 or who has touched any swarming thing or any person who
6 renders him impure – whatever his impurity – the one who
touches these things shall be impure until the evening, and
shall not eat of the sacred offerings until he has washed his
7 body in water. When the sun sets, he shall become pure again
8 and may eat of the sacred offerings, for they are his food. He
may not eat an animal found dead or one that was torn by

that a pure person who eats meat while the flesh is impure [is liable for excision]? No, we are forced to interpret the verse as describing impurity that can be removed. [The emphasis of *vetum'ato alav* – "his impurity is upon him" – suggests a state where the impurity is no longer upon him.] Hence, it must refer to a person who can be purified through immersion. [However, once food becomes impure, that state can never be corrected.]

מִמַּשְׁמָעוֹ חַיָּה לָמֵד, בְּמִי שֶׁטֻּמְאָתוֹ פּוֹרַחַת מִמֶּנּוּ הַכָּתוּב מְדַבֵּר, וְזֶהוּ הָאָדָם שֶׁיֵּשׁ לוֹ טָהֳרָה בִּטְבִילָה:

וְנִכְרְתָה – *He shall be severed:* Perhaps the text refers [not to excision which is a divine form of punishment such as dying young, but] to the offender being uprooted from the community he lives in and forced to relocate to a different locality. No, for the verse concludes with the words *I am the Lord*, meaning "I exist in all places." [There can be no separation from God just by moving from one place to another, since God is omnipresent. Hence, the severance must refer to taking the person out of the world altogether.]

וְנִכְרְתָה וְגוֹ'. יָכוֹל מִצַּד זֶה לְצַד זֶה, יִכָּרֵת מִמְּקוֹמוֹ וְיִתְיַשֵּׁב בְּמָקוֹם אַחֵר? תַּלְמוּד לוֹמַר: "אֲנִי ה'", בְּכָל מָקוֹם אֲנִי:

4 | **בְּכָל־טְמֵא־נֶפֶשׁ** – *By contact with the dead:* This refers to one who has touched a corpse. [A human corpse represents the ultimate source of impurity. A person who touches a dead body becomes a source of impurity. One who touches *that* living person becomes impure to the first degree of impurity. It is to the latter circumstance that the present verse refers: a priest who touches a person who has previously touched a corpse. The next verse mentions a priest touching an actual dead body.]

ד | **בְּכָל־טְמֵא־נֶפֶשׁ.** בְּמִי שֶׁנִּטְמָא בְּמֵת:

5 | **בְּכָל־שֶׁרֶץ אֲשֶׁר יִטְמָא־לוֹ** – *Or who has touched any swarming thing that renders him impure:* [The words "who renders him impure" limit this circumstance to one where] the creature's

ה | **בְּכָל־שֶׁרֶץ אֲשֶׁר יִטְמָא־לוֹ.** בְּשִׁעוּר הָרָאוּי לְטַמֵּא, בְּכַעֲדָשָׁה:

ד אֲנִי יְהוָה: אִישׁ אִישׁ מִזֶּרַע אַהֲרֹן וְהוּא צָרוּעַ אוֹ
זָב בַּקֳּדָשִׁים לֹא יֹאכַל עַד אֲשֶׁר יִטְהָר וְהַנֹּגֵעַ בְּכָל־
טְמֵא־נֶפֶשׁ אוֹ אִישׁ אֲשֶׁר־תֵּצֵא מִמֶּנּוּ שִׁכְבַת־זָרַע:
ה אוֹ־אִישׁ אֲשֶׁר יִגַּע בְּכָל־שֶׁרֶץ אֲשֶׁר יִטְמָא־לוֹ אוֹ
ו בְאָדָם אֲשֶׁר יִטְמָא־לוֹ לְכֹל טֻמְאָתוֹ: נֶפֶשׁ אֲשֶׁר
תִּגַּע־בּוֹ וְטָמְאָה עַד־הָעָרֶב וְלֹא יֹאכַל מִן־הַקֳּדָשִׁים
ז כִּי אִם־רָחַץ בְּשָׂרוֹ בַּמָּיִם: וּבָא הַשֶּׁמֶשׁ וְטָהֵר וְאַחַר
ח יֹאכַל מִן־הַקֳּדָשִׁים כִּי לַחְמוֹ הוּא: נְבֵלָה וּטְרֵפָה לֹא

carcass is the requisite size to transmit impurity, meaning that its volume is equal to at least that of a lentil.

אוֹ בְאָדָם – *Or any person:* This refers to a corpse.

אֲשֶׁר יִטְמָא־לוֹ – *Which renders him impure:* This refers to a priest who touches a part of the corpse which has the requisite size to transmit impurity, meaning at least the volume of an olive.

לְכֹל טֻמְאָתוֹ – *Whatever his impurity:* This last phrase serves to include a priest who touches a *zav*, a *zava*, a *nidda*, or a woman who has given birth. [All of these people are considered sources of impurity, and a second party who touches them contracts impurity to the first degree.]

6 | **נֶפֶשׁ אֲשֶׁר תִּגַּע־בּוֹ** – *The one who touches these things:* The priest need only touch one of these sources of impurity [to be barred from eating sacred offerings].

7 | **וְאַחַר יֹאכַל מִן־הַקֳּדָשִׁים** – *And may eat of the sacred offerings:* The Talmud (Yevamot 74b) teaches that this refers to *teruma* [the agricultural gifts given to priests]. That may be eaten [by the priest who was impure and immersed himself] once the sun sets.

מִן־הַקֳּדָשִׁים – *Of the sacred offerings:* When the sun sets, the purified priest may eat some of the sacred food, but not all of it.

8 | **נְבֵלָה וּטְרֵפָה לֹא יֹאכַל לְטָמְאָה־בָהּ** – *He may not eat an animal found dead or one that was torn by wild animals, becoming impure by doing so:* [The straightforward meaning of the verse

אוֹ בְאָדָם. בְּמֵת:

אֲשֶׁר יִטְמָא־לוֹ. כְּשִׁעוּרוֹ לְטַמֵּא, וְזֶהוּ כְּזַיִת:

לְכֹל טֻמְאָתוֹ. לְרַבּוֹת נוֹגֵעַ בְּזָב וְזָבָה נִדָּה וְיוֹלֶדֶת:

ו | נֶפֶשׁ אֲשֶׁר תִּגַּע־בּוֹ. בְּאֶחָד מִן הַטְּמֵאִים הַלָּלוּ:

ז | וְאַחַר יֹאכַל מִן־הַקֳּדָשִׁים. נִדְרַשׁ בִּיבָמוֹת (דף עד ע״ב) בִּתְרוּמָה, שֶׁמֻּתֶּר לֶאֱכֹל בְּהַעֲרֵב הַשֶּׁמֶשׁ:

מִן־הַקֳּדָשִׁים. וְלֹא כָּל הַקֳּדָשִׁים:

ח | נְבֵלָה וּטְרֵפָה לֹא יֹאכַל לְטָמְאָה־בָהּ. לְעִנְיַן הַטֻּמְאָה הִזְהִיר כָּאן, שֶׁאִם אָכַל נִבְלַת עוֹף

◀

wild animals, becoming impure by doing so; I am the LORD.
9 They shall keep My charge and not bear guilt and die through
it, having profaned it. I am the LORD, who makes them holy.
10 No layman may eat of the sacred offerings, nor may a priest's
11 visitor or hired laborer eat of them. But if a priest acquires a
slave for money, the slave may eat of them, and those born
12 into his household also may eat his food. If a priest's daughter
13 marries a layman, she may no longer eat of the sacred gifts. If
a priest's daughter is a widow or a divorcée, has no children,

טָהוֹר שֶׁאֵין לָהּ טֻמְאַת מַגָּע וּמַשָּׂא אֶלָּא טֻמְאַת אֲכִילָה בְּבֵית הַבְּלִיעָה, אָסוּר לֶאֱכֹל בַּקֳּדָשִׁים. וְצָרִיךְ לוֹמַר: "וּטְרֵפָה" – מִי שֶׁיֵּשׁ בְּמִינוֹ טְרֵפָה, יָצָא נִבְלַת עוֹף טָמֵא שֶׁאֵין בְּמִינוֹ טְרֵפָה:

implies that a priest may not eat kosher animals that died in these ways. However, such a prohibition applies to all Israelites, as stated in Exodus 22:30 and Deuteronomy 14:21. Hence] the prohibition here applies to contracting impurity and refers specifically to the consumption of the carcass of a kosher bird [that has not been properly slaughtered]. Such an object does not transmit impurity by being touched or by being carried, but only by being swallowed. If a priest contracts impurity in that manner, he is forbidden to subsequently eat sacred food. Now our verse mentions *terefa* [a creature torn apart by predators, or which dies from disease] as well in order to teach that the present law applies only to animals which could possibly become a *terefa*. This excludes the carcass of a non-kosher bird which can never be a *terefa*.

ט | **וְשָׁמְרוּ אֶת־מִשְׁמַרְתִּי.** מִלֶּאֱכֹל תְּרוּמָה בְּטֻמְאַת הַגּוּף:

9 | **וְשָׁמְרוּ אֶת־מִשְׁמַרְתִּי** – *They shall keep My charge:* The priests are warned against eating *teruma* while their bodies are impure.

וּמֵתוּ בוֹ. לָמַדְנוּ שֶׁהִיא מִיתָה בִּידֵי שָׁמַיִם:

וּמֵתוּ בוֹ – *And die through it:* We learn that this refers to death at the hands of heaven.

י | **לֹא־יֹאכַל קֹדֶשׁ.** בִּתְרוּמָה הַכָּתוּב מְדַבֵּר, שֶׁכָּל הָעִנְיָן דִּבֵּר בָּהּ:

10 | **לֹא־יֹאכַל קֹדֶשׁ** – *May eat of the sacred offerings:* This too refers to the consumption of *teruma*, which is the subject of this passage.

תּוֹשַׁב כֹּהֵן וְשָׂכִיר. תּוֹשָׁבוֹ שֶׁל כֹּהֵן וּשְׂכִירוֹ, לְפִיכָךְ "תּוֹשַׁב" זֶה נָקוּד פַּתָּח, לְפִי שֶׁהוּא דָּבוּק. וְאֵיזֶהוּ תּוֹשָׁב? זֶה נִרְצָע שֶׁהוּא קָנוּי לוֹ עַד הַיּוֹבֵל; וְאֵיזֶהוּ שָׂכִיר? זֶה קְנוּי קִנְיַן שָׁנִים שֶׁיּוֹצֵא בְּשֵׁשׁ, בָּא הַכָּתוּב וְלִמֵּד כָּאן שֶׁאֵין גּוּפוֹ קָנוּי לַאֲדוֹנָיו

תּוֹשַׁב כֹּהֵן וְשָׂכִיר – *A priest's visitor or hired laborer:* [The word order of this phrase is confusing. Rashi explains the syntax: The phrase means,] A *toshav* of a priest or a *sakhir* who is working for a priest. This explains why the word *toshav* is vocalized with a *pataḥ* [under the *shin*] – that indicates that the word is in the construct form [meaning "the *toshav* of the priest." Had the vowel been a *kamatz* it would have meant "a priest who

ט יֹאכַל לְטָמְאָה־בָהּ אֲנִי יהוה: וְשָׁמְרוּ אֶת־מִשְׁמַרְתִּי
וְלֹא־יִשְׂאוּ עָלָיו חֵטְא וּמֵתוּ בוֹ כִּי יְחַלְּלֻהוּ אֲנִי יהוה
י מְקַדְּשָׁם: וְכָל־זָר לֹא־יֹאכַל קֹדֶשׁ תּוֹשַׁב כֹּהֵן וְשָׂכִיר
יא לֹא־יֹאכַל קֹדֶשׁ: וְכֹהֵן כִּי־יִקְנֶה נֶפֶשׁ קִנְיַן כַּסְפּוֹ הוּא
יב יֹאכַל בּוֹ וִילִיד בֵּיתוֹ הֵם יֹאכְלוּ בְלַחְמוֹ: וּבַת־כֹּהֵן
כִּי תִהְיֶה לְאִישׁ זָר הִוא בִּתְרוּמַת הַקֳּדָשִׁים לֹא
יג תֹאכֵל: וּבַת־כֹּהֵן כִּי תִהְיֶה אַלְמָנָה וּגְרוּשָׁה וְזֶרַע

is a *toshav*"]. And what exactly is a *toshav*? The label refers to a Hebrew slave who has had his ear pierced [after fulfilling his six years of servitude and who wishes to remain enslaved, as described in Exodus 21:6]. The master acquires such a slave until the Jubilee year [when he is released]. And what is a *sakhir*? That title applies to an Israelite who is acquired for a limited time and who goes free after six years of service. The present verse teaches that the bodies of these two types of men do not actually belong to the master, which is why they are forbidden to share the priest's *teruma*.

לֶאֱכֹל בִּתְרוּמָתוֹ:

11 | **וְכֹהֵן כִּי־יִקְנֶה נֶפֶשׁ** – *But if a priest acquires a slave:* This verse refers to a Canaanite slave whose body now belongs to his master. [Since the Canaanite slave is purchased for his body, he is entitled to eat *teruma*. A Hebrew slave who is only acquired for his labor cannot.]

יא | **וְכֹהֵן כִּי־יִקְנֶה נֶפֶשׁ.** עֶבֶד כְּנַעֲנִי שֶׁקָּנוּי לְגוּפוֹ:

וִילִיד בֵּיתוֹ – *And those born into his household:* This phrase refers to children born to the priest's maidservants. This verse also teaches that because a priest's wife is acquired with his money, she too is permitted to eat *teruma*. [Betrothal to a Jewish wife is effected by giving money to the woman.] Furthermore, we learn this point from a later verse which states: *Anyone who is ritually pure in your household may eat of them* (Numbers 18:11). This is discussed in Sifrei to Parashat Koraḥ (paragraph 117).

וִילִיד בֵּיתוֹ. אֵלּוּ בְּנֵי הַשְּׁפָחוֹת. וְאֵשֶׁת כֹּהֵן אוֹכֶלֶת בִּתְרוּמָה מִן הַמִּקְרָא הַזֶּה, שֶׁאַף הִיא קִנְיַן כַּסְפּוֹ, וְעוֹד לָמֵד מִמִּקְרָא אַחֵר: ״כָּל טָהוֹר בְּבֵיתְךָ״ וְגוֹ׳ (במדבר יח, יא), בְּסִפְרֵי (קרח קיז):

12 | **לְאִישׁ זָר** – *A layman:* In this context, a "layman" refers to a Levite or a common Israelite.

יב | **לְאִישׁ זָר.** לְלֵוִי וְיִשְׂרָאֵל:

13 | **אַלְמָנָה וּגְרוּשָׁה** – *A widow or a divorcée:* If a priest's daughter married a layman who died or divorced her…

יג | **אַלְמָנָה וּגְרוּשָׁה.** מִן הָאִישׁ הַזָּר:

and returns to live in her father's house as when she was
young, she may eat her father's food again; but no layperson
14 may do so. If someone eats of the sacred gift unintentionally,
he shall make restitution to the priest, adding an extra fifth to
15 its value. The people must not profane the sacred meats that
16 Israelites bring as offerings to the LORD or incur the penalty
of iniquity by eating their sacred offerings; for I, the LORD,
make them holy."
17 18 The LORD spoke to Moshe: "Speak to Aharon, his sons, and all SHELISHI
the Israelites. Say: When anyone of the House of Israel or of
the migrants living in Israel presents an offering to the LORD

וְזֶרַע אֵין לָהּ – *And she has no children:* From that layman husband…

וְזֶרַע אֵין לָהּ. מִמֶּנּוּ:

וְשָׁבָה – *She returns:* [The priest's daughter may return to her father's table under those circumstances.] But if she had children with her husband, she is forbidden to eat *teruma* as long as the progeny are alive.

וְשָׁבָה. הָא אִם יֵשׁ לָהּ זֶרַע מִמֶּנּוּ, אֲסוּרָה בִּתְרוּמָה כָּל זְמַן שֶׁהַזֶּרַע קַיָּם:

וְכָל־זָר לֹא־יֹאכַל בּוֹ – *But no layperson may do so:* This clause does not [forbid laypeople from eating *teruma* since that was stated explicitly in verse 10. Rather, its purpose is] to permit an *onen* [a mourner whose relative has not yet been buried] to eat *teruma*. Thus, our text emphasizes that it is the state of being a non-priest that prohibits one from eating *teruma*, and not the state of bereavement.

וְכָל־זָר לֹא־יֹאכַל בּוֹ. לֹא בָא אֶלָּא לְהוֹצִיא אֶת הָאוֹנֵן שֶׁמֻּתָּר בִּתְרוּמָה, זָרוּת אָמַרְתִּי לְךָ וְלֹא אֲנִינוּת:

14 | **וְאִישׁ כִּי־יֹאכַל קֹדֶשׁ** – *If someone eats of the sacred gift:* The text continues to discuss the consumption of *teruma*.

יד | וְאִישׁ כִּי־יֹאכַל קֹדֶשׁ. תְּרוּמָה:

וְנָתַן לַכֹּהֵן אֶת־הַקֹּדֶשׁ – *He shall make restitution to the priest:* The offender must give to the priest something which can be sanctified. [The presence of the definite article in the word *hakodesh* implies that the person must return to the priest the *teruma* which he ate. Since this is impossible, he must] give him non-sacred fruit which then become *teruma*. He cannot pay the priest cash [which cannot be made holy as *teruma*.]

וְנָתַן לַכֹּהֵן אֶת־הַקֹּדֶשׁ. דָּבָר הָרָאוּי לִהְיוֹת קֹדֶשׁ, שֶׁאֵינוֹ פּוֹרֵעַ לוֹ מָעוֹת אֶלָּא פֵּרוֹת שֶׁל חֻלִּין, וְהֵן נַעֲשִׂין תְּרוּמָה:

15 | **וְלֹא יְחַלְּלוּ** – *The people must not profane:* The priests must not feed sacred food to people who are not priests.

טו | וְלֹא יְחַלְּלוּ וְגוֹ׳. לְהַאֲכִילָם לְזָרִים:

16 | **וְהִשִּׂיאוּ אוֹתָם** – *Or incur the penalty:* By feeding *teruma* to outsiders, the priests encumber themselves with sin and guilt.

טז | וְהִשִּׂיאוּ אוֹתָם. אֶת עַצְמָם יַטְעִינוּ עָוֹן, ״בְּאָכְלָם אֶת קָדְשֵׁיהֶם״

◀

אֵין לָהּ וְשָׁבָה אֶל־בֵּית אָבִיהָ כִּנְעוּרֶיהָ מִלֶּחֶם אָבִיהָ
יד תֹּאכֵל וְכָל־זָר לֹא־יֹאכַל בּוֹ: וְאִישׁ כִּי־יֹאכַל קֹדֶשׁ
בִּשְׁגָגָה וְיָסַף חֲמִשִׁיתוֹ עָלָיו וְנָתַן לַכֹּהֵן אֶת־הַקֹּדֶשׁ:
טו וְלֹא יְחַלְּלוּ אֶת־קָדְשֵׁי בְּנֵי יִשְׂרָאֵל אֵת אֲשֶׁר־יָרִימוּ
טז לַיהוָה: וְהִשִּׂיאוּ אוֹתָם עֲוֹן אַשְׁמָה בְּאָכְלָם אֶת־
קָדְשֵׁיהֶם כִּי אֲנִי יְהוָה מְקַדְּשָׁם:
יז יח וַיְדַבֵּר יְהוָה אֶל־מֹשֶׁה לֵּאמֹר: דַּבֵּר אֶל־אַהֲרֹן וְאֶל־ יח שלישי
בָּנָיו וְאֶל כָּל־בְּנֵי יִשְׂרָאֵל וְאָמַרְתָּ אֲלֵהֶם אִישׁ אִישׁ
מִבֵּית יִשְׂרָאֵל וּמִן־הַגֵּר בְּיִשְׂרָאֵל אֲשֶׁר יַקְרִיב קָרְבָּנוֹ
לְכָל־נִדְרֵיהֶם וּלְכָל־נִדְבוֹתָם אֲשֶׁר־יַקְרִיבוּ לַיהוָה

שֶׁהֻבְדְּלוּ לְשֵׁם תְּרוּמָה וְקָדְשׁוּ, וְנֶאֶסְרוּ עֲלֵיהֶן:

For that was sacred food which was set apart and established as *teruma*; it had been sanctified and thereby rendered forbidden to others.

וְהִשִּׂיאוּ אוֹתָם. זֶה אֶחָד מִשְּׁלֹשָׁה אֶתִּים שֶׁהָיָה רַבִּי יִשְׁמָעֵאל דּוֹרֵשׁ בַּתּוֹרָה שֶׁמְּדַבְּרִים בָּאָדָם עַצְמוֹ, וְכֵן: ״בְּיוֹם מְלֹאת יְמֵי נִזְרוֹ יָבִיא אֹתוֹ״(במדבר ו, יג) – הוּא יָבִיא אֶת עַצְמוֹ, וְכֵן: ״וַיִּקְבֹּר אֹתוֹ בַגַּי״(דברים לד, ו) – הוּא קָבַר אֶת עַצְמוֹ. כָּךְ נִדְרָשׁ בְּסִפְרֵי (נשא לב):

וְהִשִּׂיאוּ אוֹתָם – *Or incur the penalty:* [Although the word *otam* usually means "them,"] according to Rabbi Yishmael, the present verse represents one of three instances where *et* has a reflexive connotation ["himself,""itself,""themselves." Hence this verse would literally be translated: "or bring upon themselves the penalty etc."]. The second such case appears in the verse *On the day that the term of his nazirite vow is completed, he shall bring himself [yavi oto] to the entrance to the Tent of Meeting* (Numbers 6:13), which in context means that the *nazir* shall bring himself [and not "he shall bring him" – someone shall bring someone else]. The third example appears in the verse *He buried himself [vayikbor oto] in Moav, in a valley opposite Beit Peor* (Deuteronomy 34:6). [Although the straightforward meaning of the text seems to report that God buried Moshe, Rabbi Yishmael maintains that the word *oto*] actually means that Moshe buried himself. This is the interpretation of the Sifrei on Parashat Naso (32).

יח | **נִדְרֵיהֶם.** הֲרֵי עָלַי:

18 | **נִדְרֵיהֶם** – *Whether in fulfillment of a vow:* A vow [*neder*] is undertaken when a person states: It is incumbent upon me to bring an offering.

◀

as a burnt offering – whether in fulfillment of a vow or as a
19 freewill offering – to be acceptable on your behalf, it must be
an unblemished male from the herd, or of the sheep or goats.
20 Do not offer anything that has a blemish, for it will not be ac-
21 cepted on your behalf. When someone presents a peace sacrifice to the Lord from the herd or flock – whether because of a
spoken vow or as a freewill offering – it must be unblemished
22 to be acceptable; there shall be no blemish on it. Do not present to the Lord anything blind, injured, or maimed, or with
warts, a severe rash, or scabs. Do not place any of these on the
23 altar as a fire offering to the Lord. You may offer as a freewill
offering an ox or sheep with a limb deformed or uncloven, but

נִדְבוֹתָם – *A freewill offering:* A donation [*nedava*] is undertaken when a person states: It is incumbent upon me to bring this specific animal as an offering.

נִדְבוֹתָם. הֲרֵי זוֹ:

19 | **לִרְצֹנְכֶם** – *To be acceptable on your behalf:* [One might have thought that this word means that the sacrifice must be brought "willingly." Rashi explains that it means instead to] bring sacrifices which are suitable for obtaining appeasement from Me; those will placate Me. The Old French term for this is *apaiemant* ["appeasement"]. Now which animal is worthy of achieving that conciliation? It is *an unblemished male from the herd, or of the sheep or goats*. On the other hand, when a bird is brought as a burnt offering, it need not be male or unblemished; it is only disqualified if it is missing limbs.

יט | לִרְצֹנְכֶם. הָבִיאוּ דָּבָר הָרָאוּי לְרַצּוֹת אֶתְכֶם לְפָנַי שֶׁיְּהֵא לָכֶם לְרָצוֹן, אפיימנ"ט בְּלַעַז. וְאֵיזֶהוּ הָרָאוּי לְרָצוֹן? "תָּמִים זָכָר בַּבָּקָר בַּכְּשָׂבִים וּבָעִזִּים". אֲבָל בְּעוֹלַת הָעוֹף אֵין צָרִיךְ תַּמּוּת וְזַכְרוּת, וְאֵינוֹ נִפְסָל בְּמוּם אֶלָּא בְּחֶסְרוֹן אֵיבָר:

21 | **לְפַלֵּא־נֶדֶר** – *Because of a spoken vow:* The person wishes to fulfill a vow that he or she had expressed verbally.

כא | לְפַלֵּא־נֶדֶר. לְהַפְרִישׁ בְּדִבּוּרוֹ:

22 | **עַוֶּרֶת** – *Blind:* The term *avveret* is a noun in the feminine form meaning "blindness." The verse thus informs us that the animal "should not suffer from" [*lo yihyeh bo,* in the previous verse] the blemish of blindness.

כב | עַוֶּרֶת. שֵׁם דָּבָר שֶׁל מוּם עִוָּרוֹן בִּלְשׁוֹן נְקֵבָה, שֶׁלֹּא יְהֵא בוֹ מוּם שֶׁל עַוֶּרֶת:

אוֹ שָׁבוּר – *Injured:* [Unlike the previous term, this is an adjective, but the general sense is similar: The animal] "should not be" [*lo yihyeh*] injured.

אוֹ שָׁבוּר. לֹא יִהְיֶה:

חָרוּץ – *Maimed:* The animal's eyelid must not be split or otherwise damaged, nor may its lip be cut or maimed.

חָרוּץ. רִיס שֶׁל עַיִן שֶׁנִּסְדַּק אוֹ שֶׁנִּפְגַּם, וְכֵן שְׂפָתוֹ שֶׁנִּסְדְּקָה אוֹ נִפְגְּמָה:

יַבֶּלֶת – *Warts:* The Old French word for this is *verue* ["warts"].

יַבֶּלֶת. ורו"ה בְּלַעַז:

יט לְעֹלָה: לִרְצֹנְכֶם תָּמִים זָכָר בַּבָּקָר בַּכְּשָׂבִים וּבָעִזִּים:
כ כֹּל אֲשֶׁר־בּוֹ מוּם לֹא תַקְרִיבוּ כִּי־לֹא לְרָצוֹן יִהְיֶה
כא לָכֶם: וְאִישׁ כִּי־יַקְרִיב זֶבַח־שְׁלָמִים לַיהוָה לְפַלֵּא־
נֶדֶר אוֹ לִנְדָבָה בַּבָּקָר אוֹ בַצֹּאן תָּמִים יִהְיֶה לְרָצוֹן
כב כָּל־מוּם לֹא יִהְיֶה־בּוֹ: עַוֶּרֶת אוֹ שָׁבוּר אוֹ־חָרוּץ
אוֹ־יַבֶּלֶת אוֹ גָרָב אוֹ יַלֶּפֶת לֹא־תַקְרִיבוּ אֵלֶּה לַיהוָה
כג וְאִשֶּׁה לֹא־תִתְּנוּ מֵהֶם עַל־הַמִּזְבֵּחַ לַיהוָה: וְשׁוֹר
וָשֶׂה שָׂרוּעַ וְקָלוּט נְדָבָה תַּעֲשֶׂה אֹתוֹ וּלְנֵדֶר לֹא

גָּרָב – *A severe rash:* The term *garav* refers to a form of boils, as does the word *yallefet* ["scabs"]. The latter is related to the verse *Shimshon gripped [vayilpot] the two central pillars that the temple rested upon* (Judges 16:29). The boils are called *yalefet* because they take hold of their victim and cleave to him until his death, for there is no cure.

גָּרָב. מִין חֲזָזִית, וְכֵן ״יַלֶּפֶת״. וּלְשׁוֹן ״יַלֶּפֶת״ כְּמוֹ ״וַיִּלְפֹּת שִׁמְשׁוֹן״ (שופטים טז, כט), שֶׁאֲחוּזָה בּוֹ עַד יוֹם מִיתָה, שֶׁאֵין לָהּ רְפוּאָה:

לֹא־תַקְרִיבוּ – *Do not place any of these:* The text issues three warnings against offering blemished animals [in verses 20, 22, and 24, to teach three distinct laws]. It is forbidden to consecrate such animals as sacrifices, it is forbidden to slaughter them as such, and it is forbidden to cast the blood of these animals against the altar. [One who offers a blemished animal thereby transgresses these three prohibitions.]

לֹא־תַקְרִיבוּ. שָׁלֹשׁ פְּעָמִים (פסוקים כ, כב, כד), לְהַזְהִיר עַל הַקְדָּשָׁתָן וְעַל שְׁחִיטָתָן וְעַל זְרִיקַת דָּמָן:

וְאִשֶּׁה לֹא־תִתְּנוּ – *Do not place as a fire offering:* This represents an additional prohibition against burning these unacceptable animals on the altar.

וְאִשֶּׁה לֹא־תִתְּנוּ. אַזְהָרַת הַקְטָרָתָן:

23 | **שָׂרוּעַ** – *With a limb deformed:* This describes an animal with an unusually large limb.

כג | שָׂרוּעַ. אֵיבָר גָּדוֹל מֵחֲבֵרוֹ:

וְקָלוּט – *Or uncloven:* The hooves of such an animal are solid and undivided.

וְקָלוּט. פַּרְסוֹתָיו קְלוּטוֹת:

נְדָבָה תַּעֲשֶׂה אֹתוֹ – *As a freewill offering:* A blemished animal should be accepted as a donation for repairs to the Temple [that is, from the proceeds of its sale].

נְדָבָה תַּעֲשֶׂה אֹתוֹ. לְבֶדֶק הַבַּיִת:

וּלְנֵדֶר – *In fulfillment of a vow:* These cannot be offered on the altar.

וּלְנֵדֶר. לַמִּזְבֵּחַ:

◀

24 they will not be accepted in fulfillment of a vow. Do not offer
to the LORD an animal whose testicles are bruised, crushed,
25 torn, or cut off; and do not do such things in your land. Do
not accept such animals from a migrant as an offering of foodstuffs to your God. Because they are mutilated and blemished,
26 they will not be accepted on your behalf." The
27 LORD spoke to Moshe: "When an ox or sheep or goat is born,

לֹא יֵרָצֶה – *They will not be accepted:* What kind of an offering achieves appeasement? Only that which is consecrated for the altar.

לֹא יֵרָצֶה. אֵי זֶה הֶקְדֵּשׁ בָּא לְרַצּוֹת? הֱוֵי אוֹמֵר זֶה הֶקְדֵּשׁ הַמִּזְבֵּחַ:

24 | **וּמָעוּךְ וְכָתוּת וְנָתוּק וְכָרוּת** – *An animal whose testicles are bruised, crushed, torn, or cut off:* These conditions refer to the animal's testicles or its male organ [neither of which is explicitly stated in the Hebrew text].

כד | וּמָעוּךְ וְכָתוּת וְנָתוּק וְכָרוּת. בַּבֵּיצִים אוֹ בַּגִּיד:

מָעוּךְ – *Bruised:* The testicles have been bruised by hand.

מָעוּךְ. בֵּיצָיו מְעוּכִין בַּיָּד:

כָּתוּת – *Crushed:* The adjective represents a state beyond being bruised.

כָּתוּת. כְּתוּשִׁים יוֹתֵר מִמָּעוּךְ:

נָתוּק – *Torn:* This refers to severing the testicles to the point that the glands by which they are suspended are cut, and yet the testicles remain inside the scrotum which has not been severed.

נָתוּק. תְּלוּשִׁין בַּיָּד עַד שֶׁנִּפְסְקוּ חוּטִים שֶׁתְּלוּיִים בָּהֶן, אֲבָל נְתוּנִים הֵם בְּתוֹךְ הַכִּיס, וְהַכִּיס לֹא נִתְלַשׁ:

וְכָרוּת – *Or cut off:* With this action the testicles have been cut away while still inside the scrotum, making it appear as if it is not missing that body part.

וְכָרוּת. כְּרוּתִין בִּכְלִי וְעוֹדָן בַּכִּיס, שֶׁלֹּא יְהֵא כִּמְחֻסַּר אֵיבָר:

וּמָעוּךְ – *Bruised:* The term is rendered by the Targum as *vedimris*, which means "mashed" [a somewhat more severe condition than "bruised"].

וּמָעוּךְ. תַּרְגּוּם "וְדִימְרִיס" זֶהוּ לְשׁוֹן בְּאַרַמִּית, לְשׁוֹן כְּתִישָׁה:

וְכָתוּת – *Crushed:* The term is rendered as *vediresis* in the Targum, as in the verse *For indeed, the LORD commands and will shatter the great house to pieces [resisim, meaning "broken into thin shards"]* (Amos 6:11). We similarly find the phrase *kaneh hamrussas* – "a shattered reed" [in Shabbat 80b].

וְכָתוּת. תַּרְגּוּמוֹ "וְדִירְסִיס", כְּמוֹ "הַבַּיִת הַגָּדוֹל רְסִיסִים" (עמוס ו, יא), בְּקִיעוֹת דַּקּוֹת, וְכֵן "קָנֶה הַמְרֻסָּס" (שבת פ ע"ב) כָּתוּשׁ כְּתִיתִין:

וּבְאַרְצְכֶם לֹא תַעֲשׂוּ – *And do not do such things in your land:* [The final admonition in this sentence does not warn Israel not to offer these blemished animals as sacrifices – that has already been stated in this verse. Furthermore, the text need not

וּבְאַרְצְכֶם לֹא תַעֲשׂוּ. דָּבָר זֶה, לְסָרֵס שׁוּם בְּהֵמָה וְחַיָּה וַאֲפִלּוּ טְמֵאָה, לְכָךְ נֶאֱמַר: "בְּאַרְצְכֶם", לְרַבּוֹת כָּל אֲשֶׁר בְּאַרְצְכֶם; שֶׁאִי

כד יֵרָצֶה: וּמָעוּךְ וְכָתוּת וְנָתוּק וְכָרוּת לֹא תַקְרִיבוּ
כה לַיהוָה וּבְאַרְצְכֶם לֹא תַעֲשׂוּ: וּמִיַּד בֶּן־נֵכָר לֹא
תַקְרִיבוּ אֶת־לֶחֶם אֱלֹהֵיכֶם מִכָּל־אֵלֶּה כִּי מָשְׁחָתָם
כו בָּהֶם מוּם בָּם לֹא יֵרָצוּ לָכֶם: וַיְדַבֵּר יְהוָה
כז אֶל־מֹשֶׁה לֵּאמֹר: שׁוֹר אוֹ־כֶשֶׂב אוֹ־עֵז כִּי יִוָּלֵד וְהָיָה

emphasize that defective animals cannot serve as sacrifices "in your land," since offerings are not brought outside the land at all. Hence these words prohibit doing] this thing – castrating any domestic animal, wild beast, or bird, even those which are impure [non-kosher]. This explains the usage of the term "in your land": the prohibition extends to all animals living in your land [and not just those which are eligible to be sacrifices]. Now it is impossible to explain that the Torah here is limiting the prohibition to the land of Israel, since the act of emasculation relates to the body, and all requirements governing the body are applicable both inside the land and outside of Israel.

אֶפְשָׁר לוֹמַר לֹא נִצְטַוּוּ עַל הַסֵּרוּס אֶלָּא בָּאָרֶץ, שֶׁהֲרֵי סֵרוּס חוֹבַת הַגּוּף הוּא, וְכָל חוֹבַת הַגּוּף נוֹהֶגֶת בֵּין בָּאָרֶץ בֵּין בְּחוּצָה לָאָרֶץ:

25 | **וּמִיַּד בֶּן־נֵכָר** – *From a migrant:* If a gentile presents an animal for sacrifice in honor of God, the priest must offer it unless the specimen is blemished. For even though non-Jews are permitted to sacrifice defective animals [to God] unless the creature is actually missing a limb, that allowance only extends to shrines set up in fields. However, Israel is not to accept imperfect animals for the altar in the Tabernacle [or Temple], while perfect animal sacrifices are welcome. This is why the verse above [22:18] states: *ish ish mibeit Yisrael* – literally, "a man, a man of the House of Israel"; the repetition serves to include people who are not Israelites. Thus, gentiles are permitted to make vows and bring freewill offerings just as the Hebrews are.

כה | **וּמִיַּד בֶּן־נֵכָר.** גּוֹי שֶׁהֵבִיא קָרְבָּן בְּיַד כֹּהֵן לְהַקְרִיבוֹ לַשָּׁמַיִם, לֹא תַקְרִיבוּ לוֹ בַּעַל מוּם, וְאַף עַל פִּי שֶׁלֹּא נֶאֶסְרוּ בַּעֲלֵי מוּמִין לְקָרְבַּן בְּנֵי נֹחַ אֶלָּא אִם כֵּן מְחֻסְּרֵי אֵבֶר, זֹאת נוֹהֶגֶת בְּבָמָה שֶׁבַּשָּׂדוֹת, אֲבָל עַל הַמִּזְבֵּחַ שֶׁבַּמִּשְׁכָּן לֹא תַקְרִיבוּ; אֲבָל תְּמִימָה תְּקַבְּלוּ מֵהֶם, לְכָךְ נֶאֱמַר לְמַעְלָה: "אִישׁ אִישׁ" (פסוק יח), לְרַבּוֹת אֶת הַגּוֹיִם, שֶׁנּוֹדְרִים נְדָרִים וּנְדָבוֹת כְּיִשְׂרָאֵל:

מָשְׁחָתָם – *They are mutilated:* The Targum translates this as *ḥibbulehon* – "they are destroyed."

מָשְׁחָתָם. חִבּוּלְהוֹן:

לֹא יֵרָצוּ לָכֶם – *They will not be accepted on your behalf:* Such sacrifices will not atone for you.

לֹא יֵרָצוּ לָכֶם. לְכַפֵּר עֲלֵיכֶם:

27 | **כִּי יִוָּלֵד** – *When it is born:* This excludes a calf born via caesarean section. [Only a naturally born animal can be a sacrifice.]

כז | **כִּי יִוָּלֵד.** פְּרָט לְיוֹצֵא דֹּפֶן:

◀

it shall remain with its mother for seven days. From the eighth
day it is acceptable as a sacrifice, a fire offering to the LORD,
28 but do not slaughter an ox or sheep and its young on the same
29 day. When you sacrifice a thanksgiving offering for the LORD,
30 sacrifice it so that it will be acceptable on your behalf. It shall
be eaten on the same day – leave none of it to the morning; I
31 am the LORD. Keep My commands and fulfill them; I am the
32 LORD. Do not profane My holy name – that I may be sanctified in the midst of the Israelites. I am the LORD, who makes

28 | **אֹתוֹ וְאֶת־בְּנוֹ** – *It and its young:* The prohibition applies to the female, meaning that it is forbidden to slaughter a mother animal and on the same day to kill its offspring. The law does not apply to father animals; it is permitted to slaughter a male animal on the same day as its young. [Although the term *oto* – "him" – would seem to suggest that the rule relates to the male animal, the word is interpreted as referring to the species of ox – *shor* – and sheep – *seh*, which are masculine terms.]

כח | **אֹתוֹ וְאֶת־בְּנוֹ.** נוֹהֵג בִּנְקֵבָה, שֶׁאָסוּר לִשְׁחֹט הָאֵם וְהַבֵּן אוֹ הַבַּת, וְאֵינוֹ נוֹהֵג בִּזְכָרִים, וּמֻתָּר לִשְׁחֹט הָאָב וְהַבֵּן:

אֹתוֹ וְאֶת־בְּנוֹ – *It and its young:* [Although the phrasing implies that the prohibition is limited to killing the animal and then the offspring] it is even forbidden to first slaughter the young and subsequently the parent.

אֹתוֹ וְאֶת־בְּנוֹ. אַף בְּנוֹ וְאוֹתוֹ בַּמַּשְׁמָע:

29 | **לִרְצֹנְכֶם תִּזְבָּחוּ** – *Sacrifice it so that it will be acceptable on your behalf:* From the very start of the sacrificial procedure [that is, the slaughtering], be sure to offer the animal for the sake of its acceptance. And what criterion is necessary for the offering to be accepted? That *it shall be eaten on the same day* (22:30). Now the function of the present verse is to instruct us that the animal be slaughtered with the intention to eat the allotted portion on the same day, that is: Do not slaughter the offering while planning to eat it the next day. For if the person harbors such a disqualifying thought, the sacrifice will not gain acceptance for you. Another interpretation for the term *lirtzonekhem* – *so that it will be acceptable on your behalf:* The sacrifice must be offered with your intention. From here we learn that if one who is otherwise preoccupied happens to slaughter the animal [for example, he drops the knife and by sheer chance it slashes the animal's neck], that slaughtering invalidates the offering. And even though the text has

כט | **לִרְצֹנְכֶם תִּזְבָּחוּ.** תְּחִלַּת זְבִיחַתְכֶם הִזָּהֲרוּ שֶׁתְּהֵא לְרָצוֹן לָכֶם. וּמַהוּ הָרָצוֹן? "בַּיּוֹם הַהוּא יֵאָכֵל" (להלן פסוק ל), לֹא בָא לְהַזְהִיר אֶלָּא שֶׁתְּהֵא שְׁחִיטָה עַל מְנָת כֵּן, אַל תִּשְׁחָטוּהוּ עַל מְנָת לְאָכְלוֹ לְמָחָר, שֶׁאִם תַּחְשְׁבוּ בּוֹ מַחְשֶׁבֶת פְּסוּל לֹא יְהֵא לָכֶם לְרָצוֹן. דָּבָר אַחֵר "לִרְצֹנְכֶם", לְדַעְתְּכֶם, מִכָּאן לַמִּתְעַסֵּק שֶׁפָּסוּל בִּשְׁחִיטַת קָדָשִׁים. וְאַף עַל פִּי שֶׁפֵּרַט בַּנֶּאֱכָלִים לִשְׁנֵי יָמִים, חָזַר וּפֵרַט בַּנֶּאֱכָלִין לְיוֹם אֶחָד, שֶׁתְּהֵא זְבִיחָתָן עַל מְנָת לְאָכְלָן בִּזְמַנָּן:

◀

שִׁבְעַת יָמִים תַּחַת אִמּוֹ וּמִיּוֹם הַשְּׁמִינִי וָהָלְאָה יֵרָצֶה
כח לְקָרְבַּן אִשֶּׁה לַיהוָה: וְשׁוֹר אוֹ־שֶׂה אֹתוֹ וְאֶת־בְּנוֹ לֹא
כט תִשְׁחֲטוּ בְּיוֹם אֶחָד: וְכִי־תִזְבְּחוּ זֶבַח־תּוֹדָה לַיהוָה
ל לִרְצֹנְכֶם תִּזְבָּחוּ: בַּיּוֹם הַהוּא יֵאָכֵל לֹא־תוֹתִירוּ מִמֶּנּוּ
לא עַד־בֹּקֶר אֲנִי יהוה: וּשְׁמַרְתֶּם מִצְוֺתַי וַעֲשִׂיתֶם אֹתָם
לב אֲנִי יהוה: וְלֹא תְחַלְּלוּ אֶת־שֵׁם קָדְשִׁי וְנִקְדַּשְׁתִּי

previously made clear [in 7:18] that should one plan, when sacrificing a peace offering, to eat it beyond the designated time of two days, the Torah now discusses sacrifices which have a one-day limit for consumption, to teach that regarding these too there must be an initial intention to eat the meat within the prescribed time.

ל | בַּיּוֹם הַהוּא יֵאָכֵל. לֹא בָּא לְהַזְהִיר אֶלָּא שֶׁתְּהֵא שְׁחִיטָה עַל מְנָת כֵּן, שֶׁאִם לִקְבֹּעַ לָהּ זְמַן אֲכִילָה, כְּבָר כָּתוּב: ״וּבְשַׂר זֶבַח תּוֹדַת שְׁלָמָיו״ וְגוֹ׳ (לעיל ז, טו):

30 | בַּיּוֹם הַהוּא יֵאָכֵל – *It shall be eaten on the same day:* This verse serves to caution that the slaughter of the sacrifice must be performed on condition that the meat will be eaten on that day. The text cannot be establishing the appropriate time to eat this meat, since an earlier verse already states: *The flesh of the peace sacrifice of thanksgiving shall be eaten on the day it is offered* (7:15).

אֲנִי יהוה. דַּע מִי גָּזַר עַל הַדָּבָר וְאַל יֵקַל בְּעֵינֶיךָ:

אֲנִי יהוה – *I am the Lord:* Remember who has issued this command, and do not take it lightly.

לא | וּשְׁמַרְתֶּם. זוֹ הַמִּשְׁנָה:

31 | וּשְׁמַרְתֶּם – *Keep My commands:* This directs Israel to study the laws.

וַעֲשִׂיתֶם. זֶה הַמַּעֲשֶׂה:

וַעֲשִׂיתֶם – *And fulfill them:* Here the text enjoins the people to observe the commandments.

לב | וְלֹא תְחַלְּלוּ. לַעֲבֹר עַל דְּבָרַי מְזִידִין. מִמַּשְׁמַע שֶׁנֶּאֱמַר: ״וְלֹא תְחַלְּלוּ אֶת שֵׁם קָדְשִׁי״, מַה תַּלְמוּד לוֹמַר: ״וְנִקְדַּשְׁתִּי״? מְסֹר עַצְמְךָ וְקַדֵּשׁ שְׁמִי. יָכוֹל בְּיָחִיד? תַּלְמוּד לוֹמַר: ״בְּתוֹךְ בְּנֵי יִשְׂרָאֵל״. וּכְשֶׁהוּא מוֹסֵר עַצְמוֹ יִמְסֹר עַצְמוֹ עַל מְנָת לָמוּת, שֶׁכָּל הַמּוֹסֵר עַצְמוֹ עַל מְנָת הַנֵּס אֵין עוֹשִׂין לוֹ נֵס, שֶׁכֵּן מָצִינוּ

32 | וְלֹא תְחַלְּלוּ – *Do not profane:* Do not purposefully disobey My commands. Now since the verse states: *Do not profane My holy name*, why does it need to then say: *That I may be sanctified*? [An absence of profanation implies sanctification.] The positive statement emphasizes that a person must be prepared to sacrifice himself in order to sanctify God's name. [If one is threatened with death if he does not violate a Torah precept, he should surrender his life to avoid doing that. Thus, sanctifying the divine name is not only achieved by the passive avoidance of sin; the Jew is required to forfeit his

◀

33 you holy, who brought you out of Egypt to be your God: I am
the Lord."
23 1 2 The Lord spoke to Moshe: "Speak to the Israelites. Say: REVI'I
These are the Lord's appointed times that you shall proclaim
3 as sacred assemblies; these are My appointed times. Work
shall be done through six days, but the seventh day shall be
a Sabbath of complete rest, a sacred assembly. You shall perform no work at all; it shall be a Sabbath for the Lord in all
your dwellings.
4 These are the Lord's appointed times, sacred assemblies,
5 which you shall proclaim at their appointed times. In the first
month, the fourteenth of the month in the afternoon is the

life toward that aim, which should be viewed as an active undertaking.] Now lest we think that this obligation applies even if one is compelled to transgress the law privately, the verse states: *In the midst of the Israelites*. [It is only in public that one must choose death.] And should a Jew be required to give up his life, he should truly be prepared to die. For if such a person secretly hopes that a miracle will suddenly save his life, no such wonder will be forthcoming. Thus, we see that Ḥananya, Mishael, and Azarya did not rely on providence to rescue them, as they said to Nevukhadnetzar: *But even if He does not choose to save us, let it be known to you, O king, that we will not serve your god and we will not worship the golden figure you have erected* (Daniel 3:18). That is, these men stated their resolve that they would not engage in idolatry whether or not God saved them from the fiery furnace.

כַּחֲנַנְיָה מִישָׁאֵל וַעֲזַרְיָה שֶׁלֹּא מָסְרוּ עַצְמָן עַל מְנָת הַנֵּס, שֶׁנֶּאֱמַר: "וְהֵן לָא, יְדִיעַ לֶהֱוֵא לָךְ מַלְכָּא" וְגוֹ' (דניאל ג, יח), מַצִּיל וְלֹא מַצִּיל, "יְדִיעַ לֶהֱוֵא לָךְ" וְגוֹ':

33 | הַמּוֹצִיא אֶתְכֶם – *Who brought you out:* I redeemed you from Egypt on this condition [that you would be willing to die to sanctify My name].

לג | הַמּוֹצִיא אֶתְכֶם. עַל מְנָת כֵּן:

אֲנִי יהוה – *I am the Lord:* I can be trusted to grant your reward.

אֲנִי יהוה. נֶאֱמָן לְשַׁלֵּם שָׂכָר:

23 2 | דַּבֵּר אֶל־בְּנֵי יִשְׂרָאֵל... מוֹעֲדֵי יהוה – *Speak to the Israelites. Say: These are the Lord's appointed times:* Schedule the festivals so that the Israelites will become accustomed to observing them. Hence, we learn that [the Sanhedrin is authorized] to intercalate the year [that is, adding a thirteenth month to the calendar after Adar, the twelfth month]. Such an adjustment will allow those Jews living in exile who have uprooted

כג ב | דַּבֵּר אֶל־בְּנֵי יִשְׂרָאֵל וְגוֹ' מוֹעֲדֵי יהוה. עֲשֵׂה מוֹעֲדוֹת שֶׁיִּהְיוּ יִשְׂרָאֵל מְלֻמָּדִין בָּהֶם, שֶׁמְּעַבְּרִים אֶת הַשָּׁנָה עַל גָּלֻיּוֹת שֶׁנֶּעֶקְרוּ מִמְּקוֹמָן לַעֲלוֹת לָרֶגֶל וַעֲדַיִן לֹא הִגִּיעוּ לִירוּשָׁלַיִם:

לג בְּתוֹךְ בְּנֵי יִשְׂרָאֵל אֲנִי יהוה מְקַדִּשְׁכֶם: הַמּוֹצִיא
אֶתְכֶם מֵאֶרֶץ מִצְרַיִם לִהְיוֹת לָכֶם לֵאלֹהִים אֲנִי
יהוה:

כג א ב וַיְדַבֵּר יהוה אֶל־מֹשֶׁה לֵּאמֹר: דַּבֵּר אֶל־בְּנֵי יִשְׂרָאֵל רביעי
וְאָמַרְתָּ אֲלֵהֶם מוֹעֲדֵי יהוה אֲשֶׁר־תִּקְרְאוּ אֹתָם
ג מִקְרָאֵי קֹדֶשׁ אֵלֶּה הֵם מוֹעֲדָי: שֵׁשֶׁת יָמִים תֵּעָשֶׂה
מְלָאכָה וּבַיּוֹם הַשְּׁבִיעִי שַׁבַּת שַׁבָּתוֹן מִקְרָא־קֹדֶשׁ
כָּל־מְלָאכָה לֹא תַעֲשׂוּ שַׁבָּת הִוא לַיהוה בְּכֹל
מוֹשְׁבֹתֵיכֶם:
ד אֵלֶּה מוֹעֲדֵי יהוה מִקְרָאֵי קֹדֶשׁ אֲשֶׁר־תִּקְרְאוּ אֹתָם
ה בְּמוֹעֲדָם: בַּחֹדֶשׁ הָרִאשׁוֹן בְּאַרְבָּעָה עָשָׂר לַחֹדֶשׁ

themselves from their homes to travel to Jerusalem and to reach the city in time for Passover.

3 | שֵׁשֶׁת יָמִים – *Six days:* Why does the Torah include the Sabbath in a discussion of the festivals? In order to teach us that if one profanes the holidays [by performing forbidden labors on those days], his transgression is considered as severe as if he had violated the Sabbath. Conversely, when a person observes the holidays, he is credited as if he has kept the Sabbath.

4 | אֵלֶּה מוֹעֲדֵי יהוה – *These are the Lord's appointed times:* The earlier verse referred to intercalating the year [by adding an extra month], whereas this verse refers to sanctifying the months. [Just as the ultimate form of the year's calendar is subject to the court's deliberations, so too does the exact length of each month depend on the court acknowledging the sighting of the new moon.]

5 | בֵּין הָעַרְבָּיִם – *In the afternoon:* The afternoon starts six and a half hours into the day.

פֶּסַח לַיהוה – *The Passover sacrifice to the Lord:* This refers to the offering of the sacrifice called *Pesaḥ*.

ג | שֵׁשֶׁת יָמִים. מָה עִנְיַן שַׁבָּת אֵצֶל מוֹעֲדוֹת, לְלַמֶּדְךָ שֶׁכָּל הַמְחַלֵּל אֶת הַמּוֹעֲדוֹת מַעֲלִין עָלָיו כְּאִלּוּ חִלֵּל אֶת הַשַּׁבָּתוֹת, וְכָל הַמְקַיֵּם אֶת הַמּוֹעֲדוֹת מַעֲלִין עָלָיו כְּאִלּוּ קִיֵּם אֶת הַשַּׁבָּתוֹת:

ד | אֵלֶּה מוֹעֲדֵי יהוה. לְמַעְלָה מְדַבֵּר בְּעִבּוּר שָׁנָה, וְכָאן מְדַבֵּר בְּקִדּוּשׁ הַחֹדֶשׁ:

ה | בֵּין הָעַרְבָּיִם. מִשֵּׁשׁ שָׁעוֹת וּלְמַעְלָה:

פֶּסַח לַיהוה. הַקְרָבַת קָרְבָּן שֶׁשְּׁמוֹ פֶּסַח:

6 time for the Passover sacrifice to the Lord. The fifteenth day
of this month is the Lord's Festival of Unleavened Bread; for
7 seven days you shall eat unleavened bread. The first day shall
be a sacred assembly for you; you shall perform no laborious
8 work. And you shall present a fire offering for the Lord for
seven days; on the seventh day there shall be a sacred assembly; you shall perform no laborious work."
9 10 The Lord spoke to Moshe: "Speak to the Israelites. Say:
When you come to the land that I am giving you and reap its
11 harvest, bring the first sheaf of your harvest to the priest. He
shall display the sheaf this way and that before the Lord for
your acceptance; on the day after the day of rest the priest shall

8 | **וְהִקְרַבְתֶּם אִשֶּׁה** – *And you shall present a fire offering:* This refers to the additional offerings brought on festivals [the *musaf* sacrifices] which are discussed in Parashat Pinḥas. Why are these sacrifices mentioned here? To make the point that those additional offerings are independent of each other. [The later text reads: *You shall offer a burnt fire offering to the Lord: two young bulls, one ram, and seven yearling lambs, all unblemished* (Numbers 28:19)] and our verse states: *And you shall present a fire offering for the Lord*, meaning that the *musaf* offerings should be brought under all circumstances. If the Temple lacks bulls, the priests should nevertheless sacrifice the rams; if there are no rams, the lambs should still be offered.

ח | **וְהִקְרַבְתֶּם אִשֶּׁה וְגוֹ׳.** הֵם הַמּוּסָפִין הָאֲמוּרִים בְּפָרָשַׁת פִּינְחָס. וְלָמָּה נֶאֶמְרוּ כָּאן? לוֹמַר לְךָ שֶׁאֵין הַמּוּסָפִין מְעַכְּבִין זֶה אֶת זֶה: ״וְהִקְרַבְתֶּם אִשֶּׁה לַה׳״ – מִכָּל מָקוֹם, אִם אֵין פָּרִים הָבֵא אֵילִים, וְאִם אֵין פָּרִים וְאֵילִים הָבֵא כְּבָשִׂים:

שִׁבְעַת יָמִים – *For seven days:* [The usual term for "seven" is *shiv'a* with a *heh* at the end of the word. When a *tav* substitutes for the *heh*, it normally connotes the construct form, so that here it would suggest "a seven of days." Rashi explains:] The word *shiv'at* is a noun, such that the phrase means "a septet of days." The Old French term for this is *seteine* ["a week"]. The same interpretation applies to the word *shemonat* – connoting an octet, *sheshet* – a sextet, *ḥameshet* – a quintet, and *sheloshet* – a trio. [The author makes a similar observation in his commentary to the words *for three days* in Exodus 10:22, and *about three months later* in Genesis 38:24.]

שִׁבְעַת יָמִים. כָּל מָקוֹם שֶׁנֶּאֱמַר ׳שִׁבְעַת׳ שֵׁם דָּבָר הוּא, שָׁבוּעַ שֶׁל יָמִים, סטיינ״א בְּלַעַז. וְכֵן כָּל לְשׁוֹן שְׁמֹנַת, שֵׁשֶׁת, חֲמֵשֶׁת, שְׁלֹשֶׁת:

מְלֶאכֶת עֲבֹדָה – *No laborious work:* You may not even do work that you consider critically important to save you from suffering a financial loss. I inferred this point from the Sifra (Emor

מְלֶאכֶת עֲבֹדָה. אֲפִלּוּ מְלָאכוֹת הַחֲשׁוּבוֹת לָכֶם עֲבוֹדָה וָצֹרֶךְ, שֶׁיֵּשׁ חֶסְרוֹן כִּיס בְּבַטָּלָה שֶׁלָּהֶן, כְּגוֹן

◀

ו בֵּין הָעַרְבָּיִם פֶּסַח לַיהוָה: וּבַחֲמִשָּׁה עָשָׂר יוֹם לַחֹדֶשׁ
הַזֶּה חַג הַמַּצּוֹת לַיהוָה שִׁבְעַת יָמִים מַצּוֹת תֹּאכֵלוּ:
ז בַּיּוֹם הָרִאשׁוֹן מִקְרָא־קֹדֶשׁ יִהְיֶה לָכֶם כָּל־מְלֶאכֶת
ח עֲבֹדָה לֹא תַעֲשׂוּ: וְהִקְרַבְתֶּם אִשֶּׁה לַיהוָה שִׁבְעַת
יָמִים בַּיּוֹם הַשְּׁבִיעִי מִקְרָא־קֹדֶשׁ כָּל־מְלֶאכֶת עֲבֹדָה
לֹא תַעֲשׂוּ:
ט וַיְדַבֵּר יְהוָה אֶל־מֹשֶׁה לֵּאמֹר: דַּבֵּר אֶל־בְּנֵי יִשְׂרָאֵל
וְאָמַרְתָּ אֲלֵהֶם כִּי־תָבֹאוּ אֶל־הָאָרֶץ אֲשֶׁר אֲנִי נֹתֵן
לָכֶם וּקְצַרְתֶּם אֶת־קְצִירָהּ וַהֲבֵאתֶם אֶת־עֹמֶר
יא רֵאשִׁית קְצִירְכֶם אֶל־הַכֹּהֵן: וְהֵנִיף אֶת־הָעֹמֶר לִפְנֵי

דָּבָר הָאָבֵד. כָּךְ הֲבַנְתִּי מִתּוֹרַת כֹּהֲנִים (פרשתא יב, ח), דְּקָתָנֵי: יָכוֹל אַף חֻלּוֹ שֶׁל מוֹעֵד יְהֵא אָסוּר בִּמְלֶאכֶת עֲבוֹדָה? וְכוּ':

12:8), which derives from our verse that work of this kind is permitted on the intermediate days of the festival.

י | רֵאשִׁית קְצִירְכֶם. שֶׁתְּהֵא רִאשׁוֹנָה לַקָּצִיר:

10 | **רֵאשִׁית קְצִירְכֶם** – *The first of your harvest:* This sheaf will be the first grain cutting of the season.

עֹמֶר. עֲשִׂירִית הָאֵיפָה, כָּךְ הָיָה שְׁמָהּ, כְּמוֹ: "וַיָּמֹדּוּ בָעֹמֶר" (שמות טז, יח):

עֹמֶר – *Sheaf:* The sheaf should be comprised of an "omer of grain" which is the name for a tenth of an ephah. An earlier verse identifies this as a measurement when it states: *They measured it with an omer measure* (Exodus 16:18).

יא | וְהֵנִיף. כָּל תְּנוּפָה מוֹלִיךְ וּמֵבִיא מַעֲלֶה וּמוֹרִיד, מוֹלִיךְ וּמֵבִיא לַעֲצֹר רוּחוֹת רָעוֹת, מַעֲלֶה וּמוֹרִיד לַעֲצֹר טְלָלִים רָעִים:

11 | **וְהֵנִיף** – *He shall display:* [*Vehenif* can also be understood as "he shall wave."] All instances of waving prescribed by the Torah entail moving the object back and forth [out and in, in the four directions of the compass] in order to protect against damaging wind, and up and down as a precaution against harmful dew.

לִרְצֹנְכֶם. אִם תַּקְרִיבוּ כַּמִּשְׁפָּט הַזֶּה יִהְיֶה לְרָצוֹן לָכֶם:

לִרְצֹנְכֶם – *For your acceptance:* If you offer the sheaf this way, it will be accepted on your behalf.

מִמָּחֳרַת הַשַּׁבָּת. מִמָּחֳרַת יוֹם טוֹב הָרִאשׁוֹן שֶׁל פֶּסַח, שֶׁאִם אַתָּה אוֹמֵר שַׁבַּת בְּרֵאשִׁית, אִי אַתָּה

מִמָּחֳרַת הַשַּׁבָּת – *On the day after the day of rest:* This refers to the day following the first day of Passover [that is, on the sixteenth of Nisan]. The text cannot be referring to the Sabbath

◀

12 display it. On the day you display the sheaf this way and that,
you shall offer a yearling sheep without blemish as a burnt of-
13 fering to the LORD. Its grain offering shall be two-tenths of
an ephah of fine flour mixed with oil, a fire offering for the
LORD, a pleasing aroma; and its libation shall be a quarter
14 of a hin of wine. Until that day, until you bring this sacrifice
to your God, you shall eat no bread or roasted grain or ripe
grain. This is an everlasting statute throughout your genera-
15 tions, in all your dwellings. And from the day you
bring the sheaf of the wave offering, the day after the day of
16 rest, you shall count for yourselves seven complete weeks. To
the day after the seventh week, you shall count fifty days; and

of creation [implying that the sheaf should be brought on a Sunday] since it does not state which Sabbath in the year is signified.

יוֹדֵעַ הֵיזֶהוּ:

12 | וַעֲשִׂיתֶם... כֶּבֶשׂ – *You shall offer a sheep:* It is the sheaf of barley which creates the obligation for this offering. [The sheep mentioned in this verse does not constitute one of the day's additional *musaf* sacrifices, but is a function of the grain offering.]

יב | וַעֲשִׂיתֶם... כֶּבֶשׂ. חוֹבָה לָעֹמֶר הוּא בָּא:

13 | וּמִנְחָתוֹ – *Its grain offering:* This is the accompanying grain offering [of the sheep mentioned in the previous verse].

יג | וּמִנְחָתוֹ. מִנְחַת נְסָכָיו:

שְׁנֵי עֶשְׂרֹנִים – *Two-tenths:* This grain offering has double the usual volume. [According to Numbers 15:4–5, the standard grain offering brought with a burnt offering comprises one-tenth of an ephah of flour.]

שְׁנֵי עֶשְׂרֹנִים. כְּפוּלָה הָיְתָה:

וְנִסְכֹּה יַיִן רְבִיעִת הַהִין – *And its libation shall be a quarter of a hin of wine:* Despite the fact that this grain offering contains twice as much flour, the amount of wine is not doubled [from the usual requirement, as stated in Numbers 15:5. Even though a quarter of a hin of wine is the expected libation in this case, the text repeats this point lest we think that the wine should be increased just as the flour is].

וְנִסְכֹּה יַיִן רְבִיעִת הַהִין. אַף עַל פִּי שֶׁמִּנְחָתוֹ כְּפוּלָה, אֵין נְסָכָיו כְּפוּלִים:

14 | וְקָלִי – *Roasted grain:* Flour made of soft kernels which is dried in the oven.

יד | וְקָלִי. קֶמַח עָשׂוּי מִכַּרְמֶל רַךְ שֶׁמְּיַבְּשִׁין אוֹתוֹ בַּתַּנּוּר:

וְכַרְמֶל – *Ripe grain:* This refers to parched seeds which are called *graines* ["seeds"] in Old French.

וְכַרְמֶל. הֵן קְלָיוֹת שֶׁקּוֹרִין גרניי"ש:

יב יְהוָה לִרְצֹנְכֶם מִמָּחֳרַת הַשַּׁבָּת יְנִיפֶנּוּ הַכֹּהֵן: וַעֲשִׂיתֶם
בְּיוֹם הֲנִיפְכֶם אֶת־הָעֹמֶר כֶּבֶשׂ תָּמִים בֶּן־שְׁנָתוֹ
יג לְעֹלָה לַיהוָה: וּמִנְחָתוֹ שְׁנֵי עֶשְׂרֹנִים סֹלֶת בְּלוּלָה
בַשֶּׁמֶן אִשֶּׁה לַיהוָה רֵיחַ נִיחֹחַ וְנִסְכֹּה יַיִן רְבִיעִת
יד הַהִין: וְלֶחֶם וְקָלִי וְכַרְמֶל לֹא תֹאכְלוּ עַד־עֶצֶם הַיּוֹם
הַזֶּה עַד הֲבִיאֲכֶם אֶת־קָרְבַּן אֱלֹהֵיכֶם חֻקַּת עוֹלָם
טו לְדֹרֹתֵיכֶם בְּכֹל מֹשְׁבֹתֵיכֶם: וּסְפַרְתֶּם לָכֶם יט
מִמָּחֳרַת הַשַּׁבָּת מִיּוֹם הֲבִיאֲכֶם אֶת־עֹמֶר הַתְּנוּפָה
טז שֶׁבַע שַׁבָּתוֹת תְּמִימֹת תִּהְיֶינָה: עַד מִמָּחֳרַת הַשַּׁבָּת
הַשְּׁבִיעִת תִּסְפְּרוּ חֲמִשִּׁים יוֹם וְהִקְרַבְתֶּם מִנְחָה

בְּכֹל מֹשְׁבֹתֵיכֶם – *In all your dwellings:* The Sages of Israel have debated the interpretation of this phrase. Some scholars maintain that according to this verse, the practice of *ḥadash* [the prohibition to eat grain of the new harvest until the omer of barley has been brought] must be observed outside of Israel as well. However, others understand the significance of the words "in all your dwellings" differently: The law only takes effect once Israel has conquered, apportioned, and settled the land. [Hence, the people are living in dwellings across the country.]

בְּכֹל מֹשְׁבֹתֵיכֶם. נֶחְלְקוּ בּוֹ חַכְמֵי יִשְׂרָאֵל, יֵשׁ שֶׁלָּמְדוּ מִכָּאן שֶׁהֶחָדָשׁ נוֹהֵג בְּחוּצָה לָאָרֶץ, וְיֵשׁ אוֹמְרִים, לֹא בָא אֶלָּא לְלַמֵּד שֶׁלֹּא נִצְטַוּוּ עַל הֶחָדָשׁ אֶלָּא לְאַחַר יְרֻשָּׁה וִישִׁיבָה מִשֶּׁכְּבָשׁוּ וְחִלְּקוּ:

15 | **מִמָּחֳרַת הַשַּׁבָּת** – *The day after the day of rest:* The day after the first day of the festival.

טו | מִמָּחֳרַת הַשַּׁבָּת. מִמָּחֳרַת יוֹם טוֹב:

תְּמִימֹת תִּהְיֶינָה – *Complete weeks:* The phrase teaches that the counting of these weeks must begin in the evening. For otherwise the weeks will not be complete. [Since the sixteenth of Nisan begins in the evening, were the counting to begin in the morning, only part of that day would be included in the total.]

תְּמִימֹת תִּהְיֶינָה. מְלַמֵּד שֶׁמַּתְחִיל וּמוֹנֶה מִבָּעֶרֶב, שֶׁאִם לֹא כֵן אֵינָן תְּמִימוֹת:

16 | **הַשַּׁבָּת הַשְּׁבִיעִת** – *The seventh week:* This should be understood as the Targum renders the term: *shevuata sheviata* – "the seventh week." [The term *shabbat* should not be interpreted here as "first day of the festival" as it is in verses 11 and 15.]

טז | הַשַּׁבָּת הַשְּׁבִיעִת. כְּתַרְגּוּמוֹ: "שְׁבוּעֲתָא שְׁבִיעֲתָא":

17 then you shall present a new grain offering to the Lord. You
shall bring two loaves of bread from your dwellings made
with two-tenths of an ephah of fine flour baked with leaven,
18 as a wave offering: first produce to the Lord. Together with
the bread, you shall present seven unblemished yearling male
lambs, one young bull, and two rams – these shall be a burnt
offering for the Lord with their grain offering and their li-
19 bations, a fire offering, a pleasing aroma to the Lord. And
you shall offer one he-goat as a purification offering and two

עַד מִמָּחֳרַת הַשַּׁבָּת הַשְּׁבִיעִת תִּסְפְּרוּ. וְלֹא עַד בִּכְלָל, וְהֵן אַרְבָּעִים וְתִשְׁעָה יוֹם:

עַד מִמָּחֳרַת הַשַּׁבָּת הַשְּׁבִיעִת תִּסְפְּרוּ – *To the day after the seventh week, you shall count:* The count should continue up to the fiftieth day, but should not include it, thereby yielding a total of forty-nine days. [A count of fifty days would result not in seven full weeks, but more than that.]

חֲמִשִּׁים יוֹם וְהִקְרַבְתֶּם מִנְחָה חֲדָשָׁה לַיהוה. בְּיוֹם הַחֲמִשִּׁים תַּקְרִיבוּהָ. וְאוֹמֵר אֲנִי, זֶהוּ מִדְרָשׁוֹ, אֲבָל פְּשׁוּטוֹ: "עַד מִמָּחֳרַת הַשַּׁבָּת הַשְּׁבִיעִת שֶׁהוּא יוֹם חֲמִשִּׁים תִּסְפְּרוּ", וּמִקְרָא מְסֹרָס הוּא:

חֲמִשִּׁים יוֹם וְהִקְרַבְתֶּם מִנְחָה חֲדָשָׁה לַיהוה – *Fifty days; and then you shall present a new grain offering to the Lord:* This grain offering should be brought on the fiftieth day. Now I believe that this is the midrashic interpretation of the verse. However, the straightforward meaning of the text is: You shall count until the day after seven weeks, which is the fiftieth day. Thus, the order of the verse's phrases should be rearranged. [In Rashi's second reading, the words *ḥamishim yom* are not linked in the verse to the bringing of the grain offering, but to the counting, and to the opening words of the sentence: Until the day after the seventh week, which is the fiftieth day, you shall count.]

מִנְחָה חֲדָשָׁה. הִיא הַמִּנְחָה הָרִאשׁוֹנָה שֶׁהוּבְאָה מִן הֶחָדָשׁ. וְאִם תֹּאמַר, הֲרֵי קָרְבָה מִנְחַת הָעֹמֶר? אֵינָהּ כִּשְׁאָר כָּל הַמְּנָחוֹת, שֶׁהִיא בָּאָה מִן הַשְּׂעוֹרִים:

מִנְחָה חֲדָשָׁה – *A new grain offering:* This is the first grain offering brought from the new season's grain. And should you argue that the Omer offering [discussed above] is in fact brought earlier, that case differs from all other grain offerings, since it is comprised of barley [whereas nearly all other grain offerings are composed of wheat. Thus, this grain offering marks the start of the new wheat donations for the year.]

יז | מִמּוֹשְׁבֹתֵיכֶם. וְלֹא מִחוּצָה לָאָרֶץ:

17 | **מִמּוֹשְׁבֹתֵיכֶם** – *From your dwellings:* The flour must not be brought from wheat grown outside of the land.

לֶחֶם תְּנוּפָה. לֶחֶם תְּרוּמָה הַמּוּרָם לְשֵׁם גָּבוֹהַּ, וְזוֹ הִיא הַמִּנְחָה הַחֲדָשָׁה הָאֲמוּרָה לְמַעְלָה:

לֶחֶם תְּנוּפָה – *As a wave offering:* The adjective *tenufa* means *teruma* – "raising" [unlike the usage of the term in verse 15] for the bread is raised [distinguished] for the sake of the Almighty. This is the new grain offering mentioned above [in verse 16; it does not represent a new item].

יז חֲדָשָׁה לַיהוָה: מִמּוֹשְׁבֹתֵיכֶם תָּבִיאוּ ׀ לֶחֶם תְּנוּפָה
שְׁתַּיִם שְׁנֵי עֶשְׂרֹנִים סֹלֶת תִּהְיֶינָה חָמֵץ תֵּאָפֶינָה
יח בִּכּוּרִים לַיהוָה: וְהִקְרַבְתֶּם עַל־הַלֶּחֶם שִׁבְעַת
כְּבָשִׂים תְּמִימִם בְּנֵי שָׁנָה וּפַר בֶּן־בָּקָר אֶחָד וְאֵילִם
שְׁנָיִם יִהְיוּ עֹלָה לַיהוָה וּמִנְחָתָם וְנִסְכֵּיהֶם אִשֵּׁה רֵיחַ־
יט נִיחֹחַ לַיהוָה: וַעֲשִׂיתֶם שְׂעִיר־עִזִּים אֶחָד לְחַטָּאת

בִּכּוּרִים – *First produce:* This is the first offering brought from the new grain, even before the grain offering of jealousy [brought by a husband who suspects his wife of infidelity, as described in Numbers 5:15]. Although that offering consists of barley, it must not be brought before the two new loaves mandated here. [The Omer offering discussed earlier in this chapter is brought from barley and its sacrifice on the sixteenth of Nisan would appear to signal the start of the season for other barley grain offerings, such as that of the distrustful husband. Rashi confirms that this is not so: It is only once the wheat offering of the two loaves introduced here is brought on the holiday of Shavuot, forty-nine days later, that subsequent grain offerings of either wheat or barley can be made from the season's new crop.]

18 | **עַל־הַלֶּחֶם** – *Together with the bread:* The animals listed here are sacrificed on account of the bread; it is that which creates the obligation for these offerings.

וּמִנְחָתָם וְנִסְכֵּיהֶם – *With their grain offering and their libations:* The amounts for the accompanying grain offerings and wine libations follow the fixed rules regarding each species of animal, stated explicitly in the libation passage of Numbers 15:1–16. Namely, three-tenths of an ephah of flour is the measure for the grain offering brought along with a bull, two-tenths of an ephah is the amount when a ram is sacrificed, and one-tenth when a lamb is brought. These are the standard amounts of the grain offerings. The volumes of wine poured as libations are: half a hin of wine when a bull is sacrificed, a third of a hin when the sacrifice is a ram, and a quarter of a hin when it is a lamb.

19 | **וַעֲשִׂיתֶם שְׂעִיר־עִזִּים** – *And you shall offer one he-goat:* We might have thought that this goat and the seven lambs listed

בִּכּוּרִים. רִאשׁוֹנָה לְכָל הַמְּנָחוֹת, אַף לְמִנְחַת קְנָאוֹת הַבָּאָה מִן הַשְּׂעוֹרִים, לֹא תִקְרַב מִן הֶחָדָשׁ קֹדֶם לִשְׁתֵּי הַלֶּחֶם:

יח | עַל־הַלֶּחֶם. בִּגְלַל הַלֶּחֶם, חוֹבָה לַלֶּחֶם:

וּמִנְחָתָם וְנִסְכֵּיהֶם. כְּמִשְׁפַּט מִנְחָה וּנְסָכִים הַמְּפֹרָשִׁים בְּכָל בְּהֵמָה בְּפָרָשַׁת נְסָכִים (במדבר טו, ח-טז): שְׁלֹשָׁה עֶשְׂרֹנִים לַפָּר וּשְׁנֵי עֶשְׂרֹנִים לָאַיִל וְעִשָּׂרוֹן לַכֶּבֶשׂ – זוֹ הִיא הַמִּנְחָה. וְהַנְּסָכִים: חֲצִי הַהִין לַפָּר וּשְׁלִישִׁית הַהִין לָאַיִל וּרְבִיעִית הַהִין לַכֶּבֶשׂ:

יט | וַעֲשִׂיתֶם שְׂעִיר־עִזִּים. יָכוֹל שִׁבְעַת הַכְּבָשִׂים וְהַשָּׂעִיר הָאֲמוּרִים

20 yearling male sheep as peace sacrifices. The priest shall display
them this way and that with the bread of the first produce as
a wave offering before the Lord together with the two sheep;
21 they shall be holy to the Lord and belong to the priest. On
that day you shall make a proclamation; it shall be a sacred assembly for you; you shall perform no laborious work. This is
an everlasting statute throughout your generations in all your
22 dwellings. And when you reap the harvest of your land, do not
reap to the edge of your field or gather the gleanings of your
harvest. Leave them for the poor and for the migrant; I am the
Lord your God."

כָּאן הֵם שִׁבְעַת הַכְּבָשִׂים וְהַשָּׂעִיר הָאֲמוּרִים בְּחוּמַשׁ הַפְּקוּדִים (שם כח, כז, ל)? כְּשֶׁאַתָּה מַגִּיעַ אֵצֶל פָּרִים וְאֵילִים אֵינָן הֵם, אֱמֹר מֵעַתָּה, אֵלּוּ לְעַצְמָן וְאֵלּוּ לְעַצְמָן, אֵלּוּ קָרְבוּ בִּגְלַל הַלֶּחֶם וְאֵלּוּ לַמּוּסָפִין:

here [in the previous verse] are identical to the goat and the seven lambs described as additional [*musaf*] festival sacrifices in the book of Numbers [verses 28:27 and 28:30]. However, two bulls and one ram are also included in that later text; hence the corresponding animals in the present passage cannot represent the same sacrifices. [This is because the text in Numbers prescribes two bulls and one ram, whereas verse 18 states there must be one bull and two rams.] Thus, we must conclude that we are dealing with two different sets of sacrifices: The animals listed in Numbers are the additional festival sacrifices and the ones appearing in our text are different specimens brought in conjunction with the special Shavuot bread.

כ | **וְהֵנִיף הַכֹּהֵן אֹתָם... תְּנוּפָה.** מְלַמֵּד שֶׁטְּעוּנִין תְּנוּפָה חַיִּים. יָכוֹל כֻּלָּם? תַּלְמוּד לוֹמַר: "עַל שְׁנֵי כְּבָשִׂים":

20 | **וְהֵנִיף הַכֹּהֵן אֹתָם... תְּנוּפָה** – *The priest shall display them as a wave offering:* This verse teaches that the yearlings must be waved while they are still alive. Now perhaps all of them [the burnt offerings and the purifications brought at this time] must also be waved. No, for the verse states *together with the two sheep*. [It is only the sheep which are waved with the bread, and not the other animals.]

קֹדֶשׁ יִהְיוּ. לְפִי שֶׁשַּׁלְמֵי יָחִיד קָדָשִׁים קַלִּים, הֻזְקַק לוֹמַר בְּשַׁלְמֵי צִבּוּר שֶׁהֵם קָדְשֵׁי קָדָשִׁים:

קֹדֶשׁ יִהְיוּ – *They shall be holy:* Since the usual peace offering brought by an individual falls into the category of *kodashim kalim* [sacrifices with a lower degree of sanctity], the text needs to emphasize that communal peace offerings hold the status of *kodshei kodashim* [with the higher degree of sanctity. Indeed, the current instance is the sole case of a communal peace offering].

כ וּשְׁנֵי כְבָשִׂים בְּנֵי שָׁנָה לְזֶבַח שְׁלָמִים: וְהֵנִיף הַכֹּהֵן ׀
אֹתָם עַל לֶחֶם הַבִּכֻּרִים תְּנוּפָה לִפְנֵי יהוה עַל־שְׁנֵי
כא כְּבָשִׂים קֹדֶשׁ יִהְיוּ לַיהוה לַכֹּהֵן: וּקְרָאתֶם בְּעֶצֶם
׀ הַיּוֹם הַזֶּה מִקְרָא־קֹדֶשׁ יִהְיֶה לָכֶם כָּל־מְלֶאכֶת
עֲבֹדָה לֹא תַעֲשׂוּ חֻקַּת עוֹלָם בְּכָל־מוֹשְׁבֹתֵיכֶם
כב לְדֹרֹתֵיכֶם: וּבְקֻצְרְכֶם אֶת־קְצִיר אַרְצְכֶם לֹא־תְכַלֶּה
פְּאַת שָׂדְךָ בְּקֻצְרֶךָ וְלֶקֶט קְצִירְךָ לֹא תְלַקֵּט לֶעָנִי
וְלַגֵּר תַּעֲזֹב אֹתָם אֲנִי יהוה אֱלֹהֵיכֶם:

כב | וּבְקֻצְרְכֶם. חָזַר וְשָׁנָה לַעֲבֹר עֲלֵיהֶם בִּשְׁנֵי לָאוִין. אָמַר רַבִּי אַבְדִּימִי בְּרַבִּי יוֹסֵף, מָה רָאָה הַכָּתוּב לִתְּנָהּ בְּאֶמְצַע הָרְגָלִים, פֶּסַח וַעֲצֶרֶת מִכָּאן וְרֹאשׁ הַשָּׁנָה וְיוֹם הַכִּפּוּרִים מִכָּאן? לְלַמֶּדְךָ שֶׁכָּל הַנּוֹתֵן לֶקֶט שִׁכְחָה וּפֵאָה לֶעָנִי כָּרָאוּי, מַעֲלִין עָלָיו כְּאִלּוּ בָּנָה בֵּית הַמִּקְדָּשׁ וְהִקְרִיב עָלָיו קָרְבְּנוֹתָיו בְּתוֹכוֹ:

22 | וּבְקֻצְרְכֶם – *And when you reap:* [The obligations of this verse have previously been stated almost verbatim in 19:9.] The Torah repeats this here in order to render offenders liable for transgressing two negative commandments. Rabbi Avdimi son of Rabbi Yosef asked: Why does the text insert these agricultural laws into its discussion of the festivals, thereby separating its description of Passover and Shavuot from the holidays of Rosh Hashana [in 23:24] and Yom Kippur [23:27, and Sukkot in verse 34]? It does so in order to teach that if a farmer leaves the gleanings, his forgotten sheaves, and an uncut corner of the field for the poor as he is supposed to, the text grants him credit as if he has built the Temple and offered sacrifices in it.

תַּעֲזֹב. הַנַּח לִפְנֵיהֶם וְהֵם יְלַקְּטוּ, וְאֵין לְךָ לְסַיֵּעַ לְאֶחָד מֵהֶם:

תַּעֲזֹב – *Leave:* The owner is only required to abandon these gifts for the poor to come and collect the food for themselves. In fact, he may not assist any particular needy person [to the detriment of other poor people. Other instances of the verb *taazov* in the Torah mean "assist," as in the verse *If you see the donkey of someone who hates you, fallen under its load.... Help him – azov taazov – to release it* (Exodus 23:5). Hence Rashi emphasizes that in our verse the term holds the opposite meaning: Do not favor one poor person by helping him to gather the grain or by setting it aside for him].

אֲנִי יהוה אֱלֹהֵיכֶם. נֶאֱמָן לְשַׁלֵּם שָׂכָר:

אֲנִי יהוה אֱלֹהֵיכֶם – *I am the Lord your God:* I can be trusted to reward you for compliance with these rules.

23 24 Then the LORD spoke to Moshe: "Tell the Israelites: On the HAMISHI
first day of the seventh month, you shall observe a day of rest,
a commemoration with the sounding of the ram's horn, a sa-
25 cred assembly. You shall perform no laborious work, and you
26 shall bring close a fire offering to the LORD." The
27 LORD spoke to Moshe: "Hear: the tenth day of this seventh
month is the Day of Atonement. It shall be a sacred assembly
for you, and you shall afflict yourselves and bring a fire offer-
28 ing to the LORD. You shall perform no work at all during this
entire day, for it is the Day of Atonement, there to make atone-
29 ment for you before the LORD your God. Anyone who does
not afflict himself for this whole day shall be severed from his
30 people, and if anyone performs any work during this whole
31 day, I will annihilate that person from among his people. No
work at all may you perform; this is an everlasting statute

24 | **זִכְרוֹן תְּרוּעָה** – *A commemoration with the sounding of the ram's horn:* This text introduces the obligation of remembrance, that is, to recite on Rosh Hashana scriptural verses associated with remembrance, as well as verses mentioning the sounding of the shofar. The purpose of this is to recall the binding of Yitzḥak and the ram which was sacrificed in his stead [as detailed in Genesis chapter 22].

כד | **זִכְרוֹן תְּרוּעָה.** זִכְרוֹן פְּסוּקֵי זִכָּרוֹן וּפְסוּקֵי שׁוֹפָרוֹת, לִזְכֹּר לָכֶם עֲקֵדַת יִצְחָק שֶׁקָּרַב תַּחְתָּיו אַיִל:

25 | **וְהִקְרַבְתֶּם אִשֶּׁה** – *You shall bring close a fire offering:* This refers to the additional [*musaf*] sacrifices discussed in the book of Numbers [verses 29:1–6].

כה | **וְהִקְרַבְתֶּם אִשֶּׁה.** הַמּוּסָפִים הָאֲמוּרִין בְּחוּמַשׁ הַפְּקֻדִים (במדבר כט, א-ו):

27 | **אַךְ** – *Hear:* Whenever the Torah employs the term *akh* or *rak* ["only"], its intention is to convey some sort of limitation. In the current instance, the text implies that Yom Kippur makes atonement only for those who have repented, but not for those who have ignored that obligation.

כז | **אַךְ.** כָּל אַכִין וְרַקִּין שֶׁבַּתּוֹרָה מִעוּטִין, מְכַפֵּר הוּא לַשָּׁבִין וְאֵינוֹ מְכַפֵּר עַל שֶׁאֵינָם שָׁבִין:

30 | **וְהַאֲבַדְתִּי** – *I will annihilate:* The Torah often mentions *karet* ["excision"] without specifying what it means. By using the word "annihilate" here, our verse defines the punishment of *karet* as destruction.

ל | **וְהַאֲבַדְתִּי.** לְפִי שֶׁהוּא אוֹמֵר כָּרֵת בְּכָל מָקוֹם וְאֵינִי יוֹדֵעַ מַה הוּא, כְּשֶׁהוּא אוֹמֵר: "וְהַאֲבַדְתִּי", לִמֵּד עַל הַכָּרֵת שֶׁאֵינוֹ אֶלָּא אֲבַדּוֹן:

כג כד וַיְדַבֵּר יְהוָה אֶל־מֹשֶׁה לֵּאמֹר: דַּבֵּר אֶל־בְּנֵי חמישי
יִשְׂרָאֵל לֵאמֹר בַּחֹדֶשׁ הַשְּׁבִיעִי בְּאֶחָד לַחֹדֶשׁ
יִהְיֶה לָכֶם שַׁבָּתוֹן זִכְרוֹן תְּרוּעָה מִקְרָא־קֹדֶשׁ:
כה כָּל־מְלֶאכֶת עֲבֹדָה לֹא תַעֲשׂוּ וְהִקְרַבְתֶּם אִשֶּׁה
כו לַיהוָה: וַיְדַבֵּר יְהוָה אֶל־מֹשֶׁה לֵּאמֹר:
כז אַךְ בֶּעָשׂוֹר לַחֹדֶשׁ הַשְּׁבִיעִי הַזֶּה יוֹם הַכִּפֻּרִים הוּא
מִקְרָא־קֹדֶשׁ יִהְיֶה לָכֶם וְעִנִּיתֶם אֶת־נַפְשֹׁתֵיכֶם
כח וְהִקְרַבְתֶּם אִשֶּׁה לַיהוָה: וְכָל־מְלָאכָה לֹא תַעֲשׂוּ
בְּעֶצֶם הַיּוֹם הַזֶּה כִּי יוֹם כִּפֻּרִים הוּא לְכַפֵּר עֲלֵיכֶם
כט לִפְנֵי יְהוָה אֱלֹהֵיכֶם: כִּי כָל־הַנֶּפֶשׁ אֲשֶׁר לֹא־תְעֻנֶּה
ל בְּעֶצֶם הַיּוֹם הַזֶּה וְנִכְרְתָה מֵעַמֶּיהָ: וְכָל־הַנֶּפֶשׁ אֲשֶׁר
תַּעֲשֶׂה כָּל־מְלָאכָה בְּעֶצֶם הַיּוֹם הַזֶּה וְהַאֲבַדְתִּי
לא אֶת־הַנֶּפֶשׁ הַהִוא מִקֶּרֶב עַמָּהּ: כָּל־מְלָאכָה לֹא
תַעֲשׂוּ חֻקַּת עוֹלָם לְדֹרֹתֵיכֶם בְּכֹל מֹשְׁבֹתֵיכֶם:

לא | **כָּל־מְלָאכָה וְגוֹ'.** לַעֲבֹר עָלָיו בְּלָאוִין הַרְבֵּה, אוֹ לְהַזְהִיר עַל מְלֶאכֶת לַיְלָה כִּמְלֶאכֶת יוֹם: "מִקְרָא קֹדֶשׁ" (לעיל פסוק כז) – קַדְּשֵׁהוּ בִּכְסוּת נְקִיָּה וּבִתְפִלָּה, וְכָל שְׁאָר יָמִים טוֹבִים – בְּמַאֲכָל וּבְמִשְׁתֶּה וּבִכְסוּת נְקִיָּה וּבִתְפִלָּה:

31 | **כָּל־מְלָאכָה** – *No work at all:* [Even though the performance of labor on Yom Kippur has already been forbidden in verse 28, the present text repeats the prohibition] in order to increase the number of violations a person would commit were he or she to ignore these warnings. Alternatively, our verse might serve to equate working on the night of the holiday with similar behavior during the day itself. [Verse 23:28 emphasizes: *You shall perform no work at all during this entire day – be'etzem hayom hazeh* – a phrase often understood as relating to daylight hours.] The words "a sacred assembly" [which appear in verse 27] teach that we are to sanctify Yom Kippur by donning clean clothing and celebrating the day with prayer. By contrast, the phrase "sacred assembly" used in the context of other holidays signifies eating and drinking, as well as the wearing of festive clothes and the recitation of prayers.

◀

32 throughout your generations in all your dwellings. It is a Sabbath of complete rest for you, and you shall afflict yourselves
from the evening of the ninth day of the month: from evening
to evening shall you observe your Sabbath."
33 34 The LORD spoke to Moshe: "Tell the Israelites: From the fif- SHISHI
teenth day of this seventh month, for seven days shall be the
35 Festival of Tabernacles to the LORD. The first day shall be a
sacred assembly; on it, you shall perform no laborious work.
36 For seven days you must bring close a fire offering to the
LORD. The eighth day shall be a sacred assembly for you, and
you shall present a fire offering to the LORD. It is an assembly;
37 you shall perform no laborious work. These are the LORD's
festivals, which you shall proclaim, sacred assemblies to present a fire offering to the LORD: burnt offering, grain offering,
38 sacrifice, and libations, each on its appointed day; in addition
to the LORD's Sabbaths, and in addition to your gifts and all
your offerings in the fulfillment of vows and all the freewill
39 offerings that you give to the LORD. Hear: on the fifteenth
day of the seventh month, when you have harvested the land's

לו | **עֲצֶרֶת הִוא.** עָצַרְתִּי אֶתְכֶם אֶצְלִי, כְּמֶלֶךְ שֶׁזִּמֵּן אֶת בָּנָיו לִסְעוּדָה לְכָךְ וְכָךְ יָמִים, כֵּיוָן שֶׁהִגִּיעַ זְמַנָּן לִפָּטֵר אָמַר: בָּנַי בְּבַקָּשָׁה מִכֶּם, עַכְּבוּ עִמִּי עוֹד יוֹם אֶחָד, קָשָׁה עָלַי פְּרִישַׁתְכֶם:

36 | **עֲצֶרֶת הִוא** – *It is an assembly:* On this day I will keep you [*atzarti* – I will "stop" or "hold" you] in My company. This is akin to a king who invites his sons to a feast lasting several days. However, when the time comes for them to take their leave, the father implores them: Please, will you not stay with me for just one more day? I find your departure hard to bear.

כָּל־מְלֶאכֶת עֲבֹדָה. אֲפִלּוּ מְלָאכָה שֶׁהִיא עֲבוֹדָה לָכֶם, שֶׁאִם לֹא תַעֲשׂוּהָ יֵשׁ חֶסְרוֹן כִּיס בַּדָּבָר:

כָּל־מְלֶאכֶת עֲבֹדָה – *No laborious work:* On this day you may not perform even labor that is important work for you, meaning that neglecting the task will cause you financial loss.

לֹא תַעֲשׂוּ. יָכוֹל אַף חֻלּוֹ שֶׁל מוֹעֵד יְהֵא אָסוּר בִּמְלֶאכֶת עֲבוֹדָה? תַּלְמוּד לוֹמַר: "הִוא":

לֹא תַעֲשׂוּ – *You shall not perform:* Lest you worry that such activities may not be performed on the intermediate days of the festival, the text states: *It is an assembly.* [That is, labor may not be performed on *it* – the eighth day, but not the intermediate days.]

לז | **עֹלָה וּמִנְחָה.** מִנְחַת נְסָכִים הַקְּרֵבָה עִם הָעוֹלָה:

37 | **עֹלָה וּמִנְחָה** – *Burnt offering, grain offering:* The grain offering mentioned here refers to that which accompanies every burnt offering [and is not a distinct sacrifice of its own].

לב שַׁבַּת שַׁבָּתוֹן הוּא לָכֶם וְעִנִּיתֶם אֶת־נַפְשֹׁתֵיכֶם
בְּתִשְׁעָה לַחֹדֶשׁ בָּעֶרֶב מֵעֶרֶב עַד־עֶרֶב תִּשְׁבְּתוּ
שַׁבַּתְּכֶם׃
לג לד וַיְדַבֵּר יְהוָה אֶל־מֹשֶׁה לֵּאמֹר׃ דַּבֵּר אֶל־בְּנֵי יִשְׂרָאֵל ששי
לֵאמֹר בַּחֲמִשָּׁה עָשָׂר יוֹם לַחֹדֶשׁ הַשְּׁבִיעִי הַזֶּה חַג
לה הַסֻּכּוֹת שִׁבְעַת יָמִים לַיהוָה׃ בַּיּוֹם הָרִאשׁוֹן מִקְרָא־
לו קֹדֶשׁ כָּל־מְלֶאכֶת עֲבֹדָה לֹא תַעֲשׂוּ׃ שִׁבְעַת יָמִים
תַּקְרִיבוּ אִשֶּׁה לַיהוָה בַּיּוֹם הַשְּׁמִינִי מִקְרָא־קֹדֶשׁ
יִהְיֶה לָכֶם וְהִקְרַבְתֶּם אִשֶּׁה לַיהוָה עֲצֶרֶת הִוא
לז כָּל־מְלֶאכֶת עֲבֹדָה לֹא תַעֲשׂוּ׃ אֵלֶּה מוֹעֲדֵי יְהוָה
אֲשֶׁר־תִּקְרְאוּ אֹתָם מִקְרָאֵי קֹדֶשׁ לְהַקְרִיב אִשֶּׁה
לַיהוָה עֹלָה וּמִנְחָה זֶבַח וּנְסָכִים דְּבַר־יוֹם בְּיוֹמוֹ׃
לח מִלְּבַד שַׁבְּתֹת יְהוָה וּמִלְּבַד מַתְּנוֹתֵיכֶם וּמִלְּבַד כָּל־
נִדְרֵיכֶם וּמִלְּבַד כָּל־נִדְבֹתֵיכֶם אֲשֶׁר תִּתְּנוּ לַיהוָה׃
לט אַךְ בַּחֲמִשָּׁה עָשָׂר יוֹם לַחֹדֶשׁ הַשְּׁבִיעִי בְּאָסְפְּכֶם
אֶת־תְּבוּאַת הָאָרֶץ תָּחֹגּוּ אֶת־חַג־יְהוָה שִׁבְעַת

דְּבַר־יוֹם בְּיוֹמוֹ – *Each on its appointed day:* These should follow the prescribed laws dictated in the book of Numbers [chapters 28–29, which describe the specific additional sacrifices required for each festival].

דְּבַר־יוֹם בְּיוֹמוֹ. חֹק הַקָּצוּב בְּחוּמַשׁ הַפְּקוּדִים (במדבר כח-כט):

דְּבַר־יוֹם בְּיוֹמוֹ – *Each on its appointed day:* [The special sacrifices must be brought on the days mandated for their offering.] Once a particular festival day has passed, the opportunity to bring its sacrifices has been missed as well.

דְּבַר־יוֹם בְּיוֹמוֹ. הָא אִם עָבַר יוֹמוֹ בָּטֵל קָרְבָּנוֹ:

39 | **אַךְ בַּחֲמִשָּׁה עָשָׂר יוֹם... תָּחֹגּוּ** – *Hear: on the fifteenth day... you shall celebrate:* This holiday is celebrated by bringing a peace offering called a *korban ḥagiga*. Now do not think that this sacrifice should override the Sabbath [namely, that it should be brought on the Sabbath. Some activities which are

לט | **אַךְ בַּחֲמִשָּׁה עָשָׂר יוֹם... תָּחֹגּוּ.** קָרְבַּן שְׁלָמִים לַחֲגִיגָה. יָכוֹל תִּדְחֶה אֶת הַשַּׁבָּת? תַּלְמוּד לוֹמַר ״אַךְ״, הוֹאִיל וְיֵשׁ לָהּ תַּשְׁלוּמִין כָּל שִׁבְעָה:

produce, you shall celebrate a festival to the Lord for seven
days. The first day shall be a day of rest; the eighth day shall
40 be a day of rest. On the first day you shall take for yourselves
fruit of the majestic tree, branches of palm trees, boughs of
the leafy tree, and willows of the brook, and rejoice before the
41 Lord your God for seven days. You shall celebrate it as a festival to the Lord for seven days in the year. It shall be an everlasting statute throughout your generations; celebrate this in
42 the seventh month. For seven days you shall live in huts. All
43 those native born in Israel must live in huts, so that future generations may know that I had the Israelites live in huts when

generally forbidden on the Sabbath, such as slaughtering an animal, are permitted within the Temple as part of the sacrificial services. However, not all sacrifices that are offered on a regular weekday are subject to this leniency. The *korban ḥagiga* falls into this latter category, because] the verse states *akh* [a term indicating an exclusion, as Rashi states above. Thus, should the first day of the holiday fall on the Sabbath] this sacrifice may not be offered then, since it can be brought on any of the seven days of the festival. [In contrast, the *korban musaf* additional sacrifices which are burnt offerings are limited to their prescribed days, as Rashi points out in his previous comments.]

בְּאָסְפְּכֶם אֶת־תְּבוּאַת הָאָרֶץ. שֶׁיְּהֵא חֹדֶשׁ שְׁבִיעִי זֶה בָּא בִּזְמַן אֲסִיפָה, מִכָּאן שֶׁנִּצְטַוּוּ לְעַבֵּר אֶת הַשָּׁנִים, שֶׁאִם אֵין הָעִבּוּר, פְּעָמִים שֶׁהוּא בְּאֶמְצַע הַקַּיִץ אוֹ הַחֹרֶף:

בְּאָסְפְּכֶם אֶת־תְּבוּאַת הָאָרֶץ – *When you have harvested the land's produce:* The seventh month of the year coincides with the harvest season. [The verse does not suggest that the holiday be celebrated as the crops are actually being harvested; the activities necessary for that process are forbidden on a festival.] We learn from here that Israel is commanded to intercalate the year [by adding a thirteenth month after Adar if spring has not yet arrived. A twelve-month lunar year is shorter than a solar year, so it is necessary to add a month every few years to keep the calendar in sync with the seasons]. For if this is not done, it will sometimes happen that the festival of Sukkot will fall out during the summer or even the winter.

תָּחֹגּוּ. שַׁלְמֵי חֲגִיגָה:

תָּחֹגּוּ – *You shall celebrate:* You shall sacrifice celebratory peace offerings.

שִׁבְעַת יָמִים. אִם לֹא הֵבִיא בָּזֶה יָבִיא בָּזֶה. יָכוֹל יְהֵא מְבִיאָן כָּל שִׁבְעָה? תַּלְמוּד לוֹמַר: "וְחַגֹּתֶם אֹתוֹ", יוֹם אֶחָד בְּמַשְׁמָע וְלֹא יוֹתֵר.

שִׁבְעַת יָמִים – *For seven days:* If the *korban ḥagiga* is not brought on the first day of the festival, it should be brought on a subsequent day. Perhaps the verse mandates that this sacrifice should be offered on each of the festival's seven days? No,

יָמִים בַּיּוֹם הָרִאשׁוֹן שַׁבָּתוֹן וּבַיּוֹם הַשְּׁמִינִי שַׁבָּתוֹן:
מ וּלְקַחְתֶּם לָכֶם בַּיּוֹם הָרִאשׁוֹן פְּרִי עֵץ הָדָר כַּפֹּת
תְּמָרִים וַעֲנַף עֵץ־עָבֹת וְעַרְבֵי־נָחַל וּשְׂמַחְתֶּם לִפְנֵי
מא יְהוָה אֱלֹהֵיכֶם שִׁבְעַת יָמִים: וְחַגֹּתֶם אֹתוֹ חַג לַיהוָה
שִׁבְעַת יָמִים בַּשָּׁנָה חֻקַּת עוֹלָם לְדֹרֹתֵיכֶם בַּחֹדֶשׁ
מב הַשְּׁבִיעִי תָּחֹגּוּ אֹתוֹ: בַּסֻּכֹּת תֵּשְׁבוּ שִׁבְעַת יָמִים כָּל־
מג הָאֶזְרָח בְּיִשְׂרָאֵל יֵשְׁבוּ בַּסֻּכֹּת: לְמַעַן יֵדְעוּ דֹרֹתֵיכֶם
כִּי בַסֻּכּוֹת הוֹשַׁבְתִּי אֶת־בְּנֵי יִשְׂרָאֵל בְּהוֹצִיאִי אוֹתָם

וְלָמָּה נֶאֱמַר שִׁבְעָה? לְתַשְׁלוּמִין:

for a later verse states: *You shall celebrate it [oto, in the singular] as a festival to the Lord* (23:41), meaning: This sacrifice is required on just one day of the festival. Why then does our verse command: *You shall celebrate a festival to the Lord for seven days*? To allow fulfillment of this obligation on any of the days.

מ | פְּרִי עֵץ הָדָר. עֵץ שֶׁטַּעַם עֵצוֹ וּפִרְיוֹ שָׁוֶה:

40 | **פְּרִי עֵץ הָדָר** – *Fruit of the majestic tree:* The verse refers to a tree whose wood tastes the same as its fruit.

הָדָר. הַדָּר בְּאִילָנוֹ מִשָּׁנָה לְשָׁנָה, וְזֶהוּ אֶתְרוֹג:

הָדָר – *Majestic:* The fruit on this tree is that which lives [*hadar*, that is "can remain unpicked"] on the tree from year to year. This refers to the etrog.

כַּפֹּת תְּמָרִים. חָסֵר וָי״ו, לְלַמֵּד שֶׁאֵינָהּ אֶלָּא אַחַת:

כַּפֹּת תְּמָרִים – *Branches of palm trees:* The word *kappot* appears here without the letter *vav* [as might be expected after the *peh*] to indicate that just one is required. [The word should be read as if it was *kappat* – singular, and not *kappot* – plural. Only one lulav is used on the holiday.]

וַעֲנַף עֵץ־עָבֹת. שֶׁעֲנָפָיו קְלוּעִים כַּעֲבוֹתוֹת וְכַחֲבָלִים, וְזֶהוּ הֲדַס הֶעָשׂוּי כְּמִין קְלִיעָה:

וַעֲנַף עֵץ־עָבֹת – *Boughs of the leafy tree:* This describes a plant whose leaves are braided like ropes or cords, namely the myrtle, whose leaves run up its branches in a wave pattern as if they were intertwined.

מב | הָאֶזְרָח. זֶה אֶזְרָח:

42 | **הָאֶזְרָח** – *Native born:* The definite article *heh* refers to *the* citizen of the nation [namely, the naturally born Israelite].

בְּיִשְׂרָאֵל. לְרַבּוֹת אֶת הַגֵּרִים:

בְּיִשְׂרָאֵל – *In Israel:* This includes converts.

מג | כִּי בַסֻּכּוֹת הוֹשַׁבְתִּי. עַנְנֵי כָבוֹד:

43 | **כִּי בַסֻּכּוֹת הוֹשַׁבְתִּי** – *I had them live in huts:* This refers to the clouds of glory [which protectively hovered over the nation in the wilderness].

◀

I brought them out of the land of Egypt; I am the LORD your
44 God." Thus Moshe announced the LORD's appointed times to
the Israelites.

24 1 2 The LORD spoke to Moshe: "Command the Israelites to SHEVI'I
bring you pure oil from crushed olives for the light, to kindle
3 the lamp, every night. From evening to morning, before the
LORD, Aharon shall set it up outside the curtain of the testimony in the Tent of Meeting to burn each night. This shall be
4 a rule for all time, throughout your generations. Aharon shall
set out the lamps on the pure candelabrum each day before
the LORD.

24 2 | **צַו אֶת־בְּנֵי יִשְׂרָאֵל** – *Command the Israelites:* This is the section containing the actual commandment to light the lamps. The corresponding passage in Parashat Tetzaveh [Exodus 27:20, which states: *Command the Israelites to bring you pure oil from crushed olives for light, to kindle the lamp, every night*] was only mentioned within the broader description of the Tabernacle project in order to explain what the candelabrum would be used for. The sense of that earlier verse is: You [Moshe] will eventually order the Israelites to light the lamps in this utensil.

כד ב | **צַו אֶת־בְּנֵי יִשְׂרָאֵל.** זוֹ פָּרָשַׁת מִצְוַת הַנֵּרוֹת. וּפָרָשַׁת 'וְאַתָּה תְּצַוֶּה' (שמות כז, כ) לֹא נֶאֶמְרָה אֶלָּא עַל סֵדֶר מְלֶאכֶת הַמִּשְׁכָּן לְפָרֵשׁ צֹרֶךְ הַמְּנוֹרָה, וְכֵן מַשְׁמָע: וְאַתָּה סוֹפְךָ לְצַוּוֹת אֶת בְּנֵי יִשְׂרָאֵל עַל כָּךְ:

שֶׁמֶן זַיִת זָךְ – *Pure oil:* The process of extracting oil from olives yields three grades of the substance. The first stage [in which the fruit is pressed in a mortar] produces pure oil, as explained in the Talmud (Menaḥot 86a) and in the Sifra (13:1).

שֶׁמֶן זַיִת זָךְ. שְׁלֹשָׁה שְׁמָנִים יוֹצְאִים מִן הַזַּיִת, הָרִאשׁוֹן קָרוּי זָךְ, וְהֵן מְפֹרָשִׁין בִּמְנָחוֹת (דף פו ע״א) וּבְתוֹרַת כֹּהֲנִים (פרשתא יג, א):

תָּמִיד – *Every night:* [The term *tamid* can also be understood as "perpetual." Rashi explains that the meaning here is otherwise.] The lamps should be lit every night. We find a similar usage of the term in the verse *This is the regular [tamid] burnt offering* (Numbers 28:6), which means that this sacrifice is brought on a daily basis [and not that burnt offerings are continuously conveyed onto the altar].

תָּמִיד. מִלַּיְלָה לְלַיְלָה, כְּמוֹ: ״עֹלַת תָּמִיד״ (במדבר כח, ו) שֶׁאֵינָהּ אֶלָּא מִיּוֹם לְיוֹם:

3 | **לְפָרֹכֶת הָעֵדֻת** – *The curtain of the testimony:* This curtain hangs in front of the ark which is itself called "testimony" [on account of the tablets of the law which it holds. The phrase "Ark of the Testimony" appears, for example, in Exodus 25:22]. However, according to our Sages, the term "testimony" refers to the western lamp of the seven within the candelabrum;

ג | **לְפָרֹכֶת הָעֵדֻת.** שֶׁלִּפְנֵי הָאָרוֹן שֶׁהוּא קָרוּי עֵדוּת. וְרַבּוֹתֵינוּ דָּרְשׁוּ: עַל נֵר מַעֲרָבִי, שֶׁהוּא עֵדוּת לְכָל בָּאֵי עוֹלָם שֶׁהַשְּׁכִינָה שׁוֹרָה בְּיִשְׂרָאֵל, שֶׁנּוֹתֵן בָּהּ שֶׁמֶן כְּמִדַּת חַבְרוֹתֶיהָ, וּמִמֶּנָּה הָיָה מַתְחִיל וּבָהּ

מג מֵאֶרֶץ מִצְרָיִם אֲנִי יהוה אֱלֹהֵיכֶם: וַיְדַבֵּר מֹשֶׁה אֶת־
מֹעֲדֵי יהוה אֶל־בְּנֵי יִשְׂרָאֵל:

כד א וַיְדַבֵּר יהוה אֶל־מֹשֶׁה לֵּאמֹר: ב צַו אֶת־בְּנֵי יִשְׂרָאֵל שביעי
וְיִקְחוּ אֵלֶיךָ שֶׁמֶן זַיִת זָךְ כָּתִית לַמָּאוֹר לְהַעֲלֹת נֵר
ג תָּמִיד: מִחוּץ לְפָרֹכֶת הָעֵדֻת בְּאֹהֶל מוֹעֵד יַעֲרֹךְ
אֹתוֹ אַהֲרֹן מֵעֶרֶב עַד־בֹּקֶר לִפְנֵי יהוה תָּמִיד חֻקַּת
ד עוֹלָם לְדֹרֹתֵיכֶם: עַל הַמְּנֹרָה הַטְּהֹרָה יַעֲרֹךְ אֶת־
הַנֵּרוֹת לִפְנֵי יהוה תָּמִיד:

הָיָה מְסַיֵּם:

it is so called because it testifies to the entire world that the Divine Presence dwells within the congregation of Israel. For even though this lamp is filled with the same amount of oil as are the other six lights [it miraculously continues burning throughout the day. All seven lamps were prepared in the evening with enough oil to burn through the night. By morning six of these lamps had consumed all of their fuel, while the seventh lamp burned through the day until the next evening]. Therefore, this western lamp was first to be lit and last to be cleaned.

יַעֲרֹךְ אֹתוֹ אַהֲרֹן מֵעֶרֶב עַד־בֹּקֶר. יַעֲרֹךְ אוֹתוֹ עֲרִיכָה הָרְאוּיָה לְמִדַּת כָּל הַלַּיְלָה, וְשִׁעֲרוּ חֲכָמִים חֲצִי לֹג לְכָל נֵר וָנֵר, וְהֵן כְּדַאי אַף לְלֵילֵי תְּקוּפַת טֵבֵת, וּמִדָּה זוֹ הִקְבְּעָה לָהֶם:

יַעֲרֹךְ אֹתוֹ אַהֲרֹן מֵעֶרֶב עַד־בֹּקֶר – *Aharon shall set it up to burn each night:* Aharon should prepare the lamps with enough oil to burn throughout the night. [The instruction *me'erev ad boker* does mean that the High Priest should spend all night tending to the candelabrum.] According to the Sages, the measure of oil for each lamp was half a *log*. This sufficed for even the longest nights of the month of Tevet [which fall in the dead of winter]. The same amount of oil was used throughout the year [even during the summer, when the relatively shorter nights meant that the candles stayed lit into the daylight hours].

ד | הַמְּנֹרָה הַטְּהֹרָה. שֶׁהִיא זָהָב טָהוֹר. דָּבָר אַחֵר, עַל טָהֳרָהּ שֶׁל מְנוֹרָה, שֶׁמְּטַהֲרָהּ וּמְדַשְּׁנָהּ תְּחִלָּה מִן הָאֵפֶר:

4 | **הַמְּנֹרָה הַטְּהֹרָה** – *The pure candelabrum:* The candelabrum was pure in the sense that it was constructed out of pure gold [and not that it lacked ritual impurity]. Another interpretation: The adjective refers to the cleanliness of the utensil. The candelabrum could not be lit until it was first cleared of its ashes.

◀

5 And you shall take fine flour and bake twelve loaves, two-
6 tenths of an ephah for each loaf. You shall place them in two
columns, six to each column, on the pure table before the
7 Lord. Lay pure incense on each stack, as a remembrance
8 for the bread, as a fire offering to the Lord. Every Sabbath
he shall set it out, always, before the Lord on behalf of the
9 Israelites: an everlasting covenant. It shall belong to Aharon
and his sons. They shall eat it in a holy place because it is holy
of holies among the Lord's fire offerings, their perpetual
10 share." A man went out among the Israelites, the son
of an Israelite woman and an Egyptian man. And a fight broke
out in the camp between this son of an Israelite woman, and

6 | **שֵׁשׁ הַמַּעֲרָכֶת** – *Six to each column:* There were six loaves per column. [There were not six columns, which is a possible interpretation of the phrase.]

ו | **שֵׁשׁ הַמַּעֲרָכֶת.** שֵׁשׁ חַלּוֹת הַמַּעֲרֶכֶת הָאֶחָת:

הַשֻּׁלְחָן הַטָּהֹר – *The pure table:* The table was fashioned out of pure gold. Another interpretation: The loaves should be placed on the "purity" of the table [that is, directly on the table's top]. This means that the poles that separated the loaves in the columns must not raise the breads off the surface of the table. [This refers to the bottom two loaves which rested on the table itself; the other five items in each column were placed on horizontal pieces so that the loaves were not stacked one on top of the other.]

הַשֻּׁלְחָן הַטָּהֹר. שֶׁל זָהָב טָהוֹר. דָּבָר אַחֵר, עַל טָהֳרוֹ שֶׁל שֻׁלְחָן, שֶׁלֹּא יִהְיוּ הַסְּנִיפִין מַגְבִּיהִין אֶת הַלֶּחֶם מֵעַל גַּבֵּי הַשֻּׁלְחָן:

7 | **וְנָתַתָּ עַל־הַמַּעֲרֶכֶת** – *Lay on each stack:* [Although the definite article *heh* is used, suggesting that frankincense was placed on only one stack] the incense was added to each of the two columns. Thus, there were two incense receptacles, each holding a handful of spices.

ז | **וְנָתַתָּ עַל־הַמַּעֲרֶכֶת.** עַל כָּל אַחַת מִשְּׁתֵּי הַמַּעֲרָכוֹת; הֲרֵי שְׁנֵי בָּזִיכֵי לְבוֹנָה, מְלֹא קֹמֶץ לְכָל אַחַת:

וְהָיְתָה – *As a remembrance:* It is the frankincense itself which acts as a remembrance [and not the act of placing the incense which serves this purpose].

וְהָיְתָה. הַלְּבוֹנָה הַזֹּאת:

לַלֶּחֶם לְאַזְכָּרָה – *A remembrance for the bread:* None of the bread is actually offered up to God. [Rather, it is all consumed by the priests.] Instead, incense is burned whenever the loaves are removed from the table every Sabbath [when they are replaced with a new set of twelve breads]. The frankincense thus serves as remembrance for the bread and acts to call ◀

לַלֶּחֶם לְאַזְכָּרָה. שֶׁאֵין מִן הַלֶּחֶם לַגָּבוֹהַּ כְּלוּם, אֶלָּא הַלְּבוֹנָה נִקְטֶרֶת כְּשֶׁמְּסַלְּקִין אוֹתוֹ בְּכָל שַׁבָּת וְשַׁבָּת, וְהִיא לְזִכָּרוֹן לַלֶּחֶם, שֶׁעַל יָדָהּ הוּא נִזְכָּר לְמַעְלָה, כַּקֹּמֶץ שֶׁהוּא אַזְכָּרָה לַמִּנְחָה:

ה וְלָקַחְתָּ סֹלֶת וְאָפִיתָ אֹתָהּ שְׁתֵּים עֶשְׂרֵה חַלּוֹת
ו שְׁנֵי עֶשְׂרֹנִים יִהְיֶה הַחַלָּה הָאֶחָת: וְשַׂמְתָּ אוֹתָם
שְׁתַּיִם מַעֲרָכוֹת שֵׁשׁ הַמַּעֲרָכֶת עַל הַשֻּׁלְחָן הַטָּהֹר
ז לִפְנֵי יהוה: וְנָתַתָּ עַל־הַמַּעֲרֶכֶת לְבֹנָה זַכָּה וְהָיְתָה
ח לַלֶּחֶם לְאַזְכָּרָה אִשֶּׁה לַיהוה: בְּיוֹם הַשַּׁבָּת בְּיוֹם
הַשַּׁבָּת יַעַרְכֶנּוּ לִפְנֵי יהוה תָּמִיד מֵאֵת בְּנֵי־יִשְׂרָאֵל
ט בְּרִית עוֹלָם: וְהָיְתָה לְאַהֲרֹן וּלְבָנָיו וַאֲכָלֻהוּ בְּמָקוֹם
קָדֹשׁ כִּי קֹדֶשׁ קָדָשִׁים הוּא לוֹ מֵאִשֵּׁי יהוה חָק־
י עוֹלָם: וַיֵּצֵא בֶּן־אִשָּׁה יִשְׂרְאֵלִית וְהוּא
בֶּן־אִישׁ מִצְרִי בְּתוֹךְ בְּנֵי יִשְׂרָאֵל וַיִּנָּצוּ בַּמַּחֲנֶה בֶּן

God's attention to the loaves. In this way the burning of the spices generates a similar remembrance to that effected by the handfuls taken from grain offerings [which are then burned on the altar].

ט | וְהָיְתָה. הַמִּנְחָה הַזֹּאת, שֶׁכָּל דְּבַר הַבָּא מִן הַתְּבוּאָה בִּכְלַל מִנְחָה הוּא:

9 | **וְהָיְתָה** – *It shall belong:* This grain offering [that is, the loaves, shall belong to Aharon and his sons. Rashi refers to the loaves as a *minḥa*, a feminine term, thereby explaining the gender of the verb. Had the verse meant that the bread – *leḥem* – should be given to the priests, the text would have used the masculine form, *vehaya*]. For indeed, all items which are made out of grains fall into the category of *menaḥot* [grain offerings].

וַאֲכָלֻהוּ. מוּסָב עַל הַלֶּחֶם שֶׁהוּא לְשׁוֹן זָכָר:

וַאֲכָלֻהוּ – *They shall eat it:* The term *vaakhaluhu* refers back to the bread [mentioned in 24:7, which is masculine, corresponding to the masculine pronoun at the end of the word *akhaluhu*. Had it related to the general and feminine term *minḥa*, the verb would have been *vaakhaluha*].

י | וַיֵּצֵא בֶּן־אִשָּׁה יִשְׂרְאֵלִית. מֵהֵיכָן יָצָא? רַבִּי לֵוִי אוֹמֵר: מֵעוֹלָמוֹ יָצָא. רַבִּי בֶּרֶכְיָה אוֹמֵר: מִפָּרָשָׁה שֶׁלְּמַעְלָה יָצָא, לִגְלֵג וְאָמַר: ״בְּיוֹם הַשַּׁבָּת יַעַרְכֶנּוּ״ (לעיל פסוק ח), דֶּרֶךְ הַמֶּלֶךְ לֶאֱכֹל פַּת חַמָּה בְּכָל יוֹם,

10 | **וַיֵּצֵא בֶּן־אִשָּׁה יִשְׂרְאֵלִית** – *A man went out, the son of an Israelite woman:* From where did this man go out? Rabbi Levi taught: He left his world. [That is, his blasphemy removed him from this world, or perhaps from the next world.] Rabbi Berekhya maintains: He separated himself from this passage [that is, what is stated in the previous verses]. For the man ◀

11 an Israelite man. The Israelite woman's son blasphemed the
Name and cursed – his mother's name was Shlomit, daughter
of Divri, of the tribe of Dan – and they brought him before
12 Moshe. They placed the man in custody until the LORD's verdict would be pronounced to them.

שֶׁמָּא פַּת צוֹנֶנֶת שֶׁל תִּשְׁעָה יָמִים? בִּתְמִיהָה. וּמַתְנִיתָא אָמְרָה: מִבֵּית דִּינוֹ שֶׁל מֹשֶׁה יָצָא מְחֻיָּב. בָּא לִטַּע אָהֳלוֹ בְּתוֹךְ מַחֲנֵה דָן, אָמְרוּ לוֹ, מַה טִּיבְךָ לְכָאן? אָמַר לָהֶם: מִבְּנֵי דָן אֲנִי. אָמְרוּ לוֹ: "אִישׁ עַל דִּגְלוֹ בְאֹתֹת לְבֵית אֲבֹתָם" כְּתִיב (במדבר ב, ב), נִכְנַס לְבֵית דִּינוֹ שֶׁל מֹשֶׁה וְיָצָא מְחֻיָּב, עָמַד וְגִדֵּף:

mocked the above instruction, *Every Sabbath he shall set it out* (24:8), and said: Surely, it is customary for a king to eat freshly baked bread every single day; is it not demeaning for him to be served cold nine-day-old food? [The loaves were baked on Friday and stacked on the table's two columns on the Sabbath. A week later these breads were removed and eaten by the priests, nine days after they were baked. This disdainful attitude of the Israelite woman's son was the cause of his quarrel with the other man.] An interpretation in a *baraita* provides a third suggestion: The man left the court of Moshe where he had been found guilty of the accusation brought against him. For this man had attempted to pitch his tent within the camp of the tribe of Dan, and the members of that clan had protested. Said he: My mother comes from your tribe [hence he considered himself a Danite]. But the men of Dan turned him away, citing the verse *The Israelites shall camp, each by his banner, the ensign of his ancestral house* [*leveit avotam*, literally, "according to their fathers' houses"] [Numbers 2:2, and the man's father was an Egyptian, not a descendant of Dan]. This prompted him to enter Moshe's court for a ruling, and when the decision went against him, he stood up and blasphemed God.

בֶּן־אִישׁ מִצְרִי. הוּא הַמִּצְרִי שֶׁהָרַג מֹשֶׁה:

בֶּן־אִישׁ מִצְרִי – *The son of an Egyptian man:* The man's father was the Egyptian whom Moshe killed [as reported in Exodus 2:12. That episode refers to the antagonist as an *ish mitzri* – "an Egyptian man"].

בְּתוֹךְ בְּנֵי יִשְׂרָאֵל. מְלַמֵּד שֶׁנִּתְגַּיֵּר:

בְּתוֹךְ בְּנֵי יִשְׂרָאֵל – *Among the Israelites:* This teaches that the son of this mixed union converted [and adopted his mother's heritage].

וַיִּנָּצוּ בַּמַּחֲנֶה. עַל עִסְקֵי הַמַּחֲנֶה:

וַיִּנָּצוּ בַּמַּחֲנֶה – *And a fight broke out in the camp:* The quarrel was regarding the camp [that is, the third interpretation of the incident cited by Rashi above].

וְאִישׁ הַיִּשְׂרְאֵלִי. זֶה שֶׁכְּנֶגְדּוֹ, שֶׁמִּחָה בוֹ מִטַּע אָהֳלוֹ:

וְאִישׁ הַיִּשְׂרְאֵלִי – *And an Israelite man:* This was the opponent of the Israelite woman's son, who objected to him moving into the camp of Dan.

יא הַיִּשְׂרְאֵלִית וְאִישׁ הַיִּשְׂרְאֵלִי: וַיִּקֹּב בֶּן־הָאִשָּׁה
הַיִּשְׂרְאֵלִית אֶת־הַשֵּׁם וַיְקַלֵּל וַיָּבִיאוּ אֹתוֹ אֶל־מֹשֶׁה
יב וְשֵׁם אִמּוֹ שְׁלֹמִית בַּת־דִּבְרִי לְמַטֵּה־דָן: וַיַּנִּיחֻהוּ
בַּמִּשְׁמָר לִפְרֹשׁ לָהֶם עַל־פִּי יהוה:

11 | **וַיִּקֹּב** – *And he cursed:* His act should be interpreted as the Targum renders it – *ufaresh* – "he enunciated," meaning that the man pronounced the explicit name of God, and he cursed. He uttered the special name of God which he had heard at Mount Sinai.

יא | **וַיִּקֹּב.** כְּתַרְגּוּמוֹ: "וּפָרֵשׁ", שֶׁנָּקַב שֵׁם הַמְיֻחָד וְגִדֵּף, וְהוּא שֵׁם הַמְפֹרָשׁ שֶׁשָּׁמַע מִסִּינַי:

וְשֵׁם אִמּוֹ שְׁלֹמִית בַּת־דִּבְרִי – *His mother's name was Shlomit, daughter of Divri:* The purpose in mentioning the mother's name is to praise the rest of the nation; this woman alone prostituted herself to an Egyptian.

וְשֵׁם אִמּוֹ שְׁלֹמִית בַּת־דִּבְרִי. שִׁבְחָן שֶׁל יִשְׂרָאֵל שֶׁפִּרְסְמָהּ הַכָּתוּב לָזוֹ, לוֹמַר שֶׁהִיא לְבַדָּהּ הָיְתָה זוֹנָה:

שְׁלֹמִית – *Shlomit:* She was so called because she was a garrulous person, always saying to a passing man: Peace [*shalom*] be upon you, or wishing a group of people: May you all enjoy peace! Because she talked to everybody and had words [*devarim*] for everyone she saw [she became excessively friendly with the community and eventually inappropriately familiar with the Egyptian man].

שְׁלֹמִית. דַּהֲוַת פַּטְפְּטָה, שְׁלָם עֲלָךְ, שְׁלָם עֲלַךְ, שְׁלָם עֲלֵיכוֹן, מְפַטְפֶּטֶת בִּדְבָרִים, שׁוֹאֶלֶת בִּשְׁלוֹם הַכֹּל:

בַּת־דִּבְרִי – *Daughter of Divri:* This woman was extremely talkative [*dabranit*], speaking to everybody. This is how she ended up acting promiscuously.

בַּת־דִּבְרִי. דַּבְּרָנִית הָיְתָה, מְדַבֶּרֶת עִם כָּל אָדָם, לְפִיכָךְ קִלְקְלָה:

לְמַטֵּה־דָן – *Of the tribe of Dan:* We learn from here that a wicked person brings shame not only to himself, but also to his father, and to his whole tribe. The opposite point is derived from the verse *I have assigned to him Oholiav, son of Aḥisamakh from the tribe of Dan* (Exodus 31:6) – Oholiav's contribution to the construction of the Tabernacle brought pride not only to himself, but also to his father, and to his entire tribe.

לְמַטֵּה־דָן. מַגִּיד שֶׁהָרָשָׁע גּוֹרֵם גְּנַאי לוֹ, גְּנַאי לְאָבִיו, גְּנַאי לְשִׁבְטוֹ. כַּיּוֹצֵא בוֹ: "אָהֳלִיאָב בֶּן אֲחִיסָמָךְ לְמַטֵּה דָן" (שמות לא, ו), שֶׁבַח לוֹ, שֶׁבַח לְאָבִיו, שֶׁבַח לְשִׁבְטוֹ:

12 | **וַיַּנִּיחֻהוּ** – *They placed the man:* The son of the Israelite woman was not imprisoned with the man who had gathered wood [referring to the Sabbath violator whose arrest and punishment are described in Numbers 15:32–36] even though both incidents happened at the same time. Everyone knew that the wood gatherer was to be killed [for God had earlier

יב | **וַיַּנִּיחֻהוּ.** לְבַדּוֹ, וְלֹא הִנִּיחוּ מְקוֹשֵׁשׁ עִמּוֹ, שֶׁשְּׁנֵיהֶם הָיוּ בְּפֶרֶק אֶחָד; וְיוֹדְעִים הָיוּ שֶׁהַמְקוֹשֵׁשׁ בְּמִיתָה, אֲבָל לֹא פֹרַשׁ לָהֶם בְּאֵיזוֹ מִיתָה, לְכָךְ נֶאֱמַר: "כִּי לֹא פֹרַשׁ מַה יֵּעָשֶׂה לוֹ" (במדבר טו, לד), אֲבָל

13 14 And the LORD spoke to Moshe: "Take the one who cursed
outside the camp. All the people who heard him shall lay their
hands on his head – and then the whole community shall
15 stone him. Tell the Israelites: Anyone who curses his God
16 shall bear the sin, and anyone who blasphemes the LORD's
name shall be put to death: the whole community shall stone
him. Migrant and native born alike: one who blasphemes the
17 LORD's name shall be put to death. One who takes the life of
18 any human being shall be put to death. One who takes the
19 life of an animal shall make restitution for it: life for life. One
who injures his fellow man shall be penalized in proportion
20 to the injury inflicted: the cost of a broken bone for a broken
bone, of an eye for an eye, of a tooth for a tooth. Just as he
inflicted injury on another human being, so shall he suffer the

declared that *whoever profanes [the Sabbath] shall be put to death* (Exodus 31:14)], but the method of execution was unclear. Hence the text states: *It had not been specified what should be done to him* (Numbers 15:34). On the other hand, with regard to the blasphemer, the verse states: *They placed the man in custody until the LORD's verdict would be pronounced to them*, for the community did not know whether his behavior constituted a capital offense. [It would have been torment for the son of the Israelite woman to be held with the other man who was to be killed; that would have convinced him that he too was to die.]

בִּמְקַלֵּל הוּא אוֹמֵר ״לִפְרֹשׁ לָהֶם״, שֶׁלֹּא הָיוּ יוֹדְעִים אִם חַיָּב מִיתָה אִם לָאו:

14 | **הַשֹּׁמְעִים** – *The people who heard him:* This refers to the witnesses.

יד | הַשֹּׁמְעִים. אֵלּוּ הָעֵדִים:

כָּל – *All:* The adjective includes the judges [who had heard the blasphemy indirectly, from the witnesses].

כָּל. לְהָבִיא אֶת הַדַּיָּנִים:

אֶת־יְדֵיהֶם – *Their hands:* All of these men say to the blasphemer: Your guilt is on your head; we will not be punished for your execution because you brought this upon yourself.

אֶת־יְדֵיהֶם. אוֹמְרִים לוֹ, דָּמְךָ בְּרֹאשְׁךָ, וְאֵין אָנוּ נֶעֱנָשִׁים בְּמִיתָתְךָ שֶׁאַתָּה גָּרַמְתָּ לְךָ:

כָּל־הָעֵדָה – *The whole community:* The witnesses are to stone the sentenced person under the authority of the congregation. We learn from here the legal principle of agency. [The witnesses were to act on behalf of the nation, which would be as if everyone had stoned the sinner.]

כָּל־הָעֵדָה. בְּמַעֲמַד כָּל הָעֵדָה, מִכָּאן שֶׁשְּׁלוּחוֹ שֶׁל אָדָם כְּמוֹתוֹ:

יג יד וַיְדַבֵּר יְהוָה אֶל־מֹשֶׁה לֵּאמֹר: הוֹצֵא אֶת־הַמְקַלֵּל
אֶל־מִחוּץ לַמַּחֲנֶה וְסָמְכוּ כָל־הַשֹּׁמְעִים אֶת־יְדֵיהֶם
טו עַל־רֹאשׁוֹ וְרָגְמוּ אֹתוֹ כָּל־הָעֵדָה: וְאֶל־בְּנֵי יִשְׂרָאֵל
תְּדַבֵּר לֵאמֹר אִישׁ אִישׁ כִּי־יְקַלֵּל אֱלֹהָיו וְנָשָׂא חֶטְאוֹ:
טז וְנֹקֵב שֵׁם־יְהוָה מוֹת יוּמָת רָגוֹם יִרְגְּמוּ־בוֹ כָּל־הָעֵדָה
יז כַּגֵּר כָּאֶזְרָח בְּנָקְבוֹ־שֵׁם יוּמָת: וְאִישׁ כִּי יַכֶּה כָּל־נֶפֶשׁ
יח אָדָם מוֹת יוּמָת: וּמַכֵּה נֶפֶשׁ־בְּהֵמָה יְשַׁלְּמֶנָּה נֶפֶשׁ
יט תַּחַת נָפֶשׁ: וְאִישׁ כִּי־יִתֵּן מוּם בַּעֲמִיתוֹ כַּאֲשֶׁר עָשָׂה
כ כֵּן יֵעָשֶׂה לּוֹ: שֶׁבֶר תַּחַת שֶׁבֶר עַיִן תַּחַת עַיִן שֵׁן

15 | **וְנָשָׂא חֶטְאוֹ** – *Shall bear the sin:* A person will be punished with excision in a situation where he or she was not warned by witnesses before cursing God.

טו | **וְנָשָׂא חֶטְאוֹ.** בְּכָרֵת, כְּשֶׁאֵין הַתְרָאָה:

16 | **וְנֹקֵב שֵׁם** – *And anyone who blasphemes the Lord's name:* One is only liable if he pronounces the explicit name of God [namely, the Tetragrammaton] but not if he curses using other names of God.

טז | **וְנֹקֵב שֵׁם.** אֵינוֹ חַיָּב עַד שֶׁיְּפָרֵשׁ אֶת הַשֵּׁם, וְלֹא הַמְקַלֵּל בְּכִנּוּי:

וְנֹקֵב – *Who blasphemes:* The verb *venokev* connotes cursing, as in the verse *How can I curse [ekov] whom God has not cursed?* (Numbers 23:8).

וְנֹקֵב. לְשׁוֹן קְלָלָה, כְּמוֹ: "מָה אֶקֹּב" (במדבר כג, ח):

17 | **וְאִישׁ כִּי יַכֶּה** – *One who takes the life:* When an earlier verse states: *One person who strikes another* [*ish*, literally, "a man"] *so that he dies shall be put to death* (Exodus 21:12), that depicts culpability for killing an adult man. How do we know that one would similarly be liable for taking the life of a woman or a child? We learn that from the present verse which states: *One who takes the life of any human being.*

יז | **וְאִישׁ כִּי יַכֶּה.** לְפִי שֶׁנֶּאֱמַר: "מַכֵּה אִישׁ" וְגוֹ' (שמות כא, יב), אֵין לִי אֶלָּא שֶׁהָרַג אֶת הָאִישׁ, אִשָּׁה וְקָטָן מִנַּיִן? תַּלְמוּד לוֹמַר: "כָּל נֶפֶשׁ אָדָם":

20 | **כֵּן יִנָּתֶן בּוֹ** – *So shall he suffer the loss:* [Although the phrase *ken yinnaten bo* literally means, "the same shall be inflicted upon him,"] our Sages explained that the perpetrator is not himself actually physically harmed as punishment for his action, but that he is forced to pay monetary compensation for his crime. The victim is assessed as a slave [and the attacker pays the difference between what he would have been worth

כ | **כֵּן יִנָּתֶן בּוֹ.** פֵּרְשׁוּ רַבּוֹתֵינוּ שֶׁאֵינוֹ נְתִינַת מוּם מַמָּשׁ, אֶלָּא תַּשְׁלוּמֵי מָמוֹן – שָׁמִין אוֹתוֹ כְּעֶבֶד, לְכָךְ כָּתוּב בּוֹ לְשׁוֹן נְתִינָה, דָּבָר הַנָּתוּן מִיָּד לְיָד:

MAFTIR

21 loss. One who kills an animal shall make restitution for it; but
22 one who kills a human being shall be put to death. There shall
be one law for you, for migrant and for native born alike, for I
23 am the Lord your God." Moshe told this to the Israelites, and
so they took the blasphemer outside the camp and stoned
him. Thus the Israelites did as the Lord had commanded
Moshe.

before and after the injury]. This is why the text uses the language of *netina* – "giving": It refers to something that can be handed over from one person to another [that is, money].

כא | **וּמַכֵּה בְהֵמָה יְשַׁלְּמֶנָּה.** לְמַעְלָה דִּבֶּר בְּהוֹרֵג בְּהֵמָה, וְכָאן דִּבֶּר בְּעוֹשֶׂה בָהּ חַבּוּרָה:

21 | **וּמַכֵּה בְהֵמָה יְשַׁלְּמֶנָּה** – *One who kills an animal shall make restitution for it:* The text above [verse 18, which states: *One who takes the life of an animal* – *makkeh nefesh behema*] deals with a person who kills an animal, whereas the present verse describes merely the wounding of an animal. [Our verse omits the term *nefesh* – "life" or "soul."]

וּמַכֵּה אָדָם יוּמָת. אֲפִלּוּ לֹא הֲרָגוֹ אֶלָּא עָשָׂה בוֹ חַבּוּרָה, שֶׁלֹּא נֶאֱמַר כָּאן 'נֶפֶשׁ'. וּבְמַכֵּה אָבִיו וְאִמּוֹ דִּבֶּר הַכָּתוּב, וּבָא לְהַקִּישׁוֹ לְמַכֵּה בְהֵמָה, מַה מַּכֵּה בְהֵמָה מֵחַיִּים, אַף מַכֵּה אָבִיו מֵחַיִּים, פְּרָט לְמַכֶּה לְאַחַר מִיתָה, לְפִי שֶׁמָּצִינוּ שֶׁהַמְקַלְּלוֹ לְאַחַר מִיתָה חַיָּב, הֻצְרַךְ לוֹמַר בְּמַכֶּה שֶׁפָּטוּר. וּמַה בִּבְהֵמָה

וּמַכֵּה אָדָם יוּמָת – *But one who kills a human being shall be put to death:* Since this verse does not employ the word *nefesh* ["soul," as the text does in verse 17], we learn that the attack discussed here is one that does not result in death, but only in injury. [Even so, the perpetrator is subject to death because] the text describes the striking of one's father or mother. Hence a comparison is made between wounding one's parent and injuring an animal. Just as one is only liable for striking a living animal, so too is a son or daughter only held accountable for striking his or her parent when the latter is still alive; one

כא תַּחַת שֵׁן כַּאֲשֶׁר יִתֵּן מוּם בָּאָדָם כֵּן יִנָּתֶן בּוֹ: וּמַכֵּה מפטיר
כב בְהֵמָה יְשַׁלְּמֶנָּה וּמַכֵּה אָדָם יוּמָת: מִשְׁפַּט אֶחָד
יִהְיֶה לָכֶם כַּגֵּר כָּאֶזְרָח יִהְיֶה כִּי אֲנִי יהוה אֱלֹהֵיכֶם:
כג וַיְדַבֵּר מֹשֶׁה אֶל־בְּנֵי יִשְׂרָאֵל וַיּוֹצִיאוּ אֶת־הַמְקַלֵּל
אֶל־מִחוּץ לַמַּחֲנֶה וַיִּרְגְּמוּ אֹתוֹ אָבֶן וּבְנֵי־יִשְׂרָאֵל
עָשׂוּ כַּאֲשֶׁר צִוָּה יהוה אֶת־מֹשֶׁה:

would not be executed for hitting a dead parent. Now this had to be pointed out because we indeed find that a child remains culpable for cursing his or her parent even after the father or mother has died. In contrast, we are taught that wounding a parent's corpse is not a capital offense. Furthermore, just as one must pay for injuring an animal only when he has caused an actual wound, so too is one held liable for striking a parent only when the father or mother has suffered a wound [that is, when blood has been drawn].

בְּחַבָּלָה, שֶׁאִם אֵין חַבָּלָה אֵין תַּשְׁלוּמִין, אַף מַכֵּה אָבִיו אֵינוֹ חַיָּב עַד שֶׁיַּעֲשֶׂה בּוֹ חַבּוּרָה:

22 | אֲנִי יהוה אֱלֹהֵיכֶם – *I am the* Lord *your God:* I am the God of all of you. Just as My Name is identified with your community [of native-born Israelites], it is no less associated with the converts among you.

כב | אֲנִי יהוה אֱלֹהֵיכֶם. אֱלֹהֵי כֻּלְּכֶם, כְּשֵׁם שֶׁאֲנִי מְיַחֵד שְׁמִי עֲלֵיכֶם, כָּךְ אֲנִי מְיַחֲדוֹ עַל הַגֵּרִים:

23 | וּבְנֵי־יִשְׂרָאֵל עָשׂוּ – *Thus the Israelites did:* The people fulfilled the particulars of the commandment of stoning which are mentioned elsewhere. Specifically, the man was first pushed off a high structure. He was then stoned. Finally, his corpse was hanged up temporarily.

כג | וּבְנֵי־יִשְׂרָאֵל עָשׂוּ. כָּל הַמִּצְוָה הָאֲמוּרָה בִּסְקִילָה בְּמָקוֹם אַחֵר: דְּחִיָּה, רְגִימָה וּתְלִיָּה:

◀

HAFTARAT EMOR

EZEKIEL

5 But the priests who are Levites descended from Tzadok, who protected
the preciousness of My Sanctuary when the children of Israel strayed
from Me, they are the ones who may draw near Me in order to serve Me,
and they shall stand before Me to offer Me fat and blood: this is the word
6 of the Lord God. They are the ones who will enter My Sanctuary, and
they shall approach My table to serve Me; they shall dutifully protect My
7 precious things. This is how it shall be when they approach the gates of the
inner courtyard: they will wear linen garments, and no wool shall be upon
8 them when they serve at the gates of the inner courtyard and within. There
will be linen turbans on their heads and linen trousers on their loins; they
9 shall not gird themselves in a way that causes perspiration. And when they
leave to go to the outer courtyard – to the outer courtyard to the people –
they shall remove the garments in which they serve, leaving them in the
holy chambers, and put on other clothing, in order not to give the impression, by mingling with them wearing their holy garments, that the people
0 are equal to them in sanctity. They shall not shave their heads nor grow
their hair long in disarray; they shall keep their heads carefully trimmed.
1 Nor shall any priest drink wine when they enter the inner courtyard.
2 And they shall not take as a wife a widow or a divorcée. Rather, they shall
take as wives only virgins of the seed of the House of Israel, or a widow
3 who is the widow of a priest. And they shall teach My people the difference between the sacred and the profane and make known to them the
4 difference between impure and pure. When there is controversy, they
shall stand in judgment, adjudicating it according to My laws. And they
shall keep My teachings and My statutes at all the times I have appointed,
5 and sanctify My Sabbaths. The priest shall not approach a human corpse
and become impure because of it, though for a father or a mother, for a
son or a daughter, for a brother or for a sister who is unmarried, they may
6 become impure. After a priest's purification process begins, seven days
7 are counted for him. And on the day he comes to the Sanctuary, into the
inner courtyard to minister in the Sanctuary, he is to bring his purification
8 offering – this is the word of the Lord God. And this shall be the priests'
inheritance: I am their inheritance. Give them no territory to possess in
9 the land of Israel; I am their possession. They shall eat the grain offering
and the purification offering and the guilt offering, and everything con-
0 secrated by vow in Israel shall be theirs. The choicest of all first fruits of
every kind and every gift offering out of all your various donations belongs to the priests. And your first kneading you shall give to the priest
1 so that a blessing settles upon your home. Whether it be bird or beast,
the priests may not eat any creature that died on its own or was torn to
pieces as prey.

הפטרת אמר

ד טו וְהַכֹּהֲנִים הַלְוִיִּם בְּנֵי צָדוֹק אֲשֶׁר שָׁמְרוּ אֶת־מִשְׁמֶרֶת מִקְדָּשִׁי יחזקאל
בִּתְעוֹת בְּנֵי־יִשְׂרָאֵל מֵעָלַי הֵמָּה יִקְרְבוּ אֵלַי לְשָׁרְתֵנִי וְעָמְדוּ לְפָנַי
טז לְהַקְרִיב לִי חֵלֶב וָדָם נְאֻם אֲדֹנָי יֱהֹוִה: הֵמָּה יָבֹאוּ אֶל־מִקְדָּשִׁי
יז וְהֵמָּה יִקְרְבוּ אֶל־שֻׁלְחָנִי לְשָׁרְתֵנִי וְשָׁמְרוּ אֶת־מִשְׁמַרְתִּי: וְהָיָה
בְּבוֹאָם אֶל־שַׁעֲרֵי הֶחָצֵר הַפְּנִימִית בִּגְדֵי פִשְׁתִּים יִלְבָּשׁוּ וְלֹא־
יַעֲלֶה עֲלֵיהֶם צֶמֶר בְּשָׁרְתָם בְּשַׁעֲרֵי הֶחָצֵר הַפְּנִימִית וָבָיְתָה:
יח פַּאֲרֵי פִשְׁתִּים יִהְיוּ עַל־רֹאשָׁם וּמִכְנְסֵי פִשְׁתִּים יִהְיוּ עַל־מָתְנֵיהֶם
יט לֹא יַחְגְּרוּ בַּיָּזַע: וּבְצֵאתָם אֶל־הֶחָצֵר הַחִיצוֹנָה אֶל־הֶחָצֵר
הַחִיצוֹנָה אֶל־הָעָם יִפְשְׁטוּ אֶת־בִּגְדֵיהֶם אֲשֶׁר־הֵמָּה מְשָׁרְתִם בָּם
וְהִנִּיחוּ אוֹתָם בְּלִשְׁכֹת הַקֹּדֶשׁ וְלָבְשׁוּ בְּגָדִים אֲחֵרִים וְלֹא־יְקַדְּשׁוּ
כ אֶת־הָעָם בְּבִגְדֵיהֶם: וְרֹאשָׁם לֹא יְגַלֵּחוּ וּפֶרַע לֹא יְשַׁלֵּחוּ כָּסוֹם
כא יִכְסְמוּ אֶת־רָאשֵׁיהֶם: וְיַיִן לֹא־יִשְׁתּוּ כָּל־כֹּהֵן בְּבוֹאָם אֶל־הֶחָצֵר
כב הַפְּנִימִית: וְאַלְמָנָה וּגְרוּשָׁה לֹא־יִקְחוּ לָהֶם לְנָשִׁים כִּי אִם־בְּתוּלֹת
מִזֶּרַע בֵּית יִשְׂרָאֵל וְהָאַלְמָנָה אֲשֶׁר־תִּהְיֶה אַלְמָנָה מִכֹּהֵן יִקָּחוּ:
כג כד וְאֶת־עַמִּי יוֹרוּ בֵּין קֹדֶשׁ לְחֹל וּבֵין־טָמֵא לְטָהוֹר יוֹדִעֻם: וְעַל־רִיב
הֵמָּה יַעַמְדוּ לשפט בְּמִשְׁפָּטַי ושפטהו וְאֶת־תּוֹרֹתַי וְאֶת־חֻקֹּתַי לְמִשְׁפָּט | יִשְׁפְּטֻהוּ
כה בְּכָל־מוֹעֲדַי יִשְׁמֹרוּ וְאֶת־שַׁבְּתוֹתַי יְקַדֵּשׁוּ: וְאֶל־מֵת אָדָם לֹא
יָבוֹא לְטָמְאָה כִּי אִם־לְאָב וּלְאֵם וּלְבֵן וּלְבַת לְאָח וּלְאָחוֹת אֲשֶׁר־
כו לֹא־הָיְתָה לְאִישׁ יִטַּמָּאוּ: וְאַחֲרֵי טָהֳרָתוֹ שִׁבְעַת יָמִים יִסְפְּרוּ־לוֹ:
כז וּבְיוֹם בֹּאוֹ אֶל־הַקֹּדֶשׁ אֶל־הֶחָצֵר הַפְּנִימִית לְשָׁרֵת בַּקֹּדֶשׁ יַקְרִיב
כח חַטָּאתוֹ נְאֻם אֲדֹנָי יֱהֹוִה: וְהָיְתָה לָהֶם לְנַחֲלָה אֲנִי נַחֲלָתָם וַאֲחֻזָּה
כט לֹא־תִתְּנוּ לָהֶם בְּיִשְׂרָאֵל אֲנִי אֲחֻזָּתָם: הַמִּנְחָה וְהַחַטָּאת וְהָאָשָׁם
ל הֵמָּה יֹאכְלוּם וְכָל־חֵרֶם בְּיִשְׂרָאֵל לָהֶם יִהְיֶה: וְרֵאשִׁית כָּל־בִּכּוּרֵי
כֹל וְכָל־תְּרוּמַת כֹּל מִכֹּל תְּרוּמוֹתֵיכֶם לַכֹּהֲנִים יִהְיֶה וְרֵאשִׁית
לא עֲרִיסוֹתֵיכֶם תִּתְּנוּ לַכֹּהֵן לְהָנִיחַ בְּרָכָה אֶל־בֵּיתֶךָ: כָּל־נְבֵלָה
וּטְרֵפָה מִן־הָעוֹף וּמִן־הַבְּהֵמָה לֹא יֹאכְלוּ הַכֹּהֲנִים:

For the complete Rashi and haftara turn to the right side of this volume.

חומש קורן מקראות הדורו

HE KOREN MIKRAOT HADOROT

פרשת אמר

PARASHAT EMOR

KOREN

THE ROHR FAMILY EDITION

חומש קורן מקראות הדורות
THE KOREN MIKRAOT HADOROT

THE KOPLOW FAMILY EDITION OF PARASHAT EMOR

פרשת אמר עם מפרשים
PARASHAT EMOR WITH COMMENTARIES

TORAH TRANSLATION BY
Rabbi Lord Jonathan Sacks זצ״ל

COMMENTARIES COLLECTED AND ABRIDGED BY
Rabbi Shai Finkelstein, EDITOR-IN-CHIEF

COMMENTARIES TRANSLATED BY
Rabbi Jonathan Mishkin

MANAGING EDITOR
Rabbi Yedidya Naveh

•

KOREN PUBLISHERS JERUSALEM

The Koren Mikraot HaDorot, The Rohr Edition
Volume 28: Parashat Emor
First Edition, 2024

Koren Publishers Jerusalem Ltd.
POB 4044, Jerusalem 9104001, ISRAEL
POB 8531, New Milford, CT 06776, USA

www.korenpub.com

The Tanakh translation is excerpted from the Magerman Edition of The Koren Tanakh.

The creation of this work was made possible with the generous support of the Jewish Book Trust Inc.

Printed in ISRAEL

ISBN 978 965 7760 83 3

KMDEM01

The Rohr Family Edition of
The Koren Mikraot HaDorot
pays tribute to the memory of

Mr. Sami Rohr ז״ל
ר׳ שמואל ב״ר יהושע אליהו ז״ל

who served his Maker with joy
and whose far-reaching vision, warm open hand, love of Torah,
and love for every Jew were catalysts for the revival and growth of
vibrant Jewish life in the former Soviet Union
and in countless communities the world over

and to the memory of his beloved wife

Mrs. Charlotte Rohr (née Kastner) ע״ה
שרה בת ר׳ יקותיאל יהודה ע״ה

who survived the fires of the Shoah to become
the elegant and gracious matriarch,
first in Colombia and later in the United States,
of three generations of a family
nurtured by her love and unstinting devotion.
She found grace in the eyes of all those whose lives she touched.

Together they merited to see all their children
build lives enriched by faithful commitment
to the spreading of Torah and *Ahavat Yisrael*.

Dedicated with love by
The Rohr Family
NEW YORK, USA

"לְמַעַן יֵדְעוּ דֹרֹתֵיכֶם..."

"So that future generations may know..."

Dedicated to our
children and grandchildren,
who are the future of the Jewish people.

The Meyer G & Ellen Goodstein Koplow Foundation

CONTENTS

FOR THE COMPLETE RASHI AND HAFTARA
TURN TO THE OTHER END OF THIS VOLUME.

PUBLISHER'S PREFACE

The genius of Jewish commentary on the Torah is one of huge and critical import. Jewish life and law for millennia have been directed by our interpretations of the Torah, and each generation has looked to its rabbinic leadership for a deeper understanding of its teachings, its laws, its stories.

For centuries, *Mikraot Gedolot* have been a core part of understanding the Ḥumash; the words of Rashi, Ibn Ezra, Ramban, Rashbam, Ralbag, and other classic commentators illuminate and help us understand the Torah. But traditional editions of *Mikraot Gedolot* present only a slice in time and a small selection of the corpus of Jewish commentators. Almost every generation has produced rabbinic scholars who speak to their times, from Philo and Onkelos two thousand years ago, to Rabbi Joseph B. Soloveitchik, Rabbi Aharon Kotler, the Lubavitcher Rebbe, and Nehama Leibowitz in ours.

The Koren Mikraot HaDorot – Scriptures or Interpretations for the Generations – brings two millennia of Torah commentary into the hands and homes of Jews around the world. Readers will be able not only to encounter the classic commentators, but to gain a much broader sense of the issues that scholars grappled with in their time and the inspiration they drew from the ancient texts. We see, for example, how Philo speaks to an assimilating Greek Jewish audience in first-century Alexandria, and how similar yet different it is from Rabbi Samson Raphael Hirsch's approach to an equally assimilating nineteenth-century German readership; how the perspectives of Rabbi Soloveitchik and Rabbi Kotler differ in a post-Holocaust world; how Rav Se'adya Gaon interpreted the Torah for the Jews of Babylonia. It is an exciting journey through Jewish history via the unchanging words of the Torah.

The text of the Torah features the exceptional new translation of Rabbi Lord Jonathan Sacks, together with the celebrated and meticulously accurate Koren Hebrew text. Of course, with the exception of Rashi – for whom we present an entirely new translation in full – the commentaries are selected. We offer this anthology not to limit our reader's exploration but rather as a gateway for further learning of Torah and its commentaries on a broader and deeper level than space here permits. We discuss below how to use this book.

We must thank **Pamela and George Rohr** of New York, who recognized the unique value of *The Koren Mikraot HaDorot* and its ability to communicate historical breadth and context to the reader. For my colleagues here at Koren, we thank you; for the many generations of users who will find this a continuing source of new learning, we are forever in your debt.

We are honored to acknowledge and thank **Debra and David Magerman**, whose support for the Koren Ḥumash with Rabbi Sacks's exemplary translation and commentary laid the foundation for the core English text of this work.

Finally, I must personally thank **Rabbi Marvin Hier**, with whom I had a special breakfast some years ago at the King David Hotel. During the meal, he raised the problem that so few people knew the writings of Rabbi Joseph B. Soloveitchik and Rabbi Aharon Kotler on the Torah; and I, who had just read some of Philo's work, had the same reaction. From that conversation came the seed for this project.

HOW TO USE *THE KOREN MIKRAOT HADOROT*

The Koren Mikraot HaDorot will be a fifty-five-volume edition of the Ḥumash (one for each *parasha* plus a companion volume). Each of the fifty-four volumes of the *parashot* can be read from right to left (Hebrew opening side), and left to right (English opening side).

Opening from the Hebrew side offers:

- the full Torah text, the translation of Rabbi Sacks, and the full commentary of Rashi in both Hebrew and the new English translation
- all *haftarot* associated with the *parasha* of the volume, including Rosh Ḥodesh and special readings, both in Hebrew and English

Opening from the English side presents four sections:

- **THE TIME OF THE SAGES** – includes commentaries from the Second Temple period and the talmudic period

- **THE CLASSIC COMMENTATORS** – quotes selected explanations by Rashi as well as most of the commentators found in traditional *Mikraot Gedolot*
- **CONFRONTING MODERNITY** – selects commentaries from the eighteenth century to the close of the twentieth century
- **THE BIBLICAL IMAGINATION** – features essays surveying some of the broader conceptual ideas as a supplement to the linear, text-based commentary

The first three of these sections each feature the relevant verses, in Hebrew and English, on the page alongside their respective commentaries, in chronological order, providing the reader with a single window onto the text without excessive page turning.

In addition to being a valuable resource in a Jewish home or synagogue library, we conceived of these volumes as a weekly accompaniment in the synagogue. There is scope for the reader to study each *parasha* on a weekly basis in preparation for the reading on Shabbat. One may select a particular group of commentators for study that week, or perhaps alternate between ancient and modern viewpoints. Some readers may choose to delve into the text through verse-by-verse interpretation, while others may prefer a conceptual perspective on the *parasha* as a whole. The broad array of options for learning means this is a series which can be returned to year after year, always presenting new insights and new approaches to understanding the text.

ACKNOWLEDGMENTS

The creation of this book was possible only thanks to the small but exceptional team here at Koren Jerusalem. We are grateful to:

- Rabbi Tzvi Hersh Weinreb, שליט״א, who conceptualized the structure of the project and provides both moral and halakhic leadership at Koren
- Rabbi Shai Finkelstein, whose encyclopedic knowledge of Torah and its interpreters is equaled only by his community leadership, formerly in Memphis and today in Jerusalem
- Rabbi Yedidya Naveh, whose knowledge, organizational skills, and superb leadership brought the disparate elements together
- Rabbi Jonathan Mishkin, translator of the commentaries, who crafted a fluent, accurate, and eloquent English translation

Our design, editing, typesetting, and proofreading staff, including Tani Bayer, Esther Be'er, Tomi Mager, Adina Luber, Rabbi Dr. Tzvi Sinensky,

Dr. Yoel Finkelman, Rabbi David Debow, Tali Simon, Nechama Unterman, Ben Zion Bokser, Debbie Ismailoff, Ilana Sobel, Dvora Rhein, and Carolyn Budow Ben David, enabled an attractive, user-friendly, and accurate edition of these works.

> "One silver basin" (Numbers 7:13) was brought as a symbol of the Torah, which has been likened to wine, as the verse states: "And drink of the wine which I have mingled" (Proverbs 9:5). Because it is customary to drink wine in a basin – as we see in the verse "that drink wine in basins" (Amos 6:6) – he therefore brought a basin. "Of seventy shekels, after the shekel of the sanctuary" (Numbers 7:13). Why? Because just as the numerical value of "wine" [*yayin*] is seventy, so there are seventy modes of expounding the Torah. (Bemidbar Rabba 13:16)

Each generation produces exceptional rabbinic, intellectual leadership. It has been our purpose to enable all Jews to taste the wine of those generations, in the hope of expanding the breadth and depth of their knowledge. Torah is our greatest treasure, and we need the wisdom of those generations to better understand this bountiful gift from God. We hope that we at Koren can deepen that understanding for all who seek it.

Matthew Miller, Publisher
Jerusalem, 5784 (2024)

EDITOR'S INTRODUCTION

Over the course of millennia, the Jewish people have watched while the surrounding society and its values have changed unceasingly. For the Jews, the steadfast response to an evolving world has always been the study of Torah, specifically engagement with the weekly *parasha*. Devotees of Jewish learning have always looked to the weekly Torah portion for spiritual and intellectual guidance through life's challenges. And in every generation, commentaries on the Ḥumash have debated the precise interpretation of the verses therein. These scholars have continuously asked what message God is trying to convey to Israel and the world through the Torah's narratives and laws. Their explanations have struggled to identify the correct ways to apply its lessons to our daily lives.

Throughout, all these authors have approached the Torah text from their own unique perspectives, shaped in no small measure by the eras and environments they lived in. Naturally, the pantheon of commentaries present widely different styles in their writings. Occasionally the commentators will subject a particular verse to piercing scrutiny as a self-contained unit. At other times they present interpretations that seem to stray from the straightforward meaning of the text. Ultimately, all commentaries demand that a verse provide readers with theological meaning and direction for communal and social life.

Recognition of the wisdom embedded in the vast literature of commentary on the Torah spanning the various eras of Jewish history planted the seeds of the project whose fruit you now hold. We have called this publication ***Mikraot HaDorot*** – Readings of the Generations. This window into the world of Torah commentaries is not simply an upgrade of the classical *Mikraot Gedolot* collections, which give readers merely a handful of familiar

interpretations. *The Koren Mikraot HaDorot* instead presents a plethora of exegetical contributions, with more than forty scholars spanning Jewish teachings from the past two thousand years represented on its pages.

Each volume of the *Koren Mikraot HaDorot* series can be opened from both the right (Hebrew) side and left (English) side. The Hebrew opening side includes the Hebrew and a new English text of the *parasha*, translated by Rabbi Lord Jonathan Sacks, with a full, new translation of Rashi and the *haftarot*. The English opening side contains the bulk of the commentaries, and is divided into four parts: The first, **THE TIME OF THE SAGES**, comprises commentaries from antiquity – ranging from Philo to the Yalkut Shimoni. These figures lived mainly in the land of Israel, Egypt, and Babylonia. The second, **THE CLASSIC COMMENTATORS**, contains interpretations from the Middle Ages – starting from Rav Se'adya Gaon and Rashi and continuing through time to the work of Rabbi Shlomo Efrayim of Luntschitz, author of the *Keli Yakar*. The authors included here represent the rich traditions of both Sephardic (Spanish and North African) and Ashkenazic (central and eastern European) schools of exegesis. The third section, **CONFRONTING MODERNITY**, offers the work of both Old World and New World scholars who lived between the eighteenth and twentieth centuries. Before each of these three sections we include a time line that specifies the chronological relationships between the commentators and the places they lived.

In the final section, **THE BIBLICAL IMAGINATION**, we provide three in-depth investigations of particular ideas through the writings of the various commentaries. There are several goals to these essays. First, we aim to reveal common threads weaving across the generations of Torah scholarship. Second, we hope to illustrate how the various authors were influenced by their lives and times, and that the lessons they transmitted to their communities reflected their environments. Finally, each essay highlights for the reader some central issues that the commentaries have grappled with. We trust that this tool will facilitate the reader's understanding of the words of the commentaries themselves.

Three principles have governed the decision making in our work on *The Koren Mikraot HaDorot*:

- Chronological order: We have striven to sketch out the historical development of Torah exegesis, an enterprise that has occupied innumerable communities of Jews in far-flung lands for centuries.

- Economy of selection: In compiling the excerpts used in this work, we have gone through the authors' works and isolated those sections which most directly address the particular question, issue, or difficulty that confronted the scholar.
- Objectivity of presentation: This book presents ideas of the commentaries authentically, never censoring them or smoothing them over in light of our own positions or perspectives. We always strove to faithfully transmit the legal, conceptual, social, and ethical messages of the commentators.

The modern world constantly challenges us as individuals, as a society, and as communal leaders, teachers, and parents. The values and culture of the society that surrounds us force thinking Jews to seriously consider and reconsider their ideas and priorities on a regular basis as we struggle to find the correct path through life. Furthermore, we constantly must ask ourselves what teachings we wish to transmit to future generations. It is our hope that the *Koren Mikraot HaDorot* project will help guide its readers as they grapple with these very real problems. The world of Torah commentary is wide and deep beyond measure. It contains innumerable answers to the questions that face the individual, the family, the generation, and indeed all of humanity.

Rabbi Shai Finkelstein, Editor-in-Chief
Jerusalem, 5784 (2024)

A NOTE ON THE TRANSLATION

The terse writing style prevalent in Jewish scholarship over most of history can be difficult for the modern reader to decipher. Since our goal in the *Koren Mikraot HaDorot* series is to make thousands of years of Torah commentary accessible to a modern, English-speaking audience, we have opted for a relatively loose translation style that accurately presents the content of the Hebrew commentary while not necessarily mirroring its exact syntax. We have also resorted occasionally to paraphrase in instances where a literal translation would be opaque in English. As any student of Torah exegesis will recognize, draconian insistence on a word-for-word translation would result in an English text that was unreadable and that preserved neither the clarity nor the majesty of the original Hebrew.

Many of the commentaries' discussions focus on the meanings of words and phrases that are ambiguous in the Hebrew text of the *parasha*. The beautiful new translation of the Torah by Rabbi Lord Jonathan Sacks that we include here often dispels these ambiguities in the interest of clarity, necessarily coming down on one side or the other of a disagreement between commentators. The reader of the commentaries should therefore view the Torah translation presented here as one possible reading of the often-cryptic Hebrew original. In a similar vein, the significance of certain interpretations may seem unclear, or their points obvious, until one encounters another commentary with a starkly different read of the same verse. These contrasts, and the realization that themes and meanings we thought to be clear are actually ambiguous and multifaceted, are the essence of *The Koren Mikraot HaDorot*.

We have, as far as possible, allowed each text to speak for itself, and have left editorial comments to a minimum. Nevertheless, the commentaries often assume the reader's knowledge of other biblical episodes, midrashim,

or Hebrew grammar beyond what might be expected from the English-speaking public today. To ensure clarity, we have therefore interpolated brief editor's notes where we deemed it necessary, setting them off from the original text in square brackets.

Throughout Jewish history, the text of the Tanakh has been viewed as the apogee of the Hebrew language. For many commentators, especially those of the Middle Ages, it served as a fountain of language from which they drew numerous idioms and phrases. The result is that the Hebrew text of many commentaries is shot through with snippets of biblical prose or poetry to such an extent that almost every sentence can be viewed as a quote or allusion. Marking and citing all of these would make for a cluttered translation and would hinder rather than enhance the reader's understanding. We have therefore opted to cite only those quotes which are brought by the author as explicit evidence to further the point being made, and not those that supply only a turn of phrase.

The Hebrew side of this volume contains a complete and unabridged translation of Rashi's commentary. For those who wish to follow the *parasha* on the English side of the book, we have also reprinted many of Rashi's explanations alongside those of the other classic commentators. This will allow the reader to compare Rashi's interpretation to those of Rashbam, Ibn Ezra, and others, as well as appreciate how Rashi's commentary often serves to define the issues that will be addressed by later exegetes.

The text of the commentaries is of course abridged. We have not included ellipses to mark every point where text has been omitted, to maintain a clutter-free translation. However, we have included ellipses at points where the subject of discussion would otherwise appear to have changed abruptly and inexplicably, to save the reader confusion. We have also not adhered strictly to the original heading, or s.v. (*dibbur hamatḥil)* of every text, changing it in instances where it would help to focus the reader on those words that are the actual subject of discussion, and adding it to texts that did not originally have it.

Most of the commentaries that we quote in this series were originally organized by chapter and verse. Therefore, anyone who wishes to consult the original Hebrew text of a given commentary can simply open to the verse in question. However, not all sources are organized this way. The midrashim in particular are often ordered loosely; an important interpretation of a verse in Exodus might be found in a midrash on Deuteronomy. For the reader's convenience in locating the original Hebrew source, we have provided citations for those works not organized sequentially, as well as for commentaries

originally composed on verses other than the one under discussion. These citations can be found outside of the final punctuation at the end of the excerpt in question.

Our translation has generally relied upon the Hebrew text found in the Bar-Ilan Responsa Project and the online compendia Sefaria and AlHatorah.org, as well as the standard printed editions of commentaries not found in any of these. The Responsa Project contains more than one edition of several midrashim (Midrash Tanḥuma, Midrash Rabba, and Avot Derabbi Natan). For these works, our citations should be understood as referring to the standard editions published in Vilna and Warsaw unless otherwise indicated. Aside from this, please note:

- Passages from Philo are quoted with permission from *Rediscovering Philo of Alexandria: A First Century Torah Commentator, Volume III - Leviticus,* edited by Rabbi Michael Leo Samuel (Sarasota: First Edition Design Publishing, 2016).
- Selected commentaries of Rabbi Joseph B. Soloveitchik are printed with permission from *Chumash Mesoras HaRav,* edited by Dr. Arnold Lustiger (New York: OU Press and Ohr Publishing Inc., 2017).
- The commentaries of the Lubavitcher Rebbe are quoted from *The Torah, with an Interpolated Translation and Commentary Based on the Works of the Lubavitcher Rebbe,* edited by Rabbi Chaim Nochum Cunin and Rabbi Moshe Yaakov Wisnefsky (New York: Kehot Publication Society, 2017).
- The commentaries of Nehama Leibowitz are quoted, with generous permission, from *Studies in Vayikra (Leviticus)*, translated by Aryeh Newman (Jerusalem: World Zionist Organization Department for Torah Education and Culture in the Diaspora, 1983).

While we have thus done our best to aid the reader in finding and consulting the original Hebrew text of the commentaries we have translated, we emphasize that this is not a critical edition, and the scope and readership of the series do not permit us to fully cite every allusion and internal reference that authors make to midrashim and other commentaries. Still, we have made a supreme effort to provide citations of talmudic passages, and of course biblical verses, quoted or referred to in the material included here.

Yedidya Naveh, Managing Editor
Jerusalem, 5784 (2024)

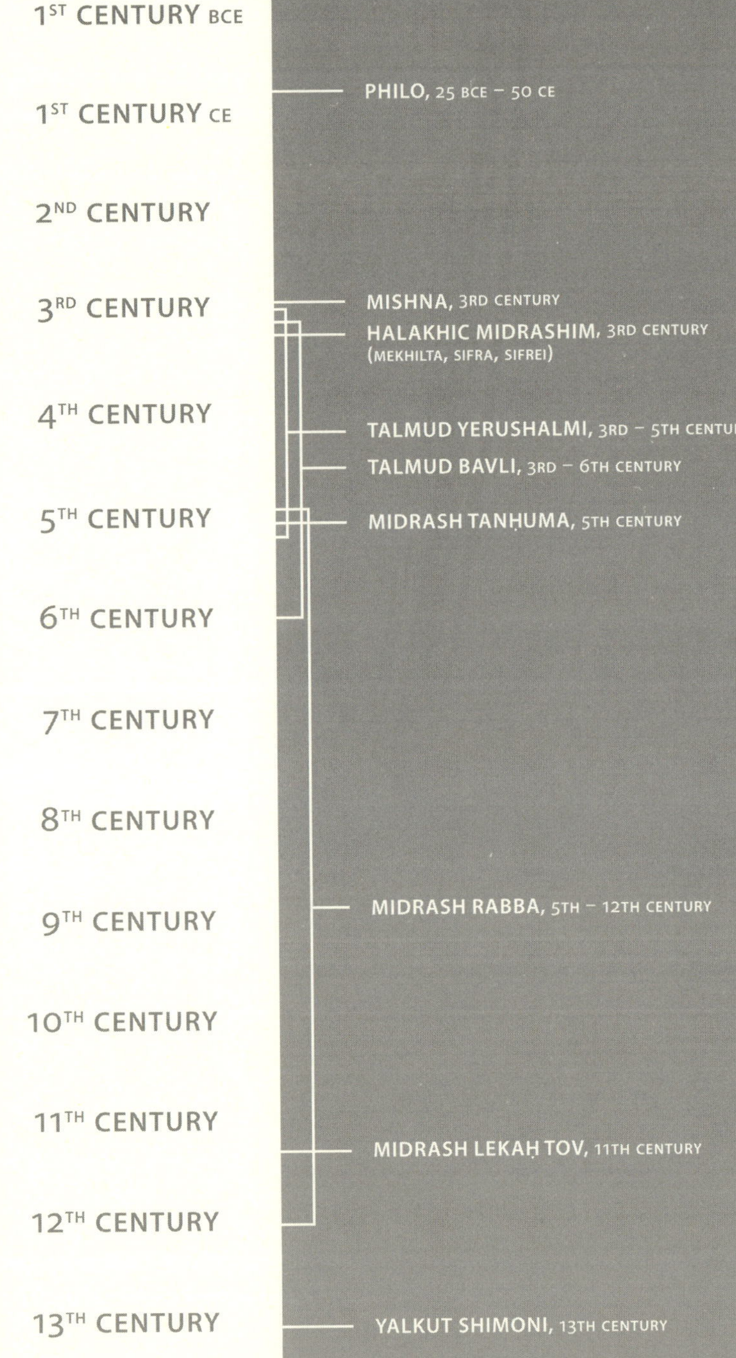

1ST CENTURY BCE
1ST CENTURY CE
PHILO, 25 BCE – 50 CE
2ND CENTURY
3RD CENTURY
MISHNA, 3RD CENTURY
HALAKHIC MIDRASHIM, 3RD CENTURY (MEKHILTA, SIFRA, SIFREI)
4TH CENTURY
TALMUD YERUSHALMI, 3RD – 5TH CENTURY
TALMUD BAVLI, 3RD – 6TH CENTURY
5TH CENTURY
MIDRASH TANḤUMA, 5TH CENTURY
6TH CENTURY
7TH CENTURY
8TH CENTURY
9TH CENTURY
MIDRASH RABBA, 5TH – 12TH CENTURY
10TH CENTURY
11TH CENTURY
MIDRASH LEKAḤ TOV, 11TH CENTURY
12TH CENTURY
13TH CENTURY
YALKUT SHIMONI, 13TH CENTURY

פרשת אמר
PARASHAT EMOR

THE **TIME** OF THE **SAGES**

כא א וַיֹּאמֶר יהוה אֶל־מֹשֶׁה אֱמֹר אֶל־הַכֹּהֲנִים בְּנֵי אַהֲרֹן וְאָמַרְתָּ יז
ב אֲלֵהֶם לְנֶפֶשׁ לֹא־יִטַּמָּא בְּעַמָּיו: כִּי אִם־לִשְׁאֵרוֹ הַקָּרֹב אֵלָיו
ג לְאִמּוֹ וּלְאָבִיו וְלִבְנוֹ וּלְבִתּוֹ וּלְאָחִיו: וְלַאֲחֹתוֹ הַבְּתוּלָה

CHAPTER 21, VERSE 1

TALMUD BAVLI

אֱמֹר אֶל־הַכֹּהֲנִים – *Speak to the priests:* The repetition of the verb *Speak...and say* teaches that both adults and minors are warned against becoming impure from a corpse. Does this mean that a parent priest must warn his children: "Do not become impure"? No, it connotes that an adult must not render minors impure through direct action. (Yevamot 114a)

TANHUMA

אֱמֹר אֶל־הַכֹּהֲנִים – *Speak to the priests:* Consider the verse *The Lord's words are pure words, like silver refined in an earthen furnace, purified seven times over* (Psalms 12:7). Thus all the warnings that the Holy One, blessed be He, issues to the people of Israel are intended to sanctify and purify them, for *the Lord's words are pure words*. Now, why does God command Moshe to speak to the priests twice? [That is, our verse contains two instances of the same verb: *emor*, "speak," and *ve'amarta*, "say."] To what might this be compared? To a royal chef who customarily enters the king's dining room. Said the monarch to him: "I hereby decree that you are never again to look at a dead body. Since you are always coming and going from my presence, I do not want you to contaminate my throne room." Similarly does the Holy One, blessed be He, order the priests who frequent the Temple not to contract impurity from a corpse, as the verse states: *No one of you shall render himself impure for any dead person among his people*. [Hence, one term of speech refers to the actual commandment, and the other relates to the reason that God orders the priests to remain pure.] (Emor 1)

אֱמֹר אֶל־הַכֹּהֲנִים – *Speak to the priests:* Rabbi Yoḥanan taught: Whenever the Torah uses the formula of *Speak...and say*, some interpretation is required. In the present instance, the first verb alludes to the fact that a priest must become impure to bury a corpse of a person who has no relatives to attend to his burial. [Although a priest is generally forbidden to touch or move dead bodies, this case is an exception, wherein the priest is obligated to bury the person if no one else is able.] By contrast, the second statement identifies the primary prohibition against a priest becoming impure from a dead body. This is the sense of the terminology *Speak...and say*. For in this world, a priest may become impure from a corpse whose burial is a mitzva, but in the future a priest will never become impure since there will be no death, as the prophet states: *He will swallow up death forever; the Lord, He will wipe every tear from every face* (Isaiah 25:8). (Emor 4)

VERSE 2

TALMUD BAVLI

כִּי אִם־לִשְׁאֵרוֹ הַקָּרֹב אֵלָיו – *Except for his nearest relatives:* The term "near relative" refers to the priest's wife. Yet a subsequent verse states: *But he shall not become impure for those he is related to by marriage, and so become profane* (21:4). We can reconcile these rules by

21 1 The Lord said to Moshe, "Speak to the priests, Aharon's sons.
Say: No one of you shall render himself impure for any dead per-
2 son among his people except for his nearest relatives: his moth-
3 er, father, son, daughter, or brother; or his virgin sister who has
remained close to him because she has not married – for her,

TALMUD BAVLI *(cont.)*

explaining that some married priests may become impure for their wives [that is, to bury them], but other married priests may not become impure for their wives. How so? A priest may become impure for a woman whom he married lawfully, but he may not become impure for a woman who is disqualified for him. (Yevamot 90b)

LEKAH TOV

כִּי אִם־לִשְׁאֵרוֹ הַקָּרֹב אֵלָיו – *Except for his nearest relatives:* The term "near relative" [*lish'ero*] is an allusion to the priest's wife, as the verse states: *A kind man does himself good, but a cruel man tears his own flesh [she'ero]* (Proverbs 11:17), while a later text there states: *He who neglects his family inherits the wind* (11:29). Just as the latter verse refers to a man's wife, so too does the earlier one relate to a wife. Another interpretation: The word *she'ero* connotes "flesh," as we read: *That is why a man leaves his father and mother and cleaves to his wife and they become one flesh* (Genesis 2:24). This is why our Sages claim that the term *she'ero* implies his wife. [That is, since the joining of flesh defines a marriage, and the word *she'er* suggests "flesh," *she'ero* is tantamount to his wife.] We similarly find this language: *You shall not expose the nakedness of your father's sister; she is of your father's flesh [she'er avikha]* (Leviticus 18:12). [Hence the word *she'er* refers to women.] **הַקָּרֹב אֵלָיו** – *His nearest:* These are the seven close relatives who are listed in the verse. Another interpretation: The term "nearest" relates to the woman: A priest may only become impure if he is married to his wife, but not if he is only betrothed to her. Based on this, the Sages rule that a priest does not become an *onen* [a unique status of mourning between the death and burial of a relative] nor may he become impure for a woman to whom he is betrothed. Furthermore, a priest does not inherit the estate of his intended bride. On the other hand, should the husband die, the woman may collect her ketubah [that is, the money of her marriage contract] from the man's property. **אֵלָיו** – *To him:* Nor may a priest become impure in order to bury a woman whom he has divorced. **וְלִבְנוֹ** – *To his son:* A priest may bury his dead son regardless of the latter's status. For example, a *mamzer* [a child born of an incestuous or adulterous union] is still considered one's son with regard to all laws. That, however, is not the case if the boy's mother is a Canaanite maidservant or other gentile woman, because lineage follows the mother in those circumstances. (58a)

VERSE 3

TALMUD BAVLI

וְלַאֲחֹתוֹ הַבְּתוּלָה – *Or his virgin sister:* Our verse excludes a woman who has been raped or seduced [since they are not virgins]. Now, we might have expected the law to also exclude a woman whose hymen was torn accidentally [via a foreign object]. Therefore, the verse

ד הַקְּרוֹבָה אֵלָיו אֲשֶׁר לֹא־הָיְתָה לְאִישׁ לָהּ יִטַּמָּא: לֹא יִטַּמָּא
ה בַּעַל בְּעַמָּיו לְהֵחַלּוֹ: לֹא־יקרחה קָרְחָה בְּרֹאשָׁם וּפְאַת יְקַרְחוּ
ו זְקָנָם לֹא יְגַלֵּחוּ וּבִבְשָׂרָם לֹא יִשְׂרְטוּ שָׂרָטֶת: קְדֹשִׁים יִהְיוּ
לֵאלֹהֵיהֶם וְלֹא יְחַלְּלוּ שֵׁם אֱלֹהֵיהֶם כִּי אֶת־אִשֵּׁי יְהוָה לֶחֶם

TALMUD BAVLI *(cont.)*

continues to describe a woman who *has not married [literally, "who has had no man"]*, thereby including only one whose state as a non-virgin was caused by a man [that is, through relations]. And in this case, the woman's status was not changed by a man but by some other means. She is therefore excluded [from the category of a non-virgin, and her brother the priest may become impure to bury her]. The term *who has remained close to him* serves to include both a betrothed sister and a grown woman. (Yevamot 60a) **לָהּ יִטַּמָּא** – *For her, he may render himself impure:* We learn from here that it is a mitzva [for a priest to become impure to bury his deceased relatives. The term mitzva is used here to imply an obligation, rather than a meritorious deed]. And if the priest is reluctant to do so, others must render him impure against his will [by forcing him to touch or carry the corpse or by pulling him into the room where the body is lying]. There was once an incident involving Yosef the priest, whose wife died on the eve of the Passover festival, yet the husband refused to become impure for her [since that would have prevented him from offering the Paschal sacrifice]. Nevertheless, his brethren the priests voted and rendered Yosef impure against his will. (Zevaḥim 100a)

VERSE 4

TALMUD YERUSHALMI

לֹא יִטַּמָּא – *But he shall not become impure:* Although a priest may not become impure *be'amav* [literally, "for his nation"], he may become impure for a corpse whose burial is a mitzva [because the body is not being tended to]. (Nazir 7:1)

VERSE 5

SIFREI DEVARIM

לֹא־יִקְרְחוּ קָרְחָה בְּרֹאשָׁם – *Priests shall not make bald patches on their heads:* A later verse warns similarly: *You are children of the Lord your God. Do not lacerate yourselves or make bald patches in the middle of your heads [bein eineikhem: literally, "between your eyes"] for the dead* (Deuteronomy 14:1). [Although our verse is directed specifically at priests, the text just cited is a warning issued to all Israelites.] Now, based on this verse, it seems that one would only be liable for tearing out the hair between his eyes. How do we know that the law would similarly be violated for removing hair elsewhere on the head? For an earlier text reads: *Priests shall not make bald patches on their heads*, which includes the entire head. Is it possible that the rules are more extensive regarding priests, considering that in general

4 he may render himself impure. But he shall not become impure
for those he is related to by marriage, and so become profane.
5 Priests shall not make bald patches on their heads, or shave off
6 the edges of their beards, or gash wounds into their flesh. They
shall be holy to their God and not profane God's name, for they
bring close the LORD's fire offerings, foodstuff offerings to their

SIFREI DEVARIM *(cont.)*

they are subject to more restrictions? Perhaps they would be held accountable for every patch that they make. And maybe removing any hair on their heads is prohibited, just as with the hair between their eyes. By contrast, with respect to a common Israelite who is not bound by as many laws as the priest, maybe he would not be punished for every single bald patch that he creates [but one set of lashes would be administered regardless of how many bald spots are made], and maybe he is warned only with respect to the hair between his eyes. No, we cannot draw such conclusions from the verbal analogy between the term "bald patches" in the verse in Deuteronomy and the use of the same term in our verse in Leviticus. Based on that similarity, we must conclude that just like a priest is held accountable for each distinct bald patch that he creates, and just like a priest is punished for all hair that he tears out, not just that which grows between his eyes, these rules apply to non-priests as well. Furthermore, just as the text in Deuteronomy teaches that an Israelite is only considered liable if he pulls out his hair in anguish over the dead, so too Leviticus prohibits a priest from pulling out his hair as an act of mourning. (Re'eh 96)

TALMUD BAVLI

לֹא יְגַלְּחוּ – *[They shall not] shave off:* We might have thought that a priest would be held accountable even if he removed his beard with scissors. Yet an earlier verse states: *Do not cut off the hair on the sides of your head or destroy the edges of your beard* (19:27). [We learn from here that one is only liable for destroying the beard to the root, which cannot be achieved using only a pair of scissors.] We might have thought that a priest would be held accountable for removing his hair with tweezers [which do extract the roots] or with small planes [since in these cases he destroys his beard]. However, our verse states: *Priests shall not shave off the edges of their beards.* [This teaches that shaving alone is prohibited, and these actions are not considered shaving.] What then is the nature of this law? The verse refers to a form of shaving that involves destruction, which we must say is that which is done with a razor. (Kiddushin 35b)

VERSE 6

LEKAH TOV

קְדֹשִׁים יִהְיוּ – *They shall be holy:* The priests will be compelled to be holy. **וְלֹא יְחַלְּלוּ שֵׁם אֱלֹהֵיהֶם** – *They shall…not profane God's name:* For it is the priests who *bring close the LORD's fire offerings*, not the Levites. **וְהָיוּ קֹדֶשׁ** – *Therefore they shall be holy:* Even priests who are blemished are holy. (59a)

ז אֱלֹהֵיהֶם הֵם מַקְרִיבִם וְהָיוּ קֹדֶשׁ: אִשָּׁה זֹנָה וַחֲלָלָה לֹא יִקָּחוּ
וְאִשָּׁה גְּרוּשָׁה מֵאִישָׁהּ לֹא יִקָּחוּ כִּי־קָדֹשׁ הוּא לֵאלֹהָיו:
ח וְקִדַּשְׁתּוֹ כִּי־אֶת־לֶחֶם אֱלֹהֶיךָ הוּא מַקְרִיב קָדֹשׁ יִהְיֶה־לָּךְ
ט כִּי קָדוֹשׁ אֲנִי יהוה מְקַדִּשְׁכֶם: וּבַת אִישׁ כֹּהֵן כִּי תֵחֵל לִזְנוֹת

VERSE 7

MISHNA

וְאִשָּׁה גְּרוּשָׁה מֵאִישָׁהּ – *A woman divorced from her husband:* If a married woman was told that her husband has died, whereupon she became betrothed to another man and subsequently her husband resurfaced, the woman is permitted to return to him. [This is because betrothal to the second man does not render the supposed widow forbidden to her initial husband.] Furthermore, if the second man had given the woman a bill of divorce, he has not thereby disqualified her from subsequently marrying into the priesthood. [That is, she is characterized merely as a widow from her first husband; she is not considered a divorcée from the second man since they were not legally married.] Rabbi Elazar ben Matya explained: The verse states: *They may not marry a woman divorced from her husband*, which indicates that a woman is not disqualified if she was divorced from a man who was not her husband [but who was merely her fiancé]. (Yevamot 10:3)

TALMUD YERUSHALMI

לֹא יִקָּחוּ – *They may not marry:* Since the prohibition is expressed in the plural, we learn that both the priest and forbidden woman are warned against an unlawful marriage. (Kiddushin 3:12)

VERSE 8

TALMUD YERUSHALMI

קָדֹשׁ יִהְיֶה־לָּךְ – *And he shall be holy to you:* Rabbi Mana cited the verse that states: *For the crown of his God's anointing oil rests upon him; I am the Lord* (21:12). It is as if God is saying: "Just as I am exalted in My greatness, so too is Aharon exceptional in his." Rabbi Avun cited the earlier verse, which reads: *And he shall be holy to you, because I, the Lord, am holy*. It is as if God is comparing Himself to Aharon: "I exist in holiness as does he." (Horayot 3:1)

TALMUD BAVLI

וְקִדַּשְׁתּוֹ – *You shall treat a priest as holy:* The academy of Rabbi Yishmael taught: When the verse states: *You shall treat a priest as holy*, it means that a priest takes precedence in all ritual matters. A priest is the first one to read from the Torah [during public readings; in our times, he receives the first *aliya*]; a priest is called upon to lead the blessings after a meal; and a priest is offered the first and best portion at a meal. (Moed Katan 28b)

YALKUT SHIMONI

וְקִדַּשְׁתּוֹ – *You shall treat a priest as holy:* The holier a person is, the greater the honor he is granted relative to someone of lesser stature. Thus, a priest takes precedence over a Levite.

7 God; therefore they shall be holy. They may not marry a woman made profane by immorality, nor may they marry a woman
8 divorced from her husband, for they are holy to their God. You
shall treat a priest as holy, for he brings close the offerings of
foodstuffs to your God. And he shall be holy to you, because
9 I, the Lord, am holy and make you holy. If the daughter of a
priest profanes herself by immorality, she profanes her father

YALKUT SHIMONI *(cont.)*

The academy of Rabbi Yishmael supported this point with the verse that reads: *You shall treat a priest as holy* – this refers to all matters of sanctity. (Emor 630)

VERSE 9

TALMUD BAVLI

כִּי תֵחֵל – *If she profanes herself:* Our Sages taught in a *baraita*: When the verse describes a priest's daughter who does something profane, does that also include the profanation [that is, the violation] of the Sabbath? No, for the full phrase is: *If she profanes herself by immorality*. Thus the Torah refers to a licentious act that qualifies as a desecration. (Sanhedrin 50b) וּבַת אִישׁ כֹּהֵן כִּי תֵחֵל לִזְנוֹת – *If the daughter of a priest profanes herself by immorality:* It was taught in a *baraita*: When the verse states: *If the daughter of a priest profanes herself by immorality*, it refers to a young woman who is betrothed. On the other hand, perhaps the text is describing the daughter of a priest who is a married woman. No, for an earlier text reads: *If a man commits adultery with a married woman, another man's wife, both the adulterer and the adulteress shall be put to death* (20:10). [The Talmud maintains that strangulation is the form of capital punishment for adultery. Strangulation is considered the least painful of the four types of execution, and it is the default mode unless the text specifies otherwise, which it does not in 20:10.] Now, that declaration covers all adulterers in the category of *the adulterer and the adulteress* [including betrothed and married women, as well as daughters of priests and of Israelites – in all cases the punishment for adultery is strangulation]. However, the Torah subsequently removed the betrothed daughter of a non-priest from the general category, and it ruled that if she has relations with a different man, she is stoned to death. [The reference is to Deuteronomy 22:23–24, which reads: *You shall bring them both to the town gate and stone them to death*.] Similarly, the Torah has removed the daughter of the priest from the general rule and given her execution through burning [as the present verse states]. Hence, just in as the exceptional case of the daughter of a non-priest who is stoned to death [instead of strangled], the Torah refers to a woman who is betrothed but not yet married, so too, when the text identifies the case of a priest's daughter who is burned to death as an exception, it refers to a woman who is betrothed but not married. [By contrast, if a married daughter of a priest commits adultery, she and her paramour will be strangled in punishment.] (Sanhedrin 51b) אֶת־אָבִיהָ הִיא מְחַלֶּלֶת – *She profanes her father also:* Rabbi Meir asked: What is the significance of the clause that states: *She profanes her father also?* This means that if her father was formerly treated in a sacred manner, he is now considered profane. If he was previously granted honor by the community, he is now disdained by them. Thus, everyone will grumble: "Cursed

י אֶת־אָבִיהָ הִיא מְחַלֶּלֶת בָּאֵשׁ תִּשָּׂרֵף: וְהַכֹּהֵן
הַגָּדוֹל מֵאֶחָיו אֲשֶׁר־יוּצַק עַל־רֹאשׁוֹ ׀ שֶׁמֶן הַמִּשְׁחָה וּמִלֵּא
אֶת־יָדוֹ לִלְבֹּשׁ אֶת־הַבְּגָדִים אֶת־רֹאשׁוֹ לֹא יִפְרָע וּבְגָדָיו לֹא
יא יִפְרֹם: וְעַל כָּל־נַפְשֹׁת מֵת לֹא יָבֹא לְאָבִיו וּלְאִמּוֹ לֹא יִטַּמָּא:

TALMUD BAVLI *(cont.)*

be this father who produced such a daughter; cursed be this father who raised such a woman; cursed be this father from whose loins this daughter emerged." (Sanhedrin 52a)

YALKUT SHIMONI

בָּאֵשׁ תִּשָּׂרֵף – *She shall be burned with fire:* Rav Mattana taught: The court would prepare a molten bar of lead. [A criminal who is to be executed with fire is not burned at the stake. Rather, the person is killed by having molten lead poured down his or her throat.] For the verse states: *She shall be burned with fire*, which includes any burning that comes from fire. But if that is so, could not actual fire be used to fulfill the requirement? Let us surround the priest's daughter with bundles of branches and burn her with them. No, for we build a verbal analogy between the cited verse and the language the text uses to describe the deaths of Aharon's sons. In our case, we find the term *serefa* ["burning"], and in the earlier passage we read: *And fire came forth from before the Lord and consumed them* (10:2). [The term *serefa* appears in verse 6 of that passage.] Just as in the earlier text the priests' souls were burned while their bodies remained intact, so too here, the daughter of the priest is burned in a way that takes her life but does not destroy her body. But let us then execute her with boiling water that has been heated by fire. No, for Rav Naḥman taught in the name of Rabba bar Avuh: Take note of the verse that states: *Love your neighbor as your own self* (19:18). That obligates us to select a kind form of death for the offender. [Even when someone must be executed, his or her dignity should be preserved. The criminal should thus be executed in the least horrible manner possible. It is assumed that using molten lead causes less pain than scalding water.] (Emor 630)

VERSE 10

SIFREI BEMIDBAR

וְהַכֹּהֵן הַגָּדוֹל מֵאֶחָיו – *The priest, the highest among his brothers:* The previous verse describes *the daughter of a priest [who] profanes herself by immorality*. Following her offense, the High Priest walks before her and proclaims: "Had you behaved in a way that emulated your ancestral mothers, you would have been privileged to produce a High Priest like me. But instead you have lost your way and squandered your honor." This explains the connection between verse 9, which states: *If the daughter of a priest profanes herself*, and the next sentence: *The priest, the highest among his brothers*. (Balak 131)

TALMUD BAVLI

וְהַכֹּהֵן הַגָּדוֹל מֵאֶחָיו – *The priest, the highest among his brothers:* What is implied by the adjective *gadol* ["higher" or "greater"]? We learn from here that the High Priest must be greater than the rest of his caste in strength, beauty, wisdom, and wealth. Other scholars

10 also; she shall be burned with fire. The priest, the
highest among his brothers, on whose head the anointing oil
has been poured and who has been ordained to wear the vest-
11 ments, shall not dishevel his hair or tear his clothes. He shall
not go near the dead; even for his father or mother he shall not

TALMUD BAVLI *(cont.)*

say: From where do we derive that if the candidate for High Priest does not possess property of his own, his brethren the priests enrich him by presenting him with gifts? For the verse refers to *the priest, the highest among his brothers*, that is, he should be raised by the estates of his brothers. (Yoma 18a) **וְהַכֹּהֵן הַגָּדוֹל מֵאֶחָיו** – *The priest, the highest among his brothers:* Our Sages taught in a *baraita*: When the verse describes *the priest, the highest among his brothers*, that refers to the High Priest; the clause that states: *On whose head the anointing oil has been poured* is an allusion to the priest anointed for war [whose role is discussed in Deuteronomy 20]; and the description that follows, *who has been ordained to wear the vestments*, relates to the High Priest who is consecrated by donning multiple garments [and who is initiated that way in the absence of anointing oil]. Regarding all three types of officials, our text warns: *He shall not dishevel his hair or tear his clothes. He shall not go near the dead* (21:10–11). (Horayot 12b) **אֶת־רֹאשׁוֹ לֹא יִפְרָע** – *He shall not dishevel his hair:* Since the verse states: *He shall not dishevel his hair or tear his clothes*, we learn that these usual mourning practices are entirely inapplicable to the High Priest. Such is the opinion of Rabbi Yehuda. However, Rabbi Yishmael maintains that although the High Priest does not rend his garments in the manner that other people, including ordinary priests, typically do – namely, from above – he does tear his clothes from below. (Horayot 12b)

VAYIKRA RABBA

וְהַכֹּהֵן הַגָּדוֹל מֵאֶחָיו – *The priest, the highest among his brothers:* Why is the High Priest called the *Kohen Gadol*? Because he is greater [*gadol*] than all other priests in five areas: wisdom, strength, beauty, wealth, and age. Regarding his appearance, the High Priest should be more handsome than his priestly brothers. The strength of the High Priest was demonstrated by Aharon, who waved twenty-two thousand Levites [to inaugurate their service] in a single day. How did he move them? He thrust them forward and backward, up and down. The High Priest must be the wealthiest priest in the caste, and if he lacks the property to receive that title, his fellow priests donate their own funds to increase his wealth. One time the priests appointed Pinḥas the stonecutter to be the next High Priest, whereupon they went to find him and discovered him hewing out stone from the earth. At that point, the priests filled the stone quarry with gold dinars on Pinḥas's behalf. And it is not just the High Priest who must be raised to this stature, but also a man appointed as Israel's king. (Margaliot, Emor 26:9)

VERSE 11

PHILO

וְעַל כָּל־נַפְשֹׁת מֵת לֹא יָבֹא – *He shall not go near the dead:* The High Priest is precluded from all outward mourning and surely with good reason. A deputy can perform the other priests'

יב וּמִן־הַמִּקְדָּשׁ לֹא יֵצֵא וְלֹא יְחַלֵּל אֵת מִקְדַּשׁ אֱלֹהָיו כִּי נֵזֶר
יג שֶׁמֶן מִשְׁחַת אֱלֹהָיו עָלָיו אֲנִי יהוה: וְהוּא אִשָּׁה בִבְתוּלֶיהָ
יד יִקָּח: אַלְמָנָה וּגְרוּשָׁה וַחֲלָלָה זֹנָה אֶת־אֵלֶּה לֹא יִקָּח כִּי

PHILO *(cont.)*

services, so that if some are in mourning, none of the customary rites need suffer. But no one else is allowed to perform the functions of a High Priest and therefore he must always continue undefiled, never coming in contact with a corpse, so that he may be ready to offer his prayers and sacrifices at the proper time without hindrance on behalf of the nation.

TALMUD BAVLI

וְעַל כָּל־נַפְשֹׁת מֵת לֹא יָבֹא – *He shall not go near the dead:* Our Sages taught in a *baraita*: To whom does the verse refer when it mandates: *He shall not go near the dead*? This text cannot be talking about persons who are unrelated to the High Priest, since that can be learned via a simple *a fortiori* argument: Since an ordinary priest cannot become impure to bury a non-family member, and yet he may become impure on behalf of a close relative, then the High Priest, who may not even become impure for his closest relatives [as our verse continues: *Even for his father or mother he shall not render himself impure*] may surely not become impure for non-relatives. Thus the clause must certainly relate to close family members. [Therefore a High Priest is prohibited from contracting impurity from any dead person, even his seven close relatives.] On the other hand, since the verse stresses that he may not become impure *for his father*, that implies that the High Priest may [must] become impure to tend to a corpse whose burial is a mitzva [because no one else is taking care of the burial]. (Nazir 47b)

LEKAḤ TOV

נַפְשֹׁת – *The dead:* The word *nafshot* appears here without the expected letter *vav* [as the penultimate letter] to teach that even a *reviit* [a certain amount] of blood that has emanated from two corpses can impart impurity in a tent [that is, an enclosed space in which the dead body lies]. (59a)

VERSE 12

MISHNA

וּמִן־הַמִּקְדָּשׁ לֹא יֵצֵא – *He shall not leave the Sanctuary:* If a relative of the High Priest dies, he may not walk behind the funeral bier [so that his grief does not lead him to clutch at the body, thereby contracting impurity]. Rather, once the members of the funeral procession are concealed from sight [by turning the corner onto the next street], the High Priest may enter the road they have just left. Then, when the company makes itself seen on the next street, the High Priest must conceal himself. He thus goes out with them in this way until the group reaches the city gates [whereupon the funeral proceeds without the High Priest. In the city of Jerusalem, the High Priest can accompany the bier at a distance in a way that conceals his involvement. However, since it would be impossible for him to hide his association from the funeral once the body leaves the city, he remains within its walls]. Such is the opinion of Rabbi Meir. Rabbi Yehuda, on the other hand, maintains that the High Priest does not even

12 render himself impure. He shall not leave the Sanctuary, profaning his God's Sanctuary, for the crown of his God's anoint-
13 ing oil rests upon him; I am the LORD. He may marry a woman
14 only in her virginity. He may not marry a widow, a divorcée,
or one profaned by immorality. He may marry only a virgin

MISHNA *(cont.)*

leave the Temple precincts, as the verse states: *He shall not leave the Sanctuary.* (Sanhedrin 2:1)

VERSE 13

TALMUD YERUSHALMI

וְהוּא – *And he:* The language emphasizes that although the High Priest must marry a virgin, such is not the case with a king or a tribal leader. However, the law does apply to the special priest anointed at a time of war. (Horayot 3:2)

TALMUD BAVLI

בִבְתוּלֶיהָ – *In her virginity:* This law excludes a grown woman whose sign of virginity has diminished. Such is the opinion of Rabbi Meir. However, Rabbi Elazar and Rabbi Shimon rule that [such] an adult woman is fit for a High Priest. (Ketubot 97b)

VERSE 14

TALMUD BAVLI

אַלְמָנָה – *A widow:* Our Sages taught in a *baraita*: The Torah's prohibition includes a married woman who was widowed as well as a betrothed woman whose fiancé has died. Is that not obvious [considering that the verse does not specify the kind of widow who is forbidden]? Nevertheless, we might have constructed the following verbal analogy between our text, which contains the word "widow," and an earlier verse, where Yehuda tells Tamar: [*"Live as a widow in your father's house until my son Shela grows up"* – Genesis 38:11]. Just as there, Tamar became a widow after her marriage to Er, so too here, perhaps the text refers only to a woman who is widowed after marriage [and not after just betrothal]. Hence, the *tanna* teaches us that this is not the case. But indeed, perhaps the inference from that comparison does represent the law. No, for the case of widowhood resembles that of divorce: Just as a divorcée is forbidden to a priest whether her husband had divorced her or only her fiancé had done so, so too may a widow not marry a High Priest whether she had been fully married or only betrothed. (Yevamot 59a)

LEKAḤ TOV

אַלְמָנָה – *A widow:* The term *almana* derives from the term *maneh*, which teaches us the amount of money promised to a widow in her ketubah [marriage contract. The standard value of a ketubah is two hundred *dinar*, the equivalent of two *maneh*. However, a widow's ketubah is worth only one hundred *dinar* or one *maneh*]. Now, since the Torah permits the common priest to marry a widow, it emphasizes that such a union is forbidden in the case of a High Priest. We learn from here that a child born to a High Priest and a widow is not a *mamzer* [the product of an incestuous or an adulterous relationship], but is nevertheless non-sacred [*ḥullin*, that is,

טו אִם־בְּתוּלָה מֵעַמָּיו יִקַּח אִשָּׁה: וְלֹא־יְחַלֵּל זַרְעוֹ בְּעַמָּיו כִּי
טז אֲנִי יְהוָה מְקַדְּשׁוֹ: וַיְדַבֵּר יְהוָה אֶל־מֹשֶׁה לֵּאמֹר: שני
יז דַּבֵּר אֶל־אַהֲרֹן לֵאמֹר אִישׁ מִזַּרְעֲךָ לְדֹרֹתָם אֲשֶׁר יִהְיֶה בוֹ
יח מוּם לֹא יִקְרַב לְהַקְרִיב לֶחֶם אֱלֹהָיו: כִּי כָל־אִישׁ אֲשֶׁר־בּוֹ
יט מוּם לֹא יִקְרָב אִישׁ עִוֵּר אוֹ פִסֵּחַ אוֹ חָרֻם אוֹ שָׂרוּעַ: אוֹ
כ אִישׁ אֲשֶׁר־יִהְיֶה בוֹ שֶׁבֶר רָגֶל אוֹ שֶׁבֶר יָד: אוֹ־גִבֵּן אוֹ־דַק
כא אוֹ תְּבַלֻּל בְּעֵינוֹ אוֹ גָרָב אוֹ יַלֶּפֶת אוֹ מְרוֹחַ אָשֶׁךְ: כָּל־אִישׁ

LEKAḤ TOV *(cont.)*

the boy is not considered a priest]. Thus, even though a common priest may marry a widow, there is a severity here in that her child with a High Priest will be non-sacred. On the other hand, there is a leniency in the case of a divorcée. That woman may marry neither a common priest nor a High Priest, whereas even if she has relations with the latter, the child that results is still not a *mamzer* but [merely] non-sacred, just as he would be if the father were a common priest. [In other words, even though there is a greater stringency attendant to a divorcée in that she can marry neither kind of priest, that does not translate into stricter treatment of her progeny. On the other hand, even though there is a leniency regarding a widow in that she may marry a common priest, should she marry a High Priest instead, the leniency does not extend to her son, thereby allowing him to live as a priest. Instead, he assumes the stringency of losing his priestly status.] **וַחֲלָלָה** – *One profaned by immortality:* This refers to a girl whose mother is disqualified from marrying a priest. [The progeny of a priest and a woman who is forbidden to him is termed a *ḥalal* if he is a boy. The outlawed woman in this instance does not refer to a relative or to a married woman but to a divorcée, or a widow if the man is the High Priest. This child cannot serve as a priest nor is he bound to the restrictions that define a priest's lifestyle. If the child is a girl, she is called a *ḥalala*, the sole implication of which is that she may not marry a priest. Similarly, if a priest has relations with a woman whom he may not marry, the woman herself becomes a *ḥalala*.] (59b)

VERSE 15

TALMUD BAVLI

וְלֹא־יְחַלֵּל זַרְעוֹ – *So that he will not profane his children:* It was taught in a *baraita*: According to Rabbi Akiva, any child of a forbidden union is termed a *mamzer* except for the progeny of a High Priest and a widow. The Sage bases this on the verse that states: *So that he will not profane his children*. Thus, although the child would be considered a *ḥalal* [non-sacred, non-priestly], that still does not make him a *mamzer*. (Kiddushin 64)

VERSE 17

TALMUD BAVLI

אִישׁ מִזַּרְעֲךָ לְדֹרֹתָם – *Any of your future descendants:* Our Sages taught in a *baraita*: When the verse bans blemished priests from the Sanctuary service, it states: *Any [ish: literally, "a man"] of your future descendants*, which teaches that a minor is unfit for Temple service

15 from his own people, so that he will not profane his children
16 among his people, for I, the Lord, sanctify him." The SHENI
17 Lord spoke to Moshe: "Tell Aharon: Any of your future descendants who has a physical blemish may not draw close to
18 present foodstuff offerings to his God. No one with a blemish
shall approach: this includes one who is blind, lame, disfigured,
19 20 or deformed; or who has a broken foot or hand; or who is a
hunchback or a dwarf, or who has a growth in his eye, a severe
21 rash, scabs, or crushed testicles. No descendant of Aharon the

TALMUD BAVLI *(cont.)*

even if he is unblemished. Such is the inference of Rabbi Elazar. At what point does the young priest become eligible to work in the Temple? Technically, that happens when he reaches puberty and grows two pubic hairs. Nevertheless, the lad's fellow priests will not allow him to participate in the Sanctuary's activities until he has attained twenty years of age. (Ḥullin 24b)

VERSE 18

TALMUD BAVLI

אִישׁ עִוֵּר – *One who is blind:* Our Sages taught in a *baraita*: A blind priest may not serve in the Temple whether he has lost his sight in both eyes or only in one. (Bekhorot 44a)

VERSE 19

LEKAḤ TOV

שֶׁבֶר רָגֶל – *A broken foot:* The ban extends to one who has a twisted foot. **שֶׁבֶר יָד** – *A broken…hand:* A priest whose fingers are bent over each other is also disqualified from service. (60a)

VERSE 20

TALMUD BAVLI

אוֹ תְבַלֻּל בְּעֵינוֹ – *Or who has a growth in his eye:* Our Sages taught in a *baraita*: The verse means that any blemish in a priest's eye disqualifies him from performing the Temple service. Based on this, the Sages ruled: If both of a priest's eyes are below [their normal location] or both of his eyes are above that place, or if one of a priest's eyes is above and the other below, or if he sees a room and an upper story as one [his vision is unfocused to the point that he sees a room on the ground floor and a room on an upper story simultaneously], or if when he speaks with his friend, a third person thinks, "He is looking at me" [then the priest is considered blemished and he is disqualified from the Temple's service]. (Bekhorot 44a)

VERSE 21

TALMUD BAVLI

כָּל־אִישׁ אֲשֶׁר־בּוֹ מוּם – *[No one] who has a physical blemish:* Our Sages taught in a *baraita*: An earlier verse reads: *Any male among Aharon's descendants may eat it as their eternal share of the Lord's fire offerings throughout their generations* (6:11), which includes blemished

אֲשֶׁר־בּוֹ מוּם מִזֶּרַע אַהֲרֹן הַכֹּהֵן לֹא יִגַּשׁ לְהַקְרִיב אֶת־אִשֵּׁי
כב יְהוָה מוּם בּוֹ אֵת לֶחֶם אֱלֹהָיו לֹא יִגַּשׁ לְהַקְרִיב׃ לֶחֶם אֱלֹהָיו
כג מִקָּדְשֵׁי הַקֳּדָשִׁים וּמִן־הַקֳּדָשִׁים יֹאכֵל׃ אַךְ אֶל־הַפָּרֹכֶת לֹא
יָבֹא וְאֶל־הַמִּזְבֵּחַ לֹא יִגַּשׁ כִּי־מוּם בּוֹ וְלֹא יְחַלֵּל אֶת־מִקְדָּשַׁי
כד כִּי אֲנִי יְהוָה מְקַדְּשָׁם׃ וַיְדַבֵּר מֹשֶׁה אֶל־אַהֲרֹן וְאֶל־בָּנָיו
וְאֶל־כָּל־בְּנֵי יִשְׂרָאֵל׃
כב א ב וַיְדַבֵּר יְהוָה אֶל־מֹשֶׁה לֵּאמֹר׃ דַּבֵּר אֶל־אַהֲרֹן וְאֶל־בָּנָיו
וְיִנָּזְרוּ מִקָּדְשֵׁי בְנֵי־יִשְׂרָאֵל וְלֹא יְחַלְּלוּ אֶת־שֵׁם קָדְשִׁי

TALMUD BAVLI *(cont.)*

priests. Now, why is this derivation necessary? It cannot be needed to teach that blemished priests may eat sacrificial meat, since the text says that explicitly: *He may eat the foodstuff offerings of his God, the holy of holies as well as the holy* (21:22). Rather, the earlier verse teaches that blemished priests may receive a share of the sacrifices [along with the other priests. Based on the present text alone we might have thought that a blemished priest is not given a portion of his own but is permitted to eat meat that a different, unblemished priest gives him. Hence, we learn that even a blemished priest receives his rightful share]. (Zevaḥim 102a)

LEKAḤ TOV

כָּל־אִישׁ אֲשֶׁר־בּוֹ מוּם – *[No one] who has a physical blemish:* The phrase *kol ish* [literally, "no man"] serves to include all other manner of blemish [beyond those listed in the previous verses], whereas the emphasis in the phrase *asher bo mum* [literally, "who has a blemish in him"] excludes a priest whose blemish has already healed. **לֹא יִגַּשׁ** – *Shall [not] draw near:* The phrase *lo yiggash* ["he shall not draw near"] appears three times in this passage to indicate that one who does so thereby violates three prohibitions for drawing near while also transgressing two warnings not to present an offering. For the verses also contain two mentions of presenting offerings. (60a)

VERSE 23

TALMUD BAVLI

אַךְ אֶל־הַפָּרֹכֶת לֹא יָבֹא – *But he may not come close to the inner curtain:* Rav Huna taught: Rav Kahana [who was a priest] supported the priests [by emphasizing their special sanctity]. For Rav Kahana taught in a *baraita*: Since the text warns that a physically imperfect priest *may not come close to the inner curtain or approach the altar, because of his blemish*, we might have thought that such persons may not even enter the area between the entrance hall and the altar [that is, the space outside] to manufacture beaten plates of gold [which are used to overlay the walls of the Holy of Holies chamber]. However, the verse opens with the term *akh* ["only"], which connotes an exclusion and hence a distinction. [That is, although a blemished priest does not have as much freedom of movement in the Temple as do his unblemished colleagues, he may enter that space for the specific purpose mentioned.]

priest who has a physical blemish shall draw near to present the
Lord's fire offerings; because of his blemish, he shall not ap-
22 proach to present an offering of foodstuffs to his God. He may
eat the foodstuff offerings of his God, the holy of holies as well
23 as the holy. But he may not come close to the inner curtain or
approach the altar, because of his blemish; he shall not profane
24 My Sanctuary; I am the Lord who makes them holy." Moshe
told this to Aharon, his sons, and all the Israelites.
22 1 2 The Lord spoke to Moshe: "Tell Aharon and his sons to take
great care with the sacred offerings that the Israelites consecrate
to Me, so that they do not profane My holy name: I am the

TALMUD BAVLI *(cont.)*

Now, although that activity should ideally be performed by unblemished priests, if there are only blemished priests available to do the job, they are permitted to do it. Similarly, it would be best if pure persons were set to this work, but impure priests may enter if needed. Still, even blemished and impure men are allowed into the holy area if they are priests, but not if they are common Israelites. (Eruvin 105a)

LEKAḤ TOV

אַךְ אֶל־הַפָּרֹכֶת לֹא יָבֹא – *But he may not come close to the inner curtain:* The text refers to the innermost chamber. **וְאֶל־הַמִּזְבֵּחַ** – *The altar:* A blemished priest may not approach the altar even though it stands outside. **לֹא יִגַּשׁ כִּי־מוּם בּוֹ** – *He may not approach…because of his blemish:* These verses warn three times that a blemished priest is not to approach and two times that he may not come close, corresponding to the five areas from which such a person is banned. For the following is taught in Tractate Taharot: There are ten areas of differing holiness…the space between the entrance hall and the altar is holy, in that blemished persons and those whose hair is disheveled may not enter that place. Thus there are these five zones where blemished priests may not appear: the space between the entrance hall and the altar, the altar itself, the Sanctuary building, the place where the curtain hangs, and the Holy of Holies chamber. **וְלֹא יְחַלֵּל אֶת־מִקְדָּשַׁי** – *He shall not profane My Sanctuary:* We learn from here that if a blemished priest neglects this law and performs the service, his actions are valid, but he has profaned the space. (60a)

VERSE 24

YALKUT SHIMONI

וַיְדַבֵּר מֹשֶׁה אֶל־אַהֲרֹן – *Moshe told this to Aharon:* Aharon's sons are to ensure that Aharon observes these rules; the sons are meant to keep an eye on each other in this regard; and the people of Israel are instructed to be vigilant with respect to the sons. (Emor 632)

CHAPTER 22, VERSE 2

TALMUD BAVLI

וְלֹא יְחַלְּלוּ – *So that they do not profane:* Rav Ḥiyya bar Avin asked Rav Yosef: From where is it derived that if an impure priest performs the Temple service, he is subject to death at the

ג אֲשֶׁר הֵם מַקְדִּשִׁים לִי אֲנִי יהוה: אֱמֹר אֲלֵהֶם לְדֹרֹתֵיכֶם
כָּל־אִישׁ ׀ אֲשֶׁר־יִקְרַב מִכָּל־זַרְעֲכֶם אֶל־הַקֳּדָשִׁים אֲשֶׁר
יַקְדִּישׁוּ בְנֵי־יִשְׂרָאֵל לַיהוה וְטֻמְאָתוֹ עָלָיו וְנִכְרְתָה הַנֶּפֶשׁ
ד הַהִוא מִלְּפָנַי אֲנִי יהוה: אִישׁ אִישׁ מִזֶּרַע אַהֲרֹן וְהוּא צָרוּעַ
אוֹ זָב בַּקֳּדָשִׁים לֹא יֹאכַל עַד אֲשֶׁר יִטְהָר וְהַנֹּגֵעַ בְּכָל־טְמֵא־
ה נֶפֶשׁ אוֹ אִישׁ אֲשֶׁר־תֵּצֵא מִמֶּנּוּ שִׁכְבַת־זָרַע: אוֹ־אִישׁ אֲשֶׁר
יִגַּע בְּכָל־שֶׁרֶץ אֲשֶׁר יִטְמָא־לוֹ אוֹ בְאָדָם אֲשֶׁר יִטְמָא־
ו לוֹ לְכֹל טֻמְאָתוֹ: נֶפֶשׁ אֲשֶׁר תִּגַּע־בּוֹ וְטָמְאָה עַד־הָעָרֶב
ז וְלֹא יֹאכַל מִן־הַקֳּדָשִׁים כִּי אִם־רָחַץ בְּשָׂרוֹ בַּמָּיִם: וּבָא
הַשֶּׁמֶשׁ וְטָהֵר וְאַחַר יֹאכַל מִן־הַקֳּדָשִׁים כִּי לַחְמוֹ הוּא:

TALMUD BAVLI *(cont.)*

hands of Heaven? Rav Yosef answered: This is learned from the verse that states: *Tell Aharon and his sons to take great care with the sacred offerings that the Israelites consecrate to Me, so that they do not profane [velo yeḥallelu] My holy name*. And we derive the punishment through a verbal analogy based on the term *ḥillul* ["desecration"] in this verse and its appearance in a subsequent text regarding *teruma* [the portion set aside for the priest, and the assumed subject of 22:9]: *They shall keep My charge and not bear guilt and die through it, having profaned it [ki yeḥalleluhu]*. Just as regarding the portion set aside for the priest, the offender is punished with death at the hands of Heaven, so too here will an impure priest who performs the Temple service face death at the hands of Heaven. (Sanhedrin 83b)

VERSE 3

TALMUD BAVLI

אֱמֹר אֲלֵהֶם – *Tell them:* The initial instruction relates to those people standing at Mount Sinai, whereas the subsequent term, "throughout the generations," refers to future generations of priests. (Bava Batra 120a)

LEKAḤ TOV

כָּל־אִישׁ – *If any descendants:* The term *ish* [literally, "man"] addresses the males. **אֲשֶׁר־יִקְרַב מִכָּל־זַרְעֲכֶם** – *Any descendant who comes near:* This serves to include females.

אֶל־הַקֳּדָשִׁים... וְנִכְרְתָה – *To the sacred offerings...shall be severed:* We learn from here that those who violate the sacred offerings face excision for their transgression.

VERSE 5

YALKUT SHIMONI

לְכֹל טֻמְאָתוֹ – *Whatever his impurity:* The term *tum'ato* ["his impurity"] is employed as one half of a verbal analogy with the following verse: *Whoever touches a corpse of a person who has died, and fails to purify himself, defiles the Lord's Tabernacle.... He remains impure; his*

3 Lord. Tell them: If any descendant of yours throughout the
generations comes near the sacred offerings that the Israelites
have consecrated to the Lord while in an impure state, he shall
4 be severed from My presence; I am the Lord. Any descendant
of Aharon who has a defiling blight of the skin or a discharge
may not eat of the sacred offerings until he becomes pure. One
who touches anything made impure by contact with the dead,
5 or who has had a seminal emission, or who has touched any
swarming thing or any person who renders him impure – what-
6 ever his impurity – the one who touches these things shall be
impure until the evening, and shall not eat of the sacred offer-
7 ings until he has washed his body in water. When the sun sets,
he shall become pure again and may eat of the sacred offerings,

YALKUT SHIMONI *(cont.)*

impurity [tum'ato] is still with him (Numbers 19:13). Just as in the later verse, the text refers to the impurity of the person and not to the impurity of the sacrificial meat, so too here, we are dealing with the impurity of the Israelite, not with the impurity of the meat. (Emor 634)

VERSE 6

TALMUD BAVLI

כִּי אִם־רָחַץ בְּשָׂרוֹ בַּמָּיִם – *Until he has washed his body in water:* The Mishna teaches: [When the ritual impurity of a *zav* – a man who had a discharge – or a leper has been completed and] he has immersed during the day and emerged from the ritual bath, he may immediately partake of the second tithe. Once the sun has set, he is permitted to eat the portion of the priest. Finally, after he has brought his atonement offering, he may eat the sacrificial food that he is eligible to consume. Now, from where do we derive these laws? Rava taught in the name of Rav Ḥisda: Three verses are written regarding the purity required for eating sacred food. First, it is written: *And he shall not eat of the sacred offerings until he has washed his body in water* (22:6), whereas if he has bathed [that is, immersed in a ritual bath], he is pure [and may partake of sacred food]. The text continues: *When the sun sets, he shall become pure again and may eat of the sacred offerings* (22:7) [which indicates that the person must wait until after sundown to eat these foods]. Third, an earlier text reads: *But if she cannot afford a sheep, she may bring two doves or two pigeons – one for the burnt offering and the other for the purification offering. The priest will then make atonement for her, and she shall be pure* (12:8). [According to this citation, a woman after childbirth is not completely pure until she has brought her offering.] How can we resolve the disparities among these texts? The first verse (22:6) permits the consumption of second tithe, the second verse (22:7) refers to the eating of the priest's portion, and the third (12:8) relates to sacrificial food. (Yevamot 74b)

VERSE 7

TALMUD YERUSHALMI

וּבָא הַשֶּׁמֶשׁ וְטָהֵר – *When the sun sets, he shall become pure again:* Rabbi Abba taught: An earlier verse states: *By the time Lot reached Tzoar, the sun had risen [yatza: literally, "had*

ח ט נְבֵלָה וּטְרֵפָה לֹא יֹאכַל לְטָמְאָה־בָהּ אֲנִי יְהוָה׃ וְשָׁמְרוּ
אֶת־מִשְׁמַרְתִּי וְלֹא־יִשְׂאוּ עָלָיו חֵטְא וּמֵתוּ בוֹ כִּי יְחַלְּלֻהוּ
י אֲנִי יְהוָה מְקַדְּשָׁם׃ וְכָל־זָר לֹא־יֹאכַל קֹדֶשׁ תּוֹשַׁב כֹּהֵן
יא וְשָׂכִיר לֹא־יֹאכַל קֹדֶשׁ׃ וְכֹהֵן כִּי־יִקְנֶה נֶפֶשׁ קִנְיַן כַּסְפּוֹ הוּא

TALMUD YERUSHALMI *(cont.)*

gone out"] over the land (Genesis 19:23), whereas here we read: *When the sun sets [uva: literally, "when it comes"], he shall become pure again.* Thus, we should compare the sun's going with its coming: Just as when the sun comes [sets] it is completely hidden from the world, so too when it goes [rises] it is totally revealed to the world. [Thus, purity is achieved at the end of sun's setting.] (Berakhot 1:1)

TALMUD BAVLI

וּבָא הַשֶּׁמֶשׁ וְטָהֵר – *When the sun sets, he shall become pure again:* It was taught in a *baraita*: The verse rules that *when the sun sets, he shall become pure again*, meaning that the setting of the sun is necessary in order for a purified priest to eat the sacrificial portions reserved for him. By contrast, failure to bring the atonement offering would not prevent him from consuming that portion. (Berakhot 2a)

VERSE 8

TALMUD BAVLI

נְבֵלָה וּטְרֵפָה – *An animal found dead or one that was torn by animals:* It was taught in a *baraita*: We might have thought that an animal carcass imparts impurity to the eater's garments once it is in his throat [as does the unslaughtered carcass of a kosher bird]. However, the verse states: *He may not eat an animal found dead or one that was torn by animals, becoming impure by doing so.* [This verse, which deals with impurity through eating, applies to] that which transfers impurity only by means of its consumption. [That is, the text refers to the kosher bird that has not been slaughtered properly and which imparts impurity only by being swallowed, not by being touched or carried. The verse therefore] excludes an animal carcass [from transferring impurity through consumption because] that transfers impurity even before one eats it [by touching or carrying it]. (Nidda 42b)

VERSE 9

TALMUD YERUSHALMI

וְשָׁמְרוּ אֶת־מִשְׁמַרְתִּי – *They shall keep My charge:* If a king of flesh and blood issues a decree, he may decide to fulfill it himself, or he may expect his subjects to execute his wishes. But the Holy One, blessed be He, acts otherwise: When He enacts a ruling, He Himself is the first to realize it, as the verse states: *They shall keep My charge. I am the Lord*, meaning: I am the Lord who was the first to observe the Torah's commandments. [For instance, God observed the Sabbath first. In general, many mitzvot are rooted in the principle of imitating God's ways, which is predicated on the assumption that God performs many mitzvot.] (Rosh Hashana 1:3)

8 for they are his food. He may not eat an animal found dead or
one that was torn by wild animals, becoming impure by doing
9 so; I am the Lord. They shall keep My charge and not bear
guilt and die through it, having profaned it. I am the Lord, who
10 makes them holy. No layman may eat of the sacred offerings,
11 nor may a priest's visitor or hired laborer eat of them. But if a
priest acquires a slave for money, the slave may eat of them, and

TALMUD BAVLI

וְשָׁמְרוּ אֶת־מִשְׁמַרְתִּי – *They shall keep My charge:* Shmuel taught: How do we know that an impure priest who eats the pure portion of a priest is subject to death at the hands of Heaven? For the verse states: *They shall keep My charge and not bear guilt and die through it.* (Sanhedrin 83a)

YALKUT SHIMONI

וְשָׁמְרוּ אֶת־מִשְׁמַרְתִּי – *They shall keep My charge:* It is the court's responsibility to warn the priests to follow these laws. **וְלֹא־יִשְׂאוּ עָלָיו חֵטְא** – *And not bear guilt…through it:* Is it perhaps the animal found dead that the text refers to? No, the verse relates to the offering itself. **וּמֵתוּ בוֹ** – *And die through it:* It is the unlawful consumption of a priest's portion that is punishable by death, not that of the second tithe. **כִּי יְחַלְּלֻהוּ** – *Having profaned it:* The verse thereby excludes a pure person who ate an impure portion of a priest. (Emor 635)

VERSE 11

TALMUD BAVLI

קִנְיַן כַּסְפּוֹ – *Acquired [with] money:* A *yavam* [a widow's brother-in-law who is a potential husband to her, and who in the present case is a priest] may not serve the woman a priest's portion. What is the reason for this? It is because the text uses the phrase *acquired with [his] money*, and it was not this man who acquired the woman [that is, who provided the money for her betrothal] but his brother. (Yevamot 58a)

LEKAḤ TOV

וְכֹהֵן כִּי־יִקְנֶה נֶפֶשׁ קִנְיַן כַּסְפּוֹ – *But if a priest acquires a slave for money:* In the event that a priest gets married or purchases Canaanite slaves, these dependents are permitted to eat the priest's portion. By contrast, how do we know that an Israelite slave may not eat a priest's portion? Because the verse refers to the acquisition of a slave, and the body of a Hebrew is not purchased. Another interpretation: If a person is partly a slave and partly free, he may not eat a priest's portion. **וִילִיד בֵּיתוֹ** – *And those born into his household:* A child born into the household [that is, a Canaanite slave who will eventually himself be a slave] may eat a priest's portion even if he has no monetary value. [The author refers to a child who suffers from a condition that will disable him from serving. Nevertheless, he may also eat a priest's portion.] How do we know that a son [whose father was a priest and whose mother was an Israelite] may continue to serve his mother a priest's portion [after the death of the father]? This may be derived from an *a fortiori* argument: If the seed of the father has the power to disqualify the mother from eating a priest's portion, then

יב יֹאכַל בּוֹ וִילִיד בֵּיתוֹ הֵם יֹאכְלוּ בְלַחְמוֹ: וּבַת־כֹּהֵן כִּי תִהְיֶה
יג לְאִישׁ זָר הִוא בִּתְרוּמַת הַקֳּדָשִׁים לֹא תֹאכֵל: וּבַת־כֹּהֵן כִּי
תִהְיֶה אַלְמָנָה וּגְרוּשָׁה וְזֶרַע אֵין לָהּ וְשָׁבָה אֶל־בֵּית אָבִיהָ

LEKAḤ TOV *(cont.)*

surely the seed of the father holds the power to allow the woman to continue eating a priest's portion. This will be found in the case of an Israelite's daughter who marries a priest and is then widowed. If she has children, she may eat a priest's portion because of them. [If an Israelite marries the daughter of a priest, she may no longer eat a priest's portion as she did in her father's house. However, if the priest dies and the widow returns home, she may once again eat it. Such is not the case if the priest had fathered a son, as 22:13 states. The existence of the father's child prevents the woman from eating a priest's portion even after the Israelite has died. Similarly, a dead priest will continue to exert his identity after his death and permit the widow to eat a priest's portion.] (60b)

VERSE 12

TALMUD BAVLI

וּבַת־כֹּהֵן כִּי תִהְיֶה לְאִישׁ זָר – *If a priest's daughter marries a layman:* [If a woman has relations with a man whom she is ineligible to marry such as a Moabite, she has thereby rendered herself unfit to subsequently marry a priest and eat his sacred portion. What is the source of this law?] Rav Yehuda taught in the name of Rav: We learn this from the verse that states: *If a priest's daughter marries a layman* [*ish zar:* literally, "a foreign man"], *she may no longer eat of the sacred gifts.* Since this woman has had relations with a man who is invalid for her, he has disqualified her from marrying into the priesthood. [The argument views the term *zar* as referring to a man who is forbidden to the woman, ignoring the word's straightforward meaning: a non-priest.] (Yevamot 68a)

VERSE 13

MISHNA

וּבַת־כֹּהֵן כִּי תִהְיֶה אַלְמָנָה – *If a priest's daughter is a widow:* If (1) the daughter of an Israelite marries a priest, she may partake of her husband's sacred portion. If (1a) the priest dies and leaves a child [a son or daughter] behind, the widow may continue to partake of his portions [on account of the child]. If (2) the woman marries a second time, now a Levite, she may eat her husband's first tithe [*maaser rishon*. However, she may not eat a priest's portion anymore, even though her son from the priest is still alive, because she has adopted the status of her second husband, who is a non-priest. Hence, had the widow not married the Levite, she could have continued to eat a priest's portion because of her son, but since she married the Levite, she cannot continue to eat it, despite the fact that her son is the child of a priest]. If (2a) the Levite dies as well and leaves a child, the widow may continue to eat first-tithe produce [on account of the child. However, even though her son from the priest is still alive, the widow may not eat a priest's portion on account of him, because the existence of the Levite's son prevents her from returning to her status as the priest's widow].

12 those born into his household also may eat his food. If a priest's
daughter marries a layman, she may no longer eat of the sacred
13 gifts. If a priest's daughter is a widow or a divorcée, has no children, and returns to live in her father's house as when she was
young, she may eat her father's food again; but no layperson

MISHNA *(cont.)*

If (3) the widow now marries an Israelite, she may no longer eat either a priest's portion or first-tithe food [due to her husband's caste]. If (3a) the third husband dies and leaves a child behind, the widow may still not eat a priest's portion or the first tithe [since the living third child links her to the Israelite]. If (3b) the child from the Israelite husband also dies [whereas the child from her marriage to the Levite remains alive], the woman may now eat the first tithe again [but not the priest's portion]. And if (2c) the child of the Levite also dies, the widow may eat the priest's portion again. However, if (1c) the child of the priest dies too, the woman may no longer partake of a priest's portion or the tithe. [Whereas the first half of the Mishna describes the effects of an Israelite's daughter marrying a priest, the second part of the text shifts to discuss the case of a priest's daughter, who as a single woman was entitled to eat the priest's portion at her father's table. This woman now marries an Israelite and forgoes that privilege.] If (4) the daughter of a priest marries an Israelite, she may no longer partake of the priest's portion. If (4a) her husband dies and he leaves behind a child, the widow may not eat a priest's portion as long as that son is alive [since the child links her to the dead husband]. If (5) the widow from the Israelite subsequently marries a Levite, she may eat her second husband's first tithe [*maaser rishon*, but she may not eat a priest's portion because her husband the Levite may not]. If (5a) the Levite husband dies, and he leaves behind a child, the widow may continue to eat the first tithe. If (6) the widow marries again, this time to a priest, she may partake of his portion. Furthermore, if (6a) the husband who is a priest dies and leaves behind a child, the woman may continue to eat a priest's portion. However, if (6b) the son from the priest dies, the woman may no longer eat a priest's portion [because she now assumes the status of her Levite husband, since his son is still alive. Hence, she can eat tithe produce due to that son]. If (5b) her son from the Levite dies, the woman may no longer partake of tithe. Finally, if (4b) the child from the Israelite dies, the widow and bereaved mother returns to her father's house, where she once again may eat the priest's portion. This is the sense of the verse that states: *[If she] returns to live in her father's house as when she was young, she may eat her father's food again*. (Yevamot 9:6)

TALMUD YERUSHALMI

וְשָׁבָה אֶל־בֵּית אָבִיהָ – *She returns to live in her father's house:* This excludes a widow who is waiting for her brother-in-law to marry her.

כִּנְעוּרֶיהָ – *As when she was young:* This phrase excludes a pregnant widow. (Yevamot 7:4)

TALMUD BAVLI

וְזֶרַע אֵין לָהּ – *She has no children:* When the verse states: *If she has no children, and returns to live in her father's house*, that seems to disqualify a woman from eating a priest's portion only if she has a child. How do we know that she would similarly be unable to

כִּנְעוּרֶיהָ מִלֶּחֶם אָבִיהָ תֹּאכֵל וְכָל־זָר לֹא־יֹאכַל בּוֹ: וְאִישׁ יד
כִּי־יֹאכַל קֹדֶשׁ בִּשְׁגָגָה וְיָסַף חֲמִשִׁיתוֹ עָלָיו וְנָתַן לַכֹּהֵן אֶת־
הַקֹּדֶשׁ: וְלֹא יְחַלְּלוּ אֶת־קָדְשֵׁי בְּנֵי יִשְׂרָאֵל אֵת אֲשֶׁר־יָרִימוּ טו
לַיהוָה: וְהִשִּׂיאוּ אוֹתָם עֲוֹן אַשְׁמָה בְּאָכְלָם אֶת־קָדְשֵׁיהֶם טז
כִּי אֲנִי יְהוָה מְקַדְּשָׁם:

TALMUD BAVLI *(cont.)*

eat a priest's portion if she has grandchildren? [If the priest's daughter's child has died but her grandchild remains alive, she would still be barred from consuming a priest's portion.] The emphasis in the verse *She has no [ein lah] children* teaches that any progeny disqualifies her from eating that food. [The teaching is based on the spelling of the word *ein* – *alef-yod-nun* – where the middle letter is not technically necessary.] Now, it would appear that it is only a legitimate child that renders the widow unable to eat a priest's portion. How do we know that an illegitimate child [such as one born through adultery] would similarly disqualify the woman from eating the food? For the verse states: *She has no [ein lah] children*, a phrase that should be read as *ayyein lah* [meaning, inquire whether she has any offspring – legitimate or otherwise]. (Yevamot 70a)

VERSE 14

TALMUD BAVLI

וְנָתַן לַכֹּהֵן אֶת־הַקֹּדֶשׁ – *He shall make restitution to the priest:* It was taught in a *baraita*: If a person eats a sacred thing in error, *he shall make restitution to the priest*. Now, the payment must comprise an item that is fit to be consecrated. As such, if a person eats leavened bread on Passover that is also a priest's portion, he is exempt from paying the monetary value of the priest's portion – not even the insubstantial value were it to be considered simply firewood. This is the opinion of Rabbi Eliezer ben Yaakov [who maintains that since the priest could not have derived benefit from the substance, he faces no financial loss]. (Pesaḥim 32a)

LEKAḤ TOV

וְאִישׁ כִּי־יֹאכַל קֹדֶשׁ – *If someone eats of the sacred gift:* The term *ish* [literally, "a man"] serves to exclude a minor. The minimum amount of unlawful eating that constitutes a violation is an olive-bulk's worth of sacred food. The term "sacred" here refers to a priest's portion, and the produce cannot have been consumed intentionally. **וְיָסַף חֲמִשִׁיתוֹ עָלָיו** – *Adding an extra fifth to its value:* The value of the principal and the fine of a fifth, when added together, should total five equal parts. [This "fifth" is thus what we might call a quarter.] **וְנָתַן לַכֹּהֵן אֶת־הַקֹּדֶשׁ** – *He shall make restitution to the priest:* The offender should give the priest superior produce in compensation. (61a)

YALKUT SHIMONI

וְיָסַף חֲמִשִׁיתוֹ עָלָיו – *Adding an extra fifth to its value:* Rabbi Yoshiya taught: The principal and the fifth together should total five parts. Rabbi Yonatan maintains: The fine should equal a fifth of the principal. [Rabbi Yoshiya's approach is called a fifth from without, *milevar*, and the

14 may do so. If someone eats of the sacred gift unintentionally,
he shall make restitution to the priest, adding an extra fifth to
15 its value. The people must not profane the sacred meats that
16 Israelites bring as offerings to the Lord or incur the penalty of
iniquity by eating their sacred offerings; for I, the Lord, make
them holy."

YALKUT SHIMONI *(cont.)*

fine equals a quarter of the principal. If the non-priest ate a sacred portion worth eighty *zuz*, he would have to pay back eighty plus a fine that is a quarter of that, for a total of one hundred *zuz*. The total is thus five-quarters of twenty, and the fine is one-fifth of that. Rabbi Yonatan's understanding is called a fifth from within, *milegav*, and is calculated as a fifth of the principal. If the principal is worth eighty *zuz*, a fifth of that is sixteen, and the total payment would be ninety-six *zuz*.] (Emor 638)

VERSE 15

TALMUD YERUSHALMI

וְלֹא יְחַלְּלוּ אֶת־קָדְשֵׁי – *They must not profane the sacred meats:* It was taught: If priests and Levites assist a farmer at his threshing floor, that does not give them the right to claim the priest's portion or the first tithe [for themselves, to the detriment of other priests and Levites]. And if the owner does give the agricultural gifts to these persons, he thereby desecrates the produce, as the verse states: *The people must not profane the sacred meats that the Israelites bring as offerings*, which is what has just been done. Thus we rule that the priest's portion does not qualify as a priest's portion, the tithe does not qualify as tithe, and dedications are not dedications. It is regarding this that the prophet says: *Her leaders arbitrate for bribes, her priests will teach for a price, and her prophets for dividends will divine* (Micah 3:11). As punishment, God will visit three sufferings upon them. (Demai 6:2)

TALMUD BAVLI

וְלֹא יְחַלְּלוּ אֶת־קָדְשֵׁי – *They must not profane the sacred meats:* Rav Aḥa bar Adda taught in the name of Rav Yehuda: If a farmer gives the priest's portion [from his produce] to a priest who is an ignoramus [the Talmud's term *am haaretz* refers to an ignorant person who is not scrupulous in his observance of the commandments], that is tantamount to placing an animal before a lion. For just as regarding that beast we can never be sure whether it will maul its prey to death and devour it right away, or whether it will kill it and consume it later, so too with respect to an ignorant priest who receives a sacred portion, it is unclear whether he will eat the produce in a state of purity or impurity. Rabbi Yoḥanan taught: If an owner gives his priest's portion to a priest who is an ignoramus, that will be the cause of the priest's death, as the verse states: *They shall keep My charge and not bear guilt and die through it, having profaned it* (22:9). The academy of Rabbi Eliezer ben Yaakov taught: He who presents an ignoramus priest with a sacred portion also brings upon him a sin of guilt [that is, he will be led to commit other infractions], as the verse warns: *Or incur the penalty of iniquity by eating their sacred offerings* (22:16). (Sanhedrin 90b)

יז וַיְדַבֵּר יְהוָה אֶל־מֹשֶׁה לֵּאמֹר: דַּבֵּר אֶל־אַהֲרֹן וְאֶל־בָּנָיו וְאֶל יח שלישי
כָּל־בְּנֵי יִשְׂרָאֵל וְאָמַרְתָּ אֲלֵהֶם אִישׁ אִישׁ מִבֵּית יִשְׂרָאֵל
וּמִן־הַגֵּר בְּיִשְׂרָאֵל אֲשֶׁר יַקְרִיב קָרְבָּנוֹ לְכָל־נִדְרֵיהֶם וּלְכָל־
יט נִדְבוֹתָם אֲשֶׁר־יַקְרִיבוּ לַיהוָה לְעֹלָה: לִרְצֹנְכֶם תָּמִים זָכָר
כ בַּבָּקָר בַּכְּשָׂבִים וּבָעִזִּים: כֹּל אֲשֶׁר־בּוֹ מוּם לֹא תַקְרִיבוּ כִּי־
כא לֹא לְרָצוֹן יִהְיֶה לָכֶם: וְאִישׁ כִּי־יַקְרִיב זֶבַח־שְׁלָמִים לַיהוָה
לְפַלֵּא־נֶדֶר אוֹ לִנְדָבָה בַּבָּקָר אוֹ בַצֹּאן תָּמִים יִהְיֶה לְרָצוֹן
כב כָּל־מוּם לֹא יִהְיֶה־בּוֹ: עַוֶּרֶת אוֹ שָׁבוּר אוֹ־חָרוּץ אוֹ־יַבֶּלֶת
אוֹ גָרָב אוֹ יַלֶּפֶת לֹא־תַקְרִיבוּ אֵלֶּה לַיהוָה וְאִשֶּׁה לֹא־תִתְּנוּ
כג מֵהֶם עַל־הַמִּזְבֵּחַ לַיהוָה: וְשׁוֹר וָשֶׂה שָׂרוּעַ וְקָלוּט נְדָבָה

VERSE 18

TALMUD BAVLI

אִישׁ אִישׁ – *When anyone:* What is the significance of the term *ish ish* [literally, "a man, a man"]? We learn from here that like Israelites, idolators too are welcome to donate a burnt offering *in fulfillment of a vow or as a freewill offering.* (Nazir 62a)

VERSE 19

LEKAḤ TOV

לִרְצֹנְכֶם – *To be acceptable on your behalf:* We do not compel the community against their will [thereby understanding the adverbial to mean willingly]. **תָּמִים זָכָר** – *An unblemished male:* It is cattle that must be male and unblemished; these criteria are not essential for birds [to be brought as sacrifices]. (61a)

VERSE 20

PHILO

כֹּל אֲשֶׁר־בּוֹ מוּם – *Anything that has a blemish:* Know that the Torah does not prescribe laws for irrational creatures per se, but for those who have mind and reason. The ultimate goal of a sacrifice is not about whether the victim has a blemish or not. Rather, the primary focus must be on the interior attitude of the offerer; it is vital that he not be defiled by any unlawful passion. Hence, the real object of concern is not the condition of the victims sacrificed – that they may have no blemish – but that of the sacrificers, who must take care not to be defiled by any unlawful passion.

LEKAḤ TOV

כֹּל אֲשֶׁר־בּוֹ מוּם – *Anything that has a blemish:* This law applies to temporary injuries as well. **לֹא תַקְרִיבוּ** – *Do not offer:* It is even forbidden to consecrate such an animal. **כִּי־לֹא לְרָצוֹן** – *It will not be accepted:* The text teaches thereby that blemished sacrifices do not secure God's favor.

17 18 The Lord spoke to Moshe: "Speak to Aharon, his sons, and all SHELISHI
the Israelites. Say: When anyone of the House of Israel or of the
migrants living in Israel presents an offering to the Lord as a
burnt offering – whether in fulfillment of a vow or as a freewill
19 offering – to be acceptable on your behalf, it must be an un-
20 blemished male from the herd, or of the sheep or goats. Do not
offer anything that has a blemish, for it will not be accepted on
21 your behalf. When someone presents a peace sacrifice to the
Lord from the herd or flock – whether because of a spoken
vow or as a freewill offering – it must be unblemished to be
22 acceptable; there shall be no blemish on it. Do not present to
the Lord anything blind, injured, or maimed, or with warts,
a severe rash, or scabs. Do not place any of these on the altar
23 as a fire offering to the Lord. You may offer as a freewill offering an ox or sheep with a limb deformed or uncloven, but they

VERSE 21

TALMUD BAVLI

כָּל־מוּם לֹא יִהְיֶה־בּוֹ – *There shall be no blemish on it:* How do we know that it is forbidden to indirectly inflict a blemish on a sacrificial animal? For it was taught in a *baraita*: When the verse states: *It must be unblemished to be acceptable*, it teaches that an animal with any sort of a defect may not be used as an offering. Now we learn from here only that the owner may not directly inflict a blemish on the animal. How do we know that he may also not indirectly create a wound on the prospective sacrifice, for example by taking some dough or a dried fig and placing it on the specimen's ear so that a dog will come and snatch it [thereby biting off part of the animal's ear]? This point is learned from the phrase *kol mum* ["any blemish." Thus the term *mum* teaches that directly causing a blemish is forbidden. The addition of the otherwise unnecessary adjective *kol* teaches that indirectly wounding the beast is also outlawed]. (Beitza 27b)

VERSE 22

VAYIKRA RABBA

עַוֶּרֶת אוֹ שָׁבוּר – *Blind or injured:* Rabbi Abba bar Yudan taught: Whatever constitutes a disqualifying blemish in an animal is nevertheless acceptable in a person. Regarding a sacrificial animal we read: *Do not present to the Lord anything blind, injured [shavur], or maimed*. But a human being in that condition is invited to approach the Almighty, as the verse states: *To God, a broken [nishbara] spirit is an offering; a crushed and broken [nishbar] heart, God, You will not spurn* (Psalms 51:19). (Margaliot, Tzav 7:2)

כד תַּעֲשֶׂה אֹתוֹ וּלְנֵדֶר לֹא יֵרָצֶה: וּמָעוּךְ וְכָתוּת וְנָתוּק וְכָרוּת
כה לֹא תַקְרִיבוּ לַיהוָה וּבְאַרְצְכֶם לֹא תַעֲשׂוּ: וּמִיַּד בֶּן־נֵכָר
לֹא תַקְרִיבוּ אֶת־לֶחֶם אֱלֹהֵיכֶם מִכָּל־אֵלֶּה כִּי מָשְׁחָתָם
כו בָּהֶם מוּם בָּם לֹא יֵרָצוּ לָכֶם: וַיְדַבֵּר
כז יְהוָה אֶל־מֹשֶׁה לֵּאמֹר: שׁוֹר אוֹ־כֶשֶׂב אוֹ־עֵז כִּי יִוָּלֵד וְהָיָה
שִׁבְעַת יָמִים תַּחַת אִמּוֹ וּמִיּוֹם הַשְּׁמִינִי וָהָלְאָה יֵרָצֶה לְקָרְבַּן

VERSE 24

TALMUD BAVLI

וּבְאַרְצְכֶם לֹא תַעֲשׂוּ – *And do not do such things in your land:* From where is it derived that castration of a man is prohibited? For the verse states: *Do not offer to the Lord an animal whose testicles are bruised, crushed, torn, or cut off; and do not do such things in your land*, meaning that you shall not do it to yourselves. Such is the teaching of Rabbi Ḥanina. (Shabbat 110b)

VERSE 25

TALMUD BAVLI

כִּי מָשְׁחָתָם בָּהֶם – *Because they are mutilated:* The school of Rabbi Yishmael taught: Whenever the Torah uses the term *hashḥata* ["corruption"], it refers to either licentiousness or idol worship. An example of this language in an instance of immorality appears in the verse that states: *God saw how corrupt [nishḥata] the earth had become, all flesh corrupting [hishḥit] its ways upon the earth* (Genesis 6:12). [This harks back to an earlier statement in that chapter: *When the sons of God saw that the daughters of man were lovely, they began to take whomever they chose to be wives to them* (6:2).] Elsewhere the term is used to describe idol worship, as we read: *Take great care for your own sake not to act in self-destruction [pen tashḥitun], making yourselves any idol, an image of any shape, any form of man or of woman* (Deuteronomy 4:15–16). Now, based on this comparison of language we can assert that any type of offering that a blemish disqualifies, matters of licentiousness and idol worship will also disqualify. By contrast, any type of offering that a blemish would not disqualify, matters of licentiousness and idol worship would also not disqualify. As such, with respect to birds that are not considered invalid if blemished – it is essential that mammal offerings be unblemished and male, but there are no such criteria with birds – that means that matters of licentiousness and idol worship should also not disqualify birds. [Thus, if a bird had been the object of bestiality or had been worshipped as a deity, it would not be disqualified as a sacrifice.] However, the verse that states: *If the offering for the Lord is to be a burnt offering of fowl, one may offer doves or pigeons [min hatorim o min benei hayona]* (Leviticus 1:14) teaches us otherwise. [The term *min*, "from," teaches that only some specimens from these categories are acceptable, to the exclusion of those birds that have been abused or worshipped.] (Ḥullin 23a)

24 will not be accepted in fulfillment of a vow. Do not offer to the
LORD an animal whose testicles are bruised, crushed, torn, or
25 cut off; and do not do such things in your land. Do not accept
such animals from a migrant as an offering of foodstuffs to
your God. Because they are mutilated and blemished, they will
26 not be accepted on your behalf." The LORD spoke
27 to Moshe: "When an ox or sheep or goat is born, it shall remain with its mother for seven days. From the eighth day it is

VERSE 27

TALMUD BAVLI

שׁוֹר אוֹ־כֶשֶׂב – *When an ox or sheep:* Our Sages taught in a *baraita*: The phrase "an ox or a sheep" serves to exclude an animal born from diverse kinds; "or a goat" serves to exclude an animal that resembles another [for example, a sheep whose parents are both sheep but it looks like a goat]. The term "is born" excludes an animal born by caesarean section; "it shall remain with its mother for seven days" excludes an animal whose time has not yet come [that is, it is not yet eight days old]; and the words *with its mother* serve to exclude an orphan. (Bekhorot 57a) **וּמִיּוֹם הַשְּׁמִינִי וָהָלְאָה** – *From the eighth day:* A newborn animal that survives its first eight days is no longer suspected of being a stillborn [that is, that it will not be viable]. (Shabbat 135b)

TANḤUMA

שׁוֹר אוֹ־כֶשֶׂב אוֹ־עֵז כִּי יִוָּלֵד – *When an ox or sheep or goat is born:* We have learned that any shofar is valid except that which comes from a cow, since the use of that type of shofar recalls Israel's sin of the golden calf. Furthermore, the Torah issues the following mandate: *If a woman approaches an animal to mate with it, you shall kill the woman and the animal; they shall both be put to death; their bloodguilt is upon them* (20:16). Now, granted that the woman should be punished for the repugnant sin she has committed. But how can the animal be said to have sinned? For the beast has acted as a stumbling block for the woman. The text therefore decrees: Do not allow the animal to wander freely through the market, thereby prompting observers to shout out: "Look! There is the animal that caused the death of so and so." This too is an illustration of the verse that states: *They will no longer be a source of trust for the House of Israel but merely a reminder of Israel's sin* (Ezekiel 29:16). Finally, consider our verse which states: *When an ox or sheep or goat is born.* Is it an ox that is born? Is the animal not a calf when it is born? However, since the text states: *They have made themselves a molten calf and are bowing down and sacrificing to it* (Exodus 32:8), our verse would rather refer to the sacrificial animal as an ox and not a calf. (Emor 8)

VAYIKRA RABBA

שׁוֹר אוֹ־כֶשֶׂב אוֹ־עֵז כִּי יִוָּלֵד – *When an ox or sheep or goat is born:* Consider the verse that states: *And God is seeking after the pursued* (Ecclesiastes 3:15). Rabbi Yehuda bar Rabbi Simon taught in the name of Rabbi Yossi bar Nehorai: The Holy One, blessed be He,

כח אִשֶּׁה לַיהוָה: וְשׁוֹר אוֹ־שֶׂה אֹתוֹ וְאֶת־בְּנוֹ לֹא תִשְׁחֲטוּ
כט בְּיוֹם אֶחָד: וְכִי־תִזְבְּחוּ זֶבַח־תּוֹדָה לַיהוָה לִרְצֹנְכֶם תִּזְבָּחוּ:

VAYIKRA RABBA *(cont.)*

will forever demand justice from those who chase and shed the blood of the pursued. We know this is so from Hevel, who was hunted by Kayin, whereas the Almighty chose Hevel, as we read: *The Lord looked favorably on Hevel and his offering* (Genesis 4:4). Avraham was pursued by Nimrod, but the Almighty chose Avraham, as we read: *You are the Lord God who chose Avram, bringing him out of Ur Kasdim and changing his name to Avraham* (Nehemiah 9:7). Israel is chased down by the nations of the world, yet the Almighty chooses Israel, as the verse states: *The Lord has chosen you of all the peoples on earth to be to Him a treasured people* (Deuteronomy 14:2). Rabbi Eliezer bar Rabbi Yosei ben Zimra taught: The same phenomenon characterizes the sacrificial animals. For the Holy One, blessed be He, declared: "The ox is pursued by the lion; the sheep is stalked by the leopard; and the goat is chased by the wolf. Thus you are not to offer Me sacrifices from among the hunters but from the hunted, as the verse states: *When an ox or sheep or goat is born...it is acceptable as a sacrifice, a fire offering to the Lord.*" (Emor 27:5) **וְהָיָה שִׁבְעַת יָמִים תַּחַת אִמּוֹ** – *It shall remain with its mother for seven days:* Why does the Torah require a seven-day waiting period before offering the young? Rabbi Yehoshua of Sikhnin taught in the name of Rabbi Levi: This may be compared to a king who enters a land and declares: "No citizen may have an audience with me before he has seen the face of my matron." In a similar way, the Holy One, blessed be He, demands: "No animal may be sacrificed unto Me before it has experienced at least one Sabbath." (Margaliot, Emor 27:10)

DEVARIM RABBA

וּמִיּוֹם הַשְּׁמִינִי וָהָלְאָה – *From the eighth day:* Why is a child circumcised on the eighth day of his life? Because the Holy One, blessed be He, has compassion for the baby, He allows him a week to build up some strength. And just as God demonstrates mercy for a person, so is He merciful toward an animal, as we read: *From the eighth day it is acceptable as a sacrifice*. Furthermore, the Torah issues this demand: *Do not slaughter an ox or sheep and its young on the same day* (22:28). (Ki Tetze 6:1)

VERSE 28

PHILO

וְשׁוֹר אוֹ־שֶׂה אֹתוֹ וְאֶת־בְּנוֹ – *An ox or sheep and its young:* It is not because creatures not yet advanced into light ought to rank equally with others, but it is in order to restrain the license of those people, whose way is to bring destruction to everything. So long as the life is still growing like a plant, it shall be reckoned as part of the parent that carries it and now is one with it. However, in the course of months, it will be severed from the common organism and it will, hopefully, become a living animal. Therefore, it is immoral to kill the mother and offspring on the same occasion and on the same day (Leviticus 22:28). By acting ethically toward other various kinds of creatures, we demonstrate the fullness of our humanity to other sentient beings who are similar to ourselves.

28 acceptable as a sacrifice, a fire offering to the Lord, but do not
29 slaughter an ox or sheep and its young on the same day. When
you sacrifice a thanksgiving offering for the Lord, sacrifice it

MISHNA

בְּיוֹם אֶחָד – *On the same day:* When the verse issues this prohibition: *Do not slaughter an ox or sheep and its young on the same day*, the day in question is linked to the preceding night. [Therefore, it is permissible to slaughter an animal during the day and its offspring on the following night since that is considered a new day.] Rabbi Shimon ben Zoma derived this point through the construction of a verbal analogy. During the description of creation, the Torah states: *And God called the light "day," and the darkness He called "night." There was evening, and there was morning – one day [yom eḥad]* (Genesis 1:5), showing that the day followed the night. Subsequently, the text uses the same term when it states: *Do not slaughter on the same day [beyom eḥad: literally, "on one day"]*. Hence, regarding the slaughter of a parent animal and its offspring, the day follows the night. (Ḥullin 5:5)

TALMUD BAVLI

וְשׁוֹר אוֹ־שֶׂה – *An ox or sheep:* Our Sages taught in a *baraita*: From where is it derived that the prohibition against slaughtering an animal and its offspring in a single day applies to sacrificial animals [and not just to nonsacred specimens]? For initially, the text states: *When an ox or sheep or goat is born…from the eighth day it is acceptable as a sacrifice, a fire offering to the Lord* (22:27), and subsequently we read: *But do not slaughter an ox or sheep and its young on the same day*. The juxtaposition of the verses teaches that the prohibition in the latter sentence applies to sacrificial animals as well. (Ḥullin 78a)

EIKHA RABBA

וְשׁוֹר אוֹ־שֶׂה אֹתוֹ וְאֶת־בְּנוֹ – *An ox or sheep and its young:* When Moshe came to the patriarchs, the elders questioned him and implored: "What has the enemy done to our children [during the Egyptian bondage]?" Moshe detailed the Israelites' suffering, saying: "Some of your descendants were killed outright; others had their hands bound behind their backs with ropes; some were chained in irons while others were stripped naked. During their exile, some of these Hebrews fell dead, to be ravaged by the birds of the sky and the beasts of the field. Still other men and women were tormented by the sun, hunger, and thirst." At once the patriarchs broke down, wailing and lamenting. Said Moshe in complaint to the Almighty: "Master of the Universe! Have You not written in Your Torah: *Do not slaughter an ox or sheep and its young on the same day*? Yet many thousands of children have been killed on the same day as their mothers, while You remain silent!" (Petiḥtot 24)

VERSE 29

SIFREI BEMIDBAR

וְכִי־תִזְבְּחוּ זֶבַח־תּוֹדָה – *When you sacrifice a thanksgiving offering:* Consider the verse that states: *Were I to hunger, I would not tell you, for Mine is the world and all that fills it* (Psalms 50:12), and the previous verse, which reads: *I know every bird of the mountains; the creatures of the fields belong to Me* (50:11). Lest we think that the Almighty eats and drinks, the

ל בַּיּוֹם הַהוּא יֵאָכֵל לֹא־תוֹתִירוּ מִמֶּנּוּ עַד־בֹּקֶר אֲנִי יהוה:
לא לב וּשְׁמַרְתֶּם מִצְוֹתַי וַעֲשִׂיתֶם אֹתָם אֲנִי יהוה: וְלֹא תְחַלְּלוּ אֶת־
שֵׁם קָדְשִׁי וְנִקְדַּשְׁתִּי בְּתוֹךְ בְּנֵי יִשְׂרָאֵל אֲנִי יהוה מְקַדִּשְׁכֶם:

SIFREI BEMIDBAR *(cont.)*

following verse asks: *Do I eat the flesh of bulls? Do I drink the blood of he-goats?* (50:13). Why then does God demand sacrifices? So that the Israelites will do His bidding [alternatively, it is for the nation's benefit]. And so does the Torah state: *When you sacrifice a thanksgiving offering for the Lord, sacrifice it so that it will be acceptable on your behalf.* (Pinḥas 143)

VAYIKRA RABBA

וְכִי־תִזְבְּחוּ זֶבַח־תּוֹדָה – *When you sacrifice a thanksgiving offering:* Rabbi Pinḥas and Rabbi Levi taught as follows, as did Rabbi Yoḥanan in the name of Rabbi Menaḥem of Galya: In messianic times, all the sacrifices will be abolished with the exception of the thanksgiving offering, which will endure forever. All expressions of gratitude will be nullified except for the thanksgiving offering, which will remain. Thus the prophet declares: *The sound of joy and the sound of happiness, the voice of the groom and the voice of the bride, the voice of those who proclaim, "Give thanks to the Lord of Hosts, for the Lord is good and His lovingkindness is forever," and the voice of those who bring offerings of thanksgiving to the House of the Lord, for I will return the captives to the land as before, says the Lord* (Jeremiah 33:11), which refers to both the verbal pronouncements of thanks as well as to the sacrifices of thanksgiving. Similarly, David says: *I must fulfill my vows to You, God; I will give thank offerings to You* (Psalms 56:13). Notice that David assumes multiple obligations: both the verbal expressions of gratitude and the donation of offerings. (Margaliot, Emor 27:12)

VERSE 31

LEKAḤ TOV

וּשְׁמַרְתֶּם מִצְוֹתַי – *Keep My commands:* This refers to God's decrees, which the Israelite has no right to challenge. **וַעֲשִׂיתֶם אֹתָם** – *And fulfill them:* The commandments must be both guarded and observed [that is, one must not only observe the commandments but also create fences to safeguard oneself from violating them]. **אֲנִי יהוה** – *I am the Lord:* I can be trusted to reward the obedient. (62a)

VERSE 32

TALMUD YERUSHALMI

וְנִקְדַּשְׁתִּי בְּתוֹךְ בְּנֵי יִשְׂרָאֵל – *That I may be sanctified in the midst of the Israelites:* Rav Avuna posed the following question to Rabbi Ammi: Is a gentile obligated to sanctify the name of God [by refusing to violate a divine commandment on pain of death]? Said he: The verse states: *That I may be sanctified in the midst of the Israelites*, showing that the people of Israel are required to sanctify the name of God, but non-Israelites have no such responsibility. Rabbi Nasa citing Rabbi Elazar based this teaching on a different verse, which states: *But may the Lord forgive your servant this: When my master comes to the temple*

30 so that it will be acceptable on your behalf. It shall be eaten
on the same day – leave none of it to the morning; I am the
31 Lord. Keep My commands and fulfill them; I am the Lord.
32 Do not profane My holy name – that I may be sanctified in the

TALMUD YERUSHALMI *(cont.)*

of Rimon to bow down there, he leans on my hand so that I must bow down in the temple of Rimon. So when I bow down in the temple of Rimon, may the Lord forgive your servant for this (II Kings 5:18). [The speaker is the Aramean general Naaman, whom Elisha permitted to engage in idolatry under the watchful eyes of his king.] We see that although an Israelite is bound to sanctify the name of God [and would be forbidden to bow down under such circumstances], a gentile has no such obligation. (Shevi'it 4:2)

TALMUD BAVLI

וְנִקְדַּשְׁתִּי בְּתוֹךְ בְּנֵי יִשְׂרָאֵל – *That I may be sanctified in the midst of the Israelites:* Rav Adda bar Ahava taught: What is the source that forbids a single person from reciting the *Kedusha* [the prayer recited by a quorum during the repetition of the *Amida*]? It is the verse that states: *That I may be sanctified in the midst of the Israelites.* We learn from here that prayers of sanctity must be recited in a quorum of at least ten people. (Berakhot 21b)

TANḤUMA

וְלֹא תְחַלְּלוּ אֶת־שֵׁם קָדְשִׁי – *Do not profane My holy name:* To what does the following verse allude: *His hair cascading curls [kevutzotav taltalim], raven black* (Song of Songs 5:11)? It suggests that even the details in the Torah that initially appear prickly as thorns [*kotzim*, meaning that they appear devoid of value] in fact hold heaps upon heaps [*tillei tillim*] of laws. On the other hand, if the Torah is misinterpreted or neglected, it can destroy the world and turn it into a *tel* [mound], as the text threatens: *It shall be an eternal ruin [tel olam], never to be rebuilt* (Deuteronomy 13:17). How might this happen? The verse cautions: *Do not profane [lo teḥallelu] My holy name,* whereas if you turn the *ḥet* of that word into a *heh* [thereby forming the phrase *lo tehallelu*, "do not praise" My holy name], the world will be wiped out. Conversely, although the psalmist sings: *Let all that breathe praise [tehallel] the Lord* (Psalms 150:6), if one turns the *heh* into a *ḥet* [forming the term *teḥallel*, "let all profane" the Lord], you will destroy the world. In another example, the familiar exhortation reads: *Listen, Israel: the Lord our God – the Lord is one [eḥad]* (Deuteronomy 6:4), whereas if one switches the *dalet* for a *resh* [to form *aḥer*, the Lord is "another"], you will destroy the world, as an earlier verse forbids: *For you must worship no other god [aḥer]* (Exodus 34:14). (Bereshit 1)

LEKAḤ TOV

וְלֹא תְחַלְּלוּ אֶת־שֵׁם קָדְשִׁי – *Do not profane My holy name:* This stresses the unification of God's name. **וְנִקְדַּשְׁתִּי בְּתוֹךְ בְּנֵי יִשְׂרָאֵל** – *That I may be sanctified in the midst of the Israelites:* If necessary, one must surrender his life to sanctify the name of God in public. Based on this, the Sages claim: If an Israelite submits his life in the belief that a miracle will be done for him, no miracle will be forthcoming. By contrast, if he has no expectation that a miracle will save his life, he will be spared by one. And so we find that Ḥananya, Mishael, and Azarya

לג הַמּוֹצִיא אֶתְכֶם מֵאֶרֶץ מִצְרַיִם לִהְיוֹת לָכֶם לֵאלֹהִים אֲנִי
יהוה:

כג א וַיְדַבֵּר יהוה אֶל־מֹשֶׁה לֵּאמֹר: דַּבֵּר אֶל־בְּנֵי יִשְׂרָאֵל וְאָמַרְתָּ רביעי
ב אֲלֵהֶם מוֹעֲדֵי יהוה אֲשֶׁר־תִּקְרְאוּ אֹתָם מִקְרָאֵי קֹדֶשׁ אֵלֶּה

LEKAḤ TOV *(cont.)*

announced their willingness for martyrdom: *O Nevukhadnetzar, we do not need to answer you at all about this matter. Behold, if He wishes, our God, whom we worship, is able to rescue us. He can rescue us from the fiery furnace as well as from your hand, O king. But even if He does not choose to save us, let it be known to you, O king, that we will not serve your god and we will not worship the golden figure you have erected* (Daniel 3:16–18). (62a)

VERSE 33

LEKAḤ TOV

הַמּוֹצִיא אֶתְכֶם מֵאֶרֶץ מִצְרַיִם לִהְיוֹת – *Who brought you out of Egypt to be:* Says God: I rescued you from Egypt on condition that you devote yourselves to the sanctification of My name. **לִהְיוֹת לָכֶם לֵאלֹהִים** – *To be your God:* I will be your God even against your will. **אֲנִי יהוה** – *I am the Lord:* I, the Lord, can be trusted to reward those who are obedient to Me. Our Sages tell the story of Trajan, who sought to kill the leaders Lulianus and his brother Pappas in Laodicea. Said he to them: "If you are from the nation of Ḥananya, Mishael, Eltzafan, and Azarya, let your God come and save you from my hand, just as He saved Ḥananya, Mishael, and Azarya from the hand of Nevukhadnetzar." Said they to him: "Ḥananya, Mishael, and Azarya were full-fledged righteous men and they were worthy of a miracle being performed for them." Even so, Trajan killed them immediately. And I hereby record the following history for posterity: The holy congregation of Mainz surrendered their lives and those of their wives and children on a single day at the start of the Shavuot festival. All these Jews were slaughtered as one to sanctify the name of the God of Israel, in the year 4856 after the creation of the world [1096 CE], when the peoples of the land became determined to rise up and capture the exalted country [in a campaign known as the First Crusade]. It is regarding these Jews and all those who suffered a similar fate that the prophet says: *Even though I pardon, I will not pardon the spilling of their blood* (Joel 4:21). (62a)

CHAPTER 23, VERSE 2

TALMUD YERUSHALMI

אֵלֶּה הֵם מוֹעֲדָי – *These are My appointed times:* How do we know that we should intercalate the year for the sake of the Jews of the Diaspora who have set out but who have not yet arrived? For the verse states: *Speak to the Israelites. Say: These are the Lord's appointed times.* [We derive from here that] the festivals should be appointed so that they can be observed by the entire nation of Israel. (Shevi'it 10:1)

TALMUD BAVLI

מִקְרָאֵי קֹדֶשׁ – *Sacred assemblies:* Rabbi Ḥiyya bar Gamda taught in the name of Rabbi Yosei ben Shaul who in turn cited Rabbi Yehuda Hanasi: The Torah relates: *Thus Moshe*

midst of the Israelites. I am the LORD, who makes you holy,
33 who brought you out of Egypt to be your God: I am the LORD."
23 1 2 The LORD spoke to Moshe: "Speak to the Israelites. Say: These REVI'I
are the LORD's appointed times that you shall proclaim as

TALMUD BAVLI *(cont.)*

announced the LORD's appointed times to the Israelites (23:44). We learn from here that the head of the court is obligated to announce: "The month is dedicated!" [Moshe's status was equivalent to that of the head of the high court [Sanhedrin], and he was the one to formally declare the appointed times of the festivals and New Moons.] In response, all the people would repeat after him: "It is sanctified! It is sanctified!" From where is that practice derived? Rav Pappa pointed to the verse that states: *That you shall proclaim them [otam] as sacred assemblies*, which should be read *attem*, "you." [Thus the word teaches that the advent of the new month is not only proclaimed by the head of the court, but also by the people.] Rav Naḥman bar Yitzḥak derived this rule from the clause that reads: *These are [hem] My appointed times*, meaning that *hem*, "they," should announce My appointed seasons. And why do we need the people to declare twice: "It is sanctified"? For the text uses the phrase "sacred assemblies" [in the plural, indicating that the masses should utter two pronouncements]. (Rosh Hashana 24a)

BEMIDBAR RABBA

אֵלֶּה הֵם מוֹעֲדָי – *These are My appointed times:* Once an idolator posed the following question to Rabbi Akiva: "Why do you Jews celebrate so many festivals? Has not the prophet proclaimed: *Your New Moons and festivals – how I hate them; they have become a burden to Me; I am weary, I cannot bear them* (Isaiah 1:14)?" The Sage answered: "Had the verse said: '*My* New Moons and *My* festivals I despise,' your attack would have been valid. In fact, however, the text reads: *Your New Moons and festivals*, referring to the holidays instituted by Yorovam, as the text relates: *And Yorovam established a festival in the eighth month, on the fifteenth day of the month, similar to the festival in Yehuda, and he ascended the altar. The sacrifice to the calves he had made took place in Beit El; he stationed at Beit El the priests he had appointed in the shrines. He ascended the altar that he had made in Beit El on the fifteenth day of the eighth month – on a date of his own invention – to establish a festival for the Israelites. And he stepped up to the altar to offer a sacrifice* (I Kings 12:32–33). On the other hand, our established festivals and New Moons will never be abolished, for they belong to the Holy One, blessed be He, as the verse states: *These are the LORD's appointed times* and *Thus Moshe announced the LORD's appointed times to the Israelites* (Leviticus 23:44). As such, these times will never be renounced, as the psalmist says: *Steady for all eternity, formed in truth and right* (Psalms 111:8)." (Pinḥas 21:25)

YALKUT SHIMONI

מִקְרָאֵי קֹדֶשׁ – *Sacred assemblies:* The verse states: *That you shall proclaim them [otam] as sacred assemblies*, which should be read as *attem*, "you." Thus you are authorized to determine the date of the new month even if you are misled by false witnesses, even if you

ג הֵם מוֹעֲדָי: שֵׁשֶׁת יָמִים תֵּעָשֶׂה מְלָאכָה וּבַיּוֹם הַשְּׁבִיעִי
שַׁבַּת שַׁבָּתוֹן מִקְרָא־קֹדֶשׁ כָּל־מְלָאכָה לֹא תַעֲשׂוּ שַׁבָּת
הִוא לַיהוה בְּכֹל מוֹשְׁבֹתֵיכֶם:
ד אֵלֶּה מוֹעֲדֵי יהוה מִקְרָאֵי קֹדֶשׁ אֲשֶׁר־תִּקְרְאוּ אֹתָם

YALKUT SHIMONI *(cont.)*

unwittingly establish the New Moon on the wrong day, and even if you do so intentionally. [In all cases, once the court establishes the day as the New Moon, it is sanctified, and God grants His consent.] (Emor 643)

VERSE 3

PHILO

וּבַיּוֹם הַשְּׁבִיעִי – *But the seventh day:* God employs the six days for the completion of the world, even though the Creator had no personal reason to do so. Human beings are different; their mortal nature demands that they rest. People require countless necessities in order to live; and no person should ever have to live his entire life in constant pursuit of his goals without ever taking time to rest on the sacred Sabbath. Would not such a recommendation only lead to man's perfection and cultivation of every virtue, culminating in unpretentious piety? The fourth commandment of the Decalogue conveys a profound truth: Always make it a point to imitate God. Let that this time in the week, when God created the world in six days for His purpose, serve as a template for you to do all of your activity. Just as God surveyed everything that He created, so too, follow God's template, and use this time well for contemplative reflection so that you may earnestly obey the law and discover happiness in your lives.

TALMUD YERUSHALMI

שַׁבָּת הִוא לַיהוה – *It shall be a Sabbath for the Lord:* Rabbi Ḥaggai taught in the name of Rabbi Shmuel bar Naḥman: Israel was given the Sabbaths and festivals solely for eating and drinking. But since the mouth thereby would be overwhelmed with too much consumption, the people were permitted to occupy themselves with Torah. Rabbi Berekhya taught in the name of Rabbi Ḥiyya: Israel was given the Sabbaths and festivals solely for the study of Torah. There is a *baraita* that supports one position or the other: What should an Israelite do on these days? He should sit and eat or he should sit and busy himself with the study of Torah. On the one hand, the verse states: *It shall be a Sabbath for the Lord.* By contrast, a later text reads: *For six days you shall eat unleavened bread and, on the seventh day, you shall hold an assembly for the Lord your God* (Deuteronomy 16:8). [The latter verse suggests that the day need not be dedicated wholly to God.] How can these texts be reconciled? Part of the day should be set aside for the study of Torah, and part of the day should be dedicated to eating and drinking. Rabbi Abbahu taught: When the verse states: *It shall be a Sabbath for the Lord*, it means that just as the Almighty rested from creative speech [in His case, creation], so too should you rest from creative speech [in our case, labor]. (Shabbat 15:3)

3 sacred assemblies; these are My appointed times. Work shall
be done through six days, but the seventh day shall be a Sabbath of complete rest, a sacred assembly. You shall perform no
work at all; it shall be a Sabbath for the LORD in all your dwellings.
4 These are the LORD's appointed times, sacred assemblies, which

LEKAḤ TOV

שֵׁשֶׁת יָמִים תֵּעָשֶׂה מְלָאכָה – *Work shall be done through six days:* What is the connection between the Sabbath and the festivals? The association teaches us that if a person transgresses the holidays, it is tantamount to violating the Sabbath. **שַׁבַּת שַׁבָּתוֹן** – *A Sabbath of complete rest:* What is the significance of the doubled term *Shabbat shabbaton* ["a Sabbath of complete rest"]? We learn from here that all the festivals are called *shabbaton*, as follows: The first day of Passover is so called in the verse that reads: *The day after the day of rest [mimoḥorat hashabbat] you shall count for yourselves seven complete weeks* (23:15). The festival of Shavuot is called *shabbat*, as we read: *To the day [mimoḥorat hashabbat] of the seventh week, you shall count fifty days* (23:16). This refers to the holiday of Shavuot, which is consecrated on the night following the forty-ninth day and is celebrated on the fiftieth day. Rosh Hashana is referred to as *shabbaton*, as the verse states: *On the first day of the seventh month, you shall observe a day of rest [shabbaton], a commemoration with the sounding of the ram's horn* (23:24). Yom Kippur is called *shabbat shabbaton* in the verse that reads: *It is a Sabbath of complete rest [shabbat shabbaton] for you* (23:32). And the first and eighth days of Sukkot are also called *shabbaton*: *Hear: On the fifteenth day of the seventh month...you shall celebrate a festival to the LORD for seven days. The first day shall be a day of rest [shabbaton]; the eighth day shall be a day of rest [shabbaton]* (23:39). Hence, the Sabbath itself is termed *shabbat shabbaton* to teach us something about all the festivals: Some are referred to as *shabbat*, others as *shabbaton*, and others as *shabbat shabbaton*. (62b)

VERSE 4

MISHNA

אֵלֶּה מוֹעֲדֵי יהוה מִקְרָאֵי קֹדֶשׁ – *These are the LORD's appointed times:* If a person has observed the New Moon but is unable to travel to Jerusalem by foot [due to an illness or difficulty walking], his neighbors may bring him to the court on a donkey or they may carry him in his bed. [This may even be done on the Sabbath if necessary.] And if witnesses are concerned that bandits may be lying in wait for them along the highway, they are permitted to carry clubs [or other weapons to protect themselves, even on the Sabbath]. If it is a long journey to Jerusalem, the witnesses may take sustenance with them, since for a walking distance of a night and a day, they may desecrate the Sabbath and go testify to determine the start of the month. This is the sense of the verse that states: *These are the LORD's appointed times, sacred assemblies, which you shall proclaim at their appointed times.* (Rosh Hashana 1:9)

ה בַּמּוֹעֲדָם׃ בַּחֹדֶשׁ הָרִאשׁוֹן בְּאַרְבָּעָה עָשָׂר לַחֹדֶשׁ בֵּין
ו הָעַרְבָּיִם פֶּסַח לַיהוָה׃ וּבַחֲמִשָּׁה עָשָׂר יוֹם לַחֹדֶשׁ הַזֶּה חַג
ז הַמַּצּוֹת לַיהוָה שִׁבְעַת יָמִים מַצּוֹת תֹּאכֵלוּ׃ בַּיּוֹם הָרִאשׁוֹן
מִקְרָא־קֹדֶשׁ יִהְיֶה לָכֶם כָּל־מְלֶאכֶת עֲבֹדָה לֹא תַעֲשׂוּ׃

MEKHILTA DERABBI SHIMON

אֵלֶּה מוֹעֲדֵי יהוה – *These are the Lord's appointed times:* What is the significance of the verse that states: *Six days shall work be done, but the seventh day is a Sabbath of complete rest, sacred to the Lord* (Exodus 31:15)? For a later verse reads: *These are the Lord's appointed times that you shall proclaim as sacred assemblies*. Now, we might have thought that just as the court holds the power to determine the festivals, so is the establishment of the Sabbath left in the hands of the people. To teach us otherwise, the text asserts: *But the seventh day is a Sabbath of complete rest, sacred to the Lord*. The determination of the Sabbath is reserved for God; its verification is not given to the court to declare. Similarly, we read: *It shall be a Sabbath for the Lord in all your dwellings* (Leviticus 23:3). The verse in Exodus continues to warn: *Whoever does any work on [the Sabbath] shall be put to death* (Exodus 31:15), and that includes any labor toward the construction of the Tabernacle. Now, when the text decrees capital punishment for the violation of the Sabbath, does that mean that the court may employ any method of execution? No, for a case study teaches that the penalty is stoning, as we read: *And the Lord said to Moshe, "The man shall be put to death. The whole community must stone him outside the camp"* (Numbers 15:35). (Shemot 31:15)

TALMUD YERUSHALMI

אֵלֶּה מוֹעֲדֵי יהוה – *These are the Lord's appointed times:* Consider the verse that states: *And what other great nation has decrees and laws as just as this entire Torah that I am setting before you today?* (Deuteronomy 4:8). What kind of a nation is this people Israel? Under usual circumstances, if the court announces that a person will be tried today but the bandits declare that the trial will be tomorrow, would the public not put their faith in the court? But the Holy One, blessed be He, behaves otherwise: If Israel's high court determines that Rosh Hashana is today, the Holy One, blessed be He, instructs His ministering angels: "Put up the dais and invite the prosecutors and the defenders, for My children have asserted that today is Rosh Hashana." However, if the court subsequently changes its mind and moves Rosh Hashana to the next day, the Holy One, blessed be He, directs His ministering angels to disassemble the platform and to dismiss the prosecutors and the defenders, explaining: "My children have changed the trial date to tomorrow." What is the reason for this? Is it not because *it is a statute for Israel, an ordinance of the God of Yaakov* (Psalms 81:5)? Thus, if something is not a statute for Israel, then it is not an ordinance for God, so to speak. Rabbi Krispa taught in the name of Rabbi Yoḥanan: In the past we would say: *These are the Lord's appointed times*, but from this point on, we say: *You shall proclaim at their appointed times*. Rabbi Ile'a taught: Says the Almighty: If Israel proclaims them, they will be My festivals; if they do not, they will not be My festivals. (Rosh Hashana 1:3)

5 you shall proclaim at their appointed times. In the first month,
the fourteenth of the month in the afternoon is the time for the
6 Passover sacrifice to the LORD. The fifteenth day of this month
is the LORD's Festival of Unleavened Bread; for seven days
7 you shall eat unleavened bread. The first day shall be a sacred

VERSE 5

PHILO

פֶּסַח לַיהוה – *The Passover sacrifice to the Lord:* As the name indicates, Passover implies "a passing over" that begins whenever the soul expresses its willingness to quit and transcend everything that is sluggish and stationary [as represented by Egypt, the land of bondage and monotony] with swiftness and haste without ever turning back. "Passover" demands that we express an energetic willingness and readiness to pass over [and leave our inner Egypt so that our passions will no longer rule us] to God our savior. On this day we express our thanksgiving to God Who brought us forth to liberty even when our ancestors nearly abandoned their hope of ever attaining it.

VERSE 6

YALKUT SHIMONI

וּבַחֲמִשָּׁה עָשָׂר יוֹם לַחֹדֶשׁ הַזֶּה – *The fifteenth day of this month:* The consumption of matza is an obligation of this day, but it is not a requirement for the festival of Sukkot. Now, logically the reverse should be true: Since the holiday of Passover does not demand the building of a sukka but does include the eating of matza, then the holiday of Sukkot, which does require a sukka, should also feature the eating of matza. To teach us otherwise, the verse emphasizes that *the fifteenth day of this month is the Lord's Festival of Unleavened Bread*. Thus, the Israelites must eat matza on that day, but they need not do so on the festival of Sukkot.

שִׁבְעַת יָמִים – *Seven days:* We might think that the consumption of matza is an obligation during all seven days of the festival. However, a later verse states: *For six days you shall eat unleavened bread and, on the seventh day, you shall hold an assembly for the Lord your God and perform no work* (Deuteronomy 16:8). Since the seventh day was included in the general statement regarding the entire week, why does the text single it out? The seventh day is mentioned specifically to teach about the rest of the festival: Just as eating matza is optional on the seventh day, so too is it voluntary during the previous six days of the holiday. Does that mean that eating matza is also optional on the first night of Passover? No, then it is mandatory, for an earlier text reads: *In the evening, you may eat only unleavened bread* (Exodus 12:18). Finally, the obligation seems to be applicable only when the Temple is standing. How do we know that even in the absence of the Temple, matza must be eaten? This is learned from the same verse, which emphasizes: *In the evening, you may eat only unleavened bread* (12:18). But if this is so, why does our text read: *For seven days you shall eat unleavened bread*? This teaches that the bread that one may eat during all seven days can also be used to fulfill one's obligation on the opening night of the holiday. This is to the exclusion of the thanksgiving offering loaves and the nazirite wafers, which may not be eaten during the seven days of the festival. (Emor 643)

ח וְהִקְרַבְתֶּם אִשֶּׁה לַיהוָה שִׁבְעַת יָמִים בַּיּוֹם הַשְּׁבִיעִי מִקְרָא־
קֹדֶשׁ כָּל־מְלֶאכֶת עֲבֹדָה לֹא תַעֲשׂוּ׃
ט וַיְדַבֵּר יְהוָה אֶל־מֹשֶׁה לֵּאמֹר׃ דַּבֵּר אֶל־בְּנֵי יִשְׂרָאֵל וְאָמַרְתָּ
אֲלֵהֶם כִּי־תָבֹאוּ אֶל־הָאָרֶץ אֲשֶׁר אֲנִי נֹתֵן לָכֶם וּקְצַרְתֶּם
אֶת־קְצִירָהּ וַהֲבֵאתֶם אֶת־עֹמֶר רֵאשִׁית קְצִירְכֶם אֶל־
יא הַכֹּהֵן׃ וְהֵנִיף אֶת־הָעֹמֶר לִפְנֵי יְהוָה לִרְצֹנְכֶם מִמָּחֳרַת

VERSE 8

MIDRASH TANNA'IM DEVARIM

כָּל־מְלֶאכֶת עֲבֹדָה לֹא תַעֲשׂוּ – *You shall perform no laborious work:* When the verse states: *On the seventh day there shall be a sacred assembly; you shall perform no laborious work*, it gives the impression that labor is only forbidden on the seventh day of the festival. How do we know that a similar restriction applies to the first day? For the previous verse reads: *The first day shall be a sacred assembly for you; you shall perform no laborious work.* Now, based on these two verses we learn that work is outlawed on the first and seventh days of the holiday; how do we know that labor is also limited on the intermediate days? For a later text reads: *For six days you shall eat unleavened bread and, on the seventh day, you shall hold an assembly for the Lord your God and perform no work* (Deuteronomy 16:8). Hence, just as labor may not be done on the seventh day, so too may it not be done on the previous six days. But if that is the case, we should say that no work whatsoever may be done on the six days, just as is the case regarding the seventh day. No, for the text emphasizes "the seventh day" to teach that it is at that time when all labor is forbidden, not during the preceding six days. Nevertheless, the intermediate days may not be treated as regular weekdays. (16:8)

VERSE 10

TANḤUMA

וַהֲבֵאתֶם אֶת־עֹמֶר – *Bring the first sheaf:* Said the Holy One, blessed be He, to the people of Israel: Shall I tell you what the difference is between you and Me? The nation of Israel grants Me one sheaf of barley once a year, as the verse states: *Bring the first sheaf [omer] of your harvest to the priest.* But I provide each Israelite with a similar amount of food, as the text states [regarding the manna]: *This is what the Lord has instructed: Each of you gather as much as you need, an omer for every person; each take enough for all the people in your tent* (Exodus 16:16). Furthermore, while the people bring their *omer* to Me but once a year, I have supplied you with your food every single day, as the text describes: *Then the Lord said to Moshe, "I am going to rain down bread from heaven. Let the people go out and gather enough for each day"* (16:4). (Buber, Beshalaḥ 23)

VAYIKRA RABBA

וַהֲבֵאתֶם אֶת־עֹמֶר – *Bring the first sheaf:* Rabbi Yannai taught: Usually, if a person buys a pound of steak in the market, how much effort must he put in and how much anxiety has

8 assembly for you; you shall perform no laborious work. And
you shall present a fire offering for the Lord for seven days;
on the seventh day there shall be a sacred assembly; you shall
perform no laborious work."
9 10 The Lord spoke to Moshe: "Speak to the Israelites. Say:
When you come to the land that I am giving you and reap its
11 harvest, bring the first sheaf of your harvest to the priest. He
shall display the sheaf this way and that before the Lord for
your acceptance; on the day after the day of rest the priest shall

VAYIKRA RABBA *(cont.)*

he to endure until he is able to grill his meal! But look what the Holy One, blessed be He, does for humanity: While people lie asleep in their beds, the Almighty blows the winds, gathers the rain clouds, grows the plants, and ripens the fruit on their behalf. And in return all the Israelite need do is pay God one sheaf of grain from his yield. Thus the text states: *Bring the first sheaf of your harvest to the priest.* (Margaliot, Emor 28:1)

VERSE 11

VAYIKRA RABBA

וְהֵנִיף אֶת־הָעֹמֶר – *He shall display the sheaf this way and that:* How was the sheaf presented? Rabbi Ḥama bar Ukva taught in the name of Rabbi Yossi bar Ḥanina: The grain was brought forward and pulled back, lifted up and taken down. The first actions of moving the sheaf to and fro acknowledge that all the land belongs to the Almighty. The second set of movements – up and down – demonstrate that both the upper and the lower worlds were created and are dependent on the Master of the Universe. Rabbi Simon bar Rabbi Yehoshua taught: The purpose of waving the offering forward and back is to combat the damage caused by harsh winds; the grain is taken up and down to counteract the harmful effects of severe dews. (Margaliot, Emor 28:5)

YALKUT SHIMONI

וְהֵנִיף אֶת־הָעֹמֶר – *He shall display the sheaf this way and that:* Israel must never take the commandment of the *omer* lightly, for it was due to the merits accrued by that practice that our forefather Avraham was privileged to inherit the land of Canaan, as we read: *And I will give you and your descendants after you the land where you now live as strangers, the whole land of Canaan, an everlasting possession.... Then God said to Avraham, "As for you, you shall keep My covenant, you and your descendants after you throughout their generations"* (Genesis 17:8–9). And to what covenant is God referring here? It is the obligation of bringing the *omer.* [This was the first injunction that the Israelites observed upon their entry to the land, and hence it is linked with the people's acquisition of the country.] Rabbi Shimon ben Lakish taught: Israel must never take the commandment of the *omer* lightly, for it is due to the merits accrued by that practice that the Holy One, blessed be He, forged peace between a husband and his wife, as we read [regarding the case of the suspected adulteress]: *Then the man shall bring his wife to the priest together with the prescribed offering for her, one-tenth of an ephah of barley flour* (Numbers 5:15). And thus the couple's reconciliation is based on

יב הַשַּׁבָּת יְנִיפֶנּוּ הַכֹּהֵן: וַעֲשִׂיתֶם בְּיוֹם הֲנִיפְכֶם אֶת־הָעֹמֶר
יג כֶּבֶשׂ תָּמִים בֶּן־שְׁנָתוֹ לְעֹלָה לַיהוָה: וּמִנְחָתוֹ שְׁנֵי עֶשְׂרֹנִים
סֹלֶת בְּלוּלָה בַשֶּׁמֶן אִשֶּׁה לַיהוָה רֵיחַ נִיחֹחַ וְנִסְכֹּה יַיִן
יד רְבִיעִת הַהִין: וְלֶחֶם וְקָלִי וְכַרְמֶל לֹא תֹאכְלוּ עַד־עֶצֶם
הַיּוֹם הַזֶּה עַד הֲבִיאֲכֶם אֶת־קָרְבַּן אֱלֹהֵיכֶם חֻקַּת עוֹלָם

YALKUT SHIMONI *(cont.)*

the virtue of bringing this grain offering. Rabbi Yehoshua ben Levi taught: Israel must never take the commandment of the *omer* lightly, for it was due to the merits accrued by that practice that the general Gidon was victorious, as the text relates: *Gidon arrived just as a man was recounting a dream to another. "I dreamed a dream," he said; "a loaf [tzelil] of barley bread came rolling through the Midianite camp – it came up to a tent, struck it, knocked it down, turned it upside down – and the tent collapsed"* (Judges 7:13). What is the significance of the term *tzelil*? Our Sages taught: That generation was devoid [*tzalul*] of righteous men, and the nation was only saved due to the merit of the barley brought to fulfill the commandment of the *omer*. (Emor 643)

VERSE 12

LEKAH TOV

וַעֲשִׂיתֶם בְּיוֹם הֲנִיפְכֶם – *On the day you display:* We learn from this verse that a person's agent is an extension of himself. For although it is the priest who displays the grain, the text uses the term *hanifekhem* ["when you" – in the plural form – "display the sheaf"]. (63a)

VERSE 13

TALMUD BAVLI

וּמִנְחָתוֹ שְׁנֵי עֶשְׂרֹנִים – *Its grain offering shall be two-tenths of an ephah:* Our Sages taught in a *baraita*: With regard to the *omer* grain offering, the verse demands that *its grain offering shall be two-tenths of an ephah*, which teaches that when a lamb is brought with the *omer*, the size of the grain offering is doubled. [As a later verse states: *And one-tenth for each of the lambs* (Numbers 29:4), the amount of flour is usually half that which is prescribed here.] Now, we might have thought that just as its meal offering is doubled, so too should its wine libation be doubled [from the usual quarter-*hin* poured out with lambs to half a *hin*]. To counter that proposal, the verse continues to say: *And its libation shall be a quarter of a hin of wine*. Still, we might argue that it is only its wine libation that is not doubled since the beverage is not mixed with the flour of the grain offering. By contrast, its oil should be doubled since that is intermingled with the flour of its grain offering. To counter this reasoning, the verse emphasizes, "And its libation," thereby teaching that all the libations in this circumstance should remain at the amount of a quarter-*hin* [just as they are with other lamb offerings]. What exactly is the textual derivation here? Rabbi Elazar explained: The word in the verse is written *veniskah* ["its libation," in the feminine: "her libation." Thus this form of the possessive pronoun would refer back to the feminine term

12 display it. On the day you display the sheaf this way and that,
you shall offer a yearling sheep without blemish as a burnt of-
13 fering to the LORD. Its grain offering shall be two-tenths of
an ephah of fine flour mixed with oil, a fire offering for the
LORD, a pleasing aroma; and its libation shall be a quarter of
14 a hin of wine. Until that day, until you bring this sacrifice to
your God, you shall eat no bread or roasted grain or ripe grain.
This is an everlasting statute throughout your generations, in

TALMUD BAVLI *(cont.)*

minḥa, "grain offering," at the start of the sentence. This means that the oil mixed with the flour is kept at a quarter of a *hin*]. However, the word is pronounced *venisko* ["its libation," in the masculine: "his libation." This form of the possessive pronoun would refer to the lamb offering itself, the masculine word *keves*. This would suggest that the wine libation that accompanies the lamb offering is a quarter of a *hin*]. How can we take both versions into account? We learn that the libation of the grain offering [that is, its oil] resembles the wine libation of the lamb: Just as the quantity of wine used is a quarter-*hin*, so too is the quantity of oil used a quarter-*hin* and no more. (Menaḥot 89b)

VERSE 14

MISHNA

לֹא תֹאכְלוּ עַד־עֶצֶם הַיּוֹם – *Until that day [you shall not] eat:* As soon as the *omer* offering was sacrificed, the produce of the year's new crop was permitted for general use immediately. By contrast, for those Israelites who lived far from Jerusalem, the new yield was permitted from midday onward [since they could not know precisely when the *omer* offering was brought]. After the Temple was destroyed, Rabbi Yoḥanan ben Zakkai instituted that grain could not be eaten throughout the entire day of waving the *omer* [the sixteenth of Nisan, and that the Israelites could partake of the new grain starting the next day]. Rabbi Yehuda responded to this claim by asking: Does not Torah law already forbid such consumption, as the verse states: *Until that day, until you bring this sacrifice to your God, you shall eat no bread or roasted grain or ripe grain*? [As the text makes clear, the new crop is prohibited on the day of the waving unless it has been permitted by the sacrifice of the offering. Why then did Rabbi Yoḥanan ben Zakkai have to establish his own rule? What the verse therefore teaches is that during the period that the Temple was extant, the new grain remained forbidden until the *omer* offering had been brought. By contrast, when the Temple no longer stood in Jerusalem – and the grain offering was not sacrificed – the new grain was prohibited "until that day," meaning, *including* that day. Hence, in the absence of the offering, it would be unlawful to eat new grain throughout the entire day of the sixteenth.] But if so, why was it permitted for Israelites who lived far from Jerusalem to eat their new crops starting at midday [during Temple times]? That was based on their trust that the members of the court would not be negligent in bringing the grain offering, and hence by noontime the sacrifice of the *omer* certainly would have been completed. (Menaḥot 10:5)

טו לְדֹרֹתֵיכֶם בְּכֹל מֹשְׁבֹתֵיכֶם: וּסְפַרְתֶּם לָכֶם יט
מִמָּחֳרַת הַשַּׁבָּת מִיּוֹם הֲבִיאֲכֶם אֶת־עֹמֶר הַתְּנוּפָה שֶׁבַע

TALMUD BAVLI

עַד הֲבִיאֲכֶם – *Until you bring:* [According to Rabbi Yehuda's opinion, as presented in the Mishna, after the destruction of the Temple, by Torah law, the new crop was forbidden every year until the entire sixteenth of Nisan had passed. However, regarding the dissenting opinion, which permits the grain on that day,] Rav and Shmuel taught: When the Temple stood, the sacrifice of the *omer* effectively permitted the new year's crop. By contrast, when the Temple no longer stood in Jerusalem, the illumination of the eastern horizon [that is, dawn on the sixteenth] permitted it. What is the reasoning behind that rule? The verse contains two apparently contradictory clauses with respect to the new crop. On the one hand, the text uses the phrase *Until you bring this sacrifice to your God* [which implies that new grain is forbidden until the offering is brought]. On the other hand, we find the term "until that day" [which suggests that the prohibition remains only until the start of the day]. How can we reconcile these instructions? The clause that states: *Until you bring this sacrifice to your God* refers to the time when the Temple stands [when consumption of the new grain is dependent on the offering of the *omer*]. By contrast, the words "until that day" relate to the era when there is no Temple [in which case the people need not wait for anything to take place on the sixteenth but may eat the new grain with the start of the day]. Rabbi Yoḥanan and Reish Lakish both taught: Even when the Temple stood, it is the illumination of the eastern horizon that allowed the Israelites to eat the year's new grain. But does the verse not state: *Until you bring this sacrifice to your God*? That teaches that [ideally one should wait to partake of the new crop until after the *omer* is brought in order] to fulfill the commandment in the optimal fashion. [Nevertheless, one is permitted to eat the grain even earlier in the day.] (Menaḥot 68a)

VERSE 15

SIFREI DEVARIM

שֶׁבַע שַׁבָּתוֹת תְּמִימֹת תִּהְיֶינָה – *Seven complete weeks:* The corresponding verse in Deuteronomy, which reads: *You shall count seven weeks* (16:9), obligates the court to observe a count. But how do we know that every Israelite is similarly required to follow this custom? For the earlier verse states: *The day after the day of rest, you shall count for yourselves seven complete weeks*, which addresses each person in the nation. (Re'eh 136:9)

TALMUD BAVLI

וּסְפַרְתֶּם לָכֶם – *You shall count for yourselves:* Our Sages taught in a *baraita*: Since the verse orders: *You shall count for yourselves*, it teaches that every Israelite is personally obligated to count these weeks. Now, the clause that states *The day after the day of rest [mimoḥorat hashabbat]* refers to the day following the first day of the festival of Passover [that is, the sixteenth of Nisan]. Or perhaps that is not what the verse means at all, but rather it connotes the day after the Sabbath of creation [that is, Sunday]. Rabbi Yosei bar Yehuda dismissed that option, citing the next verse: *You shall count fifty days* (23:16), which teaches that every time the *omer*

15 all your dwellings. And from the day you bring the
sheaf of the wave offering, the day after the day of rest, you shall

TALMUD BAVLI *(cont.)*

is counted, it should be counted for fifty days. And if we suggest that the clause *The day after the day of rest* refers to the Sabbath of creation, what emerges is that there will sometimes be a fifty-one-day period between the first day of Passover and Shavuot; in other years there will be fifty-two days between those two dates, or fifty-three days, fifty-four days, fifty-five days, or even fifty-six days. [If, for example, the first day of Passover, the fifteenth of Nisan, falls on the Sabbath, then the sixteenth of Nisan will represent both the day after the first day of the festival and the day after the Sabbath of creation. Once fifty days have been counted, the holiday of Shavuot is then celebrated. However, if the first day of Passover falls on a Friday, then according to the second system, the count would only begin on Sunday, which is already two days after the first day of Passover. After fifty days have been counted, the holiday of Shavuot would be observed fifty-one days after the first day of Passover. Hence, the length of the period between the two festivals would vary, based on the number of days between the first day of Passover and the subsequent Sunday. And should Passover start on a Sunday, the fifty days would not begin until the following week, which would push the gap between the two holidays to fifty-six days. Such an arrangement would be untenable since the Torah demands that only a fifty-day count take place every year.] The verse in question states: *And from the day you bring the sheaf of the wave offering…you shall count for yourselves seven complete weeks.* Now, if the text had only included the verse that states: *At the time when you first put sickle to standing grain, begin your count of seven weeks* (Deuteronomy 16:9), we might have thought that it would be acceptable to harvest the grain, begin the seven-week count, and then bring the *omer* offering whenever one wants. To counter that proposition, the earlier verse states: *And from the day you bring the sheaf of the wave offering…you shall count for yourselves seven complete weeks* [which indicates that the counting should start on the day that the *omer* offering is brought. And since the count must begin on the day that the *omer* is brought, the harvesting and the bringing must also take place on that day, the sixteenth of Nisan]. On the other hand, if the text had only included the verse *And from the day you bring the sheaf of the wave offering… you shall count for yourselves seven complete weeks*, we might have thought that cutting the barley, counting, and bringing the grain offering should all take place during the daytime [and not at night, since the verse emphasizes: *And from the day*.] Therefore, the verse continues to command: *You shall count for yourselves seven complete weeks.* And under what circumstances will there be seven complete weeks? That will only happen if the counting begins in the evening [at the start of the sixteenth of Nisan. By contrast, if the counting is undertaken during the day, the evening and nighttime hours will be missing, and the seven weeks will be deficient]. Abbaye taught: There is an obligation to count both days and weeks during the *omer* period. The Sages of the academy of Rav Ashi counted both days and weeks, whereas Ameimar counted only days but not weeks. For the latter maintained [that after the Temple was destroyed and the *omer* offering is no longer sacrificed, the counting that the people do] is merely in commemoration of the Temple [and hence it is sufficient to count the days]. (Menaḥot 65b)

טז שַׁבָּתוֹת תְּמִימֹת תִּהְיֶינָה: עַד מִמָּחֳרַת הַשַּׁבָּת הַשְּׁבִיעִת
תִּסְפְּרוּ חֲמִשִּׁים יוֹם וְהִקְרַבְתֶּם מִנְחָה חֲדָשָׁה לַיהוָה:
יז מִמּוֹשְׁבֹתֵיכֶם תָּבִיאוּ ׀ לֶחֶם תְּנוּפָה שְׁתַּיִם שְׁנֵי עֶשְׂרֹנִים
יח סֹלֶת תִּהְיֶינָה חָמֵץ תֵּאָפֶינָה בִּכּוּרִים לַיהוָה: וְהִקְרַבְתֶּם
עַל־הַלֶּחֶם שִׁבְעַת כְּבָשִׂים תְּמִימִם בְּנֵי שָׁנָה וּפַר בֶּן־בָּקָר
אֶחָד וְאֵילִם שְׁנָיִם יִהְיוּ עֹלָה לַיהוָה וּמִנְחָתָם וְנִסְכֵּיהֶם אִשֵּׁה
יט רֵיחַ־נִיחֹחַ לַיהוָה: וַעֲשִׂיתֶם שְׂעִיר־עִזִּים אֶחָד לְחַטָּאת
כ וּשְׁנֵי כְבָשִׂים בְּנֵי שָׁנָה לְזֶבַח שְׁלָמִים: וְהֵנִיף הַכֹּהֵן ׀ אֹתָם
עַל לֶחֶם הַבִּכֻּרִים תְּנוּפָה לִפְנֵי יהוה עַל־שְׁנֵי כְּבָשִׂים קֹדֶשׁ
כא יִהְיוּ לַיהוָה לַכֹּהֵן: וּקְרָאתֶם בְּעֶצֶם ׀ הַיּוֹם הַזֶּה מִקְרָא־

VERSE 16

YALKUT SHIMONI

עַד מִמָּחֳרַת הַשַּׁבָּת הַשְּׁבִיעִת – *To the day after the seventh week:* We might have thought that the community should count fifty days and then establish the fifty-first day as the festival of Shavuot. However, the text states: *You shall count for yourselves seven complete weeks*. Perhaps the Israelites are meant to count forty-eight days and then consecrate the forty-ninth day. No, for the verse demands: *You shall count fifty days*. How are we to understand the matter? The nation should count forty-nine days and then sanctify the fiftieth day, just as the Jubilee year constitutes the fiftieth year. (Emor 643)

VERSE 17

LEKAḤ TOV

מִמּוֹשְׁבֹתֵיכֶם – *From your dwellings:* This should not be brought from outside of the land. **לֶחֶם תְּנוּפָה** – *Loaves of bread:* The verse refers to the special wheat loaves brought on the festival of Shavuot. **שְׁתַּיִם** – *Two:* These should be made out of two-tenths of an ephah. (65a)

VERSE 20

TALMUD BAVLI

וְהֵנִיף הַכֹּהֵן אֹתָם – *The priest shall display them this way and that:* Our Sages taught in a *baraita*: When the verse instructs the priest to *display them this way and that with [al: literally, "on"] the bread of the first produce*, does that mean that the officiant should place the lambs on top of the bread for the waving? No, for the text continues to state: *Together with [al: literally, "on"] the two sheep* [which indicates that the two loaves should be on top of the lambs rather than the other way around]. But does that mean that breads should be laid on top of the lambs? Does not the earlier clause read: *Display them this way and that with [on] the bread of the first produce*? This contradiction renders the verse ambiguous, and we do not know whether the bread should be on top of the lambs or the lambs should be on top

16 count for yourselves seven complete weeks. To the day after
the seventh week, you shall count fifty days; and then you shall
17 present a new grain offering to the LORD. You shall bring two
loaves of bread from your dwellings made with two-tenths of
an ephah of fine flour baked with leaven, as a wave offering: first
18 produce to the LORD. Together with the bread, you shall present seven unblemished yearling male lambs, one young bull,
and two rams – these shall be a burnt offering for the LORD
with their grain offering and their libations, a fire offering, a
19 pleasing aroma to the LORD. And you shall offer one he-goat as
a purification offering and two yearling male sheep as peace sac-
20 rifices. The priest shall display them this way and that with the
bread of the first produce as a wave offering before the LORD
together with the two sheep; they shall be holy to the LORD
21 and belong to the priest. On that day you shall make a proclamation; it shall be a sacred assembly for you; you shall perform

TALMUD BAVLI *(cont.)*

of the bread. Nevertheless, in all other cases of waving, we find that the bread is placed above the accompanying items. So too here, the bread should be placed above the lambs. And where do we find such a circumstance in which the bread is placed on top? Rav Pappa explained: This is seen regarding the ram offered at the inauguration of the priests. (Menaḥot 62a) **קֹדֶשׁ יִהְיוּ לַיהוה לַכֹּהֵן** – *They shall be holy to the LORD and belong to the priest:* Rabbi Akiva maintains: Which item is given to the priest in its entirety? That can be only be the Shavuot loaves of bread. By contrast, Rabbi Shimon ben Nannas argues that the verse does not actually state: *Yihyu lakohen* ["They shall be to the priest"]. Rather, the text reads: *Yihyu lAdonai lakohen* [literally, "They shall be holy to the LORD, to the priest"], thereby describing something that belongs partially to God and partially to the priests. That can only refer to the sheep [which is sacrificed as a peace offering. Part of the animal is burned on the altar, while some of it is consumed by the priests]. (Menaḥot 45b)

VERSE 21

LEKAḤ TOV

וּקְרָאתֶם בְּעֶצֶם הַיּוֹם הַזֶּה – *On that day you shall make a proclamation:* This day is the fiftieth day, the day that commemorates the assembly of Israel at Mount Sinai, where they received the Torah. For our ancestors gathered at that site fifty days after they left the land of Egypt. God thus established this day of the first fruits [*bikkurim*] fifty days after the first day of Passover. Hence, the people of Israel are described in the following manner: *When I found Israel, they were as grapes in the desert; your fathers were to Me like the first [kevikkura], ripe figs of the new season* (Hosea 9:10). Now, elsewhere we find this verse: *An apple tree in the forest is my beloved among young men* (Song of Songs 2:3). For just as the apple tree produces fruit fifty days after it blossoms, so too did the nation of Israel accept the Torah fifty days after their emancipation from slavery. (65b)

קֹ֛דֶשׁ יִהְיֶ֥ה לָכֶ֖ם כָּל־מְלֶ֥אכֶת עֲבֹדָ֖ה לֹ֣א תַעֲשׂ֑וּ חֻקַּ֥ת עוֹלָ֛ם
כב בְּכָל־מֽוֹשְׁבֹתֵיכֶ֖ם לְדֹרֹֽתֵיכֶֽם׃ וּֽבְקֻצְרְכֶ֞ם אֶת־קְצִ֣יר אַרְצְכֶ֗ם
לֹֽא־תְכַלֶּ֞ה פְּאַ֤ת שָֽׂדְךָ֙ בְּקֻצְרֶ֔ךָ וְלֶ֥קֶט קְצִֽירְךָ֖ לֹ֣א תְלַקֵּ֑ט
לֶֽעָנִ֤י וְלַגֵּר֙ תַּעֲזֹ֣ב אֹתָ֔ם אֲנִ֖י יְהוָ֥ה אֱלֹהֵיכֶֽם׃
כג כד וַיְדַבֵּ֥ר יְהוָ֖ה אֶל־מֹשֶׁ֥ה לֵּאמֹֽר׃ דַּבֵּ֛ר אֶל־בְּנֵ֥י יִשְׂרָאֵ֖ל חמישי
לֵאמֹ֑ר בַּחֹ֨דֶשׁ הַשְּׁבִיעִ֜י בְּאֶחָ֣ד לַחֹ֗דֶשׁ יִהְיֶ֤ה לָכֶם֙ שַׁבָּת֔וֹן

VERSE 22

VAYIKRA RABBA

וּבְקֻצְרְכֶם אֶת־קְצִיר אַרְצְכֶם – *And when you reap the harvest of your land:* Because the nations of the world reap their entire fields [*mekhalin*, they empty the land and leave nothing for the impoverished to collect for themselves], God vows: *I will make an end [khala] of all the nations among whom I have scattered you* (Jeremiah 30:11). However, since the Israelite farmers do not clear out their entire yield, as the verse states: *Do not reap [lo tekhalleh, literally, "do not finish"] to the edge of your field or gather the gleanings of your harvest*, although God will punish the people, He promises: *But of you I will not make an end [khala]. I will discipline you justly, but I will surely not annihilate you*. And when will this take place? On Rosh Hashana, *on the first day of the seventh month* (Leviticus 23:24). (Margaliot, Emor 29:5)

YALKUT SHIMONI

וּבְקֻצְרְכֶם אֶת־קְצִיר אַרְצְכֶם – *And when you reap the harvest of your land:* Rabbi Vardimus bar Rabbi Yosei taught: Why does the Torah insert these obligations of the agricultural gifts in the middle of its discussions about the festivals? Thus, the passage first describes the holidays of Passover and Shavuot and then mentions the charitable requirements before returning to list Rosh Hashana and Yom Kippur. After all, has the text not already introduced these commandments in Parashat Kedoshim [in 19:9–10]? The Torah thereby teaches us that if a farmer leaves the fallen grains, forgotten sheaves, and corner of the field for the destitute, and he bestows upon them the tithe of the poor [in the third and sixth years of the seven-year cycle], the text gives him credit as he had brought the festival sacrifices in the rebuilt Temple. By contrast, if a landowner neglects to honor these laws, the text views it as if the Temple were standing and he did not bother bringing his offerings to the site. (Emor 645)

VERSE 24

SIFREI BEMIDBAR

זִכְרוֹן תְּרוּעָה – *A commemoration with the sounding of the ram's horn:* Why did the Sages establish the reading of the monarchy verses first, those of the remembrance texts second, and the list of shofar statements last? This sequence indicates that Israel should first coronate God as king over the nation. Once they have accepted His authority, they can turn to Him with a request for compassion and an appeal to remember them. What mechanism is used to invoke such recollection? The shofar, which signifies the call to freedom. (Behaalotekha 77)

no laborious work. This is an everlasting statute throughout
22 your generations in all your dwellings. And when you reap the
harvest of your land, do not reap to the edge of your field or
gather the gleanings of your harvest. Leave them for the poor
and for the migrant; I am the Lord your God."
23 24 Then the Lord spoke to Moshe: "Tell the Israelites: On the HAMISHI
first day of the seventh month, you shall observe a day of rest, a
commemoration with the sounding of the ram's horn, a sacred

TALMUD BAVLI

זִכְרוֹן תְּרוּעָה – *A commemoration with the sounding of the ram's horn:* From where is it derived that the shofar is not sounded on the Sabbath? Rabbi Levi bar Laḥma taught in the name of Rabbi Ḥama bar Ḥanina: The Torah contains two somewhat contradictory texts. One verse describes the festival as *a day of rest, a commemoration with the sounding of the ram's horn [zikhron teru'a: literally, "a memorial of blasts,"* which suggests that one should merely remember the shofar without sounding it]. By contrast, a later verse states: *The first day of the seventh month shall be a sacred assembly for you; you shall perform no laborious work on it. It shall be for you a day of the horn's sounding* (Numbers 29:1). [This verse implies that on this day the shofar should be blown.] But really, there is no difficulty: [The verse in which the shofar is only remembered but not heard refers to when the] festival occurs on the Sabbath. By contrast, [the verse that demands that the shofar be sounded refers to when the] holiday of Rosh Hashana falls out on a weekday. Rava argued: According to the Torah, it is permissible to sound the shofar [on Rosh Hashana when it falls out on the Sabbath], and it was the later Sages who instituted the prohibition lest a person take the shofar in hand and carry it to someone more proficient in order to learn how to use it. (Rosh Hashana 29b)

VAYIKRA RABBA

בַּחֹדֶשׁ הַשְּׁבִיעִי בְּאֶחָד לַחֹדֶשׁ – *On the first day of the seventh month:* The term *on the first [be'eḥad]* is an allusion to Avraham, as we read: *Avraham was one person [eḥad], and he inherited the land* (Ezekiel 33:24). The phrase *A commemoration with the sounding of the ram's horn* is an allusion to Yitzḥak, about whom the verse states: *Avraham went, took hold of the ram, and offered it up as a burnt offering in place of his son* (Genesis 22:13). Third, *A sacred assembly [mikra kodesh]* recalls Yaakov, as a later text reads: *Listen to Me, Yaakov, and Israel, named for Me [mekora'i]* (Isaiah 48:12). Thus God informs Israel: At the moment you mention the merits of the patriarchs before Me, you will be favored in judgment. That will take place on Rosh Hashana, *on the first day of the seventh month*. (Margaliot, Emor 29:7)

YALKUT SHIMONI

בַּחֹדֶשׁ הַשְּׁבִיעִי בְּאֶחָד לַחֹדֶשׁ – *On the first day of the seventh month:* Rabbi Berekhya used to refer to the seventh [*hashevii*] month as the month of the oath [*dishvu'a*] because it was then that the Holy One, blessed be He, swore to our forefather Avraham, as the verse states: *By My own Self I swear, says the Lord, that because you have done this and have not withheld your son, your only one* (Genesis 22:17). What need was there for an oath at that time?

כה זִכְר֥וֹן תְּרוּעָ֖ה מִקְרָא־קֹֽדֶשׁ׃ כָּל־מְלֶ֥אכֶת עֲבֹדָ֖ה לֹ֣א תַעֲשׂ֑וּ
כו וְהִקְרַבְתֶּ֥ם אִשֶּׁ֖ה לַֽיהוָֽה׃ וַיְדַבֵּ֥ר יְהוָ֖ה אֶל־מֹשֶׁ֥ה
כז לֵּאמֹֽר׃ אַ֡ךְ בֶּעָשׂ֣וֹר לַחֹדֶשׁ֩ הַשְּׁבִיעִ֨י הַזֶּ֜ה י֧וֹם הַכִּפֻּרִ֣ים ה֗וּא
מִֽקְרָא־קֹ֙דֶשׁ֙ יִהְיֶ֣ה לָכֶ֔ם וְעִנִּיתֶ֖ם אֶת־נַפְשֹֽׁתֵיכֶ֑ם וְהִקְרַבְתֶּ֥ם
כח אִשֶּׁ֖ה לַֽיהוָֽה׃ וְכָל־מְלָאכָה֙ לֹ֣א תַעֲשׂ֔וּ בְּעֶ֖צֶם הַיּ֣וֹם הַזֶּ֑ה כִּ֣י
כט י֤וֹם כִּפֻּרִים֙ ה֔וּא לְכַפֵּ֣ר עֲלֵיכֶ֔ם לִפְנֵ֖י יְהוָ֥ה אֱלֹהֵיכֶֽם׃ כִּ֤י כָל־
הַנֶּ֙פֶשׁ֙ אֲשֶׁ֣ר לֹֽא־תְעֻנֶּ֔ה בְּעֶ֖צֶם הַיּ֣וֹם הַזֶּ֑ה וְנִכְרְתָ֖ה מֵעַמֶּֽיהָ׃

YALKUT SHIMONI *(cont.)*

Rabbi Bibba Rabba said in the name of Rabbi Yoḥanan: Our forefather Avraham stood before the Almighty and petitioned: Master of the Universe! You well know that when You said to me: *"Take your son…Yitzḥak – and go to the land of Moria. There, offer him up as a burnt offering on one of the mountains"* (22:2), I considering responding: "But did You not promise me yesterday saying: *It is through Yitzḥak that your descendants will be reckoned* (21:12)? And now You order me to *offer him up as a burnt offering*?" Yet I did not say any of that but held my tongue. And so, just as I controlled myself and my passion and did not answer back, so too do I request that when Yitzḥak's progeny sin before You and commit wicked deeds, You remember the binding of their father and exercise compassion and mercy toward my progeny. I beseech You to suppress Your attribute of justice and express Your attribute of mercy when You judge Israel in the seventh month. (Emor 645)

VERSE 27

TALMUD BAVLI

מִקְרָא־קֹדֶשׁ יִהְיֶה לָכֶם – *It shall be a sacred assembly for you:* A *baraita* raised the following question: Is it possible that the day of Yom Kippur will only effect atonement in the event that the person afflicts himself, declares the day "a sacred assembly," and avoids all forbidden labor? No, the day will atone even if the person does not observe all those things, as the verse states: *It is the Day of Atonement*, meaning under all circumstances. (Shevuot 13a)

LEKAḤ TOV

אַךְ – *Hear:* In all cases, the term *akh* ["hear," but usually, "however"] indicates a limitation of some sort. In the present instance, the word alludes to the restriction of food and drink compared to the other festivals. Thus do our Sages cite the following verse and explain: *If you call the Sabbath a delight* refers to the Sabbath of creation; *the Lord's holy day to be honored* is an allusion to Yom Kippur, when there is no eating or drinking; and *If you honor it* (Isaiah 58:13) means by wearing clean and festive clothes. **בֶּעָשׂוֹר לַחֹדֶשׁ הַשְּׁבִיעִי הַזֶּה** – *The tenth day of this seventh month:* The day is dependent on the seventh month, as mentioned above. **יוֹם הַכִּפֻּרִים הוּא** – *It is the Day of Atonement:* The festival is observed

25 assembly. You shall perform no laborious work, and you shall
26 bring close a fire offering to the LORD." The LORD
27 spoke to Moshe: "Hear: the tenth day of this seventh month
is the Day of Atonement. It shall be a sacred assembly for you,
and you shall afflict yourselves and bring a fire offering to the
28 LORD. You shall perform no work at all during this entire day,
for it is the Day of Atonement, there to make atonement for
29 you before the LORD your God. Anyone who does not afflict
himself for this whole day shall be severed from his people,

LEKAḤ TOV *(cont.)*

even when no sacrifices are brought [meaning even in the absence of the Temple]. **מִקְרָא־קֹדֶשׁ יִהְיֶה לָכֶם** – *It shall be a sacred assembly for you:* The day shall be observed both in the land and outside the land. **וְעִנִּיתֶם אֶת־נַפְשֹׁתֵיכֶם** – *And you shall afflict yourselves:* This clause serves as the warning [that is, the commandment] to the Israelites to afflict themselves on Yom Kippur. (66a)

VERSE 28

TALMUD YERUSHALMI

בְּעֶצֶם הַיּוֹם הַזֶּה – *During this entire day:* Rabbi Elazar ben Yaakov taught: The phrase *During this entire day* appears both in the context of forbidden labor [in verse 28] and regarding the affliction of the Israelites' souls [in verse 29]. Just as there is no distinction in the case of labor between daytime and nighttime with respect to either the warning [the Torah forbids work at night and in the day] or the punishment [the violation of this law merits a penalty irrespective of the time that it is committed], similarly, the Torah does not distinguish in the case of affliction of the soul between the day and the night, or between the warning and the punishment. (Yoma 8:3)

VERSE 29

TALMUD BAVLI

אֲשֶׁר לֹא־תְעֻנֶּה – *Anyone who does not afflict himself:* All measures in the Torah connected to eating are set at an olive-bulk's worth of food, except for the amount of material that renders one impure. Since the verse regarding that issue changed its language, the Sages altered the measure accordingly. The proof lies in the case of Yom Kippur [where the Sages also assigned a different amount for culpability in response to the different language in the text]. What exactly does this refer to? The present verse states: *Anyone who does not afflict himself* [instead of the expected: "any person who eats on this day"]. And what is the different measure on Yom Kippur? This prohibition is only violated if a person eats the volume of a large date on the holy day. (Yoma 80a) **אֲשֶׁר לֹא־תְעֻנֶּה** – *Anyone who does not afflict himself:* Reish Lakish taught: One who eats in an excessive manner on Yom Kippur [by forcing himself to eat even when he is full] is exempt. What is the reason for that? For when the verse warns: *Anyone who does not afflict himself*, it excludes a case where a person harms himself [and thereby does not enjoy his food at all]. (Yoma 80b)

ל וְכָל־הַנֶּפֶשׁ אֲשֶׁר תַּעֲשֶׂה כָּל־מְלָאכָה בְּעֶצֶם הַיּוֹם הַזֶּה
לא וְהַאֲבַדְתִּי אֶת־הַנֶּפֶשׁ הַהִוא מִקֶּרֶב עַמָּהּ: כָּל־מְלָאכָה לֹא
לב תַעֲשׂוּ חֻקַּת עוֹלָם לְדֹרֹתֵיכֶם בְּכֹל מֹשְׁבֹתֵיכֶם: שַׁבַּת שַׁבָּתוֹן
הוּא לָכֶם וְעִנִּיתֶם אֶת־נַפְשֹׁתֵיכֶם בְּתִשְׁעָה לַחֹדֶשׁ בָּעֶרֶב
מֵעֶרֶב עַד־עֶרֶב תִּשְׁבְּתוּ שַׁבַּתְּכֶם:
לג לד וַיְדַבֵּר יהוה אֶל־מֹשֶׁה לֵּאמֹר: דַּבֵּר אֶל־בְּנֵי יִשְׂרָאֵל לֵאמֹר ששי

VERSE 30

TALMUD YERUSHALMI

וְהַאֲבַדְתִּי אֶת־הַנֶּפֶשׁ הַהִוא – *I will annihilate that person:* The verse that states: *You shall perform no work at all during this entire day* (23:28) constitutes the warning against performing labor on Yom Kippur. The punishment for violating that is stated in verse 30: *And if anyone performs any work during this whole day, I will annihilate that person from among his people*. The verse that states: *Anyone who does not afflict himself for this whole day* (23:29) represents the command to the Israelites to afflict their souls on Yom Kippur. The punishment for disobeying that command appears in the continuation of that text: *He shall be severed from his people*. And yet, there is no warning about doing labor at night and there is no stated punishment for that; furthermore, there is no direct warning regarding affliction at night nor is a penalty prescribed here. (Yoma 8:3)

VERSE 31

LEKAḤ TOV

כָּל־מְלָאכָה לֹא תַעֲשׂוּ – *No work at all may you perform:* What is the function of this verse? It cannot serve to outlaw work on Yom Kippur, since that has already been stated: *You shall perform no work at all during this entire day* (23:28). The distinction is this: The initial sentence refers to the commission of labor during the actual day of the festival, whereas verse 31 refers to avoiding work in the extended time of the day [that is, before the technical onset of Yom Kippur and after the sun has set the next day]. We learn from here that Israel is warned to desist from labor from the evening of Yom Kippur just like during the day itself. (66a)

VERSE 32

TALMUD BAVLI

וְעִנִּיתֶם אֶת־נַפְשֹׁתֵיכֶם – *And you shall afflict yourselves:* The text states: *And you shall afflict yourselves from the evening of the ninth day of the month*. Now, we might have thought that one must fast the entire day of the ninth. However, the verse continues: *From evening to evening*. And yet, if Yom Kippur actually begins in the evening, we might have thought that one need only begin to fast when it becomes dark [after nightfall, when the tenth day of the month begins]. To counter that proposition, the text says: "Of the ninth." How can these clauses be reconciled? One begins to fast on the ninth of the month while it is still daylight. We learn from here that one must extend Yom Kippur by adding time from the sacred to the profane. Based on that, we only derive that such an addition is required at the beginning

30 and if anyone performs any work during this whole day, I will
31 annihilate that person from among his people. No work at all
may you perform; this is an everlasting statute throughout your
32 generations in all your dwellings. It is a Sabbath of complete
rest for you, and you shall afflict yourselves from the evening of
the ninth day of the month: from evening to evening shall you
observe your Sabbath."
33 34 The LORD spoke to Moshe: "Tell the Israelites: From the SHISHI

TALMUD BAVLI *(cont.)*

of the festival; how do we know that Yom Kippur also must be extended at the end of the day [that is, into the eleventh]? For the verse states: *From evening to evening shall you observe your Sabbath* [which teaches that just as Yom Kippur begins before the tenth, so does it end after the tenth]. Now, all this teaches us only about Yom Kippur. From where do we derive that one must also extend the weekly Sabbath in a similar manner? We learn that point from the end of the verse, which reads: *You shall observe your Sabbath.* And how do we know that the same rule applies to other festivals? That is derived from the term "your Sabbath." [That is, the doubled phrase *tishbetu shabbattekhem* serves as a source for the extension of both Sabbaths and holidays.] How is this to be understood? Whenever there is an obligation to rest, one must add from the sacred to the profane [thereby extending the holy day at both ends]. (Rosh Hashana 9a) **בְּתִשְׁעָה לַחֹדֶשׁ** – *On the ninth day of the month:* Ḥiyya bar Rav of Difti taught: Consider the verse that states: *And you shall afflict yourselves from the evening of the ninth day of the month: from evening to evening shall you observe your Sabbath.* Now, does one fast on the ninth of Tishrei? Is the fast not observed on the tenth of the month [as mandated by 23:27]? Rather, verse 32 teaches that if a person eats and drinks on the ninth [in preparation for the fast the next day], the text ascribes him credit as if he has fasted on both the ninth and the tenth of Tishrei. (Berakhot 8b)

LEKAḤ TOV

וְעִנִּיתֶם אֶת־נַפְשֹׁתֵיכֶם – *And you shall afflict yourselves:* In five places does the Torah demand that the Israelites afflict themselves on Yom Kippur. [In addition to the two statements here in 23:27 and 23:32, the commandment appears in these verses: *On the tenth day of the seventh month, you must afflict yourselves* (16:29); *It shall be a Sabbath of complete rest for you, and on it you shall afflict yourselves* (16:31); and *The tenth day of this seventh month shall be a sacred assembly for you; you shall afflict yourselves on it and perform no work at all* (Numbers 29:7).] These five instances correspond to the five deprivations that are required on the festival: the abstention from food, drink, washing, anointing, wearing sandals, and marital relations. And should you object that this list contains six items, eating and drinking are counted as a single form of affliction.

VERSE 34

PHILO

חַג הַסֻּכּוֹת – *The festival of Tabernacles:* One possible reason for dwelling in the tents is a reminder of the long journey our ancestors had made through a wide desert, living in

בַּחֲמִשָּׁה עָשָׂר יוֹם לַחֹדֶשׁ הַשְּׁבִיעִי הַזֶּה חַג הַסֻּכּוֹת שִׁבְעַת
לה יָמִים לַיהוָה: בַּיּוֹם הָרִאשׁוֹן מִקְרָא־קֹדֶשׁ כָּל־מְלֶאכֶת עֲבֹדָה
לו לֹא תַעֲשׂוּ: שִׁבְעַת יָמִים תַּקְרִיבוּ אִשֶּׁה לַיהוָה בַּיּוֹם הַשְּׁמִינִי
מִקְרָא־קֹדֶשׁ יִהְיֶה לָכֶם וְהִקְרַבְתֶּם אִשֶּׁה לַיהוָה עֲצֶרֶת
לז הִוא כָּל־מְלֶאכֶת עֲבֹדָה לֹא תַעֲשׂוּ: אֵלֶּה מוֹעֲדֵי יהוה
אֲשֶׁר־תִּקְרְאוּ אֹתָם מִקְרָאֵי קֹדֶשׁ לְהַקְרִיב אִשֶּׁה לַיהוָה

PHILO *(cont.)*

tents for many years at each station. In times of wealth, it is most apropos to remember our humble beginnings when we were once impoverished. It is no less important for people in high positions of power to remember how we were once commoners. In times of peace, we should never forget the times of war; when the weather is tranquil, we should never forget the moments when we faced storms. When blessed with many friends, we should never forget the times when we felt alone, for in all of these examples, there is no greater pleasure than for prosperous people to remember past misfortunes. Our memory of the difficult times can be very conducive in helping us develop virtue because we understand how easily life's circumstances can change and produce a reversal of fortune. Therefore, it behooves us to thank God for all of our present blessings, as we honor God with songs and words of praise. We also beseech Him and propitiate Him with supplications that we should never be tested with hard times again.

TALMUD YERUSHALMI

חַג הַסֻּכּוֹת שִׁבְעַת יָמִים – *For seven days shall be the festival of Tabernacles:* Rabbi Eliezer taught: A person is obligated to eat fourteen meals in his sukka [over the course of the seven days of the festival], one each day and one each night. By contrast, according to the Sages, there is no fixed number of meals required during the holiday [and one may choose whether to eat any meals in the sukka] except for the meal on the evening of the first festival day of Sukkot [which one must eat there]. What is Rabbi Eliezer's reasoning? The Sage connects our text, which reads: *For seven days you shall live [teshevu] in huts* (23:42), with an earlier verse that states: *Stay [teshevu], then, at the entrance to the Tent of Meeting for seven days, day and night* (8:35). Just as in that case, the priests were ordered to treat the days like the nights, so too here the Israelites must behave during the nights as they do during the days. Rabbi Yoḥanan taught in the name of Rabbi Yishmael: With respect to the holiday of Passover, the Torah states: *The fifteenth of this month is the Lord's Festival of Unleavened Bread* (23:6), whereas regarding the holiday of Sukkot, we read: *From the fifteenth day of the seventh month, for seven days shall be the festival of Tabernacles to the Lord* (23:34). Now, just as on the holiday of Passover, it is obligatory [to eat matza] on the first night, whereas [consumption of matza] on the rest of the days is optional, so too on the holiday of Sukkot, it is obligatory [to eat in the sukka] on the first night, whereas [eating in the sukka] on the rest of the days is optional. (Sukka 2:7)

fifteenth day of this seventh month, for seven days shall be the
35 Festival of Tabernacles to the LORD. The first day shall be a
sacred assembly; on it, you shall perform no laborious work.
36 For seven days you must bring close a fire offering to the LORD.
The eighth day shall be a sacred assembly for you, and you shall
present a fire offering to the LORD. It is an assembly; you shall
37 perform no laborious work. These are the LORD's festivals,
which you shall proclaim, sacred assemblies to present a fire
offering to the LORD: burnt offering, grain offering, sacrifice,

TALMUD BAVLI

שִׁבְעַת יָמִים לַיהוה – *For seven days…to the Lord:* Mishna: Beit Shammai deems an old sukka to be invalid for the celebration of the holiday, whereas Beit Hillel rules that it is acceptable. [According to Beit Shammai, a sukka must be built explicitly for the holiday. Beit Hillel maintains that it is not necessary for the booth to be built with the festival in mind.] And what qualifies as an old sukka? A booth that is erected thirty days or more before the festival without being expressly designated for Sukkot is considered an old sukka [since it is assumed that the owner built it for some other purpose. By contrast, if it was built within thirty days of the holiday, it is clear that its purpose is for the festival]. However, if the person established the booth expressly for the sake of the festival, it is fit for use on Sukkot even if he put it up at the beginning of the previous year. [According to both Beit Shammai and Beit Hillel, the booth may be used on the festival since it was built for the sake of the festival.] Talmud: What is the rationale for Beit Shammai's opinion? The verse states: *For seven days shall be the Festival of Tabernacles [Sukkot] to the Lord,* indicating that the holiday requires a sukka that has been constructed especially for the festival. [And how does Beit Hillel interpret this verse?] According to them, that text is needed for the teaching of Rav Sheshet. For Rav Sheshet taught in the name of Rabbi Akiva: From where do we derive the prohibition of using the sukka's wood for all seven days of the festival [for some other purpose]? For the verse states: *For seven days shall be the Festival of Tabernacles to the Lord,* and it is taught in a *baraita*: Rabbi Yehuda ben Beteira says: Just as the name of Heaven takes effect upon the festival peace offering [that is, the sacrificial animal is sacred and no benefit may be derived from it before it is offered], so too does the name of Heaven take effect upon the sukka, as the verse states: *For seven days shall be the Festival of Tabernacles to the Lord.* Hence, just as the festival offering is consecrated to God, so too is the sukka consecrated to God. (Sukka 9a)

VERSE 35

LEKAḤ TOV

בַּיּוֹם הָרִאשׁוֹן מִקְרָא־קֹדֶשׁ – *The first day shall be a sacred assembly:* Sanctify the day with food and beverage and by wearing clean clothes. (66a)

VERSE 37

TALMUD BAVLI

אֲשֶׁר־תִּקְרְאוּ אֹתָם – *Which you shall proclaim:* Mishna: There was an incident in which two witnesses came and testified that they had observed the new moon at its anticipated

עֹלָה וּמִנְחָה זֶבַח וּנְסָכִים דְּבַר־יוֹם בְּיוֹמוֹ: מִלְּבַד שַׁבְּתֹת לח
יהוה וּמִלְּבַד מַתְּנוֹתֵיכֶם וּמִלְּבַד כׇּל־נִדְרֵיכֶם וּמִלְּבַד כׇּל־
נִדְבֹתֵיכֶם אֲשֶׁר תִּתְּנוּ לַיהוה: אַךְ בַּחֲמִשָּׁה עָשָׂר יוֹם לַחֹדֶשׁ לט
הַשְּׁבִיעִי בְּאׇסְפְּכֶם אֶת־תְּבוּאַת הָאָרֶץ תָּחֹגּוּ אֶת־חַג־יהוה

TALMUD BAVLI *(cont.)*

time [that is, on the night of the thirtieth day of the previous month]. However, on the following night [at the start of the thirty-first, which is often the determinant of] a full thirty-day month, the moon was not seen. Nevertheless, Rabban Gamliel accepted the witnesses' testimony [and established the New Moon on the thirtieth day]. But Rabbi Dosa ben Horkinas disagreed and said: These are false witnesses! How can they testify that a woman has given birth even as she is clearly still pregnant the next day? [If the new moon was already visible at its anticipated time, how could it not be seen a day later?] Rabbi Yehoshua said to him: I see the logic of your statement [and hence the new month should be established a day later than that accepted by Rabban Gamliel. Upon hearing that Rabbi Yehoshua had challenged his ruling] Rabban Gamliel sent a message to him: "I hereby decree that you appear before me with your staff and wallet on the day you calculate to be Yom Kippur." [By contrast, according to Rabban Gamliel, that day would already be the eleventh of Tishrei.] Subsequently, Rabbi Akiva went to Rabbi Yehoshua, who was distressed [that the head of the Sanhedrin was forcing Rabbi Yehoshua to desecrate the day that he maintained was Yom Kippur. In an attempt to console him] Rabbi Akiva said to Rabbi Yehoshua: "There is a verse that teaches us that everything that Rabban Gamliel did in sanctifying the month is done [that is, it is valid]. For the text reads: *These are the Lord's festivals, which you shall proclaim, sacred assemblies*. In this text, God asserts: Whether you have proclaimed them in their proper time or whether you have declared them not at their proper time, I have only these festivals [as they are established by the representatives of the Jewish people]." Gemara: The Mishna teaches that Rabbi Akiva went and found him distressed. But that statement is somewhat ambiguous. Who was upset at that moment: Rabbi Akiva or Rabbi Yehoshua? Come and hear what was taught in a *baraita*: Rabbi Akiva went and found Rabbi Yehoshua in a state of distress. Whereupon Rabbi Akiva said to Rabbi Yehoshua: "My teacher, for what reason are you disturbed?" Rabbi Yehoshua answered: "I would rather be sick in bed for twelve straight months than to have this decree issued against me" [which compelled him to desecrate Yom Kippur]. To this Rabbi Akiva responded: "My teacher, allow me to repeat to you something that you yourself once taught me." "Proceed," said Rabbi Yehoshua. Said he: "With respect to the festivals, the text uses the term *otam* ['them'] three times: *These are the Lord's appointed times that you shall proclaim [them] as sacred assemblies* (23:2); *These are the Lord's appointed times, sacred assemblies, which you shall proclaim [them] at their appointed times* (23:4); and *These are the Lord's festivals, which you shall proclaim [them]* (23:37). However, the three instances can be read as *attem, attem, attem* ["you," "you," "you"], which teaches that you [that is, Israel] are authorized to determine the day of the new month, even if you unwittingly establish the New Moon on the wrong day [and thus the holidays of that month are fixed in an objectively erroneous

38 **and libations, each on its appointed day; in addition to the**
Lord's Sabbaths, and in addition to your gifts and all your of-
ferings in the fulfillment of vows and all the freewill offerings
39 **that you give to the Lord. Hear: on the fifteenth day of the sev-**
enth month, when you have harvested the land's produce, you

TALMUD BAVLI *(cont.)*

way]; and you hold that power, even if you pick the wrong day intentionally; and you have the right to choose the day even if you are misled [by false witnesses. In all cases, once the court has determined the day as the New Moon, it is so sanctified, and God grants His consent to the day]." After hearing this, Rabbi Yehoshua was placated and said to him: "Akiva, you have consoled me, you have consoled me." (Rosh Hashana 25a)

YALKUT SHIMONI

עֹלָה וּמִנְחָה – *Burnt offering, grain offering:* If the burnt offering is not sacrificed, the grain offering is not brought either. Furthermore, the burnt offering must be presented before the grain offering, and if the latter is given first, it is invalid, as the verse refers to "sacrifice and libations." If the sacrifice is not offered, there are no libations brought either. Furthermore, the sacrifices must be presented before the libations, and if the latter is given first, it is invalid. **דְּבַר־יוֹם בְּיוֹמוֹ** – *Each on its appointed day:* We learn from here that the *Musaf* offerings may be brought throughout the entire day. However, once the day has passed, the time for the *Musaf* sacrifices has passed. (Emor 649)

VERSE 38

SIFREI DEVARIM

וּמִלְּבַד מַתְּנוֹתֵיכֶם – *And in addition to your gifts:* Since the verse states: *These are the Lord's festivals, which you shall proclaim, sacred assemblies to present a fire offering to the Lord: burnt offering, grain offering, sacrifice, and libations, each on its appointed day* (23:37), we might think that the only sacrifices offered on the festival are those that are a function of the day itself. How do we know that even communal sacrifices dedicated before the holiday are brought on the day, as are personal sacrifices that were consecrated before the holiday, as are those that were designated on the festival itself? For the subsequent verse reads: *And in addition to your gifts and all your offerings in the fulfillment of vows and all the freewill offerings that you give to the Lord* (23:38). (Re'eh 63)

VERSE 39

LEKAḤ TOV

אַךְ – *Hear:* The term *akh* ["hear," but usually, "however"] indicates a limitation of some sort. What does it exclude in the present instance? Beit Shammai teaches: It refers here to the festival sacrifice [the *korban ḥagiga*, a peace offering], which is presented on the intermediate days of the holiday but not on the festival day [that is, the first day]. Beit Hillel teaches: The limitation here refers to the Sabbath, such that the festival offering is brought on the festival day, but not if that day is the Sabbath. **בְּאָסְפְּכֶם אֶת־תְּבוּאַת הָאָרֶץ** – *When you have harvested the land's produce:* The text refers to the collection of all the fruit, which teaches that fruit is

שִׁבְעַת יָמִים בַּיּוֹם הָרִאשׁוֹן שַׁבָּתוֹן וּבַיּוֹם הַשְּׁמִינִי שַׁבָּתוֹן:
מ וּלְקַחְתֶּם לָכֶם בַּיּוֹם הָרִאשׁוֹן פְּרִי עֵץ הָדָר כַּפֹּת תְּמָרִים
וַעֲנַף עֵץ־עָבֹת וְעַרְבֵי־נָחַל וּשְׂמַחְתֶּם לִפְנֵי יהוה אֱלֹהֵיכֶם
מא שִׁבְעַת יָמִים: וְחַגֹּתֶם אֹתוֹ חַג לַיהוה שִׁבְעַת יָמִים בַּשָּׁנָה

LEKAḤ TOV *(cont.)*

also called *the land's produce [tevu'at haaretz: literally, "the grain of the land"].* **תָּחֹגּוּ אֶת־חַג־יהוה שִׁבְעַת יָמִים** – *Celebrate a festival to the Lord for seven days:* We learn from here that the peace offering may be brought any time during the seven days of the holiday. Based on this, the Sages rule as follows: If a person has not brought his festival offering on the first day of Sukkot, he may do so on any of the intermediate days or on the last day of the holiday. (67a)

VERSE 40

TALMUD YERUSHALMI

וּלְקַחְתֶּם לָכֶם – *You shall take for yourselves:* The verse stresses that the four species must belong to the Israelite; he does not fulfill his obligation if he has stolen the plants. Rabbi Levi taught: Any person who steals his four species is like a subject who presents a gift to the monarch which turns out to have belonged to the king in the first place. Woe to such a person whose defender has become his prosecutor! (Sukka 3:1)

TALMUD BAVLI

וּלְקַחְתֶּם לָכֶם – *You shall take for yourselves:* When the verse commands: *You shall take for yourselves*, that indicates that each Israelite must own his own set of four species. This rules out the acceptability of stolen or even borrowed specimens. (Sukka 41b) **כַּפֹּת תְּמָרִים** – Branches of palm trees: When the verse mandates the taking of *branches [kappot] of palm trees*, that means that the leaves must be bound [*kafut*]. (Sukka 32a) **וַעֲנַף עֵץ־עָבֹת** – *Boughs of the leafy tree:* The verse lists as one of the species *boughs of the leafy tree*, which refers to a tree whose leaves obscure the branches. And which tree is that? This describes the myrtle tree. (Sukka 32b)

TANḤUMA

וּלְקַחְתֶּם לָכֶם – *You shall take for yourselves:* The branches of palm trees (lulav) resembles the human spine, the boughs of the leafy tree (hadas leaves) look like a person's eyes, the willows of the brook (arava leaves) recall his lips, and the fruit of the majestic tree (etrog) stands for the heart. Said David: "There is no human organ as important as these, for they represent the whole of the body." This is what David meant when he said: *Every inch of my being declares, "O Lord, who is like You?"* (Psalms 35:10). (Emor 19) **וּלְקַחְתֶּם לָכֶם בַּיּוֹם הָרִאשׁוֹן** – *On the first day you shall take for yourselves:* Even though King Shlomo was exceptionally wise, nevertheless, he found the four species inexplicable, as he states: *Three things are too wondrous for me; four I cannot know* (Proverbs 30:18). That refers to the four plants that constitute the commandment of the lulav, whose meaning the king struggled to decipher. (Emor 20) **וּלְקַחְתֶּם לָכֶם בַּיּוֹם הָרִאשׁוֹן** – *On the first day you shall take for yourselves:* It is not because God requires these things that He has issued this commandment. Rather, the goal is to benefit the Israelites with

shall celebrate a festival to the Lord for seven days. The first
day shall be a day of rest; the eighth day shall be a day of rest.
40 On the first day you shall take for yourselves fruit of the majestic tree, branches of palm trees, boughs of the leafy tree, and
willows of the brook, and rejoice before the Lord your God
41 for seven days. You shall celebrate it as a festival to the Lord for

TANḤUMA *(cont.)*

the practice. (Buber, Emor 24) **פְּרִי עֵץ הָדָר כַּפֹּת תְּמָרִים** – *Fruit of the majestic tree, branches of palm trees:* What is the character of these four species? Some of these plants produce fruit and others do not. The fruit of the majestic tree and the branches of palm trees represent the righteous, who perform good deeds [as symbolized by their fruit]. By contrast, the boughs of the leafy tree and the willows of the brook stand for mediocre Israelites. Said the Holy One, blessed be He: The species should be bound together into a single bundle so that there should not be any disqualified persons among My people. (Buber, Emor 25)

BERESHIT RABBA

וּלְקַחְתֶּם לָכֶם בַּיּוֹם הָרִאשׁוֹן – *On the first day you shall take for yourselves:* As a reward for fulfilling the commandment *On the first day you shall take for yourselves*, God revealed Himself to Israel first, as the verse states: *I am the first and I the last; beside Me is no God* (Isaiah 44:6). (Toledot 63:8)

VAYIKRA RABBA

וּלְקַחְתֶּם לָכֶם – *You shall take for yourselves:* Between the end of Yom Kippur and the start of Sukkot, the entire nation of Israel is busy preparing commandments. While one person is building his sukka, another is collecting his four species. And then, on the first day of the festival, all the people stand before the Holy One, blessed be He, each with his lulav and his etrog, and sing God's praises. In response, the Almighty promises them: "Let bygones be bygones; from now on everybody has a clean slate." Hence Moshe instructs the Israelites: *On the first day you shall take for yourselves....* (Margaliot, Emor 30:7) **פְּרִי עֵץ הָדָר** – *Fruit of the majestic tree:* Rabbi Ḥiyya taught: What is the significance of the term *fruit of the majestic tree*? This describes a tree whose wood tastes exactly the same as its fruit, namely the etrog. Ben Azzai taught: The term *hadar* ["majestic"] connotes that this specific fruit grows, *dar* [literally, "dwells"] on the tree from one year to the next. Aquila the convert translates the word *hadar* as that which lives [*dar*] by the water. Rabbi Tarfon explained the phrase *kappot temarim* [*branches of palm trees*] to mean that the leaves must be *kafut* ["bound"], whereas if the parts of the branch are spread out, they should be tied up. Regarding the plant defined as *boughs of a leafy tree*, the branches of this specimen must cover the wood, which describes the myrtle bush. Finally, although the Torah requires *willows of the brook*, the plural of that term serves to include even trees that grow in a valley or on a hill. (Margaliot, Emor 30:8)

VERSE 41

TALMUD BAVLI

וְחַגֹּתֶם אֹתוֹ – *You shall celebrate it:* It was taught in a *baraita*: The Torah demands: *You shall celebrate it as a festival [veḥagotem oto ḥag] to the Lord for seven days*. This implies

חֻקַּת עוֹלָם לְדֹרֹתֵיכֶם בַּחֹדֶשׁ הַשְּׁבִיעִי תָּחֹגּוּ אֹתוֹ: בַּסֻּכֹּת מב
תֵּשְׁבוּ שִׁבְעַת יָמִים כָּל־הָאֶזְרָח בְּיִשְׂרָאֵל יֵשְׁבוּ בַּסֻּכֹּת:
לְמַעַן יֵדְעוּ דֹרֹתֵיכֶם כִּי בַסֻּכּוֹת הוֹשַׁבְתִּי אֶת־בְּנֵי יִשְׂרָאֵל מג

TALMUD BAVLI *(cont.)*

that the Israelite must bring a festival offering [*korban ḥagiga*] on each of the holiday's seven days. Yet the inclusion of the word *oto* ["it," in the singular form] teaches that the sacrifice is brought on one day [the first], and it need not be brought on every one of the days. Why then does the text mention the seven days of the festival? That signifies that there is redress [that is, if one neglects to bring the offering on the first day, he may fulfill the obligation on any of the subsequent days]. And how do we know that if a person has not celebrated [by bringing this peace offering] on the first day of the festival of Sukkot that he may effect that celebration throughout the pilgrimage holiday, even on the last festival day [the eighth day, Shemini Atzeret]? We learn this from the end of the verse that states: *Celebrate this [oto] in the seventh month*. [The inclusion of the term "month" teaches that the festival offering can be brought on any of the holiday days that are observed in this month. Thus, even after the seven days of Sukkot have passed, the offering can be put forth on the additional holiday day of Shemini Atzeret.] By contrast, had the verse just said: Celebrate in the seventh month [without the word *oto*], we might have thought it acceptable to celebrate by bringing the festival offering at any time during the rest of the entire month [even after Shemini Atzeret]. However, since the word *oto* is included, that indicates that the festival offering can only be brought on a festival day; the Israelite may not celebrate outside of those days. [Hence, the phrase *in the seventh month* serves to include only the day of Shemini Atzeret.] (Ḥagiga 9a)

VERSE 42

SIFREI BEMIDBAR

כָּל־הָאֶזְרָח בְּיִשְׂרָאֵל – *All those native born in Israel:* How should we understand these words? Does the verse mean to include women as well as men? No, this text serves as a prototype for whenever the Torah uses the term *ezraḥ* ["native born"]: that refers to males, not females. [Thus, women are not obligated to live in the sukka.] (Shelaḥ 112)

TALMUD BAVLI

בַּסֻּכֹּת תֵּשְׁבוּ – *You shall live in huts:* Rava taught: With this statement, the Torah commands that the Israelite leave his permanent residence and live in a temporary dwelling for seven days. And people do not make temporary dwellings taller than twenty cubits. [This is therefore the maximum height of a sukka.] (Sukka 2a) **בַּסֻּכֹּת תֵּשְׁבוּ** – *You shall live in huts:* Our Sages taught in a *baraita*: One must not dwell in a sukka that sits beneath an upper sukka, nor in one that stands beneath the branches of a tree. It is equally unacceptable to use a sukka that is constructed inside one's house. (Sukka 9a) **בַּסֻּכֹּת תֵּשְׁבוּ** – *You shall live in huts:* The Sages taught: Even though we have learned that one cannot fulfill his

seven days in the year. It shall be an everlasting statute through-
42 out your generations; celebrate this in the seventh month. For
seven days you shall live in huts. All those native born in Israel
43 must live in huts, so that future generations may know that I had
the Israelites live in huts when I brought them out of the land of

TALMUD BAVLI *(cont.)*

obligation on the first day of the festival by taking up a set of four species that belongs to someone else, the commandment to dwell in a sukka may be observed in a neighbor's booth. We learn this from the verse that states: *All those native born in Israel must live in huts [basukkot]* (23:42), which implies that the entire Israelite people could technically perform the mitzva with a single sukka. [The word *basukkot* is written here without its second *vav*; it is therefore identical to the singular form of the term, *besukkat*. This suggests that one booth could be used for *all those native born in Israel*. Now, if the value of one sukka were to be divided among the populace, no person would own a *peruta*'s worth of the structure. Hence, no one could be considered even a partial owner of that booth. Thus, the only way that the entire nation could fulfill their duty with one sukka would be to reside in a communal sukka that does not belong to any one person. We learn from here that there is no requirement to dwell specifically in one's own sukka.] (Sukka 27b) **בַּסֻּכֹּת תֵּשְׁבוּ שִׁבְעַת יָמִים** – *For seven days you shall live in huts:* Our Sages taught in a *baraita*: During the seven days of Sukkot, a person must render his sukka his permanent residence while treating his regular house as his temporary home. How should this be done? If the Israelite owns beautiful vessels, he should bring them into the hut. If he has comfortable bedding, these too should be moved into the hut. Thereafter, the family eats and drinks, relaxes in the sukka, and learns Torah there. From where is this point derived? The Sages taught in a *baraita*: The verse states: *For seven days you shall live in huts*, which means to live in the hut just as you would your house. (Sukka 27b)

VERSE 43

TALMUD BAVLI

לְמַעַן יֵדְעוּ דֹרֹתֵיכֶם – *So that future generations may know:* Rabba cited the verse that states: *So that future generations may know that I had the Israelites live in huts when I brought them out of the land of Egypt*, and taught: If a person sits in a sukka, he is aware of that fact as long as it is less than twenty cubits high. [At that size, the person can easily see the roofing.] However, if a person enters a sukka that is more than twenty cubits high, he will not be aware that he is inside a sukka because his eye does not easily see the roof. [Rabba quotes the verse because it is imperative for the Israelite to know the significance of the space he is in, something that will be difficult if he has to make a concerted effort to see the top.] (Sukka 2a) **כִּי בַסֻּכּוֹת הוֹשַׁבְתִּי אֶת־בְּנֵי יִשְׂרָאֵל** – *That I had the Israelites live in huts:* Rabbi Eliezer taught in a *baraita*: When the verse mentions the desert huts, what it really refers to are the clouds of glory that hovered over the nation. Rabbi Akiva disagreed: God actually made huts for the Israelites to live in [that is, the term "huts" should be taken literally]. (Sukka 11b)

מד בְּהוֹצִיאִי אוֹתָם מֵאֶרֶץ מִצְרָיִם אֲנִי יְהוָה אֱלֹהֵיכֶם: וַיְדַבֵּר
מֹשֶׁה אֶת־מֹעֲדֵי יְהוָה אֶל־בְּנֵי יִשְׂרָאֵל:
כד א ב וַיְדַבֵּר יְהוָה אֶל־מֹשֶׁה לֵּאמֹר: צַו אֶת־בְּנֵי יִשְׂרָאֵל וְיִקְחוּ שביעי

TANHUMA

כִּי בַסֻּכּוֹת הוֹשַׁבְתִּי אֶת־בְּנֵי יִשְׂרָאֵל – *That I had the Israelites live in huts:* Said the Holy One, blessed be He, to the people of Israel: "In this world I have commanded you to construct huts as a sign of gratitude for the shelter I provided you in the desert." This is the significance of the text that explains: *For seven days you shall live in huts… know that I had the Israelites live in huts when I brought them out of the land of Egypt.* "If you obey this directive," says God, "I will consider it as if you have repaid the favor that I did for you. Subsequently, in the next world, I will appear before you in My regality and protect you like a sukka, as the prophet predicts: *And that shelter will be shade all day from searing heat and a covering, a hiding place from the deluge, from the rain* (Isaiah 4:6)." (Buber, Emor 30)

VERSE 44

TALMUD YERUSHALMI

וַיְדַבֵּר מֹשֶׁה אֶת־מֹעֲדֵי יהוה – *Thus Moshe announced the Lord's appointed times:* Rabbi Yehuda Hanasi taught: What is the significance of the verse that states: *Thus Moshe announced the Lord's appointed times to the Israelites*? Since the Torah only explicitly states regarding the Passover sacrifice and the daily burnt offering that these must override the Sabbath, it is unclear whether the same rule applies to other communal sacrifices. [With respect to the former, the verse states: *Let the Israelites offer the Passover sacrifice at its appointed time* (Numbers 9:2). Regarding the latter, we read: *Take care to present My offering of foodstuffs – fire offerings of pleasing aroma to Me at its appointed times* – Numbers 28:2.] Thus a subsequent text states: *These you shall offer to the Lord on your festivals, in addition to your vows and freewill offerings: your burnt offerings, grain offerings, libations, and peace offerings* (29:39). Now, the matter is still unclear with respect to the *omer* and what is brought with it, and the two loaves on Shavuot and what is brought with them. However, once the text states: *Thus Moshe announced the Lord's appointed times to the Israelites*, we learn that everything is to be brought in its appointed time, even in a state of impurity. (Pesahim 7:4)

TALMUD BAVLI

וַיְדַבֵּר מֹשֶׁה אֶת־מֹעֲדֵי יהוה – *Thus Moshe announced the Lord's appointed times:* When the verse states: *Thus Moshe announced the Lord's appointed times to the Israelites*, that teaches that part of the commandment of the festivals is that the nation should publicly read the Torah portions relating to them, each one in its designated time. Our Sages taught in a *baraita*: Moshe instituted a rule whereby the people are to make halakhic inquiries and expound upon the matters of the day. Thus, Israel should occupy themselves with the laws of Passover on Passover, with the laws of Shavuot on Shavuot, and with the laws of Sukkot on Sukkot. (Megilla 32a)

44 Egypt; I am the Lord your God." Thus Moshe announced the
Lord's appointed times to the Israelites.
24 1 2 The Lord spoke to Moshe: "Command the Israelites to bring SHEVI'I
you pure oil from crushed olives for the light, to kindle the

CHAPTER 24, VERSE 2

SIFREI BEMIDBAR

צַו אֶת־בְּנֵי יִשְׂרָאֵל – *Command the Israelites:* Rabbi Shimon ben Yoḥai taught: Whenever the Torah uses the term "command," it indicates that a monetary layout is required. This is seen in the following instances: (1) *Command the Israelites to bring you pure oil from crushed olives for the light*; (2) *Command the Israelites to send away from the camp anyone who has an impure blight, or has had a discharge, or anyone made impure by contact with the dead* (Numbers 5:2); (3) *Command the Israelites to grant the Levites towns to live in, among the inheritance they will possess. Grant them also pasturelands around the towns* (35:2); and (4) *Command the Israelites; say to them: Take care to present My offering of foodstuffs – fire offerings of pleasing aroma to Me – at its appointed times* (28:2). We see that every time the verb "command" appears, there will be some expenditure involved. However, there is one exception to this rule, which is this statement regarding apportioning the land of Israel: *Command the Israelites. Say to them: As you enter the land of Canaan – this is the land that will become your possession, the land of Canaan with its borders* (34:2). Rabbi Yehuda Hanasi taught: Whenever the Torah uses the term "command," it connotes a warning, as we read: *And the Lord God commanded the man: "You are free to eat from any tree in the garden. But the Tree of Knowledge of good and evil – you may not eat from that"* (Genesis 2:16–17). (Naso 1)

VAYIKRA RABBA

צַו אֶת־בְּנֵי יִשְׂרָאֵל – *Command the Israelites:* What is implied by this praise of God [in Psalms 71:19]: *Your righteousness, God, reaches the highest heights, for You have done great things. O God, who is like You?* This refers to God's creation of the celestial spheres, as the verse states: *God made the two great lights – the greater light to rule by day and the lesser light to rule by night – and the stars* (Genesis 1:16). Who then is anything like God in the heavens, and who can possibly approximate Him on the earth? Who resembles God in His willingness to suppress His attribute of justice; and who, like the Almighty, can illuminate the skies and the ground? And even though God shines light on behalf of all the world's creatures, He still desires Israel's light, as the verse states: *Command the Israelites to bring you pure oil…for the light, to kindle the lamp, every night*. (Margaliot, Emor 31:1) צַו אֶת־בְּנֵי יִשְׂרָאֵל – *Command the Israelites:* Bar Kappara opened his discourse of this passage by citing the verse *For it is You who lights my lamp. The Lord my God lights up my darkness* (Psalms 18:29). Said the Holy One, blessed be He, to mankind: "While your lamp is in My hand, My lamp is in your hand as well. Your lamp is in My hand, as the verse states: *The Lord's lamp is a person's life* (Proverbs 20:27), whereas My lamp is in your hand, as we read: *To kindle the lamp, every night*." Thus does the Almighty promise: If Israel lights My lamp, I will light theirs, as the verse states: *Command the Israelites…* (Margaliot, Emor 31:4) וְיִקְחוּ אֵלֶיךָ – *To bring you:* Rabbi Ḥiyya taught: Israel is commanded to provide olive oil for the candelabrum. This

ג אֵלֶיךָ שֶׁמֶן זַיִת זָךְ כָּתִית לַמָּאוֹר לְהַעֲלֹת נֵר תָּמִיד׃ מִחוּץ
לְפָרֹכֶת הָעֵדֻת בְּאֹהֶל מוֹעֵד יַעֲרֹךְ אֹתוֹ אַהֲרֹן מֵעֶרֶב עַד־
ד בֹּקֶר לִפְנֵי יהוה תָּמִיד חֻקַּת עוֹלָם לְדֹרֹתֵיכֶם׃ עַל הַמְּנֹרָה
הַטְּהֹרָה יַעֲרֹךְ אֶת־הַנֵּרוֹת לִפְנֵי יהוה תָּמִיד׃
ה וְלָקַחְתָּ סֹלֶת וְאָפִיתָ אֹתָהּ שְׁתֵּים עֶשְׂרֵה חַלּוֹת שְׁנֵי עֶשְׂרֹנִים
ו יִהְיֶה הַחַלָּה הָאֶחָת׃ וְשַׂמְתָּ אוֹתָם שְׁתַּיִם מַעֲרָכוֹת שֵׁשׁ

VAYIKRA RABBA *(cont.)*

requirement cannot be fulfilled with sesame oil, walnut oil, radish oil, or almond oil, only olive oil from Israel's trees. Rabbi Avin taught: This may be compared to a king who suffered a rebellion from all his legions. Only one legion remained loyal to the monarch, whereupon the latter declared: "It is from that group of soldiers that I will now draw my generals, lieutenants, and military chiefs." Similarly did the Holy One, blessed be He, pronounce: "The olive tree brought light to the world in the time of Noaḥ," as we read: *The dove came back to him in the evening – and in its beak was a freshly picked olive leaf* (Genesis 8:11). (Margaliot, Emor 31:10) **לְהַעֲלֹת נֵר תָּמִיד** – *To kindle the lamp, every night:* Rabbi Ḥanin taught: Israel will be rewarded for lighting the perpetual lamp: They will be privileged to receive the light of the messianic king, as the psalmist pledges: *There I will make David's horn flourish; I will prepare a lamp for My anointed one* (Psalms 132:17). We further read: *I rejoiced when they said to me, "Let us go to the House of the Lord"* (Psalms 122:1). (Margaliot, Emor 31:11)

VERSE 3

TALMUD BAVLI

מִחוּץ לְפָרֹכֶת הָעֵדֻת – *Outside the curtain of the testimony:* One might ask: Why would God have any need for a candelabrum? Did He not guide the nation of Israel through the wilderness with a pillar of fire for forty years? Rather, the Tabernacle light burns as a testimony to humankind that the Divine Presence resides among the Israelites. [Hence its location outside the Holy of Holies, in the proximity of people.] And how exactly is that testimony manifested? Rav explained: That is seen in the westernmost lamp in the candelabrum. Although it was filled with the same measure of oil that the other six candles were given, nevertheless, every day the priest would light the other lamps from the flame of this one, and with it he would conclude. [The candelabrum held seven lamps, with the westernmost candle – the one closest to the Holy of Holies chamber – being exceptional. The six lamps were lit in the evening and burned through the night. In the morning, their wicks were replaced and their oil refilled in preparation for being relit the following evening. However, even though the seventh lamp was given the same amount of oil as the others, it was not extinguished in the morning but continued to burn throughout the day. When it came time to relight the entire candelabrum, the old wick of the seventh lamp, which was still burning, was used to light the flames of the other six. A new wick and additional oil were then provided for

3 lamp, every night. From evening to morning, before the Lord,
Aharon shall set it up outside the curtain of the testimony in
the Tent of Meeting to burn each night. This shall be a rule
4 for all time, throughout your generations. Aharon shall set
out the lamps on the pure candelabrum each day before the
Lord.
5 And you shall take fine flour and bake twelve loaves, two-tenths
6 of an ephah for each loaf. You shall place them in two columns,

TALMUD BAVLI *(cont.)*

the westernmost lamp, and it too was relit. This is what the Talmud means when it states that the priest concluded the arranging of the lamps with the seventh candle.] (Shabbat 22b)

VERSE 4

LEKAḤ TOV

לִפְנֵי יהוה תָּמִיד – *Each day before the Lord:* Why does the Torah juxtapose this description of the lamps with its discussion of the festivals [which appears in chapter 23]? It is based on this that our Sages maintain that there is an obligation to light candles before the Sabbath. This is why the text connects the candelabrum to the Sabbath and the holidays. (67b)

VERSE 5

PHILO

שְׁתֵּים עֶשְׂרֵה חַלּוֹת – *Twelve loaves:* The twelve loaves are placed upon the sacred table into two equal parts of six. They are placed as a memorial of the tribes, which are of a corresponding number: one half of whom, virtue, that is Leah, received as her share, having become the mother of six leaders of tribes, and the other half fell to Rachel's children and those of the other women.

TALMUD BAVLI

וְלָקַחְתָּ סֹלֶת וְאָפִיתָ אֹתָהּ – *And you shall take fine flour and bake it:* The flour of the *omer* was sifted with thirteen sifters [each one finer than the one before. It was the flour that emerged from the final sieve that was sacrificed]. The flour of the two Shavuot loaves was put through twelve sifters, and the flour of the showbread was sifted using eleven sifters. Rabbi Shimon taught: There was no fixed number of sifters for these loaves. Rather, fine flour that was completely sifted would be brought for all these offerings, as the verse states: *And you shall take fine flour and bake it,* indicating that they were required to sift the flour completely. (Menaḥot 76b)

VERSE 6

TALMUD BAVLI

עַל הַשֻּׁלְחָן הַטָּהֹר – *On the pure table:* Reish Lakish taught: What is the significance of the phrase *on the pure table before the Lord*? The verse thereby implies that the table can become impure [and hence the priests must ensure that it is pure before the twelve loaves

ז הַמַּעֲרֶכֶת עַל הַשֻּׁלְחָן הַטָּהֹר לִפְנֵי יְהוָה: וְנָתַתָּ עַל־
הַמַּעֲרֶכֶת לְבֹנָה זַכָּה וְהָיְתָה לַלֶּחֶם לְאַזְכָּרָה אִשֶּׁה לַיהוָה:
ח בְּיוֹם הַשַּׁבָּת בְּיוֹם הַשַּׁבָּת יַעַרְכֶנּוּ לִפְנֵי יְהוָה תָּמִיד מֵאֵת
ט בְּנֵי־יִשְׂרָאֵל בְּרִית עוֹלָם: וְהָיְתָה לְאַהֲרֹן וּלְבָנָיו וַאֲכָלֻהוּ
בְּמָקוֹם קָדֹשׁ כִּי קֹדֶשׁ קָדָשִׁים הוּא לוֹ מֵאִשֵּׁי יְהוָה חָק־
י עוֹלָם: וַיֵּצֵא בֶּן־אִשָּׁה יִשְׂרְאֵלִית וְהוּא בֶּן־
אִישׁ מִצְרִי בְּתוֹךְ בְּנֵי יִשְׂרָאֵל וַיִּנָּצוּ בַּמַּחֲנֶה בֶּן הַיִּשְׂרְאֵלִית

TALMUD BAVLI *(cont.)*

are placed on it]. Still, how can the table be susceptible to ritual impurity considering that it is a wooden vessel designated to rest in a fixed place and, as such, should not be subject to impurity? [This law is based on an analysis of Leviticus 11:32, which asserts that for a utensil to be subject to impurity, it must resemble a sack that is movable when it is both empty and full.] The table was occasionally moved from its spot in the Temple: It was lifted in order to display the bread to the pilgrims who had assembled in the Temple courtyard, whereupon the priests would declare: "Behold the affection with which the Almighty holds you! For God performs a weekly miracle at this table in that the bread remains as fresh when it is removed from the utensil as it was when it was placed there seven days ago." This point was taught by Rabbi Yehoshua ben Levi, who said: A great miracle was performed with the twelve loaves of showbread: They retained the same state when they were replaced as they had when they were placed. And so do we read: *So the priest gave him what was sacred, for there was no bread there but the showbread that had been removed from the Lord's presence and replaced with hot, fresh bread as soon it was taken away [ḥom beyom hillakeḥo: literally, "hot on the day it was taken away"]* (I Samuel 21:7). [This indicates that the bread David took was as hot on the day of its removal as it was when it was first baked. Hence, because the table was moved to demonstrate the fantastic nature of its bread to the populace, the rule that prevents fixed wooden vessels from becoming impure did not apply to the showbread table.] (Ḥagiga 26b)

VERSE 7

TALMUD BAVLI

וְנָתַתָּ עַל־הַמַּעֲרֶכֶת לְבֹנָה זַכָּה – *Lay pure incense on each stack:* It was taught in a *baraita*: With regard to the verse that states: *Lay pure incense on [al] each stack*, Rabbi Yehuda Hanasi taught: In this context, the preposition *al* means "adjacent to." On the other hand, perhaps the word should be understood in accordance with its literal meaning, "on." Consider the earlier text which reads: *Put in it the Ark of the Testimony, and screen [vesakkota al] the Ark with the curtain* (Exodus 40:3). [In that instance, the term *al* cannot possibly mean "on" since the curtain that separated the Sanctuary from the Holy of Holies was not placed on top of the Ark, but near it.] Here too we should say that *al* means "adjacent to." (Sota 37a)

7 six to each column, on the pure table before the Lord. Lay
pure incense on each stack, as a remembrance for the bread, as
8 a fire offering to the Lord. Every Sabbath he shall set it out, always, before the Lord on behalf of the Israelites: an everlasting
9 covenant. It shall belong to Aharon and his sons. They shall eat
it in a holy place because it is holy of holies among the Lord's
10 fire offerings, their perpetual share." A man went out
among the Israelites, the son of an Israelite woman and an
Egyptian man. And a fight broke out in the camp between

VERSE 8

LEKAḤ TOV

בְּיוֹם הַשַּׁבָּת בְּיוֹם הַשַּׁבָּת – *Every Sabbath:* Every Sabbath, Aharon would arrange the new incense and burn the substance from the previous week. **יַעַרְכֶנּוּ** – *He shall set it out:* This refers to the breads, not the poles. Rather, on Sabbath eve the priest would enter the Sanctuary, pull out the rods, and arrange them along the length of the table. After the Sabbath, Aharon would enter again and lay three rods beneath each loaf, except for the top loaves, which had two poles beneath them. [Thus each set of six loaves had a total of fourteen rods, for a total of twenty-eight dividers.] What was the purpose of these rods? They were inserted between the loaves to prevent the hot bread from becoming moldy. [The gap created by pushing the breads apart allowed air to circulate, thereby preventing mold from growing on the loaves.] Neither the arranging of the rods for the new showbread, nor their removal from the arrangement of the old showbread, overrides the Sabbath. [Thus the poles were removed from between the loaves before sundown on Friday. Then, on the Sabbath, the priest would place the new showbread on the table without the separating rods. These would be inserted between the new loaves at the conclusion of the Sabbath.] (68a)

VERSE 10

MEKHILTA DERABBI YISHMAEL

בֶּן־אִשָּׁה יִשְׂרְאֵלִית – *The son of an Israelite woman:* How do we know that in general the Israelites could not be suspected of licentiousness? For the verse states that *a man went out among the Israelites, the son of an Israelite woman and an Egyptian man*. This description is to the credit of the nation, for it stresses that this was the only Israelite woman who had relations with an outsider. (Massekhta Defisḥa 5)

TANḤUMA

וְהוּא בֶּן־אִישׁ מִצְרִי – *The son of... an Egyptian man:* In an earlier episode, the text reports: *One day, when Moshe had grown up, he went out to his people and saw their forced labor. And he noticed an Egyptian striking a Hebrew: one of his brothers* (Exodus 2:11). Who was that taskmaster? He was the father of the blasphemer, as the verse states: *A man went out among the Israelites, the son of an Israelite woman and an Egyptian man*. Thus the man whom Moshe slew was the husband of Shlomit daughter of Divri. Now, this taskmaster was in charge of 110 Israelites, and he would drive them out to work at the crack of dawn. And since the Egyptian

יא וְאִישׁ הַיִּשְׂרְאֵלִי: וַיִּקֹּב בֶּן־הָאִשָּׁה הַיִּשְׂרְאֵלִית אֶת־הַשֵּׁם
וַיְקַלֵּל וַיָּבִיאוּ אֹתוֹ אֶל־מֹשֶׁה וְשֵׁם אִמּוֹ שְׁלֹמִית בַּת־
יב דִּבְרִי לְמַטֵּה־דָן: וַיַּנִּיחֻהוּ בַּמִּשְׁמָר לִפְרֹשׁ לָהֶם עַל־פִּי
יְהוָה:

TANḤUMA *(cont.)*

was accustomed to rousing and fetching his workforce, he made himself comfortable in the Israelites' homes. This was how the man became aware of Shlomit daughter of Divri, who was a beautiful and perfect [*shelema*] woman. Since he was enamored with her, he devised a scheme to lie with her. One day, after forcing Shlomit's husband off to work, he circled back to the house and climbed into bed with the wife, while she believed it was her husband who had returned to her. When the Israelite eventually did come home, he found the taskmaster leaving the house and demanded of his wife: "Did that Egyptian touch you at all?" "He did," confessed Shlomit, "but I mistook him for you." Once the seducer realized that his behavior had been exposed, he ordered the husband to return to his labor, where the Egyptian proceeded to beat him. Meanwhile, Moshe understood the entire situation through the Divine Spirit and accosted the taskmaster, saying: "Is it not enough that you violated the man's wife, but you now are beating him to death as well?" Thus the verse states: *Looking this way and that and seeing no one [vayar ki ein ish: also, "he saw that there was no man"], he struck down the Egyptian and hid his body in the sand* (Exodus 2:12). What did Moshe see? He understood that the Egyptian was no longer a man since he deserved to be killed for his crimes. (Shemot 9)

VAYIKRA RABBA

וַיֵּצֵא בֶּן־אִשָּׁה יִשְׂרְאֵלִית – *A man went out, the son of an Israelite woman:* Rabbi Levi taught: The man went out from this world [meaning, he surrendered his life]. We find a similar use in the verse that reads: *Then the champion of the Philistine forces came forth; his name was Golyat, of Gat, and he was six cubits and a span tall* (I Samuel 17:4). Rabbi Berekhya, however, said: The man went out [that is, distanced himself] from the previous passage, which states: *And you shall take fine flour and bake twelve loaves* (Leviticus 24:5). Said this Israelite: "Any normal king would insist upon being served freshly baked bread on a daily basis. Would any self-respecting monarch eat stale bread? And yet, we learn in a Mishna [in Menaḥot 100b]: The showbread is eaten no less than nine days and no more than eleven days after it is baked." Rabbi Ḥiyya offered a third interpretation: The man went out in anger due to the Torah's positions about lineage. For initially, this person tried to pitch his tent in the camp of the tribe of Dan. But the citizens of Dan confronted him: "What do you mean by moving here with us?" Said he: "Well, I am a member of this tribe, am I not?" "No, you are not," said they, "for the text states: *The Israelites shall camp, each by his banner, the ensign of his ancestral house [leveit avotam: literally, 'according to their fathers' houses']* (Numbers 2:2). [In the present instance, the man's mother hailed from the tribe of Dan, but his father was Egyptian.] Thus the tribal association follows the father's lineage, not that of the mother." Not content with this treatment, the Israelite took the matter to Moshe's court. However, when the prophet ruled against the plaintiff, he stood up and blasphemed God. (Margaliot, Emor 32:3)

11 this son of an Israelite woman, and an Israelite man. The Israelite woman's son blasphemed the Name and cursed – his
mother's name was Shlomit, daughter of Divri, of the tribe of
12 Dan – and they brought him before Moshe. They placed the
man in custody until the LORD's verdict would be pronounced
to them.

VERSE 11

SHEMOT RABBA

וְשֵׁם אִמּוֹ שְׁלֹמִית בַּת־דִּבְרִי – *His mother's name was Shlomit, daughter of Divri:* Earlier we read: *Then Moshe said to the Israelites, "Know that the LORD has summoned by name Betzalel, son of Uri, son of Ḥur, of the tribe of Yehuda"* (Exodus 35:30). There are some people who are mentioned and blessed. Consider the subsequent verse that states: *Together with Oholiav, son of Aḥisamakh of the tribe of Dan* (35:34). The selection of Oholiav was a credit to him, his father, his family, and his entire tribe. On the other hand, there are some people who are mentioned and cursed. Such is the case of the blasphemer, who is identified in our verse: *The Israelite woman's son blasphemed the Name and cursed – his mother's name was Shlomit, daughter of Divri, of the tribe of Dan*. In this instance, the man's mother was a disgrace to her father, her family, and her entire tribe. (Vayakhel 48:1)

YALKUT SHIMONI

אֶת־הַשֵּׁם – *The Name:* This refers to the ineffable name of God, which the offender had heard at Mount Sinai. Note that the text states explicitly that the Israelite cursed, avoiding the euphemism that we find in this later text: *Navot has "blessed" God and the king!* (I Kings 21:13). We learn from here that a blasphemer many not be killed based on indirect testimony. [That is, witnesses who were present for the declaration may not say: "We heard So-and-so bless God"; rather, they must say: "We heard him curse God."] Furthermore, a transgressor will only be held accountable if he utters the actual name of God. (Emor 658)

VERSE 12

LEKAḤ TOV

וַיַּנִּיחֻהוּ בַּמִּשְׁמָר – *They placed the man in custody:* The blasphemer was not put in the same stockade with the wood gatherer [a Sabbath violator whose tale is told in Numbers 15:32–36], despite the fact that the two men committed their offenses at the same time. This was because it was clear that the wood gatherer was to be executed, since the text clearly states: *Keep the Sabbath, for it is holy to you. Whoever profanes it shall be put to death. Whoever does work on it shall be severed from his people* (Exodus 31:14). The only uncertainty in that instance was what method of capital punishment was to be used, as the verse reads: *And he was placed in custody, because it had not been specified what should be done to him* (Numbers 15:34). However, in the present case the confusion was different, as our verse states: *They placed the man in custody until the LORD's verdict would be pronounced to them*. Here, the people did not know whether the sinner deserved to be executed by his peers or whether God would kill him. (68b)

יג-יד וַיְדַבֵּר יהוה אֶל־מֹשֶׁה לֵּאמֹר: הוֹצֵא אֶת־הַמְקַלֵּל אֶל־
מִחוּץ לַמַּחֲנֶה וְסָמְכוּ כָל־הַשֹּׁמְעִים אֶת־יְדֵיהֶם עַל־רֹאשׁוֹ
טו וְרָגְמוּ אֹתוֹ כָּל־הָעֵדָה: וְאֶל־בְּנֵי יִשְׂרָאֵל תְּדַבֵּר לֵאמֹר
טז אִישׁ אִישׁ כִּי־יְקַלֵּל אֱלֹהָיו וְנָשָׂא חֶטְאוֹ: וְנֹקֵב שֵׁם־
יהוה מוֹת יוּמָת רָגוֹם יִרְגְּמוּ־בוֹ כָּל־הָעֵדָה כַּגֵּר כָּאֶזְרָח
יז בְּנָקְבוֹ־שֵׁם יוּמָת: וְאִישׁ כִּי יַכֶּה כָּל־נֶפֶשׁ אָדָם מוֹת יוּמָת:

VERSE 14

MISHNA

הוֹצֵא אֶת־הַמְקַלֵּל – *Take the one who cursed outside:* The site where criminals were stoned was situated at a remove from the court, as the verse states: *Take the one who cursed outside the camp*. [The purpose of this distance was to allow some time to elapse between the issuance of the verdict and the execution. It was hoped that in the interim, some witnesses might arrive whose favorable testimony could save the convicted from death.] (Sanhedrin 6:1)

TALMUD BAVLI

וְרָגְמוּ אֹתוֹ כָּל־הָעֵדָה – *And then the whole community shall stone him:* A man is stoned naked but a woman is not stoned naked. What is the reason for this distinction? For the verse states: *And then the whole community shall stone him*. Now, what is the significance of the term "him" [that is, what does it exclude]? We cannot suggest that only he [a man] can be stoned but that she [a woman] cannot be stoned, since a later text reads: *Then you shall take the man or woman who has done this evil act out to the town gates and stone that man or that woman to death* (Deuteronomy 17:5). Rather, the word "him" serves to exclude the condemned man's clothes: He is executed without his garments. [That is, only *he* is killed, in his natural state.] By contrast, this law does not apply to a woman: She is not stoned without her clothes on. (Sota 23b)

VERSE 15

MEKHILTA DERABBI YISHMAEL

אִישׁ אִישׁ כִּי־יְקַלֵּל – *Anyone who curses:* An earlier verse states: *One who curses his father or mother shall be put to death* (Exodus 21:17), which corresponds to this text: *Anyone who curses his God shall bear the sin*. The Torah thus equates cursing one's father and mother with blaspheming God. (Massekhta Devaḥodesh 8)

TALMUD BAVLI

אִישׁ אִישׁ כִּי־יְקַלֵּל – *Anyone who curses:* It was taught in a *baraita*: Why must the verse state: *Anyone who curses his God shall bear the sin*, considering that the text subsequently asserts: *And anyone who blasphemes the Lord's name shall be put to death* (24:16)? Based on the second verse alone, we might have thought that a person will only be liable for cursing the ineffable name of God [that is, the Tetragrammaton]. How do we know that

13 14 And the LORD spoke to Moshe: "Take the one who cursed
outside the camp. All the people who heard him shall lay their
hands on his head – and then the whole community shall stone
15 him. Tell the Israelites: Anyone who curses his God shall bear
16 the sin, and anyone who blasphemes the LORD's name shall be
put to death: the whole community shall stone him. Migrant
and native born alike: one who blasphemes the LORD's name
17 shall be put to death. One who takes the life of any human being

TALMUD BAVLI *(cont.)*

a person will similarly incur guilt if he curses using any of the other appellations as well? [The word *kinuyim*, nicknames, refers to such terms as *Raḥum*, the Merciful One, or *Ḥanun*, the Gracious One.] We learn this from the previous verse, which says: *Anyone who curses his God*, indicating that one is liable in all cases. This is the opinion of Rabbi Meir. By contrast, according to the Sages, one who curses using the ineffable name of God is liable to receive capital punishment, whereas one who curses one of God's appellations is subject to lashes for violating a prohibition. (Sanhedrin 56a)

VERSE 16

TALMUD BAVLI

בְּנָקְבוֹ־שֵׁם יוּמָת – *One who blasphemes the LORD's name shall be put to death:* It was taught in a *baraita*: Rabbi Menaḥem son of Rabbi Yosei taught: Why does the verse include the term "name" [in the final clause, where it could have simply said that one who blasphemes shall be put to death]? This serves to teach that a person who curses his father or mother will only be liable for execution if he does so using God's ineffable name. (Sanhedrin 66a)

LEKAḤ TOV

מוֹת יוּמָת – *Shall be put to death:* In the event that the offender cannot be executed by the prescribed means, the people are allowed to kill him in any other fashion. **רָגוֹם יִרְגְּמוּ־בוֹ כָּל־הָעֵדָה** – *The whole community shall stone him:* The entire populace shall act as the sinner's accusers [that is, they shall all despise him. Since the verse's instruction cannot possibly be fulfilled literally, the congregation is given the task of hating the offender]. (69a)

VERSE 17

TALMUD BAVLI

וְאִישׁ כִּי יַכֶּה כָּל־נֶפֶשׁ אָדָם – *One who takes the life of any human being:* [The verse as understood literally, and as translated here, describes a murder and an execution of the killer as his punishment. However, the Talmud maintains that the text is in fact dealing with an injury that one person causes another. Based on this approach, the text seems to suggest that if person A severs a limb from person B, the attacker's own body part is removed in return. This interpretation too is rejected, as follows:] One who commits such an offense must make a financial restitution to his victim. But perhaps the text does not demand a monetary payment but the actual death of the limb [that is, its amputation]. No, we cannot think so, for two reasons. First, verse 17, which talks about striking a person

וּמַכֵּה נֶפֶשׁ־בְּהֵמָה יְשַׁלְּמֶנָּה נֶפֶשׁ תַּחַת נָפֶשׁ׃ וְאִישׁ כִּי־יִתֵּן יח יט
מוּם בַּעֲמִיתוֹ כַּאֲשֶׁר עָשָׂה כֵּן יֵעָשֶׂה לּוֹ׃ שֶׁבֶר תַּחַת שֶׁבֶר כ
עַיִן תַּחַת עַיִן שֵׁן תַּחַת שֵׁן כַּאֲשֶׁר יִתֵּן מוּם בָּאָדָם כֵּן יִנָּתֶן
מפטיר בּוֹ׃ וּמַכֵּה בְהֵמָה יְשַׁלְּמֶנָּה וּמַכֵּה אָדָם יוּמָת׃ מִשְׁפַּט אֶחָד כא כב

TALMUD BAVLI *(cont.)*

[*ve'ish ki yakkeh kol nefesh adam*: literally, "if one smites the soul of a person"], is compared to the striking of an animal in verse 18 [*umakkeh nefesh behema*, "if one smites the soul of a beast." Since verse 21, which refers to *one who kills an animal*, refers to the actual death of an animal, verse 18 is taken as describing injuring an animal rather than killing it. Hence, verse 17 too deals with merely wounding a person, which is not a capital offense]. Second, the subsequent verse states: *Just as he inflicted injury on another human being, so shall he suffer the loss [ken yinnaten bo: literally, "so shall he be given"]*. [The argument here refers to a later discussion in the Talmud, which claims that the verb "give" connotes handing over money from one person to another.] We must therefore conclude that verse 17 demands payment. (Bava Kamma 83b) **וְאִישׁ כִּי יַכֶּה כָּל־נֶפֶשׁ אָדָם** – *One who takes the life of any human being:* Our Sages taught in a *baraita*: If ten men beat a person with ten different sticks, and the victim dies as a result of the attack, the mob is exempt for killing him [since no one person can be said to have been the murderer. This is bolstered by our verse, which stresses: *One who takes the life*]. This is so whether the miscreants struck the man all at once or one after the other. However, Rabbi Yehuda ben Beteira rules that if the pack struck the person one after the other, the villain who delivers the last blow is held accountable because he hastened [or completed] the victim's death. Rabbi Yoḥanan taught: Both of these approaches are based on the same verse: *One who takes the life of any human being [kol nefesh: literally, "any soul"] shall be put to death*. According to the Sages, the term teaches that one is only liable for murder when he takes the entire soul [also, *kol nefesh*, "all of the soul," that is, when the killer alone is responsible for the complete loss of life]. By contrast, Rabbi Yehuda ben Beteira maintains that a person can be held accountable for taking any part of a soul [even if the person has already been beaten and is close to death. The reader should note that even though the previous text from Bava Kamma 83b treats this verse as a description of injury, the present passage acknowledges that the straightforward meaning of the Torah cannot be entirely dismissed. Thus, on one level the lesson about murder can still be derived from verse 17 without conflicting with an alternative interpretation that bypasses the literal meaning of the text]. (Sanhedrin 78a)

VERSE 18

TALMUD BAVLI

וּמַכֵּה נֶפֶשׁ־בְּהֵמָה – *One who takes the life of an animal:* Our Sages taught in a *baraita*: The owner of the injured animal attends to [that is, he retains ownership of] the animal carcass [and if he wishes to, he may sell it and keep the proceeds]. What is the source of this ruling? Rabbi Ami explained: The point is based on the verse that states: *One who takes the life of an animal shall make restitution for it [yeshallemenna]*. Now, this should not be read as

18 shall be put to death. One who takes the life of an animal shall
19 make restitution for it: life for life. One who injures his fellow
20 man shall be penalized in proportion to the injury inflicted: the
cost of a broken bone for a broken bone, of an eye for an eye, of
a tooth for a tooth. Just as he inflicted injury on another human
21 being, so shall he suffer the loss. One who kills an animal shall MAFTIR
make restitution for it; but one who kills a human being shall
22 be put to death. There shall be one law for you, for migrant and

TALMUD BAVLI *(cont.)*

yeshallemenna [meaning "he shall pay money for it," such that the owner can take what he has paid for]. Rather, the word should be pronounced *yashlimenna* ["he shall complete it." Thus the animal attacker must complete the injured party's ownership, which is already partially accounted for by the right to keep and perhaps sell his animal's body]. (Bava Kamma 10b)

VERSE 20

LEKAḤ TOV

שֶׁבֶר תַּחַת שֶׁבֶר – *The cost of a broken bone for a broken bone:* Is it not possible that all these rules are meant to be taken literally? No, it is not. Consider, for example, the case of a blind man who pokes out somebody else's eye. How exactly can the thug be punished with *an eye for an eye*? Hence, we must conclude that the verse has monetary compensation in mind when it states: *Just as he inflicted injury on another human being, so shall he suffer the loss [ken yinnaten bo: literally, "so shall he be given"]*. The verb *netina* ["giving"] here should be compared with an earlier use of the term: *If two men fight and one of them hits a pregnant woman, and she miscarries but suffers no irreparable injury herself, the offender must be fined, as the woman's husband demands and as the judges rule [venatan biflilim, "according to what the judges give, hand down"]* (Exodus 21:22). Just as in that case, the punishment is a monetary one, so too here the attacker must pay for his assault. Furthermore, a later text states: *You may not accept a ransom for the life of a murderer found guilty of a capital crime; he must be put to death* (Numbers 35:31), meaning that although a murderer may not absolve his guilt through payment, one who injures the body of another may do so. (69a)

VERSE 22

TALMUD BAVLI

מִשְׁפַּט אֶחָד יִהְיֶה לָכֶם – *There shall be one law for you:* Rabbi Ḥanina taught: According to Torah law, both monetary and capital offenses should require investigation and interrogation [of witnesses], as the verse states: *There shall be one law for you*. [Thus, the legal procedures should be the same regardless of the type of case presented to the court.] Why then did the Sages rule that monetary cases do not require the vigorous interrogation of witnesses? They waived this procedure so as not to discourage potential lenders of money. [If the process of litigation in cases of monetary disputes was too demanding, people would hesitate to lend money to prospective borrowers.] (Yevamot 122b)

כג יִהְיֶה לָכֶם כַּגֵּר כָּאֶזְרָח יִהְיֶה כִּי אֲנִי יְהֹוָה אֱלֹהֵיכֶם: וַיְדַבֵּר
מֹשֶׁה אֶל־בְּנֵי יִשְׂרָאֵל וַיּוֹצִיאוּ אֶת־הַמְקַלֵּל אֶל־מִחוּץ
לַמַּחֲנֶה וַיִּרְגְּמוּ אֹתוֹ אָבֶן וּבְנֵי־יִשְׂרָאֵל עָשׂוּ כַּאֲשֶׁר צִוָּה
יְהֹוָה אֶת־מֹשֶׁה:

LEKAḤ TOV

אֲנִי יהוה – *I am the Lord:* Says God: I am privy to the confidential deliberations of your court, as the verse states: *God stands in the divine assembly; among divine beings He delivers judgment* (Psalms 82:1). The verse contains three instances of God's name, which teaches that the Divine Presence rests upon a court of three judges. [The author apparently counts the clause of *ani Adonai Eloheikhem* as three different mentions of God's name, with *ani*, "I am," being the first.] (69b)

VERSE 23

SIFREI BEMIDBAR

וַיִּרְגְּמוּ אֹתוֹ אָבֶן – *And stoned him:* With regard to the wood gatherer on the Sabbath, the text concludes: *And so, as the Lord had commanded Moshe, the whole community took him outside the camp and stoned him to death [vayirgemu oto baavanim: literally, "and they stoned him with stones"]* (Numbers 15:36). Compare that to the verse that states: *And so they took the blasphemer outside the camp and stoned him* [*vayirgemu oto aven:* literally, "and they stoned

23 for native born alike, for I am the Lord your God." Moshe told
this to the Israelites, and so they took the blasphemer outside
the camp and stoned him. Thus the Israelites did as the Lord
had commanded Moshe.

SIFREI BEMIDBAR *(cont.)*

him with a stone"]. How can we understand this disparity? The place where criminals were stoned to death was a platform that stood twice the height of an average person. One of the witnesses who testified against the offender pushes him over the edge by his hips so that he falls face up onto the ground. If the condemned person has turned over onto his chest [with his face downward], the witness turns him over onto his hips. If the person dies through his fall to the ground, the obligation to stone the transgressor is fulfilled. But if he has not died from the fall, the second witness takes the stone that has been prepared for the execution and drops it on his chest. If the person dies with the casting of this first stone, the obligation to stone him has been fulfilled. But if he does not, his stoning is completed by all the Israelites who are present, as the verse demands: *The hand of the witnesses shall be the first against him to kill him, and after theirs, the hand of all the people. You must purge the evil from your midst* (Deuteronomy 17:7). In this way, both the instruction to stone the lawbreaker with one stone and the instruction to kill him with multiple stones are fulfilled. (Shelaḥ 114)

10TH CENTURY

11TH CENTURY

RASHI, 1040 – 1105, FRANCE

12TH CENTURY

RASHBAM, 1080 – 1160, FRANCE

RABBI AVRAHAM IBN EZRA, 1089, SPAIN – 1164, ENGLAND

RABBI YOSEF BEKHOR SHOR, 12TH CENTURY, FRANCE

13TH CENTURY

RAMBAN, 1194, SPAIN – 1270, ISRAEL

RABBI ḤIZKIYA BEN MANOAḤ – *ḤIZKUNI*, 13TH CENTURY, FRANCE

14TH CENTURY

RABBEINU BAḤYA BEN ASHER, 1255 – 1340, SPAIN

RALBAG, 1288 – 1344, PROVENCE

15TH CENTURY

RABBI YITZḤAK ABARBANEL, 1437, PORTUGAL – 1508, ITALY

16TH CENTURY

RABBI OVADYA SFORNO, 1475 – 1550, ITALY

17TH CENTURY

RABBI SHLOMO EFRAYIM LUNTSCHITZ – *KELI YAKAR*, 1550, POLAND – 1619, BOHEMIA

פרשת אמר

PARASHAT EMOR

THE **CLASSIC** COMMENTATORS

כא א וַיֹּאמֶר יהוה אֶל־מֹשֶׁה אֱמֹר אֶל־הַכֹּהֲנִים בְּנֵי אַהֲרֹן וְאָמַרְתָּ יז

CHAPTER 21, VERSE 1

RASHI

אֱמֹר אֶל־הַכֹּהֲנִים – *Speak to the priests:* God instructs Moshe to both "speak to the priests" and to "say." The two verbs imply that adult priests are responsible [not only for keeping the purity laws themselves but] also for ensuring their observance by their minor sons. **בְּנֵי אַהֲרֹן** – *Aharon's sons:* Does the prohibition against becoming impure from a corpse extend to *ḥalalim*? [A *ḥalal* is one born from the unlawful union of a priest to a woman he is forbidden to marry, such as a divorcée. The *ḥalal* enjoys no privileges of the priesthood, and is subject to none of its restrictions, as Rashi's present comment notes.] No, for the verse uses the term "the priests" [thus including only priests who have not lost their status]. **בְּנֵי אַהֲרֹן** – *Aharon's sons:* These words are stated to include in the prohibition even those priests who are blemished. **בְּנֵי אַהֲרֹן** – *Aharon's sons:* However, the daughters of Aharon are not warned to avoid impurity. **לֹא־יִטַּמָּא בְּעַמָּיו** – *No one of you shall render himself impure among his people:* The restriction applies as long as the corpse remains "among his people" [that is, the dead person is being tended to by his or her fellow Israelites]. This excludes a *met mitzva*. [The term refers to a dead person who has no relatives or friends to bury him. It is incumbent upon every Israelite, including priests, to tend to this corpse.]

IBN EZRA

אֱמֹר אֶל־הַכֹּהֲנִים – *Speak to the priests:* Once the Torah has issued a general order for the Israelites and the sons of Aharon, who are a part of that collective, to strive toward holiness, the priests are now addressed directly. Since these men functioned as the servants of God, they were bound by specific restrictions. It is possible that the command "Speak to the priests" refers [not to the following verses, but rather] to the previous passage [Parashat Kedoshim, chapters 19–20], for the priests were entrusted with the Torah. [Hence it was the priests' responsibility to teach the material discussed above to the people. According to this reading, the proper translation of the verse would be: "Tell all this to the priests, Aharon's sons. And say: etc."]

BEKHOR SHOR

אֱמֹר אֶל־הַכֹּהֲנִים – *Speak to the priests:* At the end of the previous *parasha*, the text explored the difference between Israel and the nations of the world, when it stated: *I am the Lord your God, who has set you apart from all other peoples. You, then, shall set pure apart from impure animals, pure from impure birds* (20:24–25). Accordingly, Israelites were required to separate themselves from crawling and creeping creatures, from lepers, *zavim*, and *zavot*, from non-kosher beasts, and from other instances of impurity which were not prohibited to gentiles. And now, the text addresses the division between the priestly class and the average Israelite. For the priests alone must avoid contact with the human dead, aside from the five relatives who are listed here. However, the non-priest is permitted to become impure in order to bury and to attend to any dead person.

21 1 The LORD said to Moshe, "Speak to the priests, Aharon's sons.
Say: No one of you shall render himself impure for any dead

RAMBAN

אֱמֹר אֶל־הַכֹּהֲנִים – *Speak to the priests:* In my opinion, the verb *emor* ["say"] has the same connotation as *dabber* ["speak." The usual distinction between the two terms is that *dibbur* represents a general conveying of information, whereas *amira* refers to stating particular points. In the present context, the combination of *emor ve'amarta* is equivalent to *dabber*]. Thus, we find the verse which states: *Give ear to my words [amarai], LORD* [Psalms 5:2, where we would have expected the noun *devarai*].... Now, in many cases, when the Torah uses this formula: *Speak [dabber] to the Israelites. Say [ve'amarta] to them* (Leviticus 1:2), its purpose is to introduce a serious warning about a matter or to underscore the severity of the topic. Alternatively, such language signals an issue regarding which the people are prone to sin. This is the sense of the present instance: *Speak to the priests, Aharon's sons. Say: No one of you shall render himself impure* [thereby stressing that the laws which follow are extremely important]. Thus, the meaning of the verse is similar to God's command: *Speak to the Israelites. Say to them*, which suggests: Address the nation in My name and convey to them the following information. We find an explicit statement to this effect in the earlier verse which reads: *Then the LORD said to Moshe, "Go to Pharaoh and say [ve'amarta] to him: This is what the LORD says: Send My people forth, so that they may serve Me"* (Exodus 7:26). Now many commentators will argue that the formula "Speak to the Israelites" connotes a call to the people to assemble as one: Summon the masses to you so that you can teach them this material. Here too, the suggestion is that "Speak to the priests" means: Gather the priests together so that they may hear what you have to say. Now the reason that God tells Moshe to address "the priests" [instead of "Aharon and his sons"] is this: When God relates the laws of the sacrifices, the text does indeed use the conventional language of "Aharon and his sons" without identifying them as priests. This is because the emphasis there is the sanctity of the offerings or the exalted state of the Tabernacle. Here, however, when the Torah forbids these men from ever contracting impurity from a corpse, even when they are not scheduled to enter the Sanctuary, the focus is on the importance of the men themselves. This is why the text refers to them as "priests," as if to say: It is because these people are the priests of the LORD and the officials of our God that they are required to always behave with the utmost dignity, which means not coming into contact with the dead.

ABARBANEL

אֱמֹר אֶל־הַכֹּהֲנִים – *Speak to the priests:* The combination of the two verbs in this sentence – *Speak to the priests...say*, relates to the effect that the death of a loved one has on his or her relative. Due to the intense feelings of love and attachment that one might harbor for a friend, it will often be extremely difficult to bid goodbye to the deceased person. This is why the sons of Aharon, the priests, are repeatedly warned about how careful they must be not to contract impurity from *any dead person among [their] people*.... The text intentionally uses the term *nefesh* in this verse [*lenefesh lo yittamma* – "he shall not become impure for a soul"] in order to emphasize that it makes no difference whether

ב אֲלֵהֶם לְנֶפֶשׁ לֹא־יִטַּמָּא בְּעַמָּיו: כִּי אִם־לִשְׁאֵרוֹ הַקָּרֹב אֵלָיו
ג לְאִמּוֹ וּלְאָבִיו וְלִבְנוֹ וּלְבִתּוֹ וּלְאָחִיו: וְלַאֲחֹתוֹ הַבְּתוּלָה

ABARBANEL *(cont.)*

the deceased is a king of Israel, a sage endowed with outstanding wisdom, or a simple and ignorant commoner. Whenever anybody dies, the priest has to avoid the body so as not to render himself impure. At that point, the status, the greatness, or the wisdom that the person had in his life is of no significance in this regard – once the man's soul has become separated from his body, the priest must be wary of the impurity that the latter conveys. God thereby informs the priests that because their own souls are holy and cleave to the Lord, it behooves them to safeguard that sanctity to a much higher degree than the average Israelite does. This is so even though every citizen of our nation possesses inherent holiness; the sacred aspect of the priests' souls is more intense than that of the rest of the populace. That then is the sense of the command *lenefesh lo yittamma be'amav* [now to be read as: "For the protection of the priest's soul, it should not become impure due to an Israelite"]. Since the soul of the priest bears an exalted level of perfection and sanctity, it would be inappropriate for him to become impure due to the death of one of the people. Instead, it would be proper for a non-priest Israelite to bury the corpse, whereas the attendants of the Temple, the priests who approach the Almighty, ought to remain in a state of holiness that befits the sanctity and perfection of their souls. This reading is similar to that of a later verse which states: *You saw no image when the Lord spoke to you at Ḥorev out of the fire, and so take great care for your own sake* [*lenafshoteikhem*, literally, "for your souls"] (Deuteronomy 4:15) – in our context too, the word *lenefesh* should be understood as "for the benefit of the priests' souls." [That is, the word *lenefesh* refers not to the soul of the dead, but to the soul of the priest, and the preposition prefix *le* means "for" the soul of the priest, and not "from" the soul of the deceased.]

SFORNO

אֱמֹר אֶל־הַכֹּהֲנִים – *Speak to the priests:* This instruction is addressed to the priests. It relates to the previous material which introduces the topic of impurity, and draws distinctions between pure and impure animals and birds. It is the priests' obligation to understand and teach these matters to the nation, as the verse states: *To enable you to distinguish between sacred and profane, and between impure and pure, and to teach the Israelites all the statutes that the Lord has spoken to them through Moshe* (10:10–11). **וְאָמַרְתָּ אֲלֵהֶם** – *Say to them:* Aside from the laws listed above, the priests must be especially cautious to avoid impurity from the dead and the profanation of their seed [through unsuitable marriages]. For the priests are endowed with a high level of sanctity that is reserved only for them. **בְּעַמָּיו** – *Among his people:* No priest should contract impurity from a member of the nation who is not his close relative but is just one of the masses.

VERSE 2

RASHI

כִּי אִם־לִשְׁאֵרוֹ – *Except for his nearest relatives:* This refers to the priest's wife.

2 person among his people except for his nearest relatives: his
3 mother, father, son, daughter, or brother; or his virgin sister who
has remained close to him because she has not married – for her,

RABBEINU BAḤYA

לְאִמּוֹ וּלְאָבִיו – *His mother, father:* Why does the text list the mother of the common priest before the man's father, while in the case of the High Priest we read: *He shall not go near the dead; even for his father or mother he shall not render himself impure* (21:11)? It is possible that in our verse "his mother" is mentioned first because that term follows the phrase "except for his nearest relatives," which is understood as referring to the priest's wife. Thus, the text juxtaposes the permission to become impure on behalf of his two closest female relatives . For if the text had read "his father, his mother," the sequence would have been jumbled, as the male would have been situated between two females. Alternatively, the Torah begins its list with the mother since her maternity is more certain than the father's paternity. Thus, the message of the verse is that not only may a priest become impure in order to tend to his mother's burial, but he may even contract impurity from the man he believes to be his father, even when there exists a modicum of doubt that the priest is not really the son of the deceased. However, in the case of the High Priest, the text mentions the father first as if to say: Not only is the surviving priest warned not to become impure in order to bury the departed who might not actually be his father, but he may not even contract impurity from this dead woman who is undoubtedly his mother.

KELI YAKAR

לְאִמּוֹ וּלְאָבִיו – *His mother, father:* The priest's mother is not a descendant of Aharon, apart from the fact that, having attached herself to her husband's body, she is regarded as one with him. She is therefore mentioned first in this verse. For the law that the son may contract impurity from his mother who is a non-priest is more novel than the permission to inter his father the priest. On the other hand, when the text is relating to the High Priest [in verse 11], it prohibits contracting impurity from the man's dead father before his mother since it is unexpected that the official may not even become impure in order to bury his father who is a descendant of Aharon, the original High Priest.

VERSE 3

RASHI

הַקְּרוֹבָה – *Who has remained close to him:* The adjective serves to include a sister who is betrothed [but is not yet married]. **אֲשֶׁר לֹא־הָיְתָה לְאִישׁ** – *Because she has not married:* This is a woman who has not had relations with a man. **לָהּ יִטַּמָּא** – *For her, he may render himself impure:* It is an obligation [for the priest to become impure on behalf of his relatives. In contrast with the current translation, Rashi understands the text as not merely granting permission, but demanding that the priest bury his dead].

ד הַקְּרוֹבָה אֵלָיו אֲשֶׁר לֹא־הָיְתָה לְאִישׁ לָהּ יִטַּמָּא: לֹא יִטַּמָּא
ה בַּעַל בְּעַמָּיו לְהֵחַלּוֹ: לֹא־יקרחה קָרְחָה בְּרֹאשָׁם וּפְאַת יְקָרְחוּ

VERSE 4

RASHI

לֹא יִטַּמָּא בַּעַל בְּעַמָּיו לְהֵחַלּוֹ – *But he shall not become impure for those he is related to by marriage, and so become profane:* A priest may not become impure by burying his dead wife whom he was forbidden to marry, and through whom he becomes profaned as long as he lives with her. Hence the straightforward meaning of this verse is: A husband may not make himself impure for his dead wife while she is among his people, meaning that she is not a *met mitzva*, as others are able to tend to her burial. And to which wife does this restriction apply? To one who profanes him from the priesthood by being married to him. [On the other hand, the priest has an obligation to bury a lawful wife even if her relatives are available to do it.]

RASHBAM

לֹא יִטַּמָּא בַּעַל בְּעַמָּיו – *But he shall not become impure for those he is related to by marriage:* No husband who is a member the priestly caste may become impure on account of his wife. **לְהֵחַלּוֹ** – *And so become profane:* If a priest should contract impurity from his dead wife, he will thereby profane his priesthood. [That is, he will disqualify himself from engaging in priestly duties.] According to our Sages, the verse forbids a priest to contract impurity from a wife who is disqualified for him [such as a divorced woman]. However, a priest is allowed to become impure to bury his lawful wife [Yevamot 22:2].

RAMBAN

לֹא יִטַּמָּא בַּעַל בְּעַמָּיו – *But he shall not become impure for those he is related to by marriage:* The most distinguished figure in the nation should not become impure and thereby sully his honor. In other words, it is argued in the verse that as a function of the priest's stature and his position as belonging to the most religious caste of the populace, he is forbidden from becoming impure through contact with corpses. Furthermore, the text wishes to dispel the notion that the priest must only preserve his sanctity in anticipation of entering the Tent of Meeting in order to serve there. Indeed, all of the prohibitions listed in this passage relate to the very essence of the priests' exalted status.

ABARBANEL

לֹא יִטַּמָּא בַּעַל בְּעַמָּיו – *But he shall not become impure for those he is related to by marriage:* [Unlike the current translation, Abarbanel does not interpret *baal* as being associated with marriage]. The verse hereby forbids a priest [the *baal* – "master"] from contracting impurity even from a dead prince of the people [*be'amav*]. This is so even though the entire community is obligated to honor the leader. To become impure for such a cause would result in the priest's profanation; the direct consequence of becoming impure unnecessarily would be to impair the priest's sanctity. That in turn would bar the impure person from serving in the Sanctuary. Alternatively, *baal* could be referring to the priest himself; since he is a prominent leader in his nation, he must not become impure, because he would thereby profane himself.

4 **he may render himself impure. But he shall not become impure**
for those he is related to by marriage, and so become profane.
5 **Priests shall not make bald patches on their heads, or shave**
off the edges of their beards, or gash wounds into their flesh.

SFORNO

לֹא יִטַּמָּא בַּעַל בְּעַמָּיו – *But he shall not become impure for those he is related to by marriage:* The reason that a priest may only become impure through burial of one of his close relatives is that this man is in fact a *baal be'amav* ["a leader within his nation"] whose job is to understand and to teach the masses. Thus, the prophet writes: *For a priest's lips should safeguard knowledge, and the people should seek teaching from his mouth, for he is a messenger of the Lord of Hosts* (Malachi 2:7). As such, it is appropriate that this man of distinction should always act honorably so that the people will heed his instruction. What this means is that it does not behoove a priest to become profaned and thereby impair his preparation to conduct his Sanctuary duties simply to honor a dead person who is not related to him – following the opinion of our Sages [in Sanhedrin 47a] that the purpose of burial and eulogy is to do honor to the deceased. On the other hand, a priest is permitted to attend to his deceased relatives since the respect that he extends to them reflects back on him as well.

VERSE 5

RASHI

לֹא־יקרחה קָרְחָה – *Shall not make bald patches:* This may not be done as a sign of mourning for the dead. Now one might point out that the Torah also issues such a warning to the general Israelite public [when it states: *Do not make bald patches – korḥa – in the middle of your heads – bein eineikhem,* literally, "between your eyes" – *for the dead* (Deuteronomy 14:1), and surely priests as well are included in that prohibition]. And yet, because the phrase *bein eineikhem* is used in the general commandment, we might have thought that one would only be liable for tearing out his hair at that specific spot, but not anywhere else on the head. Thus, the present verse states: *On their heads*. And although this phrase is stated specifically with regard to priests, we can infer that it applies to the rest of the nation as well, through the following *gezera shava* [linguistic analogy]: The Torah uses the term *korḥa* in both the present verse and in the later one. And so, we infer that just as here the entire head is included in the prohibition, so too the subsequent text also refers to the whole head – that is, anywhere that a bald patch could be created. We also infer that just as there the prohibition is restricted to tearing out hair for the dead, that condition is necessary here as well. **וּפְאַת זְקָנָם לֹא יְגַלֵּחוּ** – *Or shave off the edges of their beards:* Because the general warning to all of Israel states: *Do not destroy the edges of your beard* (19:27), we might have thought that one who plucks out hair with tweezers or uses a file would be liable for transgressing this prohibition. Hence the present verse says: *Or shave off the edges of their beards*. Combining these two statements we conclude that a violation only occurs if a man performs an act that is considered shaving, and which also destroys the hair [by completely uprooting it]. This is only achieved by using a razor. **וּבִבְשָׂרָם לֹא יִשְׂרְטוּ שָׂרָטֶת** – *Or gash wounds into their flesh:* Because the general warning to all of Israel states: *Do not gash your body for the dead [veseret lanefesh]* [19:28, where the

ו זְקָנָם לֹא יְגַלֵּחוּ וּבִבְשָׂרָם לֹא יִשְׂרְטוּ שָׂרָטֶת: קְדֹשִׁים יִהְיוּ
לֵאלֹהֵיהֶם וְלֹא יְחַלְּלוּ שֵׁם אֱלֹהֵיהֶם כִּי אֶת־אִשֵּׁי יהוה לֶחֶם
ז אֱלֹהֵיהֶם הֵם מַקְרִיבִם וְהָיוּ קֹדֶשׁ: אִשָּׁה זֹנָה וַחֲלָלָה לֹא יִקָּחוּ

RASHI *(cont.)*

term *seret* – "gash" – is singular], we might have thought that one would be held liable for just one violation even if he gashed himself five times. Hence the present verse states: *Lo yisretu saratet* [where the term is doubled in order] to make one liable for each individual cut. Since the second word *saratet* is redundant – the text could have just said *Lo yisretu* – its presence is therefore used to teach the abovementioned point.

ABARBANEL

לֹא־יקרחה קָרְחָה – *Shall not make bald patches:* The ancient custom of the gentiles, which continues even today, was for mourners to tear their hair out in grief and shave off all the hair from their heads and beards as a sign of their sorrow. In addition, these peoples will readily cut gashes in their flesh and create wounds in their bodies and faces in order to express their sadness. In response to this, the Torah decrees that the priests, who represent God's holy nation, may not act similarly when they experience the death of a loved one: *Priests shall not make bald patches on their heads, or shave off the edges of their beards, or gash wounds into their flesh*. And even though these prohibitions apply to all Israelites, there are two reasons why the text issued a particular warning to the priests regarding this matter. First, because priests are just as human as regular Israelites, they are naturally distraught when a person who is close to them, whom they are not permitted to bury or to touch, has died. Instead, when a priest's friend or distant relative dies he will have to suffice with weeping and mourning for him. In this situation, there exists the fear that the priest will rip out his hair in his despair, believing that a Hebrew is not forbidden to do so in circumstances when he may not become impure through burying the deceased. Thus, the Torah now warns that even though the priest may not contract impurity through these dead people, he may also not gash his flesh or create a bald patch between his eyes as an expression of his misery. Second, it must be stressed that the Torah forbids any Israelite to create a bald patch on his head or beard because that was the practice of the idolaters in olden times. And earlier [in 19:25], the text forbids the planting of trees whose fruits will be credited to the false god, as I have written in my comments to Parashat Kedoshim. Now, the priests might believe that because they are servants of the Lord who are dedicated to their Temple duties and are very far removed from the threats and temptations of idolatry, they need not be concerned about such matters. The Torah therefore reminded the priests specifically that they too must always be vigilant not to be influenced by the pernicious ways and beliefs of the nations.

SFORNO

לֹא־יקרחה קָרְחָה – *Shall not make bald patches:* Even though priests are permitted to become impure for the sake of burying their close relatives, which honors the living themselves, this allowance does not extend to excessive mourning. Thus, the priest may not add to the honor of his dead by tearing out his hair or gashing his flesh.

6 They shall be holy to their God and not profane God's name,
for they bring close the LORD's fire offerings, foodstuff offer-
7 ings to their God; therefore they shall be holy. They may not
marry a woman made profane by immorality, nor may they

VERSE 6

RASHI

קְדֹשִׁים יִהְיוּ – *They shall be holy:* This is an instruction to the courts to ensure that priests maintain their sanctity [by avoiding contact with corpses].

RAMBAN

קְדֹשִׁים יִהְיוּ לֵאלֹהֵיהֶם – *They shall be holy to their God:* This statement represents a commandment to the priests to separate themselves from that which is permitted, as I have explained at length in my comments to Parashat Kedoshim (19:2). Thus, the present text cautions the priests to avoid even those circumstances that are allowed for regular Israelites. Specifically, they must remove themselves from the possibility of contracting impurity from the dead, and are forbidden to marry women who are not suitable wives for them. In short, the priests must always aim for a state of utmost purity and morality.

ḤIZKUNI

וְהָיוּ קֹדֶשׁ – *Therefore they shall be holy:* These extra words serve to include blemished priests – even they must maintain their sanctity.

ABARBANEL

וְלֹא יְחַלְּלוּ שֵׁם אֱלֹהֵיהֶם – *They shall not profane God's name:* Should a priest tear the hair out from his head and destroy his own beard, this servant of the LORD would profane his Master whom he is duty bound to honor. For it would be wholly inappropriate for a Temple official to perform his duties while in such a state, as we read: *He came as far as the entrance to the King's Gate – for no one may enter the King's Gate dressed in sackcloth* (Esther 4:2).

SFORNO

וְלֹא יְחַלְּלוּ שֵׁם אֱלֹהֵיהֶם – *They shall not profane God's name:* Even though the guidelines set forth here are geared toward honoring the priest, the latter has no right to relinquish his own prestige. For it is clear that the dignity that surrounds the priest is ultimately meant to create reverence for the Almighty. Thus, if the priest forgoes his personal honor, he thereby profanes the name of God.

VERSE 7

RASHI

זֹנָה – *By immorality:* [The literal reading suggests two different categories of women whom a priest may not marry.] A *zona* is a woman who has had relations with an Israelite whom she is forbidden to marry. This includes those with whom intimacy warrants excision [such as a brother], and those with whom intimacy is merely a prohibition, such as a *natin* [a member of the Gibeonite nation who may not marry into the nation of Israel] or a *mamzer* [a child born out of an incestuous or adulterous union who can only marry converts or other

וְאִשָּׁה גְּרוּשָׁה מֵאִישָׁהּ לֹא יִקָּחוּ כִּי־קָדֹשׁ הוּא לֵאלֹהָיו:
וְקִדַּשְׁתּוֹ כִּי־אֶת־לֶחֶם אֱלֹהֶיךָ הוּא מַקְרִיב קָדֹשׁ יִהְיֶה־לָּךְ ח
כִּי קָדוֹשׁ אֲנִי יהוה מְקַדִּשְׁכֶם: וּבַת אִישׁ כֹּהֵן כִּי תֵחֵל לִזְנוֹת ט
אֶת־אָבִיהָ הִיא מְחַלֶּלֶת בָּאֵשׁ תִּשָּׂרֵף: וְהַכֹּהֵן י
הַגָּדוֹל מֵאֶחָיו אֲשֶׁר־יוּצַק עַל־רֹאשׁוֹ ׀ שֶׁמֶן הַמִּשְׁחָה וּמִלֵּא

RASHI *(cont.)*

mamzerim. A woman who engages in such unlawful relations attains the status of *zona* and may not subsequently marry a priest]. **חֲלָלָה** – *Profane:* A *ḥalala* is a woman whose father is a priest and whose mother was forbidden to marry him. For example, the daughter of a widow who married a High Priest, or the daughter of a divorced woman who married a common priest [or obviously, a High Priest] is a *ḥalala* [and cannot herself marry a priest]. Additionally, should a woman who may not marry into the priesthood nevertheless have relations with a priest, she herself becomes a *ḥalala* [and subsequently may not marry a priest – either the man through whom she became a *ḥalala* or any other priest].

VERSE 8

RASHI

וְקִדַּשְׁתּוֹ – *You shall treat a priest as holy:* The priest should be forced to be holy. For example, if he marries a woman who is forbidden to him and refuses to divorce her, the court should administer lashes and admonish him until he complies. **קָדֹשׁ יִהְיֶה־לָּךְ** – *And he shall be holy to you:* Treat the priest with holiness, and grant him the privilege of being first in all matters. For example, invite the priest to lead the blessings at meals.

VERSE 9

RASHI

כִּי תֵחֵל לִזְנוֹת – *Profanes herself by immorality:* The verse describes the daughter of a priest who profanes herself by having unlawful relations. Specifically, this woman was either betrothed to a man or married to him and was intimate with someone else. Now although our Sages debate the matter [that is, whether the case of a priest's daughter being burned relates to a woman who was betrothed or married], all agree that Scripture is not discussing a daughter who was single. **אֶת־אָבִיהָ הִיא מְחַלֶּלֶת** – *She profanes her father also:* Through the daughter's behavior she has profaned and impugned her father's honor. For the neighbors will all say: Cursed be this man who fathered and who raised such a promiscuous daughter.

VERSE 10

RASHI

לֹא יִפְרָע – *Shall not dishevel his hair:* The High Priest may not allow his hair to grow wild in mourning for the dead. And what constitutes an unacceptable length? More than thirty days' growth creates a violation.

marry a woman divorced from her husband, for they are holy
8 to their God. You shall treat a priest as holy, for he brings close
the offerings of foodstuffs to your God. And he shall be holy
9 to you, because I, the LORD, am holy and make you holy. If the
daughter of a priest profanes herself by immorality, she pro-
10 fanes her father also; she shall be burned with fire. The
priest, the highest among his brothers, on whose head the
anointing oil has been poured and who has been ordained

RABBEINU BAHYA

וְהַכֹּהֵן הַגָּדוֹל מֵאֶחָיו – *The priest, highest among his brothers:* Because the High Priest possesses a higher level of sanctity and is expected to engage in a more intimate level of divine worship so that *he shall not leave the Sanctuary* (21:12), he is subject to greater restrictions with regard to the dead than is the common priest. Hence the High Priest is not permitted to bury and to thereby contract impurity from anybody, including his own father and mother. Furthermore, this official is only allowed to marry a suitable *virgin from his own people* (21:14). The reasoning behind this second rule is that it is appropriate for the thoughts and wishes of the High Priest's wife to be aligned with his own. Now since the High Priest ought to limit sexual contact with his wife as much as possible, he may not marry a woman who has previously been with another man, and who might pressure him to conform to the more regularly intimate lifestyle to which she was accustomed.

ABARBANEL

וְהַכֹּהֵן הַגָּדוֹל מֵאֶחָיו – *The priest, highest among his brothers:* Now that the text has listed the laws governing the lives of the common priest, it addresses rules that relate to the High Priest alone. Even though the High Priest is bound by all of the commandments which are incumbent on the regular priest, these are expanded by an additional five restrictions due to the man's higher level of holiness. The first two directives are that the High Priest may not let his hair grow long in mourning, nor may he tear his clothing in grief. In the context of these injunctions, Aharon is described as *the priest, the highest among his brothers, on whose head the anointing oil has been poured and who has been ordained to wear the vestments.* What the text means here is that the High Priest is distinguished from the rest of his class by these two features that everyone else lacks. It is only the High Priest who is anointed with oil when he assumes his office and only he is the one who wears the set of eight sacred garments that are reserved for him. In parallel to these two unique attributes held by the High Priest, he must preserve his exalted nature in two ways. Because the head of the High Priest has been adorned with anointing oil, the man *shall not dishevel his hair* as mourners are accustomed to doing. For by disobeying the injunction he will necessarily profane the sacred oil on his head. Aharon is also warned not to *tear his clothes*, an act that will sully the glory of the High Priest's holy vestments; he must never tear these garments since they are the High Priest's sacred uniform.

אֶת־יָדוֹ לִלְבֹּשׁ אֶת־הַבְּגָדִים אֶת־רֹאשׁוֹ לֹא יִפְרָע וּבְגָדָיו לֹא
יא יִפְרֹם: וְעַל כָּל־נַפְשֹׁת מֵת לֹא יָבֹא לְאָבִיו וּלְאִמּוֹ לֹא יִטַּמָּא:
יב וּמִן־הַמִּקְדָּשׁ לֹא יֵצֵא וְלֹא יְחַלֵּל אֵת מִקְדַּשׁ אֱלֹהָיו כִּי נֵזֶר
יג שֶׁמֶן מִשְׁחַת אֱלֹהָיו עָלָיו אֲנִי יהוה: וְהוּא אִשָּׁה בִבְתוּלֶיהָ
יד יִקָּח: אַלְמָנָה וּגְרוּשָׁה וַחֲלָלָה זֹנָה אֶת־אֵלֶּה לֹא יִקָּח כִּי
טו אִם־בְּתוּלָה מֵעַמָּיו יִקַּח אִשָּׁה: וְלֹא־יְחַלֵּל זַרְעוֹ בְּעַמָּיו כִּי

VERSE 11

RASHI

וְעַל כָּל־נַפְשֹׁת מֵת – *He shall not go near the dead:* The High Priest is cautioned not to enter a tent in which a corpse lies. [The preposition *al* suggests "within."] **נַפְשֹׁת מֵת** – *The dead:* [The superfluous term *nafshot* serves] to include a quarter of a *log* of blood. That amount of blood can transmit impurity to a priest who enters a tent [that is, a room] where it lies [even if the rest of the corpse is not there]. **אָבִיו וּלְאִמּוֹ לֹא יִטַּמָּא** – *Even for his father or mother he shall not render himself impure:* [The verse emphasizes that a High Priest may not become impure through contact with his deceased parents] to stress that in contrast, he may become impure in order to bury a *met mitzva* [someone who has no relatives or friends to tend to his or her burial].

VERSE 12

RASHI

וּמִן־הַמִּקְדָּשׁ לֹא יֵצֵא – *He shall not leave the Sanctuary:* Should a High Priest's parent die, he may not follow the bier during the funeral procession. Furthermore, our Sages learn from here that the High Priest continues to offer sacrifices despite the fact that he is an *onen* [a mourner whose relative has yet to be buried.] This then is the sense of the verse: Even if the High Priest's father or mother dies, he need not leave the Temple, but may continue to participate in the sacrificial services. **וְלֹא יְחַלֵּל אֵת מִקְדַּשׁ** – *He shall not...profaning his God's Sanctuary:* [If the High Priest serves in the Temple following the death of a relative] he does not thereby profane the services he performs, since the Torah has permitted him to act in the usual manner. However, the service of a regular priest would be disqualified if he works while he is an *onen* [a mourner whose relative has yet to be buried].

RAMBAN

וּמִן־הַמִּקְדָּשׁ לֹא יֵצֵא – *He shall not leave the Sanctuary:* The primary sense of this verse is that the High Priest is warned not to leave the Temple precincts while he is performing his duties there even if a relative of his has passed away. Furthermore, the High Priest must not profane the Sanctuary by walking out in the middle of the service to honor his dead loved one. [Thus, the High Priest who does exit the Temple under such circumstances will violate two prohibitions specified in our verse on "leaving" and "profaning."] Instead, this personage must regard the dignity and respect of the Temple and its sacrificial service as taking precedence above all else, including his esteem and love for the deceased. It goes

to wear the vestments, shall not dishevel his hair or tear his
11 clothes. He shall not go near the dead; even for his father or
12 mother he shall not render himself impure. He shall not leave
the Sanctuary, profaning his God's Sanctuary, for the crown
13 of his God's anointing oil rests upon him; I am the Lord. He
14 may marry a woman only in her virginity. He may not marry
a widow, a divorcée, or one profaned by immorality. He may
15 marry only a virgin from his own people, so that he will not

RAMBAN *(cont.)*

without saying that the High Priest must similarly never abandon the service for no reason, and that he will violate this prohibition if he does so. Meanwhile, the fact that the High Priest is not permitted to forgo his duties in the event of a family death means that he is allowed to continue serving while in a state of *aninut* [the grieving period prior to burial]. Therefore, since the High Priest may continue to perform his sacred work at that time, it will be an affront to and a profanation of the Temple if he neglects to do so.

VERSE 13

RAMBAN

וְהוּא אִשָּׁה בִבְתוּלֶיהָ יִקָּח – *He may marry a woman only in her virginity:* The High Priest may marry a woman only if she has never had relations with a man. Thus, the Torah uses a positive commandment [the High Priest must marry a virgin] to imply a negative commandment [he may not marry a woman who is not a virgin]. The text proceeds to declare widows and unfit women as being ineligible wives for a High Priest. This is followed by the statement: *He may marry only a virgin from his own people* (21:14), which represents a decree that the High Priest must marry. Thus, our Sages clarify that this leader is cautioned against a marrying a widow and is ordered to marry a virgin. [There are therefore two issues here: The High Priest may not marry a woman who is not a virgin; he must marry a woman and she has to be a virgin.]

VERSE 14

RASHI

וַחֲלָלָה – *One profaned by immorality:* This refers to a woman born to a mother who was disqualified from marrying a priest [and yet did].

IBN EZRA

כִּי אִם־בְּתוּלָה – *Only a virgin:* The Torah repeats this requirement in order to stress that the bride must be *from his own people*. This excludes a virgin who has been taken captive or who has converted to Judaism – these women are barred from marrying a High Priest.

VERSE 15

RASHI

וְלֹא־יְחַלֵּל זַרְעוֹ – *So that he will not profane his children:* However, should a High Priest marry a woman he is ineligible to wed, his sons will be banned from the priesthood.

טז אֲנִי יְהוָה מְקַדְּשׁוֹ: וַיְדַבֵּר יְהוָה אֶל־מֹשֶׁה לֵּאמֹר: שני
יז דַּבֵּר אֶל־אַהֲרֹן לֵאמֹר אִישׁ מִזַּרְעֲךָ לְדֹרֹתָם אֲשֶׁר יִהְיֶה בוֹ
יח מוּם לֹא יִקְרַב לְהַקְרִיב לֶחֶם אֱלֹהָיו: כִּי כָל־אִישׁ אֲשֶׁר־בּוֹ

VERSE 17

RASHI

לֶחֶם אֱלֹהָיו – *Foodstuff offerings to his God:* The term *leḥem* here [literally, "bread"] connotes the food of God. Indeed, any meal can be referred to simply as "bread," as in the verse *Beleshatzar the king made a great banquet [leḥem rav]* (Daniel 5:1).

RAMBAN

דַּבֵּר אֶל־אַהֲרֹן – *Tell Aharon:* The discriminating reader will note that in His command to Moshe here God does not adopt the formula that we find throughout all these passages: Tell Aharon and his sons. The reason is that in the previous texts the Torah was dealing with the topic of sacrifices, such as in the statement: *Instruct Aharon and his sons: This is the law of the burnt offering* (6:2), and in the subsequent verse which reads: *Tell Aharon and his sons: This is the law of the purification offering* (6:18). [Hence, the information is pertinent to the entire priestly class – Aharon and his sons together.] In the present context, however, had the text said: Tell Aharon and his sons, it would have had to continue with these words: Any man among you [that is, including Aharon himself] across the generations who has a physical blemish may not draw close. But that would have suggested the possibility that Aharon too was subject to these laws of imperfections. In fact, the first High Priest was sacred to God, a man who could be described this way: *And all of you is beauty, my love, is flawless, wholly* (Song of Songs 4:7). Instead, the Almighty presents this warning as a concern for Aharon's descendants for all of posterity. On the other hand, the later section which discusses instances of impurity contains this preface: *Tell Aharon and his sons to take great care with the sacred offerings that the Israelites consecrate to Me, so that they do not profane My holy name* (22:2). Aharon is included within that law because it is entirely possible that the High Priest might encounter impurity by touching a corpse or a dead crawling thing. [Such an occurrence would not represent any deficiency in the character or the person of Aharon the priest.] And again, when the Torah raises the case of an impure blight or an impure flow, we find the same language as above: *Any descendant of Aharon who has a defiling blight of the skin or a discharge may not eat of the sacred offerings until he becomes pure* (22:4). Here too, the verse excludes Aharon from the circumstance and limits these situations to "any descendants of Aharon" because such a thing would never happen to Aharon himself, *for he is a messenger of the Lord of Hosts* (Malachi 2:7). [The difference between an occurrence of a blight or *ziva* on the one hand, and the contraction of impurity from a dead thing on the other, is that the blight and *ziva* originate in the invalid's body and represent a flaw in the afflicted person. External impurity, however, is something that is imposed upon a person and therefore does not indicate any imperfection in him.] Now it is true that at the end of this section [dealing with blemishes] the text does read: *Moshe told this to Aharon, his sons, and all the Israelites* [21:24, a statement which seems to undermine the

profane his children among his people, for I, the Lord, sanc-
16 tify him." 17 The Lord spoke to Moshe: "Tell Aharon: SHENI
Any of your future descendants who has a physical blemish
may not draw close to present foodstuff offerings to his God.
18 No one with a blemish shall approach: this includes one who

RAMBAN *(cont.)*

author's approach]. However, the reason for this is that Moshe wanted to warn Aharon's sons to pay close attention to his teachings about this topic. In a similar way the court of Israel is cautioned to learn about the priestly blemishes [so that they can monitor the priests who wish to serve in the Temple. Thus, the latter verse does is not listing the parties who might themselves be subject to the laws of blemishes, but is referring to all those who must be familiar with these rules. Thus, "all the Israelites" will clearly never be rejected for their blemishes, just as Aharon will not].

ABARBANEL

אִישׁ מִזַּרְעֲךָ לְדֹרֹתָם – *Any of your future descendants:* When God says to Moshe: *Tell Aharon: Any of your future descendants who has a physical blemish may not draw close*, and later states, *No descendant of Aharon the priest who has a physical blemish shall draw near to present the Lord's fire offerings* (21:21), He does not mean to imply that a blemished man who is *not* among Aharon's progeny is entitled to serve in the Tabernacle! Rather, our passage is founded on the assumption that Aharon and his sons were selected to work in the Temple; they were chosen by God to be His special servants, while *any outsider who draws close to [the Tabernacle] shall be put to death* (Numbers 1:51). Now because they were selected exclusively, the priests might be led to believe that every single priest has the God-given right to serve in the Sanctuary, and that any imperfection that a man within this class is born with, or any blemish that he develops during his life, is not a reason to disqualify him from priestly duties. After all, every priest is a direct descendant of Aharon, and that in and of itself should ensure his service. Nevertheless, the Almighty here informs Moshe to teach Aharon that while God has assigned to the High Priest and his sons the task of serving in the Tabernacle, that privilege is conditional upon the person being free of all blemish. For it would be a profanation of the honor of the Divine Presence were an imperfect person *to present foodstuff offerings to his God*. The reason for this is that people who observe a blemished priest officiating in the Sanctuary will be repulsed at his appearance and detest the service he is performing. The employment of a disfigured servant is objectionable even for human kings, how much more so for the exalted One. Thus does the prophet write: *When you offer a blind animal to be sacrificed, is this no evil? And when you offer the lame and the sick, is this no evil? Offer it if you will to your governor. Would he then accept you – let you lift your face to him? So says the Lord of Hosts* (Malachi 1:8).

VERSE 18

RASHI

כִּי כָל־אִישׁ אֲשֶׁר־בּוֹ מוּם לֹא יִקְרָב – *No one with a blemish shall approach:* It would be inappropriate for a blemished priest to serve in the Temple. The reasoning behind this is

יט מ֖וּם לֹ֣א יִקְרָ֑ב אִ֤ישׁ עִוֵּר֙ א֣וֹ פִסֵּ֔חַ א֥וֹ חָרֻ֖ם א֥וֹ שָׂרֽוּעַ׃ א֣וֹ
כ אִ֔ישׁ אֲשֶׁר־יִהְיֶ֥ה ב֖וֹ שֶׁ֣בֶר רָ֑גֶל א֖וֹ שֶׁ֥בֶר יָֽד׃ אֽוֹ־גִבֵּ֣ן אוֹ־דַ֔ק
כא א֖וֹ תְּבַלֻּ֣ל בְּעֵינ֑וֹ א֤וֹ גָרָב֙ א֣וֹ יַלֶּ֔פֶת א֖וֹ מְר֥וֹחַ אָֽשֶׁךְ׃ כָּל־אִ֞ישׁ
אֲשֶׁר־בּ֣וֹ מ֗וּם מִזֶּ֙רַע֙ אַהֲרֹ֣ן הַכֹּהֵ֔ן לֹ֣א יִגַּ֔שׁ לְהַקְרִ֖יב אֶת־אִשֵּׁ֣י
כב יְהוָ֑ה מ֣וּם בּ֔וֹ אֵ֚ת לֶ֣חֶם אֱלֹהָ֔יו לֹ֥א יִגַּ֖שׁ לְהַקְרִֽיב׃ לֶ֣חֶם אֱלֹהָ֔יו

RASHI *(cont.)*

expressed in the verse *When you offer a blind animal to be sacrificed, is this no evil? And when you offer the lame and the sick, is this no evil? Offer it if you will to your governor* (Malachi 1:8). **חָרֻם** – *Disfigured:* This refers to a person whose nose is sunken between his two eyes, allowing him to apply makeup to both eyes simultaneously. **שָׂרוּעַ** – *Deformed:* A person with this blemish has one limb larger than the other. For example, he possesses one big eye and one small one, or one of his legs is longer than the other.

RAMBAN

כִּי כָל־אִישׁ אֲשֶׁר־בּוֹ מוּם – *No one with a blemish:* As the verse lists the blemishes that disqualify a priest, it begins with instances of a deficient body part: *This includes one who is blind or lame*. It then proceeds to mention cases of organs which are too small in size, such as the *ḥarum* [The Ramban accepts Rashi's interpretation of the term *ḥarum* as meaning somebody whose nose is sunken], or which are too big like the *sarua* [who has one limb larger than the other]. Afterward the text lists limbs that have been broken – even though a priest *who has a broken foot or hand* (21:19) still has an intact appendage [that is, all of the fingers and toes are still present], the fracture is sufficient to disqualify this man. The Torah next bans people with an ugly appearance like the *gibben* ["the hunchback"; the Ramban earlier defined this differently as somebody whose eyebrows are exceedingly long] or one *who has a growth in his eye* (21:20). After that, the Torah lists men whose skin is marred by blemishes, for the priest's body must be clean and smooth. Finally, the text mentions a *meroaḥ ashekh* ["one with crushed testicles"; the Ramban explains this term otherwise as a man] whose testicles are bloated with air. That defect is included even though it is frequently experienced by elderly men and does not represent a blemish in the bone or on the flesh. Our Sages have defined many other disqualifying physical maladies that are derived from these primary conditions listed by the Torah.

VERSE 20

RASHI

אוֹ־גִבֵּן – *Or who is a hunchback:* [Rashi's interpretation of this term is unlike the current translation.] The term in Old French for this part of the face is *sourcils* ["eyebrows"], and the condition described refers to a person with excessively long eyebrow hairs which lie over his eyes. **אוֹ־דַק** – *Or a dwarf:* [Rashi's interpretation of this term is unlike the current translation.] This refers to a person who has a *dok* [a membrane on top of his pupil], which is called *teile* ["eye web"] in Old French. We find this word in the verse *He spreads out the skies like a canvas [khadok]* (Isaiah 40:22). **אוֹ תְבַלֻּל** – *Or who has a growth in his eye: Tevallul* is something which

19 is blind, lame, disfigured, or deformed; or who has a broken
20 foot or hand; or who is a hunchback or a dwarf, or who has
a growth in his eye, a severe rash, scabs, or crushed testicles.
21 No descendant of Aharon the priest who has a physical blemish shall draw near to present the LORD's fire offerings; because
of his blemish, he shall not approach to present an offering of
22 foodstuffs to his God. He may eat the foodstuff offerings of his

RASHI *(cont.)*

muddles [*mevalbel*] a person's eye. It is like a white thread which extends from the white of the eye and pierces the iris – the round ring that surrounds the pupil, called *prunele* in Old French. This thread divides the iris and enters the pupil [so that the white and the black of the eye mingle]. The Targum renders the term *tevallul* as *ḥilliz* which derives from the word *ḥillazon* [a sea snail], since the thread resembles that creature. The Sages of Israel list the *tevallul* among the blemishes that disqualify a firstborn calf [from being sacrificed], referring to it as a *ḥillazon*, a snake, or a grape [since it resembles these entities]. **גָּרָב אוֹ יַלֶּפֶת** – *A severe rash, scabs:* These terms refer to various types of boils. A bout of *garav* makes the skin hard like earthenware [*ḥeres*] with boils which are dry both inside and out. The name *yallefet* relates to the Egyptian lichen. It is so called because it cleaves ever closer [*melappefet*] to the victim's skin as the condition worsens, until it kills him. This rash is moist on the outside while remaining dry on the inside. It is true that elsewhere the text refers to this type of boil as *garav*, in the verse *The LORD will afflict you with the boils of Egypt, with hemorrhoids, rashes [uvagarav], and scabs [uveḥares], from which you shall never recover* (Deuteronomy 28:27). [Since the term *ḥeres* – usually "earthenware" – refers to boils which are dry externally and internally, *garav* implies boils which are dry on the inside but moist outside.] Hence, we must explain that when the text mentions *garav* together with *ḥeres*, it is the Egyptian boils [which are wet outside] which are called *garav*. However, when the term *garav* appears in conjunction with *yallefet*, then the word *garav* connotes the thoroughly dry type of boils. This is the explanation given in the Talmud (Bekhorot 41a). **מְרוֹחַ אָשֶׁךְ** – *Crushed testicles:* The Targum renders this term as *meris paḥdin*, meaning that the sufferer's testicles are crushed. We find the word *paḥad* referring to testicles in the verse *The tendons of his testicles [paḥadav]are woven together* (Job 40:17).

VERSE 21

RASHI

כָּל־אִישׁ אֲשֶׁר־בּוֹ מוּם – *No one who has a physical blemish:* This clause serves to include people with other defects [not listed here]. **מוּם בּוֹ** – *Because of his blemish:* The priest may not serve as long as he suffers from the blemish. However, if he recovers from his condition, he is eligible to work in the Temple **לֶחֶם אֱלֹהָיו** – *Foodstuff offerings to his God:* The word *leḥem* is a general term for food.

VERSE 22

RASHI

מִקָּדְשֵׁי הַקֳּדָשִׁים – *The holy of holies:* This refers to the sacrifices with the highest degree of sanctity [such as the purification offering and the guilt offerings]. **וּמִן־הַקֳּדָשִׁים יֹאכֵל** – *He*

כג מִקָּדְשֵׁי הַקֳּדָשִׁים וּמִן־הַקֳּדָשִׁים יֹאכֵל: אַךְ אֶל־הַפָּרֹכֶת לֹא
יָבֹא וְאֶל־הַמִּזְבֵּחַ לֹא יִגַּשׁ כִּי־מוּם בּוֹ וְלֹא יְחַלֵּל אֶת־מִקְדָּשַׁי
כד כִּי אֲנִי יהוה מְקַדְּשָׁם: וַיְדַבֵּר מֹשֶׁה אֶל־אַהֲרֹן וְאֶל־בָּנָיו
וְאֶל־כָּל־בְּנֵי יִשְׂרָאֵל:
כב א ב וַיְדַבֵּר יהוה אֶל־מֹשֶׁה לֵּאמֹר: דַּבֵּר אֶל־אַהֲרֹן וְאֶל־בָּנָיו
וְיִנָּזְרוּ מִקָּדְשֵׁי בְנֵי־יִשְׂרָאֵל וְלֹא יְחַלְּלוּ אֶת־שֵׁם קָדְשִׁי

RASHI *(cont.)*

may eat the holy as well: This refers to the sacrifices with a lower degree of sanctity [such as peace offerings. One might ask why this second category has to be specified, considering that the text has already allowed a blemished priest to eat the holier type of sacrificial meat]. Had mention not been made of the lower level of offering, we might have argued that in fact the Torah only permits the blemished person to partake of the most sacred sacrifices, since there was one occasion when that type of meat was given to a non-priest. This refers to Moshe who was allowed to eat from the inaugural offerings [as stated in 8:29, despite the fact that those were a type of *kodshei kodashim*. This shows a leniency which might be extended to blemished priests]. Perhaps, however, a blemished person would not be permitted to eat the breast and thigh of the lesser types of sacrifices [the *kodashim kalim*] for we find no instance where a non-priest is given a share in these parts. This is why the Torah emphasizes that a blemished priest may eat even these. This is the interpretation found in the Talmud (Zevaḥim 101b).

VERSE 23

RASHI

אַךְ אֶל־הַפָּרֹכֶת – *But he may not come close to the inner curtain:* A blemished priest may not approach the inner curtain in order to sprinkle sacrificial blood toward it seven times. [That procedure is performed on rare occasions; see, for example, 4:17.] **וְאֶל־הַמִּזְבֵּחַ** – *Or the altar:* This refers to the outer sacrificial altar. The Sifra (3:10) explains why both of these details need be mentioned. [After all, if a blemished priest cannot serve at the altar, then he surely may not enter the Sanctuary to work there. The Sages' explanation is that the casting of the blood inside might not be viewed as an actual sacrificial service.] **וְלֹא יְחַלֵּל אֶת־מִקְדָּשַׁי** – *He shall not profane My Sanctuary:* If such a priest unlawfully serves, the work he has performed is profane and disqualified.

VERSE 24

RASHI

וַיְדַבֵּר מֹשֶׁה – *Moshe told:* Moshe related this particular commandment [regarding the service of blemished priests]. **אֶל־אַהֲרֹן... וְאֶל־כָּל־בְּנֵי יִשְׂרָאֵל** – *To Aharon, his sons, and all the Israelites:* [It appears unnecessary to communicate these laws to the Israelites, who are not required to observe them.] This warning is intended for the courts, which are responsible for overseeing the priests.

23 God, the holy of holies as well as the holy. But he may not come
close to the inner curtain or approach the altar, because of his
blemish; he shall not profane My Sanctuary; I am the Lord
24 who makes them holy." Moshe told this to Aharon, his sons,
and all the Israelites.
22 1 2 The Lord spoke to Moshe: "Tell Aharon and his sons to take
great care with the sacred offerings that the Israelites consecrate
to Me, so that they do not profane My holy name: I am the

HIZKUNI

וְאֶל־כָּל־בְּנֵי יִשְׂרָאֵל – *And to all the Israelites:* The populace had to be aware of these laws so that they would refrain from entrusting their sacrifices to blemished priests.

ABARBANEL

וַיְדַבֵּר מֹשֶׁה אֶל־אַהֲרֹן – *Moshe told this to Aharon:* Moshe indeed taught all of this material *to Aharon, his sons, and all the Israelites*. Thus, Moshe transmitted to Aharon the content that relates to him [verses 10–15], opening with the words *The priest, the highest among his brothers*. The rest of this chapter was conveyed by Moshe to Aharon's sons so that they would be familiarized with its laws. Finally, Moshe introduced these topics to the people of Israel because they are tasked with compelling the priests to maintain their sanctity. For example, should a priest marry a woman who is not suitable for him, the community must censure him [and thereby pressure him to divorce his wife]. Similarly, with regard to all of these matters, the people of Israel must ensure that the priests obey these laws and thereby preserve their holiness.

CHAPTER 22, VERSE 2

RASHI

וְיִנָּזְרוּ – *To take great care with:* The term *nezira* connotes "separation," as in the verse *For any man…who becomes estranged [veyinnazer] from me* (Ezekiel 14:7) and the verse *They fell away [nazoru ahor]* (Isaiah 1:4). The present verse warns that priests must distance themselves from the sacrifices at times when they are impure [and may not eat sacrificial meat when in that state]. Those priests must desist from *the sacred offerings that the Israelites consecrate to Me*, and that which *they consecrate to Me*, in order that *they do not profane My holy name*. The clauses of this verse must be transposed to be understood correctly. [The Hebrew original reads literally, Tell Aharon and his sons to take great care with the sacred offerings (a) that the Israelites consecrate to Me, (b) so that they do not profane My holy name, (c) that which they consecrate to Me. The first clause refers to the sacrifices that the nation brings to God, while the third clause relates to those which the priests themselves offer. According to Rashi, (c) should be inserted between (a) and (b) to teach that the service of impure priests will also defile sacrifices brought by the priestly class.] אֲשֶׁר הֵם מַקְדִּשִׁים לִי – *That which they consecrate to Me:* This refers to the sacrifices offered by the priests themselves.

ג אֲשֶׁר הֵם מַקְדִּשִׁים לִי אֲנִי יהוה: אֱמֹר אֲלֵהֶם לְדֹרֹתֵיכֶם
כָּל־אִישׁ ׀ אֲשֶׁר־יִקְרַב מִכָּל־זַרְעֲכֶם אֶל־הַקֳּדָשִׁים אֲשֶׁר
יַקְדִּישׁוּ בְנֵי־יִשְׂרָאֵל לַיהוה וְטֻמְאָתוֹ עָלָיו וְנִכְרְתָה הַנֶּפֶשׁ

RAMBAN

אֲשֶׁר הֵם מַקְדִּשִׁים לִי – *That they consecrate to Me:* According to Rashi, the text should be restructured in order to be properly interpreted: The priests should take great care with the Israelites' sacred offerings that they consecrate to Me, *and* they should not profane My holy name. Thus, the clause "that they consecrate to Me" serves to include the offerings of the priests themselves. However, even if we associate those words with the priests, there is still no need to alter the order of the phrases in this verse. For what the text is saying is that the impure priests should separate themselves from the sacred offerings that the Israelites consecrate so that they do not profane God's holy name. Furthermore, with regard to the sacred offerings that Aharon and his sons themselves consecrate to God, the priests must also not profane those [if they have become impure].

ABARBANEL

דַּבֵּר אֶל־אַהֲרֹן וְאֶל־בָּנָיו – *Tell Aharon and his sons:* Now that the Torah has completed its first set of instructions regarding the priests' obligations, namely that blemished priests are not permitted to offer sacrifices on the altar, the following chapter addresses the second type of limitation that applies to these men. Here the text warns the impure priest against eating any of the flesh from a sacrificial animal. Since we learned earlier that a priest with a physical deformity *may eat the foodstuff offerings of his God* (21:22), it became necessary to clarify that that privilege only extends to priests who are ritually pure. However, a priest who has contracted impurity is barred from consuming any meat from a sacrifice. This is the sense of the present warning to Aharon and his sons: *Take great care [yinnazeru] with the sacred offerings*. The verb connotes a separation [and derives from the term *nazir* – one who removes himself from some otherwise permitted behavior]. Thus, in the event that a priest becomes impure, he should disengage himself from the Temple proceedings and refuse to eat any sacred food. All priests must always perform their service in a state of purity and sanctity and thereby avoid desecrating the holy name of the Almighty.

SFORNO

וְיִנָּזְרוּ – *To take great care with:* Let the priests not imagine that due to their exalted status they may treat an animal that has been consecrated by an Israelite as profane. The principle suggested in the Talmud – "One who is ostracized by the student need not be ignored by the teacher" – does not apply here: [Since a pupil possesses less authority than his teacher, the latter is not subject to his subordinate's decrees. Here too, a priest might wrongfully think that an Israelite lacks the power to dedicate a sacrifice in a way that would affect him.] Rather, the priests must "take great care" not to profane the state of holiness imparted to an offering by an Israelite.

3 LORD. Tell them: If any descendant of yours throughout the generations comes near the sacred offerings that the Israelites have consecrated to the LORD while in an impure state, he shall

VERSE 3

RASHI

כָּל־אִישׁ אֲשֶׁר־יִקְרַב – *If any descendant comes near:* "Coming near" in this context refers to eating [and not merely getting close to the sacred offerings]. Indeed, we find that the Torah warns against an impure person eating sacrificial meat by using the language of "touching," as in the verse *She [a woman who has given birth] must not touch anything holy or enter the Sanctuary* (12:4). That actually represents a prohibition against eating, as the Sages learn through a *gezera shava* ["verbal analogy"]. Now it is impossible to interpret the text as saying that one who touches sacrificial meat is subject to the death penalty based on this reasoning: The Torah warns of excision with regard to eating sacred food in Parashat Tzav (in 7:20–21), a passage which twice mentions that punishment. And if a person deserved excision for merely touching holy items when impure, then surely there would be no need to refer to sentencing him for eating such foods [since eating is more severe than touching, and furthermore, one must touch food in order to eat it]. Additionally, the Sifra (4:7) argues as follows. Since one does not receive excision for touching sacred meat when impure, why does the text use the words *asher yikrav* – "who might come near"? What the verse thereby teaches is that if an impure priest eats the meat, he would only be held liable if that which renders the meat permissible for consumption [for pure priests] had already brought near [that is, had been offered on the altar. When portions of a sacrificial animal are given to the priests to eat, such as in the case of a purification offering, these may only be consumed once the relevant body parts have been sacrificed, and the blood has been cast against the altar]. The reader might wonder why the Torah threatens excision three times [that is, once in the present verse and twice in 7:20–21] with regard to an impure priest eating sacred food. The Sages explain this point in Shevuot 7a and maintain that one instance represents a general statement, and one a particular statement. [See Rashi's comments to 7:20 for a fuller analysis of this argument.] וְטֻמְאָתוֹ עָלָיו – *While in an impure state:* The verse refers to the impurity of the human being [that is, the pronouns relate to the priest who is the subject of the verse]. Still, perhaps the text is discussing the impurity of the meat itself, meaning that a pure person who eats meat while the flesh is impure [is liable for excision]? No, we are forced to interpret the verse as describing impurity that can be removed. [The emphasis of *vetum'ato alav* – "his impurity is upon him" – suggests a state where the impurity is no longer upon him.] Hence, it must refer to a person who can be purified through immersion. [However, once food becomes impure, that state can never be corrected.] וְנִכְרְתָה – *He shall be severed:* Perhaps the text refers [not to excision which is a divine form of punishment such as dying young, but] to the offender being uprooted from the community he lives in and forced to relocate to a different locality. No, for the verse concludes with the words *I am the LORD*, meaning "I exist in all places." [There can be no separation from God just by moving from one place to another, since God is omnipresent. Hence, the severance must refer to taking the person out of the world altogether.]

ד הַהוּא מִלְּפָנַי אֲנִי יהוה: אִישׁ אִישׁ מִזֶּרַע אַהֲרֹן וְהוּא צָרוּעַ
אוֹ זָב בַּקֳּדָשִׁים לֹא יֹאכַל עַד אֲשֶׁר יִטְהָר וְהַנֹּגֵעַ בְּכָל־טְמֵא־
ה נֶפֶשׁ אוֹ אִישׁ אֲשֶׁר־תֵּצֵא מִמֶּנּוּ שִׁכְבַת־זָרַע: אוֹ־אִישׁ אֲשֶׁר
יִגַּע בְּכָל־שֶׁרֶץ אֲשֶׁר יִטְמָא־לוֹ אוֹ בְאָדָם אֲשֶׁר יִטְמָא־
ו לוֹ לְכֹל טֻמְאָתוֹ: נֶפֶשׁ אֲשֶׁר תִּגַּע־בּוֹ וְטָמְאָה עַד־הָעָרֶב
ז וְלֹא יֹאכַל מִן־הַקֳּדָשִׁים כִּי אִם־רָחַץ בְּשָׂרוֹ בַּמָּיִם: וּבָא
הַשֶּׁמֶשׁ וְטָהֵר וְאַחַר יֹאכַל מִן־הַקֳּדָשִׁים כִּי לַחְמוֹ הוּא:

ABARBANEL

כָּל־אִישׁ אֲשֶׁר־יִקְרַב מִכָּל־זַרְעֲכֶם – *If any descendant of yours comes near:* It is obvious that all Israelites are warned against entering the Temple or eating sacred food while in a state of impurity. Similarly, are not all members of the nation forbidden to *eat an animal found dead or one that was torn by wild animals* (22:8)? Nevertheless, the Torah repeats these warnings with regard to the priests lest they formulate the following rationalization. The reason that a common Israelite may not enter the Tabernacle precincts when he is impure is simply because he is a non-priest. However, a priest, whose duties are performed within the Sanctuary itself, should be permitted to visit the place whether or not he is ritually pure; contracting impurity should not compel him to cease his service. To counter such an argument, the text stresses that the impure priest is suspended from duty while he is in that state. Secondly, the Torah specifically warns the priests not to consume *nevelot* or *terefot*, simply because they possess a higher level of sanctity than the rest of the nation, and as such, they must be particularly careful regarding the food they put in their mouths. Indeed, if a non-priest Israelite eats meat from an animal that has not been ritually slaughtered, he is punished with lashes. On the other hand, an impure priest who eats sacred food is subject to death. Thus, the text reiterates this proscription due to the severity of the punishment that the perpetrator incurs.

VERSE 4

RASHI

בְּכָל־טְמֵא־נֶפֶשׁ – *By contact with the dead:* This refers to one who has touched a corpse. [A human corpse represents the ultimate source of impurity. A person who touches a dead body becomes a source of impurity. One who touches *that* living person becomes impure to the first degree of impurity. It is to the latter circumstance that the present verse refers: a priest who touches a person who has previously touched a corpse. The next verse mentions a priest touching an actual dead body.]

RALBAG

אִישׁ אִישׁ מִזֶּרַע אַהֲרֹן – *Any descendant of Aharon:* From the context of this issue it is clear that the text is describing the consumption of *teruma*, and not other sacred food. Now since a subsequent verse teaches that *when the sun sets, he shall become pure again and*

4 be severed from My presence; I am the Lord. Any descendant
of Aharon who has a defiling blight of the skin or a discharge
may not eat of the sacred offerings until he becomes pure. One
who touches anything made impure by contact with the dead,
5 or who has had a seminal emission, or who has touched any
swarming thing or any person who renders him impure – what-
6 ever his impurity – the one who touches these things shall be
impure until the evening, and shall not eat of the sacred offer-
7 ings until he has washed his body in water. When the sun sets,
he shall become pure again and may eat of the sacred offerings,

RALBAG *(cont.)*

may eat of the sacred offerings (22:7), we learn that a priest who has become purified may eat *teruma* after sunset [that is, the sunset that follows his immersion in a mikveh]. This is so even though the person might still need to bring offerings to complete the process. However, the consumption of other sacred food [such as the meat from offerings] is only permitted once the requisite sacrifices have been brought to establish purification.

VERSE 5

RASHI

בְּכָל־שֶׁרֶץ אֲשֶׁר יִטְמָא־לוֹ – *Or who has touched any swarming thing that renders him impure:* [The words "who renders him impure" limit this circumstance to one where] the creature's carcass is the requisite size to transmit impurity, meaning that its volume is equal to at least that of a lentil. **אוֹ בְאָדָם** – *Or any person:* This refers to a corpse. **אֲשֶׁר יִטְמָא־לוֹ** – *Which renders him impure:* This refers to a priest who touches a part of the corpse which has the requisite size to transmit impurity, meaning at least the volume of an olive. **לְכֹל טֻמְאָתוֹ** – *Whatever his impurity:* This last phrase serves to include a priest who touches a *zav*, a *zava*, a *nidda*, or a woman who has given birth. [All of these people are considered sources of impurity, and a second party who touches them contracts impurity to the first degree.]

VERSE 6

RASHI

נֶפֶשׁ אֲשֶׁר תִּגַּע־בּוֹ – *The one who touches these things:* The priest need only touch one of these sources of impurity [to be barred from eating sacred offerings].

VERSE 7

RASHI

מִן־הַקֳּדָשִׁים – *Of the sacred offerings:* The Talmud (Yevamot 74b) teaches that this refers to *teruma* [the agricultural gifts given to priests]. That may be eaten [by the priest who was impure and immersed himself] once the sun sets. **מִן־הַקֳּדָשִׁים** – *Of the sacred offerings:* When the sun sets, the purified priest may eat some of the sacred food, but not all of it.

ח ט נְבֵלָה וּטְרֵפָה לֹא יֹאכַל לְטָמְאָה־בָהּ אֲנִי יהוה: וְשָׁמְרוּ
אֶת־מִשְׁמַרְתִּי וְלֹא־יִשְׂאוּ עָלָיו חֵטְא וּמֵתוּ בוֹ כִּי יְחַלְּלֻהוּ
י אֲנִי יהוה מְקַדְּשָׁם: וְכָל־זָר לֹא־יֹאכַל קֹדֶשׁ תּוֹשַׁב כֹּהֵן

SFORNO

כִּי לַחְמוֹ הוּא – *For they are his food:* The purified priest need not wait to complete his atonement before eating *teruma*, as our Sages have taught: Once the sun sets, he may eat *teruma* once again.

VERSE 8

RASHI

נְבֵלָה וּטְרֵפָה לֹא יֹאכַל לְטָמְאָה־בָהּ – *He may not eat an animal found dead or one that was torn by wild animals, becoming impure by doing so:* [The straightforward meaning of the verse implies that a priest may not eat kosher animals that died in these ways. However, such a prohibition applies to all Israelites, as stated in Exodus 22:30 and Deuteronomy 14:21. Hence] the prohibition here applies to contracting impurity and refers specifically to the consumption of the carcass of a kosher bird [that has not been properly slaughtered]. Such an object does not transmit impurity by being touched or by being carried, but only by being swallowed. If a priest contracts impurity in that manner, he is forbidden to subsequently eat sacred food. Now our verse mentions *terefa* [a creature torn apart by predators, or which dies from disease] as well in order to teach that the present law applies only to animals which could possibly become a *terefa*. This excludes the carcass of a non-kosher bird which can never be a *terefa*.

RAMBAN

נְבֵלָה וּטְרֵפָה לֹא יֹאכַל לְטָמְאָה־בָהּ – *He may not eat an animal found dead or one that was torn by wild animals, becoming impure by doing so:* The Torah warns priests in particular to avoid eating *nevelot* and *terefot* [even though these are forbidden to all Israelites] because contact with such carcasses imparts impurity, and if the priest becomes impure he will be forced to desist from servicing the offerings in the Tabernacle. Should that happen, the official will be unable to eat sacrificial meat unless he first immerses in a mikveh and waits until evening. The reason that this verse mentions contamination that might derive from an animal carcass is that this passage in general discusses the means by which a priest might contract impurity. [The list of sources of impurity includes cases where the contamination emanates from the priest himself, making him temporarily ineligible to serve, and instances where the priest acquires impurity from an external cause.] Verse 4 mentions specifically *a defiling blight of the skin* [*tzaraat*] and *a discharge* [*ziva*], which relates to both men and women. As well, verse 4 refers to *one who touches anything made impure by contact with the dead* or a man *who has had a seminal emission*, whereas the next sentence warns the priest *who has touched any swarming thing* to avoid the sacrificial service. This is why the text makes mention as well of *an animal found dead or one that was torn by wild animals* and cautions the priest not to eat meat from these carcasses. The reason the text warns against consumption only in the last instance [and not with regard to the "swarming things"] is that most people consider the

8 for they are his food. He may not eat an animal found dead or
one that was torn by wild animals, becoming impure by doing
9 so; I am the LORD. They shall keep My charge and not bear
guilt and die through it, having profaned it. I am the LORD, who
10 makes them holy. No layman may eat of the sacred offerings,

RAMBAN *(cont.)*

thought of eating a crawling creature as repugnant, whereas it seems less disgusting to eat *nevelot* and *terefot*. The text therefore warns against the more common situation. [The Ramban now considers the nature of a *terefa* in order to fit his understanding that this entire passage is concerned with contracting impurity.] The *terefa* that is mentioned in our text refers to an animal which has been preyed upon by a lion or a bear and has been mauled to death in a field. This must be the case, because no animal can impart impurity when it is still alive. And so, even though at the moment that the lion attacks the cow, the sheep, or the goat, it becomes a *terefa* [since it will surely die], it is still called that even after it dies. Thus, the Torah has listed all the possible sources of impurity as a warning for the priest. As for the non-kosher animal, since it has been argued that such a beast cannot be slaughtered, as I have explained in my comments to Parashat Shemini [to 11:24], it too is included in the category of the *nevela*. [That is, even if it is killed following the proper ritual slaughter used for kosher animals, a non-kosher animal will still be considered a *nevela* and a source of impurity.] This is the straightforward interpretation of this verse.

VERSE 9

RASHI

וְשָׁמְרוּ אֶת־מִשְׁמַרְתִּי – *They shall keep My charge:* The priests are warned against eating *teruma* while their bodies are impure. **וּמֵתוּ בוֹ** – *And die through it:* We learn that this refers to death at the hands of heaven.

SFORNO

אֲנִי יהוה מְקַדְּשָׁם – *I am the Lord, who makes them holy:* Because Israel has sanctified these sacrifices, I in turn have made the latter holy as well. Therefore, any priest who defiles the offerings deserves to be punished.

VERSE 10

RASHI

לֹא־יֹאכַל קֹדֶשׁ – *May eat of the sacred offerings:* This too refers to the consumption of *teruma*, which is the subject of this passage. **תּוֹשַׁב כֹּהֵן וְשָׂכִיר** – *A priest's visitor or hired laborer:* [The word order of this phrase is confusing. Rashi explains the syntax: The phrase means,] A *toshav* of a priest or a *sakhir* who is working for a priest. This explains why the word *toshav* is vocalized with a *pataḥ* [under the *shin*] – that indicates that the word is in the construct form [meaning "the *toshav* of the priest." Had the vowel been a *kamatz* it would have meant "a priest who is a *toshav*"]. And what exactly is a *toshav*? The label refers to a Hebrew slave who has had his ear pierced [after fulfilling his six years of servitude and who wishes to remain enslaved, as described in Exodus 21:6]. The master acquires such a

יא וְשָׂכִיר לֹא־יֹאכַל קֹדֶשׁ׃ וְכֹהֵן כִּי־יִקְנֶה נֶפֶשׁ קִנְיַן כַּסְפּוֹ הוּא
יב יֹאכַל בּוֹ וִילִיד בֵּיתוֹ הֵם יֹאכְלוּ בְלַחְמוֹ׃ וּבַת־כֹּהֵן כִּי תִהְיֶה
יג לְאִישׁ זָר הִוא בִּתְרוּמַת הַקֳּדָשִׁים לֹא תֹאכֵל׃ וּבַת־כֹּהֵן כִּי
תִהְיֶה אַלְמָנָה וּגְרוּשָׁה וְזֶרַע אֵין לָהּ וְשָׁבָה אֶל־בֵּית אָבִיהָ
יד כִּנְעוּרֶיהָ מִלֶּחֶם אָבִיהָ תֹּאכֵל וְכָל־זָר לֹא־יֹאכַל בּוֹ׃ וְאִישׁ
כִּי־יֹאכַל קֹדֶשׁ בִּשְׁגָגָה וְיָסַף חֲמִשִׁתוֹ עָלָיו וְנָתַן לַכֹּהֵן אֶת־
טו הַקֹּדֶשׁ׃ וְלֹא יְחַלְּלוּ אֶת־קָדְשֵׁי בְּנֵי יִשְׂרָאֵל אֵת אֲשֶׁר־יָרִימוּ

RASHI *(cont.)*

slave until the Jubilee year [when he is released]. And what is a *sakhir*? That title applies to an Israelite who is acquired for a limited time and who goes free after six years of service. The present verse teaches that the bodies of these two types of men do not actually belong to the master, which is why they are forbidden to share the priest's *teruma*.

RALBAG

תּוֹשַׁב כֹּהֵן וְשָׂכִיר – *A priest's visitor or hired laborer:* Even though the *teruma* represents the priest's food, he is not permitted to serve it to a servant unless the latter has been purchased and is the priest's possession.

VERSE 11

RASHI

וְכֹהֵן כִּי־יִקְנֶה נֶפֶשׁ – *But if a priest acquires a slave:* This verse refers to a Canaanite slave whose body now belongs to his master. [Since the Canaanite slave is purchased for his body, he is entitled to eat *teruma*. A Hebrew slave who is only acquired for his labor cannot.] **וִילִיד בֵּיתוֹ** – *And those born into his household:* This phrase refers to children born to the priest's maidservants. This verse also teaches that because a priest's wife is acquired with his money, she too is permitted to eat *teruma*. [Betrothal to a Jewish wife is effected by giving money to the woman.] Furthermore, we learn this point from a later verse which states: *Anyone who is ritually pure in your household may eat of them* (Numbers 18:11). This is discussed in Sifrei to Parashat Koraḥ (paragraph 117).

VERSE 12

RASHI

לְאִישׁ זָר – *A layman:* In this context, a "layman" refers to a Levite or a common Israelite.

VERSE 13

RASHI

אַלְמָנָה וּגְרוּשָׁה – *A widow or a divorcée:* If a priest's daughter married a layman who died or divorced her… **וְזֶרַע אֵין לָהּ** – *And she has no children:* From that layman husband… **וְשָׁבָה** – *She returns:* [The priest's daughter may return to her father's table under those

11 nor may a priest's visitor or hired laborer eat of them. But if a
priest acquires a slave for money, the slave may eat of them, and
12 those born into his household also may eat his food. If a priest's
daughter marries a layman, she may no longer eat of the sacred
13 gifts. If a priest's daughter is a widow or a divorcée, has no children, and returns to live in her father's house as when she was
young, she may eat her father's food again; but no layperson
14 may do so. If someone eats of the sacred gift unintentionally,
he shall make restitution to the priest, adding an extra fifth to
15 its value. The people must not profane the sacred meats that

RASHI *(cont.)*

circumstances.] But if she had children with her husband, she is forbidden to eat *teruma* as long as the progeny are alive. **וְכָל־זָר לֹא־יֹאכַל בּוֹ** – *But no layperson may do so:* This clause does not [forbid laypeople from eating *teruma* since that was stated explicitly in verse 10. Rather, its purpose is] to permit an *onen* [a mourner whose relative has not yet been buried] to eat *teruma*. Thus, our text emphasizes that it is the state of being a non-priest that prohibits one from eating *teruma*, and not the state of bereavement.

VERSE 14

RASHI

וְאִישׁ כִּי־יֹאכַל קֹדֶשׁ – *If someone eats of the sacred gift:* The text continues to discuss the consumption of *teruma*. **וְנָתַן לַכֹּהֵן אֶת־הַקֹּדֶשׁ** – *He shall make restitution to the priest:* The offender must give to the priest something which can be sanctified. [The presence of the definite article in the word *hakodesh* implies that the person must return to the priest the *teruma* which he ate. Since this is impossible, he must] give him non-sacred fruit which then become *teruma*. He cannot pay the priest cash [which cannot be made holy as *teruma*.]

VERSE 15

RASHI

וְלֹא יְחַלְּלוּ – *The people must not profane:* The priests must not feed sacred food to people who are not priests.

BEKHOR SHOR

וְלֹא יְחַלְּלוּ – *The people must not profane:* The people must not treat the sacred meats as *ḥol* ["profane" or "secular"].

RAMBAN

וְלֹא יְחַלְּלוּ – *The people must not profane:* The priests must not profane the meat by serving it to non-priest Israelites. If they do so, the priests will *incur the penalty of iniquity* (22:16) when the recipients eat the holy food that has been separated as *teruma*, since it has been consecrated and has become forbidden to them.

טז לַיהוָה: וְהִשִּׂיאוּ אוֹתָם עֲוֺן אַשְׁמָה בְּאׇכְלָם אֶת־קׇדְשֵׁיהֶם
כִּי אֲנִי יְהוָה מְקַדְּשָׁם:
יז יח וַיְדַבֵּר יְהוָה אֶל־מֹשֶׁה לֵּאמֹר: דַּבֵּר אֶל־אַהֲרֹן וְאֶל־בָּנָיו וְאֶל יח שלישי
כׇּל־בְּנֵי יִשְׂרָאֵל וְאָמַרְתָּ אֲלֵהֶם אִישׁ אִישׁ מִבֵּית יִשְׂרָאֵל
וּמִן־הַגֵּר בְּיִשְׂרָאֵל אֲשֶׁר יַקְרִיב קׇרְבָּנוֹ לְכׇל־נִדְרֵיהֶם וּלְכׇל־

VERSE 16

RASHI

וְהִשִּׂיאוּ אוֹתָם – *Or incur the penalty:* By feeding *teruma* to outsiders, the priests encumber themselves with sin and guilt. For that was sacred food which was set apart and established as *teruma*; it had been sanctified and thereby rendered forbidden to others. **וְהִשִּׂיאוּ אוֹתָם** – *Or incur the penalty:* [Although the word *otam* usually means "them,"] according to Rabbi Yishmael, the present verse represents one of three instances where *et* has a reflexive connotation ["himself," "itself," "themselves." Hence this verse would literally be translated: "or bring upon themselves the penalty etc."]. The second such case appears in the verse *On the day that the term of his nazirite vow is completed, he shall bring himself [yavi oto] to the entrance to the Tent of Meeting* (Numbers 6:13), which in context means that the *nazir* shall bring himself [and not "he shall bring him" – someone shall bring someone else]. The third example appears in the verse *He buried himself [vayikbor oto] in Moav, in a valley opposite Beit Peor* (Deuteronomy 34:6). [Although the straightforward meaning of the text seems to report that God buried Moshe, Rabbi Yishmael maintains that the word *oto*] actually means that Moshe buried himself. This is the interpretation of the Sifrei on Parashat Naso (32).

ABARBANEL

וְהִשִּׂיאוּ אוֹתָם עֲוֺן אַשְׁמָה – *Or incur the penalty of iniquity:* It is the priests' obligation to safeguard the sanctity of the sacred food and to make sure that it is not treated lightly by being served to those who may not eat it or by consuming it in a state of impurity. This is the sense of the commandment *The people must not profane the sacred meats that Israelites bring* [in verse 15]. The text itself explains what exactly must be protected by using the phrase *et asher yarimu lAdonai* [literally, "that which is raised to the Lord"], which refers to *teruma* that is lifted up for the glory of the Almighty. The people thus rely on the priests to conduct themselves with sanctity regarding these foods. The text continues to warn that the priests will *incur the penalty of iniquity* if they are lax in their handling and eating of the *teruma*, or if they feed it to non-priests. For instead of facilitating God's promise of *I, the Lord, make them holy*, they will have profaned Him. It is possible to connect the clause *or incur the penalty of iniquity [vehissiu avon ashma]* to an earlier verse which states: *The goat shall carry all their iniquities upon itself [venasa et kol avonotam] to a desolate place* (16:22), meaning: The Israelites have burdened the priests with the threat of iniquity by placing upon them the task of guarding the sacred food. [Because they have entrusted that duty to the priests, if the Israelites eat the *teruma* they thereby cause the priests to sin by not fulfilling their responsibility.]

16 Israelites bring as offerings to the LORD or incur the penalty of
iniquity by eating their sacred offerings; for I, the LORD, make
them holy."
17 18 The LORD spoke to Moshe: "Speak to Aharon, his sons, and all SHELISHI
the Israelites. Say: When anyone of the House of Israel or of the
migrants living in Israel presents an offering to the LORD as a
burnt offering – whether in fulfillment of a vow or as a freewill

VERSE 18

RASHI

נִדְרֵיהֶם – *Whether in fulfillment of a vow:* A vow [*neder*] is undertaken when a person states: It is incumbent upon me to bring an offering. **נִדְבוֹתָם** – *A freewill offering:* A donation [*nedava*] is undertaken when a person states: It is incumbent upon me to bring this specific animal as an offering.

IBN EZRA

וּמִן־הַגֵּר בְּיִשְׂרָאֵל – *Or of the migrants living in Israel:* The text reminds us that with regard to vow offerings and freewill offerings, the same set of rules apply to native-born Israelites and to foreigners in their midst. For the Torah states: *One law and one rule, for you and for the migrant who lives among you* (Numbers 15:16).

RAMBAN

לְכָל־נִדְרֵיהֶם וּלְכָל־נִדְבוֹתָם – *Whether in fulfillment of a vow or as a freewill offering:* When somebody pledges: I vow to bring a sacrifice, that constitutes a *neder* – a vow offering. However, if he procures an animal and states: I undertake to bring this beast as a sacrifice, he has just declared his decision to bring a *nedava* – a freewill offering. This is how Rashi distinguishes between the two forms of offerings. Now I will offer the following interpretation based on the language of the subsequent verse which states: *Whether because of a spoken vow* [*lefalei*, "to utter a vow"] *or as a freewill offering* (22:21). This is terminology that we find elsewhere, such as in the passage describing libations: *Whether it be a burnt offering or a sacrifice to fulfill a spoken vow [lefalei neder], or brought as a freewill offering, or a festival offering* (Numbers 15:3); with respect to valuations: *When a person makes a spoken vow [ki yafli neder] to the* LORD *to give the equivalent of the value of a person* (Leviticus 27:2); and in the context of a nazirite commitment: *Speak to the Israelites. Say: When a man or a woman takes a special vow [ki yafli lindor], the vow of a nazirite, to separate him or herself to the* LORD (Numbers 6:2). The explanation for this is that a person declares a *neder* in situations that are beyond his control, turning to the LORD for assistance in his hour of trouble or need, saying: If you, God perform a wonder [*peleh*] on my behalf and rescue me from my travail, I will bring a burnt offering or a peace offering as an acknowledgment of Your aid. This sort of approach is reflected in the following narratives: *Yaakov then made a vow. "If God will be with me…"* (Genesis 28:20); *When the Canaanite king of Arad, dwelling in the Negev, heard that the Israelites were coming by the way of Atarim, he attacked the Israelites and took captives. And the Israelites vowed to the* LORD*: If You give this people over into our hands, we will utterly destroy their towns* (Numbers 21:1–2); and *Then they lifted Yona up and cast him out*

יט נִדְבוֹתָם אֲשֶׁר־יַקְרִיבוּ לַיהוָה לְעֹלָה: לִרְצֹנְכֶם תָּמִים זָכָר
כ בַּבָּקָר בַּכְּשָׂבִים וּבָעִזִּים: כֹּל אֲשֶׁר־בּוֹ מוּם לֹא תַקְרִיבוּ כִּי־

RAMBAN *(cont.)*

into the sea, and the sea ceased raging and grew still. And the men were filled with a great fear of the Lord, and they offered up a sacrifice to the Lord, and made vows (Jonah 1:15–16). Now our Sages ask about the difference between a vow offering and a freewill offering [in Mishna Kinnim 1:1]: What constitutes a *neder*? If somebody announces: I hereby pledge to bring a burnt offering – that is a vow. However, if he states: I hereby dedicate this animal as a burnt offering, he has promised to bring a *nedava* – a freewill offering. And what distinguishes one type of undertaking from the other? If the animal that has been selected for a vow offering dies or is stolen, the donor is responsible to replace it. But that definition by the Sages is merely a practical matter. [The Sages' technical explanation does not at first appear to correspond to the Ramban's understanding that a *neder* – vow offering, is pledged in a moment of trouble, whereas a *nedava* – freewill offering, is promised as an expression of joy or contentment. Nevertheless, the Ramban maintains that the nature of the *neder* reflects the language that a person uses when he pronounces it.] For it is usual when someone utters a vow in a difficult time to say: If the Almighty will be with me, I vow to bring a burnt offering or a peace offering! [In that circumstance of anxiety, the person is focusing on himself and his hardship; he is not thinking about any specific animal that he might use to honor his pledge.] Therefore, that declaration would not be termed a *nedava* – a freewill offering [or a donation, because the anxious person has no particular gift in mind as yet]. On the other hand, when an Israelite allocates an animal and dedicates it for a sacrifice, he does so because right then the spirit moves him to part with this possession as a gesture to the Lord. In the present context, the Torah relates that when a person presents a burnt offering or a peace offering, either to fulfill a *neder* pronounced during a moment of hope or worry, or as a sign of their heart's generosity, the specimen must be free of all blemishes. The text applies this rule to both forms of promises since we might have thought that only in the case of the *neder* is it necessary that the animal be in perfect condition [since it is linked to the donor's plea] whereas a *nedava* can be somewhat less than ideal [since it is merely a gift]. This is the explanation of our verse.

RALBAG

וּמִן־הַגֵּר בְּיִשְׂרָאֵל – *Or of the migrants living in Israel:* The verse refers to a righteous convert who is like an Israelite with regard to all of the Torah's commandments, as the text makes clear on multiple occasions.

ABARBANEL

וּמִן־הַגֵּר בְּיִשְׂרָאֵל – *Or of the migrants living in Israel:* Since it was not unusual for foreigners to present blemished vow offerings and freewill offerings at the Temple, the text warns the priests not to accept such donations. Indeed, it is even possible that these outsiders would intend to demean the altar by giving imperfect specimens, because they are corrupt gentiles. In other words, members of the other nations hold warped beliefs and considering

19 offering – to be acceptable on your behalf, it must be an un-
20 blemished male from the herd, or of the sheep or goats. Do not
offer anything that has a blemish, for it will not be accepted on

ABARBANEL *(cont.)*

that the donors themselves are flawed, that is perhaps reflected in their blemished sacrifices. The strangers' animals and their utensils mirror their owners, and that is the sense of the verse *Because they are mutilated and blemished, they will not be accepted on your behalf [lakhem]* (22:25). That is, even though the gentile's intentions might be honorable, his offering is unsuitable due to its imperfection. Therefore, it will not be acceptable for you [*lakhem*], who are the priests of the Lord, to service such an offering and thereby desecrate My name. Now, since *an ox or sheep or goat* is like a stillborn when it is first born, and it is not perfect or whole, the text juxtaposes the law of verse 27, where it states: *It shall remain with its mother for seven days*, to the prohibition of blemished animals. Thus, the calf must remain with its mother for a week until it gains some strength, and should not be brought to the Temple before that time has passed. For during its first few days the animal is like a flawed specimen and cannot serve as *a fire offering to the Lord.*

SFORNO

אֲשֶׁר יַקְרִיב קָרְבָּנוֹ – *Presents an offering:* Once the text has finished discussing the [conditions incumbent on the] priests who service the sacrifices and the sanctity of these men, it proceeds to describe the flawless nature that is required for the animals themselves.

לְכָל־נִדְרֵיהֶם וּלְכָל־נִדְבוֹתָם – *Whether in fulfillment of a vow or as a freewill offering:* The Israelite might imagine that since his freewill offering is essentially a donation, which he is under no obligation whatsoever to bring, it should be acceptable to present any sort of gift that he wishes, even if it is blemished. Indeed, the prophet reacts to this notion with the following criticism: *When you offer a blind animal to be sacrificed, is this no evil? And when you offer the lame and the sick, is this no evil? Offer it if you will to your governor. Would he then accept you – let you lift your face to him? So says the Lord of Hosts* (Malachi 1:8).

VERSE 19

RASHI

לִרְצֹנְכֶם – *To be acceptable on your behalf:* [One might have thought that this word means that the sacrifice must be brought "willingly." Rashi explains that it means instead to] bring sacrifices which are suitable for obtaining appeasement from Me; those will placate Me. The Old French term for this is *apaiemant* ["appeasement"]. Now which animal is worthy of achieving that conciliation? It is *an unblemished male from the herd, or of the sheep or goats*. On the other hand, when a bird is brought as a burnt offering, it need not be male or unblemished; it is only disqualified if it is missing limbs.

SFORNO

תָּמִים זָכָר – *An unblemished male:* The sacrifice must be perfect because *the Rock, His work is whole, and all His ways are justice* (Deuteronomy 32:4); hence God demands perfection.

כא לֹא לְרָצוֹן יִהְיֶה לָכֶם: וְאִישׁ כִּי־יַקְרִיב זֶבַח־שְׁלָמִים לַיהוָה
לְפַלֵּא־נֶדֶר אוֹ לִנְדָבָה בַּבָּקָר אוֹ בַצֹּאן תָּמִים יִהְיֶה לְרָצוֹן
כב כָּל־מוּם לֹא יִהְיֶה־בּוֹ: עַוֶּרֶת אוֹ שָׁבוּר אוֹ־חָרוּץ אוֹ־יַבֶּלֶת
אוֹ גָרָב אוֹ יַלֶּפֶת לֹא־תַקְרִיבוּ אֵלֶּה לַיהוָה וְאִשֶּׁה לֹא־תִתְּנוּ
כג מֵהֶם עַל־הַמִּזְבֵּחַ לַיהוָה: וְשׁוֹר וָשֶׂה שָׂרוּעַ וְקָלוּט נְדָבָה
כד תַּעֲשֶׂה אֹתוֹ וּלְנֵדֶר לֹא יֵרָצֶה: וּמָעוּךְ וְכָתוּת וְנָתוּק וְכָרוּת

VERSE 21

RASHI

לְפַלֵּא־נֶדֶר – *Because of a spoken vow:* The person wishes to fulfill a vow that he had expressed verbally.

SFORNO

וְאִישׁ כִּי־יַקְרִיב זֶבַח־שְׁלָמִים לַיהוה – *When someone presents a peace sacrifice to the Lord:* Even though these sacrifices fall into the category of *kodashim kalim* [offerings with a lower degree of sanctity] and they can be either male or female, as the verse states above: *If one's sacrifice is a peace offering, and brought from the herd, whether male or female, the animal one offers before the Lord must be without blemish* (3:1), the specimen must still be flawless. The Torah itself explains why this is so: *Do not present to the Lord anything blind, injured, or maimed* (22:22), for it is dishonorable to offer to God something that is disfigured. Our passage adds a second aspect of this admonition when it states: *Do not place any of these on the altar as a fire offering to the Lord.* Thus, in the event that an animal has become blemished after it has been consecrated, the donors may not even present its sacrificial parts on the altar because it is inappropriate to offer to the Almighty that which is repulsive to Him.

VERSE 22

RASHI

עַוֶּרֶת – *Blind:* The term *avveret* is a noun in the feminine form meaning "blindness." The verse thus informs us that the animal "should not suffer from" [*lo yihyeh bo,* in the previous verse] the blemish of blindness. **אוֹ שָׁבוּר** – *Injured:* [Unlike the previous term, this is an adjective, but the general sense is similar: The animal] "should not be" [*lo yihyeh*] injured. **חָרוּץ** – *Maimed:* The animal's eyelid must not be split or otherwise damaged, nor may its lip be cut or maimed. **יַבֶּלֶת** – *Warts:* The Old French word for this is *verue* ["warts"]. **גָּרָב** – *A severe rash:* The term *garav* refers to a form of boils, as does the word *yallefet* ["scabs."] The latter is related to the verse *Shimshon gripped [vayilpot] the two central pillars that the temple rested upon* (Judges 16:29). The boils are called *yalefet* because they take hold of their victim and cleave to him until his death, for there is no cure. **לֹא־תַקְרִיבוּ** – *Do not place any of these:* The text issues three warnings against offering blemished animals [in verses 20, 22, and 24, to teach three distinct laws]. It is forbidden to consecrate such animals as sacrifices, it is forbidden to slaughter them as such, and it is forbidden to cast the blood of these

21 your behalf. When someone presents a peace sacrifice to the
LORD from the herd or flock – whether because of a spoken
vow or as a freewill offering – it must be unblemished to be
22 acceptable; there shall be no blemish on it. Do not present to
the LORD anything blind, injured, or maimed, or with warts,
a severe rash, or scabs. Do not place any of these on the altar
23 as a fire offering to the LORD. You may offer as a freewill offering an ox or sheep with a limb deformed or uncloven, but they
24 will not be accepted in fulfillment of a vow. Do not offer to the
LORD an animal whose testicles are bruised, crushed, torn,

RASHI *(cont.)*

animals against the altar. [One who offers a blemished animal thereby transgresses these three prohibitions.] **וְאִשֶּׁה לֹא־תִתְּנוּ** – *Do not place as a fire offering:* This represents an additional prohibition against burning these unacceptable animals on the altar.

VERSE 23

RASHI

שָׂרוּעַ – *With a limb deformed:* This describes an animal with an unusually large limb. **וְקָלוּט** – *Or uncloven:* The hooves of such an animal are solid and undivided. **נְדָבָה תַּעֲשֶׂה אֹתוֹ** – *As a freewill offering:* A blemished animal should be accepted as a donation for repairs to the Temple [that is, from the proceeds of its sale]. **וּלְנֶדֶר** – *In fulfillment of a vow:* These cannot be offered on the altar. **לֹא יֵרָצֶה** – *They will not be accepted:* What kind of an offering achieves appeasement? Only that which is consecrated for the altar.

SFORNO

נְדָבָה תַּעֲשֶׂה אֹתוֹ – *You may offer as a freewill offering:* Because the blemishes in these animals are readily visible, we might have thought that such specimens should even be rejected as a donation toward the repair of the House [that is, the Temple]. Therefore, the Torah teaches that these animals are indeed acceptable for that purpose since no part of the donation is actually offered on the altar. The only sanctity that the blemished beast possesses is embodied in its monetary value; after the animal is dedicated, it is sold, thereby losing all holiness. [The money received for it is then used to pay for alterations to the Temple or to purchase items to be used in its functioning.]

VERSE 24

RASHI

וּמָעוּךְ וְכָתוּת וְנָתוּק וְכָרוּת – *An animal whose testicles are bruised, crushed, torn, or cut off:* These conditions refer to the animal's testicles or its male organ [neither of which is explicitly stated in the Hebrew text]. **מָעוּךְ** – *Bruised:* The testicles have been bruised by hand. **כָּתוּת** – *Crushed:* The adjective represents a state beyond being bruised. **נָתוּק** – *Torn:* This refers to severing the testicles to the point that the glands by which they are suspended are cut, and yet the testicles remain inside the scrotum which has not been severed.

כה לֹא תַקְרִיבוּ לַיהוָה וּבְאַרְצְכֶם לֹא תַעֲשׂוּ: וּמִיַּד בֶּן־נֵכָר
לֹא תַקְרִיבוּ אֶת־לֶחֶם אֱלֹהֵיכֶם מִכׇּל־אֵלֶּה כִּי מׇשְׁחָתָם
כו בָּהֶם מוּם בָּם לֹא יֵרָצוּ לָכֶם: וַיְדַבֵּר
כז יְהוָה אֶל־מֹשֶׁה לֵּאמֹר: שׁוֹר אוֹ־כֶשֶׂב אוֹ־עֵז כִּי יִוָּלֵד וְהָיָה
שִׁבְעַת יָמִים תַּחַת אִמּוֹ וּמִיּוֹם הַשְּׁמִינִי וָהָלְאָה יֵרָצֶה לְקׇרְבַּן

RASHI *(cont.)*

וְכָרוּת – *Or cut off:* With this action the testicles have been cut away while still inside the scrotum, making it appear as if it is not missing that body part. **וּמָעוּךְ** – *Bruised:* The term is rendered by the Targum as *vedimris*, which means "mashed" [a somewhat more severe condition than "bruised"]. **וְכָתוּת** – *Crushed:* The term is rendered as *vediresis* in the Targum, as in the verse *For indeed, the Lord commands and will shatter the great house to pieces* [*resisim*, meaning "broken into thin shards"] (Amos 6:11). We similarly find the phrase *kaneh hamerussas* – "a shattered reed" [in Shabbat 80b]. **וּבְאַרְצְכֶם לֹא תַעֲשׂוּ** – *And do not do such things in your land:* [The final admonition in this sentence does not warn Israel not to offer these blemished animals as sacrifices – that has already been stated in this verse. Furthermore, the text need not emphasize that defective animals cannot serve as sacrifices "in your land," since offerings are not brought outside the land at all. Hence these words prohibit doing] this thing – castrating any domestic animal, wild beast, or bird, even those which are impure [non-kosher]. This explains the usage of the term "in your land": the prohibition extends to all animals living in your land [and not just those which are eligible to be sacrifices]. Now it is impossible to explain that the Torah here is limiting the prohibition to the land of Israel, since the act of emasculation relates to the body, and all requirements governing the body are applicable both inside the land and outside of Israel.

RALBAG

וּבְאַרְצְכֶם לֹא תַעֲשׂוּ – *And do not do such things in your land:* Do not imagine that the Torah prohibits the castration of animals just because it is wrong to offer such damaged specimens to the Lord. We would then infer that in a situation when an animal is not dedicated to the Almighty, such an act would be acceptable. The fact is that even outside the framework of the Temple, in areas that are not reserved for God but belong to the Israelites, this repugnant treatment of an animal is prohibited. The reason for this decree is that it is sinful to destroy the animal's means of reproduction. For God has associated His name with undertaking to preserve every animal species. This explains why the commandment is applicable outside of the land of Israel as well; it is clear that this is in no way a matter that is connected or bound to the holy soil.

VERSE 25

RASHI

וּמִיַּד בֶּן־נֵכָר – *From a migrant:* If a gentile presents an animal for sacrifice in honor of God, the priest must offer it unless the specimen is blemished. For even though non-Jews are permitted to sacrifice defective animals [to God] unless the creature is actually missing a

25 or cut off; and do not do such things in your land. Do not accept such animals from a migrant as an offering of foodstuffs
to your God. Because they are mutilated and blemished, they
26 will not be accepted on your behalf." The LORD
27 spoke to Moshe: "When an ox or sheep or goat is born, it
shall remain with its mother for seven days. From the eighth

RASHI *(cont.)*

limb, that allowance only extends to shrines set up in fields. However, Israel is not to accept imperfect animals for the altar in the Tabernacle [or Temple], while perfect animal sacrifices are welcome. This is why the verse above [22:18] states: *ish ish mibeit Yisrael* – literally, "a man, a man of the House of Israel"; the repetition serves to include people who are not Israelites. Thus, gentiles are permitted to make vows and bring freewill offerings just as the Hebrews are. **מָשְׁחָתָם** – *They are mutilated:* The Targum translates this as *ḥibbulehon* – "they are destroyed." **לֹא יֵרָצוּ לָכֶם** – *They will not be accepted on your behalf:* Such sacrifices will not atone for you.

VERSE 27

RASHI

כִּי יִוָּלֵד – *When it is born:* This excludes a calf born via caesarean section. [Only a naturally born animal can be a sacrifice.]

BEKHOR SHOR

וְהָיָה שִׁבְעַת יָמִים תַּחַת אִמּוֹ – *It shall remain with its mother for seven days:* It is not immediately clear whether the young will survive. Furthermore, anything that emerges from an impure or a filthy environment must be separated before it can be introduced to the camp of the Divine Presence. We find that a similar distancing is imposed on the *zav*, the leper, and a person who has come into contact with a corpse.

RALBAG

שׁוֹר אוֹ־כֶשֶׂב אוֹ־עֵז – *An ox or sheep or goat:* We learn from here that it is permissible to raise upon the altar only purebred animal specimens. It is unlawful to sacrifice the product of two crossbred species, since such a beast will not be *an ox or sheep or goat*. Thus, the Sages maintain that an animal serves as an acceptable offering only if it resembles its kind. This excludes, for example, the young of a goat that looks like a sheep, since that is not a lamb, but not clearly a goat either. **כִּי יִוָּלֵד** – *Is born:* The verb teaches that an animal represents a viable offering only if it is born in the natural way, and not if it emerges as a caesarean birth. Since that is not the normal way for the young to be born, it signals a type of deficiency – and this could be the reason that it could not be born in the usual fashion. Such a case might also indicate that the calf's formation in the womb was not yet complete and for some reason it still attempted to come out. Perhaps the animal fetus was not receiving sufficient sustenance, or it suffered from some other condition like those that lead to miscarriage. **וְהָיָה שִׁבְעַת יָמִים תַּחַת אִמּוֹ** – *It shall remain with its mother for seven days:* This rule teaches that is appropriate for a young animal to have a mother, and that makes it suitable

כח אִשֶּׁה לַיהוָה: וְשׁוֹר אוֹ־שֶׂה אֹתוֹ וְאֶת־בְּנוֹ לֹא תִשְׁחֲטוּ
כט בְּיוֹם אֶחָד: וְכִי־תִזְבְּחוּ זֶבַח־תּוֹדָה לַיהוָה לִרְצֹנְכֶם תִּזְבָּחוּ:

RALBAG *(cont.)*

for the altar. However, if the mother were to be slaughtered the day before its young is born, the calf would be unfit as a sacrifice. Furthermore, the emergence of the young in that circumstance [that is, if after being killed the mother is opened to take out its fetus] would not represent a usual birth. Thus, it seems that just like offspring that is born via a caesarean procedure is not born under ideal conditions and is therefore not suitable for the altar, similarly an orphan animal is also rejected. Now this does not mean that the mother must be alive for seven days, because the continued existence of the adult does nothing to ensure the perfection of the young after its birth. For it is entirely possible for the calf, the lamb, or the kid to suckle from a different female which is not its mother to no discernible detriment.

וּמִיּוֹם הַשְּׁמִינִי וָהָלְאָה – *From the eighth day:* The purpose of this law is that when an animal young is born it is not immediately clear that the calf will survive, even if its birth is a normal one and it seems healthy. Seven days are required to determine its viability. This is why it is prohibited to slaughter an animal before seven days have passed.

SFORNO

שׁוֹר אוֹ־כֶשֶׂב – *An ox or sheep:* Our text has now finished listing all the types of blemishes that disqualify animals from being offered as sacrifices, resulting in their rejection from the altar. While it is possible that a perfectly formed animal might be worth a *sela*, whereas an animal with an imperfection could fetch twice as much due to its size or weight, nevertheless any flawed specimen is banned. Indeed, perhaps a blemished animal would make an acceptable and welcome gift to a human king. Nevertheless, because God is described as *The Rock, His work is whole, and all His ways are justice* (Deuteronomy 32:4), what He desires is wholeness and perfection in the offerings that are burned before Him, as well as in the servants who perform the sacrifice. Thus, the animal that is raised to the altar must retain its natural perfection, while the priest who services the offering should have achieved a divine perfection through striving to imitate his Creator as much as possible. After the text has established these qualifications, it sets limitations on the times for an offering, teaching that one must not bring the animal too early or sacrifice it at an inappropriate hour. First, the Torah stipulates that the youngest age for an animal to be sacrificed is eight days, and then it prohibits killing an animal and its calf on the same day. Furthermore, the text warns against harboring thoughts of eating sacrificial meat beyond the allotted time, a rule which applies to offerings with a lesser degree of sanctity as well. The thanksgiving offering is mentioned again to stress that even though it represents a type of peace offering, the consumption of its meat is also limited to one day and one night, in contrast to other peace offerings which may be eaten over the course of two days and an intervening night.

VERSE 28

RASHI

אֹתוֹ וְאֶת־בְּנוֹ – *It and its young:* The prohibition applies to the female, meaning that it is forbidden to slaughter a mother animal and on the same day to kill its offspring. The

day it is acceptable as a sacrifice, a fire offering to the Lord,
28 but do not slaughter an ox or sheep and its young on the same
29 day. When you sacrifice a thanksgiving offering for the Lord,

RASHI *(cont.)*

law does not apply to father animals; it is permitted to slaughter a male animal on the same day as its young. [Although the term *oto* – "him" – would seem to suggest that the rule relates to the male animal, the word is interpreted as referring to the species of ox – *shor* – and sheep – *seh*, which are masculine terms.] **אֹתוֹ וְאֶת־בְּנוֹ** – *It and its young:* [Although the phrasing implies that the prohibition is limited to killing the animal and then the offspring] it is even forbidden to first slaughter the young and subsequently the parent.

ABARBANEL

אֹתוֹ וְאֶת־בְּנוֹ – *It and its young:* When the text warns, *Do not slaughter an ox [shor] or sheep [seh] and its young on the same day*, the term *shor* refers to both the male and the female of the species. This explains the verse's usage of the masculine pronoun *oto* ["it" or "he"]. Now according to our tradition, the young of an animal is far more attached to its mother than it is to its father. For not only can we not be sure of the male's paternal relationship to the young animal, but the calf itself will recognize only its mother and not its father. Therefore, even though the text is expressed in the masculine, the phrase *oto ve'et beno* refers to a mother and her young. The term *seh* includes sheep lambs and goat kids. Indeed, the words *oto ve'et beno*, which as we have said are in the masculine, refer to the person doing the slaughtering which is most likely a man and not a woman. Thus, it is as if the Torah is appealing to the human's sense of compassion not to kill the mother and its young together. For that would be an extremely cruel and unfeeling act, similar to the murder of one's own beloved son.

VERSE 29

RASHI

לִרְצֹנְכֶם תִּזְבָּחוּ – *Sacrifice it so that it will be acceptable on your behalf:* From the very start of the sacrificial procedure [that is, the slaughtering], be sure to offer the animal for the sake of its acceptance. And what criterion is necessary for the offering to be accepted? That *it shall be eaten on the same day* (22:30). Now the function of the present verse is to instruct us that the animal be slaughtered with the intention to eat the allotted portion on the same day, that is: Do not slaughter the offering while planning to eat it the next day. For if the person harbors such a disqualifying thought, the sacrifice will not gain acceptance for you. Another interpretation for the term *lirtzonekhem* – *so that it will be acceptable on your behalf:* The sacrifice must be offered with your intention. From here we learn that if one who is otherwise preoccupied happens to slaughter the animal [for example, he drops the knife and by sheer chance it slashes the animal's neck], that slaughtering invalidates the offering. And even though the text has previously made clear [in 7:18] that should one plan, when sacrificing a peace offering, to eat it beyond the designated time of two days, the Torah now discusses sacrifices which have a one-day limit for consumption, to teach that regarding these too there must be an initial intention to eat the meat within the prescribed time.

ל בַּיּ֥וֹם הַהוּא֙ יֵאָכֵ֔ל לֹא־תוֹתִ֥ירוּ מִמֶּ֖נּוּ עַד־בֹּ֑קֶר אֲנִ֖י יְהוָֽה׃
לא וּשְׁמַרְתֶּם֙ מִצְוֺתַ֔י וַעֲשִׂיתֶ֖ם אֹתָ֑ם אֲנִ֖י יְהוָֽה׃ וְלֹ֤א תְחַלְּלוּ֙ אֶת־
לב שֵׁ֣ם קָדְשִׁ֔י וְנִ֨קְדַּשְׁתִּ֔י בְּת֖וֹךְ בְּנֵ֣י יִשְׂרָאֵ֑ל אֲנִ֥י יְהוָ֖ה מְקַדִּשְׁכֶֽם׃

SFORNO

לִרְצֹנְכֶם תִּזְבָּחוּ – *Sacrifice it so that it will be acceptable on your behalf:* When someone brings this sacrifice he must intend and plan that its meat will be eaten on that very day. This is because, says God: *I am the Lord* (22:30), and therefore My deeds are characterized as perfection, which means that there must be boundaries to that which is associated with Me. These may not be crossed either at the start or at the end.

VERSE 30

RASHI

בַּיּוֹם הַהוּא יֵאָכֵל – *It shall be eaten on the same day:* This verse serves to caution that the slaughter of the sacrifice must be performed on condition that the meat will be eaten on that day. The text cannot be establishing the appropriate time to eat this meat, since an earlier verse already states: *The flesh of the peace sacrifice of thanksgiving shall be eaten on the day it is offered* (7:15). **אֲנִי יהוה** – *I am the* Lord: Remember who has issued this command, and do not take it lightly.

VERSE 31

RASHI

וּשְׁמַרְתֶּם מִצְוֹתַי – *Keep My commands:* This directs Israel to study the laws. **וַעֲשִׂיתֶם אֹתָם** – *And fulfill them:* Here the text enjoins the people to observe the commandments.

IBN EZRA

וּשְׁמַרְתֶּם מִצְוֹתַי – *Keep My commands:* Your hearts should be committed to the laws. **וַעֲשִׂיתֶם אֹתָם אֲנִי יהוה** – *And fulfill them; I am the Lord:* I will scrutinize your hearts and I will see everything that you do.

RAMBAN

וּשְׁמַרְתֶּם מִצְוֹתַי – *Keep My commands:* This admonition cautions Israel to observe the guidelines regarding blemished animals. Israelites must not offer specimens which have not yet been alive for eight days or whose mothers have been slaughtered on that very day. Thus, the nation must bring sacrifices and thanksgiving offerings such that they *will be acceptable on [their] behalf* (22:29). In addition to this advice about offerings, this verse urges obedience to all the commandments. It is thereby repeating an earlier statement which reads: *Keep all My decrees and laws and fulfill them; I am the Lord* (19:37).

VERSE 32

RASHI

וְלֹא תְחַלְּלוּ – *Do not profane:* Do not purposefully disobey My commands. Now since the verse states: *Do not profane My holy name,* why does it need to then say: *That I may be*

30 sacrifice it so that it will be acceptable on your behalf. It shall
be eaten on the same day – leave none of it to the morning; I
31 am the LORD. Keep My commands and fulfill them; I am the
32 LORD. Do not profane My holy name – that I may be sanctified

RASHI *(cont.)*

sanctified? [An absence of profanation implies sanctification.] The positive statement emphasizes that a person must be prepared to sacrifice himself in order to sanctify God's name. [If one is threatened with death if he does not violate a Torah precept, he should surrender his life to avoid doing that. Thus, sanctifying the divine name is not only achieved by the passive avoidance of sin; the Jew is required to forfeit his life toward that aim, which should be viewed as an active undertaking.] Now lest we think that this obligation applies even if one is compelled to transgress the law privately, the verse states: *In the midst of the Israelites*. [It is only in public that one must choose death.] And should a Jew be required to give up his life, he should truly be prepared to die. For if such a person secretly hopes that a miracle will suddenly save his life, no such wonder will be forthcoming. Thus, we see that Ḥananya, Mishael, and Azarya did not rely on providence to rescue them, as they said to Nevukhadnetzar: *But even if He does not choose to save us, let it be known to you, O king, that we will not serve your god and we will not worship the golden figure you have erected* (Daniel 3:18). That is, these men stated their resolve that they would not engage in idolatry whether or not God saved them from the fiery furnace.

IBN EZRA

וְלֹא תְחַלְּלוּ אֶת־שֵׁם קָדְשִׁי – *Do not profane My holy name:* This injunction is addressed to the sons of Aharon, since this whole paragraph contains guidelines for the priests: It is they who are commanded not to *slaughter an ox or sheep and its young on the same day* (22:28) either for themselves or on the Israelites' behalf. It is also possible that the verse which states: *When you sacrifice a thanksgiving offering for the LORD, sacrifice it so that it will be acceptable on your behalf* (22:29), is also directed to the sons of Aharon. Proof for this interpretation lies in the subsequent statement: *Speak to the Israelites* [23:2, which shows that the preceding material was not spoken to the nation at large, but to the priests]. A second proof appears in the words *That I may be sanctified in the midst of the Israelites*. [If this verse were spoken to all of the people rather than to only the priests, it would read: That I may be sanctified in your midst].

RAMBAN

וְלֹא תְחַלְּלוּ אֶת־שֵׁם קָדְשִׁי – *Do not profane My holy name:* The people of Israel will avoid such disrespect by heeding the prophet's admonition: *Cursed is the knave who has a ram in his flock but pledges and sacrifices a damaged animal to the LORD* (Malachi 1:14). Similarly are the sons of Aharon warned above *to take great care with the sacred offerings… so that they do not profane [God's] holy name* (22:2) by becoming impure or by serving while blemished. **וְנִקְדַּשְׁתִּי בְּתוֹךְ בְּנֵי יִשְׂרָאֵל** – *That I may be sanctified in the midst of the Israelites:* According to our Sages, this reflects a positive commandment. [That is, the sanctification of God will not merely result if the people do not profane God's name; there must be an active effort on their part to grant the Almighty this respect.] God will thus be sanctified if Israel's

לג הַמּוֹצִיא אֶתְכֶם מֵאֶרֶץ מִצְרַיִם לִהְיוֹת לָכֶם לֵאלֹהִים אֲנִי
יהוה:
כג א ב וַיְדַבֵּר יהוה אֶל־מֹשֶׁה לֵּאמֹר: דַּבֵּר אֶל־בְּנֵי יִשְׂרָאֵל וְאָמַרְתָּ רביעי
אֲלֵהֶם מוֹעֲדֵי יהוה אֲשֶׁר־תִּקְרְאוּ אֹתָם מִקְרָאֵי קֹדֶשׁ אֵלֶּה

RAMBAN *(cont.)*

observes His laws even to the point of surrendering their lives rather than violate the Torah. The chapter ends with the reminder: *I brought you out of Egypt to be your God*, which represents the foundation of the entire corpus of commandments: It is appropriate for Israel to sanctify God's name and His Torah because once the Almighty redeemed them from the Egyptian slavery, they became His own servants.

ABARBANEL

וְנִקְדַּשְׁתִּי בְּתוֹךְ בְּנֵי יִשְׂרָאֵל – *That I may be sanctified in the midst of the Israelites:* Says God: Since I have sanctified you, it is inappropriate for you priests to *profane My holy name* among the people of Israel. Now the proof that this comment is addressed to the priests lies in the clause *That I may be sanctified in the midst of the Israelites*. Thus, God plans to be made holy within the populace who will honor and revere Him when they see that the priests themselves are holy and preserve their purity.

SFORNO

וְלֹא תְחַלְּלוּ אֶת־שֵׁם קָדְשִׁי – *Do not profane My holy name:* Says God to the people of Israel: Since you are witness to the perfection of My achievements, you must realize that you have been sanctified to walk in My ways. Therefore, you must not profane My holy name by committing inadequate and despicable acts. Do not fulfill the prophet's prediction when he states: *There, in whichever nations they came to, they desecrated My holy Name because it was said of them, "These are the Lord's people, and they have left His land"* (Ezekiel 36:20). **וְנִקְדַּשְׁתִּי בְּתוֹךְ בְּנֵי יִשְׂרָאֵל** – *That I may be sanctified in the midst of the Israelites:* I will be sanctified when I perform miracles on behalf of the nation as I have pledged to do when I said: *Now am I hereby making a covenant. Before your entire people I will perform such wonders as never have been performed anywhere on earth* (Exodus 34:10). The reason for that is that *I am the Lord, who makes you holy.*

VERSE 33

RASHI

הַמּוֹצִיא אֶתְכֶם – *Who brought out:* I redeemed you from Egypt on this condition [that you would be willing to die to sanctify My name].

אֲנִי יהוה – *I am the Lord:* I can be trusted to grant your reward.

IBN EZRA

הַמּוֹצִיא אֶתְכֶם – *Who brought out:* The verse ends with the phrase "I am the Lord," which parallels the opening of the Ten Commandments. For this message is the basis of all the commandments.

in the midst of the Israelites. I am the LORD, who makes you
33 holy, who brought you out of Egypt to be your God: I am the
LORD."
23 1 2 The LORD spoke to Moshe: "Speak to the Israelites. Say: These REVI'I
are the LORD's appointed times that you shall proclaim as

ABARBANEL

הַמּוֹצִיא אֶתְכֶם – *Who brought out:* Let the Israelites always remember that the Almighty has brought them out of Egypt in order to be their God: He is their LORD. For by accepting the commandments, we accept the authority of the Lawgiver.

SFORNO

לִהְיוֹת לָכֶם לֵאלֹהִים – *To be your God:* I emancipated you from Egypt in order to be your direct leader; there shall be no intermediary between us as long as you walk in My holy ways. Thus, a later text warns: *Do not learn the ways of the nations; do not fear heavenly portents, even if the nations fear them* (Jeremiah 10:2). **אֲנִי יהוה** – *I am the LORD:* Because I am immutable, I will treat you in the future in the same way as I did in the past, on condition that your transgressions do not create a rift between us, as the prophet promises: *As in the days when you came out of Egypt, I will show My wonders* (Micah 7:15).

CLASSIC COMMENTATORS

CHAPTER 23, VERSE 2

RASHI

דַּבֵּר אֶל־בְּנֵי יִשְׂרָאֵל...מוֹעֲדֵי יהוה – *Speak to the Israelites. Say: These are the Lord's appointed times:* Schedule the festivals so that the Israelites will become accustomed to observing them. Hence, we learn that [the Sanhedrin is authorized] to intercalate the year [that is, adding a thirteenth month to the calendar after Adar, the twelfth month]. Such an adjustment will allow those Jews living in exile who have uprooted themselves from their homes to travel to Jerusalem and to reach the city in time for Passover.

RASHBAM

אֲשֶׁר־תִּקְרְאוּ אֹתָם מִקְרָאֵי קֹדֶשׁ – *That you shall proclaim as sacred assemblies:* The Torah hereby demands that Israel declare these festivals as sacred times. Whenever the term *keria* ["proclamation"] is used in conjunction with the holidays, it refers to the establishment of a particular time. Thus, we find the verse: *He has called [kara] a solemn assembly against me* (Lamentations 1:15).

IBN EZRA

אֵלֶּה הֵם מוֹעֲדָי – *These are My appointed times:* The verse refers to the Sabbath, and the noun is in the plural since a year has many Sabbaths in it.

RAMBAN

דַּבֵּר אֶל־בְּנֵי יִשְׂרָאֵל – *Speak to the Israelites:* The topic of the festivals is no more relevant to the priestly class than it is to the rest of the Israelite population, which is why the substance of the present chapter is not addressed to Aharon and to his sons, but to the people of Israel as a whole. The case would be otherwise if this chapter discussed the

RAMBAN *(cont.)*

additional [*musaf*] offerings which would fall under the priests' purview. Nevertheless, the national holidays are described here in the book of Leviticus because these are days of sacrifices [and thus the subject fits with the overall orientation of the book], a characteristic that the text alludes to in its repeated phrase *And you shall present a fire offering for the Lord* (23:8). [These words appear as well in verses 25, 27, and 36.] Indeed, at the end of this passage we read: *These are the Lord's festivals, which you shall proclaim, sacred assemblies to present a fire offering to the Lord: burnt offering, grain offering, sacrifice, and libations, each on its appointed day* (23:37), although the Torah does not mention here the additional sacrifices that are specific to the holidays. The reason for that omission is that God did not wish the people to bring the *musaf* sacrifices during their sojourn in the desert. Instead, after the book of Numbers lists the families who are to enter the land of Israel and concludes that *the land shall be apportioned to them for inheritance by the tally of their names* (Numbers 26:53), it subsequently details all of the *musaf* offerings that the nation is to sacrifice upon their entry into the land and for all posterity. This explains why, with regard to Yom Kippur, the Torah proclaims: *And as the Lord commanded Moshe, so it was done* (Leviticus 16:34), meaning: In the case of that festival alone, the procedures of the day were observed even in the wilderness. Now our chapter does talk about the Omer sheep [brought with the barley sheaf on the sixteenth of Nisan, as introduced in verses 12 and 13], as well as the lambs that are sacrificed on Shavuot [which accompanied the two special loaves of the holiday, as mentioned in verse 18]. But that is because it is clear that these were only brought within the land along with their respective grain offerings, as we read: *When you come to the land that I am giving you and reap its harvest* (23:10). [Hence these examples do not violate the author's rule that the chapter is devoted to the celebration of the festivals in the desert.] However, the days themselves were observed all along in the wilderness. Now, why does the text include the observance of the Sabbath in its list of the Lord's festivals [in verse 3]? This is because the Sabbath is also an appointed time that should be proclaimed as a sacred assembly. Before proceeding to discuss the aggregate of holidays, the Torah separates that group from the Sabbath by again stating: *These are the... appointed times, which you shall proclaim as sacred assemblies*. That statement emphasizes that the festivals should be commemorated regardless of what day of the week they fall out on. This of course is in contrast to the Sabbath, which need not be proclaimed at an appointed time because it occurs on the same day – the seventh – every single week. According to the Sages [as stated in the Sifra], the clause *which you shall proclaim as sacred assemblies* refers to the intercalations of the months and the year. Thus, the nation is directly involved in establishing the times for the festivals. Now it seems to me that our verse, *These are the Lord's appointed times that you shall proclaim as sacred assemblies; these are My appointed times*, serves as an introduction to the content regarding the festivals that appears below. This material starts with the statement: *In the first month, the fourteenth of the month* (23:5). However, verse 4 repeats this preface because the Sabbath has been mentioned in the interim. [Thus, neither verse 2, which precedes the reminder of the Sabbath in verse 3, nor verse 4 which follows it, include the seventh day in their general exclamations about "appointed times."] Hence, what verse 2 means is that *these are the Lord's appointed times* [the festivals] when it is forbidden to perform *melekhet avoda* [constructive labor]. In contrast, the Sabbath must be

RAMBAN (cont.)

observed as a day "of compete rest" when no work whatsoever may be done [whereas certain labors that are forbidden on the Sabbath may be done on the festivals for the purpose of the preparation of food]. Indeed, the Torah repeatedly issues admonitions to observe the Sabbath [so that the present case should not seem unusual]. The juxtaposition of the Sabbath with the festivals teaches that this leniency which allows the cooking of food may not be relied on should a holiday fall out on a Sabbath. **מִקְרָאֵי קֹדֶשׁ** – *Sacred assemblies:* The signification of this term is that the festivals are times when the entire community is summoned to gather together in order to sanctify the holiday. For the Torah commands the Israelites to assemble in the House of God at these special times and there to publicly make the day holy through prayers and praises of the Almighty. The celebratory and hallowed nature of the day is enhanced by the wearing of clean garments and by feasting, as is related in our tradition: *Then Neḥemya, His Excellency the governor...said to all the people, "Today is sacred to the Lord, your God. You should neither mourn nor weep"....* *"Now go and feast on delicacies, drink sweet things, and send servings of food to those who have none – for this day is sacred to our Lord. Do not be sorrowful, for rejoicing in the Lord is your strength and shelter"* (Nehemiah 8:9–10). What emerges is that the phrase "sacred assemblies" [*mikra'ei kodesh*] refers to the summoning of the people, as in the verse *These were the ones chosen from the community [keru'ei ha'eda], princes of their ancestral tribes* (Numbers 1:16). The Targum, however, identifies a different association, and connects the phrase to the verse *Then Yaakov called for his sons and said, "Gather together so that I can tell you what will happen [asher yikra] to you in the days to come"* (Genesis 49:1). Based on this, *mikra'ei kodesh* connotes a sacred event – whatever day the festival falls on should be made a consecrated occasion. Finally, our Sages explain the words *mikra'ei kodesh* as follows: Commemorate these days [*ar'em* – "make them an occasion"] with food, beverages, and clean garments. In other words, the festival days should not be treated like regular weekdays, but as sacred happenings, wherein celebratory meals and festive dress demonstrate their significance and the shift to the holy from the profane. This is also the Targum's approach.

RABBEINU BAḤYA

אֵלֶּה הֵם מוֹעֲדָי – *These are My appointed times:* This discussion of the festivals includes the observance of the Sabbath because that too is defined as an "appointed time." Note that regarding the seventh day the verse states: *It shall be a Sabbath for the Lord in all your dwellings* (23:3), but does not state: This is an everlasting statute throughout your generations in all your dwellings [language that we find several times in this chapter, such as in verse 14, with respect to the festivals]. For had the text said that in the context of the Sabbath, it would have meant that no labor would be permitted wherever Israel dwelled through the ages, and even in the Temple. The present phrasing means that creative labor is banned on the Sabbath only in places where the Israelites live, but not in the Temple.

ABARBANEL

מוֹעֲדֵי יהוה – *These are the Lord's appointed times:* Since the Sabbath is not described here as a separate institution [but as one of Israel's sacred days], the text does not mention the sacrifices that are specific to the day. These are discussed in other places in the Torah. We also

ג הֵם מוֹעֲדָי: שֵׁשֶׁת יָמִים תֵּעָשֶׂה מְלָאכָה וּבַיּוֹם הַשְּׁבִיעִי
שַׁבַּת שַׁבָּתוֹן מִקְרָא־קֹדֶשׁ כָּל־מְלָאכָה לֹא תַעֲשׂוּ שַׁבָּת
הִוא לַיהוה בְּכֹל מוֹשְׁבֹתֵיכֶם:
ד אֵלֶּה מוֹעֲדֵי יהוה מִקְרָאֵי קֹדֶשׁ אֲשֶׁר־תִּקְרְאוּ אֹתָם
ה בְּמוֹעֲדָם: בַּחֹדֶשׁ הָרִאשׁוֹן בְּאַרְבָּעָה עָשָׂר לַחֹדֶשׁ בֵּין

ABARBANEL *(cont.)*

do not find here the phrase *be'etzem hayom hazeh* [literally, "on this selfsame day," which appears several times in this chapter, such as in verse 28], because those words are reserved for holidays that occur at specific times during the year. The Sabbath, however, is observed repeatedly throughout the course of the year, every seven days. Finally, the sanctity of any given Sabbath does not derive from a holy event that happened specifically on that day. Rather, the Sabbath serves as a remembrance for the first Sabbath of creation.

SFORNO

מוֹעֲדֵי יהוה – *These are the Lord's appointed times:* At this point, the Torah has finished discussing the topic of sacrifices and has laid down laws for the people who service the Tabernacle offerings. The purpose of that entire system is to welcome the Divine Presence into the midst of the Israelite people, as we read earlier: *This shall be the regular burnt offering throughout your generations at the entrance of the Tent of Meeting before the Lord. There I will meet with you, there I will speak to you* (Exodus 29:42). The text now begins its discussion of the festivals, teaching that Israel must accept the cessation of everyday work at those times, including a complete avoidance of labor on the Sabbath and Yom Kippur. Such undertakings should be replaced with the study of Torah and matters of sanctity, as we read earlier: *Six days you shall work, and carry out all your labors, but the seventh is a Sabbath to the Lord your God* (Exodus 20:9–10). This means that one should lay down his hoe and his sickle and devote himself entirely to the Almighty. On the other holidays, it is only creative [non-food-related] work that must be avoided. The purpose of that is to encourage the people to celebrate the day with their Creator and focus on holy things, as the Sages maintain: The festival should be evenly divided between spiritual enhancement and physical enjoyment. When that balance is achieved, the Divine Presence will most assuredly rest upon Israel, as the psalmist declares: *God stands in the divine assembly* (Psalms 82:1). Thus, the sacred assemblies [*mikra'ei kodesh*] are times when the populace gathers for sacred pursuits, for a gathering of the nation is called *mikra*, as in the verse *New Moon and Sabbath, the feast days you proclaim [kero mikra]* (Isaiah 1:13).

VERSE 3

RASHI

שֵׁשֶׁת יָמִים – *Six days:* Why does the text include the Sabbath in a discussion of the festivals? In order to teach us that if an individual profanes the holidays [by performing

3 sacred assemblies; these are My appointed times. Work shall
be done through six days, but the seventh day shall be a Sabbath of complete rest, a sacred assembly. You shall perform
no work at all; it shall be a Sabbath for the LORD in all your
dwellings.
4 These are the LORD's appointed times, sacred assemblies, which
5 you shall proclaim at their appointed times. In the first month,
the fourteenth of the month in the afternoon is the time for the

RASHI *(cont.)*

forbidden labors on those days], his transgression is considered as severe as if he had violated the Sabbath. Conversely, when a person observes the holidays, he is credited as if he has kept the Sabbath.

VERSE 4

RASHI

אֵלֶּה מוֹעֲדֵי יהוה – *These are the LORD's appointed times:* The earlier verse referred to intercalating the year [by adding an extra month], whereas this verse refers to sanctifying the months. [Just as the ultimate form of the year's calendar is subject to the court's deliberations, so too does the exact length of each month depend on the court acknowledging the sighting of the new moon.]

RABBEINU BAḤYA

אֵלֶּה מוֹעֲדֵי יהוה – *These are the LORD's appointed times:* The text now begins to describe the festivals of Israel, a number of celebrations associated with the essence of God, symbolized by His personal name [the LORD]. The topic is introduced with the term *elleh* ["These are"] which signifies something permanent. Thus, the holidays will never be annulled, but will be celebrated as long as this physical world endures as it is currently configured. And so does a later verse state: *It is for us and our children to eternity to keep all the words of this Law* (Deuteronomy 29:28).

VERSE 5

RASHI

בֵּין הָעַרְבָּיִם – *In the afternoon:* The afternoon starts six and a half hours into the day. **פֶּסַח לַיהוה** – *The Passover sacrifice to the LORD:* This refers to the offering of the sacrifice called *Pesaḥ*.

ḤIZKUNI

בֵּין הָעַרְבָּיִם פֶּסַח – *In the afternoon for the Passover sacrifice:* This refers to the afternoon preceding the first day of the Passover holiday. That night is the time properly called *Pesaḥ* because that is when Israel occupies itself with the sacrifice of that name. However, the rest of the festival after the first night is called the Festival of Unleavened Bread.

ו הָעַרְבָּיִם פֶּסַח לַיהוה: וּבַחֲמִשָּׁה עָשָׂר יוֹם לַחֹדֶשׁ הַזֶּה חַג
ז הַמַּצּוֹת לַיהוה שִׁבְעַת יָמִים מַצּוֹת תֹּאכֵלוּ: בַּיּוֹם הָרִאשׁוֹן
מִקְרָא־קֹדֶשׁ יִהְיֶה לָכֶם כָּל־מְלֶאכֶת עֲבֹדָה לֹא תַעֲשׂוּ:
ח וְהִקְרַבְתֶּם אִשֶּׁה לַיהוה שִׁבְעַת יָמִים בַּיּוֹם הַשְּׁבִיעִי מִקְרָא־
קֹדֶשׁ כָּל־מְלֶאכֶת עֲבֹדָה לֹא תַעֲשׂוּ:

ABARBANEL

פֶּסַח לַיהוה – *The Passover sacrifice to the Lord:* The Torah begins its discussion of the festivals with Passover since it comes first in the calendar. Passover also serves as the foundation for all of the other holidays. The Ramban is correct when he writes that each of the year's special events is addressed in a separate section in the text because this chapter introduces something new regarding every festival, details that have not yet appeared in the Torah. Thus, it seems to me that this explains why the mention of Passover is not preceded by the statement: The Lord spoke to Moshe [as is the case for other festivals, in verses 9, 23, 26, and 33], for there is no novel addition here to our understanding of that holiday. Indeed, the Almighty already recounted the particulars of this festival at great length in Parashat Bo [Exodus 12:1–20 and 12:43–51] and in other places. Nothing new about the holiday is said in the present context; its inclusion represents merely a remembrance of the festival.

VERSE 8

RASHI

וְהִקְרַבְתֶּם אִשֶּׁה – *And you shall present a fire offering:* This refers to the additional offerings brought on festivals [the *musaf* sacrifices] which are discussed in Parashat Pinḥas. Why are these sacrifices mentioned here? To make the point that those additional offerings are independent of each other. [The later text reads: *You shall offer a burnt fire offering to the Lord: two young bulls, one ram, and seven yearling lambs, all unblemished* (Numbers 28:19)] and our verse states: *And you shall present a fire offering for the Lord*, meaning that the *musaf* offerings should be brought under all circumstances. If the Temple lacks bulls, the priests should nevertheless sacrifice the rams; if there are no rams, the lambs should still be offered. **שִׁבְעַת יָמִים** – *For seven days:* [The usual term for "seven" is *shiv'a* with a *heh* at the end of the word. When a *tav* substitutes for the *heh*, it normally connotes the construct form, so that here it would suggest "a seven of days." Rashi explains:] The word *shiv'at* is a noun, such that the phrase means "a septet of days." The Old French term for this is *seteine* ["a week"]. The same interpretation applies to the word *shemonat* – connoting an octet, *sheshet* – a sextet, *ḥameshet* – a quintet, and *sheloshet* – a trio. [The author makes a similar observation in his commentary to the words *for three days* in Exodus 10:22, and *about three months later* in Genesis 38:24.] **מְלֶאכֶת עֲבֹדָה** – *No laborious work:* You may not even do work that you consider critically important to save you from suffering a financial loss. I inferred this point from the Sifra (Emor 12:8), which derives from our verse that work of this kind is permitted on the intermediate days of the festival.

6 Passover sacrifice to the LORD. The fifteenth day of this month
is the LORD's Festival of Unleavened Bread; for seven days you
7 shall eat unleavened bread. The first day shall be a sacred as-
8 sembly for you; you shall perform no laborious work. And you
shall present a fire offering for the LORD for seven days; on the
seventh day there shall be a sacred assembly; you shall perform
no laborious work."

RAMBAN

כָּל־מְלֶאכֶת עֲבֹדָה לֹא תַעֲשׂוּ – *You shall perform no laborious work:* The term *melekhet avoda* ["laborious work"] connotes any forbidden labor that is not required for the preparation of food. We can understand that definition based on the following texts. (1) *Six days you shall work [taavod], and carry out all your labors [melakhtekha]* (Exodus 20:9); (2) *The Egyptians embittered their lives with... all kinds of tasks [avoda] in the fields* (Exodus 1:14); (3) *I will turn toward you, and you will be tilled [ne'evadtem] and sown* (Ezekiel 36:9); and (4) *Kayin was a worker [oved] of the land* (Genesis 4:2). [Hence, *avoda* connotes work that is done in the fields rather than in the kitchen. It is the former that is forbidden on the festivals, rather than the latter.] However, labor that is performed directly for the sake of eating is considered *melekhet hanaa* ["beneficial work"] rather than *melekhet avoda* ["laborious work"]. The Torah makes this distinction clear in an earlier discussion of Passover where the text initially states: *The first day shall be a sacred assembly and the seventh day shall be a sacred assembly. On them no work [melakha] may be done* [Exodus 12:16, which suggests that all manner of labor is forbidden]. However, the verse continues to qualify that prohibition: *But preparing the food for everyone to eat. That alone may you do.* This clarification is abridged in the Torah's presentation of the other festivals, where the text simply commands: *You shall perform no laborious work [melekhet avoda]* (in 23:21, 25, 35, and 36), thereby proscribing any work which is not directly necessary for the preparation of food. Thus, the reader will never find the term *kol melakha* ["all labor"] stated in relation to the festivals [since not *all* labor is forbidden]. Nor does the Torah explicitly permit labor for the preparation of food, since that is implied by the prohibition of *melekhet avoda* [which is unrelated to food preparation]. Nevertheless, the following mention of the Festival of Unleavened Bread does not appear to fit this model: *For six days you shall eat unleavened bread and, on the seventh day, you shall hold an assembly for the LORD your God and perform no work [melakha]* (Deuteronomy 16:8). [As the term *melekhet avoda* is not used in this text, this suggests that no labor may be done on the last day of Passover, including that which is restricted to food preparation.] The explanation for this exception is that the Torah has already defined and permitted what may be done on the seventh day of the festival [in Exodus 12:16, cited above]. Hence, there was no need for the full phrase *melekhet avoda* to be used subsequently when the word *avoda* would suffice. Even so, note that the text does not emphasize that *kol melakha* ["all labor"] must be avoided, as it does above in verse 23:3 with respect to the Sabbath, a phrase that will recur below in the context of Yom Kippur [in 23:28. In contrast to the other holidays, food may not be prepared on the Sabbath or on Yom Kippur]. However, the verse in Deuteronomy (16:8) refers back to the type of labor about which the Torah has already warned Israel. [That is, *melekhet avoda*, in Exodus 12:16.]

ט וַיְדַבֵּר יְהוָה אֶל־מֹשֶׁה לֵּאמֹר: דַּבֵּר אֶל־בְּנֵי יִשְׂרָאֵל וְאָמַרְתָּ
אֲלֵהֶם כִּי־תָבֹאוּ אֶל־הָאָרֶץ אֲשֶׁר אֲנִי נֹתֵן לָכֶם וּקְצַרְתֶּם
אֶת־קְצִירָהּ וַהֲבֵאתֶם אֶת־עֹמֶר רֵאשִׁית קְצִירְכֶם אֶל־

SFORNO

וְהִקְרַבְתֶּם אִשֶּׁה לַיהוה שִׁבְעַת יָמִים – *And you shall present a fire offering for the Lord for seven days:* By commanding that Israel *present a fire offering for the Lord for seven days*, the Torah teaches that the intermediate days of the Passover festival should not be treated as completely profane [that is, with no holy character at all]. Since these five days are celebrated with a communal additional [*musaf*] offering in addition to the usual daily sacrifice, just like on the festival days [*yom tov*], it is clear that these days are part of the holiday. Now the Torah does not here describe the nature of the intermediate day *musaf* sacrifices, just as it does not elaborate on the *musaf* services of any of the other holidays. [That is a topic which is addressed fully in Numbers chapters 28 and 29.] In a similar way does the text, in the case of Sukkot, state succinctly: *For seven days you must bring close a fire offering to the Lord* (23:36), to indicate that the six intermediate days of that festival are also sacred to a degree. With respect to Rosh Hashana we read: *You shall bring close a fire offering to the Lord* (23:25), and that refers to the additional sacrifice commemorating Rosh Ḥodesh, as we read later: *This will be in addition to the monthly burnt offering with its grain offering* (Numbers 29:6). [Rosh Hashana of course has no intermediate days, and hence the "fire offering" mentioned in connection with that holiday must refer to something else, namely the *musaf* offering for the New Moon of Tishrei, which coincides with Rosh Hashana.] On the other hand, in the present chapter's discussion of the Sabbath, Shavuot, and Yom Kippur, there is no allusion at all to the *musaf* offerings that are brought on those days. For when the verse states regarding Yom Kippur: *You shall bring a fire-offering to the Lord*, that is not a reference to the *musaf* sacrifice but to the burnt offerings and the purification offerings that the High Priest and the community present on the Day of Atonement, as detailed in Parashat Aḥarei Mot [chapter 16]. The reader will notice that text employs a single statement of address: *The Lord spoke to Moshe: "Speak to the Israelites"* (23:1–2) to present the Sabbath [in verse 3], the Passover sacrifice [verse 5], and the Festival of Unleavened Bread [verse 6]. This is because God commanded Israel regarding each of those occasions before the revelation of the Torah. In contrast to those three occasions, each of the other festivals is here given its own introduction. Our chapter's discussion of Shavuot opens with a description of the Omer offering [in verses 10–13], since the moment it is brought signals the beginning of the grain harvest, and it is when the counting of the seven weeks starts. Both of these issues are reflected in the names of the holiday which is referred to as *the Festival of the Harvest* (Exodus 23:16), and *the Festival of Weeks* (Exodus 34:22). On this day, the Israelites express their gratitude to the Almighty for *the weeks reserved for harvest* (Jeremiah 5:24). For the purpose of the pilgrimage festivals is to engage in prayer and thanksgiving, just as Passover is dedicated to acknowledging the ripening of the grain, and appreciating the Lord's emancipation of our ancestors. And since the success of the harvest depends on the weather conditions from the time that the crops begin to ripen until they are reaped, the prophet states: *Let us revere the Lord our God who has given us rain, early and late, in*

9 The Lord spoke to Moshe: "Speak to the Israelites. Say:
10 When you come to the land that I am giving you and reap its

SFORNO *(cont.)*

the proper time, who protects for us the weeks reserved for harvest (Jeremiah 5:24). Therefore, the Omer offering, which takes place at the beginning of the ripening season, represents the nation's recognition of God's assistance; it is as if the first fruits of the field have been given back to the owner in thanks. Meanwhile, the animal sacrifice which accompanies the grain offering signals a petition for the future; the forty-nine days of counting are an opportunity to pray [throughout this period for the prosperity of the yield]; and the Festival of the Harvest [Shavuot itself] represents the ultimate moment of gratitude for the bounty that the fields have provided. Subsequently, the Festival of Gathering [Sukkot] culminates the cycle with a statement acknowledging the richness of the harvest.

VERSE 10

RASHI

רֵאשִׁית קְצִירְכֶם – *The first of your harvest:* This sheaf will be the first grain cutting of the season. **עֹמֶר** – *Sheaf:* The sheaf should be comprised of an "omer of grain" which is the name for a tenth of an ephah. An earlier verse identifies this as a measurement when it states: *They measured it with an omer measure* (Exodus 16:18).

BEKHOR SHOR

וַהֲבֵאתֶם אֶת־עֹמֶר רֵאשִׁית קְצִירְכֶם – *Bring the first sheaf of your harvest:* It is only permissible to eat the grains of the year's new harvest once a tribute from that yield has been presented to God. The Omer offering is brought from barley. We know this because the term *aviv* is used in connection with this offering [an earlier verse reads: *If you bring a grain offering of first produce to the Lord, it shall be brought as soon as it ripens on the stalk – aviv* (2:14), alluding to the Omer], and we know that *aviv* relates to that grain from the verse *By then the flax and barley had been destroyed, because the barley was ripe [aviv] and the flax in bud* (Exodus 9:31). Just as in the Egyptian plague the crop in question was barley, so too here, the commandment relates to barley. The measurement of an omer represents a tenth of an ephah [as stated explicitly in Exodus 16:36]. Since an omer of grain can produce a tenth of an ephah of flour, that measurement is referred to as an omer.

RAMBAN

דַּבֵּר אֶל־בְּנֵי יִשְׂרָאֵל וְאָמַרְתָּ אֲלֵהֶם – *Speak to the Israelites. Say:* All of the following sections, each one dealing with a different festival, contain a new commandment relating to that holiday, aside from the general requirements to make these times days of rest and holiness. This is why the distinct paragraphs are all prefaced with the words "Speak to the Israelites." Recognize that the day on which the holiday of Shavuot is celebrated is dependent on the counting of the Omer. That explains why those two topics are linked [and why Shavuot is not similarly introduced in verse 16 with the formula "Speak to the Israelites"]. Furthermore, since the Day of Remembrance [Rosh HaShana] and Yom Kippur both fall in the same month and both festivals address the same theme of repentance from transgression, the

יא הַכֹּהֵן: וְהֵנִיף אֶת־הָעֹמֶר לִפְנֵי יהוה לִרְצֹנְכֶם מִמָּחֳרַת
יב הַשַּׁבָּת יְנִיפֶנּוּ הַכֹּהֵן: וַעֲשִׂיתֶם בְּיוֹם הֲנִיפְכֶם אֶת־הָעֹמֶר
יג כֶּבֶשׂ תָּמִים בֶּן־שְׁנָתוֹ לְעֹלָה לַיהוה: וּמִנְחָתוֹ שְׁנֵי עֶשְׂרֹנִים
סֹלֶת בְּלוּלָה בַשֶּׁמֶן אִשֶּׁה לַיהוה רֵיחַ נִיחֹחַ וְנִסְכֹּה יַיִן

RAMBAN *(cont.)*

preface to Yom Kippur is shortened to *The Lord spoke to Moshe*, without the accompanying command "Tell the Israelites." In other words, the initial order *Tell the Israelites* (23:24) relating to Rosh Hashana suffices for both holidays. Even so, the Torah describes these two days in separate paragraphs because they represent distinct issues.

VERSE 11

RASHI

וְהֵנִיף – *He shall display:* [*Vehenif* can also be understood as "he shall wave."] All instances of waving prescribed by the Torah entail moving the object back and forth [out and in, in the four directions of the compass] in order to protect against damaging wind, and up and down as a precaution against harmful dew. **לִרְצֹנְכֶם** – *For your acceptance:* If you offer the sheaf this way, it will be accepted on your behalf. **מִמָּחֳרַת הַשַּׁבָּת** – *On the day after the day of rest:* This refers to the day following the first day of Passover [that is, on the sixteenth of Nisan]. The text cannot be referring to the Sabbath of creation [implying that the sheaf should be brought on a Sunday] since it does not state which Sabbath in the year is signified.

RAMBAN

מִמָּחֳרַת הַשַּׁבָּת – *On the day after the day of rest:* According to the tradition as presented by the Sages, when the Torah uses the phrase "the day after the day of rest" [*mimoḥorat hashabbat*], it refers to the day following the first day of the festival [and does not mean, as was suggested by the Sadducees, the day after the Sabbath, that is, Sunday]. In light of that reading, the progression of these verses makes perfect sense. At first, the text commands [in verses 6–8] that the Festival of Unleavened Bread be celebrated for seven days in the first month of the year, of which the opening and the concluding days of the holiday shall each be a day of rest [*shabbaton*] when "no laborious work" may be performed. Following this instruction, the Torah states [in verses 9–11] that when the nation enters the land of Israel, they shall present the Omer on the day after that "day of rest" [*shabbat*]. That refers to the first day of rest mentioned here [that is, the first day of Passover, described in verse 7 as a rest day]. Furthermore, the significance of this passage is that the Omer should only be brought when Israel resides in the land, and not in the wilderness or outside the land [should the populace be exiled from their home]. Nevertheless, the subsequent usage of the term *shabbat* in this passage, in the verse *To the day after the seventh week [ad mimoḥorat hashabbat hasheviit]* (23:16) and in the verse *You shall count for yourselves seven complete weeks [sheva shabbatot temimot]* (23:15) cannot similarly connote the first festival day of Passover. In these cases, the word *shabbat* means "week," which is how the Targum translates it. What emerges is that in verse 15, which contains two references to

11 harvest, bring the first sheaf of your harvest to the priest. He
shall display the sheaf this way and that before the LORD for
your acceptance; on the day after the day of rest the priest shall
12 display it. On the day you display the sheaf this way and that,
you shall offer a yearling sheep without blemish as a burnt of-
13 fering to the LORD. Its grain offering shall be two-tenths of
an ephah of fine flour mixed with oil, a fire offering for the
LORD, a pleasing aroma; and its libation shall be a quarter of

RAMBAN *(cont.)*

the word *shabbat*, the term is used in two different ways. Indeed, some commentators praise such writing as stylistically eloquent. Another example of two homonyms within the same verse appears in the text *He had thirty sons who rode on thirty donkeys [ayarim] and owned thirty villages [ayarim]* (Judges 10:4). A later verse supports our interpretation of 23:15 here when it states: *You shall count seven weeks [shavuot]* [Deuteronomy 16:9, instead of employing the word in our text, *shabbatot*, showing that they mean the same thing]. The reason that a week is termed "a sabbath" is that every set of seven days includes a Shabbat in it. As well, the days of the week are all reckoned in relation to the Sabbath. [Sunday is referred to as *yom rishon beShabbat* –the first day toward the next Sabbath; Monday is called *yom sheni beShabbat* – the second day toward the next Sabbath, and so on.] Hence, the group of seven days together are named a *shabbat* ["week," thereby identifying the focus of the entire set as the Sabbath]. The Sages noted that this language is very common, as in the statement [in Ketubot 2a]: City courts convene twice a *shabbat* ["week"].

VERSE 12

RASHI

וַעֲשִׂיתֶם... כֶּבֶשׂ – *You shall offer a sheep:* It is the sheaf of barley which creates the obligation for this offering. [The sheep mentioned in this verse does not constitute one of the day's additional *musaf* sacrifices, but is a function of the grain offering.]

VERSE 13

RASHI

וּמִנְחָתוֹ – *Its grain offering:* This is the accompanying grain offering [of the sheep mentioned in the previous verse]. **שְׁנֵי עֶשְׂרֹנִים** – *Two-tenths:* This grain offering has double the usual volume. [According to Numbers 15:4–5, the standard grain offering brought with a burnt offering comprises one-tenth of an ephah of flour.] **וְנִסְכֹּה יַיִן רְבִיעִת הַהִין** – *And its libation shall be a quarter of a hin of wine:* Despite the fact that this grain offering contains twice as much flour, the amount of wine is not doubled [from the usual requirement, as stated in Numbers 15:5. Even though a quarter of a hin of wine is the expected libation in this case, the text repeats this point lest we think that the wine should be increased just as the flour is].

ḤIZKUNI

וּמִנְחָתוֹ שְׁנֵי עֶשְׂרֹנִים – *Its grain offering shall be two-tenths of an ephah:* This grain offering comprises twice as much flour because it signals the start of the harvest season. The

יד רְבִיעִת הַהִין: וְלֶחֶם וְקָלִי וְכַרְמֶל לֹא תֹאכְלוּ עַד־עֶצֶם
הַיּוֹם הַזֶּה עַד הֲבִיאֲכֶם אֶת־קָרְבַּן אֱלֹהֵיכֶם חֻקַּת עוֹלָם
טו לְדֹרֹתֵיכֶם בְּכֹל מֹשְׁבֹתֵיכֶם: וּסְפַרְתֶּם לָכֶם יט
מִמָּחֳרַת הַשַּׁבָּת מִיּוֹם הֲבִיאֲכֶם אֶת־עֹמֶר הַתְּנוּפָה שֶׁבַע

ḤIZKUNI *(cont.)*

excess amount of material symbolizes the hope for a blessed and bountiful yield. And since a sheep comprising the *musaf* offering is usually accompanied by a grain offering that is but a single tenth of an ephah [as mandated by Numbers 15:4], the amounts of grain offerings for the respective sacrifices are delineated in our prayers [in order to highlight this difference]. According to some commentators, one of the two-tenths is the Omer that is brought with the yearling sheep, and the second of the tenths is the usual tenth brought as a grain offering. Support for this interpretation can be found in the fact that the libation is still *a quarter of a hin of wine*, as it is in other cases of sheep sacrifices. But this understanding is incorrect because these two-tenths of an ephah are composed of wheat, as the verse states: *Fine flour [solet] mixed with oil*, and we have a tradition that *solet* always connotes wheat. On the other hand, the Omer is cut from stalks of barley.

ABARBANEL

וּמִנְחָתוֹ שְׁנֵי עֶשְׂרֹנִים – *Its grain offering shall be two-tenths of an ephah:* Since it would be inappropriate to bring a barley offering by itself, the Torah orders that it be accompanied by the sacrifice of a single sheep along with its attendant grain offering of "two-tenths of an ephah." Now it seems to me that the logical basis for this sacrifice is as follows. First, God has commanded that Israel bring the Omer offering as the first fruits of the barley harvest, for all initial produce should be delivered to the House of the Lord. There is an allusion to this offering: Upon their emancipation from Egypt all of the Israelites resembled cattle; hence the donation comprises barley [which is animal feed]. Now throughout the holiday of Passover, seven lambs were sacrificed every day [as mandated by Numbers 28:19]. These corresponded to the duration of the festival, which is seven days. The number of sheep matched the number of Passover days to indicate that the law prohibiting leaven applies equally to every day of the holiday. Hence, this week is referred to as the Festival of Unleavened Bread. On the other hand, the first day of Passover is singled out since it is the only one of the seven on which the Omer is brought; this offering is not repeated on any of the other Passover days. In recognition of this unique event, the Torah instructs Israel to bring *a yearling sheep without blemish as a burnt offering to the Lord* – the one sheep corresponds to the one-time offering of the Omer and to the first day of the festival, which is also unique. Furthermore, since offerings of barley are generally considered inferior, the donation of the Omer might seem somewhat disrespectful to the Almighty. To compensate for that apparent affront, the Torah instructs that an additional "two-tenths of an ephah of flour" be brought as well. This is the same wheat flour that accompanies all the usual sheep sacrifices. Similarly, these should represent "a fire offering for the Lord," meaning that it is not a handful of flour that is burned as a remembrance; rather, the entire batch

14 **a hin of wine. Until that day, until you bring this sacrifice to**
your God, you shall eat no bread or roasted grain or ripe grain.
This is an everlasting statute throughout your generations, in
15 **all your dwellings. And from the day you bring the**
sheaf of the wave offering, the day after the day of rest, you shall

ABARBANEL *(cont.)*

is consumed. The message is therefore that even though barley – which is not considered as desirable as wheat – is brought here to symbolize Israel, which is like a scattered flock, the accompanying grain offering is not only superlative and unsullied, but its amount is twice as much as is normally presented. For soon the nation will gather to accept the Torah. We might also say that the additional tenth of an ephah signifies a blessing for the grain harvest. There is also no doubt that there was a greater amount of oil mixed in with the doubled flour. This is the reason behind this sacrifice.

VERSE 14

RASHI

וְקָלִי – *Roasted grain:* Flour made of soft kernels which is dried in the oven. **וְכַרְמֶל** – *Ripe grain:* This refers to parched seeds which are called *graines* ["seeds"] in Old French. **בְּכֹל מֹשְׁבֹתֵיכֶם** – *In all your dwellings:* The Sages of Israel have debated the interpretation of this phrase. Some scholars maintain that according to this verse, the practice of *ḥadash* [the prohibition to eat grain of the new harvest until the omer of barley has been brought] must be observed outside of Israel as well. However, others understand the significance of the words "in all your dwellings" differently: The law only takes effect once Israel has conquered, apportioned, and settled the land. [Hence, the people are living in dwellings across the country.]

VERSE 15

RASHI

מִמָּחֳרַת הַשַּׁבָּת – *The day after the day of rest:* The day after the first day of the festival. **תְּמִימֹת תִּהְיֶינָה** – *Complete weeks:* The phrase teaches that the counting of these weeks must begin in the evening. For otherwise the weeks will not be complete. [Since the sixteenth of Nisan begins in the evening, were the counting to begin in the morning, only part of that day would be included in the total.]

RAMBAN

וּסְפַרְתֶּם לָכֶם – *You shall count for yourselves:* This injunction is similar to the subsequent verse which reads: *You shall take for yourselves fruit of the majestic tree, branches of palm trees* (23:40), meaning that both the counting and the taking are incumbent upon every person. Thus, each Israelite must verbally count this period and keep track of its days. Such is the tradition as taught to us by the Sages. On the other hand, consider the verse which states regarding the *zav*: *When the man with the discharge is purified of it, he shall count seven days for his purification* (15:13), or that which we read with respect to the *zava*: *When the woman's discharge ends, she shall count seven days; after that, she will be purified* (15:28). In

טז שַׁבָּתוֹת תְּמִימֹת תִּהְיֶינָה: עַד מִמָּחֳרַת הַשַּׁבָּת הַשְּׁבִיעִת
תִּסְפְּרוּ חֲמִשִּׁים יוֹם וְהִקְרַבְתֶּם מִנְחָה חֲדָשָׁה לַיהוָה:

RAMBAN *(cont.)*

these instances, the man or the woman is entitled to remain impure as long as they do not forget their condition [and inadvertently enter the Temple precincts or eat sacred food while they are still in a state of impurity. Since the *zav* and *zava* are under no obligation to purify themselves, they need not count their clean days out loud, in contrast to the Israelite who must reckon the days of the Omer]. Elsewhere, the Torah describes the tallying of the Jubilee years as follows: *And you shall count off seven Sabbaths of years – seven times seven years – so that the seven Sabbath cycles total forty-nine years* (25:8). In this instance, it is a matter of primary importance to remember the number of the current year [although there exists no requirement for the people to actually state that detail orally]. Indeed, the Sifra maintains that the Jubilee years should be announced by the court. I do not know if that means that the Sanhedrin in Jerusalem was required to reckon the year within the fifty, and to identify which seven-year cycle had been reached, in addition to reciting a blessing. Such a procedure would parallel the counting of the days and the weeks that are noted during the Omer. Alternatively, perhaps the court is merely required to know the number of every year and ultimately to sanctify the fiftieth year. Now what is the significance of the clause *This is an everlasting statute throughout your generations, in all your dwellings*, which is mentioned in conjunction with the prohibition of the new grain [in 23:14], and with regard to resting from work that is required on the Festival of Shavuot [as stated in 23:21]? The inclusion of these statements is necessary since the former is dependent on the waving of the Omer and the latter is linked to the presentation of new grain offerings. [The year's new grain may not be eaten until the barley offering has been brought and waved. Fifty days later, on Shavuot, *the bread of the first produce [is brought] as a wave offering* (23:20) in the form of two special loaves. Subsequently, verse 21 instructs that "no laborious work" shall be done on the holiday. Now we might have thought that in a situation where no Omer is brought, no new grain may be eaten, and that when the two loaves are similarly absent, all work may be performed on the day of Shavuot.] To counter this reasoning, the Torah declares that even after the people of Israel have been exiled from their land and the waving of the Omer and the grain offering are no longer practiced, these prohibitions still apply – it is forbidden to eat new grain everywhere [until the sixteenth of Nisan, even when there is no Omer offering. As well, no labor may be done on Shavuot even though the two loaves are not brought anymore. The author is thereby explaining why the Torah emphasizes that these laws remain in force in all times and places]. Similarly, this clause does not appear in the case of Rosh Hashana [because there is no reason to think that the laws of that festival are contingent on the Temple]. Moreover, the Torah does not state in the case of Sukkot [that the commandments of the four species, living in booths, and avoidance of labor are in force] "in all of your dwellings." Both mentions of time and place appear in the discussion of Yom Kippur [in verse 31]. This is because Parashat Aḥarei Mot has associated our atonement with the sacrificial services. It was therefore necessary for the present text to stress that the prohibitions [of eating and working]

16 count for yourselves seven complete weeks. To the day after
the seventh week, you shall count fifty days; and then you shall

RAMBAN *(cont.)*

remain relevant to the holy day always and in all places that Israelites live. For the day of Yom Kippur is intended to cleanse the soul from its transgressions through affliction and the cessation of work. Thus, the absence of sacrifices on the day is not an impediment to receiving absolution from the Lord. Finally, the Torah does not demand that the Festival of Unleavened Bread be commemorated in all generations and dwellings. Nevertheless, an earlier text does include both points: *Safeguard the unleavened bread.... You shall observe this day for all generations; it is an everlasting law.... Eat nothing leavened. Wherever you may live, you shall eat unleavened bread* (Exodus 12:17 and 20). It was necessary to mandate that the festival be celebrated throughout time and in all places since we might have thought that the Passover holiday is founded upon and depends on the Passover sacrifice, as the verse states: *They shall eat the meat that night, roasted over a fire; with unleavened bread and bitter herbs they shall eat it* (Exodus 12:8). Hence the Torah teaches us otherwise.

VERSE 16

RASHI

הַשַּׁבָּת הַשְּׁבִיעִת – *The seventh week:* This should be understood as the Targum renders the term: *shevuata sheviata* – "the seventh week." [The term *shabbat* should not be interpreted here as "first day of the festival" as it is in verses 11 and 15.] **עַד מִמָּחֳרַת הַשַּׁבָּת הַשְּׁבִיעִת תִּסְפְּרוּ** – *To the day after the seventh week, you shall count:* The count should continue up to the fiftieth day, but should not include it, thereby yielding a total of forty-nine days. [A count of fifty days would result not in seven full weeks, but more than that.] **חֲמִשִּׁים יוֹם וְהִקְרַבְתֶּם מִנְחָה חֲדָשָׁה לַיהוה** – *Fifty days; and then you shall present a new grain offering to the Lord:* This grain offering should be brought on the fiftieth day. Now I believe that this is the midrashic interpretation of the verse. However, the straightforward meaning of the text is: You shall count until the day after seven weeks, which is the fiftieth day. Thus, the order of the verse's phrases should be rearranged. [In Rashi's second reading, the words *ḥamishim yom* are not linked in the verse to the bringing of the grain offering, but to the counting, and to the opening words of the sentence: Until the day after the seventh week, which is the fiftieth day, you shall count.] **מִנְחָה חֲדָשָׁה** – *A new grain offering:* This is the first grain offering brought from the new season's grain. And should you argue that the Omer offering [discussed above] is in fact brought earlier, that case differs from all other grain offerings, since it is comprised of barley [whereas nearly all other grain offerings are composed of wheat. Thus, this grain offering marks the start of the new wheat donations for the year.]

ḤIZKUNI

תִּסְפְּרוּ חֲמִשִּׁים יוֹם – *You shall count fifty days:* A blessing should be recited upon the counting of these days because their progression is uninterrupted. This is not so in the case of the menstruating woman, with regard to whom the text states: *When the woman's discharge ends, she shall count seven days; after that, she will be purified* (15:28). No blessing is required in that instance because it is possible that the woman's clean days will be broken up by the

יז מִמּוֹשְׁבֹתֵיכֶם תָּבִיאוּ ׀ לֶחֶם תְּנוּפָה שְׁתַּיִם שְׁנֵי עֶשְׂרֹנִים

ḤIZKUNI *(cont.)*

appearance of blood, in which case all the previous days will be discounted. That would result in a *berakha levatala*, a "futile blessing." [From the author's discussion it appears that he is referring to the recitation of a blessing at the start of the Omer count, and not to the repetition of that blessing on all subsequent days.]

KELI YAKAR

וְהִקְרַבְתֶּם מִנְחָה חֲדָשָׁה לַיהוה – *And then you shall present a new grain offering to the Lord:* Offering the new grain symbolizes the anniversary of the revelation of the Torah because every time one studies its contents, they must be as fresh, novel, and exciting to him as if the material had just now been conveyed to the nation by God at Mount Sinai. Naturally, the reader might ask why the text does not explicitly identify the Festival of Shavuot as a commemoration of the imparting of the Torah. It is similarly noteworthy that the holiday of Rosh Hashana is not identified as the Day of Judgment. Indeed, there is one explanation that satisfies both issues. When considering His presentation of the Torah, God did not wish to limit the affirmation of that event to a single day. This is because it is incumbent upon the Israelite to imagine on every day that God has spoken to him right now and commanded him to fulfill His laws and practices. Our Sages [in Eruvin 54b] compare the study of the Torah to a baby suckling at his mother's breast. Just as the child continually finds new tastes in the milk that nourishes him, so too does the Jew continually discover new ideas in the text of God's word. It is therefore appropriate that those people who occupy themselves with seeking the depth of the Torah's meaning regard every day as a commemoration of its revelation. Hence, it is not wholly fitting to mark but a single day as significant for acknowledging the receipt of the Torah. Again, the Sages remark that a person should never consider the Torah's message to be an ancient and timeworn communication that he is tired of perusing. Rather, the Israelite must forever seek new dimensions of understanding that are concealed in the profundities of the Torah's verses. All of this explains why the emphasis in the text regarding Shavuot is not about the national experience at Mount Sinai, but about the bringing of the new grain to the Temple. The Torah itself represents an "offering of new grain" every single day. We can apply the same reasoning to the Torah's presentation of the Rosh Hashana festival, where the text makes no reference to its fundamental characteristic as the Day of Judgment. The Torah omits this ascription lest throughout the year one continues to commit multiple transgressions with the intention of repenting as the day approaches on which God ascends His throne to examine every person's behavior. Instead, it behooves every Israelite to imagine that the Almighty considers humanity's sins on a daily basis and regularly records the misdeeds performed by His creations. If a person thinks in this way, he will spend every single day in contrition and repentance.

VERSE 17

RASHI

מִמּוֹשְׁבֹתֵיכֶם – *From your dwellings:* The flour must not be brought from wheat grown outside of the land. **לֶחֶם תְּנוּפָה** – *As a wave offering:* The adjective *tenufa* means

17 **present a new grain offering to the LORD. You shall bring two**
loaves of bread from your dwellings made with two-tenths of
an ephah of fine flour baked with leaven, as a wave offering: first

RASHI *(cont.)*

teruma – "raising" [unlike the usage of the term in verse 15] for the bread is raised [distinguished] for the sake of the Almighty. This is the new grain offering mentioned above [in verse 16; it does not represent a new item].

בִּכּוּרִים – *First produce:* This is the first offering brought from the new grain, even before the grain offering of jealousy [brought by a husband who suspects his wife of infidelity, as described in Numbers 5:15]. Although that offering consists of barley, it must not be brought before the two new loaves mandated here. [The Omer offering discussed earlier in this chapter is brought from barley and its sacrifice on the sixteenth of Nisan would appear to signal the start of the season for other barley grain offerings, such as that of the distrustful husband. Rashi confirms that this is not so: It is only once the wheat offering of the two loaves introduced here is brought on the holiday of Shavuot, forty-nine days later, that subsequent grain offerings of either wheat or barley can be made from the season's new crop.]

IBN EZRA

מִמּוֹשְׁבֹתֵיכֶם – *From your dwellings:* Since peace offerings are slaughtered on the Festival of Shavuot, which is a day of sacred assembly, we learn that it is permissible to slaughter animals on any holiday [for the consumption of meat]. This is in contrast to the Sadducees' approach.

RAMBAN

חָמֵץ תֵּאָפֶינָה – *Baked with leaven:* The text commands that the two Shavuot loaves be made with leaven [in contrast to the vast majority of grain offerings which must be unleavened] because these breads represent an expression of gratitude to God for sustaining the meteorological conditions necessary for a successful harvest. Note that the thanksgiving offering is also accompanied by leavened bread. [Ten loaves out of the forty which are prepared for this sacrifice are leavened.] It is possible that the general prohibition of presenting leavened grain offerings [as recorded earlier in 2:11] alludes to the [sour] attribute of Justice, which has been termed *hametz*, in the same way that wine which has become sour is referred to as *ḥometz yayin* and *ḥometz sheikhar* [for example in Numbers 6:3]. The word itself is related to the language of this verse: *My God, rescue me from the hands of the wicked, from the grip of the evil and the violent [ḥometz]* (Psalms 71:4), because when wine and other alcohol have turned rancid, it is as if their taste has been violently seized from them, thereby rendering them unfit for drinking. We find a similar idea in the verse which states: *When my heart was sour [yitḥametz] and my conscience pricked* (Psalms 73:21), suggesting that the poet's mind was enraged and depleted of its usual reason. Now since the sacrifices are brought for the glory of the Almighty, it is inappropriate for them to be tainted by any substance that significantly alters their nature or taste. Similarly, it would be unsuitable for offerings to be flavored by a taste that is wholly sweet like honey [and hence, the contrasting attribute of Mercy should also not be completely embraced.

יח סֹלֶת תִּהְיֶינָה חָמֵץ תֵּאָפֶינָה בִּכּוּרִים לַיהוה: וְהִקְרַבְתֶּם
עַל־הַלֶּחֶם שִׁבְעַת כְּבָשִׂים תְּמִימִם בְּנֵי שָׁנָה וּפַר בֶּן־בָּקָר
אֶחָד וְאֵילִם שְׁנָיִם יִהְיוּ עֹלָה לַיהוה וּמִנְחָתָם וְנִסְכֵּיהֶם אִשֵּׁה
יט רֵיחַ־נִיחֹחַ לַיהוה: וַעֲשִׂיתֶם שְׂעִיר־עִזִּים אֶחָד לְחַטָּאת
כ וּשְׁנֵי כְבָשִׂים בְּנֵי שָׁנָה לְזֶבַח שְׁלָמִים: וְהֵנִיף הַכֹּהֵן ׀ אֹתָם
עַל לֶחֶם הַבִּכֻּרִים תְּנוּפָה לִפְנֵי יהוה עַל־שְׁנֵי כְּבָשִׂים קֹדֶשׁ

RAMBAN *(cont.)*

Indeed, honey too is forbidden as the earlier citation from 2:11 makes clear]. Instead, sacrifices should be characterized by elements that represent a mixture of qualities, which is how our Sages describe God's creation of the world: When the Almighty formed the universe, He brought together the attributes of judgment and compassion in order to do so. Now it is fitting to celebrate the Festival of Shavuot, the anniversary of the Torah's revelation, with a grain presentation that resembles the thanksgiving offering. The Sages refer to the mystical symbolism of this matter when they assert: Even though all sacrifices will be annulled in messianic times, this will not apply to the thanksgiving offering, which will endure for all eternity. For the latter includes both leavened and unleavened breads, a state which corresponds to the World to Come [in which the attributes of justice and mercy will coexist].

RALBAG

מִמּוֹשְׁבֹתֵיכֶם – *From your dwellings:* We have learned that the two Shavuot loaves must be baked from wheat that was grown in the land of Israel. This is derived from the fact that the text does not use the phrase "from all of your dwellings"; the grain has to be taken from particular and special places where the Israelites live [that is, only from the Holy Land]. Each of the two loaves is prepared from one-tenth of an ephah of flour, which is produced from the new year's grain. Thus, the Torah refers to the breads as "a new grain offering to the Lord" (23:16).

SFORNO

חָמֵץ תֵּאָפֶינָה – *Baked with leaven:* The Omer offering served as the donation of the first fruits of the season's barley, while the two loaves on Shavuot represented the first fruits of the year's wheat crop. This explains the association of this holiday with the first fruits, as a later verse states: *The day of first produce, when you bring an offering of new grain to the Lord on your Festival of Weeks, shall be a sacred assembly for you* (Numbers 28:26). The present verse identifies the bread as the "first produce to the Lord" because once it is offered, subsequent grain offerings to God can be brought from the new year's yields. When Israel offers these loaves, they express their gratitude to the Almighty for the favorable weather conditions during the harvest, which preserved the viability of the wheat. This is why the two loaves are made leavened, just like some of the breads which accompany the standard thanksgiving offering.

18 produce to the LORD. Together with the bread, you shall present seven unblemished yearling male lambs, one young bull,
and two rams – these shall be a burnt offering for the LORD
with their grain offering and their libations, a fire offering, a
19 pleasing aroma to the LORD. And you shall offer one he-goat as
a purification offering and two yearling male sheep as peace sac-
20 rifices. The priest shall display them this way and that with the
bread of the first produce as a wave offering before the LORD
together with the two sheep; they shall be holy to the LORD

VERSE 18

RASHI

עַל־הַלֶּחֶם – *Together with the bread:* The animals listed here are sacrificed on account of the bread; it is that which creates the obligation for these offerings. **וּמִנְחָתָם וְנִסְכֵּיהֶם** – *With their grain offering and their libations:* The amounts for the accompanying grain offerings and wine libations follow the fixed rules regarding each species of animal, stated explicitly in the libation passage of Numbers 15:1–16. Namely, three-tenths of an ephah of flour is the measure for the grain offering brought along with a bull, two-tenths of an ephah is the amount when a ram is sacrificed, and one-tenth when a lamb is brought. These are the standard amounts of the grain offerings. The volumes of wine poured as libations are: half a hin of wine when a bull is sacrificed, a third of a hin when the sacrifice is a ram, and a quarter of a hin when it is a lamb.

VERSE 19

RASHI

וַעֲשִׂיתֶם שְׂעִיר־עִזִּים – *And you shall offer one he-goat:* We might have thought that this goat and the seven lambs listed here [in the previous verse] are identical to the goat and the seven lambs described as additional [*musaf*] festival sacrifices in the book of Numbers [verses 28:27 and 28:30]. However, two bulls and one ram are also included in that later text; hence the corresponding animals in the present passage cannot represent the same sacrifices. [This is because the text in Numbers prescribes two bulls and one ram, whereas verse 18 states there must be one bull and two rams.] Thus, we must conclude that we are dealing with two different sets of sacrifices: The animals listed in Numbers are the additional festival sacrifices and the ones appearing in our text are different specimens brought in conjunction with the special Shavuot bread.

VERSE 20

RASHI

וְהֵנִיף הַכֹּהֵן אֹתָם... תְּנוּפָה – *The priest shall display them as a wave offering:* This verse teaches that the yearlings must be waved while they are still alive. Now perhaps all of them [the burnt offerings and the purifications brought at this time] must also be waved. No, for the verse states *together with the two sheep.* [It is only the sheep which are waved with

כא יִהְיוּ לַיהוָה לַכֹּהֵן: וּקְרָאתֶם בְּעֶצֶם ׀ הַיּוֹם הַזֶּה מִקְרָא־
קֹדֶשׁ יִהְיֶה לָכֶם כָּל־מְלֶאכֶת עֲבֹדָה לֹא תַעֲשׂוּ חֻקַּת עוֹלָם

RASHI *(cont.)*

the bread, and not the other animals.] **קֹדֶשׁ יִהְיוּ** – *They shall be holy:* Since the usual peace offering brought by an individual falls into the category of *kodashim kalim* [sacrifices with a lower degree of sanctity], the text needs to emphasize that communal peace offerings hold the status of *kodshei kodashim* [with the higher degree of sanctity. Indeed, the current instance is the sole case of a communal peace offering].

RALBAG

וְהֵנִיף הַכֹּהֵן אֹתָם – *The priest shall display them this way and that:* The priest must wave the sheep around while they are still alive; this movement of the animals should be done after that performed with *the bread of the first produce*. Alternatively, the verse might be ordering that the sheep and the breads be displayed at the same time. That approach would recall an earlier instruction which reads: *The priest shall send its remembrance up in smoke – some of the crushed new grain and oil together with all of the incense – as a fire offering to the Lord* (2:16). The verse states that *the priest shall display them this way and that with* [*al*, usually "upon"] *the bread of the first produce* to indicate that these loaves hold greater significance than the sheep. Nevertheless, during this ritual of waving, the loaves should be laid upon the two animals [and not the other way around].

VERSE 21

ḤIZKUNI

וּקְרָאתֶם בְּעֶצֶם הַיּוֹם הַזֶּה – *On that day you shall make a proclamation:* Why does the Torah not specify the month of the year and the date within that month that the Festival of Shavuot is meant to be celebrated, in contrast to all of the other holidays where that information is provided? Had the text stated the exact date for Shavuot, the people would not bother to count out the seven weeks. Rather, they would just make sure to observe the festival on its designated day. And yet, there is great significance to the practice of counting the days and the weeks of the Omer, as I have discussed above. Since we do reckon the time starting from the cutting of the barley offering, the fiftieth day will inevitably occur on the sixth of Sivan, which is the anniversary of God's pronouncement of the Ten Commandments. Finally, because the purpose of counting these seven weeks is to reach the holiday of Shavuot, the moment when the Omer is reaped is not considered a special time which would warrant the recitation of the *Sheheḥeyanu* blessing.

ABARBANEL

מִקְרָא־קֹדֶשׁ יִהְיֶה לָכֶם – *It shall be a sacred assembly for you:* Why does the Torah not provide any explanation for the institution of this festival, or state directly that Shavuot commemorates the day that God gave Israel His Torah? The answer to this is that the holiday was not established as a remembrance of that event. For the divine Torah that the nation possesses and the prophecy that has accompanied the law are themselves testimony to

21 **and belong to the priest. On that day you shall make a procla-**
mation; it shall be a sacred assembly for you; you shall perform
no laborious work. This is an everlasting statute throughout

ABARBANEL *(cont.)*

the revelation; there was really no need to set aside a particular date to remember the Almighty's communication to the people. The fact is that the Festival of Shavuot marks the beginning of the wheat harvest in the land of Israel. And just as the holiday of Sukkot signals the end of the gathering in of the crops, so does the process of collecting the season's yield start in the time of Shavuot. It was the wish of the Almighty that the Israelites express their gratitude to the One who feeds all living creatures at the time when they begin to take in the grain, which represents human sustenance. This occurs when they bring home the first wheat which ripens around the time of Shavuot. Similarly, when the task is completed at the end of the summer, it is fitting to celebrate a second holiday for that same purpose [that is, Sukkot]. Now there is of course no doubt that the Torah was given to the Israelite nation on the date of their first Shavuot in the wilderness. But even so, God did not command that the experience at Mount Sinai be memorialized by means of a festival. We find a parallel phenomenon regarding the holiday of Rosh Hashana, about which our prayers state: This is the day when You began Your creation of the universe; it is a remembrance for the world's very first day. And even though that assertion is a true one, we do not claim that God has ordered *the sounding of the ram's horn* (23:24) to serve as a remembrance for His formation of the world. Instead, Rosh Hashana is defined as the "Day of Judgment." [That characterization of Rosh Hashana also does not appear in the Torah, but is an expression used by the Sages.] In like manner, although the Festival of Shavuot does take place on the day of the Torah's revelation, we have not been ordered to celebrate the day in order to remember that encounter with the Divine. Rather, the Torah's focus is on the agricultural aspect of the season, namely the start of the wheat harvest. Here then is the corresponding statement regarding our holiday that appears in Parashat Mishpatim: *Likewise, keep the Festival of the Harvest, of the first fruits of the produce that you sowed in the field. Keep the Festival of Ingathering at the end of the year* (Exodus 23:16), whereas Parashat Ki Tisa reads as follows: *Observe the Festival of Weeks, of the first fruits of wheat harvest, as well as the Festival of Ingathering at the close of the year* (Exodus 34:22). Thirdly, Parashat Pinḥas presents the holiday this way: *The day of first produce, when you bring an offering of new grain to the Lord on your Festival of Weeks, shall be a sacred assembly for you* (Numbers 28:26). And finally, in the book of Deuteronomy, Shavuot is mentioned in Parashat Re'eh: *You shall count seven weeks. At the time when you first put sickle to standing grain, begin your count of seven weeks. And then celebrate the Festival of Weeks to the Lord your God* (Deuteronomy 16:9–10). In these instances, the text refers to Shavuot as the "Festival of Weeks"; the commandment associated with the day relates only to the bringing of the first fruits and not at all to a remembrance of the giving of the Torah. This then is the significance of the phrase *be'etzem hayom hazeh* ["on that day" or "on that selfsame day"]. The verse here emphasizes the essence [*itzumo*] of the day, and the first fruits that are donated then. The holiday's importance is not based on an earlier event.

כב בְּכָל־מוֹשְׁבֹתֵיכֶם לְדֹרֹתֵיכֶם: וּבְקֻצְרְכֶם אֶת־קְצִיר אַרְצְכֶם
לֹא־תְכַלֶּה פְּאַת שָׂדְךָ בְּקֻצְרֶךָ וְלֶקֶט קְצִירְךָ לֹא תְלַקֵּט
לֶעָנִי וְלַגֵּר תַּעֲזֹב אֹתָם אֲנִי יהוה אֱלֹהֵיכֶם:
כג כד וַיְדַבֵּר יהוה אֶל־מֹשֶׁה לֵּאמֹר: דַּבֵּר אֶל־בְּנֵי יִשְׂרָאֵל חמישי
לֵאמֹר בַּחֹדֶשׁ הַשְּׁבִיעִי בְּאֶחָד לַחֹדֶשׁ יִהְיֶה לָכֶם שַׁבָּתוֹן

SFORNO

חֻקַּת עוֹלָם בְּכָל־מוֹשְׁבֹתֵיכֶם – *This is an everlasting statute in all your dwellings:* Even though no manner of sacrifices are offered in the Israelites' settlements in exile, the practices of counting the Omer and keeping the sanctity of Shavuot shall still be observed.

VERSE 22

RASHI

וּבְקֻצְרְכֶם – *And when you reap:* [The obligations of this verse have previously been stated almost verbatim in 19:9.] The Torah repeats this here in order to render offenders liable for transgressing two negative commandments. Rabbi Avdimi son of Rabbi Yosef asked: Why does the text insert these agricultural laws into its discussion of the festivals, thereby separating its description of Passover and Shavuot from the holidays of Rosh Hashana [in 23:24] and Yom Kippur [23:27, and Sukkot in verse 34]? It does so in order to teach that if a farmer leaves the gleanings, his forgotten sheaves, and an uncut corner of the field for the poor as he is supposed to, the text grants him credit as if he has built the Temple and offered sacrifices in it. **תַּעֲזֹב** – *Leave:* The owner is only required to abandon these gifts for the poor, who have to come and collect the food for themselves. In fact, he may not assist any particular needy person [to the detriment of other poor people. Other instances of the verb *taazov* in the Torah mean "assist," as in the verse *If you see the donkey of someone who hates you, fallen under its load.... Help him – azov taazov – to release it* (Exodus 23:5). Hence Rashi emphasizes that in our verse the term holds the opposite meaning: Do not favor one poor person by helping him to gather the grain or by setting it aside for him]. **אֲנִי יהוה אֱלֹהֵיכֶם** – *I am the* Lord *your God:* I can be trusted to reward you for compliance with these rules.

IBN EZRA

וּבְקֻצְרְכֶם אֶת־קְצִיר אַרְצְכֶם – *And when you reap the harvest of your land:* Why does the text repeat these laws of agricultural charity that have already appeared in this book? [Leviticus 19:9–10 introduces these obligations and indeed prefaces the commandments with the clause *When you reap the harvest of your land*...] The reason for this is straightforward. Since the Festival of Shavuot marks the beginning of the wheat harvest, the Torah reminds the farmer: In these exciting times of reaping, do not forget that which I have commanded you to do on such an occasion.

RAMBAN

וּבְקֻצְרְכֶם אֶת־קְצִיר אַרְצְכֶם – *And when you reap the harvest of your land:* It seems to me that this verse relates back to the earlier discussion regarding the reaping of the Omer

22 your generations in all your dwellings. And when you reap the
harvest of your land, do not reap to the edge of your field or
gather the gleanings of your harvest. Leave them for the poor
and for the migrant; I am the Lord your God."
23 24 Then the Lord spoke to Moshe: "Tell the Israelites: On the HAMISHI
first day of the seventh month, you shall observe a day of rest, a
commemoration with the sounding of the ram's horn, a sacred

RAMBAN *(cont.)*

that appears at the start of this paragraph [in verse 10]. Thus, the present text issues this instruction to the people of Israel: When you enter your land and the time arrives to cut down the first grains of the year, *do not reap to the edge of your field* [that is, do not harvest the corner of the field] and present that barley as the Omer. Furthermore, you must not *gather the gleanings of your harvest* either. In other words, the harvesting of the Omer cannot override these negative commandments that are intended to provide for the poor.

SFORNO

וּבְקֻצְרְכֶם – *And when you reap:* Now that the Israelite has expressed his gratitude for the success of his harvest, he is cautioned to observe the commandments which will ensure his prosperity, namely the laws of the fallen gleanings and of the corner of the field. **אֲנִי יהוה אֱלֹהֵיכֶם** – *I am the Lord your God:* The Almighty declares: I am both the God of the harvesters and the God of the impoverished gatherers, who sustain themselves with the forgotten grains and the edge of the field. Thus, I will treat well those who honor My will and take care of the less fortunate.

VERSE 24

RASHI

זִכְרוֹן תְּרוּעָה – *A commemoration with the sounding of the ram's horn:* This text introduces the obligation of remembrance, that is, to recite on Rosh Hashana scriptural verses associated with remembrance, as well as verses mentioning the sounding of the shofar. The purpose of this is to recall the binding of Yitzḥak and the ram which was sacrificed in his stead [as detailed in Genesis chapter 22].

RASHBAM

זִכְרוֹן תְּרוּעָה – *A commemoration with the sounding of the ram's horn:* Through the blowing of the shofar, Israel will be remembered by the Almighty. And so it is promised in a later verse: *When you go to war against an enemy who is attacking you in your land, you shall blow short blasts on the trumpets to be remembered before the Lord your God, to be delivered from your enemies* (Numbers 10:9).

RAMBAN

זִכְרוֹן תְּרוּעָה – *A commemoration with the sounding of the ram's horn:* The phrase *zikhron terua* ["a commemoration with the sounding of the ram's horn"] is synonymous with a later term: *The first day of the seventh month shall be a sacred assembly for you; you shall perform*

כה זִכְרוֹן תְּרוּעָה מִקְרָא־קֹדֶשׁ: כָּל־מְלֶאכֶת עֲבֹדָה לֹא תַעֲשׂוּ
כו וְהִקְרַבְתֶּם אִשֶּׁה לַיהוָה: וַיְדַבֵּר יהוה אֶל־מֹשֶׁה
כז לֵאמֹר: אַךְ בֶּעָשׂוֹר לַחֹדֶשׁ הַשְּׁבִיעִי הַזֶּה יוֹם הַכִּפֻּרִים הוּא
מִקְרָא־קֹדֶשׁ יִהְיֶה לָכֶם וְעִנִּיתֶם אֶת־נַפְשֹׁתֵיכֶם וְהִקְרַבְתֶּם

RAMBAN *(cont.)*

no laborious work on it. It shall be for you a day of the horn's sounding [yom terua] (Numbers 29:1). The Torah thus commands that on this day the people of Israel should sound the shofar and thereby be remembered before the Almighty, as is pledged in the continuation of that passage: *When you go to war against an enemy who is attacking you in your land, you shall blow short blasts on the trumpets to be remembered before the Lord your God, to be delivered from your enemies* (Numbers 10:9). It should be pointed out that it is stated in Parashat Behaalotekha: *And on your days of rejoicing, your festivals and New Moons, you shall blow the trumpets over your burnt offerings and your peace offerings* (Numbers 10:10), whereas in the present context the Torah merely commands the "sounding of the ram's horn" [without initially linking it to any sacrifices]. It is only in the subsequent verse that we read: *And you shall bring close a fire offering to the Lord* (Leviticus 23:25). It would therefore seem that the sounding described in the book of Numbers is not the same practice that our text is referring to. For the call that Israel is told to make there is produced by trumpets and is closely associated with offerings. The sounding on Rosh Hashana, on the other hand, is not made while sacrifices are being brought, and indeed, the entire nation is required to blow the shofar. [Clearly, the populace would not be burning sacrifices throughout the country as they fulfill their obligation of sounding the ram's horn.] In fact, at the time when the Torah introduces this commandment, God had not yet ordered Moshe to fashion any trumpets. Finally, any unspecified playing of a *terua* refers to a shofar, as a later verse clarifies: *Then you shall sound the ram's horn [shofar terua]* [25:9, in the context of the Jubilee year. Although the present translation describes the Rosh Hashana commandment as *a commemoration with the sounding of the ram's horn*, that is, the shofar, the Hebrew is unclear, demanding only *zikhron terua* – "commemoration with a sounding." Hence, the Ramban explains that this *terua* is performed with a shofar in contrast to the declaration in Numbers, which is made with a trumpet fashioned out of silver.] Now the text does not explain the reason for this custom: Why must we create a sounding on the first day of the seventh month? Furthermore, the Torah does not tell us why the nation needs to be remembered before God on this date more than at any other time of the year. And thirdly, why is this day characterized as "a sacred assembly"? The explanation for all of this lies in the fact that this festival falls on the first day of the month that includes Yom Kippur. It is clear that on Rosh Hashana, the Almighty sits in judgment and examines the behavior of all of humankind. Ten days following that, God suspends the punishment of His servants [and forgives people who have repented]. And so, the text alludes to the meaning of Rosh Hashana, corresponding to the teachings of Israel's prophets and their holy ancestors.

25 assembly. You shall perform no laborious work, and you shall
26 bring close a fire offering to the LORD." The LORD
27 spoke to Moshe: "Hear: the tenth day of this seventh month
is the Day of Atonement. It shall be a sacred assembly for you,
and you shall afflict yourselves and bring a fire offering to the

ABARBANEL

שַׁבָּתוֹן – *A day of rest:* Whenever the Torah uses the term *shabbaton* it refers to a day on which the Jews enjoy a true sense of quiet and tranquility, when they are untroubled by worries or anxious thoughts. For example, Israel undertakes the celebration of Sukkot with the peace of mind that follows the gathering of all their crops [which is why the word appears in verse 39]. This explains why we do not find the word *shabbaton* in conjunction with the Shavuot festival: At that time the nation is still thinking about the grain that remains out in the fields. It is for this same reason that the Passover holiday is not identified as a *shabbaton*, as I have explained.

SFORNO

זִכְרוֹן תְּרוּעָה – *A commemoration with the sounding of the ram's horn: The sounding of the ram's horn* announces the glory of the king which causes the people to rejoice, as the verse states: *Sing for joy to God, our might; shout out to the God of Yaakov* (Psalms 81:2). The call of the shofar celebrates the ascent of the Almighty to His throne of justice, as tradition teaches. This is expressed in the continuation of that chapter: *Sound the ram's horn on the New Moon, on our feast day when the moon is full, for it is a statute for Israel, an ordinance of the God of Yaakov* (Psalms 81:4–5). It is appropriate for humanity to take joy in the fact that our King exercises His righteousness by exonerating us when He judges the world. And so do we read: *For the LORD is our judge, the LORD our lawgiver, the LORD our King – and He will rescue us* (Isaiah 33:22).

VERSE 25

RASHI

וְהִקְרַבְתֶּם אִשֶּׁה – *You shall bring close a fire offering:* This refers to the additional [*musaf*] sacrifices discussed in the book of Numbers [verses 29:1–6].

VERSE 27

RASHI

אַךְ – *Hear:* Whenever the Torah employs the term *akh* or *rak* ["only"], its intention is to convey some sort of limitation. In the current instance, the text implies that Yom Kippur makes atonement only for those who have repented, but not for those who have ignored that obligation.

RASHBAM

אַךְ בֶּעָשׂוֹר – *Hear: the tenth day:* On all of the other festivals, the Israelite people are permitted to perform work for the preparation of food and are only forbidden to engage

כח אִשֶּׁה לַיהוָה: וְכָל־מְלָאכָה לֹא תַעֲשׂוּ בְּעֶצֶם הַיּוֹם הַזֶּה כִּי

RASHBAM *(cont.)*

in laborious activity. However, since Yom Kippur is a day of affliction, the nation is warned against doing any *work at all during this entire day* [23:28, that is, they may not cook food on this particular holiday].

BEKHOR SHOR

אַךְ בֶּעָשׂוֹר – *Hear: the tenth day:* All of the holidays possess the character of a "sacred assembly," which requires the Israelites to eat, to drink, to be happy, and to enjoy themselves. But with respect to Yom Kippur, the text states: *akh be'asor* – on "the tenth day of this seventh month" [*akh* usually means "however" and connotes an exception]. The sacred nature of the day is expressed through bringing multiple sacrifices. And instead of celebrating the day with physical pleasure, the people are enjoined to afflict themselves in the manner defined by the Sages.

RAMBAN

אַךְ בֶּעָשׂוֹר – *Hear: the tenth day:* The usual usage of the term *akh* ["however"] represents the confirmation of a matter, as in the verse: *Then Moshe was afraid; "Surely [akhen]," he thought, "the thing has become known"* (Exodus 2:14), and in this text: *But [akhen] you shall die like mere men; you will fall like any prince* (Psalms 82:7). In the present context, our verse states: *Akh – the tenth day of this seventh month is the Day of Atonement*, meaning: This is an actual and true pledge that although the first of the seventh month serves as the Day of Judgment, the tenth will indeed effect atonement. For this reason, the nation should afflict themselves and *perform no work at all during this entire day*.

ABARBANEL

אַךְ בֶּעָשׂוֹר לַחֹדֶשׁ הַשְּׁבִיעִי הַזֶּה – *Hear: the tenth day of this seventh month:* Indeed, why was the tenth day of the seventh month singled out as a time for forgiveness, atonement, and the deliverance of our protected nation from the wrath of the celestial court? There are several reasons for this distinction. First, God created the world in the month of Tishrei according to Rabbi Eliezer [in contrast to Rabbi Yehoshua's opinion that the universe was formed in Nisan]. Our Sages have taught us that on this very date the first man repented for his sin and was forgiven. For even though the Almighty did not permit Adam to return to the Garden of Eden, he once again found favor in God's eyes and was granted a share in the World to Come. Second, the Sages teach that our forefather Avraham was circumcised on the day of Yom Kippur. It is on the basis of that covenant that the patriarch's descendants are sanctified and continue to perform their ancestor's work in their service of God. The third reason for the day's selection appears in Pirkei Derabbi Eliezer, where we read that Moshe ascended Mount Sinai on the first day of Elul [the sixth month] to receive the second set of tablets. He remained there in the presence of the Divine for forty days and forty nights, completing his stay in that realm on the very day of Yom Kippur. In remembrance of that event, the tenth of Tishrei has remained forever after as a propitious time for forgiveness and atonement, since that was when the Lord forgave Israel for their crime of the golden calf. Fourth, the following encounter took place on the day of Yom Kippur: *Then the Lord said, "Look, there is a place by Me where*

28 Lord. You shall perform no work at all during this entire day,
for it is the Day of Atonement, there to make atonement for

ABARBANEL *(cont.)*

you may stand on the rock, and while My glory passes by I will put you in a cleft of the rock, and I will shield you with My hand until I have passed" (Exodus 33:20–21). It was then that the Holy One, blessed be He, taught Moshe the thirteen attributes of compassion [as expressed in Exodus 34:6–7]. The tenth of the month thereby acquired a degree of sanctity by which it could serve as an time for repentance, confession, forgiveness, and absolution. It is a day on which these thirteen divine qualities are recited and recalled for the sake of effecting atonement for those of Israel's sinners who have abandoned their unlawful ways. Israelites who return to the proper path of the Torah thereby emulate their original ancestor Adam, who cleaved to the Almighty following his offense. They connect to Avraham, who was circumcised on Yom Kippur, and strive for the exoneration of their desert fathers, whose wrongdoing with the golden calf was pardoned on this date. Furthermore, the combination of absorbing the Torah's teachings which were inscribed on the stone tablets and the recollection of God's thirteen attributes of mercy that Moshe learned on the mountain on Yom Kippur will serve to bring the nation back into God's good graces.

VERSE 28

RAMBAN

כִּי יוֹם כִּפֻּרִים הוּא – *For it is the Day of Atonement:* In the current chapter the text states: *You shall afflict yourselves and bring a fire offering to the Lord* (23:27), while in Parashat Aḥarei Mot the Torah implies that Israel's atonement depends upon the sacrifices of the day and on the ritual of the goat that is sent away. It is to clarify that apparent discrepancy that the text subsequently states: *You shall perform no work at all during this entire day* [*be'etzem hayom hazeh*, literally, "on this selfsame day"] – for it is the essence of the day itself that effects atonement on Yom Kippur, quite aside from the absolution which is achieved through the offerings. [Hence, the verse emphasizes: *It is – hu – the Day of Atonement*: Yom Kippur itself possesses this power, independent of what Israel does on the day.] In a similar fashion we read above: *Until that day [ad etzem hayom hazeh]* (23:14), with regard to the eating of the season's new grain, meaning that no fresh grain may be eaten until the essential nature of the day expresses itself – through the bringing of the Omer as an offering to the Lord. What emerges is that even if the Omer is not offered [for example, following the destruction of the Temple], the commandment remains applicable to the day of the sixteenth. Thus, new grain is forbidden before this day, but is permitted after it. This explains why that verse concludes this way: *This is an everlasting statute throughout your generations, in all your dwellings*, as I have written. [Even though the restrictions on Yom Kippur and Shavuot appear to be reliant on the respective Temple services performed on these days, they are in fact primarily functions of the days on which these holidays occur.]

RALBAG

כִּי יוֹם כִּפֻּרִים הוּא – *For it is the Day of Atonement:* We learn from here that the day of Yom Kippur itself effects atonement even if the sacrifices of the holiday are not offered. This

כט יוֹם כִּפֻּרִים הוּא לְכַפֵּר עֲלֵיכֶם לִפְנֵי יְהוָה אֱלֹהֵיכֶם: כִּי כָל־
הַנֶּפֶשׁ אֲשֶׁר לֹא־תְעֻנֶּה בְּעֶצֶם הַיּוֹם הַזֶּה וְנִכְרְתָה מֵעַמֶּיהָ:
ל וְכָל־הַנֶּפֶשׁ אֲשֶׁר תַּעֲשֶׂה כָּל־מְלָאכָה בְּעֶצֶם הַיּוֹם הַזֶּה
לא וְהַאֲבַדְתִּי אֶת־הַנֶּפֶשׁ הַהִוא מִקֶּרֶב עַמָּהּ: כָּל־מְלָאכָה לֹא
לב תַעֲשׂוּ חֻקַּת עוֹלָם לְדֹרֹתֵיכֶם בְּכֹל מֹשְׁבֹתֵיכֶם: שַׁבַּת שַׁבָּתוֹן
הוּא לָכֶם וְעִנִּיתֶם אֶת־נַפְשֹׁתֵיכֶם בְּתִשְׁעָה לַחֹדֶשׁ בָּעֶרֶב
מֵעֶרֶב עַד־עֶרֶב תִּשְׁבְּתוּ שַׁבַּתְּכֶם:
לג לד וַיְדַבֵּר יְהוָה אֶל־מֹשֶׁה לֵּאמֹר: דַּבֵּר אֶל־בְּנֵי יִשְׂרָאֵל לֵאמֹר ששי
בַּחֲמִשָּׁה עָשָׂר יוֹם לַחֹדֶשׁ הַשְּׁבִיעִי הַזֶּה חַג הַסֻּכּוֹת שִׁבְעַת
לה יָמִים לַיהוָה: בַּיּוֹם הָרִאשׁוֹן מִקְרָא־קֹדֶשׁ כָּל־מְלֶאכֶת עֲבֹדָה
לו לֹא תַעֲשׂוּ: שִׁבְעַת יָמִים תַּקְרִיבוּ אִשֶּׁה לַיהוָה בַּיּוֹם הַשְּׁמִינִי
מִקְרָא־קֹדֶשׁ יִהְיֶה לָכֶם וְהִקְרַבְתֶּם אִשֶּׁה לַיהוָה עֲצֶרֶת

RALBAG *(cont.)*

makes sense since the purpose of the offerings is merely to direct us toward repentance. And if we can reach that state of contrition and self-improvement without the assistance of the sacrifices, it is reasonable that the essence of the day should absolve the sinner.

VERSE 30

RASHI

וְהַאֲבַדְתִּי – *I will annihilate:* The Torah often mentions *karet* ["excision"] without specifying what it means. By using the word "annihilate" here, our verse defines the punishment of *karet* as destruction.

VERSE 31

RASHI

כָּל־מְלָאכָה – *No work at all:* [Even though the performance of labor on Yom Kippur has already been forbidden in verse 28, the present text repeats the prohibition] in order to increase the number of violations a person would commit were he or she to ignore these warnings. Alternatively, our verse might serve to equate working on the night of the holiday with similar behavior during the day itself. [Verse 23:28 emphasizes: *You shall perform no work at all during this entire day – be'etzem hayom hazeh* – a phrase often understood as relating to daylight hours.] The words "a sacred assembly" [which appear in verse 27] teach that we are to sanctify Yom Kippur by donning clean clothing and celebrating the day with prayer. By contrast, the phrase "sacred assembly" used in the context of other holidays signifies eating and drinking, as well as the wearing of festive clothes and the recitation of prayers.

29 you before the Lord your God. Anyone who does not afflict
himself for this whole day shall be severed from his people,
30 and if anyone performs any work during this whole day, I will
31 annihilate that person from among his people. No work at all
may you perform; this is an everlasting statute throughout your
32 generations in all your dwellings. It is a Sabbath of complete
rest for you, and you shall afflict yourselves from the evening of
the ninth day of the month: from evening to evening shall you
observe your Sabbath."
33 34 The Lord spoke to Moshe: "Tell the Israelites: From the fif- SHISHI
teenth day of this seventh month, for seven days shall be the
35 Festival of Tabernacles to the Lord. The first day shall be a
sacred assembly; on it, you shall perform no laborious work.
36 For seven days you must bring close a fire offering to the Lord.
The eighth day shall be a sacred assembly for you, and you shall
present a fire offering to the Lord. It is an assembly; you shall

IBN EZRA

כָּל־מְלָאכָה – *No work at all:* The text reiterates that no work may be done on Yom Kippur in order to add that *this is an everlasting statute throughout [the] generations.*

VERSE 32

ḤIZKUNI

תִּשְׁבְּתוּ שַׁבַּתְּכֶם – *You shall observe your Sabbath:* The term "sabbath" here refers to Yom Kippur which has been given to Israel as a day of rest and a sacred assembly. In contrast to that, the seventh day of the week is not described as a "Sabbath for Israel" but as *a Sabbath for the Lord* (23:3). For the weekly Sabbath commemorates God's cessation from creation.

VERSE 36

RASHI

עֲצֶרֶת הִוא – *It is an assembly:* On this day I will keep you [*atzarti* – I will "stop" or" "hold" you] in My company. This is akin to a king who invites his sons to a feast lasting several days. However, when the time comes for them to take their leave, the father implores them: Please, will you not stay with me for just one more day? I find your departure hard to bear. **כָּל־מְלֶאכֶת עֲבֹדָה** – *No laborious work:* On this day you may not perform even labor that is important work for you, meaning that neglecting the task will cause you financial loss. **לֹא תַעֲשׂוּ** – *You shall not perform:* Lest you worry that such activities may not be performed on the intermediate days of the festival, the text states: *It is an assembly.* [That is, labor may not be performed on *it* – the eighth day, but not the intermediate days.]

RASHBAM

עֲצֶרֶת הִוא – *It is an assembly:* The term *atzeret* connotes the stopping [*atzirat*] and avoidance of work.

לז הִוא כָּל־מְלֶאכֶת עֲבֹדָה לֹא תַעֲשׂוּ: אֵלֶּה מוֹעֲדֵי יהוה
אֲשֶׁר־תִּקְרְאוּ אֹתָם מִקְרָאֵי קֹדֶשׁ לְהַקְרִיב אִשֶּׁה לַיהוה
לח עֹלָה וּמִנְחָה זֶבַח וּנְסָכִים דְּבַר־יוֹם בְּיוֹמוֹ: מִלְּבַד שַׁבְּתֹת
יהוה וּמִלְּבַד מַתְּנוֹתֵיכֶם וּמִלְּבַד כָּל־נִדְרֵיכֶם וּמִלְּבַד כָּל־

RAMBAN

עֲצֶרֶת הִוא – *It is an assembly:* Our text alludes to a mystical matter here relating to the creation of time. In the Ten Commandments we read: *For in six days the Lord made heaven and earth, the sea, and all that they contain, and He rested on the seventh day* (Exodus 20:11). Initially, each of the six days of the week was partnered with another day, whereas the Sabbath was left unpaired. This is why the people of Israel were designated as the Sabbath's companion as that verse states: *And earth.* [That is, the Sabbath was given an earthly partner: the Jewish people.] This in turn is represented by the eighth day. [That is, the nation is thus equivalent to the eighth day and hence the partner of the seventh – the Sabbath]. Furthermore, the eighth day [of Sukkot] is termed *atzeret* because all work had ceased [*ne'etzar*] by that time. Now the Almighty commands that the Festival of Unleavened Bread be celebrated for seven days and that the first and last of these be treated as sacred, even though the entire holiday is holy and God's presence is among the people. In addition, forty-nine days, meaning seven weeks, are to be counted, corresponding to the seven days of creation. The eighth day [really, the fiftieth – Shavuot, which is parallel to the eighth day following the seven "days" of the Omer] should also be holy, just like the eighth day of Sukkot is. Therefore, the forty-nine days of the Omer are akin to the intermediate days of the Sukkot festival – the six days between the first holy day and the eighth day [of Shemini Atzeret]. This "eighth" day commemorates the giving of the Torah when God revealed His great fire to the Israelite people and sounded His voice for them to hear. It is for this reason that our Sages will always refer to Shavuot as "Atzeret," for it is like the eighth day of the Sukkot festival which the text itself calls by that name [here in verse 36].

SFORNO

עֲצֶרֶת הִוא – *It is an assembly:* The idea of *atzira* [literally, "ceasing"] does not merely imply the stoppage of usual labor. Rather, it suggests that the nation spend some time in the holy places where they should serve God, either through prayer or through sacrifices. We find a similar usage of the term in a later verse which reads: *Meanwhile, one of Sha'ul's servants had been detained [ne'etzar] there before the Lord; his name was Doeg the Edomite* (I Samuel 21:8), as well as in the text *Sanctify a fast day, convene an assembly [atzara]* (Joel 1:14) and in this verse *"Declare a holy assembly [atzara] for Baal," said Yehu, and so it was proclaimed* (II Kings 10:20). Therefore, the day that follows the Sukkot festival, when all of the celebrations have reached their pinnacle, should itself be recognized as a holy day. At that point, the populace should remain in their sacred location and revel in the joy of Torah and good deeds, as we read: *Let Israel rejoice in its Maker; let the children of Zion exult in their King* (Psalms 149:2). Now since the fiftieth day after the emancipation from Egypt marked the revelation of the Torah, when all of Israel assembled together for the worship of

37 perform no laborious work. These are the Lord's festivals,
which you shall proclaim, sacred assemblies to present a fire
offering to the Lord: burnt offering, grain offering, sacrifice,
38 and libations, each on its appointed day; in addition to the
Lord's Sabbaths, and in addition to your gifts and all your offerings in the fulfillment of vows and all the freewill offerings

SFORNO *(cont.)*

the Lord, our Sages have termed the Festival of Shavuot *Atzeret*. Still, the Torah itself does not use that name for the holiday, due to the fact that the nation sullied the gathering following their experience, as we read: *So the Israelites stripped themselves of their finery from Mount Ḥorev onward* (Exodus 33:6).

VERSE 37

RASHI

עֹלָה וּמִנְחָה – *Burnt offering, grain offering:* The grain offering mentioned here refers to that which accompanies every burnt offering [and is not a distinct sacrifice of its own]. **דְּבַר־יוֹם בְּיוֹמוֹ** – *Each on its appointed day:* These should follow the prescribed laws dictated in the book of Numbers [chapters 28–29, which describe the specific additional sacrifices required for each festival]. **דְּבַר־יוֹם בְּיוֹמוֹ** – *Each on its appointed day:* [The special sacrifices must be brought on the days mandated for their offering.] Once a particular festival day has passed, the opportunity to bring its sacrifices has been missed as well.

ḤIZKUNI

אֵלֶּה מוֹעֲדֵי יהוה – *These are the Lord's festivals:* The Torah repeats this declaration [which was previously made in verse 2] for the sake of the eighth day [Shemini Atzeret] regarding which the text does not mandate that Israel bring "a fire offering to the Lord." Hence, the present verse expresses the general requirement that all festivals be accompanied by such a sacrifice. Furthermore, the earlier description of the Sabbath [in verse 3] similarly omits any mention of that offering. This is why the present text states: *In addition to the Lord's Sabbaths.* **לְהַקְרִיב אִשֶּׁה לַיהוה עֹלָה** – *To present a fire offering to the Lord: burnt offering:* Each of the festivals must be celebrated with a *burnt offering, grain offering, sacrifice [zevaḥ], and libations,* where the term *zevaḥ* generally connotes all sacrifices. For just as the communal peace offerings are partially eaten by the priests, so too are parts of the purification offerings given for consumption by the priests.

RALBAG

אֲשֶׁר־תִּקְרְאוּ אֹתָם מִקְרָאֵי קֹדֶשׁ – *Which you shall proclaim, sacred assemblies:* This clause in the text is intended to exclude the Sabbath, since after the seventh day is mentioned [in verse 3], the Torah proceeds to introduce the festivals with these words: *These are the Lord's appointed times, sacred assemblies* (23:4). And now that the text has finished listing this material, it summarizes the topic by saying that the holidays that it has just mentioned are the special times to which the preface was referring, those days which Israel is required to proclaim.

לט נִדְבֹתֵיכֶם אֲשֶׁר תִּתְּנוּ לַיהוָה: אַךְ בַּחֲמִשָּׁה עָשָׂר יוֹם לַחֹדֶשׁ
הַשְּׁבִיעִי בְּאָסְפְּכֶם אֶת־תְּבוּאַת הָאָרֶץ תָּחֹגּוּ אֶת־חַג־יהוָה
שִׁבְעַת יָמִים בַּיּוֹם הָרִאשׁוֹן שַׁבָּתוֹן וּבַיּוֹם הַשְּׁמִינִי שַׁבָּתוֹן:
מ וּלְקַחְתֶּם לָכֶם בַּיּוֹם הָרִאשׁוֹן פְּרִי עֵץ הָדָר כַּפֹּת תְּמָרִים
וַעֲנַף עֵץ־עָבֹת וְעַרְבֵי־נָחַל וּשְׂמַחְתֶּם לִפְנֵי יהוָה אֱלֹהֵיכֶם

VERSE 39

RASHI

אַךְ בַּחֲמִשָּׁה עָשָׂר יוֹם... תָּחֹגּוּ – *Hear: on the fifteenth day...you shall celebrate:* This holiday is celebrated by bringing a peace offering called a *korban ḥagiga*. Now do not think that this sacrifice should override the Sabbath [namely, that it should be brought on the Sabbath. Some activities which are generally forbidden on the Sabbath, such as slaughtering an animal, are permitted within the Temple as part of the sacrificial services. However, not all sacrifices that are offered on a regular weekday are subject to this leniency. The *korban ḥagiga* falls into this latter category, because] the verse states *akh* [a term indicating an exclusion, as Rashi states above. Thus, should the first day of the holiday fall on the Sabbath] this sacrifice may not be offered then, since it can be brought on any of the seven days of the festival. [In contrast, the *korban musaf* additional sacrifices which are burnt offerings are limited to their prescribed days, as Rashi points out in his previous comments.] **בְּאָסְפְּכֶם אֶת־תְּבוּאַת הָאָרֶץ** – *When you have harvested the land's produce:* The seventh month of the year coincides with the harvest season. [The verse does not suggest that the holiday be celebrated as the crops are actually being harvested; the activities necessary for that process are forbidden on a festival.] We learn from here that Israel is commanded to intercalate the year [by adding a thirteenth month after Adar if spring has not yet arrived. A twelve-month lunar year is shorter than a solar year, so it is necessary to add a month every few years to keep the calendar in sync with the seasons]. For if this is not done, it will sometimes happen that the Festival of Sukkot will fall out during the summer or even the winter. **תָּחֹגּוּ** – *You shall celebrate:* You shall sacrifice celebratory peace offerings. **שִׁבְעַת יָמִים** – *For seven days:* If the *korban ḥagiga* is not brought on the first day of the festival, it should be brought on a subsequent day. Perhaps the verse mandates that this sacrifice should be offered on each of the festival's seven days? No, for a later verse states: *You shall celebrate it [oto, in the singular] as a festival to the Lord* (23:41), meaning: This sacrifice is required on just one day of the festival. Why then does our verse command: *You shall celebrate a festival to the Lord for seven days*? To allow fulfillment of this obligation on any of the days.

RASHBAM

אַךְ בַּחֲמִשָּׁה עָשָׂר יוֹם – *Hear: on the fifteenth day:* While the days of Rosh Hashana and Yom Kippur serve as times of remembrance and atonement, the Festival of Sukkot was instituted as a week of happiness and gratitude. During that holiday, the Israelite people acknowledge that God had assisted them in filling their granaries with bounty during the preceding harvest. [The author thereby explains the adverb *akh* – usually "however" – that starts this verse: The objective of Sukkot differs from that of the previous two holidays.]

39 that you give to the Lord. Hear: on the fifteenth day of the seventh month, when you have harvested the land's produce, you
shall celebrate a festival to the Lord for seven days. The first
day shall be a day of rest; the eighth day shall be a day of rest.
40 On the first day you shall take for yourselves fruit of the majestic tree, branches of palm trees, boughs of the leafy tree, and
willows of the brook, and rejoice before the Lord your God

BEKHOR SHOR

אַךְ בַּחֲמִשָּׁה עָשָׂר יוֹם – *Hear: on the fifteenth day:* Certainly the atmosphere during all of the festivals should be one of happiness. However, the character of Sukkot is even more joyous. For at that point the populace will have completely "harvested the land's produce," and all of the crops will be safely stored away, thereby granting the nation a sense of contentment and tranquility. They will experience then no other feeling than gladness and gratification, as a later text reads: *For seven days, celebrate before the Lord your God… for the Lord your God will grant you blessing in all your harvest and in all the work of your hands, and you shall be wholly joyful [akh sameaḥ]* (Deuteronomy 16:15). Thus, the Torah prescribes a single emotion, that of happiness, for the people when Sukkot arrives. Furthermore, by the time the festival begins, Yom Kippur has passed, meaning that the Israelites' sins have been forgiven. That too will contribute to the people's joy.

SFORNO

אַךְ בַּחֲמִשָּׁה עָשָׂר יוֹם – *Hear: on the fifteenth day:* The Torah has now listed all of its festivals and presented the general practices that are to be observed on each of them as sacred assemblies: Each of the holidays requires an additional [*musaf*] offering, as the verse states: *These are the Lord's festivals, which you shall proclaim, sacred assemblies to present a fire offering to the Lord* (23:37). But now the text returns to a discussion of Sukkot with the words *Hear* [*akh*, usually "however"]: *on the fifteenth day*, thereby declaring that this festival differs from the other special days in a number of ways. First, the eighth day of this holiday is to be celebrated as a holy time, as the verse reads: *The eighth day shall be a day of rest* (23:39). This stands in stark contrast to all other times: It is the *seventh* day of the week which is holy; the *seventh* day of Passover which is celebrated as a sacred day; the *seventh* month of the year and the *seventh* year of the agricultural cycle are both recognized as sacred [whereas there is no significance to the eighth stage in these cases]. Second, the Festival of Sukkot demands a change of venue, as we read: *For seven days you shall live in huts* [23:42, which is highly irregular and not found in regard to any of the other holidays]. Last, there is an obligation on Sukkot to take up the four species, as the text [in the next verse] mandates: *On the first day you shall take for yourselves fruit of the majestic tree…* [Thus, the word *akh* identifies this festival as different in several ways from the other holidays.]

VERSE 40

RASHI

פְּרִי עֵץ הָדָר – *Fruit of the majestic tree:* The verse refers to a tree whose wood tastes the same as its fruit. **הָדָר** – *Majestic:* The fruit on this tree is that which lives [*hadar*, that

מא שִׁבְעַת יָמִים: וְחַגֹּתֶם אֹתוֹ חַג לַיהוָה שִׁבְעַת יָמִים בַּשָּׁנָה
מב חֻקַּת עוֹלָם לְדֹרֹתֵיכֶם בַּחֹדֶשׁ הַשְּׁבִיעִי תָּחֹגּוּ אֹתוֹ: בַּסֻּכֹּת
תֵּשְׁבוּ שִׁבְעַת יָמִים כָּל־הָאֶזְרָח בְּיִשְׂרָאֵל יֵשְׁבוּ בַּסֻּכֹּת:
מג לְמַעַן יֵדְעוּ דֹרֹתֵיכֶם כִּי בַסֻּכּוֹת הוֹשַׁבְתִּי אֶת־בְּנֵי יִשְׂרָאֵל

RASHI *(cont.)*

is "can remain unpicked"] on the tree from year to year. This refers to the etrog. **כַּפֹּת תְּמָרִים** – *Branches of palm trees:* The word *kappot* appears here without the letter *vav* [as might be expected after the *peh*] to indicate that just one is required. [The word should be read as if it was *kappat* – singular, and not *kappot* – plural. Only one lulav is used on the holiday.] **וַעֲנַף עֵץ־עָבֹת** – *Boughs of the leafy tree:* This describes a plant whose leaves are braided like ropes or cords, namely the myrtle, whose leaves run up its branches in a wave pattern as if they were intertwined.

KELI YAKAR

וּשְׂמַחְתֶּם לִפְנֵי יהוה אֱלֹהֵיכֶם – *And rejoice before the* Lord *your God:* The people of Israel cannot truly rejoice unless they are united in a single congregation. This is especially notable during the festivals because those assemblies are inherently conducive to happiness. Thus, the Torah warns the nation not to engage in the sort of celebrations in which degenerate people revel, where the chief goals are to slaughter and consume many animals and to drink wine to excess. That kind of festivity will usually result in conflict, and indeed indulgence in such gaiety led to the destruction of both the first and the second Israelite Temples. These tragedies were accompanied by the exile of the nation from their homeland, as the verse states: *For you will go forth in joy* (Isaiah 55:12). [The phrase "go forth" is understood by the author as leaving the land of Israel.] Thus does the Talmud maintain [in Kiddushin 81a]: The vulnerable time of the year is the festival [since men and women gather together then and that inevitably leads to licentiousness]. Should the Jews not commemorate their holidays for the sake the Lord, they will suffer all manner of damage and illness. As the wise man writes: *"Delirium," I called laughter; asked of joy, "What comes of this?"* (Ecclesiastes 2:2). On the other hand, it is appropriate for the nation to enjoy a common happiness when peace reigns among them, as that verse continues: *The mountains and the hills will break out in song before you as all the wild trees clap their hands* (Isaiah 55:12). The "mountains" refer to the heads of the community who lead the people in all matters of holiness; the youth must not be allowed to overrule their elders, which is what happened in the episode of the spies. The clause *all the wild trees* [*atzei hasadeh*, literally, the trees of the field] *will clap their hands* alludes to the four classes of people, who in turn are symbolized by the four species of plants used on the Sukkot festival – all of these are taken from the fields. Together, the variegated groups within Israel will join hands in celebration of the Lord. In a different rabbinic text [Vayikra Rabba 30:4], the Sages address the verse which states: *Let the fields revel, and all they contain, then [az] all the trees of the forest will sing for joy* (Psalms 96:12), by relating the text to the four species. According to that midrash, the word *az*, spelled with an *alef* [signifying "one," and a *zayin* with

41 for seven days. You shall celebrate it as a festival to the LORD for
seven days in the year. It shall be an everlasting statute through-
42 out your generations; celebrate this in the seventh month. For
seven days you shall live in huts. All those native born in Israel
43 must live in huts, so that future generations may know that I had

KELI YAKAR *(cont.)*

a value of seven] hints at the *lulav*, which is taken up for all seven days of the festival in the Temple, but only on the first day throughout the land.

VERSE 42

RASHI

הָאֶזְרָח – *Native born:* The definite article *heh* refers to *the* citizen of the nation [namely, the naturally born Israelite]. **בְּיִשְׂרָאֵל** – *In Israel:* This includes converts.

RASHBAM

כָּל־הָאֶזְרָח – *All those native born:* Even those who own houses are required to *live in huts*. [The term "all" includes the wealthy.]

RAMBAN

כָּל־הָאֶזְרָח בְּיִשְׂרָאֵל יֵשְׁבוּ בַּסֻּכֹּת – *All those native born in Israel must live in huts:* This statement places an obligation on every single member of the Israelite people – all citizens, from the important leader down to the lowly commoner – to "live in huts." Furthermore, it does not suffice for one person in the household to move into the sukka while the rest of the family remains in the house. Rather, everybody must dwell in the booth throughout the entire week. It is also possible that the text extends the commandment to all those people who live comfortably in houses, to the exclusion of seafarers and other travelers who are exempt from this law.

RALBAG

כָּל־הָאֶזְרָח בְּיִשְׂרָאֵל יֵשְׁבוּ בַּסֻּכֹּת – *All those native born in Israel must live in huts:* The reader must not deduce from this statement that the true convert is not obligated to reside in a sukka. For a convert to Judaism is required to observe all of the Torah's commandments, just like any native-born Israelite. This is something that the text makes quite clear on multiple occasions. Rather, the verse mentions the *ezraḥ* ["native born"] citizen, since we might have thought that a certain class of people should in fact be excused from this practice. I refer to the leaders and ministers among the population: Do not imagine that they are too important and dignified to move into a flimsy hut for a week. Surely they should be dwelling within fancy edifices and sturdy and elaborate mansions! To counter such a suggestion, the Torah states that this commandment devolves upon all Israelites equally.

VERSE 43

RASHI

כִּי בַסֻּכּוֹת הוֹשַׁבְתִּי – *I had them live in huts:* This refers to the clouds of glory [which protectively hovered over the nation in the wilderness].

מד בְּהוֹצִיאִי אוֹתָם מֵאֶרֶץ מִצְרָיִם אֲנִי יְהוָה אֱלֹהֵיכֶם: וַיְדַבֵּר
מֹשֶׁה אֶת־מֹעֲדֵי יְהוָה אֶל־בְּנֵי יִשְׂרָאֵל:
כד א ב וַיְדַבֵּר יְהוָה אֶל־מֹשֶׁה לֵּאמֹר: צַו אֶת־בְּנֵי יִשְׂרָאֵל וְיִקְחוּ שביעי

RASHBAM

כִּי בַסֻּכּוֹת הוֹשַׁבְתִּי אֶת־בְּנֵי יִשְׂרָאֵל – *That I had the Israelites live in huts:* The straightforward meaning of this text is accepted in Sukka 11b, where it is argued that this assertion should be taken literally. [The opposing position claims that "huts" refers to the protective clouds of glory that God placed above the Israelite camp.] This then is the sense of the later verse which states: *You shall keep the Festival of Tabernacles for seven days, after you have gathered the produce from your threshing floor and winepress* (Deuteronomy 16:13), meaning: Once they have brought in the harvest from their land and the silos are brimming with produce – grain, wine, and oil – Israel should dwell in huts. If they do that, they will remember that God provided the people with booths in the wilderness for forty years when they lived without permanent settlements outside of their inherited country. This will naturally lead the people to give thanks to the Lord who has granted them the land of Israel along with bountiful granaries and storehouses. The nation must take heed of the following advice: *You might be tempted to say to yourself, "My power, the strength of my own hand, have brought me this great wealth." But remember the Lord your God, for it is He who gives you the power to do great things, upholding the covenant that He swore to your ancestors, as He is doing on this day* (Deuteronomy 8:17–18). It is to dispel such an attitude that the Israelites are required to leave their homes, that are filled with the riches of the season's yield. They move into huts to help them remember that their ancestors had very little in the wilderness – no houses to dwell in, and no granaries full of harvested crops. Thus, the Holy One, blessed be He, established the Festival of Sukkot precisely at the time when the threshing floor and the winepress have been at their busiest. This prevents the farmer or the vintner from declaring: It is my power and my strength which have brought me the great wealth that my home and hearth represent.

VERSE 44

RAMBAN

וַיְדַבֵּר מֹשֶׁה אֶת־מֹעֲדֵי יהוה אֶל־בְּנֵי יִשְׂרָאֵל – *Thus Moshe announced the Lord's appointed times to the Israelites:* What is the import of this verse? The reader will recall that the previous chapters [21 and 22] comprise prohibitions that are directed to Aharon and his sons; the text contains material that God conveyed to Moshe for the purpose of instructing the High Priest and the common priests. On occasion the text does mention that the information was given to the nation at large as well. For example, at the end of the Torah's consideration of priestly blemishes, we read: *Moshe told this to Aharon, his sons, and all the Israelites* (21:24). For even though God's command to the prophet was exclusive to Aharon and his progeny, as the text states: *Tell Aharon: Any of your future descendants who has a physical blemish may not draw close to present foodstuff offerings to his God* (21:17), Moshe decided to relate the issue to the court of Israel as well. Perhaps the reason for this is that in general, a person with a physical defect will try to conceal it. Likewise, a priest with a blemish will fear being barred

the Israelites live in huts when I brought them out of the land of
44 Egypt; I am the LORD your God." Thus Moshe announced the
LORD's appointed times to the Israelites.
24 1 2 The LORD spoke to Moshe: "Command the Israelites to bring SHEVI'I
you pure oil from crushed olives for the light, to kindle the lamp,

RAMBAN (cont.)

from the Temple service, since that would be a dreadful embarrassment to him. Therefore, the Sanhedrin was directed [to monitor the priests' entry and eagerness to work in the Sanctuary]. In the present context, however, the festivals of the LORD were presented to the entire nation of Israel as a single community; there is no more attention given to teaching this topic to the sons of Aharon than to anybody else. The reason for that, of course, is that the rules of the holidays apply equally to everybody: All members of the populace must rest on the Sabbaths and the festivals; everybody must declare these days to be sacred assemblies. Furthermore, the only sacrifices that are discussed in conjunction with the festivals are the Omer offering [in verse 12–13] and the two loaves of bread on Shavuot [in verse 18–20], for it is those grain offerings that are the central focus of the holiday itself. [Hence the focus in our chapter is not really the holiday sacrifices, for which the priests would be solely responsible.] However, in the text that introduces the main offerings of Yom Kippur, we read: *"Tell your brother Aharon," said the LORD to Moshe, "that he may not come at any time into the holy place inside the inner curtain in front of the cover on the Ark"* (16:2).

CHAPTER 24, VERSE 2

RASHI

צַו אֶת־בְּנֵי יִשְׂרָאֵל – *Command the Israelites:* This is the section containing the actual commandment to light the lamps. The corresponding passage in Parashat Tetzaveh [Exodus 27:20, which states: *Command the Israelites to bring you pure oil from crushed olives for light, to kindle the lamp, every night*] was only mentioned within the broader description of the Tabernacle project in order to explain what the candelabrum would be used for. The sense of that earlier verse is: You [Moshe] will eventually order the Israelites to light the lamps in this utensil. **שֶׁמֶן זַיִת זָךְ** – *Pure oil:* The process of extracting oil from olives yields three grades of the substance. The first stage [in which the fruit is pressed in a mortar] produces pure oil, as explained in the Talmud (Menaḥot 86a) and in the Sifra (13:1). **תָּמִיד** – *Every night:* [The term *tamid* can also be understood as "perpetual." Rashi explains that the meaning here is otherwise.] The lamps should be lit every night. We find a similar usage of the term in the verse *This is the regular [tamid] burnt offering* (Numbers 28:6), which means that this sacrifice is brought on a daily basis [and not that burnt offerings are continuously conveyed onto the altar].

RASHBAM

וְיִקְחוּ אֵלֶיךָ שֶׁמֶן זַיִת זָךְ – *To bring you pure olive oil:* The Torah repeats this material [after originally introducing the laws of the candelabrum in Exodus chapter 27] because this utensil was placed next to the table in order to illuminate the showbreads, which in turn are now discussed. Thus, the whole passage here focuses on the table and its arrangement. The oil is used for casting light on it, and the loaves are to be displayed on it.

ג אֵלֶ֜יךָ שֶׁ֣מֶן זַ֥יִת זָ֛ךְ כָּתִ֖ית לַמָּא֑וֹר לְהַעֲלֹ֥ת נֵ֖ר תָּמִֽיד׃ מִחוּץ
לְפָרֹ֨כֶת הָעֵדֻ֜ת בְּאֹ֣הֶל מוֹעֵ֗ד יַעֲרֹךְ֩ אֹת֨וֹ אַהֲרֹ֜ן מֵעֶ֧רֶב עַד־
ד בֹּ֛קֶר לִפְנֵ֥י יהוה תָּמִ֑יד חֻקַּ֥ת עוֹלָ֖ם לְדֹרֹתֵיכֶֽם׃ עַ֚ל הַמְּנֹרָ֣ה
הַטְּהֹרָ֔ה יַעֲרֹ֖ךְ אֶת־הַנֵּר֑וֹת לִפְנֵ֥י יהוה תָּמִֽיד׃

RAMBAN

וְיִקְחוּ אֵלֶיךָ שֶׁמֶן זַיִת זָךְ – *To bring you pure olive oil:* There are two reasons why the Torah includes a review of the Tabernacle lights. Firstly, the earlier commandment that introduces the lamps reads: *Command the Israelites to bring you pure oil from crushed olives for light, to kindle the lamp, every night* (Exodus 27:20), thereby requesting that any Israelite who owns pure oil suitable for lighting should donate it to the Sanctuary project along with the other donations that were made. And indeed, some people heeded this call, as we subsequently read: *The leaders brought rock crystal stones… together with spices and oil for the light* (Exodus 35:27–28). Now even though the Torah does say: *This shall be a rule for all time for the Israelites, throughout their generations* [Exodus 27:21, which would imply that all of the oil used to light the lamps was collected from individual donors], that statement refers in fact to the eternal obligation to light the candelabrum. [The full verse reads: *From evening to morning, before the Lord, Aharon and his sons shall set the lamp to burn in the Tent of Meeting, outside the curtain that veils the Ark of the Testimony. This shall be a rule for all time for the Israelites, throughout their generations.*] At this point, however, the oil that the tribal chiefs had originally supplied had been depleted, and that prompted the present instruction: The Israelite community was ordered to provide for all generations "pure oil from crushed olives," just like the initial donation. [The nation was required to collect funds from the public, which were to be used for purchasing or producing new oil.] We find a similar command in a different context, where the text reads: *Tell the Israelites to bring you [veyikḥu elekha] a cow, completely red, without blemish, on which no yoke has been laid* (Numbers 19:2). Thus, the phrase "bring you" in the case of the olive oil also means: Seek it out and buy it with money from the national treasury [as opposed to asking private people who have the oil, or indeed, the red cow, to donate it]. Secondly, the previous passage states only that *Aharon and his sons shall set the lamp*, and that could mean either that they are to light the lamps within the candelabrum or even to do so without the candelabrum, if for example that utensil should happen to be broken or lost. Such was the case when the Israelites returned from the Babylonian exile. Nevertheless, the present text states quite clearly: *Aharon shall set out the lamps on the pure candelabrum each day before the Lord* (24:4), which teaches that the lamps may only be lit if they have been placed in a pure candelabrum.

VERSE 3

RASHI

לְפָרֹכֶת הָעֵדֻת – *The curtain of the testimony:* This curtain hangs in front of the ark which is itself called "testimony" [on account of the tablets of the law which it holds. The phrase "Ark of the Testimony" appears, for example, in Exodus 25:22]. However, according to our Sages, the term "testimony" refers to the western lamp of the seven within the candelabrum;

3 every night. From evening to morning, before the LORD, Aharon
shall set it up outside the curtain of the testimony in the Tent
of Meeting to burn each night. This shall be a rule for all time,
4 throughout your generations. Aharon shall set out the lamps on
the pure candelabrum each day before the LORD.

RASHI *(cont.)*

it is so called because it testifies to the entire world that the Divine Presence dwells within the congregation of Israel. For even though this lamp is filled with the same amount of oil as are the other six lights [it miraculously continues burning throughout the day. All seven lamps were prepared in the evening with enough oil to burn through the night. By morning six of these lamps had consumed all of their fuel, while the seventh lamp burned through the day until the next evening]. Therefore, this western lamp was first to be lit and last to be cleaned. **יַעֲרֹךְ אֹתוֹ אַהֲרֹן מֵעֶרֶב עַד־בֹּקֶר** – *Aharon shall set it up to burn each night:* Aharon should prepare the lamps with enough oil to burn throughout the night. [The instruction *me'erev ad boker* does mean that the High Priest should spend all night tending to the candelabrum.] According to the Sages, the measure of oil for each lamp was half a *log*. This sufficed for even the longest nights of the month of Tevet [which fall in the dead of winter]. The same amount of oil was used throughout the year [even during the summer, when the relatively shorter nights meant that the candles stayed lit into the daylight hours].

SFORNO

יַעֲרֹךְ אֹתוֹ אַהֲרֹן – *Aharon shall set it up:* Although throughout the generations any common priest was permitted to light the candelabrum lamps and to burn the daily incense, which is the tradition according to our Sages, Aharon himself was instructed to perform these two duties while he served as the High Priest. The reason for this is that during the nation's sojourn in the wilderness, the status of the Tabernacle [even on a regular day] was equivalent to its condition on Yom Kippur in perpetuity. Thus, with regard to Yom Kippur the text states: *For in a cloud above the cover I appear* (16:2), whereas, this is the general description of the Sanctuary: *The LORD's cloud was over the Tabernacle by day, and fire was in it at night, in view of all the House of Israel through all their journeys* (Exodus 40:38). [Hence, God's presence was manifested over the Tabernacle at all times in the desert, as if every day were Yom Kippur.] It was therefore appropriate for the burning of the incense and the lighting of the lamps, both of which took place inside the holy chamber of the Sanctuary, to be performed by the High Priest, since that official would subsequently do so on Yom Kippur throughout the ages.

VERSE 4

RASHI

הַמְּנֹרָה הַטְּהֹרָה – *The pure candelabrum:* The candelabrum was pure in the sense that it was constructed out of pure gold [and not that it lacked ritual impurity]. Another interpretation: the adjective refers to the cleanliness of the utensil. The candelabrum could not be lit until it was first cleared of its ashes.

ה וְלָקַחְתָּ סֹלֶת וְאָפִיתָ אֹתָהּ שְׁתֵּים עֶשְׂרֵה חַלּוֹת שְׁנֵי עֶשְׂרֹנִים
ו יִהְיֶה הַחַלָּה הָאֶחָת: וְשַׂמְתָּ אוֹתָם שְׁתַּיִם מַעֲרָכוֹת שֵׁשׁ
ז הַמַּעֲרָכֶת עַל הַשֻּׁלְחָן הַטָּהֹר לִפְנֵי יהוה: וְנָתַתָּ עַל־
הַמַּעֲרֶכֶת לְבֹנָה זַכָּה וְהָיְתָה לַלֶּחֶם לְאַזְכָּרָה אִשֶּׁה לַיהוה:
ח בְּיוֹם הַשַּׁבָּת בְּיוֹם הַשַּׁבָּת יַעַרְכֶנּוּ לִפְנֵי יהוה תָּמִיד מֵאֵת
ט בְּנֵי־יִשְׂרָאֵל בְּרִית עוֹלָם: וְהָיְתָה לְאַהֲרֹן וּלְבָנָיו וַאֲכָלֻהוּ
בְּמָקוֹם קָדֹשׁ כִּי קֹדֶשׁ קָדָשִׁים הוּא לוֹ מֵאִשֵּׁי יהוה חָק־
י עוֹלָם: וַיֵּצֵא בֶּן־אִשָּׁה יִשְׂרְאֵלִית וְהוּא בֶּן־
אִישׁ מִצְרִי בְּתוֹךְ בְּנֵי יִשְׂרָאֵל וַיִּנָּצוּ בַּמַּחֲנֶה בֶּן הַיִּשְׂרְאֵלִית

VERSE 6

RASHI

שֵׁשׁ הַמַּעֲרָכֶת – *Six to each column:* There were six loaves per column. [There were not six columns, which is a possible interpretation of the phrase.] **הַשֻּׁלְחָן הַטָּהֹר** – *The pure table:* The table was fashioned out of pure gold. Another interpretation: The loaves should be placed on the "purity" of the table [that is, directly on the table's top]. This means that the poles that separated the loaves in the columns must not raise the breads off the surface of the table. [This refers to the bottom two loaves which rested on the table itself; the other five items in each column were placed on horizontal pieces so that the loaves were not stacked one on top of the other.]

VERSE 7

RASHI

וְנָתַתָּ עַל־הַמַּעֲרֶכֶת – *Lay on each stack:* [Although the definite article *heh* is used, suggesting that frankincense was placed on only one stack] the incense was added to each of the two columns. Thus, there were two incense receptacles, each holding a handful of spices. **וְהָיְתָה** – *As a remembrance:* It is the frankincense itself which acts as a remembrance [and not the act of placing the incense which serves this purpose]. **לַלֶּחֶם לְאַזְכָּרָה** – *A remembrance for the bread:* None of the bread is actually offered up to God. [Rather, it is all consumed by the priests.] Instead, incense is burned whenever the loaves are removed from the table every Sabbath [when they are replaced with a new set of twelve breads]. The frankincense thus serves as remembrance for the bread and acts to call God's attention to the loaves. In this way the burning of the spices generates a similar remembrance to that effected by the handfuls taken from grain offerings [which are then burned on the altar].

VERSE 9

RASHI

וְהָיְתָה – *It shall belong:* This grain offering [that is, the loaves, shall belong to Aharon and his sons. Rashi refers to the loaves as a *minḥa*, a feminine term, thereby explaining the

5 And you shall take fine flour and bake twelve loaves, two-tenths
6 of an ephah for each loaf. You shall place them in two columns,
7 six to each column, on the pure table before the Lord. Lay
pure incense on each stack, as a remembrance for the bread, as
8 a fire offering to the Lord. Every Sabbath he shall set it out, always, before the Lord on behalf of the Israelites: an everlasting
9 covenant. It shall belong to Aharon and his sons. They shall eat
it in a holy place because it is holy of holies among the Lord's
10 fire offerings, their perpetual share." A man went
out among the Israelites, the son of an Israelite woman and
an Egyptian man. And a fight broke out in the camp between

RASHI *(cont.)*

gender of the verb. Had the verse meant that the bread – *leḥem* – should be given to the priests, the text would have used the masculine form, *vehaya*]. For indeed, all items which are made out of grains fall into the category of *menaḥot* [grain offerings]. **וַאֲכָלֻהוּ** – *They shall eat it:* The term *vaakhaluhu* refers back to the bread [mentioned in 24:7, which is masculine, corresponding to the masculine pronoun at the end of the word *akhaluhu*. Had it related to the general and feminine term *minḥa*, the verb would have been *vaakhaluha*].

VERSE 10

RASHI

וַיֵּצֵא בֶּן־אִשָּׁה יִשְׂרְאֵלִית – *A man went out, the son of an Israelite woman:* From where did this man go out? Rabbi Levi taught: He left his world. [That is, his blasphemy removed him from this world, or perhaps from the next world.] Rabbi Berekhya maintains: He separated himself from this passage [that is, what is stated in the previous verses]. For the man mocked the above instruction, *Every Sabbath he shall set it out* (24:8), and said: Surely, it is customary for a king to eat freshly baked bread every single day; is it not demeaning for him to be served cold nine-day-old food? [The loaves were baked on Friday and stacked on the table's two columns on the Sabbath. A week later these breads were removed and eaten by the priests, nine days after they were baked. This disdainful attitude of the Israelite woman's son was the cause of his quarrel with the other man.] An interpretation in a *baraita* provides a third suggestion: The man left the court of Moshe where he had been found guilty of the accusation brought against him. For this man had attempted to pitch his tent within the camp of the tribe of Dan, and the members of that clan had protested. Said he: My mother comes from your tribe [hence he considered himself a Danite]. But the men of Dan turned him away, citing the verse *The Israelites shall camp, each by his banner, the ensign of his ancestral house* [*leveit avotam*, literally, "according to their fathers' houses"] [Numbers 2:2, and the man's father was an Egyptian, not a descendant of Dan]. This prompted him to enter Moshe's court for a ruling, and when the decision went against him, he stood up and blasphemed God. **בֶּן־אִישׁ מִצְרִי** – *The son of an Egyptian man:* The man's father was the Egyptian whom Moshe killed [as reported in Exodus 2:12. That episode refers to the antagonist as an *ish Mitzri* – "an Egyptian man"]. **בְּתוֹךְ בְּנֵי יִשְׂרָאֵל** – *Among the Israelites:* This teaches

RASHI *(cont.)*

that the son of this mixed union converted [and adopted his mother's heritage]. **וַיִּנָּצוּ בַּמַּחֲנֶה** – *And a fight broke out in the camp:* The quarrel was regarding the camp [that is, the third interpretation of the incident cited by Rashi above]. **וְאִישׁ הַיִּשְׂרְאֵלִי** – *And an Israelite man:* This was the opponent of the Israelite woman's son, who objected to him moving into the camp of Dan.

IBN EZRA

וַיֵּצֵא בֶּן־אִשָּׁה יִשְׂרְאֵלִית – *A man went out, the son of an Israelite woman:* The protagonist of this tale went out from his tent. We find similar language in this later episode: *Datan and Aviram came out and stood at the openings of their tents* (Numbers 16:27). **בֶּן־אִישׁ מִצְרִי** – *The son of an Egyptian man:* The man's father was a convert to Judaism. **וְאִישׁ הַיִּשְׂרְאֵלִי** – *And an Israelite man:* The grammatical construction here is akin to that in this verse: *But a traveler came to the house of the rich man [le'ish he'ashir]* (II Samuel 12:4). [Because the adjective *ashir* is prefaced with the definite article *heh*, we would expect the noun to also be definite: *la'ish he'ashir*. Similarly here, the more usual form would be *ha'ish haYisre'eli* – the Israelite (the) man. Ibn Ezra is pointing out several exceptions to this rule.] We find another instance in the text which reads: *God blessed the seventh day [yom hashevi'i] and sanctified it* [Genesis 2:3, instead of *hayom hashevi'i*). It remains unclear how this narrative is connected to the previous material. It is possible that the blasphemer uttered inappropriate statements regarding the showbread, the oil, or the sacrifices.

BEKHOR SHOR

וְהוּא בֶּן־אִישׁ מִצְרִי – *The son of an Egyptian man:* It was the man's heritage which led him to curse the Name. For the Egyptians were accustomed to scorning the Almighty, as we read: *But Pharaoh said, "Who is this Lord that I should obey Him and send Israel forth? I do not know the Lord, and I will not send Israel forth"* (Exodus 5:2).

RAMBAN

וַיֵּצֵא בֶּן־אִשָּׁה יִשְׂרְאֵלִית – *A man went out, the son of an Israelite woman:* The *man went out among the Israelites [betokh Benei Yisrael]*. [The sequence of the clauses in the Hebrew original makes the matter unclear: A son of an Israelite woman went out, and he was the son of an Egyptian, among the Israelites. Thus, these last words perhaps refer to the father who was living within the Israelite community. The Ramban argues instead that they represent an adverbial clause identifying where the man went.] We find a similar expression in a later book: *And he walked out to the middle of the town [betokh ha'ir], crying out, a great and bitter cry* (Esther 4:1). [As in the case of Mordekhai] here too the man left his tent or his home and entered the public square – "among the Israelites," where he fought with his foe. The text stresses that the altercation took place "in the camp" to explain why many people were present and happened to hear the blasphemer's exclamation. The bystanders then seized the offender and *brought him before Moshe* (24:11) in his tent. Now according to the Sages, this incident is recorded here in the text because this man "went out" [that is, he disparaged] the above teaching regarding the fire offering of the Lord

RAMBAN *(cont.)*

[the showbread, discussed in verse 7]. When he heard that, the Israelite man rebuked him, they quarreled, and in his anger the son of the Egyptian issued his curse.

ḤIZKUNI

בְּתוֹךְ בְּנֵי יִשְׂרָאֵל – *Among the Israelites:* According to Rashi, the passage teaches that this son of the Egyptian man had converted to Judaism. Now the reader might recall an earlier comment that Rashi makes regarding the verse *Looking this way and that and seeing no one, he struck down the Egyptian and hid his body in the sand* (Exodus 2:12). Writes that author: Moshe saw that this Egyptian would produce no offspring who would convert. [The implication being that had Moshe believed that the Egyptian taskmaster would father a child who would convert, he would not have killed him. How then can Rashi now argue that the person in the present incident was the son of that wicked Egyptian who had actually joined Israel's faith?] We might resolve the contradiction by suggesting that when Moshe confronted the taskmaster, Shlomit daughter of Divri was already pregnant. It was then that Moshe intuited through divine inspiration that this man who would convert would father no further offspring, and so he killed him. So far, we have seen nothing to commend about this blasphemer [that might have influenced Moshe to ensure he would be born], and that is why it is pointed out that he converted [in an act of solidarity with Israel]. Now one might ask: Since this man was the son of an Israelite woman, why did he have to convert? Does the rule not state that if a gentile has relations with a Jewish woman, the resulting child is considered a Jew? Hence, we must say that the law whereby a child's lineage follows the mother only took effect after the giving of the Torah. In the present instance, the Egyptian man consorted with the Israelite woman prior to the revelation, when a child's ethnicity still followed the father. This explains why the son of this mixed union required conversion.

ABARBANEL

וַיֵּצֵא בֶּן־אִשָּׁה יִשְׂרְאֵלִית – *A man went out, the son of an Israelite woman:* In earlier passages we have read the Torah's warnings about preserving the honor due to God and the prohibitions against deprecating Him. The Israelite people as a whole were cautioned regarding this matter, and the priests in particular were issued their own specific commandments of respect. The three classes of Israelites, Levites, and priests have been instructed to observe the festivals of the Lord, to tend to the lighting of the Sanctuary lamps, and to arrange the twelve showbread loaves on the Tabernacle table. The goal of all these rituals is to glorify God and to refrain from desecrating His name. The text therefore now provides an instance of the violation of these rules with an actual incident of an Israelite who dared to blaspheme the name of God. As a punishment for such effrontery, God orders that he be stoned to death. And in fact, the community at large is rebuked for not having immediately executed this sinner. This then is the sense of the introductory statement, *A man went out* – he thereby removed himself from the acceptable norm of revering God and chose instead to profane His name. Thus, this man separated himself from the congregation of Israel and ignored its guiding principles. It is also possible that the verb "went out" refers to the fact that this son of Shlomit was still a young man, and he left the familiar surroundings of his home environment and went out into the wider public sphere in order to explore the world beyond his family.

יא וְאִישׁ הַיִּשְׂרְאֵלִי: וַיִּקֹּב בֶּן־הָאִשָּׁה הַיִּשְׂרְאֵלִית אֶת־הַשֵּׁם
וַיְקַלֵּל וַיָּבִיאוּ אֹתוֹ אֶל־מֹשֶׁה וְשֵׁם אִמּוֹ שְׁלֹמִית בַּת־
יב דִּבְרִי לְמַטֵּה־דָן: וַיַּנִּיחֻהוּ בַּמִּשְׁמָר לִפְרֹשׁ לָהֶם עַל־פִּי
יְהוָה:
יג וַיְדַבֵּר יְהוָה אֶל־מֹשֶׁה לֵּאמֹר: הוֹצֵא אֶת־הַמְקַלֵּל אֶל־
יד מִחוּץ לַמַּחֲנֶה וְסָמְכוּ כָל־הַשֹּׁמְעִים אֶת־יְדֵיהֶם עַל־רֹאשׁוֹ

VERSE 11

RASHI

וַיִּקֹּב – *And he cursed:* His act should be interpreted as the Targum renders it – *ufaresh* – "he enunciated," meaning that the man pronounced the explicit name of God, and he cursed. He uttered the special name of God which he had heard at Mount Sinai. **וְשֵׁם אִמּוֹ שְׁלֹמִית בַּת־דִּבְרִי** – *His mother's name was Shlomit, daughter of Divri:* The purpose in mentioning the mother's name is to praise the rest of the nation; this woman alone prostituted herself to an Egyptian. **שְׁלֹמִית** – *Shlomit:* She was so called because she was a garrulous person, always saying to a passing man: Peace [*shalom*] be upon you, or wishing a group of people: May you all enjoy peace! Because she talked to everybody and had words [*devarim*] for everyone she saw [she became excessively friendly with the community and eventually inappropriately familiar with the Egyptian man]. **בַּת־דִּבְרִי** – *Daughter of Divri:* This woman was extremely talkative [*dabberanit*], speaking to everybody. This is how she ended up acting promiscuously. **לְמַטֵּה־דָן** – *Of the tribe of Dan:* We learn from here that a wicked person brings shame not only to himself, but also to his father, and to his whole tribe. The opposite point is derived from the verse *I have assigned to him Oholiav, son of Aḥisamakh from the tribe of Dan* (Exodus 31:6) – Oholiav's contribution to the construction of the Tabernacle brought pride not only to himself, but also to his father, and to his entire tribe.

VERSE 12

RASHI

וַיַּנִּיחֻהוּ – *They placed the man:* The son of the Israelite woman was not imprisoned with the man who had gathered wood [referring to the Sabbath violator whose arrest and punishment are described in Numbers 15:32–36] even though both incidents happened at the same time. Everyone knew that the wood gatherer was to be killed [for God had earlier declared that *whoever profanes [the Sabbath] shall be put to death* (Exodus 31:14)], but the method of execution was unclear. Hence the text states: *It had not been specified what should be done to him* (Numbers 15:34). On the other hand, with regard to the blasphemer, the verse states: *They placed the man in custody until the Lord's verdict would be pronounced to them*, for the community did not know whether his behavior constituted a capital offense. [It would have been torment for the son of the Israelite woman to be held with the other man who was to be killed; that would have convinced him that he too was to die.]

11 this son of an Israelite woman, and an Israelite man. The Israelite woman's son blasphemed the Name and cursed – his
mother's name was Shlomit, daughter of Divri, of the tribe of
12 Dan – and they brought him before Moshe. They placed the
man in custody until the LORD's verdict would be pronounced
to them.
13 14 And the LORD spoke to Moshe: "Take the one who cursed
outside the camp. All the people who heard him shall lay their
hands on his head – and then the whole community shall stone

ḤIZKUNI

לְפְרֹשׁ לָהֶם עַל־פִּי יהוה – *Until the LORD's verdict would be pronounced to them:* The people conjectured that the man would have to be stoned to death based on the following reasoning. Since an earlier text states: *Since he has cursed his father or mother, his bloodguilt is upon him* (20:9), one could reasonably infer that this man who cursed God should be punished in a similar fashion. However, because no punishment can be imposed through deduction, the nation had to wait *until the LORD's verdict would be pronounced to them.*

VERSE 14

RASHI

הַשֹּׁמְעִים – *The people who heard him:* This refers to the witnesses. **כָּל** – *All:* The adjective includes the judges [who had heard the blasphemy indirectly, from the witnesses]. **אֶת־יְדֵיהֶם** – *Their hands:* All of these men say to the blasphemer: Your guilt is on your head; we will not be punished for your execution because you brought this upon yourself.

כָּל־הָעֵדָה – *The whole community:* The witnesses are to stone the sentenced person under the authority of the congregation. We learn from here the legal principle of agency. [The witnesses were to act on behalf of the nation, which would be as if everyone had stoned the sinner.]

IBN EZRA

וְסָמְכוּ כָל־הַשֹּׁמְעִים – *All the people who heard him shall lay their hands:* The witnesses to the offense were to place their hands on the sinner's head because he was being executed based on their testimony.

ABARBANEL

הוֹצֵא אֶת־הַמְקַלֵּל אֶל־מִחוּץ לַמַּחֲנֶה – *Take the one who cursed outside the camp:* There were many Israelites who heard the blasphemer utter his despicable words but refused to act spontaneously and kill the transgressor. These passive bystanders thereby incurred great blame for their inaction. Therefore, it was appropriate for every single person who had heard the interjection to place his hands upon the head of the offender and thereby expiate his guilt by saying to him: Your blood is on your own head and not on ours [a reference to II Samuel 1:16]. All of those who heard the treachery then stoned the sinner to death without mercy. Thus, God avenged Himself against the man who belittled His honor.

טו וְרָגְמוּ אֹתוֹ כָּל־הָעֵדָה׃ וְאֶל־בְּנֵי יִשְׂרָאֵל תְּדַבֵּר לֵאמֹר
טז אִישׁ אִישׁ כִּי־יְקַלֵּל אֱלֹהָיו וְנָשָׂא חֶטְאוֹ׃ וְנֹקֵב שֵׁם־
יהוה מוֹת יוּמָת רָגוֹם יִרְגְּמוּ־בוֹ כָּל־הָעֵדָה כַּגֵּר כָּאֶזְרָח
יז בְּנָקְבוֹ־שֵׁם יוּמָת׃ וְאִישׁ כִּי יַכֶּה כָּל־נֶפֶשׁ אָדָם מוֹת יוּמָת׃
יח יט וּמַכֵּה נֶפֶשׁ־בְּהֵמָה יְשַׁלְּמֶנָּה נֶפֶשׁ תַּחַת נָפֶשׁ׃ וְאִישׁ כִּי־יִתֵּן
כ מוּם בַּעֲמִיתוֹ כַּאֲשֶׁר עָשָׂה כֵּן יֵעָשֶׂה לּוֹ׃ שֶׁבֶר תַּחַת שֶׁבֶר

ABARBANEL *(cont.)*

Now the Almighty also castigated the public which had demonstrated leniency toward the blasphemer and was prepared to excuse his behavior. This is the meaning of the following verse: *Tell the Israelites: Anyone* [*ish, ish*, literally, "a man, a man"] *who curses his God shall bear the sin* (24:16), meaning: This law applies equally to an Egyptian and to a Jew – the identity of the person who curses the object of his worship is irrelevant. For if the gentile defames the deity of his nation and his country, he shall bear the sin against that god, but he shall not be punished by us – let that particular entity strike him down! However, should a person *blaspheme the Lord's name* (24:16), referring to the hallowed name of the Creator, *he shall be put to death: the whole community shall stone him. Migrant and native born alike*. In other words, whether the culprit is an Israelite citizen or is a convert from among the Egyptian people, or from some other nation, he *who blasphemes the Lord's name shall be put to death* (24:16). Indeed, if a person does not hail from the community of Israel, what right does he have to even utter the name of our God? Thus, if he goes so far as to curse the venerable name of the Almighty with his mouth and his lips, he surely deserves to die! Since the man in question was an Egyptian, why did he not simply curse one of his own Egyptian deities instead of encroaching into the center of the Israelite camp only to profane our national God?

VERSE 15

RASHI

וְנָשָׂא חֶטְאוֹ – *Shall bear the sin:* A person will be punished with excision in a situation where he or she was not warned by witnesses before cursing God.

VERSE 16

RASHI

וְנֹקֵב שֵׁם – *And anyone who blasphemes the name:* One is only liable if he pronounces the explicit name of God [namely, the Tetragrammaton] but not if he curses using other names of God. **וְנֹקֵב** – *Who blasphemes:* The verb *venokev* connotes cursing, as in the verse *How can I curse [ekov] whom God has not cursed?* (Numbers 23:8).

IBN EZRA

כָּל־הָעֵדָה – *The whole community:* This term refers to the distinguished members of society, the leaders of the Israelite people.

15 him. Tell the Israelites: Anyone who curses his God shall bear
16 the sin, and anyone who blasphemes the LORD's name shall be
put to death: the whole community shall stone him. Migrant
and native born alike: one who blasphemes the LORD's name
17 shall be put to death. One who takes the life of any human be-
18 ing shall be put to death. One who takes the life of an animal
19 shall make restitution for it: life for life. One who injures his
fellow man shall be penalized in proportion to the injury in-
20 flicted: the cost of a broken bone for a broken bone, of an eye
for an eye, of a tooth for a tooth. Just as he inflicted injury on

ḤIZKUNI

כַּגֵּר כָּאֶזְרָח – *Migrant and native born alike:* Since the main actor in this tale was a convert and this entire passage was recorded as a result of his offense, the *ger* ["convert" or "outsider"] is mentioned first in this pair.

VERSE 17

RASHI

וְאִישׁ כִּי יַכֶּה – *One who takes the life:* When an earlier verse states: *One person who strikes another* [*ish*, literally "a man"] *so that he dies shall be put to death* (Exodus 21:12), that depicts culpability for killing an adult man. How do we know that one would similarly be liable for taking the life of a woman or a child? We learn that from the present verse which states: *One who takes the life of any human being.*

IBN EZRA

וְאִישׁ כִּי יַכֶּה כָּל־נֶפֶשׁ אָדָם – *One who takes the life of any human being:* The text opens this list of offenses with an offender who intentionally attacks somebody outside the context of a war. The law applies whether the murderer's victim is a foreigner or a native Israelite.

VERSE 18

RAMBAN

וּמַכֵּה נֶפֶשׁ־בְּהֵמָה – *One who takes the life of an animal:* The Torah does not mean that the slain animal should actually be replaced with a different animal, so that the criminal is compelled to buy a new animal for the owner of the dead beast. [Even though the text reads "life for life," this is not meant to be taken literally.] Rather, the guilty party must compensate the victim with money equal to the damage he has done. This interpretation applies as well to the subsequent statements: *The cost of a broken bone for a broken bone, of an eye for an eye,* and so on. This is the opinion of our Sages [in Bava Kamma 83b. In all cases, the criminal must pay the difference between the value of the animal before and after the assault.]

VERSE 20

RASHI

כֵּן יִנָּתֶן בּוֹ – *So shall he suffer the loss:* [Although the phrase *ken yinnaten bo* literally means, "the same shall be inflicted upon him,"] our Sages explained that the perpetrator is not

עַיִן תַּחַת עַיִן שֵׁן תַּחַת שֵׁן כַּאֲשֶׁר יִתֵּן מוּם בָּאָדָם כֵּן יִנָּתֶן
כא כב בּוֹ: וּמַכֵּה בְהֵמָה יְשַׁלְּמֶנָּה וּמַכֵּה אָדָם יוּמָת: מִשְׁפַּט אֶחָד מפטיר
כג יִהְיֶה לָכֶם כַּגֵּר כָּאֶזְרָח יִהְיֶה כִּי אֲנִי יהוה אֱלֹהֵיכֶם: וַיְדַבֵּר
מֹשֶׁה אֶל־בְּנֵי יִשְׂרָאֵל וַיּוֹצִיאוּ אֶת־הַמְקַלֵּל אֶל־מִחוּץ
לַמַּחֲנֶה וַיִּרְגְּמוּ אֹתוֹ אָבֶן וּבְנֵי־יִשְׂרָאֵל עָשׂוּ כַּאֲשֶׁר צִוָּה
יהוה אֶת־מֹשֶׁה:

RASHI *(cont.)*

himself actually physically harmed as punishment for his action, but that he is forced to pay monetary compensation for his crime. The victim is assessed as a slave [and the attacker pays the difference between what he would have been worth before and after the injury]. This is why the text uses the language of *netina* – "giving": It refers to something that can be handed over from one person to another [that is, money].

VERSE 21

RASHI

וּמַכֵּה בְהֵמָה יְשַׁלְּמֶנָּה – *One who kills an animal shall make restitution for it:* The text above [verse 18, which states: *One who takes the life of an animal – makkeh nefesh behema*] deals with a person who kills an animal, whereas the present verse describes merely the wounding of an animal. [Our verse omits the term *nefesh* – "life" or "soul."] **וּמַכֵּה אָדָם יוּמָת** – *But one who kills a human being shall be put to death:* Since this verse does not employ the word *nefesh* ["soul," as the text does in verse 17], we learn that the attack discussed here is one that does not result in death, but only in injury. [Even so, the perpetrator is subject to death because] the text describes the striking of one's father or mother. Hence a comparison is made between wounding one's parent and injuring an animal. Just as one is only liable for striking a living animal, so too is a son or daughter only held accountable for striking his or her parent when the latter is still alive; one would not be executed for hitting a dead parent. Now this had to be pointed out because we indeed find that a child remains culpable for cursing his or her parent even after the father or mother has died. In contrast, we are taught that wounding a parent's corpse is not a capital offense. Furthermore, just as one must pay for injuring an animal only when he has caused an actual wound, so too is one held liable for striking a parent only when the father or mother has suffered a wound [that is, when blood has been drawn].

VERSE 22

RASHI

אֲנִי יהוה אֱלֹהֵיכֶם – *I am the Lord your God:* I am the God of all of you. Just as My Name is identified with your community [of native-born Israelites], it is no less associated with the converts among you.

21 another human being, so shall he suffer the loss. One who kills MAFTIR
an animal shall make restitution for it; but one who kills a hu-
22 man being shall be put to death. There shall be one law for you,
for migrant and for native born alike, for I am the LORD your
23 God." Moshe told this to the Israelites, and so they took the
blasphemer outside the camp and stoned him. Thus the Israelites did as the LORD had commanded Moshe.

RABBEINU BAḤYA

כִּי אֲנִי יהוה אֱלֹהֵיכֶם – *For I am the Lord your God:* Declares the Almighty: If you follow these laws then I will be *the Lord your God*. Based on this positive statement, we can infer the negative. [That is, if Israel neglects the commandments, the Lord will not be their God.] For should a person not obey the Torah's mandates he will thereby distance himself from his God and essentially deny His existence. It is a widely accepted idea that all of Israel's beliefs and all of our statutes represent an interpretation of the Torah. Thus, the Torah's laws are its foundational element. Therefore, should a Jew not occupy himself with the particulars of the law, he profanes the name of God. Furthermore, if others have the opportunity to reproach a sinner and fail to do so, they too are guilty of desecrating the divine name. And that is tantamount to displaying reverence for idolatry, to disparaging the Torah of Moshe, and to depleting the wealth of their fellow Israelites. This is because the security and welfare of the entire world depend on the Torah's laws, and the Holy One, blessed be He, has bestowed these rules upon Israel alone, as the psalmist writes: *He has declared His words to Yaakov, His statutes and laws to Israel. He has done this for no other nation; such laws they do not know. Halleluya!* (Psalms 147:19–20).

VERSE 23

RASHI

וּבְנֵי־יִשְׂרָאֵל עָשׂוּ – *Thus the Israelites did:* The people fulfilled the particulars of the commandment of stoning which are mentioned elsewhere. Specifically, the man was first pushed off a high structure. He was then stoned. Finally, his corpse was hanged up temporarily.

IBN EZRA

וּבְנֵי־יִשְׂרָאֵל עָשׂוּ – *Thus the Israelites did:* From that day onward, the Israelites implemented these laws with regard to one who injures his fellow.

RAMBAN

וּבְנֵי־יִשְׂרָאֵל עָשׂוּ – *Thus the Israelites did:* As soon as Moshe announced the verdict with respect to the offender, the people *took the blasphemer outside the camp and stoned him*. Furthermore, all of the Israelites executed the sentence in order to obey and to fulfill God's commandment to Moshe. The nation was not motivated by feelings of hatred for the son of the Egyptian who had fought with the Israelite; their sole intention was to expunge the pollution from their midst.

18TH CENTURY

RABBI ḤAYYIM IBN ATTAR – *OR HAḤAYYIM*,
1696, MOROCCO – 1743, ISRAEL

19TH CENTURY

RABBI YAAKOV TZVI MECKLENBURG – *HAKETAV VEHAKABBALA*,
1785 – 1865, GERMANY

SHADAL, 1800 – 1865, ITALY

RABBI SAMSON RAPHAEL HIRSCH,
1808 – 1888, GERMANY

MALBIM, 1809 – 1879, UKRAINE

RABBI NAFTALI TZVI YEHUDA BERLIN – *HAAMEK DAVAR*, 1816, BELARUS – 1893, POLAND

20TH CENTURY

RABBI DAVID TZVI HOFFMAN,
1843, HUNGARY – 1926, GERMANY

RABBI MEIR SIMḤA OF DVINSK – *MESHEKH ḤOKHMA*, 1843, LITHUANIA – 1926, LATVIA

RABBI JOSEPH B. SOLOVEITCHIK,
1903, LITHUANIA – 1993, USA

RABBI MENACHEM MENDEL SCHNEERSON – THE LUBAVITCHER REBBE,
1902, UKRAINE – 1994, USA

NEHAMA LEIBOWITZ,
1905, LATVIA – 1997, ISRAEL

פרשת אמר

PARASHAT EMOR

CONFRONTING
MODERNITY

כא א וַיֹּאמֶר יהוה אֶל־מֹשֶׁה אֱמֹר אֶל־הַכֹּהֲנִים בְּנֵי אַהֲרֹן וְאָמַרְתָּ יז
ב אֲלֵהֶם לְנֶפֶשׁ לֹא־יִטַּמָּא בְּעַמָּיו: כִּי אִם־לִשְׁאֵרוֹ הַקָּרֹב אֵלָיו

CHAPTER 21, VERSE 1

RABBI SAMSON RAPHAEL HIRSCH

אֱמֹר אֶל־הַכֹּהֲנִים בְּנֵי אַהֲרֹן – *Speak to the priests, Aharon's sons:* Our *parasha* opens with unusual wording, "speak to the priests" [*emor el hakohanim*]. This verb, "speak" [*emor*], is distinct from the usual opening verb, "tell" [*dabber*]. The expected verb, *dabber*, connotes a brief presentation of material, a general instruction of the law in question. The verb *emor* here introduces a full detailed exposition, such that the listener will gain an understanding of the matter at hand. The act of *dabber* ["tell"] is not synonymous with the experience of *emor* ["speak"]. When a person undertakes "telling" he articulates an idea and expresses himself even in the absence of an audience. But a person who engages in "saying" has captured his listener's attention. As such, when a person is alone, he can "tell" or "declaim" all he wants; but he cannot "speak" unless he has company. "Telling" gives a precise formulation to his thoughts, but "speaking" appeals directly to another person's heart and communicates ideas for his companion's approval. It is therefore "speaking" that introduces here a fully developed and detailed explanation of the duties and definitions of being a priest. **בְּעַמָּיו** – *Among his people:* All twelve of Israel's tribes are commanded to assume responsibility for burying the dead. However, Aharon's tribe, the priestly clan, represents the only group which must stand apart and observe from a distance. The priests must not touch a dead person or contact any body parts that impart impurity. Neither may a priest enter a room which contains a corpse [since the shared space also conveys impurity; see Numbers 19:14]. Still, this prohibition applies only when the corpse is "among his people." This condition limits a priest's passivity to cases where the dead person is found in proximity to the community so that there are other Israelites who can attend to his burial. However, in the case of an unattended corpse [the *met mitzva*] which a priest might chance upon, lying abandoned on the road, a priest is forbidden to ignore the corpse. He is required to take upon himself the burial of his fellow Israelite, even though he will necessarily become impure in the process. This law teaches us the extreme degree of value in acting righteously toward a neglected and unidentified body. We find here a manifestation of the living Torah that is Judaism: The ultimate goal of the Torah is to educate a person to be humane, a mensch.

HAAMEK DAVAR

אֶל־הַכֹּהֲנִים בְּנֵי אַהֲרֹן – *To the priests, Aharon's sons:* [The author seeks to explain the redundancy in this verse. Why does it need to specify both priests and Aharon's sons? Are not priests, by definition, Aharon's sons?] In a subsequent verse, the Hebrew term identifying the priest suggests something different. In the context of a priest's limitations on burying a relative, the Torah states: *But he shall not become impure for those he is related to by marriage* [*baal be'amav*, 21:4. Here the priest is called *baal*, a master, and that might give rise to a totally different interpretation of these verses]. The term *baal* refers to a distinguished member of the community, as in the verse, *The citizens of Yeriḥo [baalei Yeriḥo] fought against you* (Joshua 24:11). There are many similar instances. Now, we might

21 1 The LORD said to Moshe, "Speak to the priests, Aharon's sons.
Say: No one of you shall render himself impure for any dead
2 person among his people except for his nearest relatives: his

HAAMEK DAVAR *(cont.)*

have thought that this entire section which excludes people of a certain status from being involved in burial also includes eminent Israelites. Had the verse only addressed these laws to the "priests" we still may have come to that conclusion because occasionally the term "priests" also refers to important Israelites, leaders of towns [despite not being Aharon's descendants]. We find such a usage in the verse which reads: *And David's sons were priests* [II Samuel 8:18, where the title cannot be meant literally since David belonged to the tribe of Yehuda]. To dispel this proposition the text clarifies that the prohibition is directed to "the priests, Aharon's sons." [Israelite noblemen cannot claim an exemption from the duty to bury the dead, explaining that it is beneath their dignity and that they are similarly considered priests. Only hereditary priests, Aharon's sons, are exempt.]

MESHEKH ḤOKHMA

אֱמֹר אֶל־הַכֹּהֲנִים – *Speak to the priests:* Rabbi Avraham Ibn Ezra is correct when he observes that the instructions here, which discuss specific laws limited to the priesthood, relate to the previous material [chapter 20], which discusses the punishments for illicit relations, which are applicable to the entire nation. This is because the priests were tasked with guarding the Torah. [This general imperative to guard the Torah has many aspects. The priests were the teachers and interpreters of the law. See Deuteronomy 21:5, for example: *The priests, sons of Levi, shall step forward, for it is them the LORD your God has chosen to minister to Him…and to decide all cases of dispute and assault.* They also set a standard. The *Meshekh Ḥokhma* will connect this role of the priests to the enforcement of the punishments for illicit unions just described.] This understanding, that priests have a hand in the guarding and preservation of the integrity of the Torah's laws, finds a lovely support in the Rambam's *Hilkhot Sanhedrin* (14:11), where he writes: At the moment that a priest is occupied in burning a sacrifice on the altar, that is when the Supreme Court judges capital cases. This explains why the preceding text, which outlines the punishments for incest and adultery, is juxtaposed here with God's command to "speak to the priests": the enforcement of the laws governing licentiousness relate to the time and fact of the priests being occupied with the Temple service.

RABBI JOSEPH B. SOLOVEITCHIK

לְנֶפֶשׁ לֹא־יִטַּמָּא – *No one of you shall render himself impure for any dead person:* Corpse impurity [*tum'at met*] is due not to organic but to spiritual destruction. It is the expression of human anxiety and terror, human helplessness in the face of a mocking Satan. Corpse impurity is the result of the traumatic experience that dislocates man's self, I-awareness and existential security. Death lurks in the shadows. Death defeats everyone, great or small, clever or simple. *All is as it is for all. The same fate awaits the righteous and the wicked* (Ecclesiastes 9:2). Corpse impurity represents not just an experience of ugliness, but the human situation, the tragic and absurd human destiny.

ג לְאִמּוֹ וּלְאָבִיו וְלִבְנוֹ וּלְבִתּוֹ וּלְאָחִיו: וְלַאֲחֹתוֹ הַבְּתוּלָה
ד הַקְּרוֹבָה אֵלָיו אֲשֶׁר לֹא־הָיְתָה לְאִישׁ לָהּ יִטַּמָּא: לֹא יִטַּמָּא
ה בַּעַל בְּעַמָּיו לְהֵחַלּוֹ: לֹא־יקרחה קָרְחָה בְּרֹאשָׁם וּפְאַת יִקְרְחוּ

VERSE 3

SHADAL

אֲשֶׁר לֹא־הָיְתָה לְאִישׁ – *Because she has not married:* If the sister has had relations with a man, then she presumably has sons who will be able to attend to their mother's burial. The Torah here describes the most common situation, since most women who have been intimate with a man have given birth to children. However, if the sister does not have any sons, then perhaps her husband will bury her under the obligation of an unattended corpse [*met mitzva*]. Alternatively, the man might hire others to undertake the task.

HAAMEK DAVAR

הַקְּרוֹבָה אֵלָיו – *Who has remained close to him:* [The author wants to explain the meaning of the expression "who has remained close to him," which in Hebrew is *hakerova elav*, meaning simply, a relative. But since she is a sister, she is obviously a relative. If so, why does the Torah include this extra descriptive phrase?] It was customary in ancient times for an orphan sister to be guided by her brother's advice until she could be married off. As such, a girl is brought up with a close connection to her brother lest the siblings' father die. [The phrase *hakerova elav* expresses this added dimension of the relationship of a brother to his sister, that he is a potential stand-in for a parent.]

VERSE 4

HAAMEK DAVAR

לֹא יִטַּמָּא בַּעַל בְּעַמָּיו – *But he shall not become impure for those he is related to by marriage:* [According to the understanding of the Sages, this verse prohibits a priest from defiling himself over the burial of a wife, if that wife were someone the priest was prohibited to marry. The *Haamek Davar* wants to explain the plain meaning of the verse, especially the use of the strange expression *baal be'amav* to indicate a wife. He suggests that the verse is teaching a moral point.] The phrase *baal be'amav* indicates an important personage, as I wrote earlier (on 21:1). The force of this verse then becomes: An important person should not get his hands dirty with a burial if that activity results in his becoming profane [*leheḥalo*], but otherwise an important person should certainly undertake that lowly task. Thus, a priest is exempt from burial, not because it is beneath his dignity but only because it causes his status as a priest to become profaned due to its involvement with impurity. This is not a concern for other prominent people. The text therefore teaches that it is fitting for a person of eminence to engage in the menial task of burying a fellow from "among his people," whether the deceased was himself somebody deserving of honor while alive, or was a lower-class commoner who would have served this august man. [*Baal be'amav* translates literally as "a master among his people" and carries the sense that even an important person should remain responsible and in a sense equal to those from among his compatriots.]

3 mother, father, son, daughter, or brother; or his virgin sister
who has remained close to him because she has not married –
4 for her, he may render himself impure. But he shall not become
impure for those he is related to by marriage, and so become
5 profane. Priests shall not make bald patches on their heads, or
shave off the edges of their beards, or gash wounds into their

VERSE 5

RABBI SAMSON RAPHAEL HIRSCH

לֹא־יקרחה קָרְחָה בְּרֹאשָׁם – *Priests shall not make bald patches on their heads:* There is a very good reason why the Torah repeats these three prohibitions here, specifically in the context of the priesthood. [Two warnings regarding these matters have already been issued to the general Israelite nation, while the third one is mentioned in Deuteronomy. In Parashat Kedoshim we read: *Do not cut off the hair on the sides of your head or destroy the edges of your beard. Do not gash your body for the dead* – 19:27–28. The third text, from Deuteronomy 14:1, commands: *Do not lacerate yourselves or make* – *lo tasimu* – *bald patches in the middle of your heads for the dead.* Although various details of the law are learned from the wording in each instance, Rabbi Hirsch is seeking a more thematic reason which necessitates these three prohibitions being mentioned in the context of priesthood.] Based on the verse from Deuteronomy, we learn that this prohibition applies only when the person is mourning his dead. Furthermore, the usage of the verb *tasimu* [literally, "place," rather than "make"] in that text suggests that the Torah objects not to the action itself but to the result of the deed. We are not dealing primarily with an action which expresses the mourner's anguish. In fact, the forbidden removal of hair through some sort of paste causes no pain in the least. These lacerations are not for the mourner but for the dead, as the verse states: *Do not gash your body for the dead* (19:28). The verse in Deuteronomy mentions a location for these forbidden lacerations and bald patches as "the middle of your heads" [*bein eineikhem*], even though they may not be placed anywhere on the head. This is the same location as for tefillin, which suggests that these markings are similarly considered signs that are intended to occupy the mourner's attention. Based on all this, we may suggest that the bald patch, like the gash on the skin, wrongly symbolizes that the worth of his body has become diminished by the death. Now that his beloved relative or friend has passed away, the bereaved survivor believes that his own body too has lost value. What emerges is that the bald space and the slash are signs of defeat, a tribute of submission to the deity of death whose power is supreme and inescapable. Once we understand that, it becomes clear why the Torah again relates the prohibitions on the priestly class, even though it should be obvious that if the nation at large may not do these things, this applies to the descendants of Aharon as well. It would seem that the laws in question are connected to the ban against a priest contracting impurity, something that relates only to this group of Israelites. In both its ancient and modern iterations, idolatry inevitably links religion with death. According to such a philosophy, the deity's domain begins at the point where the human's reign ends. This is why the dying process and the resultant death exist as the main realms of the false gods, entities which rule over the world of the deceased. These are not gods of life – they

ה זָקְנָם לֹא יִגַלְּחוּ וּבִבְשָׂרָם לֹא יִשְׂרְטוּ שָׂרָטֶת: קְדֹשִׁים יִהְיוּ
לֵאלֹהֵיהֶם וְלֹא יְחַלְּלוּ שֵׁם אֱלֹהֵיהֶם כִּי אֶת־אִשֵּׁי יהוה לֶחֶם
ו אֱלֹהֵיהֶם הֵם מַקְרִיבִם וְהָיוּ קֹדֶשׁ: אִשָּׁה זֹנָה וַחֲלָלָה לֹא יִקָּחוּ
וְאִשָּׁה גְּרוּשָׁה מֵאִישָׁהּ לֹא יִקָּחוּ כִּי־קָדֹשׁ הוּא לֵאלֹהָיו:

RABBI SAMSON RAPHAEL HIRSCH *(cont.)*

might kill, but they never resurrect. This heathen force dispatches death and its heralds, illness and destitution, so that the human being will learn to dread the deity's unyielding force and acknowledge that he has no weapons to combat his invariable end. All of this explains why idolatrous temples are constructed in the midst of cemeteries, and why their priests are most often found ministering to the dead. It is in such surroundings that the purveyors of these dreary and hopeless faiths can most successfully peddle their misguided religion, as they appeal to the weeping eyes and play on the crushed hearts of the mourner. Thus do these idolators bear upon their bodies the sign of death, the insignia of a death cult which the person believes rules over all other forces in the world. This badge of death demonstrates his perpetual awareness and fealty to his ultimate end. Because the infliction of such a marker represents an obvious religious acknowledgement, it is most fitting that it is the priest himself who should adopt the symbolism. But of course, the priests of Israel must portray a completely different mentality and attitude: The understanding we have described has no connection to the Torah's conception of God and is utterly foreign to the faith of Israel. Our God, who guides the priest in his leadership of the populace, is the God of life. The Almighty's most exalted manifestation lies not in His mastery of death which destroys life and the strength it boasts. The opposite is true: The influence of God in this world is seen in the power that is present within the freedom of life; it is felt in the exhilaration that is vitality and revitalization. Thus does God sustain man and encourage him toward liberty and eternal life. It should be clear to all that Judaism's focus is not on how to die; it trains its adherents how to live. Indeed, the Torah way teaches the Israelites how to defeat death even while they are still alive. How can we overcome the lack of liberty found in subjugation to the physical temptations, those that target man's weakness by enticing his sense? By living every moment one is granted under the framework of eternal existence, one serves God. And so does the Torah prompt its readers to strive for a life of thought and will, creativity and productivity, while not ignoring that enjoyment too is permitted. It is this idea that forms the foundational message of the Lord's Sanctuary. The priests who serve at that site should at all times present to their charges, the Israelites, the Torah's emphasis on life; they must never succumb to the lazy, bleak, and desperate religion of death.

VERSE 6

HAAMEK DAVAR

קְדֹשִׁים יִהְיוּ לֵאלֹהֵיהֶם – *They shall be holy to their God:* This verse enjoins the priests with a mission, that "they shall be holy." [The *Haamek Davar* is connecting this verse to the general theme of holiness which has characterized the preceding chapters and in particular the charge to the entire nation, "be holy" – 19:2. That holiness was to be achieved by the

6 flesh. They shall be holy to their God and not profane God's
name, for they bring close the LORD's fire offerings, foodstuff
7 offerings to their God; therefore they shall be holy. They may
not marry a woman made profane by immorality, nor may they
marry a woman divorced from her husband, for they are holy

HAAMEK DAVAR *(cont.)*

saintly behaviors detailed in those chapters and in particular a certain sexual abstinence highlighted by Rashi in his commentary on that verse: Separate yourselves from forbidden sexual relations. But this raises a problem when addressed to the priests. How should they separate and distinguish themselves from the rest of the nation?] Holiness means abstinence and separation from people for the sake of God. It means behaviors which succeed in glorifying the name of God [creating a *kiddush Hashem*]. Therefore, this charge, "they shall be holy," enjoins the priests to excel in moral saintliness, in modesty, and in other positive character traits. This is opposed to distinguishing themselves through elitism, arrogance, and a "holier than thou" attitude, which bring no glorification of God's name. **וְלֹא יְחַלְּלוּ שֵׁם אֱלֹהֵיהֶם** – *And not profane God's name:* Priests will profane God's name [cause a *ḥillul Hashem*] if they fail to act with exemplary behavior and do not demonstrate the excellence of character befitting a priest. Therefore, this verse is not concerned with outright violations that would apply to any Israelite, but with those behaviors which cause the reputation of God, the priests, and God's people to be diminished. The Talmud (Yoma 86a) gives examples of how people desecrate God's name through certain acts that are inappropriate but not forbidden, such as buying meat and not paying for it immediately. So too, here the Torah warns against profaning the name of God through deeds unbefitting a priest. **וְהָיוּ קֹדֶשׁ** – *Therefore they shall be holy:* The text hereby promises that if a priest distinguishes himself from those around him with excellent behavior and character, and he does this for the sake of heaven [and not to be elitist] then "he shall be holy" in the eyes of the people. The people will recognize the priests' distinctive and elevated conduct and treat them with honor and reverence.

VERSE 7

RABBI SAMSON RAPHAEL HIRSCH

לֹא יִקָּחוּ – *They may not marry:* Why does the text repeat the prohibition? [The verse states: "May not marry," and again: "nor may they marry," when a single mention could have sufficed.] We learn from here that the responsibility for maintaining the wholesomeness of the priests' unions devolves not only on these men themselves, but on the community as a whole. This is implied by the next verse, which charges the entire nation to treat the priests properly, "You shall treat a priest as holy." Chief among the people responsible for safeguarding the propriety of priestly marriages are the women who must refuse a marriage that violates the sanctity of a priest. Therefore, the verse repeated the words "may not marry" in reference to "a woman made profane by immorality" and again in reference to a divorcée, as if to say that each of these different women must ensure that these weddings do not take place. If we take as a whole the details that govern the specialized life of the priest, we

ח וְקִדַּשְׁתּוֹ כִּי־אֶת־לֶחֶם אֱלֹהֶיךָ הוּא מַקְרִיב קָדֹשׁ יִהְיֶה־לָּךְ
ט כִּי קָדוֹשׁ אֲנִי יהוה מְקַדִּשְׁכֶם: וּבַת אִישׁ כֹּהֵן כִּי תֵחֵל לִזְנוֹת
י אֶת־אָבִיהָ הִיא מְחַלֶּלֶת בָּאֵשׁ תִּשָּׂרֵף: וְהַכֹּהֵן
הַגָּדוֹל מֵאֶחָיו אֲשֶׁר־יוּצַק עַל־רֹאשׁוֹ | שֶׁמֶן הַמִּשְׁחָה וּמִלֵּא
אֶת־יָדוֹ לִלְבֹּשׁ אֶת־הַבְּגָדִים אֶת־רֹאשׁוֹ לֹא יִפְרָע וּבְגָדָיו לֹא

RABBI SAMSON RAPHAEL HIRSCH *(cont.)*

realize that this clan bears its own holy mission, which is to inculcate in the people a proper understanding of their God. This they do by constantly reminding the populace what the true principles of their lives ought to be. This is why a priest is forbidden to contract impurity from a corpse since he thereby preserves in everyone's minds the belief in the One true God, who is unique, personal, and entirely free, and the nature of man as a completely free ethical agent. [Rabbi Hirsch emphasizes the freedom of both God and man in order to explain that just like God is unconstrained by death, so too are people unconstrained by forces leading to sin or to unhappy homes. People have the power to direct their lives toward the ideals of life, morality, and domestic happiness.] It is these ideas which must remain the basis for our entire lives. Hence the priest may not marry *a woman made profane by immorality, nor a woman divorced from her husband.* We learn from here that the essential values of fidelity and modesty inside a home life sanctified with peace and felicity serve as the bases for every Jewish home and are the goals to which we aspire. The priest must strive to exemplify these ideals even in his private life, outside of his work in the Temple. [The Torah understands that death, sin, and divorce are an inevitable part of a community's life. Nevertheless, it enjoins the priests to live a life distanced from these things in order to remind us of the ideal life and direct our efforts toward life, morality, and felicitous marriages.]

HAAMEK DAVAR

כִּי־קָדֹשׁ הוּא לֵאלֹהָיו – *For they are holy to their God:* Since the priests are holy men, it behooves them to marry appropriate women, who will not lead their husbands astray.

VERSE 8

OR HAḤAYYIM

וְקִדַּשְׁתּוֹ – *You shall treat a priest as holy:* Why does the text refer to a single priest as "a priest" rather than a plural collect of priests? [Verses 21:5–7 spoke of priests in the plural: "Priests shall not make," "They shall be holy," and "They may not marry."] The Sages extrapolate from this verse that in the event that a priest refuses to divorce his unlawfully wedded wife, the community must beat and pressure him until he agrees to do so (Yevamot 88b). [This is the explication of the imperative directed to the non-priest concerning the priest, *vekiddashto*, literally, "you shall make him holy" by making sure his marriage is proper.] Now based on the explanation for this commandment given by the verse itself, namely that the priest *brings close the offerings of foodstuffs to your God*, we might have thought that if there were many other suitable priests who can serve in the Temple besides this scofflaw, he need not be harassed to reform. Hence, the text uses the singular form to teach that even a solitary priest

8 to their God. You shall treat a priest as holy, for he brings close
the offerings of foodstuffs to your God. And he shall be holy
9 to you, because I, the LORD, am holy and make you holy. If the
daughter of a priest profanes herself by immorality, she pro-
10 fanes her father also; she shall be burned with fire. The
priest, the highest among his brothers, on whose head the
anointing oil has been poured and who has been ordained

OR HAHAYYIM *(cont.)*

who has violated these guidelines must be coerced into behaving properly. **אֲנִי יהוה מְקַדִּשְׁכֶם** – *I the LORD…make you holy:* This clause appears to be the reason why the court must compel a priest to divorce his unlawful wife. [Among the prohibited unions outlawed by the Torah, some will not produce a valid marriage if attempted. For example, a man who betroths his sister has achieved nothing; no divorce is required, because there is no union. Other matches that are forbidden result in a binding marriage even though a law has been violated. Thus, a priest who betroths a divorced woman has created a marital bond although it is illegal. It must be severed with divorce.] For it is through the sanctity of the priest that God allows His Divine Presence to rest in Israel's midst, and sanctifies the nation. If there is no priest, there will be no service and no Temple, and God will not manifest Himself within Israel. [This is why the Israelites have a responsibility to monitor the priests' marriages. They also have a role in ensuring that the Divine Presence continues to dwell in their midst.]

RABBI SAMSON RAPHAEL HIRSCH

כִּי קָדוֹשׁ אֲנִי יהוה מְקַדִּשְׁכֶם – *Because I, the LORD, am holy and make you holy:* The holiness of the Israelite nation is not impaired by a recalcitrant priest. [Even if a priest violates the sanctity of his position by an improper marriage, that does not hamper the holiness of the nation. The nation receives its holy status directly from God; it is not mediated through the priesthood.] Indeed, the opposite is true; the root and the purpose of the priestly class's holiness is to serve as the basis of the people's own sanctity. The holiness of life which is represented by the priest is brought to fruition by the state as a whole, of which the priests are a part.

HAAMEK DAVAR

כִּי־אֶת־לֶחֶם אֱלֹהֶיךָ הוּא מַקְרִיב – *For he brings close the offerings of foodstuffs to your God:* If a priest is not suited for his job and therefore cannot bring *close the offerings of foodstuffs to your God*, he puts the Israelite's livelihood in jeopardy. [One of the benefits of properly conducted service in the Temple is that the blessings of prosperity are bestowed upon the nation. Therefore, it is of immediate concern to the nation that priests are suited for their job.] And since the priest in turn is supported by the donations of the public, the masses have the right and the power to preserve their benefits from being impaired by a wayward priest.

VERSE 10

RABBI SAMSON RAPHAEL HIRSCH

אֲשֶׁר־יוּצַק עַל־רֹאשׁוֹ שֶׁמֶן הַמִּשְׁחָה – *On whose head the anointing oil has been poured:* The High Court of seventy-one judges, which is the ultimate representative of the national polity,

CONFRONTING MODERNITY

יא יִפְרֹם: וְעַל כָּל־נַפְשֹׁת מֵת לֹא יָבֹא לְאָבִיו וּלְאִמּוֹ לֹא יִטַּמָּא:
יב וּמִן־הַמִּקְדָּשׁ לֹא יֵצֵא וְלֹא יְחַלֵּל אֵת מִקְדַּשׁ אֱלֹהָיו כִּי נֵזֶר

RABBI SAMSON RAPHAEL HIRSCH *(cont.)*

installs the High Priest by placing anointing oil on his head. That in turn authorizes him to wear the sacred vestments of the High Priesthood. His investiture transforms this official into the representative of Israel's highest moral ideal, which means that he is no longer treated as a private person. Rather, even his personal life becomes dedicated to the national ideal. And since the High Priest is called upon to express only the positive aspects of sanctity and life, he must therefore shunt aside any other contradictory emotion or expression which might hinder that positive expression. Understood as a collective idea that spans all of Jewish history, the community of Israel is indeed immortal; it cannot die. As the representative of that eternal, ahistorical idea, the High Priest may not outwardly mourn. Because the High Priest has been crowned with anointing oil, his head may never display any modicum of grief or mourning, even for a fleeting moment. Even when faced with the loss of a loved one, he may not tear his holy uniform in anguish like a normal Israelite would. And even when the High Priest's closest relative has died, it is forbidden for the man to approach the body. Nevertheless, the institution of the High Priesthood is itself superseded by the needs of an unattended corpse on the road. Finally, even when he is in a state of *aninut* [acute mourning prior to the burial of a relative] the High Priest may not abandon his post. For his continuous task is to exemplify life and its joys under all circumstances. The source of this existential happiness must be the Lord. And the Temple, established by God, remains the locus of his bliss and preserves it forever. Of course, none of this means that the High Priest is required to purge all human emotions from his heart. The passing of a family member need not flit past his consciousness without registering a tremor in his heart. As we will learn below, the High Priest must serve as a model for the people in all matters of family and marriage. He is an exemplar of life whose formal expectations and outward expressions surpass the rest of his priestly brethren. Nevertheless, he is not asked to model coldhearted indifference. He is indeed an *onen*, a person mourning, and that does have some impact on his public demeanor. Although he continues to perform the sacrificial service, he may not eat from the sacred animals' flesh. Although he does not rend his clothing in the manner that the average mourning Israelite does, he does make a tear lower down, near the hem. And even though the High Priest may not walk behind the funeral bier with the rest of the escort, he does accompany the group from a distance until the party reaches the town gates. As the Talmud teaches: The High Priest waits until the mourners have turned off of one street before he enters it, and continues this way until the procession has left the city. The High Priest is called upon, even while his heart is grieving for the deceased and his mind is preoccupied with thoughts of death, to represent to the entire community the overwhelming powers of life and joy. For the Almighty is the source for all living beings, and the celebration of that fact serves as the foundation for His Sanctuary. It is that message which emanates from the center of the religion, and it is the High Priest as the faith's primary servant who must convey that concept always and forever.

to wear the vestments, shall not dishevel his hair or tear his
11 clothes. He shall not go near the dead; even for his father or
12 mother he shall not render himself impure. He shall not leave
the Sanctuary, profaning his God's Sanctuary, for the crown
of his God's anointing oil rests upon him; I am the Lord.

VERSE 11

HAAMEK DAVAR

וְעַל כָּל־נַפְשֹׁת מֵת לֹא יָבֹא – *He shall not go near the dead:* The High Priest is barred from joining the congregation in eulogizing the dead and in accompanying the body to its burial. Thus the Mishna teaches (Sanhedrin 18a): If the High Priest loses a relative, he must not walk behind the bier during the funeral, but must keep at a distance and around the corner behind the procession. Nevertheless, the official is permitted to leave his house in order to partially escort the dead. Of course, that allowance is granted only if the High Priest is at home during the funeral, whereas if he is occupied in the Temple service at the time, *he shall not leave the Sanctuary* (21:12).

THE LUBAVITCHER REBBE

וְעַל כָּל־נַפְשֹׁת מֵת לֹא יָבֹא – *He shall not go near the dead:* If there is no one else that can bury this corpse, the High Priest must leave the most sacred part of the Tabernacle on the holiest day of the year in order to do so. This teaches us, firstly, that taking care of our fellow Jews' crucial needs takes precedence over tending to our own spiritual tasks. Secondly, we sometimes encounter people who may be figuratively considered "unattended, lifeless bodies," i.e., people who pay no attention to the spiritual side of life and who have no one else to guide them in this regard. In such cases, we must seize the opportunity to assist them, reminding ourselves that even the High Priest is required to disregard his most sublime responsibilities on the holy day of Yom Kippur in order to bury an unattended corpse. We, in contrast, have both the obligation and the privilege of not merely attending to a "lifeless" person but reviving him.

VERSE 12

HAAMEK DAVAR

כִּי נֵזֶר שֶׁמֶן מִשְׁחַת אֱלֹהָיו עָלָיו – *For the crown of his God's anointing oil rests upon him:* The reason that a High Priest who is an *onen* may not halt his duties in the Temple and thereby profane the service is that *the crown of his God's anointing oil rests upon him*. [*Aninut*, the stage of being an *onen*, is the most acute stage of mourning. It begins with the passing of the relative and ends once the deceased is buried.] Now, in general an acute mourner is forbidden to perform the sacrifices because it would be inappropriate for him to stand before the Lord while under severe distress. Hence, an Israelite too is forbidden to eat sacred food in such a condition – he is sharing meat from the table of the Almighty, and it is incongruous for the bereaved to take a seat in the dining room of the king. The High Priest, on the other hand, cleaves to the Divine Presence, and therefore it is appropriate for him to adopt a cheerful face and disposition even in a situation of *aninut*.

יג שֶׁמֶן מִשְׁחַת אֱלֹהָיו עָלָיו אֲנִי יהוה: וְהוּא אִשָּׁה בִבְתוּלֶיהָ
יד יִקָּח: אַלְמָנָה וּגְרוּשָׁה וַחֲלָלָה זֹנָה אֶת־אֵלֶּה לֹא יִקָּח כִּי
טו אִם־בְּתוּלָה מֵעַמָּיו יִקַּח אִשָּׁה: וְלֹא־יְחַלֵּל זַרְעוֹ בְּעַמָּיו כִּי

VERSE 14

RABBI SAMSON RAPHAEL HIRSCH

כִּי אִם־בְּתוּלָה מֵעַמָּיו יִקַּח אִשָּׁה – *He may marry only a virgin from his own people:* The High Priest must marry someone who is "from his own people." This does not limit her to being a descendant of Aharon, or even belonging to the tribe of Levi, but rather she must be a woman from any one of the Israelite tribes. We have earlier noted that it is incumbent upon the High Priest to be a married man. Now, the prohibitions imposed upon this official are stricter and more expansive than those governing the life of the common priest. For the regular priest is only forbidden to marry a *zona*, a *ḥalala*, and a divorcée. [A *zona* refers to a woman who has engaged in relations with someone forbidden to her. A *ḥalala* refers to a woman born of a union between a priest and someone he was forbidden to marry. But the High Priest may not marry any woman who has previously been with another man, even a widow or a non-virgin who has never married.] The lawful unions which limit all priests demonstrate a commitment to the cardinal principles of the Israelite marriage: modesty, the sanctity of the priesthood, harmony, and felicity. [Priests must distance themselves from a woman who has been divorced, for example, because divorce, although sometimes necessary, still represents discord, which is inconsonant with the values that a priestly marriage is being mandated to at least formally represent.] These ideals are taken a step forward with regard to the High Priest: This man's relationship to his wife expresses a unity of hearts and souls. The High Priest and the High Priest's wife must be united in purpose, share the same outlooks, philosophies, and life goals, the type of harmony that is desirable between every husband and wife. This is why the High Priest may not marry a widow and why he must wed a virgin. In other words, this man's sanctity must be complemented by a woman who has never accustomed herself to another man, who has never been influenced by the habits and thinking of some other Israelite. Indeed, this wife is selected while she is still young enough not to have harbored any thoughts about a man who is not her eventual husband.

HAAMEK DAVAR

כִּי אִם־בְּתוּלָה מֵעַמָּיו יִקַּח אִשָּׁה – *He may marry only a virgin from his own people:* Why does verse 13 order that the High Priest must *marry a woman only in her virginity* [when it could have simply said that he must marry a virgin? What is the significance of the term *isha*, meaning woman]? We learn from here that the High Priest's wife must be a woman enlightened with the knowledge of God. [Corresponding to the term *ish*, an *isha* is similarly a person of distinction.] She must be steeped in reverence for God, even though she is still a virgin and quite young in years. Now, verse 14 repeats the requirement of a High Priest to marry a virgin, but describes the woman somewhat differently: *a virgin from his own people*. These words expand the possibilities for the High Priest's bride. For even though the High Priest

13 14 He may marry a woman only in her virginity. He may not marry a widow, a divorcée, or one profaned by immorality. He may
15 marry only a virgin from his own people, so that he will not
profane his children among his people, for I, the LORD, sanctify

HAAMEK DAVAR *(cont.)*

must strive to select a woman with purity and clarity of thought, should no such suitable person be found, he may wed a virgin who is simply "from his own people." This emphasizes that the High Priest is forbidden to serve while unmarried. Hence, he is allowed to marry even a simple girl from the common folk as long as she is a virginal Israelite.

VERSE 15

RABBI SAMSON RAPHAEL HIRSCH

וְלֹא־יְחַלֵּל זַרְעוֹ בְּעַמָּיו – *So that he will not profane his children among his people:* According to Torah law, a *ḥalal* [a child born from a priest's unlawful union with a forbidden woman] is identical to a *zar* [a non-priest] in all matters relating to the Temple and its holy things. He is forbidden even from partaking of *teruma*, priestly food. Nevertheless, a priest who has married a woman he should not have married does not himself assume the status of *ḥalal*, even though he has thereby profaned [*ḥillel*] his children, who do assume the status of a *ḥalal*. This father remains a member of the priesthood, but he is barred from participating in the Temple service until he divorces his prohibited wife. [Despite the fact that a priest may not marry a divorcée, for example, nevertheless, should he betroth her, the union is sinful but nonetheless valid and requires a divorce to be dissolved. That priest can be restored to the Temple service if he does dissolve that forbidden marriage.] We must point out that Israel's priesthood is not a profession which a person chooses. Rather, the institution represents a life destiny, a calling which God ordains upon the priest at birth. [In the case of a *ḥalal* his designation as a priest at birth is prevented and can never be recovered.] A priest's ability to fulfill his task might be temporarily suspended, but it can never be abrogated. It therefore becomes the priest's primary obligation to overcome any factor that has invalidated him from the Almighty's service. A priest who has been born in purity as a descendant of Aharon will never stop being a priest, and the mission he has been assigned remains a lifelong pursuit. The one exception to this rule is the priest who has engaged in idolatry. He is forever banned from priestly service. The same sort of description may be applied to Judaism as a whole, where the Israelite nation acts as priests on behalf of humanity. A person who is born a Jew can never forsake his destiny. Judaism is not a faith that the Jew willingly decides to embrace – it is thrust upon him by the Almighty as his life's definition at birth. A naturally born Jew cannot walk away from the responsibilities that this identity imposes any more than a priest can stop being one. Thus do our Rabbis assert (Sanhedrin 44a): A Jew is always a Jew regardless of any sin he might commit. Of course, a rebellious person might estrange himself from this mission; he might reject it in spirit, in thought, or in practice. He might utterly turn his back on his people and their traditions. And if he does so, he loses the right to participate in those activities which are reserved for a loyal Jew. Nevertheless, the path of return is always available to any Jew. His life's

טו אֲנִי יְהוָה מְקַדְּשׁוֹ׃ וַיְדַבֵּר יְהוָה אֶל־מֹשֶׁה לֵּאמֹר׃ שני
יז דַּבֵּר אֶל־אַהֲרֹן לֵאמֹר אִישׁ מִזַּרְעֲךָ לְדֹרֹתָם אֲשֶׁר יִהְיֶה בוֹ
יח מוּם לֹא יִקְרַב לְהַקְרִיב לֶחֶם אֱלֹהָיו׃ כִּי כָל־אִישׁ אֲשֶׁר־בּוֹ
יט מוּם לֹא יִקְרָב אִישׁ עִוֵּר אוֹ פִסֵּחַ אוֹ חָרֻם אוֹ שָׂרוּעַ׃ אוֹ
כ אִישׁ אֲשֶׁר־יִהְיֶה בוֹ שֶׁבֶר רָגֶל אוֹ שֶׁבֶר יָד׃ אוֹ־גִבֵּן אוֹ־דַק
כא אוֹ תְּבַלֻּל בְּעֵינוֹ אוֹ גָרָב אוֹ יַלֶּפֶת אוֹ מְרוֹחַ אָשֶׁךְ׃ כָּל־אִישׁ
אֲשֶׁר־בּוֹ מוּם מִזֶּרַע אַהֲרֹן הַכֹּהֵן לֹא יִגַּשׁ לְהַקְרִיב אֶת־אִשֵּׁי
כב יְהוָה מוּם בּוֹ אֵת לֶחֶם אֱלֹהָיו לֹא יִגַּשׁ לְהַקְרִיב׃ לֶחֶם אֱלֹהָיו
כג מִקָּדְשֵׁי הַקֳּדָשִׁים וּמִן־הַקֳּדָשִׁים יֹאכֵל׃ אַךְ אֶל־הַפָּרֹכֶת לֹא
יָבֹא וְאֶל־הַמִּזְבֵּחַ לֹא יִגַּשׁ כִּי־מוּם בּוֹ וְלֹא יְחַלֵּל אֶת־מִקְדָּשַׁי

RABBI SAMSON RAPHAEL HIRSCH *(cont.)*

destiny as a Jew having been established for him at birth, God's continuous calling remains in force such that his duty to return in spirit, in thought, and in action never ends.

VERSE 17

MESHEKH ḤOKHMA

אִישׁ מִזַּרְעֲךָ לְדֹרֹתָם אֲשֶׁר יִהְיֶה בוֹ מוּם – *Any of your future descendants who has a physical blemish:* It seems to me that the Torah's system of sacrifices belongs to the realm of *ḥukkim* ["statutes"], meaning: laws which defy human rationale and inquiry. It is for this reason that in its discussions of this topic the text consistently employs the Tetragrammaton [the four-letter ineffable name of God]. In this way the Torah defends itself against the appearance that different sacrifices are being offered to different deities [as one might wrongfully have concluded if God had been referred to by His various appellations. See Menaḥot 110a]. In a similar vein, the Torah is concerned that during a priest's service he might wonder about principles of faith or doubt the legitimacy or efficacy of his duties. The Torah commands all Israelites *to love the Lord your God and to serve Him with all your heart and with all your soul* (Deuteronomy 11:13). Now, it is surely inappropriate for a priest to deny the existence of God; the sacrifices that such a person offers are naturally invalid. On the other hand, it would be impractical and wrong to rely on a prophet to reveal what is truly going on in the head of a non-believing priest. For it is not God's way to expose a person's hidden sins. Therefore, the Almighty devised a scheme to prevent priests who harbor heretical thoughts from participating in the Tabernacle's services. Any priest with a blemish, even one who is utterly righteous and faithful, will be disqualified from serving. Such is the divine decree due to God's hidden plan and does not reflect any impropriety on the part of the blemished priest. However, if a priest truly does not believe in the purpose of the sacrifices or harbors doubts about the faith, God sees to it that he will develop an outward blemish. This

16 him." 17 The LORD spoke to Moshe: "Tell Aharon: Any SHENI
of your future descendants who has a physical blemish may not
18 draw close to present foodstuff offerings to his God. No one
with a blemish shall approach: this includes one who is blind,
19 lame, disfigured, or deformed; or who has a broken foot or
20 hand; or who is a hunchback or a dwarf, or who has a growth
21 in his eye, a severe rash, scabs, or crushed testicles. No descendant of Aharon the priest who has a physical blemish shall draw
near to present the LORD's fire offerings; because of his blemish, he shall not approach to present an offering of foodstuffs
22 to his God. He may eat the foodstuff offerings of his God, the
23 holy of holies as well as the holy. But he may not come close
to the inner curtain or approach the altar, because of his blemish; he shall not profane My Sanctuary; I am the LORD who

MESHEKH ḤOKHMA *(cont.)*

will successfully remove him from the roster of priests who serve at the altar of the LORD. In this way nobody will know the treachery festering in the inner recesses of the priest's heart. This is because "no one with a blemish shall approach" – it is a blanket ban and clearly not a function of apostasy. A priest who is without a doubt a righteous and religious person, or a person who was born with a defect long before he could be guilty of any impious thoughts are all included in the ban. God does not decide whether a person will develop into a good person or a wicked one. [That choice is granted to every person, and so at birth everyone is blameless even though he may be blemished.]

VERSE 19

HAAMEK DAVAR

שֶׁבֶר רָגֶל – *A broken foot:* This is also a visible blemish. [The *Haamek Davar* understands the listing of blemishes to proceed in order from the most severe to the least. The previous verse included the blind, lame, disfigured, or deformed, as all of those are obvious defects and often congenital. This verse lists the broken foot or hand, blemishes a level down because] nobody is born with such a condition and the fracture can be healed. [A broken foot is distinct from lameness in this way.] The phrase *asher yihyeh* ["one who has"] indicates that the priest is considered blemished even if his broken foot is detectable only when he walks in the service of his duties, but otherwise cannot be detected. [Even where the blemish is only functional and not aesthetic, it still disqualifies the priest. The author is noting the difference in language from the previous verse, which states: *asher bo mum* – "with a blemish." In the case of a broken bone, a person may heal completely, leaving no trace of injury even in the way that person moves, returning the priest to full service. But that might also not be the case, and a person may be someone "who has" a blemish, meaning his function is impaired.]

כד כִּי אֲנִי יהוה מְקַדְּשָׁם: וַיְדַבֵּר מֹשֶׁה אֶל־אַהֲרֹן וְאֶל־בָּנָיו
וְאֶל־כָּל־בְּנֵי יִשְׂרָאֵל:
כב א ב וַיְדַבֵּר יהוה אֶל־מֹשֶׁה לֵּאמֹר: דַּבֵּר אֶל־אַהֲרֹן וְאֶל־בָּנָיו
וְיִנָּזְרוּ מִקָּדְשֵׁי בְנֵי־יִשְׂרָאֵל וְלֹא יְחַלְּלוּ אֶת־שֵׁם קָדְשִׁי
ג אֲשֶׁר הֵם מַקְדִּשִׁים לִי אֲנִי יהוה: אֱמֹר אֲלֵהֶם לְדֹרֹתֵיכֶם
כָּל־אִישׁ ׀ אֲשֶׁר־יִקְרַב מִכָּל־זַרְעֲכֶם אֶל־הַקֳּדָשִׁים אֲשֶׁר
יַקְדִּישׁוּ בְנֵי־יִשְׂרָאֵל לַיהוה וְטֻמְאָתוֹ עָלָיו וְנִכְרְתָה הַנֶּפֶשׁ

VERSE 24

MALBIM

וַיְדַבֵּר מֹשֶׁה אֶל־אַהֲרֹן וְאֶל־בָּנָיו – *Moshe told this to Aharon [and to] his sons:* Despite the fact that God instructed Moshe: *Tell Aharon* (21:17), Moshe went on to tell "his sons, and all the Israelites." [The conjunctive *vav* in that phrase, *ve'el banav ve'el kol benei Yisrael*, seems to imply a parsing of the verse that separates the command to tell Aharon from the fact that Moshe did inform the others.] For it was Moshe's hope that each group would supervise and monitor themselves and the other groups. The court of Israel would monitor the participation of the officials in the Temple, and in addition, the priests would warn and supervise each other.

CHAPTER 22, VERSE 2

RABBI SAMSON RAPHAEL HIRSCH

קָדְשֵׁי בְּנֵי־יִשְׂרָאֵל...אֲשֶׁר הֵם מַקְדִּשִׁים לִי – *The sacred offerings that the Israelites consecrate to Me:* On several occasions our chapter refers to the sacrifices as *the sacred offerings that the Israelites consecrate to Me*. If we are not mistaken, the Torah is thereby warning the priests that they must not err through spiritual arrogance. These officials must never come to see themselves as the primary focus of the Temple or reach a point where they act disparagingly toward the ordinary non-priests who are bringing the offerings. When the common Israelite hands his offering over to the priest to be serviced, the role of the latter is to attend to the religious needs of the people, while at the same time humbly accepting the material benefits to himself of these sacrifices. Woe to the priest who services a world of sanctity but who is himself bereft of sanctity! As such, the Temple's staff is hereby informed that the entire Sanctuary and all of its sacrifices – with the exception of the priests' own offerings – are sanctified only through the will of the ordinary non-priest. Either the will of the Israelite community as a whole or the will of a specific Israelite has invested these beasts and other ordinary objects with the sanctity that renders them offerings. At the very moment that the priest services the congregation's offering or that of a single Israelite, he is realizing the holy intentions that were formed in the hearts of the people. And if we are correct in this approach, then we can make sense of the following clause from this verse: *So that they do not profane My holy name*. The priest is enjoined in this verse to take great care with sacred objects, which are a manifestation of the holy intentions of ordinary Israelites. A

24 makes them holy." Moshe told this to Aharon, his sons, and all
the Israelites.
22 1 2 The LORD spoke to Moshe: "Tell Aharon and his sons to take
great care with the sacred offerings that the Israelites consecrate
to Me, so that they do not profane My holy name: I am the
3 LORD. Tell them: If any descendant of yours throughout the
generations comes near the sacred offerings that the Israelites
have consecrated to the LORD while in an impure state, he shall

RABBI SAMSON RAPHAEL HIRSCH *(cont.)*

lack of care and humility with these objects is tantamount to profaning God's holy name. Why is God's name a good metaphor? Even if the lowest member of the Jewish nation writes God's name with the proper intention, he invests that name, and the text it occupies, with intense holiness requiring tremendous care. So too, when a simple Jew dedicates an object to the Temple by virtue of his directed thought and words, and the priest then takes that object into his hands, he must treat it with the utmost reverence, for it is a holy object, dedicated to an expression of divinity. The priests must treat all holy objects with the utmost humility, modesty, and sincerity that is fitting for the name of God, just as they must treat every sacred animal.

RABBI DAVID TZVI HOFFMAN

וְלֹא יְחַלְּלוּ אֶת־שֵׁם קָדְשִׁי – *So that they do not profane My holy name:* A blemished priest is permanently prevented from offering sacrifices, as the previous chapter makes quite clear: *No descendant of Aharon the priest who has a physical blemish shall draw near to present the LORD's fire offerings* (21:21). In that verse, the injunction is stated clearly without added emphasis: The priest shall not "draw near" [*yiggash*]. But this chapter opens with a prohibition which is stated with extra emphasis: *Take great care with the sacred offerings* (22:2). The reason is that here the ban is only temporary, as it is a function of the priest's impurity, and hence he must be particularly conscientious about staying away from sacred objects that he is otherwise accustomed to handling. This verse has an odd construction [that is not readily apparent in the English translation]. The clause, *that they consecrate to Me* [*asher hem makdishim li*] relates back to *the sacred offerings of the Israelites*. [The translation smooths out the problem by rendering the English continuous: *With the sacred offerings that the Israelites consecrate to Me*. In the Hebrew, however, the two phrases are separated by the directive, *so that they do not profane My holy name.*] It is possible that this jumbled text teaches that the profanation of God's name is intertwined with the desecration of the offerings. For everything holy is dedicated "to Me," so that the desecration of a sacred object affects God's name.

VERSE 3

RABBI SAMSON RAPHAEL HIRSCH

וְנִכְרְתָה הַנֶּפֶשׁ הַהִוא מִלְּפָנַי – *He shall be severed from My presence:* This clause is found nowhere else in the Torah. We find instead such expressions as, "he shall be severed from his nation." In the present instance it seems that this language is tied to the transgression

ד הַהִוא מִלְּפָנַי אֲנִי יְהוָה: אִישׁ אִישׁ מִזֶּרַע אַהֲרֹן וְהוּא צָרוּעַ
אוֹ זָב בַּקֳּדָשִׁים לֹא יֹאכַל עַד אֲשֶׁר יִטְהָר וְהַנֹּגֵעַ בְּכָל־טְמֵא־
ה נֶפֶשׁ אוֹ אִישׁ אֲשֶׁר־תֵּצֵא מִמֶּנּוּ שִׁכְבַת־זָרַע: אוֹ־אִישׁ אֲשֶׁר
יִגַּע בְּכָל־שֶׁרֶץ אֲשֶׁר יִטְמָא־לוֹ אוֹ בְאָדָם אֲשֶׁר יִטְמָא־
ו לוֹ לְכֹל טֻמְאָתוֹ: נֶפֶשׁ אֲשֶׁר תִּגַּע־בּוֹ וְטָמְאָה עַד־הָעָרֶב
ז וְלֹא יֹאכַל מִן־הַקֳּדָשִׁים כִּי אִם־רָחַץ בְּשָׂרוֹ בַּמָּיִם: וּבָא
הַשֶּׁמֶשׁ וְטָהֵר וְאַחַר יֹאכַל מִן־הַקֳּדָשִׁים כִּי לַחְמוֹ הוּא:
ח ט נְבֵלָה וּטְרֵפָה לֹא יֹאכַל לְטָמְאָה־בָהּ אֲנִי יְהוָה: וְשָׁמְרוּ
אֶת־מִשְׁמַרְתִּי וְלֹא־יִשְׂאוּ עָלָיו חֵטְא וּמֵתוּ בוֹ כִּי יְחַלְּלֻהוּ

RABBI SAMSON RAPHAEL HIRSCH *(cont.)*

of consuming sacred meat while in a state of impurity. Says the Lord: because this priest ignored My significance when he serviced the sacrifice and neglected to see My holy name stamped on Israel's consecrated offerings, it is only just that *he shall be severed from My presence*. These words thus reflect the profound desecration of God's name that occurs if an impure priest eats sacred meat.

VERSE 4

RABBI DAVID TZVI HOFFMAN

אִישׁ אִישׁ מִזֶּרַע אַהֲרֹן – *Any descendant of Aharon:* Why does the text shift from using the second person in the previous verse to speaking in the third person here? The previous verse reads: *If any descendant of yours*, whereas this verse states: *Any descendant of Aharon*. The Torah does this to avoid giving the impression of cursing the priests. It would have appeared rude and insulting had the text turned directly to Aharon and said: "Any descendant of yours who has a defiling blight…"

VERSE 7

RABBI SAMSON RAPHAEL HIRSCH

כִּי לַחְמוֹ הוּא – *For they are his food:* "His food," referred to here, is *teruma*. [*Teruma* is a tithe, approximately 2 percent, that every Israelite gives directly to the priest from his agricultural produce.] It is considered "his food," i.e., the priest's food, because it is a holy gift which is meant to sustain him and his household. The Israelite gives the priest this produce directly. This contrasts with other gifts which the priests receive only indirectly, from the table of the Almighty.

VERSE 9

RABBI SAMSON RAPHAEL HIRSCH

וְשָׁמְרוּ אֶת־מִשְׁמַרְתִּי – *They shall keep My charge:* This is the significance of the clause *they shall keep My charge*: It relates back to the earlier statement, *for they are his food* (22:7). It

4 be severed from My presence; I am the LORD. Any descendant
of Aharon who has a defiling blight of the skin or a discharge
may not eat of the sacred offerings until he becomes pure. One
who touches anything made impure by contact with the dead,
5 or who has had a seminal emission, or who has touched any
swarming thing or any person who renders him impure – what-
6 ever his impurity – the one who touches these things shall be
impure until the evening, and shall not eat of the sacred offer-
7 ings until he has washed his body in water. When the sun sets,
he shall become pure again and may eat of the sacred offerings,
8 for they are his food. He may not eat an animal found dead or
one that was torn by wild animals, becoming impure by doing
9 so; I am the LORD. They shall keep My charge and not bear
guilt and die through it, having profaned it. I am the LORD, who

RABBI SAMSON RAPHAEL HIRSCH *(cont.)*

is clear that the bread in the basket of the Israelite differs from similar bread that reaches the priest's table. This is because non-sanctified bread represents the fruit of the farmer's labor, produce which has been blessed by God. By contrast, the *teruma* [agricultural gift] which the citizen has bestowed upon the priest has been entrusted to him as a reminder of the sacred duties vested upon him. This food serves as a warning to the priest to diligently fulfill the responsibilities which the Almighty has assigned to him. Nevertheless, it seems that the primary source of food for the priest and his family is based on the allowance from the Torah called *terumat maaser* ["a donation from the tithe"]. This is produce which the Israelite people indirectly provide to the priestly caste; it is given as a fixed percentage of the farmer's yield. After the owner brings a tenth of his harvest to the Levite, thereby giving him a tithe of his grain, wine, and oil, the receiving Levite takes a tenth of that tenth and passes it along to the priest as a tithe called *terumat maaser*. It is acceptable for the Israelite to himself separate a tenth of the produce from the tenth that he has set aside for the Levite and then to give this *terumat maaser* directly to the priest. Nevertheless, the custom is generally for the Levite to bestow this gift to the priest. Hence, even if the Israelite does deliver the goods to the priest, he is really giving him a share of what the Levite should have first received. What emerges from this system is an awareness in the mind of the Levite that the Sanctuary of the Torah, over which the priest presides, is elevated above him in a hierarchy of value and is prior to his task as a Levite. [The word *teruma* – "donation" – derives from the word *leharim*, meaning "to lift up" or "exalt." The fact that the priest's sustenance is "lifted up" and out of the Levite's portion symbolizes the primary importance of the Temple in the hierarchy of the nation's institutions.] The Levite soberly understands that his entire existence and position within the nation is only justified and only sustains any purpose as a function of his submission to the primacy of the holiness of the Temple before the LORD. The priest receives the food that sustains him and must subsequently treat it as a sacred item. And yet, the priest is not given that produce directly by the growers of the crops; it comes from the Levite, who hands it to him. This in turn teaches the priest that his

י אֲנִי יְהוָה מְקַדְּשָׁם: וְכָל־זָר לֹא־יֹאכַל קֹדֶשׁ תּוֹשַׁב כֹּהֵן
יא וְשָׂכִיר לֹא־יֹאכַל קֹדֶשׁ: וְכֹהֵן כִּי־יִקְנֶה נֶפֶשׁ קִנְיַן כַּסְפּוֹ הוּא
יב יֹאכַל בּוֹ וִילִיד בֵּיתוֹ הֵם יֹאכְלוּ בְלַחְמוֹ: וּבַת־כֹּהֵן כִּי תִהְיֶה
יג לְאִישׁ זָר הִוא בִּתְרוּמַת הַקֳּדָשִׁים לֹא תֹאכֵל: וּבַת־כֹּהֵן כִּי
תִהְיֶה אַלְמָנָה וּגְרוּשָׁה וְזֶרַע אֵין לָהּ וְשָׁבָה אֶל־בֵּית אָבִיהָ

RABBI SAMSON RAPHAEL HIRSCH *(cont.)*

existence, status, and function are all founded on the Levite's holy ground. For the priestly clan is considered the choicest part of the Levite tribe. It becomes the priest's role to carry the distinction and distinctive functions of the Levite tribe. This is the tribe whose founding father, Levi, set alight the spiritual flame of the nation with courage and force. When the Jewish nation had sinned with the golden calf, this tribe alone followed Moshe and heeded his cry, as the verse reports: *So Moshe stood at the gate of the camp and said, "Who is for the Lord? Come to me!" All the Levites rallied round him* (Exodus 32:26). At that very moment the tribe of Levi was crowned as the Lord's representatives and as the defender of His will for all generations. Thus, the priests would do well to remember all of this; even after the family of Aharon become the nation's priests they do not stop being Levites. And even though their material survival is dependent on other people, in the realm of Torah teaching and inspiration they must remain fiercely independent. As they guide the Israelites and issue rulings, the priests must never waver, never try to curry favor, and never display any partiality. As they present the Torah to the nation – and if need be, even against the nation – the priests must always keep in mind that they are not fed by the people so that they will accede to popular demands or give their blessing to every whimsy. Instead, when the average citizen looks at a priest he should see a faithful agent of the Torah, the highest human ideal, even though this representative of God might appear to oppose him at that moment. Indeed, so does Moshe, the most important of all Levites, say of his tribe: *He said of his father and mother, 'I do not regard them,' ignored his brothers, and did not acknowledge his children – instead keeping Your word, and guarding close Your covenant* (Deuteronomy 33:9). The bread which the Levites grant the priests is sacred; it is holy to the Temple of the Torah. And those men who receive this gift thereby become commissioned and devoted to the Sanctuary service and its high ideals. This bread must enable them to "keep My charge," and not become obsequious and servile out of fear of challenging the hands that feed them. Unfortunate is the priest whose holy meal does not in turn sanctify him and make him ever more devoted to his holy role! Woe to the priest whose slice of bread does not summon him to perform his exalted task. And pity the priest who desecrates this food while ignoring its message for his special mission. Thus does our text warn: *They shall keep My charge and not bear guilt and die through it, having profaned it.* For although the priest is served his bread so that he may live, if he defiles it instead, it will become a fatal poison.

HAAMEK DAVAR

וְשָׁמְרוּ אֶת־מִשְׁמַרְתִּי – *They shall keep My charge:* The text refers to *teruma* as "My charge" because this produce has been entrusted to the priest in order to strengthen

10 makes them holy. No layman may eat of the sacred offerings,
11 nor may a priest's visitor or hired laborer eat of them. But if a
priest acquires a slave for money, the slave may eat of them, and
12 those born into his household also may eat his food. If a priest's
daughter marries a layman, she may no longer eat of the sacred
13 gifts. If a priest's daughter is a widow or a divorcée, has no children, and returns to live in her father's house as when she was
young, she may eat her father's food again; but no layperson

HAAMEK DAVAR *(cont.)*

him in the service of God's Torah and keep him in a state of sanctity. [That is, not only is the priest meant to protect the holiness of the *teruma*, but the food serves to protect him too and maintain the priest's status of purity.] The verse warns that this duty must not cause the priest to stubble, for if he does not preserve the importance of the *teruma*, he will bear guilt and will "die through it," meaning: he will be killed at the hands of heaven.

כִּי יְחַלְּלֻהוּ – *Having profaned it:* The priest will thereby desecrate the sanctity of the food. However, if the priests had not been given these holy items, they would not risk bearing guilt or death through them. As the verse says: *They shall keep My charge and not bear guilt and die through it*, as a consequence of their neglecting this charge. [This verse speaks to the increased stakes and risks the priesthood entails.]

VERSE 10

MALBIM

וְכָל־זָר לֹא־יֹאכַל קֹדֶשׁ – *No layman may eat of the sacred offerings:* The noun *zar* ["layman," or better in this context, "outsider"] expresses a relative outsideness. [He is outside whatever institution is being addressed.] For example, we find this usage of the word in the verse, *The two of us live together – there was no one else [ein zar, literally, "there was no stranger"] in the house besides us, just the two of us in the house* [I Kings 3:18. Here the term *zar* refers to anyone besides those living in the house]. Similarly, we read: *When brothers live together, and one of them dies without a son, his widow shall not be married to a stranger [le'ish zar] outside the family* (Deuteronomy 25:5), where the word *zar* signifies: anyone who is not a brother. Another relative sense is given by the prophet with this threat: *Foreigners [zarim] will stand up to pasture your flocks, children of strangers your farm and vineyard laborers* (Isaiah 61:5), where *zarim* refers to people of other nations. A *zar* can refer to someone who is outside the possibility of marriage: a *mamzer*, who may not marry into the nation at large. We might have thought that this was the sense of *zar* being used in this verse, that *mamzerim* were prohibited from eating of this food but an ordinary Israelite may eat of it. However, the verse broadened the sense of *zar* with the addition of the word *kol zar*, to imply "all strangers, any type of outsider." Therefore, we know that this verse means to exclude anyone outside the priesthood from partaking of these sacred offerings. *No layman [kol zar] may eat of the sacred offerings*, thereby excluding all manner of outsiders from consuming the priestly gifts. In this case even the Levite and the Israelite are considered foreigners.

יד כִּנְעוּרֶיהָ מִלֶּחֶם אָבִיהָ תֹּאכֵל וְכׇל־זָר לֹא־יֹאכַל בּוֹ׃ וְאִישׁ
כִּי־יֹאכַל קֹדֶשׁ בִּשְׁגָגָה וְיָסַף חֲמִשִׁיתוֹ עָלָיו וְנָתַן לַכֹּהֵן אֶת־
טו הַקֹּדֶשׁ׃ וְלֹא יְחַלְּלוּ אֶת־קׇדְשֵׁי בְּנֵי יִשְׂרָאֵל אֵת אֲשֶׁר־יָרִימוּ
טז לַיהוָה׃ וְהִשִּׂיאוּ אוֹתָם עֲוֺן אַשְׁמָה בְּאׇכְלָם אֶת־קׇדְשֵׁיהֶם
כִּי אֲנִי יְהוָה מְקַדְּשָׁם׃
יז יח וַיְדַבֵּר יְהוָה אֶל־מֹשֶׁה לֵּאמֹר׃ דַּבֵּר אֶל־אַהֲרֹן וְאֶל־בָּנָיו וְאֶל יח שלישי
כׇּל־בְּנֵי יִשְׂרָאֵל וְאָמַרְתָּ אֲלֵהֶם אִישׁ אִישׁ מִבֵּית יִשְׂרָאֵל
וּמִן־הַגֵּר בְּיִשְׂרָאֵל אֲשֶׁר יַקְרִיב קׇרְבָּנוֹ לְכׇל־נִדְרֵיהֶם וּלְכׇל־

VERSE 16

RABBI SAMSON RAPHAEL HIRSCH

וְהִשִּׂיאוּ אוֹתָם עֲוֺן אַשְׁמָה – *Or incur the penalty of iniquity:* We have already explored the meaning behind the term *asham* ["guilt"], and concluded that it derives from the concept of *shemama* ["desolation." The Hebrew word for "iniquity" in this verse is *ashma*, which is elsewhere translated as "guilt"]. This refers to the spiritual desolation that an offender can expect as a result of his transgression. In our comments on an earlier text we have pointed out that the Torah will often criticize as an *asham* an act that demonstrates indifference to sacred items or which involves a sin with the Sanctuary itself. [See verses 5:14–26. There the Torah details the series of offenses for which one would bring a guilt offering – an *asham*. These offenses include inadvertently making use of or benefiting from a sacred object.] In such circumstances the callousness of the Israelite is compounded by the desire to enrich himself at the sanctum's expense. The Torah in this passage thus insists that a person will enjoy prosperity only if he first shows respect and deference to that which has been consecrated to the Lord. He can enjoy personal wealth only if he zealously guards the boundary between what is his and what belongs to God. No benefit will devolve to him from appropriating wealth that is not his, only desolation. Hence, in the present context, as the text completes its discussion about the laws of *teruma*, it stresses that the boundaries which set off the property of the priest and the realm of the holy set a limit to the strictly utilitarian view that one's hard-earned bread is meant to serve his own economic interests. A Jew must be on guard lest he breach this boundary, whether through carelessness or deliberate neglect, and instead place a portion of his earnings beyond any immediate self-interest. The fruit which has been harvested and prepared for the homeowner's table may not be eaten until the farmer acknowledges his subordination to the Sanctuary of the Torah, and the crops' subordination as well. The farmer recognizes that the Sanctuary and the priests who service it exist on a more exalted plane than he, and that these institutions take priority over the private lives of the citizenry. [Rabbi Hirsch is explaining the derivation of the word *teruma*, from the Hebrew root *resh-vav-mem*, meaning to elevate and prioritize.] Every morsel of *teruma*, which the Israelite has in fact grown, must be treated as forbidden to him as

14 may do so. If someone eats of the sacred gift unintentionally,
he shall make restitution to the priest, adding an extra fifth to
15 its value. The people must not profane the sacred meats that
16 Israelites bring as offerings to the Lord or incur the penalty of
iniquity by eating their sacred offerings; for I, the Lord, make
them holy."
17 18 The Lord spoke to Moshe: "Speak to Aharon, his sons, and all SHELISHI
the Israelites. Say: When anyone of the House of Israel or of
the migrants living in Israel presents an offering to the Lord
as a burnt offering – whether in fulfillment of a vow or as a

RABBI SAMSON RAPHAEL HIRSCH *(cont.)*

a non-priest, and as such stands as a stark sign of his subordinate status. Now, although the proper treatment of *teruma* is critical for the common Israelite, it is even more crucial that the priest and his own household exercise great caution when handling this holy food. Not only does *teruma* remind the Israelite that first priority must be given to the Temple, it brings this message home to the priest and his household as well and with even greater force. He too must recall that the Temple and its service is the fundamental condition upon which his own flourishing depends. For even the produce of a priest's own garden is forbidden for consumption before he has separated the *teruma* and the tithe from it. That, then, is the warning to the priest: It is insufficient for him to represent the Sanctuary of the Torah to the people; he must just as much represent the Temple to himself.

HAAMEK DAVAR

וְהִשִּׁיאוּ אוֹתָם עֲוֹן אַשְׁמָה בְּאָכְלָם אֶת־קָדְשֵׁיהֶם – *Or incur the penalty of iniquity by eating their sacred offerings:* The verse here refers to the sacred flesh of sacrificial animals that have been brought to effect atonement. Indeed, the Sages express the connection between the consumption of the meat and the atonement being effected with the following formula: While the priests eat the meat, the donors receive their absolution. If the priests are not cautious regarding their consumption of this food [and eat it in a state of impurity], the Israelites who have brought the offering will not attain atonement. In this way it will be the priests' fault should the people retain their level of iniquity. Thus the verse means to say, "the priests will bear responsibility for the people's unresolved iniquity."

VERSE 18

RABBI SAMSON RAPHAEL HIRSCH

וּמִן־הַגֵּר בְּיִשְׂרָאֵל – *Or of the migrants living in Israel:* With this text the Torah allows non-Israelites to donate freewill offerings. And since this point is made with respect to burnt offerings, we find support for the rule that foreigners are permitted to bring only burnt offerings to the Temple. Thus, the Talmud (Menaḥot 73b) asserts: When the verse refers to *an offering to the Lord as a burnt offering,* it teaches that outsiders may present only burnt offerings to Israel's Temple. Therefore, should such a non-Jew announce his intention to sacrifice a peace offering, the officiating priests must treat it as a burnt offering

יט נִדְבוֹתָם אֲשֶׁר־יַקְרִיבוּ לַיהוה לְעֹלָה: לִרְצֹנְכֶם תָּמִים זָכָר
כ בַּבָּקָר בַּכְּשָׂבִים וּבָעִזִּים: כֹּל אֲשֶׁר־בּוֹ מוּם לֹא תַקְרִיבוּ כִּי־
כא לֹא לְרָצוֹן יִהְיֶה לָכֶם: וְאִישׁ כִּי־יַקְרִיב זֶבַח־שְׁלָמִים לַיהוה
לְפַלֵּא־נֶדֶר אוֹ לִנְדָבָה בַּבָּקָר אוֹ בַצֹּאן תָּמִים יִהְיֶה לְרָצוֹן
כב כָּל־מוּם לֹא יִהְיֶה־בּוֹ: עַוֶּרֶת אוֹ שָׁבוּר אוֹ־חָרוּץ אוֹ־יַבֶּלֶת
אוֹ גָרָב אוֹ יַלֶּפֶת לֹא־תַקְרִיבוּ אֵלֶּה לַיהוה וְאִשֶּׁה לֹא־תִתְּנוּ

RABBI SAMSON RAPHAEL HIRSCH *(cont.)*

anyway. The philosophy behind this rule is the gentiles' fundamental attitude toward sacrifices, which is that an animal offering symbolizes the petitioner's total submission of himself to the Almighty. A non-Israelite does not conceive of the idea that is unique to our people, that which is expressed through the peace offering; I refer to the understanding that a Jew can serve the Lord through the joy of material pleasures which are mandated by His command. [The Jewish donor of a peace offering, but not of a burnt offering, enjoys the consumption of part of the meat of the peace offering.]

HAAMEK DAVAR

אֲשֶׁר־יַקְרִיבוּ לַיהוה לְעֹלָה – *Present an offering to the Lord as a burnt offering:* [This verse, which introduces those who bring burnt offerings, differs significantly from the introduction at the beginning of Leviticus. There the donor is called *adam*, whereas here the donor is called *ish*. The term *adam* refers to a distinguished person, a leader, "one in a thousand," whereas the term *ish* can refer to an ordinary person. This, then, alludes to the different purposes for which a burnt offering is brought, depending on who the donor is and what he is capable of. In addition, this verse combines plural verb-subject agreement with singular verb-subject agreement: *asher yakriv* – "anyone presents," in singular, but *yakrivu* – "they present," in plural.] A burnt offering has two possible purposes. When offered alone by a person of learning, or by a leader, the donor wishes to grasp the understanding of the Lord for himself. Alternatively, the person might be incapable of such a lofty attainment and hence his burnt offering is simply attached to vow or freewill peace offerings offered by others. In such a case he adds additional force with his burnt offering to the pleas and entreaties of those peace offerings which are seeking to propitiate God to bless His people with peace and the ability to earn a decent livelihood. This explains why the verb *yakrivu* ["they present"] appears here in the plural. The sense of the verse therefore is this: *when anyone presents [asher yakriv, in the singular]* and joins *an offering* [*korbano*] to *a vow or as a freewill offering*, that is, of other people [perhaps in the form of a communal offering], *that they present [asher yakrivu] to the Lord*. Thus, this added sacrifice is brought in the form of a burnt offering. What emerges is that the term *le'ola* ["as a burnt offering," at the end of the verse] performs two functions. It is as if the text had written: He who presents his sacrifice as a burnt offering to the Lord, for the sake of grasping an understanding of

19 freewill offering – to be acceptable on your behalf, it must be
an unblemished male from the herd, or of the sheep or goats.
20 Do not offer anything that has a blemish, for it will not be ac-
21 cepted on your behalf. When someone presents a peace sacrifice to the LORD from the herd or flock – whether because of a
spoken vow or as a freewill offering – it must be unblemished
22 to be acceptable; there shall be no blemish on it. Do not present to the LORD anything blind, injured, or maimed, or with
warts, a severe rash, or scabs. Do not place any of these on the

HAAMEK DAVAR *(cont.)*

the LORD; he furthermore joins company with those who present a vow or freewill offering. The donor thereby participates as well in the vow offerings of the many, and simultaneously adopts the goal of the peace offering as well.

VERSE 20

HAAMEK DAVAR

כִּי־לֹא לְרָצוֹן יִהְיֶה לָכֶם – *For it will not be accepted on your behalf:* You will not succeed through it [the blemished sacrifice] in attaining your goal of finding favor with God, which is expressed as being "accepted on your behalf," referring to having your prayers accepted by the LORD.

VERSE 21

RABBI SAMSON RAPHAEL HIRSCH

לְפַלֵּא־נֶדֶר – *A spoken vow:* The term *peleh* refers to an act of God which He performs solely as a manifestation of His all-powerful will. This deed takes place in a manner independent of and unconstrained by the natural order of things, and as such stands apart from the world as it already exists. Analogously, a *neder* is a function of a person's free will. It creates an obligation or restriction which is independent of and stands apart from the system of existing commandments which already obligate and restrict his behavior. Thus, an Israelite who utters a vow undertakes a new duty or binds himself to a pledge as an autonomous agent.

VERSE 22

SHADAL

וְאִשֶּׁה לֹא־תִתְּנוּ מֵהֶם עַל־הַמִּזְבֵּחַ לַיהוה – *Do not place any of these on the altar as a fire offering to the LORD:* The donor must not reason as follows: Since this sacrifice is not a burnt offering but a peace offering, the majority of which will be consumed by the owners, why should it matter to me that the animal is blemished? If I am the one consuming it, then I can decide for myself whether I find the blemish problematic. The text therefore concludes with this clause: *Do not place any of these on the altar as a fire offering to the LORD,* meaning: Even though this animal may be mostly consumed by its owner, it is still "a fire offering to the LORD." Its fats and blood are still "a fire offering," as they are burned on the altar in offering to the Almighty, and as such it is only appropriate that they be unblemished.

כג מֵהֶם עַל־הַמִּזְבֵּחַ לַיהוָה: וְשׁוֹר וָשֶׂה שָׂרוּעַ וְקָלוּט נְדָבָה
כד תַּעֲשֶׂה אֹתוֹ וּלְנֵדֶר לֹא יֵרָצֶה: וּמָעוּךְ וְכָתוּת וְנָתוּק וְכָרוּת
כה לֹא תַקְרִיבוּ לַיהוָה וּבְאַרְצְכֶם לֹא תַעֲשׂוּ: וּמִיַּד בֶּן־נֵכָר
לֹא תַקְרִיבוּ אֶת־לֶחֶם אֱלֹהֵיכֶם מִכָּל־אֵלֶּה כִּי מָשְׁחָתָם
כו בָּהֶם מוּם בָּם לֹא יֵרָצוּ לָכֶם: וַיְדַבֵּר

VERSE 23

RABBI SAMSON RAPHAEL HIRSCH

נְדָבָה תַּעֲשֶׂה אֹתוֹ – *You may offer as a freewill offering:* Our verse makes a noteworthy distinction between the invalidity of a blemished animal in fulfillment of a vow [*neder*] versus its acceptability with regard to a freewill offering [*nedava*]. This needs to be understood in contrast to the earlier verses, which invalidate a blemished animal with regard to both a freewill offering and in fulfillment of a vow: *Whether in fulfillment of a vow or as a freewill offering.... Do not offer anything that has a blemish, for it will not be accepted on your behalf* (22:18–20). In order to resolve this disparity, we must understand the difference between dedicating the value of an object and dedicating the object itself. When a person consecrates a *nedava*, he dedicates the value of the object to the Temple coffers, the *bedek habayit*. A blemished specimen is a valid *nedava*, because whatever monetary value it represents now belongs to the Temple. [This specimen will not be sacrificed on the altar but will be sold, and the funds it brings will be given toward Temple repairs.] Of course, the defect in the animal will lower its value, but then it was only ever dedicated for the sake of its monetary worth and on condition that it could fetch some sort of money. In the case of a *neder*, on the other hand, the determination of the donor to bring an offering is a reflection of the Israelite's personal wishes and his desire to dedicate himself – his efforts and personality – to God. It is for this reason that an imperfect animal cannot symbolize the wholehearted and complete intention of the donor. That is why the defective beast *will not be accepted in fulfillment of a vow*. In a similar vein, the Sages teach (Temura 6a) that it is forbidden to donate a whole, unblemished animal for the sake of Temple repair [*bedek habayit* – the Temple coffers], since a perfect specimen should be a viable sacrifice instead. These two laws stand as eternal truisms that our will and dedication to fulfill God's command always transcend the importance of the physical structure of outward manifestation of the Temple. On the one hand, one may not consecrate unblemished animals for their funds. Such animals must fulfill their higher purpose as actual sacrifices. And on the other hand, the fact that a blemished animal is not acceptable in fulfillment of a vow expresses the idea that the dedication and submission of a person's life efforts, symbolized by blood and flesh, cannot be properly represented by a blemished animal. Submission to the will of the Lord bears a value that far surpasses the physical magnificence and beauty that is applied to the Temple. After all, does such devotion not demonstrate the main purpose and goal of the physical Sanctuary to begin with? The Israelite must not for a moment forget the essence of the Temple even regarding the usage of a solitary object. And so do the Sages state (Shevuot 16a): Rabbi Yehoshua taught: I have heard that one sacrifices offerings on the

23 altar as a fire offering to the Lord. You may offer as a freewill
offering an ox or sheep with a limb deformed or uncloven, but
24 they will not be accepted in fulfillment of a vow. Do not offer
to the Lord an animal whose testicles are bruised, crushed,
25 torn, or cut off; and do not do such things in your land. Do
not accept such animals from a migrant as an offering of foodstuffs to your God. Because they are mutilated and blemished,
26 they will not be accepted on your behalf." The

RABBI SAMSON RAPHAEL HIRSCH *(cont.)*

altar even if there is no Temple, and one partakes of the offerings of the most sacred order in the Temple even if there are no curtains, and one partakes of offerings of lesser sanctity and second-tithe produce in Jerusalem even if there is no wall surrounding the city. This is due to the fact that the initial consecration sanctified the Temple and Jerusalem for their time and also sanctified them forever. Thus, acts of sacrifice and dedication always surpass in importance the physical building. The same may be said with respect to a synagogue: Its walls may be on the verge of collapse, and yet if the members of the congregation who attend this house of prayer are prepared to affirm their covenant with the Almighty, then the quorum's devotion to the Torah elevates the place above even the most splendid edifice which is devoid of such loyal believers. A magnificent building empty of sincere prayer holds no value compared to a dilapidated space filled with genuine devotion.

VERSE 24

MALBIM

וּבְאַרְצְכֶם לֹא תַעֲשׂוּ – *And do not do such things in your land:* It is forbidden to sacrifice such defective specimens in the Temple, whereas across the land the prohibition refers to the castration of any animal. [But use of such animals may still be permitted in the land. *Do not do such things*, but you may benefit from such things, outside the Temple.]

HAAMEK DAVAR

וּמָעוּךְ – *An animal whose testicles are bruised:* The blemishes listed here are unlike other physical defects, for it would be insulting to present such a defective animal even to a distinguished person. And so does the prophet argue: *When you offer a blind animal to be sacrificed, is this no evil? And when you offer the lame and the sick, is this no evil? Offer it if you will to your governor. Would he then accept you – let you lift your face to him? So says the Lord of Hosts* (Malachi 1:8). On the other hand, a castrated animal is not repugnant; in fact the opposite is true. A sterilized ox is considered superior [as a draft or a riding animal, since its aggression has been suppressed]. Nevertheless, as a sacrificial beast, such a specimen is deemed to be flawed. **וּבְאַרְצְכֶם לֹא תַעֲשׂוּ** – *And do not do such things in your land:* Do not perform such procedures on animals for the sake of fattening them up and thereby increasing their value. That is an unacceptable tactic even if the intention is to sell the animal and donate the funds to the treasury for Temple repairs, as a freewill offering; that sort of donation is still forbidden.

כו יְהוָה אֶל־מֹשֶׁה לֵּאמֹר: שׁוֹר אוֹ־כֶשֶׂב אוֹ־עֵז כִּי יִוָּלֵד וְהָיָה
שִׁבְעַת יָמִים תַּחַת אִמּוֹ וּמִיּוֹם הַשְּׁמִינִי וָהָלְאָה יֵרָצֶה לְקָרְבַּן

VERSE 27

RABBI SAMSON RAPHAEL HIRSCH

וְהָיָה שִׁבְעַת יָמִים תַּחַת אִמּוֹ – *It shall remain with its mother for seven days:* The Hebrew words *taḥat immo* [here translated as "shall remain with its mother"] can be interpreted in two ways: "under the protection of" or "in place of." [The law derives two different conditions from this phrase. It disqualifies an orphan which has not spent a moment with its mother, but it allows an infant which has not spent the full seven days with the mother because the mother died in the middle. Rabbi Hirsch will make the point that each of these opposite conditions, one which limits the suitability of an animal for sacrifice and one which expands the suitability, comes from two different readings of the words *taḥat immo.*] Since the law derives from the term *taḥat immo* that an animal born without a mother is disqualified from being a sacrifice, it implies a reading of the words in the sense of "under the protection of." The animal must experience a state of being under the actual protection of its mother in order to qualify as a sacrifice. But when an animal is born as an orphan, it has never enjoyed being "under the protection of" its mother and is therefore disqualified. The Talmud (Ḥullin 38b) describes the situation of the orphaned animal as one which never enjoyed its mother's protection even for a moment: The adult was pulled to death, while the young was pulled to life, and hence mother and child spent not even one moment together. Because there was never a moment when the animal could be considered *taḥat immo*, "under the protection of," it becomes invalid as an offering. The Torah elsewhere describes the requirement of an animal to stay with its mother with slightly different language: *Likewise with your oxen and sheep; let them stay with their mothers [im immo] for seven days, and on the eighth, give them over to Me* (Exodus 22:29). Thus, this requirement to "remain with its mother" referred to in this verse with the words *taḥat immo* is similar to the words *im immo* from the verse in Exodus. They both refer to the actual state of being "together with," such that the young animal benefits from the warmth and the nourishment that its mother's body can provide. However, the Sifra contrasts the words *im immo* with the words *taḥat immo* in order to learn something different. It argues that had the verse wanted to teach that a young animal must benefit from the warmth and nourishment of its mother for a full seven days, it should have used the words *im immo*, meaning "together with" the mother. Since the verse switched to the more ambiguous expression *taḥat immo*, it must be teaching that there is no need for the animal to be together with its mother for all seven days. All that is required by these words is that the animal live for seven days, with or without the protection of its mother. The sense of the phrase *taḥat immo* changes. According to the Sifra it is being read as "in place of." The young animal has taken the place of the mother, here in this world of living creatures. Based on this reading, our verse does not in fact demand that the mother remain alive with its offspring for seven days. Rather, the verse requires that we leave the animal alone for the first seven days of its life regardless of whether it is benefiting from the mother's protection. Following this

27 LORD spoke to Moshe: "When an ox or sheep or goat is born,
it shall remain with its mother for seven days. From the eighth

RABBI SAMSON RAPHAEL HIRSCH *(cont.)*

reading, during the first week of life an animal is always considered *taḥat immo*, whether the mother is alive or not, because that is the way of the world; a fledgling in its first week of life tends to be at its mother's side. The owner may not curtail this initial period of an animal's life even for the important purpose of dedicating it as an offering. Both readings insist that the natural order be respected and this normal and important period of maternal-infant bonding be left undisturbed for at least a moment. [Whether the bonding extends for the entire seven days or whether the mother dies before it is completed, either way, this period in which the bonding normally occurs must be respected.] By contrast, an orphan animal that was denied this possibility entirely does reflect some sort of inherent deficiency and is therefore disqualified as an offering.

MESHEKH ḤOKHMA

שׁוֹר אוֹ־כֶשֶׂב אוֹ־עֵז כִּי יִוָּלֵד – *When an ox or sheep or goat is born:* One of the aims within the world of idolatry was the attempt to appease the various deities which the ancients imagined influenced their world. People of the nations would therefore demonstrate their devotion by self-destructive behavior dedicated to their gods. They would destroy son and daughter, and they would slash and gash their own bodies in dedication to the celestial entities. They were guided by their gods' perceived cruel interest in human suffering. And so does the prophet write: *Men who offer sacrifices must kiss calves* (Hosea 13:2). This was the reigning conception until God in His mercy enlightened humanity with His Torah and issued commandments which are geared toward the development of the Israelites and the perfection of their own condition; the laws are in no way intended to benefit God Himself, as the following text asks rhetorically: *If you sin, do you affect Him at all? Even as your iniquities multiply, do you do anything to Him? If you are in the right, what do you give Him; what does He accept from you?* (Job 35:6–7). For the Almighty is clothed entirely in righteousness. The LORD has invested His Torah with the principles of constant compassion and graciousness for humankind across all strata of society. For instance, the nation is required to sanctify the priest, as we read: *You shall treat a priest as holy* (21:8); to make the Levite happy, as the verse demands: *And rejoice before the LORD your God – you and your sons and daughters, your male and female slaves, and the Levites living in your towns* (Deuteronomy 16:11); and to provide financially for the Israelite, as mandated by this text: *If there be a poor person among your kinsfolk in any of your towns… Open your hand generously and freely lend him enough to answer all his needs* (Deuteronomy 15:7–8). We must refrain from selling a Hebrew into servitude, as we read: *For they are My servants whom I brought out from Egypt: they cannot be sold as slaves* (25:42), and if certain circumstances do lead to enslavement, *over your brother Israelites you may not rule so harshly* (25:46). The community is ordered to sustain resident aliens, as the verse states: *If your brother becomes poor and is struggling, extend him support – a migrant or visitor also – that he may live among you* (25:35). We are further required to care for a Canaanite servant, whom a master is not permitted to shame. And even an animal must not be abused, as the verse states: *You shall*

כח אִשֶּׁה לַיהוָה: וְשׁוֹר אוֹ־שֶׂה אֹתוֹ וְאֶת־בְּנוֹ לֹא תִשְׁחֲטוּ

MESHEKH ḤOKHMA *(cont.)*

not see your kinsman's donkey or ox fallen on the road and ignore it. Help him to lift it (Deuteronomy 22:4). Should the Israelite come to eat the meat of his animal, that does not excuse him from displaying a measure of mercy to the cow or the sheep. Hence, the Torah issues various decrees for the sake of the animals; it is only the pain of death which the Torah allows, since that of course is inevitable if the thing is to be eaten. As such, the verse states: *Do not muzzle an ox while it is treading out the grain* (Deuteronomy 25:4), while a different text extends the luxury of rest to both the servant and the animal: *The seventh is a Sabbath to the Lord your God. On it, do no work at all – neither you, nor your son or daughter, your male or female servant, your ox, your donkey, nor any of your livestock* (Deuteronomy 5:14). Finally, the preservation of human life overrides the entire Torah. This lesson is derived from the verse: *Keep My statutes and laws, for by them a person shall live; I am the Lord* (18:5). In summary, the entirety of the Torah and all of its commandments evince compassion, grace, and righteousness – all of which are hallmarks of the Lord and of His Torah. In our passage the Torah again states which animals constitute acceptable sacrifices, specifying that these species are commonplace domesticated animals, easily found within the Israelites' settlement. God has not troubled the people to risk the dangers of the wilderness to trap wild and rare beasts for the altar. The text then decrees (see 22:27) that a young animal becomes suitable as an offering only following its first seven days that it has spent suckling from its mother. This is because God extends His mercy even to the souls of the animal kingdom. We see this concern as well in the law which states: *Do not slaughter an ox or sheep and its young on the same day* (22:28). In their interpretation of this verse, the Sages (Vayikra Rabba 27:11) cite the maxim: *The righteous man knows his beast's needs* (Proverbs 12:10) and claim: This is illustrated by God, who forbids the killing of a parent and child animal on the same day. We learn from these cases that the Almighty takes no personal interest in sacrifices, nor does He derive any benefit from our offerings. All that God wants is for people to act righteously and to walk in His ways. This is the sense of the clause, *sacrifice it so that it will be acceptable on your behalf [lirtzonekhem]* (22:29): An Israelite is pressured to bring sacrifices [since they are for his own good], until he willingly agrees [*rotzeh*]. Israel must not imagine that the sacrificial system is a barbaric one. Instead, the people's focus should be these statements: *Keep My commands and fulfill them; I am the Lord. Do not profane My holy name* (22:31–32). For God's good name and reputation testify to His eternal existence and His care in sustaining all of His world's creatures. The Almighty does not desire the destruction of His life forms, heaven forbid, since that would lead to the desecration of His good and sacred name. On the other hand, the people of Israel are issued this warning: Do not imagine that if your enemies compel you to violate My laws and to defile My name, that your own lives take precedence over that. Such is not the case! Indeed, that text cautions: *Do not profane My holy name – that I may be sanctified in the midst of the Israelites* (22:32). This expresses the requirement for a Jew to relinquish his life for the honor and

day it is acceptable as a sacrifice, a fire offering to the Lord,

MESHEKH HOKHMA *(cont.)*

sanctification of God's name. For it is a great honor for the Almighty when His commandments are so firmly established and embedded in the hearts of the nation that they are not easily breached. However, were God's law an expression of brutality, it would in fact be a profanation of His name to observe it. The fact is that there is no such character attendant upon the Torah's commandments; it is only wicked individuals, who wish to disparage the law and God's name, who portray His word as one of savagery. In conclusion, it is incumbent upon us to sanctify the name of God and to offer ourselves as burnt offerings on the altar and the fires of faith. We will thereby enlighten the eyes of the remaining Israelites and teach them how to serve the Master of all life.

THE LUBAVITCHER REBBE

וְהָיָה שִׁבְעַת יָמִים תַּחַת אִמּוֹ – *It shall remain with its mother for seven days:* The mystical meaning of this law is as follows: "Mother" signifies the intellect, since the intellect "gives birth" to the emotions. When the intellect recognizes the virtue of something or someone, it "gives birth" to the emotion of love for it; when it recognizes the undesirability or harmfulness of something or someone it "gives birth" to the emotion of hatred or fear for it, and so on. The "animal" signifies the emotions, since animals are driven by their instinctive emotions rather than by intellect. When an emotion is first "born" it must be matured by the intellect. This process takes place over the course of seven "days" i.e., it is a sevenfold process – one for each of the seven basic emotions. Only after the emotions have been matured are they fit to be "an offering for God" i.e., worthy of becoming part of the psyche of a human being dedicated to God's service.

VERSE 28

RABBI SAMSON RAPHAEL HIRSCH

שׁוֹר אוֹ־שֶׂה אֹתוֹ וְאֶת־בְּנוֹ – *An ox or sheep and its young:* This law recognizes a humane dimension within the life of an animal. The fact that this law, which forbids the slaughter of a mother and child on the same day, applies to non-sacred meat as well, that is, when the animal is being killed for the sake of a regular meat meal, teaches us that the dining-room table in the Jewish home resembles an altar with regard to its ethical function. Nevertheless, the Torah forbids only the ritual slaughter of this pair together, while still allowing one to kill the beasts one after the other in any other manner including puncturing the neck. It seems evident that ultimately the text is not trying to promote compassion for the animal's feelings. Rather, the reason behind this commandment is this: At the moment that the Israelite is transforming the life of an animal into his protein by causing its death [where proper slaughter is the only valid method which allows animal meat to be eaten], the Torah grants the young another day of life due to its mother, or alternately, allows the mother to live another day on account of its young. This in turn should remind a person of his humaneness, just as he is preparing to absorb the animal's essence into his own.

כט בְּיוֹם אֶחָד: וְכִי־תִזְבְּחוּ זֶבַח־תּוֹדָה לַיהוָה לִרְצֹנְכֶם תִּזְבָּחוּ:
ל בַּיּוֹם הַהוּא יֵאָכֵל לֹא־תוֹתִירוּ מִמֶּנּוּ עַד־בֹּקֶר אֲנִי יְהוָה:
לא ושְׁמַרְתֶּם מִצְוֹתַי וַעֲשִׂיתֶם אֹתָם אֲנִי יְהוָה: וְלֹא תְחַלְּלוּ אֶת־
לב שֵׁם קָדְשִׁי וְנִקְדַּשְׁתִּי בְּתוֹךְ בְּנֵי יִשְׂרָאֵל אֲנִי יְהוָה מְקַדִּשְׁכֶם:

VERSE 29

SHADAL

לִרְצֹנְכֶם תִּזְבָּחוּ – *So that it will be acceptable on your behalf:* What will make this sacrifice acceptable? When the Israelite makes sure to include many others to partake of its meat such that together they finish the meat in time, with nothing left over to the morning.

HAAMEK DAVAR

וְכִי־תִזְבְּחוּ זֶבַח־תּוֹדָה לַיהוה – *When you sacrifice a thanksgiving offering for the Lord:* At first glance this text seems to offer nothing new that has not already been said in Parashat Tzav (see 7:11–15) within the Torah's discussion of the peace offering. The Sages proposed various interpretations about what this verse adds. Still, the straightforward meaning of the text has something to teach us. To begin with, the reader must realize that the thanksgiving offering is not obligatory but is voluntary. [The language of the verse, "when you sacrifice," indicates a voluntary motivation.] Usually, a thanksgiving offering is reserved for a person who has been blessed with a miraculous form of salvation; nevertheless, we learn from here that one can volunteer a thanksgiving offering even absent any specific event demanding thanks. [The law defines four specific events as salvations which ought to be marked with a large gathering around a thanksgiving sacrifice, at which time the saved person recounts the event. The four cases are someone who: was released from captivity, completed a dangerous journey by sea or through a desert, or was healed from injury. The verses in Parashat Tzav relate more to a case when a person brings his thanksgiving offering in response to an event. And hence, the language there is phrased more as an imperative.] The rescued man is encouraged to recount God's kindness to him during the celebratory meal, during which he serves the multiple loaves of bread that accompany this sacrifice. I have explained this matter in my commentary to Parashat Tzav. [According to the author's essay on 7:13, the donor of this offering is encouraged to invite many guests to the feast he throws to mark his salvation. At that time he speaks about and thereby publicizes the greatness God has displayed on his behalf. However, this verse, coming as it does in close proximity to a detailed discussion of all the holidays, relates to a different situation when it was customary for the Israelites to bring a thanksgiving offering.] This verse addresses the voluntary thanksgiving offerings which augment the sacrifices brought on the festival of Sukkot. They are not in recognition of a past miracle, but because of the breads which are a fitting prelude to the rain that will hopefully fall after the holiday. According to the Talmud (Rosh Hashana 15a), it is on Sukkot that God decrees how much rain will fall in the upcoming season, and rain of course is directly responsible for the successful harvest in the land. The prophet describes this phenomenon when he writes: *Come to Beit El and sin, to the Gilgal and sin greatly. Bring your sacrifices in the morning and your tithes*

28 but do not slaughter an ox or sheep and its young on the same
29 day. When you sacrifice a thanksgiving offering for the LORD,
30 sacrifice it so that it will be acceptable on your behalf. It shall
be eaten on the same day – leave none of it to the morning; I
31 am the LORD. Keep My commands and fulfill them; I am the
32 LORD. Do not profane My holy name – that I may be sanctified

HAAMEK DAVAR *(cont.)*

on the third day. Burn your thanksgiving offering of leaven; call for donations; let it be heard, for this is what you love doing, children of Israel, says the LORD God. Yet I gave you clean teeth in all your cities, a lack of bread in your places, but you did not return to Me, says the LORD. And I held back the rain from you three months before the harvest, caused rain to fall on one city and not another; one plot will be rained upon, and one in which there will be no rain will wither away (Amos 4:4–7). This then was the practice of the Israelites [to offer thanksgiving sacrifices with their many loaves during Sukkot as an appeal for rain. Amos asserts that these offerings are hardly sufficient; God will weigh the nation's request against the transgressions that the people have committed, before determining the amount of rain that the land will receive].

This then is the sense of our verse, which refers to a "thanksgiving offering for the LORD" [with added emphasis on "for the LORD" and not for some other, extraneous purpose]: The verse cautions that these voluntary thanksgiving offerings should be brought out of proper motivation, for the sake of entreating God to bless the coming year with rain. They should not be simply "what you love doing," as the prophet Amos warned against. [The Sukkot festival celebrated the end of the harvest and could be marked as a time of cornucopia, when people delighted in the plentiful food. The *Haamek Davar* reads Amos as admonishing the people to direct their thanksgiving to God as an entreaty for the prosperity to continue, and not as a self-satisfied celebration of plenty.]

VERSE 30

HAAMEK DAVAR

בַּיּוֹם הַהוּא יֵאָכֵל – *It shall be eaten on the same day:* Even though this thanksgiving offering is not brought so that the donor might relate the miracle that he has enjoyed [but is sacrificed on Sukkot as an appeal to rain], there is nevertheless one law that governs all thanksgiving offerings. [This explains why the text repeats this particular detail here.]

VERSE 32

RABBI SAMSON RAPHAEL HIRSCH

וְנִקְדַּשְׁתִּי בְּתוֹךְ בְּנֵי יִשְׂרָאֵל – *That I may be sanctified in the midst of the Israelites:* The will of God must serve as the supreme and sacred value for the Israelite people; its importance should tower over all other concerns. God's sacred will must form the precondition for all of our actions, and His command is to be obeyed under all circumstances. We must realize through the life we lead what it is that a sacrifice symbolizes. The blood that is the Israelite's life force, representing all his inclinations and pursuits, his physical abilities, his wealth, his possessions, his goals and wishes, the joy of his existence, the life force which animates every one of his limbs must all be sacrificed on the altar of the LORD. We must dedicate

לג הַמּוֹצִיא אֶתְכֶם מֵאֶרֶץ מִצְרַיִם לִהְיוֹת לָכֶם לֵאלֹהִים אֲנִי
יהוה:
כג א ב וַיְדַבֵּר יהוה אֶל־מֹשֶׁה לֵּאמֹר: דַּבֵּר אֶל־בְּנֵי יִשְׂרָאֵל וְאָמַרְתָּ רביעי
אֲלֵהֶם מוֹעֲדֵי יהוה אֲשֶׁר־תִּקְרְאוּ אֹתָם מִקְרָאֵי קֹדֶשׁ אֵלֶּה

RABBI SAMSON RAPHAEL HIRSCH *(cont.)*

everything to His sacred and divine will and only then can we achieve human perfection. Thus will we serve as models, representing the true role of a Jew "in the midst of the Israelites." This locating of the total dedication required of a Jew to "the midst of the Israelites" posits that the nation of Israel itself functions as a living organism, a whole in which all of the various parts are interconnected and interdependent and united around a single will, which is to sanctify God's "holy name." When a Jew loyally fulfills his obligation and willingly offers his sacrifices, he thereby encourages his neighbors to rise to that same level of faithfulness. On the other hand, when a Jew transgresses the word of God, he not only sabotages his own divinely ordained duty but causes others to stumble, as they are empowered to learn from his rebellious example. The Torah's call to its adherents to dedicate and sanctify all their aspirations and goals is exemplified by the act of offering an animal sacrifice. This is synonymous with the Torah's call to sanctify God's name, *that I may be sanctified in the midst of the Israelites*. This call sometimes requires the ultimate sacrifice of dying for the sanctification of God's holy name. The ability of a Jew to answer this call wholeheartedly represents the historical strength of the Jewish people. The annals of Jewish history in the diaspora are illuminated by the faithful who answered this test when called. I refer to all of the righteous, holy, and pure-hearted Jews, all of the sacred communities who have dedicated their lives for the sanctification of God's name, the beloved and tender lives which were not distanced in death. [Here Rabbi Hirsch is quoting from the familiar prayers recited at memorials.] These men and women who lived their lives with the singular purpose of loving the Almighty and who wished to glimpse the pleasantness of His ways did not flinch when that singular purpose required their life. Even in their deaths they maintained that selfsame ultimate purpose. They were lighter than eagles and mightier than lions in their zeal to fulfill the Lord's will and the desires of their Creator. These were the people whose complete commitment to God's will reached the summit of human achievement as they embodied the total dedication expressed by a sacrifice. They donated their lives and their personal hopes on the altar of God. For they were prepared to devote every future and planned act of theirs, all their possessions, their joy of life to the message of the Torah. And so did they testify to the absolute power of the Torah to govern the heart of every Jew. They thereby conveyed the lesson to all future generations regarding the appropriate way for a Jew to understand and to fulfill the present commandment to "not profane My holy name."

RABBI JOSEPH B. SOLOVEITCHIK

וְנִקְדַּשְׁתִּי בְּתוֹךְ בְּנֵי יִשְׂרָאֵל – *That I may be sanctified in the midst of the Israelites:* After the destruction of the Temple, the honor of the nation had to be restored. Daniel, Ḥananya,

in the midst of the Israelites. I am the Lord, who makes you
33 holy, who brought you out of Egypt to be your God: I am the
Lord."
23 1 2 The Lord spoke to Moshe: "Speak to the Israelites. Say: These REVI'I
are the Lord's appointed times that you shall proclaim as

RABBI JOSEPH B. SOLOVEITCHIK *(cont.)*

Mishael, and Azarya restored the honor of the Jewish people by defying Nevukhadnetzar and refusing to bow down to an idol (Daniel chapter 1). The general principle that a person must give up his life rather than transgress certain commands [*yehareg ve'al yaavor*] includes the concept that the honor of Israel should not be diminished. That is why the Rambam includes all the different forms of profaning God's name in the same chapter: idolatry, illicit relationships, and murder, as well as a scholar who acts in a way that brings shame on Torah and himself. All share in diminishing the honor of the Children of Israel.

THE LUBAVITCHER REBBE

וְנִקְדַּשְׁתִּי בְּתוֹךְ בְּנֵי יִשְׂרָאֵל – *That I may be sanctified in the midst of the Israelites:* The word for "in the midst of" also means "within," meaning that persistently meditating on God's transcendence will allow this renewed enthusiasm to penetrate our hearts, saturating our consciousness with love of God.

CHAPTER 23, VERSE 2

OR HAḤAYYIM

אֵלֶּה הֵם מוֹעֲדָי – *These are My appointed times:* Why does the text, at the end of the verse, repeat this introductory phrase: *appointed times*? Secondly, why must our passage again command the observance of the Sabbath [considering that the Torah has already discussed this day multiple times, e.g., Exodus 20:8, 31:15, and Leviticus 19:3]? Finally, how can we explain the fact that immediately after the current mention of the Sabbath, the verse once again states: *These are the Lord's appointed times* (23:4)? The interpretation of our text is as follows: At first the chapter declares that the celebration of the festivals will depend primarily on the times that are determined by Israel's court, which establishes the new month. [This then is the sense of the opening clause: *These are the Lord's appointed times* – that will depend upon the determination of the new moon – *that you shall proclaim.*] And yet, the Torah was concerned lest we think that the timing of the Sabbath might also be a function of a court decision. Perhaps a court could also delay the onset of the Sabbath just like it can delay the onset of a new month. Perhaps if the judges agreed, the court could have the power to sanctify one Sunday evening as the Sabbath. To counter that supposition the text states again: *These are My appointed times. Work shall be done through six days* (23:2–3), meaning: These Sabbath days are appointed times that the Creator has proclaimed, and they are not subject to change. [In this reading, the end of verse 2 should be understood as a preface to verse 3, rather than as a reiteration of the earlier statement in verse 2 itself. This reading emphasizes that they are "My appointed times" and are not given to court determination.]

RABBI SAMSON RAPHAEL HIRSCH

אֵלֶּה הֵם מוֹעֲדָי – *These are My appointed times:* When God states: *These are My appointed times*, this stresses that these festivals will be declared according to a unique system which includes the decisions of human courts. The holiday of *Aviv* [Passover], that of the reaping of the first fruits [Shavuot], and that of the harvest [Sukkot] are entirely distinct from seasonal celebration [common among pagans, marking solstices and equinoxes]. These festivals should not in any way be interpreted as celebrations of spring, summer, and autumn. These are not occasions to mark astronomically significant events, common to all sun cults whose intent it was to glorify Mother Nature. [While the Hebrew calendar contains provisions to make sure that Passover fell around the vernal equinox, it is decidedly not a celebration of that notable day when day and night are of equal length. Passover is a unique holiday celebrated during the spring but is not a celebration of the spring.] In the exact same way, we must resist identifying the commemoration of the New Moon as a manifestation of moon worship. Instead, the renewal of the moon corresponds to our national reinvigoration. [The declaration of a new month is coordinated with the lunar conjunction but is not a celebration of that astronomical occurrence. It is an event that helps us mark the passage of time, but is not significant in and of itself. So too, the vernal equinox helps the court align Passover with the correct season, but there is no need to mark that event.] Similarly, the festivals that take place in the seasons of the spring, the summer, and the autumn, are nothing but sacred assemblies [*mikra'ei kodesh*, literally, "holy callings"]. For with the advent of these holidays, the people are called to assemble, to step away from the framework of nature, and to distance themselves from the field and the forest. Changing their farming clothes to their urban wear, the Israelites are beckoned to ascend to Jerusalem and to enter the Sanctuary, which represents the Torah of the Lord. Such a gesture stands as a vocal negation of pagan ideas, which are devoted to the veneration of sun and stream. In direct opposition to the glorification of the natural world, our Temple worshippers declare that the blessings mankind receives do not rely upon the independent sphere of the sun, which directs the passage of the seasons. It is not to that body that we owe gratitude for ripening the grain on the stalks and the fruits on the trees. For the sun does not choose whether or not to fill our granaries with produce, it is only the Lord acting under His free will, who judges humanity with righteousness and kindness. Thus, if the Israelites have fulfilled God's Torah, which resides in His Sanctuary, He will in return cause our fields to blossom in the spring, He will allow our fruits to ripen in the summer, and He will stock our silos with a bountiful harvest in the autumn. In recognition of this fact, that our blessings do not flow from blind nature but from adherence to the moral and social demands of the Torah, which encompass every sphere of human endeavor, the Jewish people must submit to the rule of the Almighty in all these areas of behavior.

HAAMEK DAVAR

אֵלֶּה הֵם מוֹעֲדָי – *These are My appointed times:* On the surface, this verse seems somewhat verbose. However, the message of our text is this: Just as the festival days are sacred assemblies for the people of Israel, as I will explain below, so too are these holidays sacred assemblies for God, so to speak, with respect to the manner in which the Almighty conducts the affairs of the world. Thus God has established several different new years as times to make

HAAMEK DAVAR *(cont.)*

certain determinations for the upcoming year, as the Talmud states (Rosh Hashana 16a): At four times of the year the world is judged: On Passover judgment is passed concerning the grain; on Shavuot judgment is passed regarding fruits that grow on trees; on Rosh Hashana all of humanity passes before the Almighty like sheep; and on the festival of Sukkot the world is judged concerning the rainfall of the coming year. As such, the meaning of our verse is this: *These are the Lord's appointed times that you shall proclaim as sacred assemblies* with respect to what relates to us. The verse emphasizes that these are to be Israel's festivals to the exclusion of all others. [Thus, each of the Torah's festivals plays its own specific role in God's determination of the fate of Israel in the coming year. Even though the courts have some leeway in determining the exact dates of these festivals, nevertheless, the Jewish nation may label as sacred assemblies only those days which the Almighty identifies here.]

RABBI DAVID TZVI HOFFMAN

אֵלֶּה הֵם מוֹעֲדָי – *These are My appointed times:* Just as the form of Israel's festivals relies on the Sabbath for its definition, so too does the nature of these holidays resemble the character of the Sabbath. The origin of the Sabbath relates back to the formation of the world. Upon His completion of the universe after six days of creation, God blessed the seventh day and sanctified it. In commemoration of that event, after man has toiled for six days, he too honors and sanctifies the seventh day as a period of rest and holiness. With that weekly tribute, the Israelite acknowledges that God is the Creator and Master of everything. Now, beyond the recognition of God as first cause, it becomes equally important for the nation to agree to and proclaim the role that the Almighty plays as a continuous guardian of Israel and as their redeemer in history. We acknowledge that the Lord has chosen us and directs our affairs continuously. Whereas the Sabbath is the time to consider God as Creator, the celebration of the festivals recalls the Almighty as the primary actor in Jewish history. On the one hand, the holidays are connected to those joyous annual agricultural events, namely: the start of the grain harvest, the end of the harvest, and the gathering in of the crops from the fields. On the other hand, the festivals are designed to preserve the memory of particular historical occurrences in the life of the Israelite nation, specifically: the exodus of the people from Egypt, the revelation of the Torah at Mount Sinai, and God's care and protection of the masses during their sojourn in the desert… These two parallel organizing narratives, agricultural and historical, are not, as a superficial approach might conclude, in opposition to one another. Rather, they are closely related and complementary. For it is precisely at those times of the year when the people experience their highest level of contentment, when they revel in their wealth and their blessings, that the nation must acknowledge the role of the Almighty in achieving this wealth. At those moments the Israelites recall their historical milestones, which they know were successfully conducted not through the efforts of their ancestors. They must admit certain fundamental truths related to each historical event if they are to properly appreciate the natural abundance that the harvest brings. They must first admit, in connection with the exodus from Egypt, that their achievements are not their own, and that only through divine assistance are the Jewish people able to enjoy their independence. Only through God's involvement can one benefit from *my power, and the strength of my own hand*

CONFRONTING MODERNITY

ג הֵ֖ם מוֹעֲדָֽי׃ שֵׁ֣שֶׁת יָמִים֮ תֵּעָשֶׂ֣ה מְלָאכָה֒ וּבַיּ֣וֹם הַשְּׁבִיעִ֗י
שַׁבַּ֤ת שַׁבָּתוֹן֙ מִקְרָא־קֹ֔דֶשׁ כׇּל־מְלָאכָ֖ה לֹ֣א תַעֲשׂ֑וּ שַׁבָּ֥ת
הִוא֙ לַיהֹוָ֔ה בְּכֹ֖ל מוֹשְׁבֹֽתֵיכֶֽם׃

RABBI DAVID TZVI HOFFMAN *(cont.)*

(Deuteronomy 8:17). The Israelites must next appreciate, in connection with the holiday of Shavuot and the giving of the Torah, that there are treasures far more valuable than the new year's grain. The asset that they were given on that first Shavuot must be cherished, preserved, and developed. Finally, in connection with the festival of Sukkot, the people must learn that they can truly celebrate their bounty only when they acknowledge their vulnerability and place themselves and all their property under the complete protection of the Lord.

RABBI JOSEPH B. SOLOVEITCHIK

אֵלֶּה הֵם מוֹעֲדָי – *These are My appointed times:* To modern man, a day is not a living entity. We do not associate the term "day" with substance or content; it is not a subject to which attributes can be ascribed or traits predicated. To the scientist, time is a mathematical concept. Modern physics has combined time with space, rendering time as empty as space, merely one coordinate of a system within which we try to model the universe. To Judaism, in contrast, time is a living entity. There is substance and essence to time. Time is not a void but a reality. One can ascribe attributes such as "joyous" or "sad" to time just as one can ascribe these attributes to people. One can refer to a day as evil, meaning that the day itself is cursed. When we refer to a holy day, we do not merely signify that it is a day in which man somehow experiences holiness. The day itself has an inner endowment, a charisma hidden in its very substance. It has suddenly become a metaphysical entity.

VERSE 3

HAKETAV VEHAKABBALA

שַׁבָּת הִוא לַיהוה – *It shall be a Sabbath for the Lord:* The term *shabbat* connotes rest and the cessation of and respite from work. And it seems to me that the word also includes a sense of investigation and reflection, as in the verses which state: *I turned again [veshavti] and saw empty breath beneath the sun* (Ecclesiastes 4:7), and: *After I turned back [shuvi], I was remorseful* (Jeremiah 31:18). These texts correspond to the rabbinic phrase *yishuv hadaat* ["peace of mind"]. Therefore, we might suggest that the Sabbath day is a time devoted to spiritual development and religious contemplation. On this holy day of the week the Israelite should clear his mind of extraneous thoughts and focus on matters pertaining to his relationship with Almighty God. Thus do the Sages say: The Lord granted Israel the Sabbath so that they might occupy themselves with the study of the Torah.

RABBI SAMSON RAPHAEL HIRSCH

בְּכֹל מוֹשְׁבֹתֵיכֶם – *In all your dwellings:* Because the Sabbath day is a fixed institution, it is observed wherever Jews live and throughout the world's scattered communities. In contrast,

3 sacred assemblies; these are My appointed times. Work shall
be done through six days, but the seventh day shall be a Sabbath of complete rest, a sacred assembly. You shall perform
no work at all; it shall be a Sabbath for the Lord in all your
dwellings.

RABBI SAMSON RAPHAEL HIRSCH *(cont.)*

celebration of the festivals relies on the nation and on the declaration of the New Moon by court, representing the people. The Sanhedrin sanctifies the month from Jerusalem, which stands as the center of Israel's national life. On the other hand, the holiness of the Sabbath preceded the formation of the Israelite people and hence its advent on a weekly basis does not require the agency of the nation. Instead, it is mankind which is summoned to submit to the Creator of the world, whose domain is recalled by the recognition of the Sabbath. Wherever a person may find himself within God's world, the Sabbath accompanies him into the realm of the divine. And as the Israelite crosses the threshold between Friday and the Sabbath, he is invited to yield control over his life, offer it up to the Almighty, and thereby recognize God as the ultimate sovereign.

MALBIM

וּבַיּוֹם הַשְּׁבִיעִי שַׁבַּת שַׁבָּתוֹן – *But the seventh day shall be a Sabbath of complete rest:* The Torah really should not have included the Sabbath in the present list of Israel's festivals, for the simple reason that holiness is inherent in the seventh day, and the Sabbath need not be sanctified by the court [unlike the festivals, which are determined by human establishment of the New Moon]. The reason that the text opens this discussion with the Sabbath is the concern that the people might take the holiness of the festivals lightly, reasoning that these days are proclaimed by the nation. Hence, the Torah equates sanctity of festivals with that of the Sabbath, and treats them as a single group in terms of their character and substance. Thus, any violation of the festivals is tantamount to the profanation of the Sabbath.

HAAMEK DAVAR

שַׁבַּת שַׁבָּתוֹן – *A Sabbath of complete rest:* The term *shabbaton* suggests that the scope of the resting should be limited. [According to the author, the *vav-nun* suffix – *on*, indicates a reduction.] This explains the usage of the word *shabbaton* in the context of festivals, because forbidden labor is less restricted on festivals. Certain food preparations which are forbidden on the Sabbath are permitted during festivals. In contrast, when the Torah discusses the Sabbath of creation [that is, the seventh day of every week], we find always the term *shabbat* without the diminutive suffix. The appearance in the present verse of the expanded phrase *shabbat shabbaton* does not connote that the extent of forbidden labors should be diminished, because the regular word *shabbat* is still used. Rather, the presence of the word *shabbaton* in this case serves to limit the extent of the day in that the length of the day itself is bounded; the Torah does not demand that extra time be added to the start or to the end of this *shabbat shabbaton*. [The *Haamek Davar* explains that the extra time we add to the Sabbath is not mandated by Torah law.]

ד אֵלֶּה מוֹעֲדֵי יהוה מִקְרָאֵי קֹדֶשׁ אֲשֶׁר־תִּקְרְאוּ אֹתָם
ה בְּמוֹעֲדָם: בַּחֹדֶשׁ הָרִאשׁוֹן בְּאַרְבָּעָה עָשָׂר לַחֹדֶשׁ בֵּין
ו הָעַרְבָּיִם פֶּסַח לַיהוה: וּבַחֲמִשָּׁה עָשָׂר יוֹם לַחֹדֶשׁ הַזֶּה חַג

VERSE 4

RABBI JOSEPH B. SOLOVEITCHIK

אֲשֶׁר־תִּקְרְאוּ אֹתָם בְּמוֹעֲדָם – *Which you shall proclaim at their appointed times:* The role of man in the endowment of holiness is a central theme in halakha. For example, if a scribe writes a Torah scroll and does not explicitly note the sanctity of the Tetragrammaton while writing the Name, neither the Name nor the scroll have any sanctity. The loftiness of the text itself makes no difference; if the scribe does not write the Name having in mind that he is writing for the purpose of vesting holiness in the scroll, even the ultimate expression of faith itself, the *Shema*, becomes profane. A Torah scroll is invested with holiness by man. A sacrifice is consecrated by man's designation. Whether sanctity is vested in physical matter or in time, we find few instances where man is not the active participant in the establishment of holiness.

THE LUBAVITCHER REBBE

אֲשֶׁר־תִּקְרְאוּ אֹתָם בְּמוֹעֲדָם – *Which you shall proclaim at their appointed times:* The three pilgrim festivals mark the key points of the agriculture cycle. Allegorically, God refers to the Jewish people as His "produce." Just as a farmer sows grain in the earth in order to reap a much greater return, God "sows" Jewish souls in the physical world in order to enable them to accomplish much more than they can in their spiritual abode. The verse states: *Which you shall proclaim at their appointed times*; we are only able to accomplish this, however, by "designating" the festivals, which here means preparing for them spiritually, so that we can experience their holiness "at their appointed times."

VERSE 5

RABBI SAMSON RAPHAEL HIRSCH

בַּחֹדֶשׁ הָרִאשׁוֹן – *In the first month:* The month of *Aviv* ["spring," referring to the month of Nisan] is the month of redemption, which is why this month begins the year. It is the month which births the Jewish nation: *This month shall be to you the beginning of months; the opening of the year, this month will be for you* (Exodus 12:2). The fourteenth day of this month marks the anniversary of the people's last day of slavery in Egypt. The afternoon of that date transitions into the day of salvation. The waning rays of sunlight on that day herald the arrival of *the Passover sacrifice to the Lord*. This moment returns us to that fateful time when the future of every Israelite household was weighed in the balance, deciding between life or death, slavery or freedom. Therefore, it behooves the nation to repeat the behavior of their ancestors during that original Passover, when the people held out great hope for the birth of their nation. When the family gathers for the sacrifice of the Passover offering, they must sanctify their home and the souls of all of its members. In that way they will return to Israel's original state of receiving God's leadership along with His gift of life and liberty.

4 These are the LORD's appointed times, sacred assemblies, which
5 you shall proclaim at their appointed times. In the first month,
the fourteenth of the month in the afternoon is the time for the
6 Passover sacrifice to the LORD. The fifteenth day of this month
is the LORD's Festival of Unleavened Bread; for seven days you

VERSE 6

HAAMEK DAVAR

חַג הַמַּצּוֹת לַיהוה שִׁבְעַת יָמִים – *The LORD's Festival of Unleavened Bread for seven days:* The holiday is called the "Festival of Unleavened Bread" because the LORD has commanded that matzot, unleavened bread, be eaten during this festival. Similarly, the holiday of Sukkot is so termed, as the verse states: *For seven days shall be the Festival of Tabernacles [hasukkot] to the LORD* (23:34), because of its essence. [That is, these holidays are named after the commandments which define them. During the holiday of Sukkot Jews are commanded to live in huts called Sukkot.] On the other hand, in Exodus a different terminology is used. Shavuot is called the *Festival of the Harvest* (Exodus 23:16), and Sukkot is referred to as *the Festival of Ingathering* (Exodus 23:16). There, the holidays are identified with the time of year in which they are celebrated and not the main activity that characterizes their observance. Let us consider why the text uses different formulae in this chapter's language. Here the verse presents the phrase "seven days" after the term "to the LORD." [The Hebrew reads: *ḥag hamatzot lAdonai shiv'at yamim* – which would translate more literally as "the Festival of Unleavened Bread for the LORD – seven days."] However, in the mention of the Sukkot holiday in our chapter, the order of those words is switched [*ḥag hasukkot shiv'at yamim lAdonai* – literally, "the festival of Tabernacles seven days for the LORD. See 23:34]. The explanation for this relates to my earlier comments (see Exodus 13:6), where I argue that when the Torah refers to *ḥag hamatzot*, that really only describes the first day [the fifteenth of the month, since that is the only time when the Torah demands that matzot be eaten along with the Passover sacrifice]. By contrast, the text always labels the entire week of Sukkot as *ḥag hasukkot* [since the requirement to dwell in the sukka holds for all seven days]. With regard to Passover, we should parse the verse as follows: *The fifteenth day of this month is…the Festival of the Unleavened Bread*, meaning, this one-day holiday "is the LORD's." [This explains why the phrase "is the LORD's" follows immediately after mention of the holiday and interrupts mention of the seven days.] The verse continues: *For seven days you shall eat unleavened bread.* [According to the Sages, it is permissible but not obligatory to eat matza throughout the subsequent six days. The concluding six days do not take the name "Festival of Unleavened Bread."] In contrast, *ḥag hasukkot* – the festival of Sukkot, continues for *shiv'at yamim*, every day of which there is an obligation to dwell in the hut. [The verse regarding Sukkot is therefore phrased to place the name of the holiday continuous with the seven straight days of its observance with the dedication "to the LORD" following only at the end – *ḥag hasukkot shiv'at yamim lAdonai*.]

THE LUBAVITCHER REBBE

חַג הַמַּצּוֹת לַיהוה שִׁבְעַת יָמִים – *The LORD's Festival of Unleavened Bread for seven days:* The two names, "Festival of Unleavened Bread" and "Passover," reflect two different perspectives

CONFRONTING MODERNITY

ז הַמַּצּ֖וֹת לַיהוָ֑ה שִׁבְעַ֥ת יָמִ֖ים מַצּ֥וֹת תֹּאכֵֽלוּ׃ בַּיּוֹם֙ הָֽרִאשׁ֔וֹן
מִקְרָא־קֹ֖דֶשׁ יִהְיֶ֣ה לָכֶ֑ם כָּל־מְלֶ֥אכֶת עֲבֹדָ֖ה לֹ֥א תַעֲשֽׂוּ׃
ח וְהִקְרַבְתֶּ֥ם אִשֶּׁ֛ה לַיהוָ֖ה שִׁבְעַ֣ת יָמִ֑ים בַּיּ֤וֹם הַשְּׁבִיעִי֙ מִקְרָא־
קֹ֔דֶשׁ כָּל־מְלֶ֥אכֶת עֲבֹדָ֖ה לֹ֥א תַעֲשֽׂוּ׃
ט וַיְדַבֵּ֥ר יְהוָ֖ה אֶל־מֹשֶׁ֥ה לֵּאמֹֽר׃ דַּבֵּ֞ר אֶל־בְּנֵ֤י יִשְׂרָאֵל֙ וְאָמַרְתָּ֣
אֲלֵהֶ֔ם כִּֽי־תָבֹ֣אוּ אֶל־הָאָ֗רֶץ אֲשֶׁ֤ר אֲנִי֙ נֹתֵ֣ן לָכֶ֔ם וּקְצַרְתֶּ֖ם
אֶת־קְצִירָ֑הּ וַהֲבֵאתֶ֥ם אֶת־עֹ֛מֶר רֵאשִׁ֥ית קְצִירְכֶ֖ם אֶל־
יא הַכֹּהֵֽן׃ וְהֵנִ֧יף אֶת־הָעֹ֛מֶר לִפְנֵ֥י יְהוָ֖ה לִרְצֹנְכֶ֑ם מִֽמָּחֳרַת֙

THE LUBAVITCHER REBBE *(cont.)*

on the holiday. God wishes to stress the uniqueness of the Jewish people; He therefore focuses on the unleavened bread – matza. Matza recalls how the Jews left Egypt in such haste that they did not have time to let their dough rise, highlighting their implicit faith in God and their willingness to follow Him wherever He directed them to go. We, on the other hand, relate to the holiday as an opportunity to praise God and thank Him; we therefore refer to it as Passover, recalling God's great miracles, particularly when He "passed over" the Jewish houses and brought His plagues only upon the Egyptians.

VERSE 10

RABBI SAMSON RAPHAEL HIRSCH

כִּי־תָבֹאוּ אֶל־הָאָרֶץ – *When you come to the land:* The obligation to donate the omer of barley only comes into effect once the nation enters the land of Israel (Menaḥot 84a). At that point the people will have gained not only their freedom but also national independence, something that is obtained only when that nation successfully settles their territory. It is then that the nation will reap the harvest of their land, and that which their own soil has produced will be properly earned and rightfully possessed. **וַהֲבֵאתֶם אֶת־עֹמֶר** – *Bring the sheaf:* The obligation here is to donate an omer's worth of the first harvest to the Temple. This amount of grain would suffice to feed a single person for one day, a fact we know from an earlier text [discussing the manna]: *This is what the Lord has instructed: Each of you gather as much as you need, an omer for every person* (Exodus 16:16). The sheaves of barley are presented to the priest, who represents the nation in the Temple of the Lord. The overarching philosophy here is that food which the ground has sprouted and which the sun has ripened does not actually belong to the farmer who has nurtured its growth and development. Rather, this grain has been grown for the sake of the Torah of God's Sanctuary, through which every Jew plays their proper role. The primacy of Torah must be asserted such that this dedicated omer must be "the first sheaf of [Israel's] harvest." The reaping of any other grain which will be used for the citizens' personal benefit may not precede this grain, which is dedicated to the Temple.

7 shall eat unleavened bread. The first day shall be a sacred as-
8 sembly for you; you shall perform no laborious work. And you
shall present a fire offering for the LORD for seven days; on the
seventh day there shall be a sacred assembly; you shall perform
no laborious work."
9 10 The LORD spoke to Moshe: "Speak to the Israelites. Say:
When you come to the land that I am giving you and reap its
11 harvest, bring the first sheaf of your harvest to the priest. He
shall display the sheaf this way and that before the LORD for
your acceptance; on the day after the day of rest the priest shall

MESHEKH ḤOKHMA

כִּי־תָבֹאוּ אֶל־הָאָרֶץ – *When you come to the land:* What we see here is further evidence for God's desire that the Israelite people not become completely immersed in the pecuniary and materialistic concerns of agriculture. To counter that tendency, the Creator attached multiple commandments to every stage of the growing process. These practices focus the farmers' thoughts more upon the LORD and less upon the right time to spread manure. The tillers of the soil and the gatherers of the crops are thereby primed toward spiritual perfection as they cleave to the Almighty and put their physical achievements in perspective. Thus, God orders the Israelites to donate an omer of grain at the start of the harvest, and to present two special loaves of bread at the festival of Shavuot. When the grains of the field are cut down, the corner of the land should not be touched, but left for the poor to take home. During the actual harvest, fallen gleanings must not be picked up. The fundamental principle here is that during the start, the middle, and the end of the harvesting activities, our productive enterprise is devoted to the LORD and our products are dedicated to the poor. Fruit and grain must be granted to the impoverished, an attitude which will instill compassion and kindness in the hearts of the owners. That in turn will bring the Israelite to the state of contentment and perfection necessary for reaching the spiritual heights God has designed for him. It is for this reason that our text repeats the laws of agricultural charity which already appear in Parashat Kedoshim (19:9–10) – it is imperative to instill in our hearts this most basic idea.

VERSE 11

SHADAL

מִמָּחֳרַת הַשַּׁבָּת – *On the day after the day of rest:* According to *The Kuzari* [by Rabbi Yehuda Halevi, in 3:41 of that book], we should concede to the Karaites that the term *mimoḥorat hashabbat* probably should be taken at face value as meaning on the day after the Sabbath of Creation [that is, on Sunday]. Nevertheless, some of our judges and the Sanhedrin believed that the text mentions "the day after *shabbat*" only as an instance of when the grain could be cut, not when it was required to be cut. This verse gives the nation license to cut the omer of barley on any day they want, and it was the men of the Sanhedrin who established that this should be undertaken on the second day of Passover. The reader should understand that Rabbi Avraham Ibn Ezra's verbose presentation on this matter is

יב הַשַּׁבָּת יְנִיפֶנּוּ הַכֹּהֵן: וַעֲשִׂיתֶם בְּיוֹם הֲנִיפְכֶם אֶת־הָעֹמֶר
יג כֶּבֶשׂ תָּמִים בֶּן־שְׁנָתוֹ לְעֹלָה לַיהוָה: וּמִנְחָתוֹ שְׁנֵי עֶשְׂרֹנִים
סֹלֶת בְּלוּלָה בַשֶּׁמֶן אִשֶּׁה לַיהוָה רֵיחַ נִיחֹחַ וְנִסְכֹּה יַיִן
יד רְבִיעִת הַהִין: וְלֶחֶם וְקָלִי וְכַרְמֶל לֹא תֹאכְלוּ עַד־עֶצֶם
הַיּוֹם הַזֶּה עַד הֲבִיאֲכֶם אֶת־קָרְבַּן אֱלֹהֵיכֶם חֻקַּת עוֹלָם
טו לְדֹרֹתֵיכֶם בְּכֹל מֹשְׁבֹתֵיכֶם: וּסְפַרְתֶּם לָכֶם יט

SHADAL *(cont.)*

merely circumlocution, since that commentator fundamentally agrees with *The Kuzari* on this issue: The term *shabbat* in this verse should be understood literally, as referring to the Sabbath. Still, the Torah does not actually insist that the Omer be cut and brought on a Sunday; the ritual of waving the grain can be performed on any day of the week – the Sabbath is only mentioned as an example. This is how Ibn Ezra understands the term *lirtzonekhem* ["for your acceptance," that is, whenever you want – *rotzeh*].

RABBI SAMSON RAPHAEL HIRSCH

מִמָּחֳרַת הַשַּׁבָּת – *On the day after the day of rest:* We must confess that nowhere does the Torah refer to a festival day [a *yom tov*] as *shabbat*. [The difficulty here is that according to tradition the Omer is cut and presented on the day following the first day of Passover, that is, on the sixteenth of Nisan. Outside sects, however, have claimed that the term *shabbat* should be taken literally, as "the Sabbath," which means that the barley has to be donated the day after that, namely, on Sunday. *Shabbat* is translated here as "day of rest" to support the rabbinic reading that it refers to the first day of Passover, on which we rest.] Furthermore, although the text refers to "the day after the day of rest," it does not specify whether this means the first day of the festival or the last. This is despite the fact that the seventh day also bears the nature of a *shabbaton*. [The seventh and final day of Passover is observed as a holiday and a day when we cease from most productive labors. The term *shabbaton* is not actually used in the context of Passover. Verse 8 employs the phrase *mikra kodesh* to refer to the last day of the festival, as the text does in verse 7 regarding the first day. Curiously, both festival days associated with Sukkot, which share the same level of sanctity as their corresponding days on Passover, are called *shabbaton* in verse 39.] Naphtali Herz Wessely argues that if the Torah had intended for the Omer to be brought on the day after the seventh day of Passover, it would not have used the term *mimoḥorat hashabbat*, but *mimoḥorat heḥag* [the day after the entire seven-day festival]. Perhaps we can explain the Sages' approach to the language in this verse with the following consideration. The previous sentence identifies the Omer as "the first sheaf of your harvest," a description which teaches that it is forbidden to harvest any grain from the new crop before the Omer barley has been offered, or has at least been reaped. A subsequent text reads: *Until that day, until you bring this sacrifice to your God, you shall eat no bread or roasted grain or ripe grain* [23:14. This verse refers to the prohibition to partake of any of the new crop until the specific day of the Omer offering has passed]. Put together,

12 display it. On the day you display the sheaf this way and that,
you shall offer a yearling sheep without blemish as a burnt of-
13 fering to the LORD. Its grain offering shall be two-tenths of
an ephah of fine flour mixed with oil, a fire offering for the
LORD, a pleasing aroma; and its libation shall be a quarter of
14 a hin of wine. Until that day, until you bring this sacrifice to
your God, you shall eat no bread or roasted grain or ripe grain.
This is an everlasting statute throughout your generations, in
15 all your dwellings. And from the day you bring the

RABBI SAMSON RAPHAEL HIRSCH *(cont.)*

we learn that the fields must be allowed to rest until the day of the Omer has passed. Even though the grains stand ripe on their stalks, their harvest must wait; they may not be cut down and eaten. This cessation of agricultural activity can also be called a *shabbat*, as the Torah later states in the context of the Sabbatical Year, when the land lies fallow: *But the seventh year shall be to the land a Sabbath of complete rest, a Sabbath to the LORD* (25:4). Based on this, the fifteenth of Nisan represents the last day of rest and idleness of the land, a form of Sabbath. Therefore, the sixteenth, which is the day the Omer is reaped and brought to the Temple, is called *mimoḥorat hashabbat* – the day after the cessation of work. [Hence the word *shabbat* does not mean "the day that is *yom tov*," but a period of inactivity, which culminates with the first day of *yom tov*.]

HAAMEK DAVAR

מִמָּחֳרַת הַשַּׁבָּת – *On the day after the day of rest:* The phrase refers to the day after the first Passover *yom tov* ["festival," meaning, the day after the fifteenth of the month. The author asks why this terminology is chosen to describe the date]. The Torah refers to this day as *shabbat* because in this context, where we are discussing Temple offerings, there is no essential difference between the Sabbath and the festivals. On both of these occasions, specific obligatory sacrifices are brought that are mandated due to the days themselves, whereas vow and freewill offerings may not be brought then. And despite the fact that there is still a distinction between the Sabbath and the festivals with respect to the burnt offering of appearance [*re'iya*] and the pilgrimage [*ḥagiga*] offering [a peace offering, both of which are only brought on the festivals and not on the Sabbath], that still represents only a single detail. In general, in the context of sacrifices, it is fitting to call a festival *shabbat*. Outside the Temple, however, the terminology of *shabbaton* serves to distinguish festivals from the Sabbath. The word *shabbaton* teaches that the extent of forbidden labors normally operative on the Sabbath is curtailed, and that certain labors related to food preparation are permitted on festivals.

VERSE 15

HAKETAV VEHAKABBALA

וּסְפַרְתֶּם לָכֶם – *You shall count for yourselves:* The term *lakhem* ["for yourselves"] does not appear here merely as a superfluous flourish, which is the first impression one gets. Rather,

CONFRONTING MODERNITY

מִמָּחֳרַת הַשַּׁבָּת מִיּוֹם הֲבִיאֲכֶם אֶת־עֹמֶר הַתְּנוּפָה שֶׁבַע

HAKETAV VEHAKABBALA *(cont.)*

this reflexive pronoun holds a critical place in this sentence. The term teaches that these seven weeks are not meant to be counted purely to keep track of the number of days that have passed, which is what the masses generally think. Rather, the act of counting the Omer days is intended as a mechanism for improving the quality of every facet of the Jew's life, both the theoretical and the practical. The language here recalls God's original summons to Avraham: *Go [lekh lekha, literally, "go for yourself"] – from your land, your birthplace, and your father's house – to the land that I will show you* (Genesis 12:1). The reflexive pronoun *lekha* within that command also connotes that the "going" is not just for the sake of what is accomplished by the migration but that this "going" also holds an advantage and benefits the person being addressed. Indeed, Rashi comments on the verse that this migration will be for your good and to your benefit. The following verse makes this point explicitly: *I will make you a great nation, and I will bless you and make your name great. You will become a blessing* (Genesis 12:2). In the present context, God instructs the Israelites to count forty-nine days from the Omer until Shavuot as part of a schedule of self-improvement. The nation should use those seven weeks to sanctify and to purify themselves as best they can, cleansing their hearts from inherent desires and base thoughts. For when the Torah says to count, it does not simply require the people to reckon the number of days and weeks between point A and point B. Instead, it is encouraging the nation to contemplate their lives and the providence which governs them, as in the verse which states: *When You number my every step, You do not even wait for my sin* (Job 14:16), and the verse *Is it not true that He watches my ways and counts my every step?* (Job 31:4). The meaning of these declarations is not the assertion that the Almighty tallies people's steps, but to state that God observes the nature of man's every movement. We find a similar phenomenon in the obligations discussed earlier in the book: *When the man with the discharge is purified of it, he shall count seven days for his purification* (15:13) and: *When the woman's discharge ends, she shall count seven days; after that, she will be purified* (15:28). Again, there is no purpose to marking these days just to note the passing of time; the aim is to identify the quality of these periods and note whether or not they are free of bodily issue. And so it is in our case: The Torah hereby commands the people to take stock of themselves, to calculate which elements of their character they wish to preserve and what wicked dimensions need to be expunged. No action should be taken until the person has carefully weighed his personality and determined which parts are good and which are bad. In this sense the exercise of *sefirat ha'omer* [counting the seven weeks] is akin to measuring out a prescription – one must calculate the amount of medicine he is to ingest to ensure its efficacy.

RABBI SAMSON RAPHAEL HIRSCH

וּסְפַרְתֶּם לָכֶם – *You shall count for yourselves:* The Torah commands its adherents to count the days of the calendar starting from the date of their national liberation and independence. What does this tell us if not that this impressive accomplishment is not the end point but just the beginning of Israel's national aspirations? This counting provides the nation with

sheaf of the wave offering, the day after the day of rest, you shall

RABBI SAMSON RAPHAEL HIRSCH *(cont.)*

a method geared toward attaining these elevated purposes. By counting seven weeks, the people activate the educational power of seven Sabbaths on their daily and working lives. On seven successive Sabbaths Israel is to accept the reign of the LORD's kingship, which essentially means acknowledging that the world, which sometimes appears to be controlled by man and which sometimes rules over him, is actually under the complete command of the Almighty, Creator of the Universe. Through this counting the Jewish people will reflect and come to realize that our political emancipation along with our physical possession of territory which enables and forms the basis for our independence and self-determination must be purified seven times over with the spiritual ideal exemplified and lived-out through the Sabbath. It is only following that process that the Israelites will be capable of commemorating that achievement that the counting leads to. As we have said, the reckoning begins from the moment of the nation's redemption and acquisition of their land [under Yehoshua's command, the Israelites entered the land of Israel on the tenth of Nisan, just prior to the celebration of Passover], and carries toward the true purpose of national liberation and settlement of the promised land. For those were only preliminary steps for receiving and realizing God's Torah. It should be clear to all that the acceptance of the Torah requires preparation, that which must be readied by the Sabbath. For what is the fundamental meaning behind the seventh day if not the submission of man to the will of the LORD, and the joyous recognition and agreement to bow in service to Him? The reader will remember that the creation of the Sabbath preceded the nation of Israel, and the holy day's reintroduction to Israelite history came [when God mandated the Sabbath's observance just after the salvation from Egypt, as described in Exodus chapter 16] before the revelation of the Torah. Through the cessation of labor on the holy day the Israelites are trained to subordinate their own immediate needs to the will of the Almighty. The Sabbath liberates a person from his obsessive anxiety over his livelihood. It is thus the Sabbath which enables the nation to transform their freedom into servitude of the LORD as His nation.

MESHEKH ḤOKHMA

וּסְפַרְתֶּם לָכֶם מִמָּחֳרַת הַשַּׁבָּת – *The day after the day of rest you shall count for yourselves:* According to the Zohar, the purpose of this counting is to spiritually prepare the nation of Israel for receiving the Torah. This counting should be compared to that of the *zava*. [If a woman has a genital discharge unrelated to menstruation she is termed a *zava*. Once the discharge ends, she counts seven days before being permitted to have relations with her husband. That count is mandated by the Torah and shares much in common with the Omer count. *When the woman's discharge ends, she shall count seven days; after that, she will be purified.* See 15:28. The *Meshekh Ḥokhma* is utilizing the symbolic idea that the revelation on Mount Sinai was akin to a wedding which united the people of Israel and God. In both cases a counting period anticipates the union and also marks the sloughing off of impediments that hampered the union.] Now, of course, the primary purpose of accepting the Torah is to observe the commandments therein. The only reason that the LORD executed a face-to-face encounter with the people of Israel was to demand that the nation fulfill

טז שַׁבָּתוֹת תְּמִימֹת תִּהְיֶינָה: עַד מִמָּחֳרַת הַשַּׁבָּת הַשְּׁבִיעִת
תִּסְפְּרוּ חֲמִשִּׁים יוֹם וְהִקְרַבְתֶּם מִנְחָה חֲדָשָׁה לַיהוָה:

MESHEKH ḤOKHMA *(cont.)*

the law of the Almighty forever after. The main thing is this: Even when the Israelites are sighing and moaning under the travails of their exile, as they endure the scattered nature of their existence and their assimilation into the nations, they must still adhere to every detail of the Torah's statutes. The Jews must steadfastly distinguish themselves from the gentiles in all ways of life based on the dictates of our holy Torah. This is exactly what the text means when it states: *Be holy to Me, for I the Lord am holy, and I have set you apart from all other peoples to be My own* (20:26). Therefore, God decrees that this count start from Israel's day of respite. [This verse marks the beginning of the Omer count as *the day after the day of rest* referring to the day after the first day of Passover, meaning, on the sixteenth of Nisan. In what sense is the first day of Passover understood to be a "day of rest," a *shabbat*? And why is that terminology used here?] Some commentators explain the word *shabbat* to be referring to the first day of Passover based on this verse, which uses the verb *tashbitu*, related to *shabbat*, in referring to the removal of unleavened bread: *For seven days you shall eat unleavened bread. By the first day you shall have removed [tashbitu] leaven from your houses* (Exodus 12:15). For even though leavened bread may be eaten throughout the year and need not be avoided, during the Passover festival this food is barred from Israel's borders. This represents a key instruction for Israel to accept the Torah and to observe it especially when they are absorbed into foreign environments. The Israelites will thereby be able to maintain their identity. [Thus, the counting of the Omer begins from the day that the Israelites have distanced themselves from the diet that they maintain throughout the year. That in turn teaches us that when the Jewish people find themselves embedded among the nations of the world, they too must remove themselves from what they are used to, namely, the gentiles. It also relates to the idea that we must be a separate and distinct nation and uniquely attracted to and attracted by those we are permitted to marry.]

RABBI JOSEPH B. SOLOVEITCHIK

וּסְפַרְתֶּם לָכֶם מִמָּחֳרַת הַשַּׁבָּת – *The day after the day of rest, you shall count for yourselves:* Judaism is not only an experience, but also a way of thinking, a *modus cogitandi*. Mathematics and physics stand mainly for a methodology, a singular way of interpreting nature: quantification of the qualitative contents, converting the latter into a relational system, or the duplication or bifurcation of reality. The laws are the results of this singular mode of thinking. The same is true of halakha. The latter requires disciplined thought. It has its own unique approach to reality – both physical and spiritual. It has its own method of forming value judgments and moral norms. And, truthfully, halakhic logic, our methodology, does not lag behind most modern methods of philosophical analysis. As far as the arts of defining, formulating, inferring, categorizing, and systematizing are concerned, we are as progressive as the most advanced formal logic. Of course, the halakhic way of thinking and valuing manifests itself in action, in laws pertaining to the external deeds and inner impulses. However, what lies at the root is Torah, a divine mode of thinking in all its

16 **count for yourselves seven complete weeks. To the day after the seventh week, you shall count fifty days; and then you shall**

RABBI JOSEPH B. SOLOVEITCHIK *(cont.)*

strangeness and otherness. Counting is symbolic of our halakhic thinking, in that both demand precision and continuity. The mathematical series is a continuous one. There is a systematic transition from one to another; one cannot leap from position to position. Our halakhic thinking behaves in a similar manner; it is orderly, precise cognition. There is no arbitrariness and no haphazard conclusions; logical necessity reigns supreme. An erroneous count, or omission of one position, suspends the whole count. One cannot jump from three to five; one must move though position four. In a word, halakhic thinking is like mathematical thinking. Each detail is extremely important. The Jew who approaches Mount Sinai to receive the Torah is rooted in the ancient past, while he or she is at the same time committed to a future which is pre-experienced as a reality. One's mind is precise and exact, pedantic as to the component parts, and also beholds an exalted vision of the whole. All this is symbolized by counting the Omer. A slave who is capable of appreciating each day, of grasping its meaning and worth, of weaving every thread of time into a glorious fabric, quantitatively stretching over the period of seven weeks but qualitatively forming the warp and woof of centuries of change, is eligible for Torah. He has achieved freedom. Qualitative-time consciousness is comprised of two elements. First, the appreciation of the enormous implications inherent in the fleeting moments of the present. No fraction of time, however infinitesimal, should slip through the fingers, left unexploited; for eternity may depend upon the brief moment. Second, qualitative-time consciousness involves the vicarious experience, while in the present, of the past and future. No distance, however removed, should separate one's time consciousness from the dawn of one's group or from the eschatological destiny and infinite realization of one's cherished ideals.

VERSE 16

RABBI SAMSON RAPHAEL HIRSCH

תִּסְפְּרוּ חֲמִשִּׁים יוֹם – *You shall count fifty days:* During this period the Israelites count forty-nine days, which comprise seven sets of seven days each, at the end of which they enter the fiftieth day in a transformed state. For during those seven weeks, a person completely sloughs off his constrained, limited self, immersed and dependent on an impure sensualism, and on that fiftieth day, he emerges pure and ready to embrace ethical freedom. It is in this sense that the fiftieth year of the agricultural cycle corresponds to the fiftieth day of the Omer counting. The function of the Jubilee Year is the rejuvenation of the Jewish nation based on the foundation of internal social freedom. In a similar vein, the fiftieth day of the annual reckoning contributes to the nation's inherent moral freedom, to the freedom of the people and to their external independence. For it is only under those conditions that Israel can properly receive its Torah from the hands of the Lord, on the route to developing complete liberty and independence. And even though national freedom can be received through passive means, simply as a gift from the Almighty, the version of ethical freedom that we strive for can be achieved only through diligent effort. That is the goal of the seven-week project.

יז מִמּוֹשְׁבֹתֵיכֶם תָּבִיאוּ ׀ לֶחֶם תְּנוּפָה שְׁתַּיִם שְׁנֵי עֶשְׂרֹנִים
יח סֹלֶת תִּהְיֶינָה חָמֵץ תֵּאָפֶינָה בִּכּוּרִים לַיהוָה: וְהִקְרַבְתֶּם
עַל־הַלֶּחֶם שִׁבְעַת כְּבָשִׂים תְּמִימִם בְּנֵי שָׁנָה וּפַר בֶּן־בָּקָר
אֶחָד וְאֵילִם שְׁנָיִם יִהְיוּ עֹלָה לַיהוָה וּמִנְחָתָם וְנִסְכֵּיהֶם אִשֵּׁה
יט רֵיחַ־נִיחֹחַ לַיהוָה: וַעֲשִׂיתֶם שְׂעִיר־עִזִּים אֶחָד לְחַטָּאת
כ וּשְׁנֵי כְבָשִׂים בְּנֵי שָׁנָה לְזֶבַח שְׁלָמִים: וְהֵנִיף הַכֹּהֵן ׀ אֹתָם
עַל לֶחֶם הַבִּכֻּרִים תְּנוּפָה לִפְנֵי יְהוָה עַל־שְׁנֵי כְּבָשִׂים קֹדֶשׁ

THE LUBAVITCHER REBBE

תִּסְפְּרוּ חֲמִשִּׁים יוֹם – *You shall count fifty days:* The lesson of "counting" and "polishing," the process of spiritual refinement and maturation, continues past Shavuot and applies the whole year round. We should always be counting; every day, even every hour, must be valued as an opportunity for further spiritual growth. At the end of each day, we should know what we accomplished that day and what still remains to be done.

VERSE 17

SHADAL

מִמּוֹשְׁבֹתֵיכֶם תָּבִיאוּ – *You shall bring...from your dwellings:* The phrase "from your dwellings" serves to include any place within the whole land of Israel as a possible location from which to bring this offering. You are instructed to find the site, anywhere in the land, where the grain first ripens. It is there that the people should harvest the "first produce to the Lord."

THE LUBAVITCHER REBBE

סֹלֶת תִּהְיֶינָה חָמֵץ תֵּאָפֶינָה – *Fine flour baked with leaven:* Indeed, in the Temple the overwhelming majority of grain offerings are unleavened, and even the few leavened ones that are prescribed are explicitly prohibited from being offered on the altar. In contrast, when we leave the Temple precincts in order to fulfill our divine mission in the material world, which is naturally apathetic or even antagonistic to divine consciousness, we have to evince at least a modicum of self-assertion in order to impose our divine vision on a reluctant or inimical world. Therefore, outside the Temple, leavened bread is permitted.

VERSE 19

RABBI SAMSON RAPHAEL HIRSCH

וּשְׁנֵי כְבָשִׂים בְּנֵי שָׁנָה לְזֶבַח שְׁלָמִים – *And two yearling male sheep as peace sacrifices:* As the text states, these two sheep are sacrificed as peace offerings. In fact, these represent the only instance of communal peace offerings across the spectrum of the sacrificial system. [Peace offerings are offered by individuals as a thanksgiving offering or as a voluntary donation. The donors partake of their meat. This is the only instance when the peace offerings are brought by the community and when, consequently, none of the meat goes to an individual Israelite. Instead, all the meat is consumed by priests.] And because there

17 present a new grain offering to the Lord. You shall bring two
loaves of bread from your dwellings made with two-tenths of
an ephah of fine flour baked with leaven, as a wave offering: first
18 produce to the Lord. Together with the bread, you shall present seven unblemished yearling male lambs, one young bull,
and two rams – these shall be a burnt offering for the Lord
with their grain offering and their libations, a fire offering, a
19 pleasing aroma to the Lord. And you shall offer one he-goat as
a purification offering and two yearling male sheep as peace sac-
20 rifices. The priest shall display them this way and that with the
bread of the first produce as a wave offering before the Lord
together with the two sheep; they shall be holy to the Lord

RABBI SAMSON RAPHAEL HIRSCH *(cont.)*

is a pair of these animals, they relate not only to the nation as a corporate unit but also to the individual citizens. [In certain other offerings, a single animal represents the nation. In this case, representing the collective nation with more than a single animal expresses the awareness of the individuals that compose the nation.] We should also say that the two sheep serve as a complement to the two special leavened loaves that are also brought on Shavuot. Together, these sheep and breads express a celebration of national independence. This independence is won through the agency of Torah instruction and for the sake of furthering that selfsame Torah, and is vouchsafed by a land dedicated to Torah. Inside this framework of a land and polity dedicated to Torah the individual Jew becomes worthy of his leavened loaf, the bread of independence. At the same time the sheep represent the citizen's joy and holy pleasure living under the watchful eye of the Lord, his shepherd. These two sheep are brought by the nation as a whole and not, as is usually the case, by private Israelites. As such, they do not represent the happiness of the individual donor with his lot. Rather, the animals remind the nation as a whole of its collective destiny, to continue to vouchsafe joy and prosperity to its citizens through an independent land and polity which adhere scrupulously to the Torah. For this reason, this offering is considered *kodshei kodashim* [an offering of a greater level of sanctity, which cannot be eaten by non-priests]. For, like the burnt offering and the purification offering, which relate to the atonement of improper actions, this offering too relates to the highest sanctity of our actions [and less to the joy and prosperity that our proper actions are meant to bring about]. As such, the sheep are slaughtered in the north of the courtyard, and their flesh can be eaten only by males of the priesthood, just like the purification offering.

VERSE 20

HAAMEK DAVAR

עַל לֶחֶם הַבִּכֻּרִים – *With the bread of the first produce:* What is the significance of the term *al* in the phrase *al leḥem habikkurim* ["with the bread of the first produce"? The Hebrew word *al* literally means "on," but here it is translated in context as "with"]. In the present context the word *al* connotes "for the purpose of." It means that these two sheep, together with

כא יִהְיוּ לַיהוָה לַכֹּהֵן: וּקְרָאתֶם בְּעֶצֶם ׀ הַיּוֹם הַזֶּה מִקְרָא־
קֹדֶשׁ יִהְיֶה לָכֶם כָּל־מְלֶאכֶת עֲבֹדָה לֹא תַעֲשׂוּ חֻקַּת עוֹלָם

HAAMEK DAVAR *(cont.)*

the loaves, were waved back and forth for a purpose [that the *Haamek Davar* will explain later in this comment]. The verse concludes with the clause, *they shall be holy to the Lord*, referring to the two sheep which have been displayed, or more specifically to the specimens' sacrificial parts. Subsequently the flesh of these animals shall "belong to the priest," as will the breads. Now, why indeed are these peace offerings displayed in this manner along with the loaves of the first produce? In the case of a standard peace offering, the animal's breast and thigh are waved together with the fats such that both together are dedicated to God. Following this display, the breast and thigh are granted to the priests while the fats are dedicated to the altar. In the present instance as well, the two male sheep are taken up with the two loaves in order to unite them into one whole which is altogether dedicated to the Lord. [This constitutes another sense for the preposition *al* – "together with."] With regard to both the bread and the animals, parts of these items are raised onto the altar, and parts are given as gifts to the priests. Such is the straightforward meaning of the text. Now we will also bring a homiletic sense. On the festival of Shavuot the nation brought these peace offerings along with leavened bread (see 23:17). The purpose was to ward off unfavorable winds and damaging dew, which harm the yearly harvest. [The author refers to the following explanation from Menaḥot 62a: Rabbi Ḥama bar Ukva taught in the name of Rabbi Yosei bar Ḥanina: The priest extends the lambs forward and brings them back in order to request a halt to harmful winds which come from all directions. Similarly, he raises and lowers the offerings in order to put a halt to harmful dews that descend from above.] This too is the significance of the practice on Sukkot, when individual Israelites bring their thanksgiving offerings, which are a type of peace offering, accompanied by leavened bread [ten out of the forty loaves brought with this sacrifice are leavened]. Such was the Israelite practice on Sukkot, to propitiate God for favorable rains in the upcoming season, as we have discussed above [see comments on 22:29]. The difference, however, is that on Sukkot each Israelite would offer his own sacrifice, because the amount of rain that falls on a person's fields is a function of his merits. And so do the Sages proclaim (Taanit 9a): Rain falls on behalf of individuals. By contrast, wind and dew are not a function of individuals and their merits but of the nation as a whole. This explains why the present peace offering, which is a uniquely communal peace offering, was brought and waved on Shavuot. It sought to entreat the Lord on behalf of the entire nation for favorable winds and dew, which affect the nation as a whole.

VERSE 21

MESHEKH ḤOKHMA

מִקְרָא־קֹדֶשׁ יִהְיֶה לָכֶם – *It shall be a sacred assembly for you:* The religion of God is replete with both commandments which bind the Jewish people to their Father in heaven, and mandates which strengthen the ties between individual Israelites. The former category includes such things as tzitzit, tefillin, and mezuza, and the latter category includes practices

21 **and belong to the priest. On that day you shall make a procla-**
mation; it shall be a sacred assembly for you; you shall perform
no laborious work. This is an everlasting statute throughout

MESHEKH ḤOKHMA *(cont.)*

like neighborly kindness, *terumot*, and tithes. This distinction sets up an interesting way to understand the difference between the Sabbath and festivals. The Sabbath aligns more with those commandments which connect individuals and families directly to God. Certain instructions regarding the Sabbath were given in connection with the gathering of manna in the desert: *Understand that the Lord has given you a Sabbath – that is why He gave you two days' bread on the sixth day. You shall each rest where you are: let no man depart from where he is on the seventh day* (Exodus 16:29). The emphasis here is on the private celebration of the Sabbath of each family alone in their own home. Indeed, it is forbidden on the Sabbath to transport anything between the public domain and the private domain, a halakha which further isolates people. The preparation of food is also not permitted on this day. Therefore, every Israelite person is encouraged to spend the Sabbath alone at home, sitting and studying the Torah. The contemplation of God's word stands as the primary means available to a person for connecting to the Almighty. As each person contemplates and connects to the truth of a common living God, we become united indirectly through that God and common purpose. Thus does the midrash (Vayikra Rabba 4:6) state: Because the sons of Yaakov all serve the same God, they are referred to as a single soul. The Torah's festivals, by contrast, present a much more direct mechanism for bringing the Israelite people together. Food preparation beyond the basic necessities for one's family is halakhically justified, because a Jew needs to be prepared lest a thousand guests suddenly descend upon one's home. Indeed, the Talmud (Pesaḥim 46b) rules that one is not punished for cooking on a festival just for the purpose of preparing food for consumption on the next day, since the excess food can always be served to company. Furthermore, the celebration of the pilgrimage festivals centers around Israelites traveling from around the country to the city of Jerusalem, where they rejoice in the holiday along with new and old acquaintances alike. It is for this reason that objects may be carried outside on a festival and why all food preparation is permitted then. For if these activities were banned [as they are on the Sabbath], the people would find it difficult to bond and to unite with each other. An examination of the festival of Passover, however, reveals its nature as something in between the full-blown national unity of a festival and the more isolated, family-centered nature of the Sabbath. The reader will recall that the name of the holiday derives from a singular moment in the exodus narrative: *It is the Passover [pesaḥ] sacrifice to the Lord who passed over [pasaḥ] the houses of the Israelites in Egypt, for He struck the Egyptians; but our homes, He spared* (Exodus 12:27). At that time, the Israelites were not fully integrated into a complete nation. Indeed, the people were more aptly described as solitary households, as the verse emphasizes: *None of you shall leave by the doors of your houses until morning* (Exodus 12:22). Nevertheless, the Hebrews were all truly acting in concert, as every family brought its own Passover sacrifice and everybody shared the same belief in a single Master – the Lord, God of Israel. Thus, the Passover offering comes with this particular guideline: Only persons who had

בְּכָל־מוֹשְׁבֹתֵיכֶם לְדֹרֹתֵיכֶם: וּבְקֻצְרְכֶם אֶת־קְצִיר אַרְצְכֶם כב
לֹא־תְכַלֶּה פְּאַת שָׂדְךָ בְּקֻצְרֶךָ וְלֶקֶט קְצִירְךָ לֹא תְלַקֵּט
לֶעָנִי וְלַגֵּר תַּעֲזֹב אֹתָם אֲנִי יהוה אֱלֹהֵיכֶם:

MESHEKH ḤOKHMA *(cont.)*

preregistered for the offering may partake of it. It was not permitted to just show up and join in. Here we see the nature of Passover being organized around individual homes, but also all those homes being united through their common devotion to God. We see another reflection of the alignment of Passover with the more atomized nature of the Sabbath rest in the way the start of the Omer count is expressed by the Torah: *The day after the day of rest [mimoḥorat hashabbat], you shall count for yourselves seven complete weeks* (23:15). This verse instructs us to start counting on the sixteenth of Nisan, which is the day after the first day of Passover, which is referred to here as a *shabbat*. Following the first day of Passover, the nation begins a seven-week journey whose goal it is to more fully integrate these individual households into a nation. From marking the Passover side by side, they are to prepare for the moment when they will be forged into a nation that will experience together the great revelation at Har Sinai at the culmination of this seven-week period on Shavuot. Significantly, this chapter repeats the commandments of agricultural charity in the context of this seven-week, nation-building, process of Omer-counting: *And when you reap the harvest of your land, do not reap to the edge of your field or gather the gleanings of your harvest. Leave them for the poor and for the migrant* (23:22). Of course, in all nations of the world the citizens are tied to each other as a matter of common custom and interests. These unifying aspects derive from a shared history, or from the unique features of a common geography and temperament. Not so, for the children of Yaakov. Our national bond is so mighty because we have been given God's Torah as our code of law. And through the consensus leadership and interpretive authority of our Sages, we continue to direct our lives in obedience to God's precepts and thereby enjoy God's providence. God continues to contract with His people and to give them authority to interpret His will. We thus have the following surprising midrash (Devarim Rabba 2:14), which reports this conversation: When ministering angels assemble before God and ask him when Rosh Hashana will fall out this year and when Yom Kippur will, God says to them: Why are you asking Me? Let us all descend to the Israelite court, and there we will learn what days they have determined for these festivals. Indeed, where do we find the first example of rabbinic activity and the nation's obligation to follow the understandings of their religious leaders as part of the Oral Law? This event occurred on the sixth day of Sivan [as Israel prepared to receive the Torah at Mount Sinai]. Thus does the Talmud (Shabbat 87a) interpret the text which reads: *The Lord said to Moshe, "Go to the people and consecrate them today and tomorrow; let them wash their clothes and be ready for the third day, for on that third day the Lord will descend on Mount Sinai before all the peoples' eyes"* (Exodus 19:10–11). Moshe added one day [for the people to get ready to meet God] based on his own perception. We have here a case of the Israelite people becoming united in this magnificent way [that is, through the general acceptance of rabbinic authority, which has the effect of connecting the nation to the Almighty].

22 your generations in all your dwellings. And when you reap the
harvest of your land, do not reap to the edge of your field or
gather the gleanings of your harvest. Leave them for the poor
and for the migrant; I am the LORD your God."

THE LUBAVITCHER REBBE

מִקְרָא־קֹדֶשׁ יִהְיֶה לָכֶם – *It shall be a sacred assembly for you:* While both Passover and Sukkot are celebrated for an entire week, Shavuot lasts only one day. This is because Shavuot is the annual reliving of the revelation that took place when the Torah was given on Mount Sinai. This experience of God's infinite essence transcends the limitations of time; we therefore do not require a full week to assimilate it into the complete array of our emotions.

VERSE 22

OR HAḤAYYIM

וּבְקֻצְרְכֶם אֶת־קְצִיר אַרְצְכֶם – *And when you reap the harvest of your land:* The reader might ask: Why does the Torah repeat these agricultural laws of charity in the midst of its discussion about the festivals? [The mitzvot of *leket*, which is leaving fallen stalks for the poor, and *pe'ah*, which is leaving a corner of the crops uncut, were already commanded in 19:9.] Perhaps the presence of these rules here teaches that even the field from which the omer of barley has been cut is subject to the obligations of *leket* and *pe'ah*. For we might have reasoned that since the first produce of this area was harvested for an offering, that should exempt the rest of the field from these requirements. Our verse teaches us that the matter is otherwise; even in a field used for a Temple offering, the laws of *leket* and *pe'ah* apply. [There are three primary obligations that limit the thoroughness with which a farmer can harvest his crops. These obligations ensure that there are remainders for the poor. The third obligation, *shikheḥa*, is not mentioned here. This command, mentioned in Deuteronomy 24:19, instructs a farmer who has forgotten a bundle of grain in his field, not to go back and get it but to leave it for the poor.] The supposed importance of this field might lead us to consider its exemption from *leket* and *pe'ah*, for these two laws represent functions of the field alone. But since the commandment of *shikheḥa* is a function of the farmer's behavior, we would have never have reasoned in the first place that the importance of this field, providing as it does a Temple offering, exempts its farmer from the obligation of *shikheḥa*. And since we never thought to exempt the farmer of this field from that command, the Torah had no reason to disabuse us of that erroneous thought like it did with *leket* and *pe'ah*.

RABBI SAMSON RAPHAEL HIRSCH

וּבְקֻצְרְכֶם אֶת־קְצִיר אַרְצְכֶם – *And when you reap the harvest of your land:* At this time of year, the nation of Israel takes its first cutting of the year from its fields and heads off with it to the Sanctuary of the Torah. At the religious center the grain is displayed before the LORD. And on the anniversary of God's gift of the Torah to His people, Israel presents two special loaves at the site. It is then that they renew their vow to fulfill their obligations as the nation of the Torah. For the bounty that God has granted to the nation as a whole needs

כג כד וַיְדַבֵּר יְהוָה אֶל־מֹשֶׁה לֵּאמֹר: דַּבֵּר אֶל־בְּנֵי יִשְׂרָאֵל חמישי
לֵאמֹר בַּחֹדֶשׁ הַשְּׁבִיעִי בְּאֶחָד לַחֹדֶשׁ יִהְיֶה לָכֶם שַׁבָּתוֹן

RABBI SAMSON RAPHAEL HIRSCH *(cont.)*

to provide every member of this nation with honor and dignity. In the land of Israel, governed by the Torah, the produce which the soil yields and the fruits of the people's labor are not reserved for the benefit of propertied citizens alone. Rather, even the dispossessed and the migrants share a claim in the harvest. Their sustenance and well-being is an obligation for the rich and a right for the poor. This is the relationship and duty that emerges from the commandment to leave the field's corner uncut [*pe'ah*] and to leave the dropped stalks for the poor [*leket*. Both of these commands are related here in the context of the Omer count and barley harvest].

VERSE 24

SHADAL

זִכְרוֹן תְּרוּעָה – *A commemoration with the sounding of the ram's horn:* The purpose of "the sounding of the ram's horn" is to ensure that everybody knows that this day is Rosh Hashana. In a similar way, the shofar is blown at the start of the Jubilee Year to announce the advent of that significant year. And in order to distinguish the sounding of the ram's horn in the Jubilee Year from all other years, when it is heard on Rosh Hashana, the Torah orders us to blow the shofar announcing the Jubilee on Yom Kippur (see 25:9).

RABBI SAMSON RAPHAEL HIRSCH

יִהְיֶה לָכֶם שַׁבָּתוֹן – *You shall observe a day of rest:* The careful reader will have detected a difference between the present verse and the introductions of the other festivals. In connection with Passover, we read: *In the first month, the fourteenth of the month…is the time for the Passover sacrifice* (23:5). Yom Kippur shares a similar pattern: *The tenth day of this seventh month is the Day of Atonement* (23:27). Sukkot as well: *From the fifteenth day of this seventh month…shall be the festival of Tabernacles to the Lord* (23:34). In each of these three cases the Torah begins by defining the nature of the day and then details the method of its observance. The present verse does not follow that pattern. It jumps right into the method, *you shall observe a day of rest*, and only afterward defines the nature of the day, declaring it *a commemoration with the sounding of the ram's horn*. This distinct introduction to the seventh month reflects the different nature of the observances to be held this month. We are not called upon to recall and commemorate any sort of gifts that the Lord has bestowed upon us this month. The words *you shall observe a day of rest* introduce the holidays of Tishrei, on which we are called upon to cease the normal flow of activity, and instead we are invited to be reflective, look inward, and work on ourselves.

HAAMEK DAVAR

זִכְרוֹן תְּרוּעָה – *A commemoration with the sounding of the ram's horn:* The following text appears in Parashat Behaalotekha: *When you go to war against an enemy who is attacking you in your land, you shall blow short blasts [vehare'otem – terua] on the trumpets to be*

23 24 Then the LORD spoke to Moshe: "Tell the Israelites: On the ḤAMISHI
first day of the seventh month, you shall observe a day of rest, a
commemoration with the sounding of the ram's horn, a sacred

HAAMEK DAVAR *(cont.)*

remembered before the LORD your God, to be delivered from your enemies. And on your days of rejoicing, your festivals and New Moons, you shall blow [utkatem – tekia] the trumpets over your burnt offerings and your peace offerings. They will be a reminder of you before your God. I am the LORD your God (Numbers 10:9–10). Now, we have a well-known tradition (Rosh Hashana 34a) which states that every sounding of a *tekia* is accompanied by a *terua*, and every *terua* is preceded and is followed by a *tekia*. [Thus, the familiar pattern of shofar blasts on Rosh Hashana are all variations of *tekia-terua-tekia*. But why does the Torah refer only to a *terua* in the context of war, and mentions just the *tekia* regarding moments of happiness?] The Torah mentions only the *terua* of war and the *tekia* of happiness in allusion to the differing purposes of these clarion calls. In celebratory times the primary emotion is happiness, and that is expressed by the triumphant *tekia* sound. Nevertheless, *teruot* are also blown in order to temper that jubilation and arouse a sense of caution, reflection, and restraint. For the nation must guard themselves against overconfident triumphalism and take care lest they create a situation where their "joy ends in misery" (Proverbs 14:13). In contrast to that, during difficult times of war and other tribulations, the main sounding is of the *terua* [which encourages Israel to be on guard and watch their behavior]. In that case it is the *tekia* which serves as the complementary call. Despite the worry and fear which might grip the people with the onset of war, the confidence of the *tekia* sound is meant to dispel despair and hold out hope for redemption. Returning to our own text we find that the Torah refers to Rosh Hashana as a *yom terua* [in Numbers 29:1, which states: *It shall be for you a day of the horn's sounding*. [Although the English translates a generic "horn's sounding," the Hebrew signals the fear-inducing *terua* sound.] For the main goal of a *terua* is to shake up the listeners, break through their blithe confidence that all is well, and serve them with *hit'orerut* [a wake-up call] on the Day of Judgment. The present text expands its description of Rosh Hashana to *zikhron terua – a commemoration with the sounding of the ram's horn*. The word *zikhron* [translated as "commemoration" from the root meaning "memory"] adds emphasis to the fact that the day is not just about sounding the horn correctly but about being reflective and recalling the purpose of what a *terua* sound is meant to evoke. This explains why the verse first introduces the festival this way: *You shall observe [yihyeh lakhem, literally, "it shall be for you"] a day of rest*. The message here is piercing and direct: Take an hour of respite from all of your labor and your worldly concerns and just contemplate that this day is a *zikhron terua*. In this way the Torah distinguishes its presentation of Rosh Hashana from that of all the other holidays where we find the usage of the term *shabbaton*, meaning simply: a day of rest, when no strenuous labor may be performed. However, in its discussion of Rosh Hashana the text adds the term *lakhem* [in its phrase *yihyeh lakhem shabbaton*] to stress that every Israelite should reserve time for himself or herself during the day to focus on the purpose of the *terua* and allow that to arouse feelings of penitence and a need for personal improvement.

כה זִכְרוֹן תְּרוּעָה מִקְרָא־קֹדֶשׁ: כָּל־מְלֶאכֶת עֲבֹדָה לֹא תַעֲשׂוּ
כו וְהִקְרַבְתֶּם אִשֶּׁה לַיהוה: וַיְדַבֵּר יהוה אֶל־מֹשֶׁה
כז לֵּאמֹר: אַךְ בֶּעָשׂוֹר לַחֹדֶשׁ הַשְּׁבִיעִי הַזֶּה יוֹם הַכִּפֻּרִים הוּא
מִקְרָא־קֹדֶשׁ יִהְיֶה לָכֶם וְעִנִּיתֶם אֶת־נַפְשֹׁתֵיכֶם וְהִקְרַבְתֶּם
כח אִשֶּׁה לַיהוה: וְכָל־מְלָאכָה לֹא תַעֲשׂוּ בְּעֶצֶם הַיּוֹם הַזֶּה כִּי

VERSE 27

OR HAḤAYYIM

מִקְרָא־קֹדֶשׁ יִהְיֶה לָכֶם – *It shall be a sacred assembly for you:* What is the significance of the phrase *yihyeh lakhem* ["it shall be for you"]? It is understood that even if Israel does not consecrate this tenth day of Tishrei as Yom Kippur, and even if the people do not afflict themselves on that day, nevertheless, the day will remain the Day of Atonement irrespective of the people's behavior. [That is, the essence of the day itself holds the power of absolution and serves to cleanse Israel of its sins, whether they are aware of this power or not.] Therefore, when the people do consecrate the day with a sacred assembly and do observe its various deprivations, those actions "shall be for you" – *yihyeh lakhem.* Since they are not needed to trigger the day's absolving powers, they are counted entirely to the credit of the people observing the fast and gathering in sacred assembly.

HAKETAV VEHAKABBALA

יוֹם הַכִּפֻּרִים הוּא – *It is the Day of Atonement:* Why does the Torah label this day "*Yom Hakippurim*" in the plural [literally, "the day of atonements"] instead of using the singular, *yom kappara* [day of atonement]? The language reflects the existence of different levels of repentance. There are, for example, some people who return to God out of a sense of fear that they will be punished for their transgressions. In such a circumstance the person's sin is not completely erased from the record, but leaves an impression on the offender's soul. As our Sages teach (Yoma 86b), when one expresses remorse for deliberate iniquities, they are treated as inadvertent errors [but the repentance does not erase the sin entirely]. On the other hand, there are people for whom repentance is an expression of devotion to God and an embrace of the truth. The trespasses of such a man or woman are wiped clean, as the Sages also teach in that same discussion: Intentional violations, when abandoned, are considered as merits. [With this higher form of repentance intentional violations are erased entirely and even converted to merits.] Thus, in recognition of these two forms of contrition, the day is called *Yom Hakippurim* to reflect its double nature.

RABBI SAMSON RAPHAEL HIRSCH

בֶּעָשׂוֹר לַחֹדֶשׁ הַשְּׁבִיעִי הַזֶּה – *The tenth day of this seventh month:* We must explain why the Day of Atonement is situated within the seventh month of the Jewish calendar. The explanation for this takes into account the events that are marked in the preceding months, for those are times which lay the groundwork for a person's relationship with the Almighty. In the first month of the year [Nisan] the Israelite leaves the land of Egypt along with his ancestors. In the third month [Sivan] he stands at attention by the foot of Mount Sinai together with

25 assembly. You shall perform no laborious work, and you shall
26 bring close a fire offering to the Lord." The Lord
27 spoke to Moshe: "Hear: the tenth day of this seventh month
is the Day of Atonement. It shall be a sacred assembly for you,
and you shall afflict yourselves and bring a fire offering to the
28 Lord. You shall perform no work at all during this entire day,

RABBI SAMSON RAPHAEL HIRSCH *(cont.)*

generations of his people to receive the Torah of his life from the Lord. What emerges is that the year until this point is characterized for this person as a Jewish year, and hence atonement can only be effected in the seventh month. It is only then that he can receive God's ultimate kindness and the highest degree of graciousness that a person can hope for. But consider a Jew who treats Tishrei as the first month of the year. He is a person who has not commemorated Passover and Shavuot; he has not celebrated redemption or revelation. And hence this Israelite does not count his year according to the Jewish calendar – he expresses no awareness or concern for the messages of Nisan and Sivan. How can such a person, who has spent the past six months in a non-Jewish frame of mind, have the temerity to request absolution when Yom Kippur comes around? That attitude is nothing less than blasphemy against the Lord and a deception against himself. Note as well that the Day of Atonement occurs only on the tenth day of the seventh month, after a week and a half of preparation. The beginning of the month is marked by *a commemoration with the sounding of the ram's horn* (23:24), which takes place on the first day. That experience is intended to create a change in the person's priorities. The call of the shofar should free the Israelite to return to the Lord. The subsequent nine days are devoted to effecting this personal transformation, one that pulls the person closer to his God. It is in that state of readiness that the Jew approaches the Almighty on the tenth day of the seventh month; he is a new man, imbued with a new character. It is only thus that the tenth of the month can truly serve as this person's Yom Kippur, because, as our Sages teach (Shevuot 13a), this holy day will effect atonement only for those people who have repented for their sins. Recall that the tenth of Tishrei was the date on which God related to Moshe the extent of His graciousness. It was on that day that the prophet received the new set of tablets containing the same message that was written on the original, broken tablets. These newly inscribed stones signaled to the nation the Lord's great compassion, thereby ensuring the people of a future that they had almost squandered with the sin of the golden calf. As a result of that moment the tenth of Tishrei is stamped throughout history as a time characterized by the Almighty's great kindness. For the tremendous truth was then revealed that even one who has fallen into the deepest pit of transgression can return to God and thereby merit His grace through recognition of one's sin, remorse, and repentance. Such kindness is manifested by God's willingness and ability to erase a person's past and ignore the consequences of his behavior. And this is why the tenth day of the seventh month stands as historical evidence of the power of atonement.

VERSE 28

HAAMEK DAVAR

כִּי יוֹם כִּפֻּרִים הוּא – *For it is the Day of Atonement:* This is the reason that you must afflict yourselves. For it is the Day of Atonement, and fasting is advantageous to absolution.

כט יוֹם כִּפֻּרִים הוּא לְכַפֵּר עֲלֵיכֶם לִפְנֵי יהוה אֱלֹהֵיכֶם: כִּי כָל־
הַנֶּפֶשׁ אֲשֶׁר לֹא־תְעֻנֶּה בְּעֶצֶם הַיּוֹם הַזֶּה וְנִכְרְתָה מֵעַמֶּיהָ:
ל וְכָל־הַנֶּפֶשׁ אֲשֶׁר תַּעֲשֶׂה כָּל־מְלָאכָה בְּעֶצֶם הַיּוֹם הַזֶּה
לא וְהַאֲבַדְתִּי אֶת־הַנֶּפֶשׁ הַהִוא מִקֶּרֶב עַמָּהּ: כָּל־מְלָאכָה לֹא
לב תַעֲשׂוּ חֻקַּת עוֹלָם לְדֹרֹתֵיכֶם בְּכֹל מֹשְׁבֹתֵיכֶם: שַׁבַּת שַׁבָּתוֹן
הוּא לָכֶם וְעִנִּיתֶם אֶת־נַפְשֹׁתֵיכֶם בְּתִשְׁעָה לַחֹדֶשׁ בָּעֶרֶב
מֵעֶרֶב עַד־עֶרֶב תִּשְׁבְּתוּ שַׁבַּתְּכֶם:

RABBI DAVID TZVI HOFFMAN

כִּי יוֹם כִּפֻּרִים הוּא – *For it is the Day of Atonement:* Why did God select the tenth day of the month of Tishrei to serve as Israel's annual Day of Atonement? We are persuaded by the approach of [the gentile scholars] Ewald and Keil. Yom Kippur acts as preparation for the holiday of Sukkot. The latter in turn represents a time of great happiness, when the people celebrate the blessings and the bounty that the Lord has granted them. At the end of gathering in the harvest, the nation wishes to express its gratitude and to rejoice in the proximity of the Almighty. However, such acknowledgement is possible only after the Israelites have reconciled themselves to God through a renewed commitment to God's ways and having been purged of transgression. Only following this Day of Atonement can the people unite with the Lord, having absolved themselves of sin. Through remorse and repentance, fasting and cessation of labor, the nation becomes worthy of cleaving to God, ready and able to experience the pure joy of the upcoming festival.

The matter may be compared to the state of the Israelites in Egypt when God commanded them to prepare, on the tenth of Nisan, a lamb for their Passover sacrifice in anticipation of their departure from the land on the fifteenth. Similarly, here, the tenth of Tishrei serves as groundwork for the upcoming festival of Sukkot on the fifteenth. Nevertheless, this approach should not be interpreted as robbing Yom Kippur of its independent significance. Rather, our point is that this powerful time of self-reflection and abnegation, this Day of Atonement, on which the nation as a collective takes stock and effects self-transforming change, is positioned on the calendar so that the results of this process of repentance feed directly into the joy that follows on the festival of Sukkot. God agrees on this wondrous day, through His mercy and power, to wipe out the consequences of our sins, conditioned upon our proper repentance. This is the historical legacy of this gift of atonement.

VERSE 31

MESHEKH ḤOKHMA

כָּל־מְלָאכָה לֹא תַעֲשׂוּ – *No work at all may you perform:* Even though the text twice forbids the performance of labor on Yom Kippur (see 23:28, 31) and twice demands that the Israelites fast on this day (see 23:27, 32), note that the Torah states only after its warning against labor that *this is an everlasting statute throughout your generations*. Why did the Torah add

for it is the Day of Atonement, there to make atonement for
29 you before the Lord your God. Anyone who does not afflict
himself for this whole day shall be severed from his people,
30 and if anyone performs any work during this whole day, I will
31 annihilate that person from among his people. No work at all
may you perform; this is an everlasting statute throughout your
32 generations in all your dwellings. It is a Sabbath of complete
rest for you, and you shall afflict yourselves from the evening of
the ninth day of the month: from evening to evening shall you
observe your Sabbath."

MESHEKH ḤOKHMA *(cont.)*

this emphasis to forbidden labor but not in the context of affliction? It would seem that this omission is an allusion to the Yom Kippur that took place when the First Temple was consecrated. According to the Talmud (Yoma 9a) the nation did not fast during Shlomo's celebrations of that structure; only labor was restricted, not the enjoyment of food. Thus, the description of an "everlasting statute" was applied only to work performed on the Day of Atonement but not to fasting, because on one significant occasion fasting was not required. As such, it was not correct to describe this prohibition as demanded "throughout your generations."

VERSE 32

RABBI SAMSON RAPHAEL HIRSCH

מֵעֶרֶב עַד־עֶרֶב – *From evening to evening:* The halakha forbids fasting on the ninth of Tishrei with a force equivalent to that for the requirement of fasting on the tenth. This duality, that makes eating and drinking on one day just as important as not eating and not drinking on the next day, is a hallmark of a Jewish ethic. [This verse seems to require fasting from the evening of the ninth of Tishrei even though Yom Kippur is limited to the tenth of Tishrei: *You shall afflict yourselves from the evening of the ninth day of the month*. The Sages instead interpret this verse to mean that it is as important to eat on the ninth in preparation for Yom Kippur as it is to fast on the tenth.] As the Sages (Yoma 81b) expressed the point: The Torah grants credit to a person who eats and drinks on the ninth of the month as if he has fasted on both the ninth and the tenth of Tishrei. Now, if fasting were a unidimensional attempt to appease a wrathful god, if the purpose of self–inflicted pain and discomfort was to somehow mollify the rage of a vengeful deity, then it would seem that the more pain the better. If the point is self-flagellation, then clearly double the affliction from a two-day fast is more of what such a god wants from us. But our conception of this day, expressed by the halakha requiring our eating on the ninth, completely gives lie to this immoral and anti–Jewish thinking. The Jewish God is not ever interested in our pain. On the contrary, fasting serves a positive purpose. Indeed, the mandate to eat prior to Yom Kippur reveals the fast's true significance, which is to focus our thoughts on repentance and atonement, our task of the moment. That is something that can be effected only on the day of the tenth, which explains why fasting is limited to that day.

לג לד וַיְדַבֵּר יְהוָה אֶל־מֹשֶׁה לֵּאמֹר: דַּבֵּר אֶל־בְּנֵי יִשְׂרָאֵל לֵאמֹר ששי
בַּחֲמִשָּׁה עָשָׂר יוֹם לַחֹדֶשׁ הַשְּׁבִיעִי הַזֶּה חַג הַסֻּכּוֹת שִׁבְעַת
לה יָמִים לַיהוָה: בַּיּוֹם הָרִאשׁוֹן מִקְרָא־קֹדֶשׁ כָּל־מְלֶאכֶת עֲבֹדָה
לו לֹא תַעֲשׂוּ: שִׁבְעַת יָמִים תַּקְרִיבוּ אִשֶּׁה לַיהוָה בַּיּוֹם הַשְּׁמִינִי
מִקְרָא־קֹדֶשׁ יִהְיֶה לָכֶם וְהִקְרַבְתֶּם אִשֶּׁה לַיהוָה עֲצֶרֶת

VERSE 34

RABBI SAMSON RAPHAEL HIRSCH

בַּחֲמִשָּׁה עָשָׂר יוֹם לַחֹדֶשׁ הַשְּׁבִיעִי הַזֶּה – *From the fifteenth day of this seventh month:* The first day of this month is observed as "a commemoration with the sounding of the ram's horn" (23:24), a time for startling and rousing the public to abandon its sinful ways. Next, on the tenth day of the month, Israel stands before the Lord as a community impoverished by a dearth of merit, a people whose right to endure is a tenuous one. And then comes the fifteenth of Tishrei during which we experience the fruits of Yom Kippur's atonement. On this festival we build our huts throughout the land as an expression of security in the Almighty's continued protection. Simultaneously, we take in our hands representative fruits from the soil of the land of Israel to celebrate before God in recognition of our continued existence and creative capacity. For although our sinful past had prevented us from full living and productivity, Yom Kippur erased that hindrance, whereupon Sukkot celebrates the return of the land's vitality and fecundity. On Sukkot the nation merits the greatest of earthly assets, the ability to celebrate in the presence of the Lord. Notice that where the Torah mandates a single day to sound the shofar, and just one day of fasting and repenting, it demands that the Israelites devote seven full days to the festival of Sukkot. Thus, we are granted a full cycle of days to rejoice in our huts with the produce of the land. Such is the typical and true Torah approach: A person need not wallow in a broken and humbled spirit; rather, he should enjoy his life with a strong and upright posture, the correct deportment for the Jewish person. It is with positivity and purpose that the Jew traverses the course of the annual calendar. It is with a head held high that he faithfully fulfills his Torah obligations.

HAAMEK DAVAR

בַּחֲמִשָּׁה עָשָׂר יוֹם לַחֹדֶשׁ הַשְּׁבִיעִי הַזֶּה – *From the fifteenth day of this seventh month:* Let us contrast the present verse, which uses the term *hazeh* ["this," in the phrase *from the fifteenth day of this seventh month*] to a subsequent text, listing the festivals' additional sacrifices, which omits this word: *The fifteenth day of the seventh month shall be a sacred assembly for you* (Numbers 29:12). This disparity can be explained by the fact that in our paragraph the Torah mentions the offerings of the individual (see 23:37–38) along with its discussion of the four species (see 23:40), both of which are efficacious in producing rain over the coming year. Furthermore, all of this is dependent on the sounding of the shofar on the Rosh Hashana that precedes it. Thus does the psalmist write: *Sound the ram's horn on the New Moon, on our feast day [ḥagenu] when the moon is full* (Psalms 81:4), where the feast day in question is that of

33 34 The Lord spoke to Moshe: "Tell the Israelites: From the fif- SHISHI
teenth day of this seventh month, for seven days shall be the
35 Festival of Tabernacles to the Lord. The first day shall be a
sacred assembly; on it, you shall perform no laborious work.
36 For seven days you must bring close a fire offering to the Lord.
The eighth day shall be a sacred assembly for you, and you shall
present a fire offering to the Lord. It is an assembly; you shall

HAAMEK DAVAR *(cont.)*

Sukkot. For we find that the term *ḥag* without specification refers to the festival of Sukkot, in contrast to Rosh Hashana, which is never called *ḥag*. What emerges is that the day of Rosh Hashana serves as preparation for the festival of Sukkot, when the heavenly court determines how much water the land is to receive over the coming year. That, of course, has a direct effect on the subsistence of the nation. The prophet refers to this when he writes: *They will not pour wine in offering to the Lord, nor will their sacrifices find favor with Him; like the bread of grievers it will be; all who eat of it will be defiled, for their bread is merely to feed their hunger and will not be brought to the House of the Lord. What then will you offer on festival days, on days of sacrifice to the Lord?* (Hosea 9:4–5). The force of these verses means that since the sacrifices are not being brought for noble purposes, "what then will you offer on festival days?" – that is, on Rosh Hashana, and "what will you offer...on days of sacrifice" – Sukkot. For it is on those days that the sustenance of the nation is determined. Based on all of this we can understand why the current verse identifies Tishrei as "this seventh month": The power of Sukkot is dependent on what is achieved on Rosh Hashana, when the shofar is sounded and the nation is remembered for good before the Almighty. On the other hand, the seventy bulls that are offered over the course of Sukkot (see Numbers chapter 29) correspond to the seventy nations of the world, as the Talmud (Sukka 55b) maintains. And hence, there is no reason for that passage to refer to Tishrei as "this month" [thereby connecting Sukkot to Rosh Hashana which begins the seventh month] since the success of the world's gentiles is in no way conditional upon Israel's behavior on the preceding Rosh Hashana.

VERSE 36

RABBI SAMSON RAPHAEL HIRSCH

עֲצֶרֶת הִוא – *It is an assembly:* The celebration on the eighth day [Shemini Atzeret] not only signals the end of the festivals occurring in the seventh month, it also represents the last holiday of the whole year. [Ḥanukka and Purim, which follow in the ninth and twelfth month respectively, are rabbinic creations.] That fact encapsulates the entire character of Shemini Atzeret: On this day we summon all of the decisions and clarity that we have formulated during the seventh month and indeed over the course of the previous twelve months. This is the moment when we decide to remain within the domain of the divine, and to maintain the spiritual gains that we have labored so hard to acquire. In this way we hope that the religious growth we have heretofore experienced will not diminish or dissipate when our normal lives resume after the holiday. Instead, Israel will hold fast to the renewed bonds that they have forged with the Almighty for the duration of the months

לז הִוא כָּל־מְלֶאכֶת עֲבֹדָה לֹא תַעֲשׂוּ: אֵלֶּה מוֹעֲדֵי יהוה
אֲשֶׁר־תִּקְרְאוּ אֹתָם מִקְרָאֵי קֹדֶשׁ לְהַקְרִיב אִשֶּׁה לַיהוה
לח עֹלָה וּמִנְחָה זֶבַח וּנְסָכִים דְּבַר־יוֹם בְּיוֹמוֹ: מִלְּבַד שַׁבְּתֹת
יהוה וּמִלְּבַד מַתְּנוֹתֵיכֶם וּמִלְּבַד כָּל־נִדְרֵיכֶם וּמִלְּבַד כָּל־
לט נִדְבֹתֵיכֶם אֲשֶׁר תִּתְּנוּ לַיהוה: אַךְ בַּחֲמִשָּׁה עָשָׂר יוֹם לַחֹדֶשׁ
הַשְּׁבִיעִי בְּאָסְפְּכֶם אֶת־תְּבוּאַת הָאָרֶץ תָּחֹגּוּ אֶת־חַג־יהוה
שִׁבְעַת יָמִים בַּיּוֹם הָרִאשׁוֹן שַׁבָּתוֹן וּבַיּוֹם הַשְּׁמִינִי שַׁבָּתוֹן:
מ וּלְקַחְתֶּם לָכֶם בַּיּוֹם הָרִאשׁוֹן פְּרִי עֵץ הָדָר כַּפֹּת תְּמָרִים
וַעֲנַף עֵץ־עָבֹת וְעַרְבֵי־נָחַל וּשְׂמַחְתֶּם לִפְנֵי יהוה אֱלֹהֵיכֶם

RABBI SAMSON RAPHAEL HIRSCH *(cont.)*

to come. [Rabbi Hirsch is playing with the meaning of the word *Atzeret*. This root relates to *otzar*, meaning a treasure or a stored-up resource, and also relates to the word *atzor*, meaning to stop or to prevent from escape. Thus, the spiritual treasures of the entire year are stored up on this last day of the year and hopefully held fast so that they do not dissipate over the mundane days that follow.]

HAAMEK DAVAR

עֲצֶרֶת הִוא – *It is an assembly:* What is the fundamental purpose of the pilgrimage festivals? By instituting these holidays, God wished for the people of Israel to assemble in the city of Jerusalem and to make an appearance in the Temple courtyard there. The goal of such gatherings is in turn for the populace to be exposed to the ethical teachings and wisdom of the priests who greet them. After all, Jerusalem stands as the primary source of the word of the Lord, and the Israelites are thus meant to learn the proper ways to behave in their private lives when they return to their communities. Now, during the first days of the Sukkot festival the pilgrims were occupied with the appearance [*re'iya*] offering, the pilgrimage [*ḥagiga*] offering, and the various freewill and vow sacrifices they had brought with them on their journey. These latter peace offerings were brought by the people during the intermediate days of the holiday to fulfill the commitments they had undertaken during the previous months. But by the time of the last day of the festival, the Israelites had by and large discharged their sacrificial obligations. It was only the rare person who had not yet brought his pilgrimage offering on the first day who was now required to offer it on the last day. Furthermore, if an Israelite had neglected to donate his freewill or vow offerings on any of the intermediate days, he would not be permitted to do so on the eighth day, which is also a festival [that is, a *yom tov*, when nonobligatory sacrifices are not accepted]. It is only the *shalmei simḥa* [a peace offering of joy] which is brought on this day. What this means is that all of Israel was free on the last day to attend Torah lessons and to receive rebuke and moral teachings from their spiritual leaders. This then explains why this eighth [*shemini*] day is referred to as Shemini Atzeret. [The *Haamek Davar* is playing

37 perform no laborious work. These are the Lord's festivals,
which you shall proclaim, sacred assemblies to present a fire
offering to the Lord: burnt offering, grain offering, sacrifice,
38 and libations, each on its appointed day; in addition to the
Lord's Sabbaths, and in addition to your gifts and all your offerings in the fulfillment of vows and all the freewill offerings
39 that you give to the Lord. Hear: on the fifteenth day of the seventh month, when you have harvested the land's produce, you
shall celebrate a festival to the Lord for seven days. The first
day shall be a day of rest; the eighth day shall be a day of rest.
40 On the first day you shall take for yourselves fruit of the majestic tree, branches of palm trees, boughs of the leafy tree, and
willows of the brook, and rejoice before the Lord your God

HAAMEK DAVAR *(cont.)*

with the Hebrew meaning of Atzeret, which also means to stop – *atzor*. On this day the people finally stop – *otzerim* – from their busy schedules of mundane affairs and even the busy demands of their sacrificial obligations. They finally have time to assemble in Jerusalem for the sake of hearing words of Torah.]

VERSE 38

HAAMEK DAVAR

מִלְּבַד שַׁבְּתֹת יהוה – *In addition to the Lord's Sabbaths:* The term *milevad* means "prior to." [The term *milevad* is translated here twice as "in addition to," but the *Haamek Davar* understands this term to take on different senses in the verse. The first instance, referring to the Sabbaths, he translates as "prior to." Thus, this verse instructs that the additional [*musaf*] offerings special to the Sabbath are brought "prior to" the festival offerings detailed in the previous verse. This follows the general rule that the more frequently brought sacrifice is offered prior to the less frequent sacrifice. Since the Sabbath offerings are more frequent, they take priority over the festival offerings.] However, the second instance of *milevad*, in the phrase *umilevad mattenoteikhem* ["and in addition to your gifts"], the word means "subsequent to." [That is, the vow and freewill offerings are brought after the festival's additional sacrifices.] This explains the phrase at the end of the verse, *that you give [asher tittenu, literally, "that you will give"] to the Lord*, which is expressed in future tense. [Thus, these freewill offerings will be offered only after the festival offerings of the previous verse are complete.]

VERSE 40

RABBI SAMSON RAPHAEL HIRSCH

וּלְקַחְתֶּם לָכֶם בַּיּוֹם הָרִאשׁוֹן – *On the first day you shall take for yourselves:* On the tenth of the month of Tishrei the Jewish people are commanded to afflict [*le'anot*] their souls. Simultaneously, we admit to the Lord that we are morally impoverished [*aniyyim*], for we have squandered our rights to food and drink, and hence the basic conditions for our continued survival. This acknowledgement of our state, and the confession before the

מא שִׁבְעַת יָמִים: וְחַגֹּתֶם אֹתוֹ חַג לַיהוה שִׁבְעַת יָמִים בַּשָּׁנָה
מב חֻקַּת עוֹלָם לְדֹרֹתֵיכֶם בַּחֹדֶשׁ הַשְּׁבִיעִי תָּחֹגּוּ אֹתוֹ: בַּסֻּכֹּת
תֵּשְׁבוּ שִׁבְעַת יָמִים כָּל־הָאֶזְרָח בְּיִשְׂרָאֵל יֵשְׁבוּ בַּסֻּכֹּת:

RABBI SAMSON RAPHAEL HIRSCH *(cont.)*

Almighty, are what bring us to atonement; they bring a halt to all of the past factors that had threatened to sever our future. But now the nation is summoned to a new level of existence, and we must heed that call and become a part of the Lord's eternal people. The seven days of the Sukkot festival are dedicated to the awareness of a brighter future and the renewed right to live within the nation of God. This stands as the polar opposite of the severance and destruction from the people of Israel [which is a threat expressed for violation of Yom Kippur in verse 30]. Thus, after the Lord calls upon the Israelites to afflict themselves (see 23:27) on the tenth of the month, He issues a very different type of demand regarding the fifteenth of Tishrei: "Take for yourselves." That is the language of renewal of our rights and indeed our duties and hope, as the people go into the fields and gather for themselves the products of God's soil. On the Day of Atonement Israel's lot was affliction and fasting; now we are graced with the greatest possible fate available to man on this earth: the invitation to celebrate in the presence of the Lord. And so does our verse state: *Take for yourselves...and rejoice before the Lord your God for seven days.*

RABBI JOSEPH B. SOLOVEITCHIK

וּשְׂמַחְתֶּם לִפְנֵי יהוה אֱלֹהֵיכֶם – *Rejoice before the Lord your God:* Sukkot is the holiday that is most closely associated with the Oral Law. Only through the Oral Law can we identify the words [in the verse] with an *etrog*. [The Written Law simply lists the "fruit of the majestic tree." It is only through the oral tradition that we can link this majestic tree to the citron fruit known as an *etrog*.] The Sadducees and Pharisees argued about very basic rules involving the Sukkot festival, such as the command regarding the willows and the water libations. Indeed, what is a sukka? What should its height be? The vast majority of the halakhot defining a sukka were transmitted as *halakha leMoshe miSinai* [a tradition passed down directly from Moshe from what he learned orally at Mount Sinai]. Sukkot is therefore the festival of the Oral Law. Sukkot is also the holiday most clearly associated with the concept of joy [*simḥa*] (see Deuteronomy 16:13–14), precisely because of its proximity to Yom Kippur.

The *simḥa* of Sukkot derives from the communal forgiveness of sin that Israel experiences during Yom Kippur. The celebration of that forgiveness actually takes place during Sukkot. What motivated this celebration? There was no wine and no meat at the Celebration of Water Drawing [*Simḥat Beit Hasho'eva*], only water. [On the weekday nights of the intervening days of Sukkot great revelry would take place around the drawing of the water for the next day's water libation.] The celebration was not motivated by a successful harvest. Rather, this joy [*simḥa*] was an expression of the ability to "rejoice before the Lord your God" (Deuteronomy 12:12). When a Jew senses that he is before his God, it makes no difference if the year was a good year or a bad one, if he is poor or rich, comfortable or suffering. If one is "before the Lord" there is *simḥa*: the rejoicing one feels in the shadow of the Divine Presence, symbolized by the *sekhakh* [the loose, dry branches forming the temporary roof] of

41 for seven days. You shall celebrate it as a festival to the Lord for
seven days in the year. It shall be an everlasting statute through-
42 out your generations; celebrate this in the seventh month. For
seven days you shall live in huts. All those native born in Israel

RABBI JOSEPH B. SOLOVEITCHIK *(cont.)*

the sukka. Personal circumstances do not affect this rejoicing; it could be raining or sunny, he may be healthy or in physical pain. When he is "before the Lord" there is only jubilation.

VERSE 41

HAAMEK DAVAR

בַּחֹדֶשׁ הַשְּׁבִיעִי – *In the seventh month:* Since verse 39 has already identified the seventh month as the time for the Sukkot festival, why does this verse repeat this detail: *Celebrate this in the seventh month*? The initial description of the holiday connects it to the agricultural stage: *When you have harvested the land's produce you shall celebrate a festival to the Lord* (23:39). Hence, we might have thought that in the event that the gathering of the harvest has been delayed into the eighth month, Sukkot too should be put off until Marḥeshvan. This was in fact what Yorovam did in his time (see I Kings 12:32). To counter such a proposition, the Torah now emphasizes that the festival must be observed "in the seventh month."

RABBI DAVID TZVI HOFFMAN

וְחַגֹּתֶם אֹתוֹ חַג לַיהוה – *You shall celebrate it as a festival to the Lord:* Just as at the end of its discussion of Yom Kippur the Torah emphasizes that *this is an everlasting statute throughout your generations* (23:31), so too here does the text make a similar statement. In this verse we read: *It shall be an everlasting statute throughout your generations* to stress that the celebration of Sukkot does not depend on the gathering in of the country's crops. The observation of this festival remains an eternal commandment independent of the agricultural circumstances.

VERSE 42

HAAMEK DAVAR

כָּל־הָאֶזְרָח בְּיִשְׂרָאֵל יֵשְׁבוּ בַּסֻּכֹּת – *All those native born in Israel must live in huts:* Why does this verse repeat the injunction to live in huts, stating it first generally and second with reference to the "native born"? This repetition emphasizes that the purpose of living in huts applies to everyone. According to the straightforward meaning of the law, an Israelite must repair from his usual, sturdy, brick-and-mortar home into less stable shelters for the duration of the festival. The lesson to the landed and successful farmers is to not take their prosperity for granted and become indifferent to their independence and security. These happy residents of the land, surrounded as they are by their recently completed homes, must recall that indeed they are not really landowners within Israel, but are more akin to foreigners. Thus does David exclaim: *For to You we are but passersby, mere transients like all our ancestors; our days are like shadows over the earth* (I Chronicles 29:15). Based on this, one might argue that in fact the obligation to live in a sukka falls exclusively on Israelites who possess lands of their own. These are people who have finished gathering in the season's produce; their hearts are full with contentment and joy and in danger of becoming complacent. Whereas, this thinking goes, the

HAAMEK DAVAR *(cont.)*

poor vagrant does not truly require the commandment of the sukka. To counter such a proposition, the Torah emphasizes that *kol ha'ezraḥ* ["all those native born"] – every single native Israelite – must live in a hut in celebration of this festival, landed citizens and migrant workers alike. Thus, when the next verse states: *So that future generations may know that I had the Israelites live in huts when I brought them out of the land of Egypt*, that comment is directed toward the misfortunate elements of society who might not own a parcel of soil within the land of Israel and who might despair of ever enjoying a share of the good life. Hence, these poor people are told that the commandment of the sukka serves to remind the populace that the entire nation lived in huts when God took Israel out of Egypt. And despite such humble and sparse circumstances the Israelites were still able to celebrate in the joy of their emancipation. Thus does God declare: *I am the Lord your God* (23:43), meaning: I constantly direct your history and I will forever protect you; nothing will prevent Me from bestowing My beneficence and My blessing upon the people, even for those who lack a homestead of their own. Living in huts is a reminder that one does not need land to benefit from God's goodness. Let us further consider the text's usage of the term *ezraḥ* in the verse, *All those native born [kol ha'ezraḥ] in Israel must live in huts*. Normally, the word *ezraḥ* comes in contradistinction to the word *ger*, and means a resident and not a foreigner. Here, however, the expansive term "all those native born [*kol ha'ezraḥ*]" means to include everyone, as the Talmud (Sukka 28b) confirms that even *gerim* ["non-native citizens"] must live in huts during the festival. Why then does the Torah imply with this terminology that the commandment devolves primarily upon "native born" Israelites? To understand this point we should note that the text juxtaposes the obligation to dwell in a hut to the instruction to take hold of four species on this same festival [as instructed in verse 40: *On the first day you shall take for yourselves fruit of the majestic tree, branches of palm trees, boughs of the leafy tree, and willows of the brook, and rejoice before the Lord your God for seven days*]. Now, it would seem to us that the Torah should have introduced the requirement of the huts first, in order to explain why this festival is called Sukkot, and only then should it have described the waving of the four plant species, which is an important activity on the day but does not define the name of the holiday. Thus, it is clear that both commandments of the hut and the species are a function of the same central concept which gets at the essence of this festival. I refer the reader to the midrash from Vayikra Rabba (30:2) which is built on this verse: *In Your presence is fullness of joy; at Your right hand, bliss for evermore* [Psalms 16:11. The Hebrew word here translated as "evermore" is *netzaḥ*. In addition to connoting an eternity, the term also carries the meaning of victory. Perhaps the core idea is the reign of an idea that is so powerful that it will be sovereign evermore]. The midrash, based on this verse, describes an Israelite with the four species in hand like a warrior returning victorious from battle. For it was common practice for the valiant soldier to carry a *lulav* and to wave it in triumph. We find such a similar celebratory display recorded in this text which describes the transport of the Ark in the time of David: *And David and all the House of Israel reveling before the Lord with all kinds of instruments of cypress wood, lyres, harps, timbrels, sistra, and cymbals* (II Samuel 6:5). According to Bemidbar Rabba (4:20), celebrants who lacked musical instruments at that procession marched with their branches of palm trees, *lulavim*. Furthermore, as I have already written, the text alludes to the fact that on the

HAAMEK DAVAR *(cont.)*

day of Yom Kippur the Israelite people wage a battle against the spiritual forces of temptation. On Sukkot we celebrate emerging victorious, with divine forgiveness, from that battle against those evil tempters. This metaphor continues with the way that combat soldiers live throughout the time of conflict – the battalions are not billeted in well-furnished homes during their service; they sleep in tents out in the fields. This is why God orders the nation to dwell in huts for the duration of the festival, so that the Israelites might relive the experience of their ancestors who charged out of bondage following the crushing defeat of their enemy. Then too our fathers were like armed fighters girded for confrontation. This is how the Jewish people must always think and act following Yom Kippur: as if they have emerged victorious from war. It is because of all this that the commandments of the *lulav* and the sukka are directed primarily to the native-born citizens of Israel, as I have written in my comments to Parashat Aḥarei Mot. [See the *Haamek Davar* on 16:29. There, he argues that only entrenched members of the nation go out to battle for their homeland; foreigners do not participate in such campaigns.] In conclusion, the practice of dwelling in the sukka holds two purposes for the people of Israel. First, for each individual Hebrew, it serves to strengthen faith and certainty that God provides for human beings' basic needs. This is why God commanded everyone, not just the landed farmers, to displace himself from his permanent home and to live in temporary dwellings for seven days. [As the author explains at the start of this essay, the goal of the sukka is to both temper the self-satisfaction and complacency of the wealthy around their bounty and to give hope to the dispossessed that everyone has access to divine munificence. It is channeled not only through fruit of the field.] Second, the aim of the sukka is to remind the nation, the collective, that the Lord protects them during times of attack, just as Israel emerged victorious from the struggles of the wilderness. Finally, it seems that this dual messaging of the nature of a sukka reflects a well-known tannaitic debate (Sukka 11b): In describing the Israelites' living conditions in the desert, the verse states: *I had the Israelites live in huts when I brought them out of the land of Egypt* (23:43)? Does the word "huts" refer to actual booths made out of wood and canvas, or does it describe the clouds of glory that hovered over the nation during their desert stay? The fact is that both claims are correct. For forty years the Israelite families lived in tent-like huts. [That relates to the author's first interpretation here: Each individual must take to heart the message of the festival on a personal level.] And in addition, the whole congregation was at that time united under the practices of prayer and Torah study that spread as protective clouds above the community. In that way the people were like soldiers who camp in tents during a conflict. [This reflects the general sense of guardianship that God exercised over the entire camp on Israel's behalf.]

MESHEKH ḤOKHMA

בַּסֻּכֹּת תֵּשְׁבוּ שִׁבְעַת יָמִים – *For seven days you shall live in huts:* Within the divine Torah we find some commandments which do indeed demand that a person defy his natural inclinations. Others complement human inclinations and serve to enhance and purify the person's desires. We will return below to an expression of that idea. Now, the mandate to dwell in the sukka for seven days sits firmly within those obligations that counter our natural desires. Consider the farmer who has just spent his entire summer out in the fields. After preparing

מג לְמַעַן יֵדְעוּ דֹרֹתֵיכֶם כִּי בַסֻּכּוֹת הוֹשַׁבְתִּי אֶת־בְּנֵי יִשְׂרָאֵל
מד בְּהוֹצִיאִי אוֹתָם מֵאֶרֶץ מִצְרָיִם אֲנִי יהוה אֱלֹהֵיכֶם: וַיְדַבֵּר
מֹשֶׁה אֶת־מֹעֲדֵי יהוה אֶל־בְּנֵי יִשְׂרָאֵל:

MESHEKH ḤOKHMA *(cont.)*

the ground by plowing the soil, sowing the seeds, and hoeing the weeds, this man works hard to reap his crops and bundle the grain. Later he toils to haul the produce out of the fields, whereupon he fills his granaries with the harvest. How does this Israelite feel when the process is finally complete? Surely, he is proud of the fruits that his efforts have borne, but he is also looking forward to a long and well-deserved rest in the comfort of his home. And yet, it is precisely at this moment that the Torah demands that he leave the four walls of his sturdy, secure, and luxurious house, and move into a flimsy, shaky, and uncomfortable hut that is exposed to all the elements he has just escaped! Such a mandate goes completely against human nature and feelings, at least from a material perspective. It is for this reason that our Sages maintain that that the festival [*ḥag*] of Sukkot should be celebrated for the Lord, such that the sukka itself should be treated with the same sanctity as a pilgrimage [*ḥagiga*] offering [that is, the sacrifice offered on this holiday]. The hut should be considered as holy, meaning that for the duration of the week, it is forbidden to derive any benefit from the wood of the booth [including both its walls and its roofing. In other words, because the Israelite's relocation to the sukka is not really something desirable from his perspective, the mitzva should be viewed as a total dedication to the will of God, distinct from the will of the person, who wants something different]. Nevertheless, as I have mentioned above, there are some commandments which do align with human nature. The precise and excellent details of these laws take a natural human inclination and direct it in a way that accords with divine wisdom. For example, when people celebrate the end of the harvest season they universally fashion garlands for themselves from the grasses of the fields and hold up grain stalks to rejoice in the success of the earth's plants. Still, the Torah guides this natural and universal expression of celebration and limits the type and extent of plants to four specific species in accordance with divine wisdom. Take hold of these, says the text, *and rejoice before the Lord your God for seven days*. Now, there is a practical distinction between the way we treat the wood of the sukka, which is a mitzva that counters our natural inclination, and the way we treat an *etrog*, which aligns with our natural desires. It is for this reason that use of wood from a sukka is entirely off limits, for God's name has been associated with it, making it akin to a sacrifice. [It is elevated outside the realm of human uses.] But an *etrog* is not entirely off limits; it may be smelled though not eaten. It is set aside to be used for a mitzva, but without associating it with the name of the Lord. In a similar vein, a sukka, which is counter to natural inclinations, requires increased mental preparation in order to properly designate it as a mitzva object, whereas the four species requires less. [The unnatural sukka requires increased intentionality, but a more natural member of the four species is ready to use as is.] This is why the Torah uses the verb *taaseh* ["you shall do," or "strive"] in the context of Sukkot: *You shall keep [taaseh] the Festival of Tabernacles for seven days* (Deuteronomy 16:13). This imperative gets translated into the halakhic

43 **must live in huts, so that future generations may know that I had
the Israelites live in huts when I brought them out of the land of
44 Egypt; I am the LORD your God." Thus Moshe announced the
LORD's appointed times to the Israelites.**

MESHEKH ḤOKHMA *(cont.)*

requirements of a suitable sukka. It must be built for the purpose of *sukkot* and cannot be repurposed from something already existing. However, when it comes to the four species, whose incorporation into the holiday celebrations is completely instinctive and welcome, there is no real effort required to use them. In fact, the four items may be taken up even if they are not bound together [which is the ideal way to hold them]. Or it may be slightly pruned in order to make it acceptable on *yom tov* itself. [Thus, one is permitted to pluck off berries from a myrtle branch which has too many berries to render it fit for use even on the festival day. This is permitted only after the fact and only from a branch which is no longer attached to a tree.]

THE LUBAVITCHER REBBE

בַּסֻּכֹּת תֵּשְׁבוּ שִׁבְעַת יָמִים – *For seven days you shall live in huts:* The sukka is unique among the Torah's commandments in that it is the only one that we physically enter; the sukka surrounds us on all sides. This property of the sukka is a physical manifestation of the divine energy that the sukka embodies: God's transcendence.

VERSE 44

RABBI DAVID TZVI HOFFMAN

וַיְדַבֵּר מֹשֶׁה אֶת־מֹעֲדֵי יהוה – *Thus Moshe announced the LORD's appointed times:* In their Targum's of this verse both Onkelos and Yonatan ben Uziel write: Moshe announced the *seder* ["sequence," or "arrangement"] of the LORD's appointed times and taught the material to the Israelites. It would seem that these Aramaic translators saw in this concluding verse the following allusion: In addition to the laws of the festivals that appear in the body of the Torah text, God taught our teacher Moshe the rules regarding the determination of the New Moon and the establishment of the holiday times. The prophet learned about the intercalation of the years and conveyed all of this information to the nation. Based on this understanding, we can attribute to the words "thus Moshe announced" a reference to the Oral Law regarding Israel's calendar of festivals. Now, the fact is that it is difficult to explain the straightforward meaning of this verse. Why does the text emphasize specifically here that Moshe transmitted God's statutes to the people of Israel? Curiously a parallel statement also serves to summarize the laws of the festivals in the book of Numbers, *And Moshe told the Israelites all that the LORD had commanded him* (Numbers 30:1). We find a similar declaration earlier in our book with respect to the priestly guidelines: *Moshe told this to Aharon, his sons, and all the Israelites* (21:24). In that context the Torah reveals that although the content of that passage had been given directly to the priests, Moshe transmitted it to the nation as well. However, the presence of this concluding sentence in the present case is surprising. Has not verse 2 already instructed Moshe: *Speak to the Israelites. Say: These are the LORD's appointed times*? [That is, it was clear that Moshe was supposed to transmit the descriptions of the

כד א ב וַיְדַבֵּר יְהוָה אֶל־מֹשֶׁה לֵּאמֹר: צַו אֶת־בְּנֵי יִשְׂרָאֵל וְיִקְחוּ שביעי
ג אֵלֶיךָ שֶׁמֶן זַיִת זָךְ כָּתִית לַמָּאוֹר לְהַעֲלֹת נֵר תָּמִיד: מִחוּץ
לְפָרֹכֶת הָעֵדֻת בְּאֹהֶל מוֹעֵד יַעֲרֹךְ אֹתוֹ אַהֲרֹן מֵעֶרֶב עַד־
ד בֹּקֶר לִפְנֵי יְהוָה תָּמִיד חֻקַּת עוֹלָם לְדֹרֹתֵיכֶם: עַל הַמְּנֹרָה
הַטְּהֹרָה יַעֲרֹךְ אֶת־הַנֵּרוֹת לִפְנֵי יְהוָה תָּמִיד:
ה וְלָקַחְתָּ סֹלֶת וְאָפִיתָ אֹתָהּ שְׁתֵּים עֶשְׂרֵה חַלּוֹת שְׁנֵי עֶשְׂרֹנִים

RABBI DAVID TZVI HOFFMAN *(cont.)*

holiday to the nation.] Furthermore, why does the text not include a corresponding exclamation at the end of chapter 20 [following the list of forbidden unions and the punishments for violating those laws]? The meaning behind this issue can be found within the rabbinic writings of the Sifra, which maintain that Moshe taught the Israelites about each festival during the course of the year, when the time came for their celebration. This point is made even more clear by the Sifrei on Deuteronomy 16:1: After Moshe learned about the holiday cycle at Mount Sinai he presented the rules to the people of Israel and then reviewed the relevant laws with the advent of each festival. According to this approach our verse means that Moshe told the nation about these special times immediately after he himself had learned about them. He did this even though he knew he would have to revisit the material throughout the year. Nevertheless, at first Moshe taught his disciples about the holidays in a general sense and then elaborated on each topic separately.

CHAPTER 24, VERSE 2

OR HAHAYYIM

וְיִקְחוּ אֵלֶיךָ שֶׁמֶן זַיִת זָךְ – *To bring you pure olive oil:* Why does the text juxtapose the description of the candelabrum to its discussion of the Sukkot festival? Perhaps this relates to the teaching offered by our Sages regarding the candelabrum in the next verse, *Aharon shall set it up outside the curtain of the testimony in the Tent of Meeting to burn each night* (24:3). Why is the location of the candelabrum related to the curtain of the testimony? It is evident that the Almighty had no need for the light of the Tabernacle lamps. After all, during the nation's forty-year sojourn in the wilderness the people were guided by the illumination of God Himself! Rather, the verse alludes to the fact that the candelabrum serves as a testament to the entire world that the Lord's presence continues to shine among Israel. [This was evident through the miracle of the eternal flame, the western lamp of the candelabrum which burned eternally.] In their comments to that statement, the Tosafists clarified that God did not illuminate the desert trek with the ordinary light of the sun. Instead, through the miraculous clouds of glory, God hid the scorching sun, but also provided comfortable ambient lighting. Through this divine light, the Israelites were able to glimpse that which is normally concealed and could see through opaque containers. This then was the clever message that the Almighty wished to convey by shifting from the topic of Sukkot directly to the Tabernacle lamps. For when the verse states: *So that future generations may*

24 1 2 The Lord spoke to Moshe: "Command the Israelites to bring SHEVI'I
you pure oil from crushed olives for the light, to kindle the
3 lamp, every night. From evening to morning, before the Lord,
Aharon shall set it up outside the curtain of the testimony in
the Tent of Meeting to burn each night. This shall be a rule
4 for all time, throughout your generations. Aharon shall set
out the lamps on the pure candelabrum each day before the
Lord.
5 And you shall take fine flour and bake twelve loaves, two-tenths

OR HAḤAYYIM *(cont.)*

know that I had the Israelites live in huts when I brought them out of the land of Egypt (23:43), that refers to the clouds of glory that God spread above the nation's camp to protect them in the desert and provide miraculously for their needs, including lighting. Similarly, the purpose of the seven lamps in the Tabernacle was a testament to the presence of God in the midst of His nation, and not to provide ordinary light.

VERSE 3

MESHEKH ḤOKHMA

מִחוּץ לְפָרֹכֶת הָעֵדֻת – *Outside the curtain of the testimony:* In the corresponding statement in Parashat Tetzaveh we read regarding the lamp: *Aharon and his sons shall set it up to burn in the Tent of Meeting, outside the curtain that veils [asher al, literally, "that is on"] the Ark of the Testimony* [Exodus 27:21. This contrasts with the present verse, which describes the same curtain as simply "the curtain of the testimony" without stating that it veils anything]. Now, it makes sense that here, following the discussion of the holidays, that the Torah omits mention of the veiling. For according to a report in Yoma (54a), during the pilgrimage festivals the priests would pull back the curtain and reveal the golden cherubs of the Ark cover to the assembled masses. "Look!" they would declare, "how much you are beloved to the Almighty!" During the festivals, for a time at least, the curtain did not veil the Ark of the Testimony. There is another explanation for this juxtaposition which takes note of the difference between the present instruction, which is issued only to Aharon, and the earlier directive, which is given to "Aharon and his sons." With respect to the service of the High Priest, the Jerusalem Talmud (Ḥagiga 2:4) maintains that it was only on the Sabbaths and the festivals that the High Priest donned the priestly vestments and offered the communal sacrifices in the Temple. This explains why, immediately after the text's presentation of the festivals, the present chapter addresses just Aharon and not his sons. For it was then that the High Priest brought the sacrifices and arranged and lit the lamps within the Sanctuary.

VERSE 5

RABBI SAMSON RAPHAEL HIRSCH

וְלָקַחְתָּ סֹלֶת – *And you shall take fine flour:* The twelve showbread loaves symbolize national prosperity, while the table describes the source of that abundance and why exactly the Israelite people enjoy such material success. The design of the table demonstrates the conditions for

ו יִהְיֶה הַחַלָּה הָאֶחָת: וְשַׂמְתָּ אוֹתָם שְׁתַּיִם מַעֲרָכוֹת שֵׁשׁ
ז הַמַּעֲרָכֶת עַל הַשֻּׁלְחָן הַטָּהֹר לִפְנֵי יהוה: וְנָתַתָּ עַל־
הַמַּעֲרֶכֶת לְבֹנָה זַכָּה וְהָיְתָה לַלֶּחֶם לְאַזְכָּרָה אִשֶּׁה לַיהוה:
ח בְּיוֹם הַשַּׁבָּת בְּיוֹם הַשַּׁבָּת יַעַרְכֶנּוּ לִפְנֵי יהוה תָּמִיד מֵאֵת
ט בְּנֵי־יִשְׂרָאֵל בְּרִית עוֹלָם: וְהָיְתָה לְאַהֲרֹן וּלְבָנָיו וַאֲכָלֻהוּ

RABBI SAMSON RAPHAEL HIRSCH *(cont.)*

a flourishing national economy that follows from the life and character of the Jewish state. The table's solid wooden core represents industrious free growth, but it is circumscribed by a golden band representing the necessary limits within which economic activity must be bounded. The golden framework supporting the loaves represents the law, which demarcates limits and protects the integrity of the loaves. As the loaves themselves, the *leḥem hapanim* [literally, "the bread of faces"], are described as having faces, the showbread expresses the necessary fraternity which similarly contributes to a thriving economy. Nevertheless, there is one communal attribute which these verses emphasize above everything with respect to both the table and the candelabrum. This essential component for the creation and maintenance of Israelite society is critical on both a material and a spiritual level; this characteristic defines the national illumination that is signified by the burning lamps, and the national sustenance that is symbolized by the table of twelve breads. I refer to the quality of purity, a term which refers to ethical flawlessness. In the absence of morality there can be no spiritual growth, and material wealth becomes impossible. The Torah therefore demands that the lamps be arranged on *the pure candelabrum* (24:4), and that the breads be laid out on *the pure table before the Lord* (24:6). It is only thus that these utensils can be placed within the Sanctuary of the Torah. It is only a pure candelabrum that can sustain the light of God, and it is only a pure table that can carry the bread of God's bountiful promise.

VERSE 6

RABBI DAVID TZVI HOFFMAN

וְשַׂמְתָּ אוֹתָם שְׁתַּיִם מַעֲרָכוֹת – *You shall place them in two columns:* The two columns of showbreads corresponded to the twelve names of Israel's tribes, which were engraved on *the two stones on the shoulder pieces of the ephod* (Exodus 28:12), worn by the High Priest. These too were arranged in two columns of six. [Each onyx stone contained the names of six tribes.] In the present instance as well, the twelve loaves were stacked in two columns.

VERSE 7

RABBI SAMSON RAPHAEL HIRSCH

וְהָיְתָה לַלֶּחֶם – *For the bread:* The twelve showbread loaves are prepared without oil, which means that they do not signify luxury, but only basic and necessary income. The sense of contentment and well-being expressed by the table is not from the loaves themselves but from the addition of frankincense. Only once the basic bread is spiced with this external ingredient does the combination represent the bread of well-being. This

6 of an ephah for each loaf. You shall place them in two columns,
7 six to each column, on the pure table before the LORD. Lay
pure incense on each stack, as a remembrance for the bread,
8 as a fire offering to the LORD. Every Sabbath he shall set it out,
always, before the LORD on behalf of the Israelites: an ever-
9 lasting covenant. It shall belong to Aharon and his sons. They

RABBI SAMSON RAPHAEL HIRSCH *(cont.)*

then serves admirably as the special bread of the Jew – he is rich not by virtue of partaking in luxury items but by being satisfied with his lot. The Israelite's contentment follows not from the wealth of his material possessions but from a spiritual satisfaction due to his relationship with the LORD.

VERSE 8

RABBI SAMSON RAPHAEL HIRSCH

יַעַרְכֶנּוּ – *He shall set it out:* The subject of this command is Aharon, who is mentioned by name in verse 3 in the discussion of the candelabrum. [This verse returns to third person and therefore picks up the subject named earlier.] This reference indicates the strong connection between the arrangement of the lamps and the presentation of the loaves, namely: The people of Israel must forever submit to the will of the LORD with respect to both their spiritual and their material development. **לִפְנֵי יהוה תָּמִיד** – Always before the *LORD*: Because the loaves are to have a continuous presence in the Sanctuary, they are referred to as *leḥem hapanim*, bread placed before the LORD, bread to which God directs His attention perpetually. This is the bread of the Almighty's special providence over the nation of Israel.

According to our tradition the western lamp of the candelabrum and the twelve showbread loaves share a common characteristic. The divine protection which Israel enjoys is represented to the world by this particular lamp which was never extinguished. The bread too incorporates a continuous feature, in that it remains fresh and warm throughout the week that it sits on the table. That too announces to the rest of humanity that God eternally takes interest and demonstrates care for the material requirements of the Israelite people. And so states the Talmud (Menaḥot 29a): A great miracle was performed for the showbread: It retained exactly the same freshness when it was replaced after seven days as it had when it was first baked.

HAAMEK DAVAR

בְּרִית עוֹלָם – *An everlasting covenant:* The text here refers to the covenant of the Sabbath, which demands that the Israelites not work to support themselves on that day. Rather, on the seventh day the people must enjoy themselves as the nation of the LORD based on what they have prepared during the week. For His part, God honors this contract with Israel by providing His bounty to the people during the coming week. This agreement is symbolized by the showbread loaves, which were placed on the table just before the Sabbath day and were blessed later, when they were eaten at the end of the following week. It is from these breads that God's blessings spread to all the residents of the land of Israel.

בְּמָקוֹם קָדֹשׁ כִּי קֹדֶשׁ קָדָשִׁים הוּא לוֹ מֵאִשֵּׁי יְהוָה חָק־
י עוֹלָם׃ וַיֵּצֵא בֶּן־אִשָּׁה יִשְׂרְאֵלִית וְהוּא בֶּן־
אִישׁ מִצְרִי בְּתוֹךְ בְּנֵי יִשְׂרָאֵל וַיִּנָּצוּ בַּמַּחֲנֶה בֶּן הַיִּשְׂרְאֵלִית
יא וְאִישׁ הַיִּשְׂרְאֵלִי׃ וַיִּקֹּב בֶּן־הָאִשָּׁה הַיִּשְׂרְאֵלִית אֶת־הַשֵּׁם
וַיְקַלֵּל וַיָּבִיאוּ אֹתוֹ אֶל־מֹשֶׁה וְשֵׁם אִמּוֹ שְׁלֹמִית בַּת־
יב דִּבְרִי לְמַטֵּה־דָן׃ וַיַּנִּיחֻהוּ בַּמִּשְׁמָר לִפְרֹשׁ לָהֶם עַל־פִּי
יְהוָה׃

VERSE 10

OR HAHAYYIM

וַיֵּצֵא בֶּן־אִשָּׁה יִשְׂרְאֵלִית – *A man went out… the son of an Israelite woman:* The significance of the verb *vayetze* ["he went out"] here should be understood in light of the earlier verse which reads: *So I told them, "Who has gold? Take it off." They gave it to me, I threw it into the fire – and out came [vayetze] this calf* [Exodus 32:24. In that case, Aharon had not intentionally fashioned a golden calf; it just emerged out of the fire on its own]. In the same manner, this Israelite woman had not meant to perform such an ignoble act [as to have relations with an Egyptian man]. Rather, through the inadvertent forbidden act of Shlomit daughter of Divri, this blighted child was born. Our Sages describe that the Egyptian taskmaster had ordered Shlomit's husband out to work in the fields whereupon the brute stole into her house and slept with the wife. All along, the woman believed that it was her own husband who had returned to her. As a result of this union the blemished offspring of this tale was conceived. To emphasize the mother's lack of culpability, the text equates her with her son's opponent by using similar language to describe them: *this son of an Israelite woman, and an Israelite man*. Just as the Israelite man was without guilt, so too was Shlomit daughter of Divri an innocent victim. Now the text writes that the Israelite woman's son "went out among the Israelites" to teach that he was the lone bastard within the Israelite community. [The Jewish people preciously guarded the integrity of their marriages.] Furthermore, we learn from this phrase "among the Israelites" the cause of his frustration: He had difficulty finding a place among them. Whenever he attempted to settle down in a neighborhood, he was told to get out: You are not one of us! According to the Sages, the clause indicates that this person did attempt to join the community and be a member "among the Israelites," by converting to Israel's faith. All these approaches are words of the living God.

SHADAL

וַיֵּצֵא בֶּן־אִשָּׁה יִשְׂרְאֵלִית – *A man went out… the son of an Israelite woman:* Once the Torah has finished discussing a range of commandments whose observance honors the Lord, including the sacrifices, the festivals, and the priestly guidelines, the text describes the punishment of the blasphemer. The latter represents the extreme negation of honoring God. Note that the Torah had not directly prohibited the offense that this man commits.

shall eat it in a holy place because it is holy of holies among
10 the LORD's fire offerings, their perpetual share." A man
went out among the Israelites, the son of an Israelite woman
and an Egyptian man. And a fight broke out in the camp be-
11 tween this son of an Israelite woman, and an Israelite man. The
Israelite woman's son blasphemed the Name and cursed – his
mother's name was Shlomit, daughter of Divri, of the tribe of
12 Dan – and they brought him before Moshe. They placed the
man in custody until the LORD's verdict would be pronounced
to them.

SHADAL *(cont.)*

For the verse which states: *Do not curse a judge* [*elohim lo tekallel* – Exodus 22:27 – which could also mean, "Do not curse God"] refers to the courts rather than to the Almighty. The reason that the text did not introduce such a prohibition is that it was inconceivable that any Israelite could ever curse the LORD. Indeed, the Torah would never have bothered to forbid this sort of behavior if the event reported, wherein the son of an Egyptian man perpetrated this abomination, had not actually taken place. But once the offense did occur the Torah pronounced its warning against blasphemy (see 24:16). The matter is included here as a conclusion to the broader topic of the sanctification of the LORD's name.

VERSE 11

OR HAḤAYYIM

וְשֵׁם אִמּוֹ שְׁלֹמִית בַּת־דִּבְרִי – *His mother's name was Shlomit, daughter of Divri:* The reader might rightfully ask why the text does not mention this woman's name at the start of this passage [in verse 10]. Why does her name appear only once her son the offender is brought before Moshe? There are two ways to answer this question. The first approach is complimentary to the mother. The verse could be rendered more literally, preserving the order of the clauses as, "They brought him before Moshe, and his mother's name was Shlomit, daughter of Divri." This demonstrates that the criminal's mother was among the appalled crowd who heard the blasphemy, apprehended her son and brought him to justice. The second interpretation is critical of this woman: After the sinner was hauled before Moshe it became necessary to publicize who exactly his mother was. Shlomit actually tried to protect her son out of sympathy for him, whereas the wise man warns: *The "compassion" of the wicked is but cruelty* (Proverbs 12:10). Thus, the text names Shlomit daughter of Divri in conjunction with her son's arrest to equate their unbecoming behavior.

VERSE 12

THE LUBAVITCHER REBBE

וַיַּנִּיחֻהוּ בַּמִּשְׁמָר – *They placed the man in custody:* The Torah does not forbid incarceration. The court is allowed to imprison criminals or suspected criminals when they [the judges] find it necessary. But it never prescribes incarceration as a punishment.

יג
יד וַיְדַבֵּר יהוה אֶל־מֹשֶׁה לֵּאמֹר: הוֹצֵא אֶת־הַמְקַלֵּל אֶל־
מִחוּץ לַמַּחֲנֶה וְסָמְכוּ כָל־הַשֹּׁמְעִים אֶת־יְדֵיהֶם עַל־רֹאשׁוֹ
טו וְרָגְמוּ אֹתוֹ כָּל־הָעֵדָה: וְאֶל־בְּנֵי יִשְׂרָאֵל תְּדַבֵּר לֵאמֹר
טז אִישׁ אִישׁ כִּי־יְקַלֵּל אֱלֹהָיו וְנָשָׂא חֶטְאוֹ: וְנֹקֵב שֵׁם־
יהוה מוֹת יוּמָת רָגוֹם יִרְגְּמוּ־בוֹ כָּל־הָעֵדָה כַּגֵּר כָּאֶזְרָח

VERSE 15

RABBI JOSEPH B. SOLOVEITCHIK

אִישׁ אִישׁ כִּי־יְקַלֵּל אֱלֹהָיו – *Anyone who curses his God:* The Torah considered blasphemy to be a very severe violation, considering the irreverent remark a grave sin. Yet, do we punish an insect that bites us? Does it arouse our wrath? Do we feel hurt by the barking of a dog? Certainly not. Why, then, is the omniscient, eternal creator and sustainer of the universe, whose will is the source of all cosmic dynamics, concerned with a nonsensical indignity uttered by a stupid, weak, transient being, "here today, tomorrow in the grave"? If we are not angry at the mosquito, why should God punish the blasphemer with death? God punishes the blasphemer not because of the indignity to Him, but because by making such a statement, man destroys his own *tzelem Elohim*, his Godly image. He destroys not only his own *tzelem Elohim*, but the *tzelem Elohim* reflected in the universe. Nature, the universe, is as such a moral being. The Rambam in his *Guide of the Perplexed* (1:72) refers to the cosmos as a "macro-anthropos," one large individuality, a personality. Blasphemy destroys the *tzelem Elohim* not only of the person himself, but of the "macro-anthropos." The universe reflects the glory, the image of God. "Shall bear the sin" – the blasphemer is burdened with sin; he has brought about a destructive change in his personality. The moment that he makes the sacrilegious statement he is no longer rooted in the Almighty. But the destructive effect is not limited to him; it is destructive for the entire universe.

VERSE 16

HAAMEK DAVAR

כַּגֵּר כָּאֶזְרָח – *Migrant and native born alike:* The Torah teaches that there is no difference whether a migrant or a native-born person blasphemes; their punishment is the same – death. [The *Haamek Davar* elaborates on why it was necessary to equate them. In general, we understand the obligations of the Torah to apply equally to everyone. His explanation sheds important light on why the marginal identity of the blasphemer was a key point of the story.] The text juxtaposes the crime of blasphemy to the crime of taking a human life [which is reviewed in verse 17]. This teaches that these two matters are eternal concerns that are critical for the endurance of the world. Recognize that a person bears the image of God and thereby, by his very existence, maintains the cosmos. Thus a murderer upsets the cosmic order and deserves to die. Similarly, the pronouncement of the name of the Lord vitalizes the world. This concept is supported by God's own pledge: *Wherever I cause My name to be invoked, I will come to you and I will bless you* (Exodus 20:21),

13 14 And the Lord spoke to Moshe: "Take the one who cursed
outside the camp. All the people who heard him shall lay their
hands on his head – and then the whole community shall stone
15 him. Tell the Israelites: Anyone who curses his God shall bear
16 the sin, and anyone who blasphemes the Lord's name shall be
put to death: the whole community shall stone him. Migrant
and native born alike: one who blasphemes the Lord's name

HAAMEK DAVAR *(cont.)*

which signifies the honor of the Almighty. Cursing God does the opposite of vitalizing; it is tantamount to slaying a fellow Israelite, for both acts strike at the basic foundations of the world's existence. Now the argument could be made that the impression that an ordinary commoner makes on the world, should he say the name of God in the middle of the street, cannot be nearly as potent as the effect which ensues when the High Priest utters the Tetragrammaton in the Temple courtyard as part of the Yom Kippur service. And if that assessment is correct, it would be reasonable to impose a far lighter punishment upon a lowly blasphemer who curses the Almighty than the execution which is prescribed here. We might suggest that this son of an Egyptian man should have been treated leniently for his offense [since how much damage could this base person cause to the fabric of the universe with his objectionable speech? Indeed, perhaps the Torah includes this detail of the man's lineage in order to suggest the lower significance of his crime]. Finally, the Torah stresses that the transgression took place "in the camp" (24:10); the son of Divri was not within the Sanctuary courtyard when he committed his sin. As such, even if the man had proclaimed God's ineffable name for the sake of praising Him, that would not have engendered as positive and affirming an impact on the world as if he had done so inside the Tabernacle. Consequently, the fact that he did not bless God's name but cursed it, should not have led to his execution. In order to completely counter this argument, the Torah warns both the *ger* ["migrant" or "foreigner"], who is not a particularly distinguished member of society, and the *ezraḥ* ["native-born Israelite"], who is, against blaspheming God's name. Thus, since the son of the Israelite woman exclaimed the name of God, and instead of using the opportunity to advance and augment the existence of the world he used his speech to impair life, he surely deserved to "be put to death." Just as we understand that a murder devastates life in this world, no matter who perpetrates the crime, so too, we must understand that blasphemy is equally devasting to the fabric of the cosmos, no matter who does the cursing.

THE LUBAVITCHER REBBE

וְנֹקֵב שֵׁם־יהוה – *Anyone who blasphemes the Lord's name:* The word for "pronounce" literally means "to puncture." [The Hebrew for blaspheme is *nokev shem*, literally, to pronounce the name of." The word *nokev* also means to puncture.] Failure to observe any given commandment drills a hole, so to speak, in God's name, draining it of its divine energy. Instead of sustaining and spiritually invigorating all the spiritual and physical worlds, this divine energy is wasted and may even bolster negativity. Such an act warrants a death penalty, for it, too, has drained the lifeblood of existence.

CONFRONTING MODERNITY

יז בְּנָקְבוֹ־שֵׁם יוּמָת: וְאִישׁ כִּי יַכֶּה כָּל־נֶפֶשׁ אָדָם מוֹת יוּמָת:
יח יט וּמַכֵּה נֶפֶשׁ־בְּהֵמָה יְשַׁלְּמֶנָּה נֶפֶשׁ תַּחַת נָפֶשׁ: וְאִישׁ כִּי־יִתֵּן
כ מוּם בַּעֲמִיתוֹ כַּאֲשֶׁר עָשָׂה כֵּן יֵעָשֶׂה לּוֹ: שֶׁבֶר תַּחַת שֶׁבֶר
עַיִן תַּחַת עַיִן שֵׁן תַּחַת שֵׁן כַּאֲשֶׁר יִתֵּן מוּם בָּאָדָם כֵּן יִנָּתֶן
כא כב בּוֹ: וּמַכֵּה בְהֵמָה יְשַׁלְּמֶנָּה וּמַכֵּה אָדָם יוּמָת: מִשְׁפַּט אֶחָד מפטיר

VERSE 18

RABBI SAMSON RAPHAEL HIRSCH

וּמַכֵּה נֶפֶשׁ־בְּהֵמָה – *One who takes the life of an animal:* All of these laws and concepts have already been presented in Parashat Mishpatim, which describes the judicial principles for constructing a civil society. In that passage as well, a sharp distinction is drawn between causing death or damage to a person versus to an animal. Both here and in Exodus the Torah makes clear the qualitive, irreducible difference between the life of a human and that of an animal. Taking the life of the former forfeits one's own life, whereas taking the life of an animal creates a monetary debt. In the present text, however, this essential distinction follows from an even more basic principle. The story of the blasphemer forms a sort of preamble to the current discussion of damage and death caused to people and animals. It roots the difference between them in a fundamental principle and shows how the distinction between man and beast follows as a corollary. This archetypical philosophic concept forms the necessary presupposition for all legal theory, for a true anthropology of humankind and an understanding of the human personality. This critical axiom then, is the autonomous agency of the divine personality. If one denies God's autonomous will, then there is no possibility of justice; it becomes a deceitful illusion. Law posits legal rights which cannot be recognized unless humans have agency, ethical freedom. And humans cannot be understood to have agency, if it is denied to the Creator of all. A person who denies God's autonomous personality cannot conceive of a world operating according to justice, but only naked power. This is a world governed by blind forces, physical forces, mechanical forces, political-economic forces, even organic forces. Justice and moral reasoning factor not at all. All that matters is the man who wields the biggest stick; the profound implication of justice is beyond his grasp. Thus, we must insist on a Creator who possesses freedom Himself, and who has bestowed some of that spirit to His creation, humanity, to exercise wisely as a function of its God-given moral agency.

MESHEKH ḤOKHMA

וּמַכֵּה נֶפֶשׁ־בְּהֵמָה יְשַׁלְּמֶנָּה – *One who takes the life of an animal shall make restitution for it:* We might ask why this law does not appear in Parashat Mishpatim [which does discuss violence perpetrated by one animal against another]. The reason is that the present passage includes an attack against a non-Jew's beast as well as that of an Israelite. This explains why verse 21 states: *But one who kills a human being shall be put to death [yumat]*

17 shall be put to death. One who takes the life of any human be-
18 ing shall be put to death. One who takes the life of an animal
19 shall make restitution for it: life for life. One who injures his
fellow man shall be penalized in proportion to the injury in-
20 flicted: the cost of a broken bone for a broken bone, of an eye
for an eye, of a tooth for a tooth. Just as he inflicted injury on
21 another human being, so shall he suffer the loss. One who kills MAFTIR
an animal shall make restitution for it; but one who kills a hu-
22 man being shall be put to death. There shall be one law for you,
for migrant and for native born alike, for I am the LORD your

MESHEKH ḤOKHMA *(cont.)*

instead of the more forceful *mot yumat* ["shall surely die"]. The phrasing in this passage, *shall be put to death [yumat]*, refers to death at the hands of heaven, as in the following examples which all refer to death at the hands of heaven: *Appoint Aharon and his sons to attend to the priestly duties; any outsider who draws close will die [yumat]* (Numbers 3:10), and: *I give you your priestly service as a gift, but any outsider who draws close will die [yumat]* (Numbers 18:7). This means that if an Israelite kills a non-Jew, his case is tried by a heavenly tribunal rather than by a human court, and his punishment is meted out by the hands of heaven.

VERSE 22

MESHEKH ḤOKHMA

מִשְׁפַּט אֶחָד יִהְיֶה לָכֶם – *There shall be one law for you:* This statement means that one law applies to "the migrant and…native born alike" in the realm of monetary infractions as well as in capital offenses. Nevertheless, the two parties are not equal with respect to acting as judges, for a foreigner can adjudicate capital cases of other outsiders, but he is not permitted to try an Israelite for a capital offense. He is permitted to try Israelites in momentary matters (see Yevamot 102a). Perhaps the equivalence of *for migrant and for native born alike* can be understood differently. Our verse should be seen in light of the general passage which relates to the honor of the Almighty, and thus addresses such matters as cursing God and those rules dealing with homicide in which everyone is treated the same. However, here too, we find a distinction. The Talmud asserts (Sanhedrin 71b) that if a gentile curses God and then converts to Judaism, he would be exempt from punishment, since his trial procedure has changed and the death penalty to which he is subject has also changed. Nevertheless, we can assert the equivalence when the crimes were committed against a Jew, before the *ger* converted. That is the sense of the term *lakhem* – "for you." *Ger* and *ezraḥ* are equal when they have sinned against Jews, "for you" [literally, "to you"]. Thus, in ancient times, if a Noahide killed a Jew or committed adultery with a married Jewish woman and then converted, he would still be subject to death after his conversion.

כג יִהְיֶה לָכֶם כַּגֵּר כָּאֶזְרָח יִהְיֶה כִּי אֲנִי יְהוָה אֱלֹהֵיכֶם׃ וַיְדַבֵּר
מֹשֶׁה אֶל־בְּנֵי יִשְׂרָאֵל וַיּוֹצִיאוּ אֶת־הַמְקַלֵּל אֶל־מִחוּץ
לַמַּחֲנֶה וַיִּרְגְּמוּ אֹתוֹ אָבֶן וּבְנֵי־יִשְׂרָאֵל עָשׂוּ כַּאֲשֶׁר צִוָּה
יְהוָה אֶת־מֹשֶׁה׃

23 God." Moshe told this to the Israelites, and so they took the
blasphemer outside the camp and stoned him. Thus the Israelites did as the LORD had commanded Moshe.

פרשת אמר

PARASHAT EMOR

THE **BIBLICAL** IMAGINATION

RABBI SHAI FINKELSTEIN

THE OX, THE SHEEP, AND THE GOAT

In Parashat Emor, the Torah commands that sacrifices be brought from relatively few types of animals, as we read: "When an ox or sheep or goat is born, it shall remain with its mother for seven days. From the eighth day it is acceptable as a sacrifice, a fire offering to the LORD" (22:27). The reference to these specific beasts raises several questions. First, considering that it is a valid sacrificial specimen, why is the calf not mentioned among the animals that comprise acceptable offerings? Second, why are the ox, sheep, and goat specified here? These questions, especially the second, could have been asked regardless of where the Torah had chosen to present this selection. That leads us to a third difficulty: Why does the text list these animals in the middle of Parashat Emor, and why does it provide this list specifically within the context of the restriction on their age?

Commenting on our verse, Vayikra Rabba quotes Rabbi Yaakov ben Zavdi, who cites another verse in connection with ours. The prophet Yeḥezkel utters a pledge to the nation of Israel: "They will no longer be a source of trust for the House of Israel but merely a reminder of Israel's sin in turning to them, and they will know that I am the Lord GOD" (Ezekiel 29:16). According to Rabbi Yaakov ben Zavdi, Yeḥezkel teaches that the angels who minister to God cover their "feet" with their wings because angels' feet resemble those of a calf, and they do not wish to evoke a memory of Israel's transgression with the golden calf. The midrash proceeds to argue that this same consideration is reflected in the type of animal horn that may be used to fashion the shofar sounded on Rosh Hashana. The horns of all kosher animals are acceptable for the shofar with the lone exception of the cow's horn, which would similarly recall the sin of the golden calf. Why would the Jewish people wish to mention their terrible offense as they seek to evoke the merit associated with the binding of Yitzḥak? This is the second instance when we make a conscious effort not to reference the golden calf.

The midrash further refers to two other instances of such sensitivity. First, if a man accuses his wife of adultery and compels her to drink the bitter waters of the *sota*, the wife is not permitted to drink from the same cup that another similarly unfortunate woman previously drank from. If that were allowed, people would recall the first wife as well and her licentiousness, which would cause her unnecessary suffering. Second, if a woman copulates with an animal, both are killed, even though beast cannot sin, lest the community point to the creature wandering through the market and end up gossiping about their neighbor's wrongdoing. After discussing these cases, the midrash draws a connection be-

tween this idea of suppressing the memory of a sin also to the list of animals that we presented at the start of this essay:

> Why does the verse state: "When an ox or sheep or goat is born"? Is it an ox that is born? Is the animal not a calf when it is born? Rather, since the text states: "They have made themselves a molten calf and are bowing down and sacrificing to it" (Exodus 32:8), our verse would rather refer to the sacrificial animal as an ox and not a calf.

The Torah's list omits any mention of the calf, even though it is at times perfectly acceptable to bring such an animal as an offering. It only mentions an ox, which began as a calf. All this reflects the divine wish to preserve Israel's honor by not recalling our darkest hour.

The midrash offers several essential messages. From God's perspective, the sin of the golden calf ought to be erased from memory for the Almighty does not wish for that misdeed to prevent Israel's spiritual growth. The people of Israel have understood that kindness and have given it expression in their Oral Law, specifically regarding the laws of the shofar and *sota*. It is also possible that the Sages are engaging in anti-Christian polemic. The Church has long argued that Israel's sin of the golden calf can be neither forgotten nor forgiven. The Sages therefore maintain an opposing view, portraying God Himself as trying to set that tragic experience behind Him.

The next passage in Vayikra Rabba emphasizes a different message. This text opens with the following citation from Ecclesiastes: "That which has been is already here, and that which will be has already been. And God is seeking after the pursued" (Ecclesiastes 3:15). Based on this verse, Rav Huna teaches in the name of Rav Yosef: "God always takes the side of the pursued."

To this Rabbi Yehuda bar Rabbi Simon adds that not only does God stand up for the pursued, but He also exacts retribution from the pursuers for the blood of their victims. Rabbi Yehuda bar Rabbi Simon supports his argument with a range of cases from Scripture, including Hevel, Noaḥ, Avraham, Yitzḥak, Yaakov, Yosef, Moshe, David, and Sha'ul, all of whom were preyed upon, and all of whom were selected for special treatment by the Almighty. Their experiences correspond to the fate of the Jewish people. We too have been hounded relentlessly by the nations, yet we too are God's chosen people.

Next, Rabbi Eliezer bar Rabbi Yosei bar Zimra enters the discussion, drawing the following curious parallel:

> The same phenomenon characterizes the sacrificial animals. For the Holy One, blessed be He, declared: "The ox is pursued by the lion; the sheep is

> stalked by the leopard; and the goat is chased by the wolf. Thus you are not to offer Me sacrifices from among the hunters but from the hunted, as the verse states: "When an ox or sheep or goat is born...it is acceptable as a sacrifice, a fire offering to the LORD."

According to Rabbi Eliezer bar Rabbi Yosei bar Zimra, the ox, sheep, and goat are accepted as sacrifices specifically because they are the weaker creatures that are hunted by their stronger counterparts in the animal kingdom. Underlying the idea of an animal offering is the human approach to God and the desire to dwell under His protective wings. These three animals are not predators but victims of nature's violent creatures. This is why the ox, sheep, and goat were chosen by God. The allegorical comparison between these animals and the people of Israel is clear. The Jewish people have long found themselves in a state of exile, where they must contend with rapacious gentiles, implicitly raising questions about our status as God's favored nation. The midrash therefore reinforces our claim to be the chosen people. What is more, this title does not merely confirm our status as a pursued nation; it represents an intimidating message to our enemies. God demands retribution from the pursuers for the blood of their victims. And so the list of permissible sacrificial animals serves as the midrash's starting point as it justifies God's selection of Israel as His treasured people. At the same time, the author attempts to console the Jews for the harsh experiences that exile has thrust upon us.

For the midrash, then, the Torah's choice to specify the ox, sheep, and goat is anything but anomalous. The absence of the calf underscores God's desire to protect the dignity of Israel. And the selection of these three non-predatory animals implicitly points to God's selection of the Jewish people and His promise to not only protect us but also to exact vengeance from our enemies.

THE PLACEMENT OF THE FESTIVALS

The opening chapters in Parashat Emor are consistent with what we have come to expect in the book of Leviticus: They address laws that are particular to the priests' lives and careers, and they address matters of purity and impurity alongside definitions of acceptable sacrifices. Yet there is a sudden shift as the Torah changes course when it begins its discussion of the festival laws:

> The Lord spoke to Moshe: "Speak to the Israelites. Say: These are the Lord's appointed times that you shall proclaim as sacred assemblies; these are My appointed times. Work shall be done through six days, but the seventh day shall be a Sabbath of complete rest, a sacred assembly. You shall perform no work at all; it shall be a Sabbath for the Lord in all your dwellings. These are the Lord's appointed times, sacred assemblies, which you shall proclaim at their appointed times. In the first month, the fourteenth of the month in the afternoon is the time for the Passover sacrifice to the Lord." (23:1–5)

The position of this chapter in the midst of Parashat Emor and as the book of Leviticus nears its conclusion raises two questions. First, is there some contextual connection between the plethora of details that precede the presentation of the festivals in the text? We might similarly inquire why chapter 24 includes the tale of the blasphemer; is that too linked in some way to the main themes of this book?

Our second line of investigation centers on the internal structure of the passage regarding the festivals. Long ago, our Sages recognized a fundamental distinction between the Sabbath and the festivals. The seventh day of the week was created long before the appearance of Israel and exists independently of the nation. The holidays, on the other hand, are all dimensions of Jewish life, and their commemoration relies on Israel's declaration of the New Moon and establishment of the calendar. Why, then, do they appear together in chapter 23?

In his comments to our chapter, Rashi cites the Sifra, which noted our second problem centuries ago. He writes:

> Why does the text include the Sabbath in a discussion of the festivals? In order to teach us that if one profanes the holidays [by performing forbidden labors on those days], his transgression is considered as severe as if he had violated the Sabbath. Conversely, when a person observes the holidays, he is credited as if he has kept the Sabbath.

For the Sifra and Rashi, the inclusion of the Sabbath in the Torah's discussion of the festivals serves to enhance and reinforce the populace's perception of the holidays by granting to these days the character and authority of the Sabbath. In general, people are reluctant to attribute to the festivals as much importance as they give the Sabbath; hence it is necessary to stress the significance of these occasions as well. According to this approach, there is no contextual link between the Sabbath and festivals. Rather, the Sabbath is included in this chapter purely to bolster the nation's association with the holidays.

In his commentary, the Ramban directs his attention to our first question. According to him, the holidays are presented alongside the discussion of the sacrifices in the book of Leviticus even though the topic of the festivals is no more relevant to the priestly class than it is to the rest of the Israelite population. That is why the substance of this chapter is not addressed to Aharon and his sons but to the people of Israel as a whole. The Torah lists the festivals in Leviticus because these are times when a unique set of sacrifices is offered.

The Ramban maintains that the mention of the festivals following information about the sacrificial system is not meant to convey the message that these times in the calendar are more closely connected to the priests than they are to the other tribes of Israel. Rather, the entire nation maintains the same relationship with the holidays. With the advent of the festivals, the people are required to offer new sacrifices that have been set apart in order to deepen Israel's relationship with God. This opportunity to bond with the Almighty is available to every Jew.

The Ramban then proceeds to explore the idea of the national assemblies that take place during the pilgrimage festivals, and, in a different manner, on the Sabbaths. The primary function of these gatherings is to cement the nation's union with God:

> Our Sages ask why the Torah includes this reiteration of the Sabbath within its discussion of the festivals considering that the seventh day is not really a holiday like the other times mentioned here. According to the Sages, the inclusion of the Sabbath serves to define the notion of a "sacred assembly." The signification of this term is that the festivals are times when the entire community is summoned to gather together in order to sanctify the holiday. For the Torah commands the Israelites to assemble in the House of God at these special times and there to publicly make the day holy through prayers and praises of the Almighty. The celebratory and hallowed nature of the day is enhanced by the wearing of clean garments and by feasting, as is related in our tradition: "Then Neḥemya, His Excellency the governor… said to all the people, 'Today is sacred to the Lord, your God. You should neither mourn nor weep'…. 'Now go and feast on delicacies, drink sweet things, and send

> servings of food to those who have none – for this day is sacred to our Lord. Do not be sorrowful, for rejoicing in the Lord is your strength and shelter'" (Nehemiah 8:9–10). What emerges is that the phrase "sacred assemblies" [*mikra'ei kodesh*] refers to the summoning of the people, as in the verse "These were the ones chosen from the community [*keru'ei ha'eda*], princes of their ancestral tribes" (Numbers 1:16).

There is great power inherent in the idea that the people of Israel gather in unity on the holidays to express their desire to bond with the Almighty, not just as individuals but as an entire nation. Perhaps the connection between that aim and the commandments of the sacrifices – which at first glance appear to be limited in their application to the priests – is that the pilgrimage festivals serve as the antithesis to that apparent exclusivity. The passage regarding these special times of the year testifies to the fact that the congregation of Israel in the house of God creates a bond with Him that is as strong as anything the priests can effect through their daily duties. Judaism is not reserved for a particular segment of society. The Torah is a way of life that God wishes to be followed by every one of us.

With this, the Ramban resolves the two questions we raised above. This chapter, which is devoted to the festivals, is connected to the overall theme of the book of Leviticus, namely the sacrifices, in that through the holidays, the task of drawing close to the Almighty devolves equally on all the people of Israel. That which the priests are privileged to do and to achieve on a regular basis is available to every man and woman when the holidays are celebrated. In addition, the commandments associated with the Sabbath are recalled in this section about the festivals because they too are related to the overall objective of instilling a closer relationship with God through the unification of Israel and through serving the Almighty as a united nation.

Let us now consider the approach of Rabbi Ovadya Sforno:

> At this point, the Torah has finished discussing the topic of sacrifices and has laid down laws for the people who service the Tabernacle offerings. The purpose of that entire system is to welcome the Divine Presence into the midst of the Israelite people, as we read earlier: "This shall be the regular burnt offering throughout your generations at the entrance of the Tent of Meeting before the Lord. There I will meet with you, there I will speak to you" (Exodus 29:42).

The text now begins its discussion of the festivals, teaching that Israel must accept the cessation of everyday work at those times, including complete avoidance of labor on the Sabbath and Yom Kippur. Such undertakings should be

replaced with the study of Torah and matters of sanctity, as we read earlier: "Six days you shall work, and carry out all your labors, but the seventh is a Sabbath to the LORD your God" (Exodus 20:9–10). This means that one should lay down his hoe and his sickle and devote himself entirely to the Almighty. On the other holidays, it is only creative [non-food-related] work that must be avoided. The purpose of that is to encourage the people to celebrate the day with their Creator and focus on holy things, as the Sages maintain: The festival should be evenly divided between spiritual enhancement and physical enjoyment. When that balance is achieved, the Divine Presence will most assuredly rest upon Israel, as the psalmist declares: "God stands in the divine assembly" (Psalms 82:1). Thus, the sacred assemblies [*mikra'ei kodesh*] are times when the populace gathers for sacred pursuits, for a gathering of the nation is called *mikra*, as in the verse "New Moon and Sabbath, the feast days you proclaim [*kero mikra*]" (Isaiah 1:13).

In Sforno's opinion, the laws of the sacrifices and practices of the festivals share the same goal of inviting the Divine Presence into the midst of the nation. The Israelite people's aim can be achieved by various means. First, the priestly caste devote their lives to the Temple service in order to guarantee that God's presence is manifest in Jerusalem and throughout the land. Curiously, the celebration of the festivals demands a sort of passivity on the part of the people, which results from the cessation of work on holy days. At the same time, the Israelite strives for personal and spiritual elevation as he occupies himself with the study of Torah and the performance of holy deeds. Third, the Israelite is invited to balance these religious activities with the physical manifestations of celebration, namely eating and drinking. And so the festivals provide to the entire nation the opportunity to grow close to God as they engage in benefiting both their souls and their bodies. On these days, the Divine Presence rests among us due to our overcoming the challenges in the perpetual struggle of guiding our lives down the correct paths presented by our Torah. For that is the invitation posed by our faith, which urges us to forge a life combining the spiritual and material dimensions.

For Sforno, the placement of the festival list does not appear where it does as an antithesis to the sacrifices. Instead, the holidays represent the other side of the coin, in which we welcome the Divine Presence into the earthly realm. Can there be a more potent way of transforming our secular day-to-day lives into a sacred national project?

There is one further idea implicit in Sforno's presentation, which connects the list of the festivals to the incident of the blasphemer at the end of Parashat Emor. Even without a full analysis of that episode, the straightforward meaning of the text makes several points clear. The son of the Egyptian man and the Israelite woman is categorized by the Torah as "the other," someone who fails to find a proper place in society. In other words, the Sabbath and the festivals,

which are designed to bring the citizens of Israel together, failed to achieve their purpose in this case. In this way, the story of the blasphemer serves as a wake-up call to the Israelite community. There are times when we can be so focused on the spiritual areas of life – the *kodesh* – that we neglect the summons of the *mikra,* the call of community, which obligates us to join our hands and hearts with all of our fellow Jews.

THE SABBATH AND THE FESTIVALS

Parashat Emor expands the Torah's presentation of the festivals, identifying the features that characterize the different holidays. In this essay, we will focus on the framework in which the festivals are mentioned. Chapter 23 opens its discussion about these familiar days in the following way:

> The LORD spoke to Moshe: "Speak to the Israelites. Say: These are the LORD's appointed times that you shall proclaim as sacred assemblies; these are My appointed times. Work shall be done through six days, but the seventh day shall be a Sabbath of complete rest, a sacred assembly. You shall perform no work at all; it shall be a Sabbath for the LORD in all your dwellings. These are the LORD's appointed times, sacred assemblies, which you shall proclaim at their appointed times." (23:1–4)

This paragraph raises an interesting question, based on the differing natures of the Sabbath and the festivals regarding their sanctity and, indeed, their very origins. The holiness of the seventh day is fixed and eternal, which is why it is God who makes the Sabbath sacred. On the other hand, a holiday becomes holy because of the collaboration between God and the nation. Hence our blessings on holidays use the phrasing "He who sanctifies Israel and the festivals." The Sabbath was instituted following the Almighty's six days of creation, whereas the holidays are determined based on the nation's declaration of the New Moon, and hence they are a function of Israel's holiness and the task that has been assigned to them. How then can the Torah speak about "the LORD's appointed times" and then immediately insert the commandment of the Sabbath? What is the connection between the Sabbath and the festivals that the Torah is attempting to develop here?

Let us recall that the phenomenon of the Sabbath appears in multiple places throughout the Torah, embedded within a wide range of contexts. Here is a partial list of such occurrences: (1) At the beginning of the second chapter of the book of Genesis, God first sanctifies this day on behalf of all mankind. (2) Chapter 16 of Exodus describes Israel's initial encounter with the Sabbath during the introduction of the manna and the demand that the people have faith in God. (3) The Ten Commandments appear in chapter 20 of Exodus, where the Sabbath is presented as the foundation of the acknowledgment of God as the creator and sustainer of the world. (4) Chapter 23 of the same book includes

the Sabbath as part of its presentation of humanitarian principles and the establishment of a well-functioning society. (5) Near the end of the book, in chapter 31, the Torah again includes the Sabbath within the broader discussion of the Tabernacle's construction. (6) And in chapter 19 of the present book of Leviticus, we find the Sabbath associated with Jewish education and parental respect. That brings us to our chapter in Parashat Emor, where the Sabbath is identified as one of our holy times. We can explain the presence of the Sabbath here, as an introduction to the festivals, in one of several ways.

First, the power and ability of the Israelite people to sanctify the festivals stems from the fact that God already imbued holiness into the Sabbath at the start of creation. Following the formation of the material world, the Almighty created the concept known as "holiness of time," a phenomenon that bears a particular purpose and character. Subsequently, the task of sanctifying time was granted to Israel just prior to their emancipation from Egypt. In this way, God allowed the Israelite people to become partners in the enterprise of making time holy. Consequently, it becomes clear that the inclusion of the Sabbath in the chapter on the festivals was necessary because the seventh day serves as the foundation for the whole notion of sacred time. The nation subsequently borrowed this concept and applied it to our calendar of holidays.

Second, the institution of the Sabbath is not completely distinct from the festivals – that is, the *moadim* – for the term *mo'ed*, "time," is not only a synonym for "holiday." It also signifies *hitvaadut* or "assembly." This refers to the gathering of family, community, and nation for the sake of drawing close to God. In this way, the Sabbath is the prototype of a Jewish gathering. On that day, the Sabbath acquires a quality of spiritual and educational inspiration that is similarly reflected in the festivals. It is for this reason that the Torah opens its discussion of the holidays by first mentioning the Sabbath.

Third, in an earlier verse we read: "The Israelites shall keep the Sabbath, making it a day of rest throughout their generations as a covenant forever" (Exodus 31:16). What exactly does the Torah mean when it asks Israel to "make the Sabbath"? The straightforward meaning is that the nation is instructed to "observe" the seventh day. There is, however, another possible approach. Even though the sanctity of the Sabbath has existed from the beginning of time, in the absence of any Jews to relate to it, it is viewed as just Saturday, and there is nothing special about it aside from its being the first day of the weekend. The Sabbath can be "made" only by the individual Jew who observes it with an apprehension of all its components. These elements of a spiritually satisfying day include social dimensions as well as by times devoted to matters of faith and morality. The Sabbath requires no testimony of witnesses and no declaration of the court. Instead, it is the behavior of each Jewish family within its home that constitutes the Sabbath day. In this way, the people of Israel subordinate their will within

the national project of associating themselves with the sacred, that has existed since the seventh day of creation.

This interpretation of the Sabbath raises the question as to how we are to transmit the significance of these concepts to the next generation. Merely abstaining from work on the seventh day does not create an atmosphere of rest; tranquility is an independently positive status. The peacefulness of the Sabbath enables us to conduct our lives of action, and not just because this one day reenergizes us for the coming week. Rather, on the Sabbath we pause and we contemplate the very purpose of our lives, thereby compelling us to contemplate what exactly we are working toward. This point is set forth in the writings of Rabbi Tzadok of Lublin, in chapter 7 of his work *Yisrael Kedoshim*:

> The wicked Haman inflicted the evil eye over the sacred times of the Israelite people. For the whole of the Jewish year is founded on the Sabbath day, and it is that which incurred the envy of this villain, the enemy who understood that the foundation of our holiness rests on the respite and the relaxation that we enjoy on the Sabbath. Based on that, we can extend the sanctity of the Sabbath to the entire week of activity. This allows our people to occupy ourselves with Torah and labor without bothering with the more mundane matters of this world. All our efforts are thereby blessed, as the Talmud states [in Berakhot 32b] regarding our ancient and righteous ancestors. Such peace of mind, however, is not available to the gentiles, who must toil day and night to earn their bread. Meanwhile, the Israelite people eat and drink and are merry, as they spend their hours in song and praises of the Almighty. This, of course, contrasts with the nations of the world, who fritter away their time with frivolities. Now since the true temperament of a man is revealed after he has imbibed alcohol, it is imperative to drink wine in celebration of the downfall of the hated Haman. It is then that we recall that it was through that man's drinking that he attempted to attack the sanctity of the Israelite people. Recall also the maxim that states: When wine goes in, secrets come out. For it was in Haman's inebriated state that he revealed his recognition that the Jewish people represent a sacred nation bound to the holiness of God. Furthermore, he knew that we draw our spirituality from the special and unique quality of the Sabbath, a holiness that has existed from the beginning of time. It is the Sabbath that is the wellspring for all sacred times in the Jewish lifecycle. Furthermore, these holy days serve to imbue every day of the year with holiness, even if that might not be easily apparent.

Haman never truly understood the secret of the Sabbath and its associated Jewish holidays. He could not truly internalize how our people attains sanctity by sitting around and doing nothing once a week. But indeed, the Sabbath is the

source of all blessing for the Israelite nation. For it is specifically by avoiding labor that we learn to emulate the Holy One, blessed be He, who rested on the seventh day of creation. And it is precisely by understanding the essential nature of the Sabbath day that the Jewish people elevate an otherwise mundane existence, transforming it into an exalted state of holiness.

For commentaries and the Biblical Imagination turn to the left side of this volume.